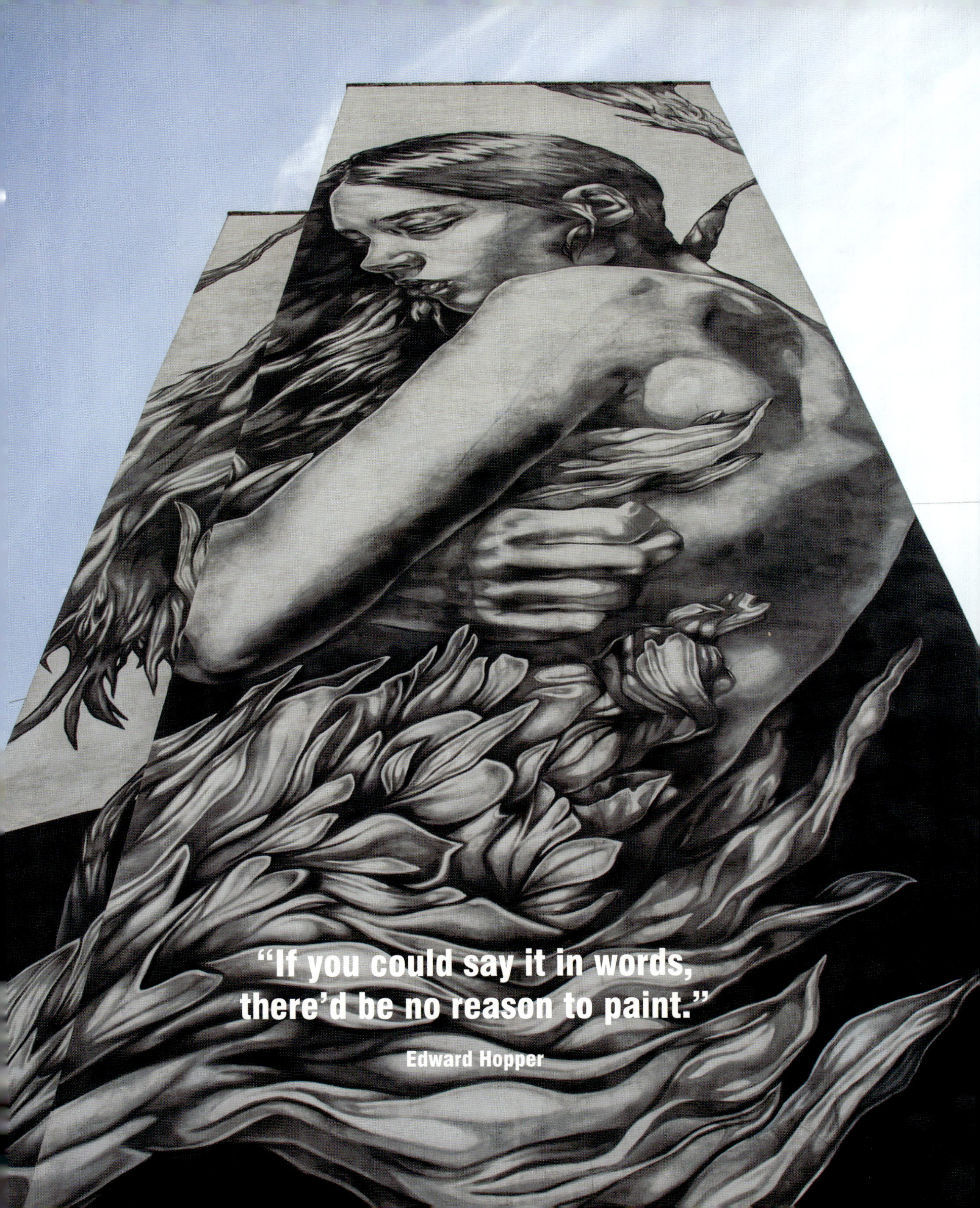

"If you could say it in words,
there'd be no reason to paint."
Edward Hopper

A catalogue record for this book is available from the British Library.

First Edition 2019
First published in Great Britain in 2019
by Carpet Bombing Culture.
An imprint of Pro-actif Communications
www.carpetbombingculture.co.uk
Email: books@carpetbombingculture.co.uk
©Carpet Bombing Culture. Pro-actif Communications

Photography by Julio Ashitaka
Essays by Patrick Potter

ISBN: 978-1908211-79-8

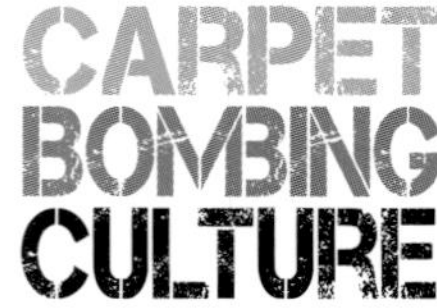

www.carpetbombingculture.co.uk

COLOSSUS

Julio Ashitaka

DREAMING OUT LOUD.
THE MURAL
IS THE BORDER WHERE THE
URBAN WORLD
TOUCHES IT'S DREAMS OF ITSELF. IT IS THE WINDOW ONTO
NARNIA, THE LOOKING GLASS,
THE THIN PLACE. WHEN IT WORKS IT ALLOWS US
TO ESCAPE,
FOR A MOMENT, FROM LANGUAGE.

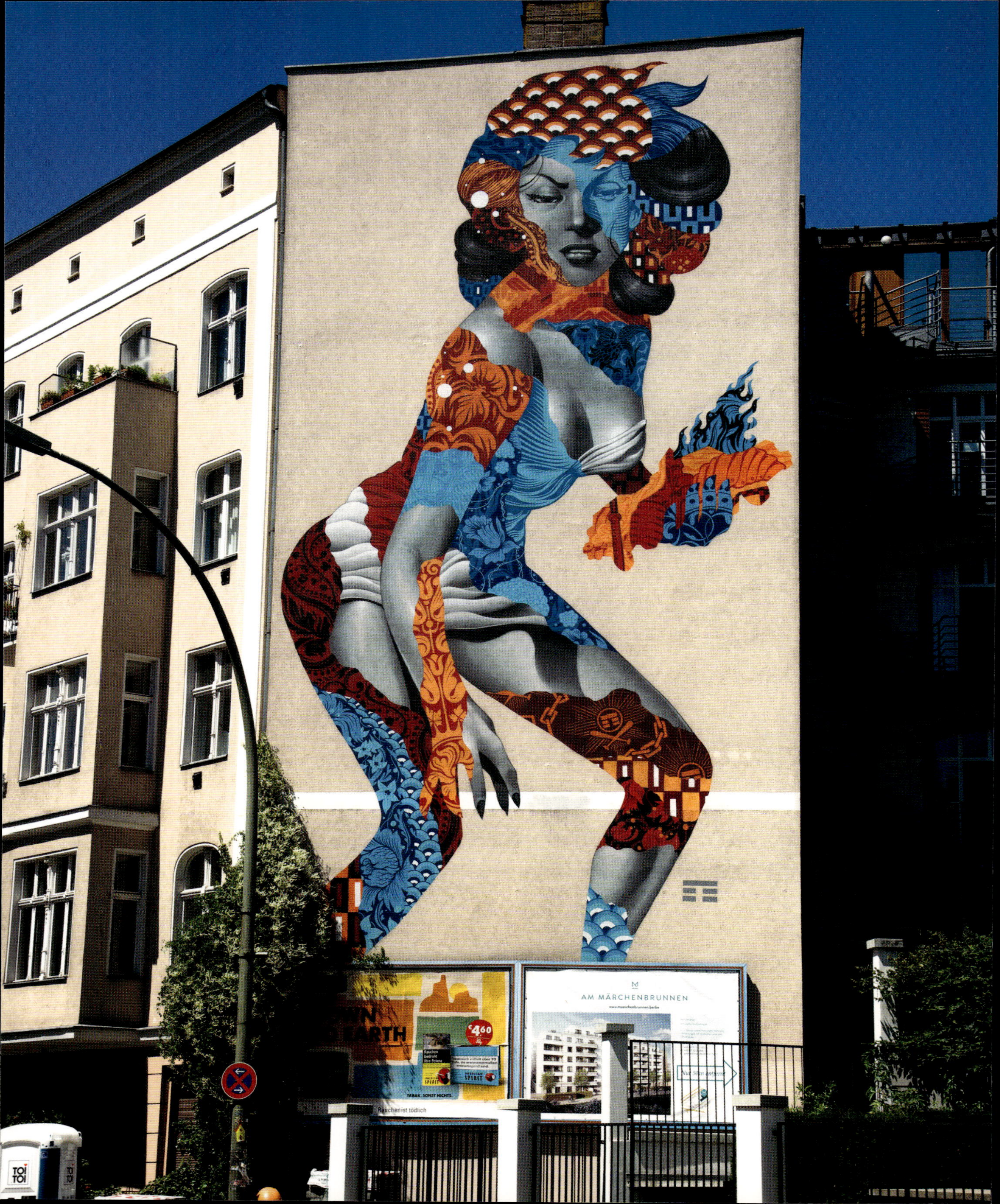

AM MÄRCHENBRUNNEN
TOI TOI

Introduction

The first time I saw graffiti was about 20 years ago during the 1990's. It was colourful tagging on a dirty wall in my home town in Japan. I couldn't read it, but the vivid graffiti deeply embedded itself in my memory.

In the 1990's the Internet was not as developed as it is today. It was hard to find out information on street art. A lot of time has passed by since then. After undertaking a trip to Latin America, I decided to travel back to Japan via Europe. It was here, while working in Lodz, Poland that I came across large scale street art for the very first time, a giant-sized 20 metres tall work of art and on further discovery I realized that large scale murals were not confined to a single place.

Following on from Lodz I began to research the European street art scene via the internet, discovering there were literally hundreds of epic large scale murals spread throughout Europe. That was the catalyst for my intention to track down and document these works.

I travelled from Lodz to Berlin, Berlin to Vienna, Vienna to Budapest - my quest had begun. Throughout Europe the painting styles are incredibly diverse, each artist has their own unique technique. Figurative, abstract, geometric and photo-realistic. Travelling throughout Europe became like a visit to an open-air art museum.

During the time I've spent documenting these images more than a hundred street art works have disappeared for various reasons including the demolishing of buildings, repainting of buildings and the extension of buildings. New work painted over old work. Street art does not last forever. It can disappear in weeks, months or years or conversely still be around decades later. They appear and disappear repeatedly.

This book documents my travels between 2018 and 2019. The QR codes included with each city are there so that you too can witness the creativity and spectacle of European street art. Oh, and one last thing, should you arrive at the location and not find the piece of work that I have documented, its highly likely that you might find a new gem waiting for you!

Julio Ashitaka

VIENNA

AUSTRIA

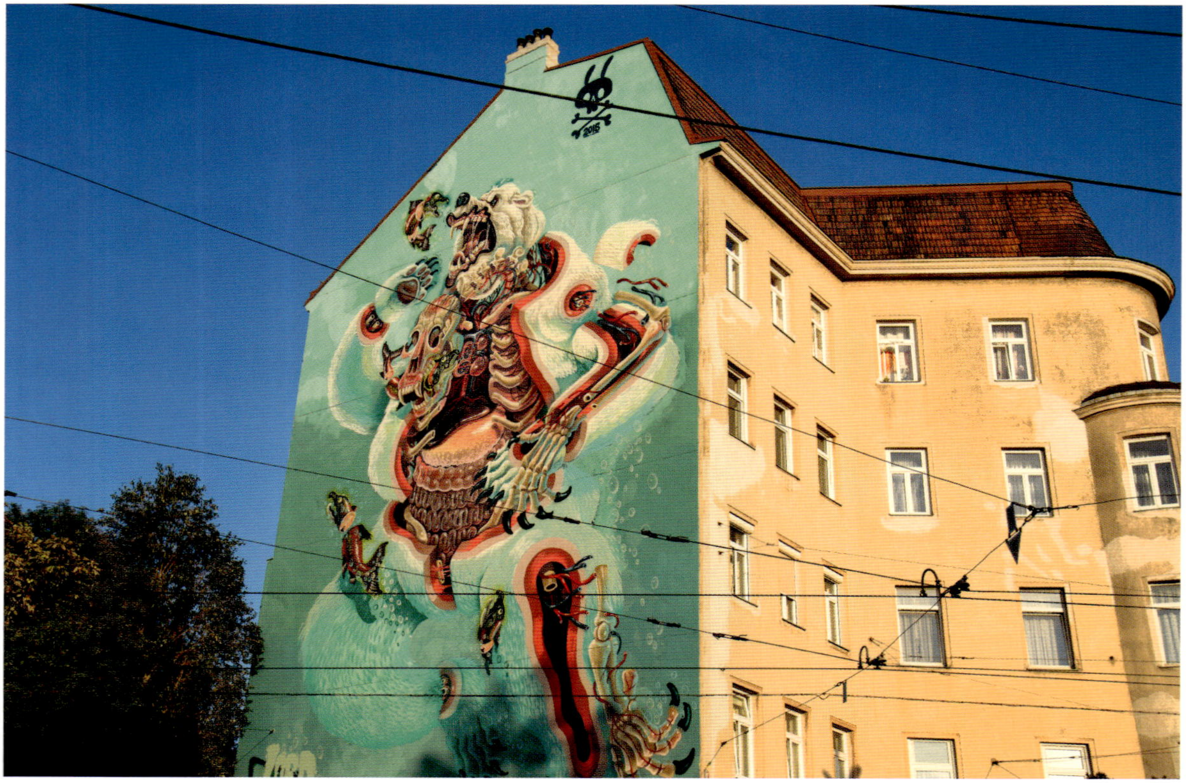

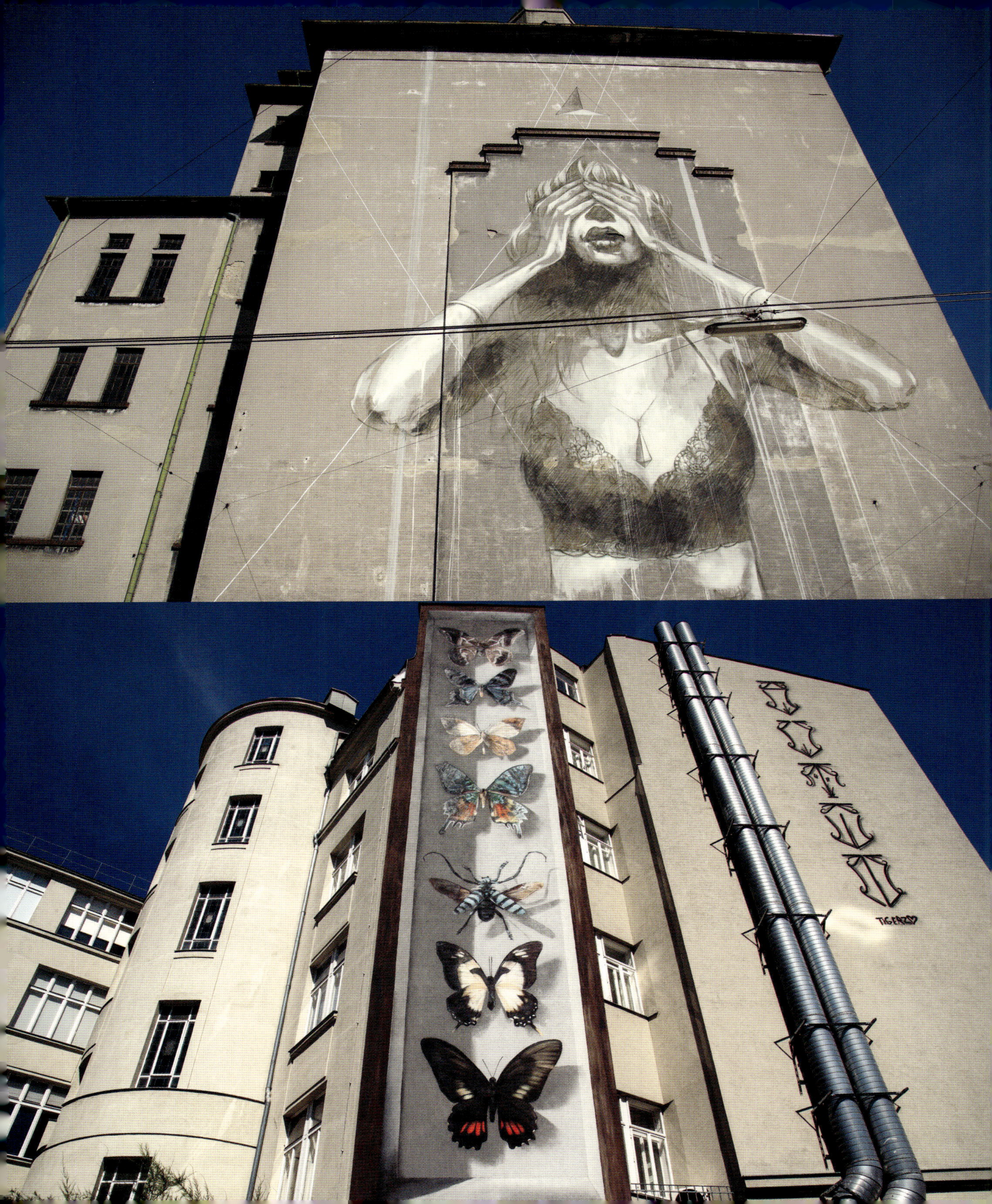
TIGER♥

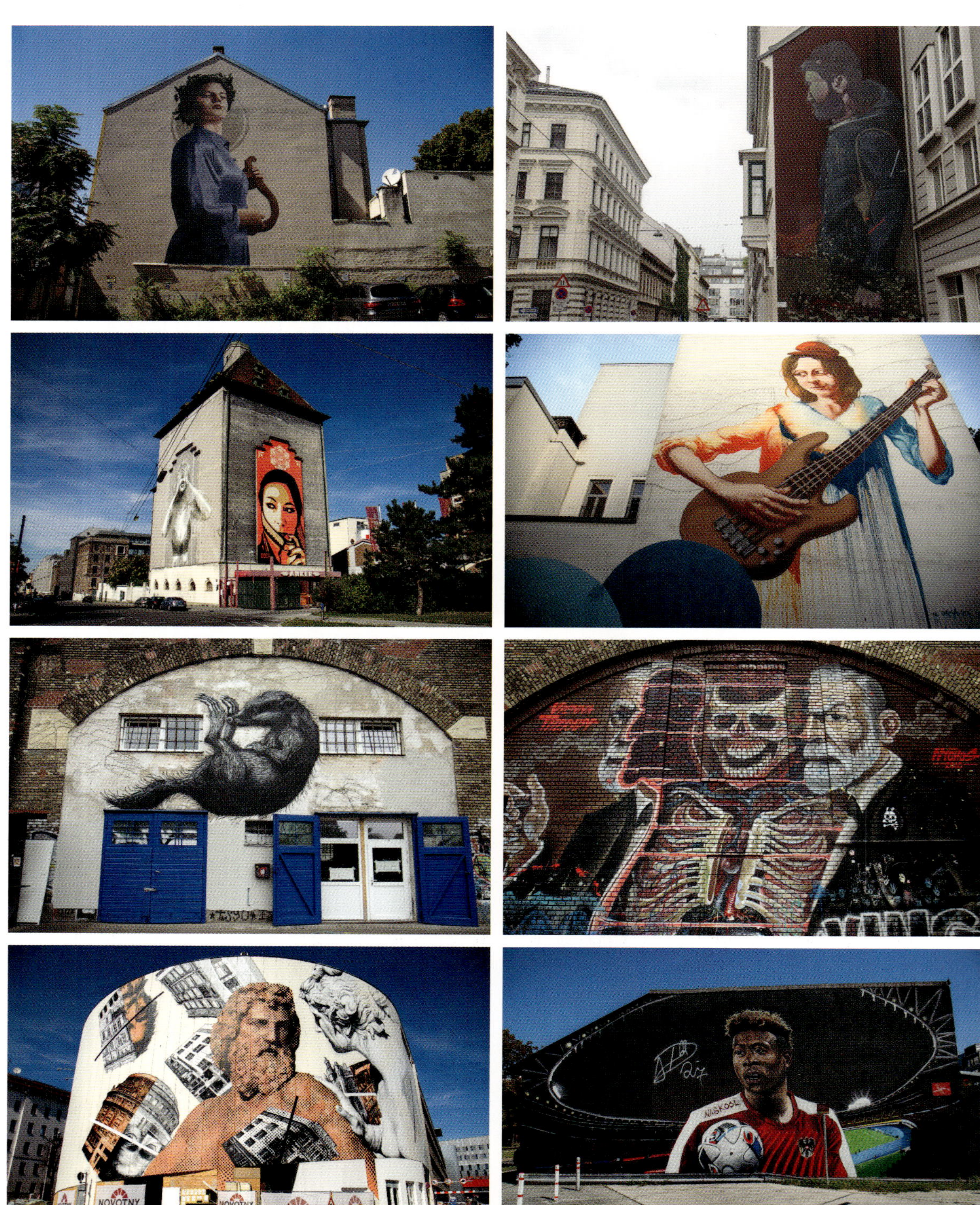

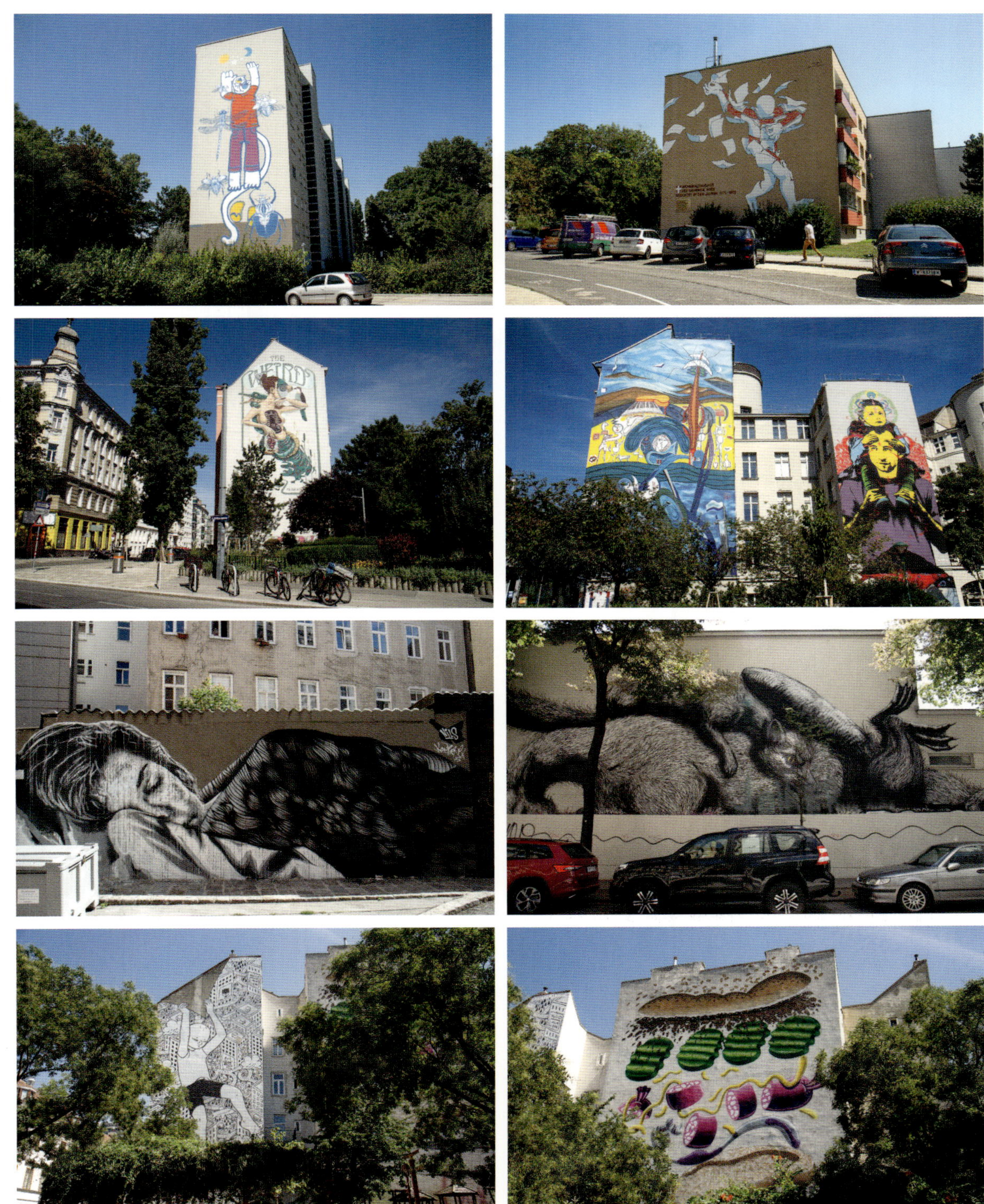

BERLIN

GERMANY

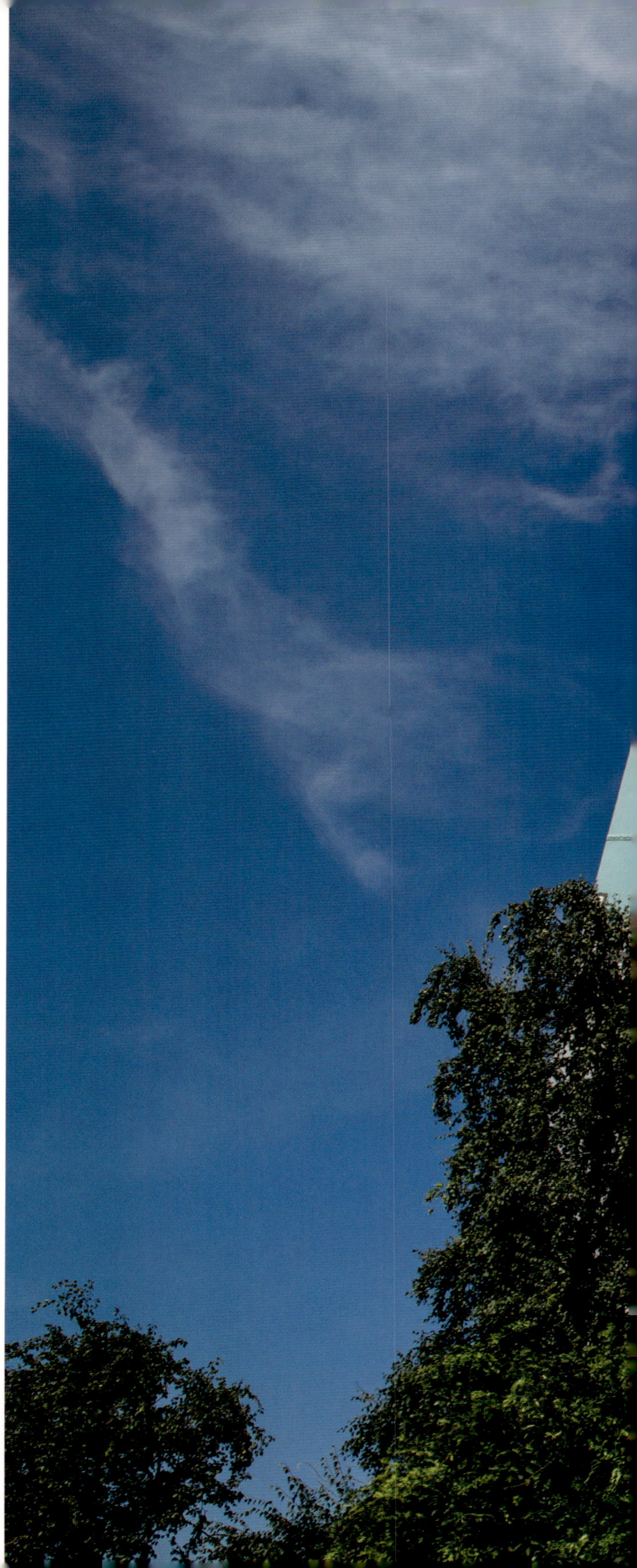

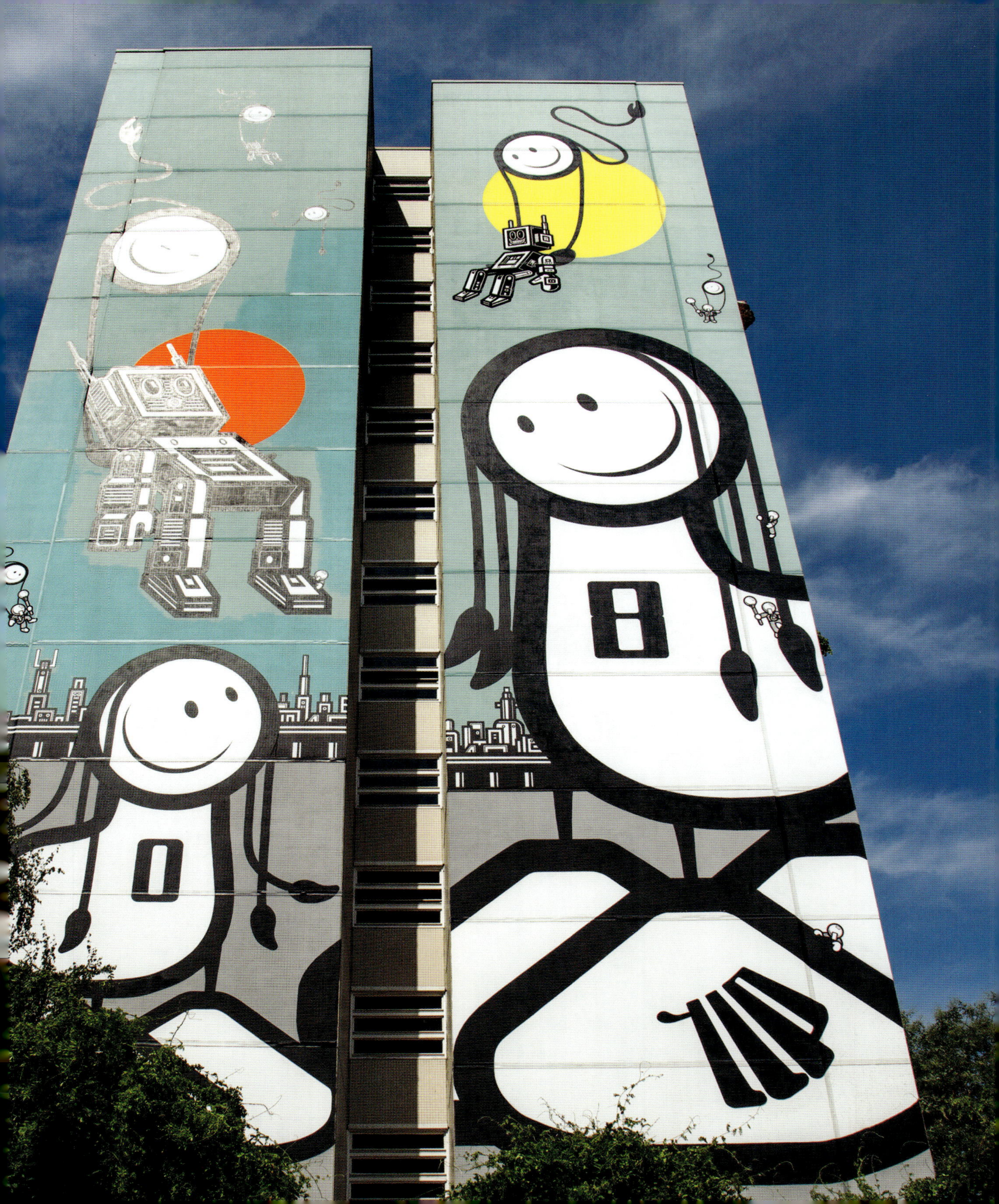

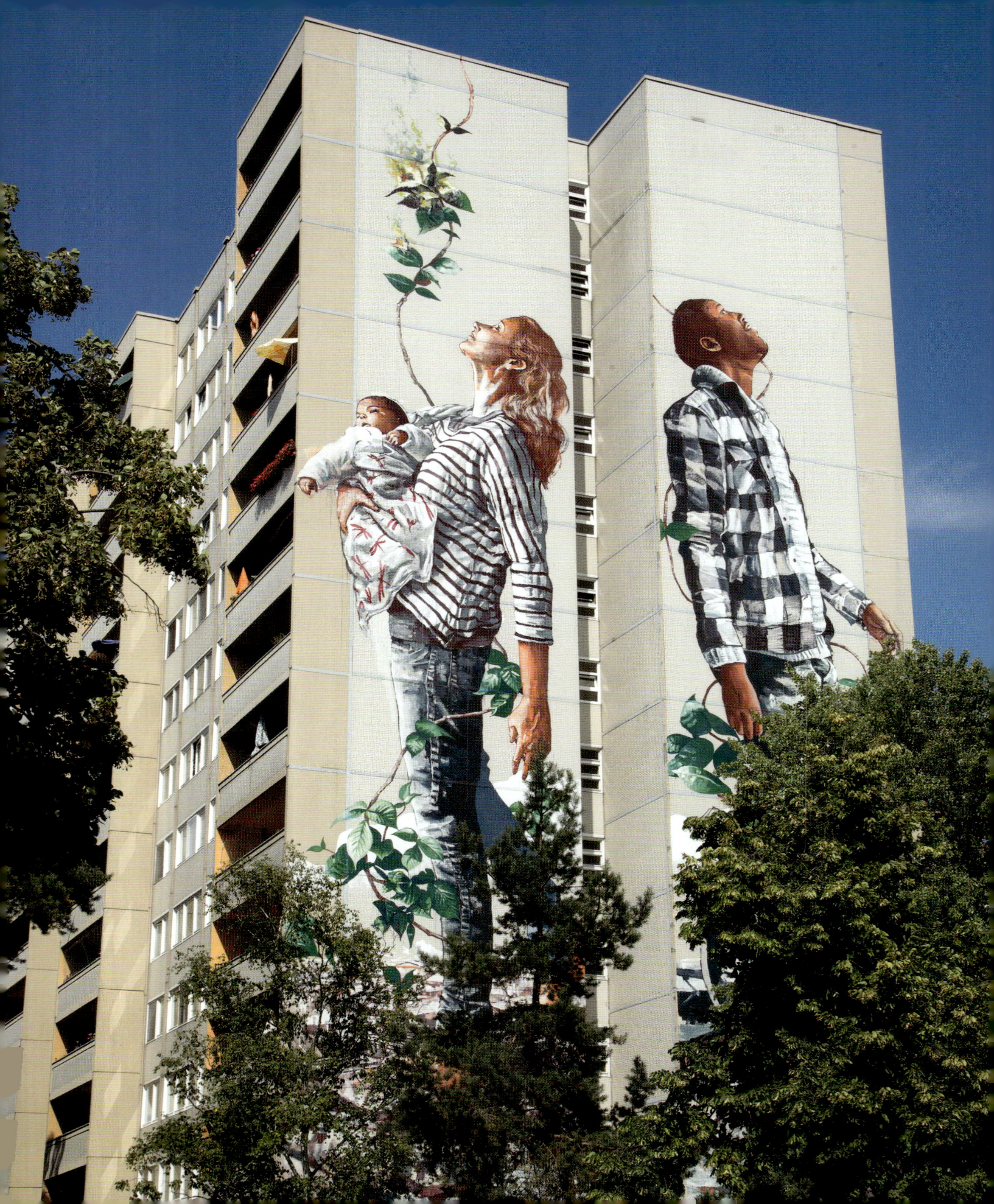

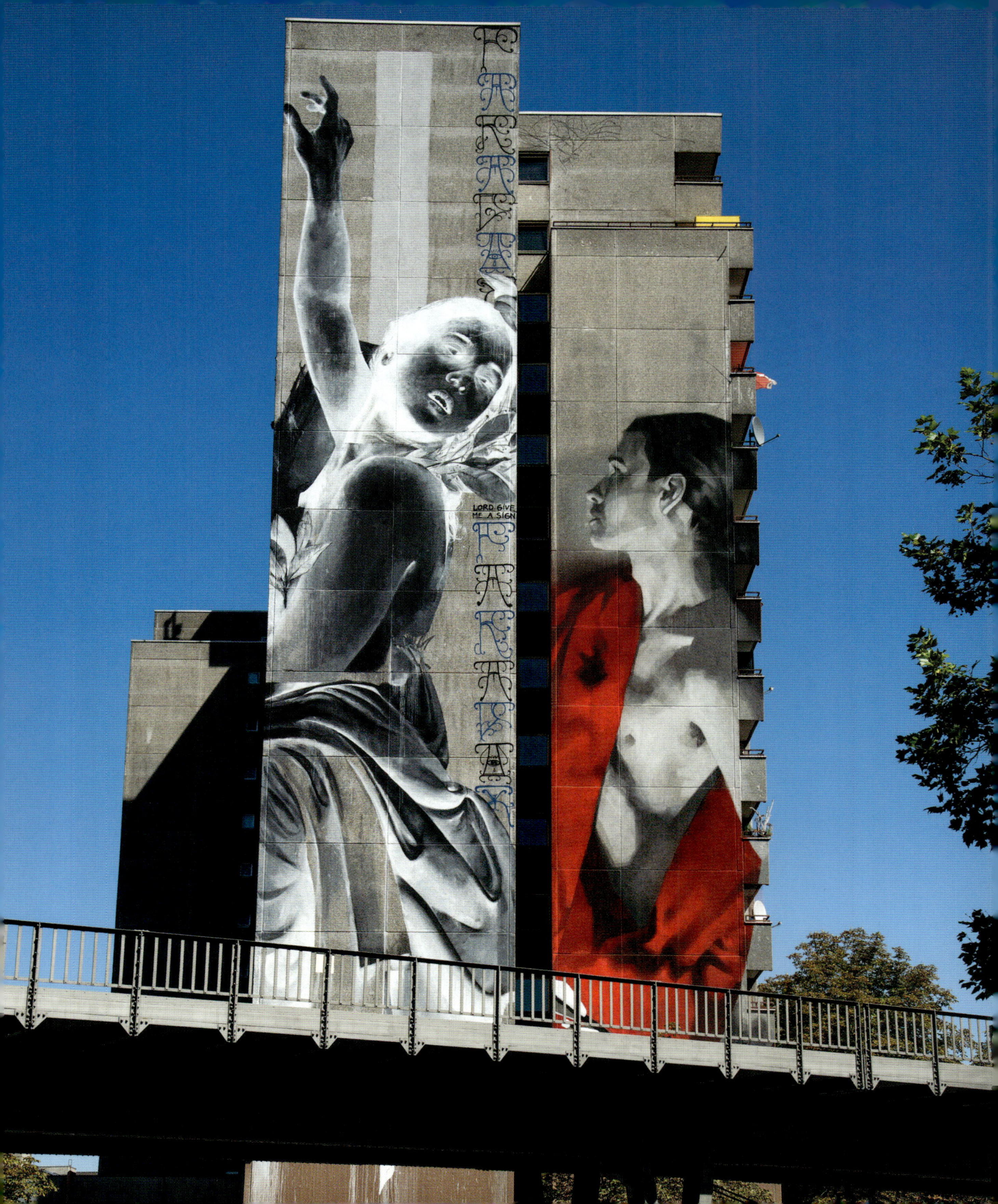

LORD GIVE
ME A SIGN

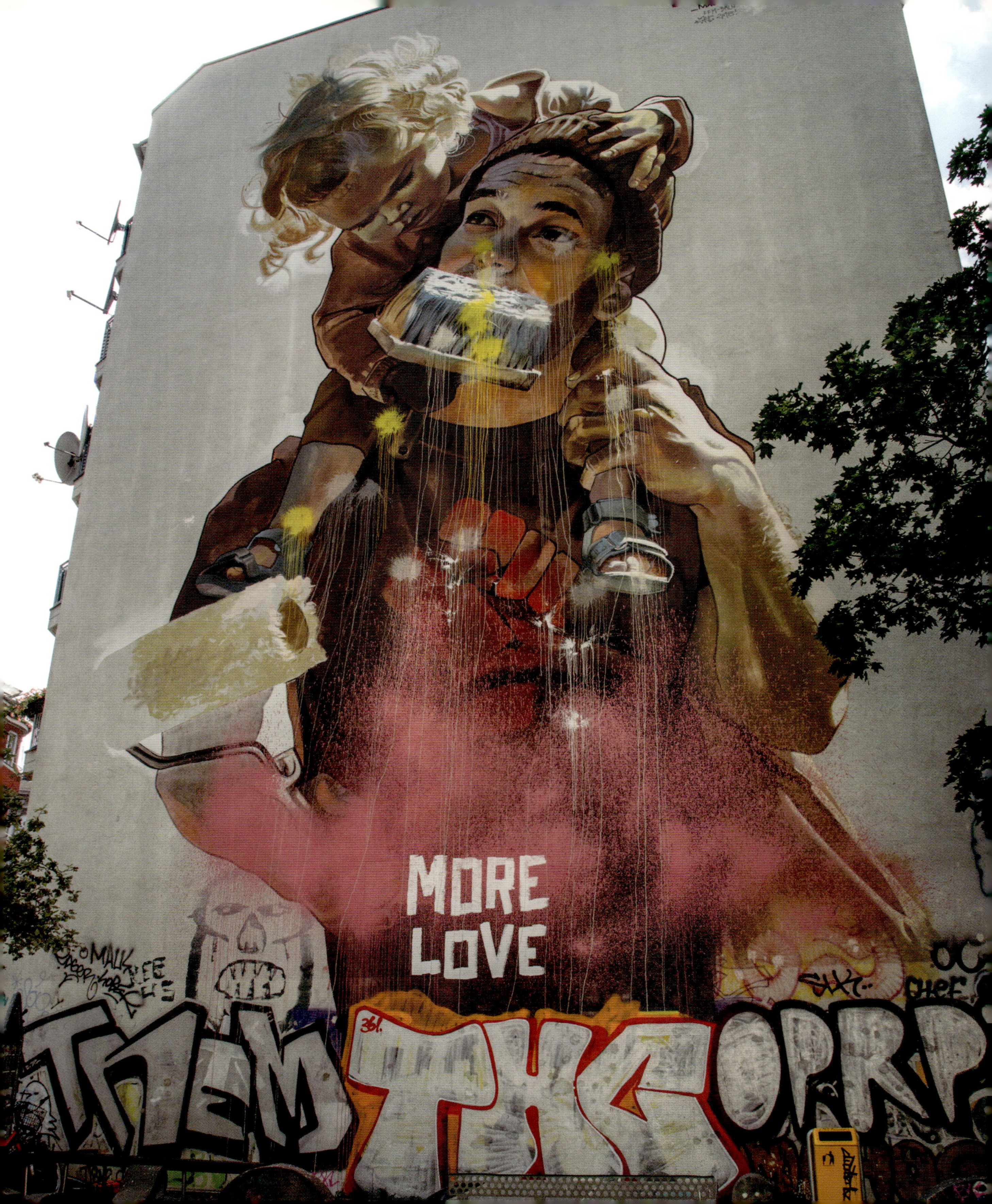

MORE
LOVE

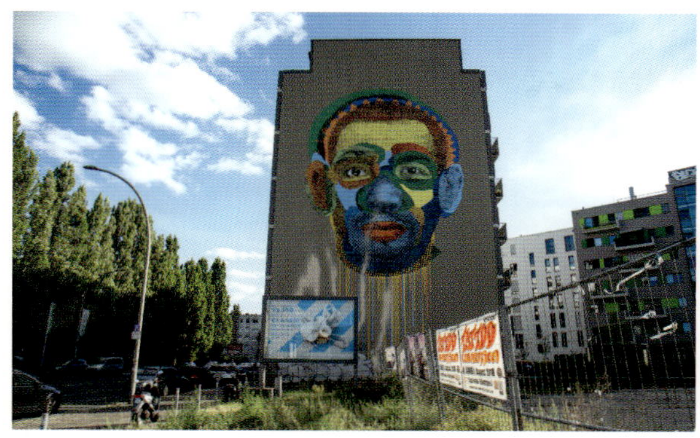
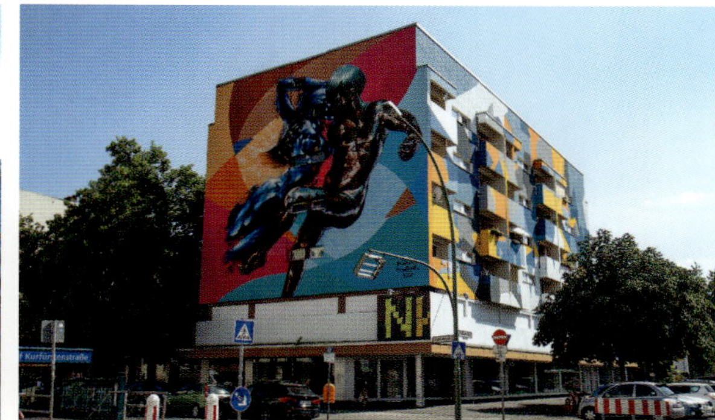
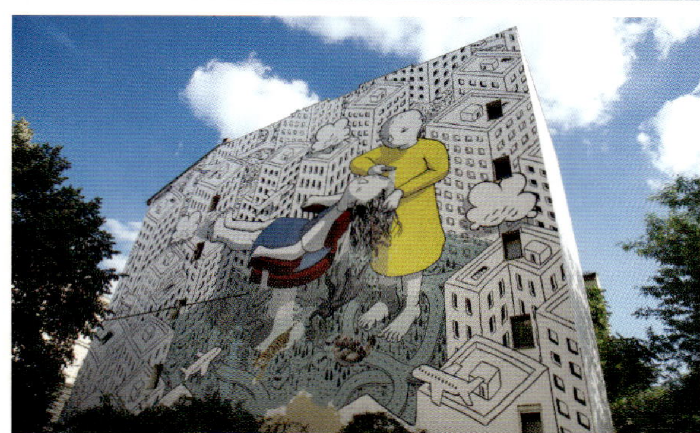
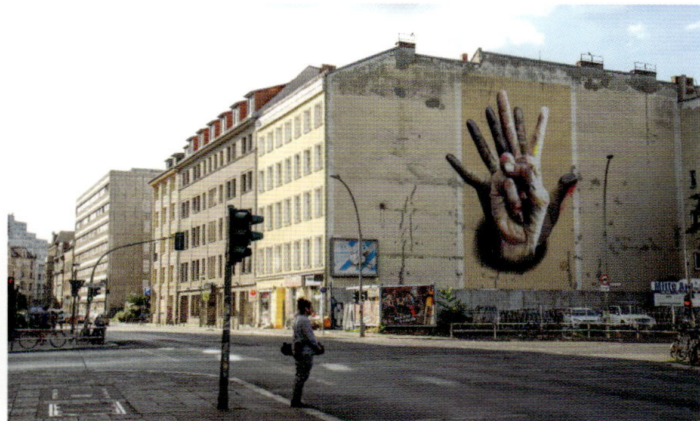
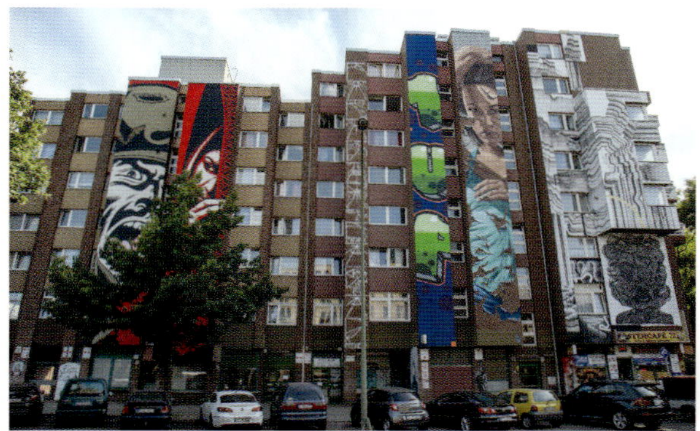
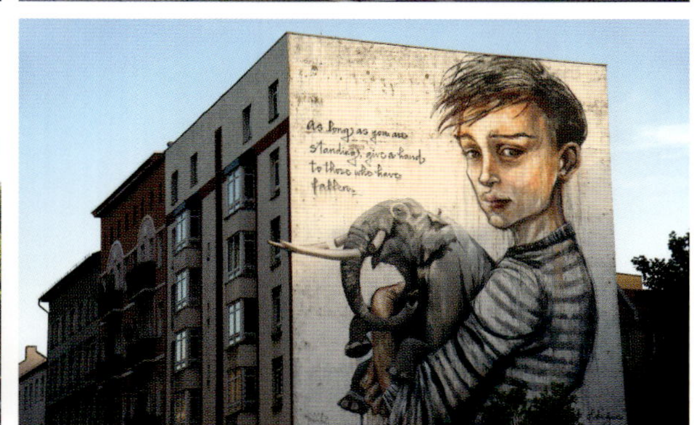
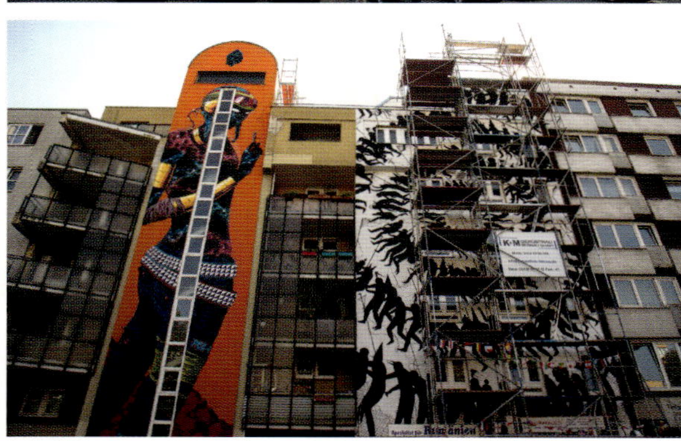
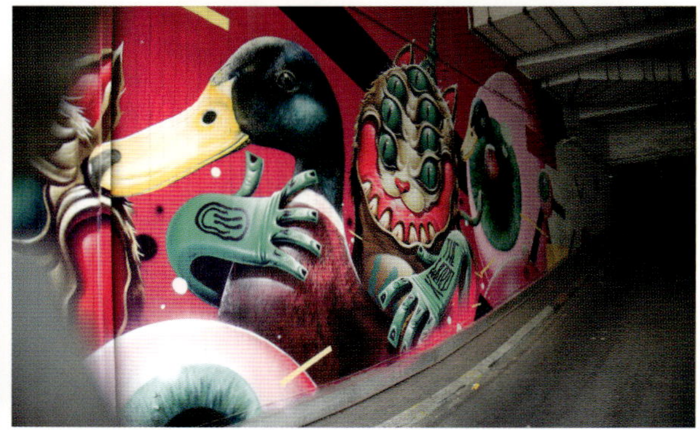

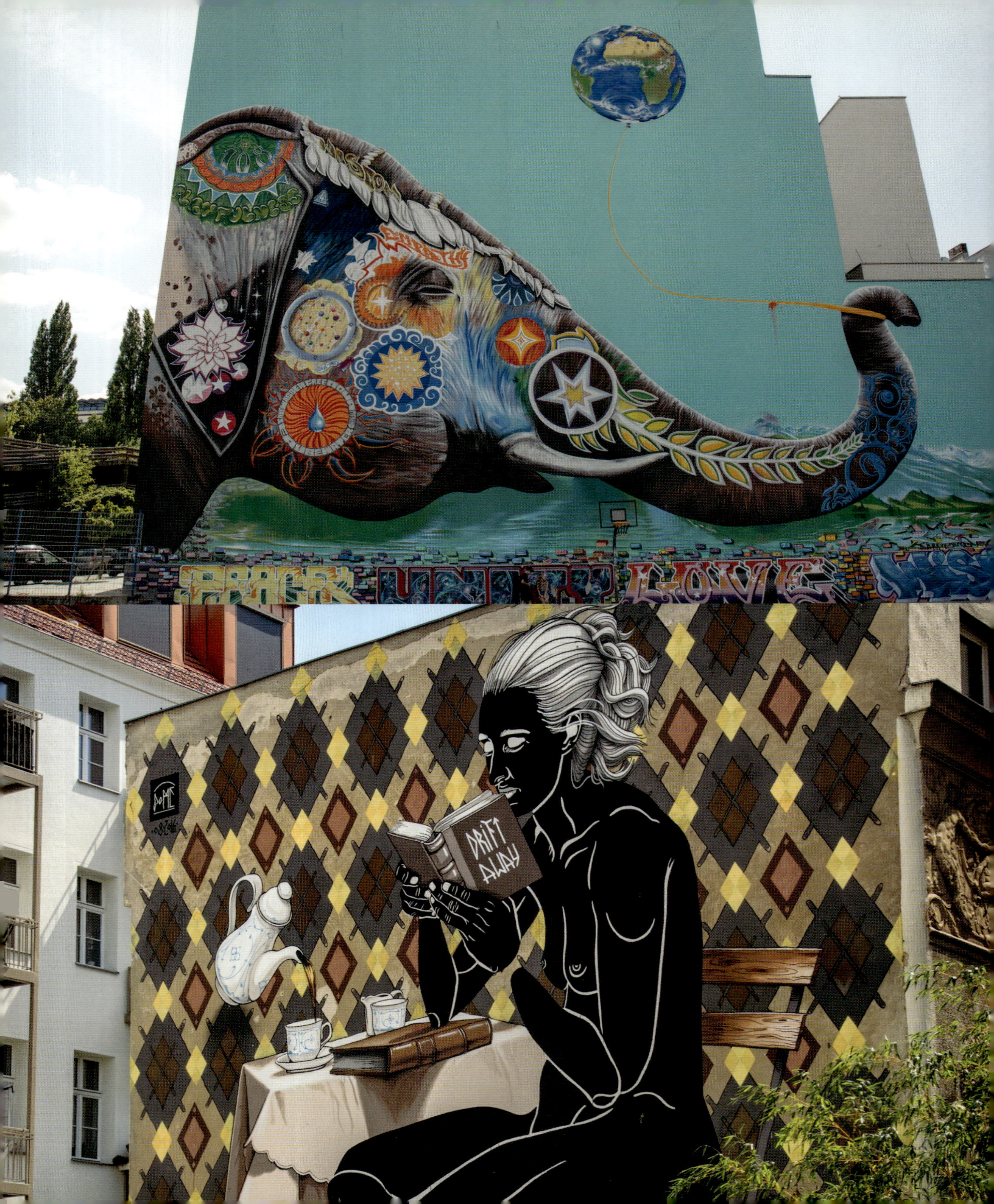

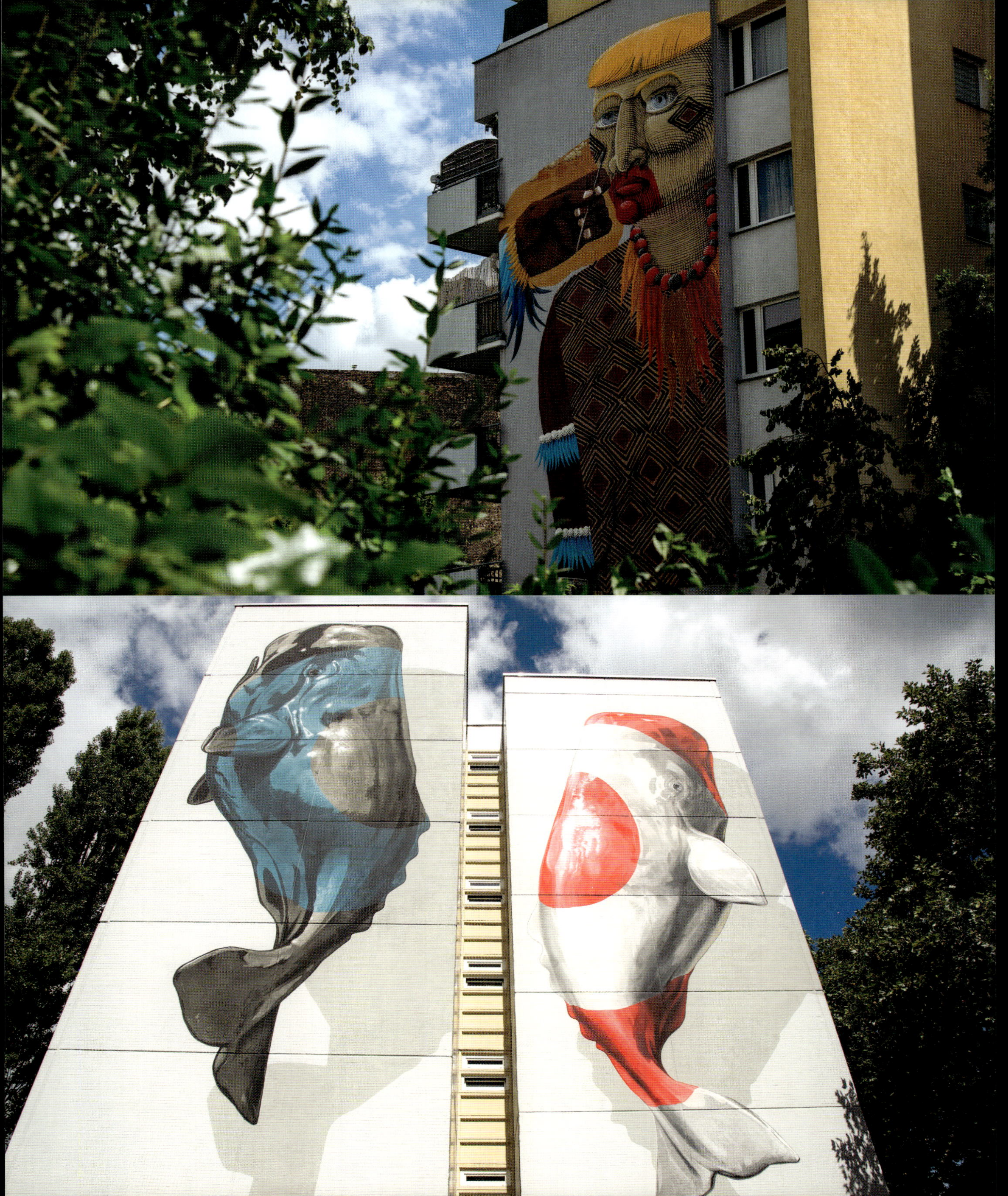

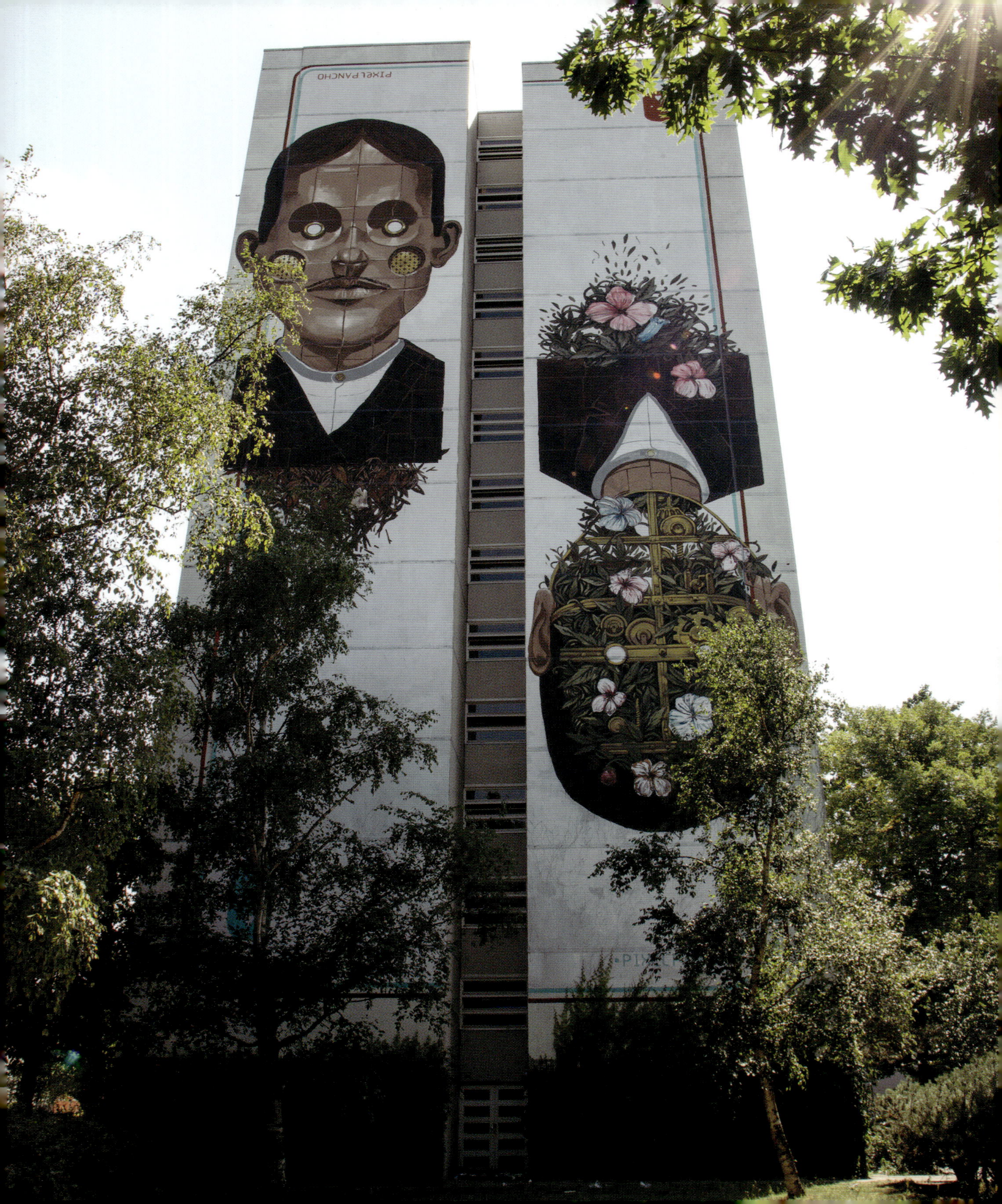
PIXEL PANCHO

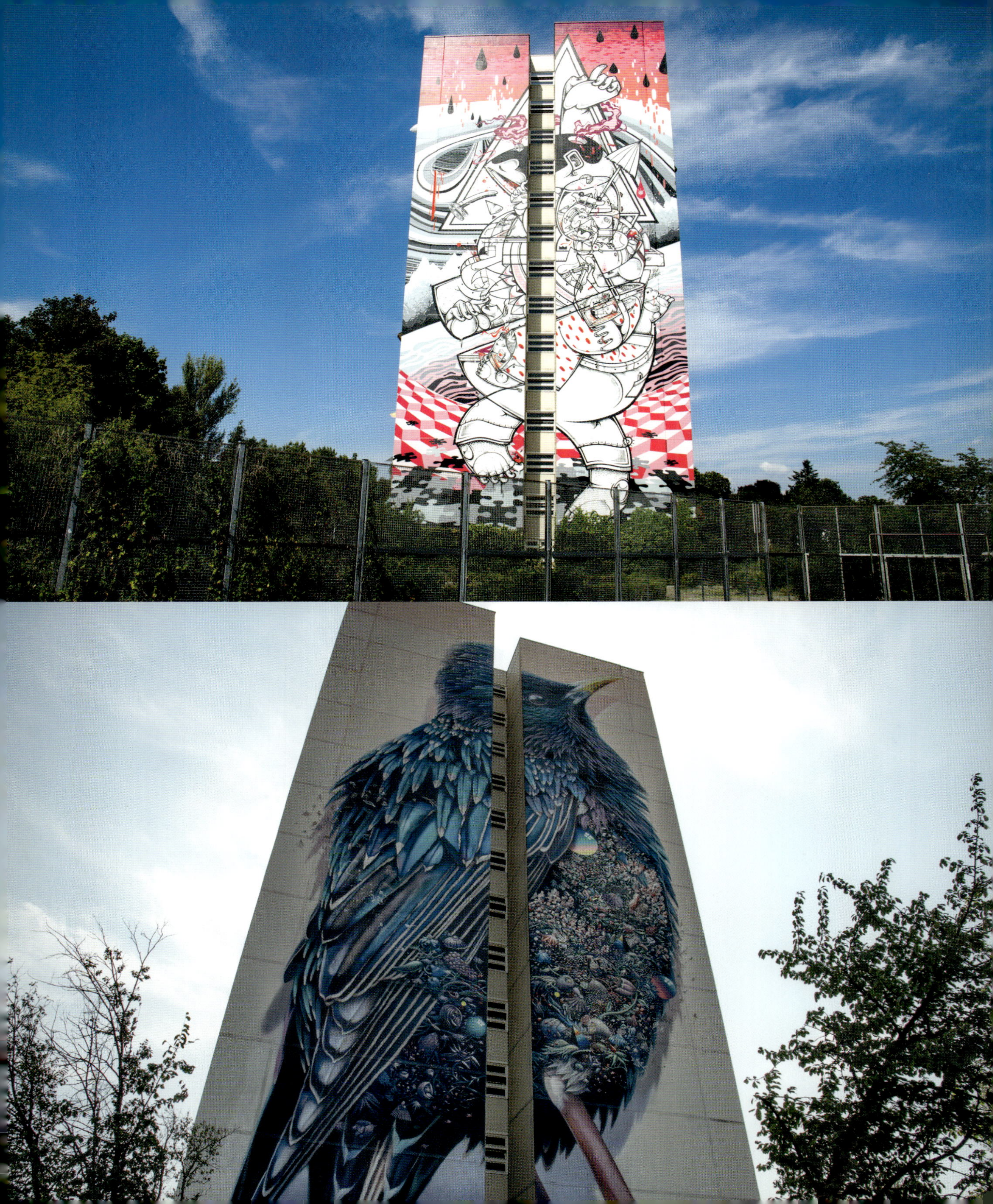

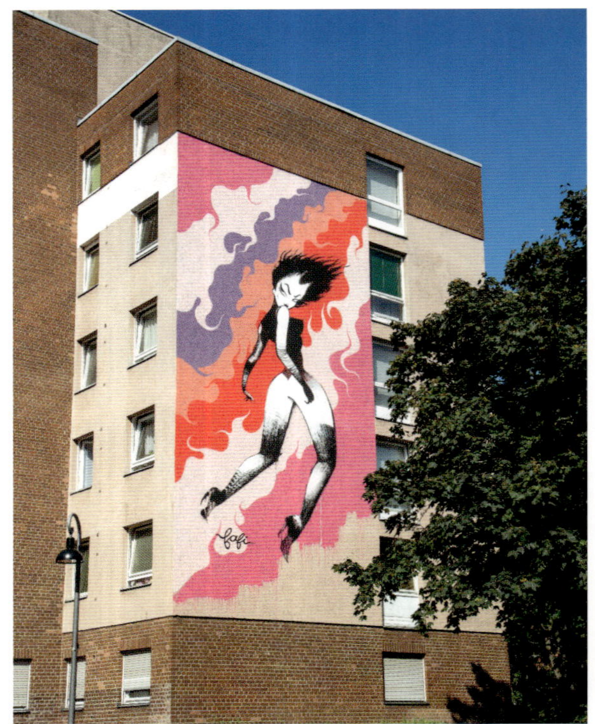

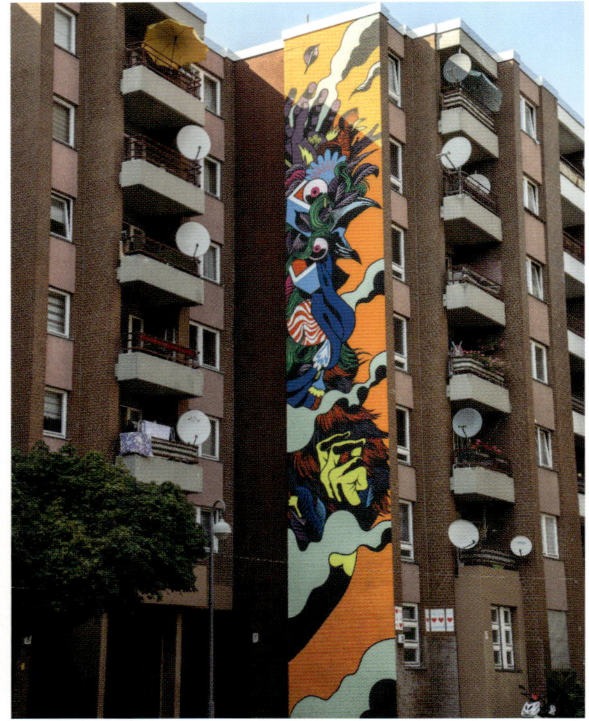

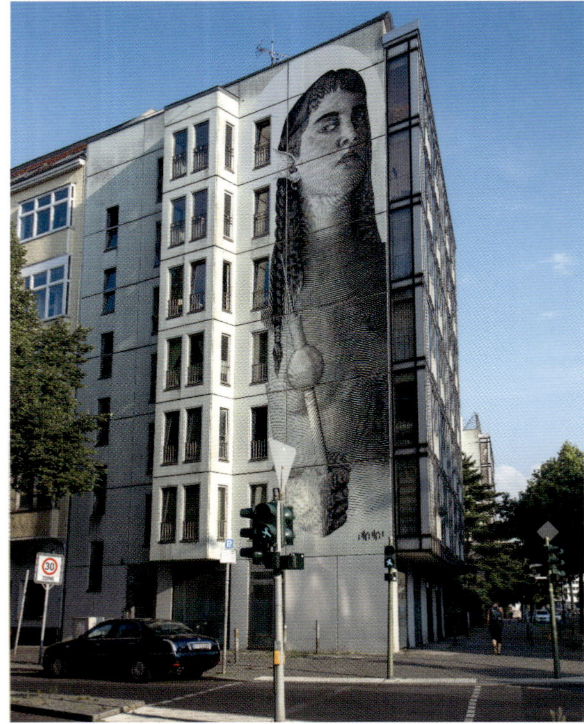

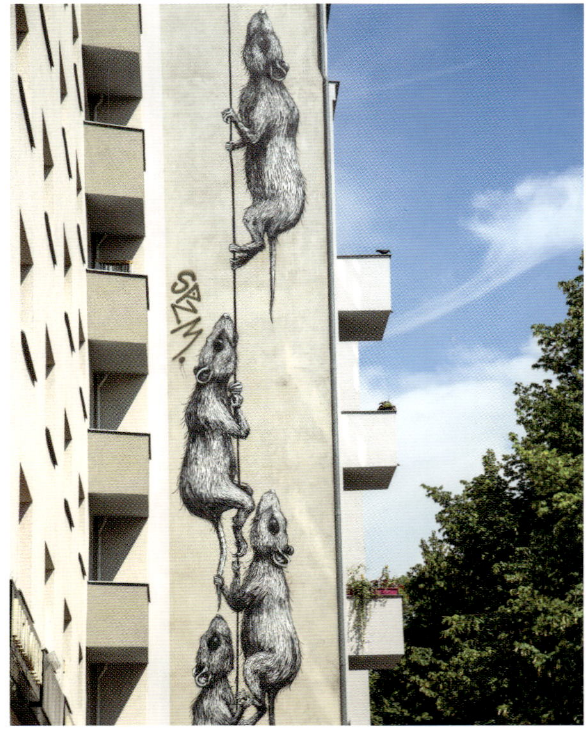

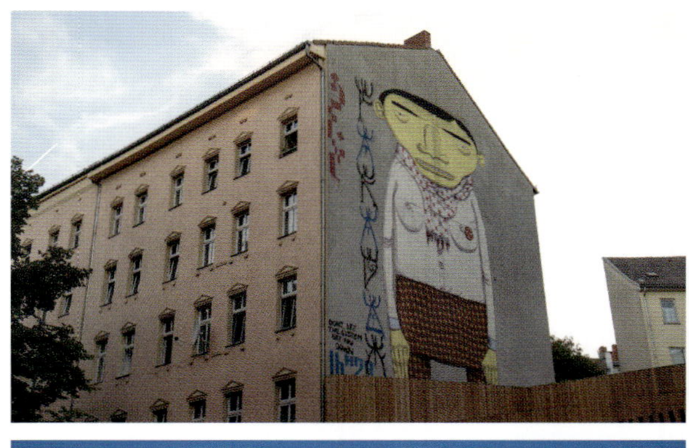
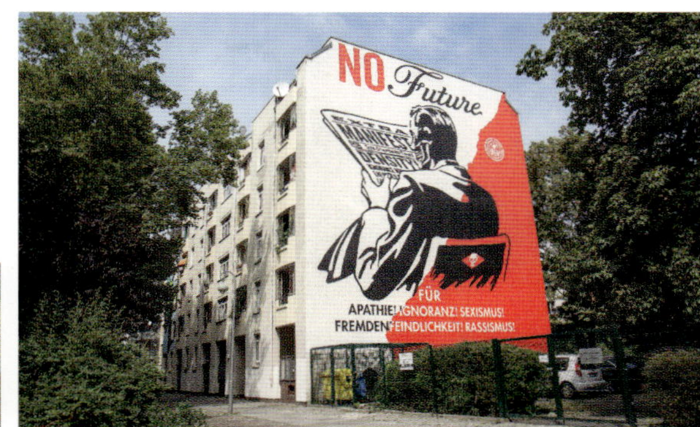

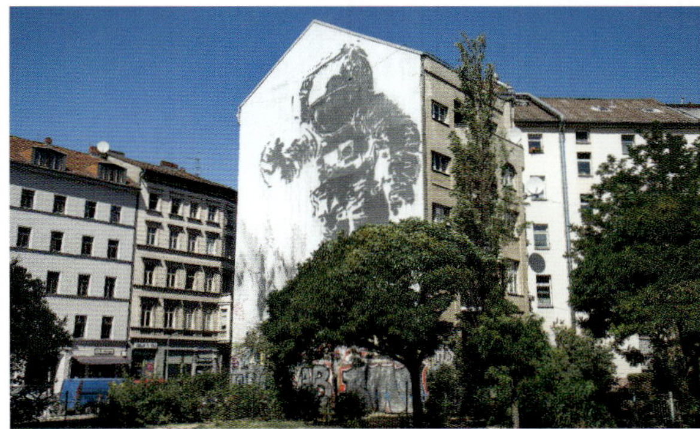
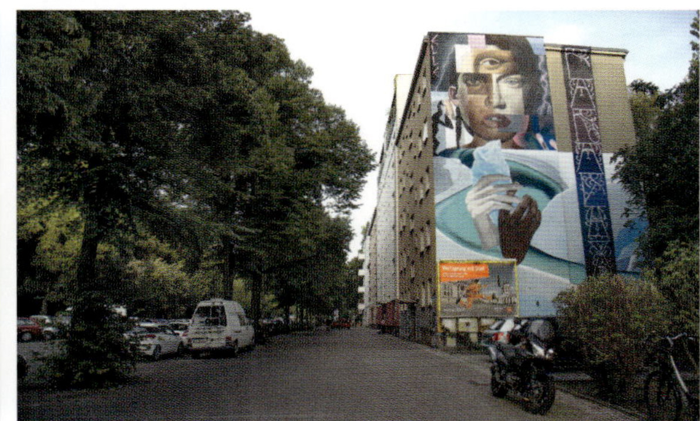

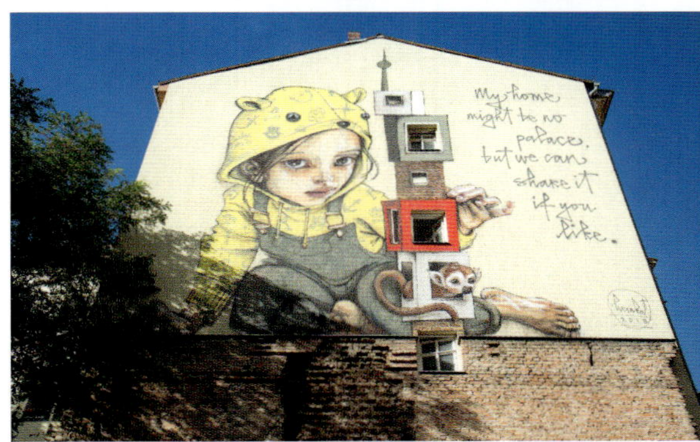
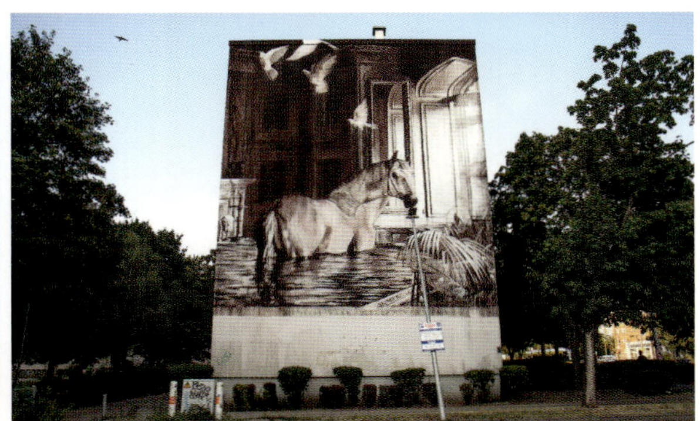

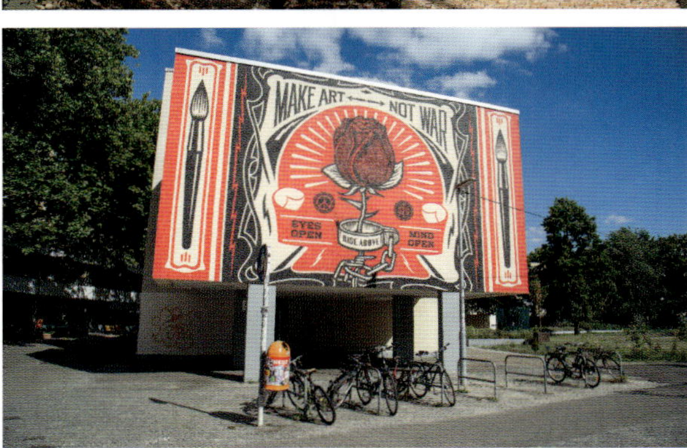
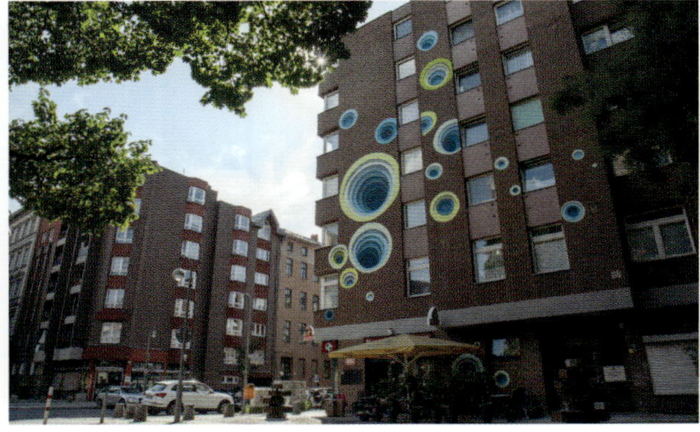

An Historical Perspective on Mural Painting

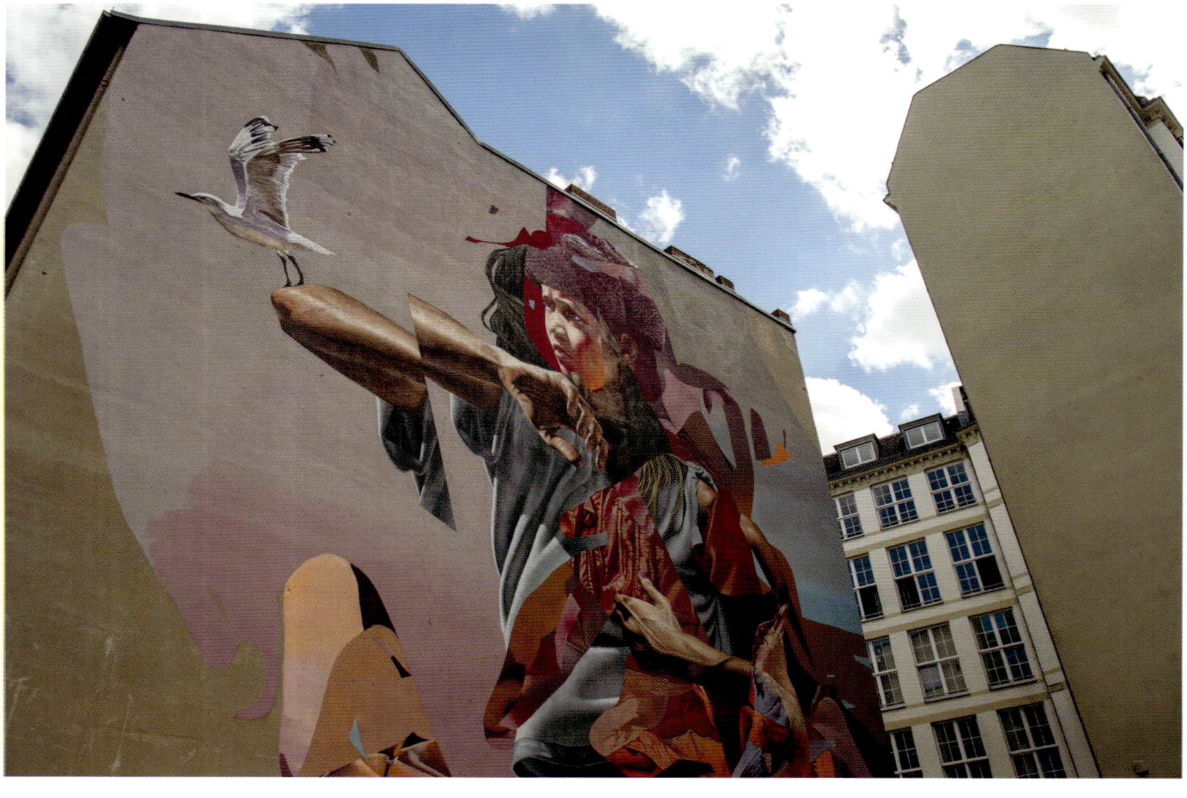

Mural, 'A painting or work of art executed on a wall', came to English from French, from the Latin 'Muralis' meaning 'of a wall'. It is the oldest form of visual art that we know of, with some cave paintings dating back to 30,000 BC. The mural was a major feature of ancient Egyptian culture, Minoan civilisation and the classical Roman world, with the most striking example being the murals preserved in the volcanic ash of Pompeii.

Mural, 'A painting or work of art executed on a wall', came to English from French, from the Latin 'Muralis' meaning 'of a wall'. It is the oldest form of visual art that we know of, with some cave paintings dating back to 30,000 BC. The mural was a major feature of ancient Egyptian culture, Minoan civilisation and the classical Roman world, with the most striking example being the murals preserved in the volcanic ash of Pompeii.

In the dark ages of medieval Europe, art was religious, or it was heretical. Muralism belonged to the church, who indeed owned all the elements of life that were not directly linked to survival, that is to say 'culture'. The power of painting at that time must have been immense, if it was the only representation that you saw, being an illiterate peasant, of the sublime world of ideas. Older still, the Keralan traditional of Fresco depicted an intense otherworld of colorful gods and miracles.

In the late middle-ages, the cultural rebirth sparked by the rediscovery of classical culture from ancient Rome and Greece, inspired colossal feats of wall art, especially in Italy, home of the Renaissance. These are frescoes like the Sistine Chapel that still have the power to stun even our jaded and image saturated eyes. And they show us worlds from our imaginations, heaven and hell, places we cannot go except through art.

In the modern world, as people were negotiating new ideological landscapes, ideas of National Identity, Class Struggle, the tension between Tradition and Change, muralism became of these struggles in Mexico. After a tremendously violent 19th century, Mexico was looking for an identity that could reconcile it's inner tensions.

The great muralists, Diego Rivera, José Clemente Orozco and David Alfaro Siqueiros, were backed by the post-revolutionary government to paint a new unified Mexico into existence. The most colossal of these works was the interior of the National Palace in Mexico city, depicting the history of Mexico from pre-columbian civilisation to the 1920's.

Murals have been a vital part of Latin American politics ever since. They have been associated with revolutionary movements and they continue to play a part in building communities and offering positive identities to neighbourhoods in US cities. This political muralism also flourished in Eastern Bloc communism, and in the Northern Irish troubles. Art in the street can never escape politics.

"I know too that the powerful fear art, whatever its form, when it does this, and that amongst the people such art sometimes runs like a rumour and a legend because it makes sense of what life's brutalities cannot, a sense that unites us, for it is inseparable from a justice at last. Art, when it functions like this, becomes a meeting-place of the invisible, the irreducible, the enduring, guts and honour." - John Berger

The Modern World as we know it was born in Paris, and Modern Art was its first child. Photography raised the question, why bother painting realistic representations? Artists rebelled against the "académie française des beaux arts" that tried to regulate the boundaries of French art just as the explosion of experimentation of the 'Fin de Siecle' approached. The Modern Era gave us the first wave of commercial art. Modernist giants like Alfons Mucha painted advertising and product artwork as well as traditional works of fine art. Paris was already covered in Billboards, Poster Art, Branding and bright lights by the turn of the century. Art got out of it's oppressive relationship with the church and leapt into bed with capitalism.

Then came the avant gardes, not content for art to become so rapidly the slave of the new middle class, they rebelled. From the Cubists onwards, art movements threw their carefully aimed aesthetic bombs at the heart of bourgeois society, believing that they could fight a revolution on the plane of art. A hundred years later, few have the dizzying self-confidence, the self-destructive zeal of the original avant-gardes and their manifestos seem to us like naive teenage iconoclasm. Who among us could still be shocked by a Dali or a Picasso?

Many avant gardes aligned themselves with the Communist International, but Soviet Communism would soon decide that formal experimentation was decadent and would advocate the Socialist Realist style, a stylised and heroic portrayal of The People enjoying their socialist utopia. Socialist Realism remains an aesthetic influence on many of the muralists in this book, if not a political one.

Fast forward seventy years and a new generation of young artists were celebrating the death of that world. As the Soviet Bloc collapsed in the late 1980's, one of the most famous galleries of street art in the world was created on both sides of the Berlin Wall. A kilometre of the wall, known as the East Side gallery, is kept as a memorial to the division of the city after WW2.

Karl Marx's dream ended in repression, a society of secret police and constant espionage in East Berlin. When it collapsed, the idea of the End of History emerged. There would be no more march towards a brighter future, no more grand narratives - we were in the best of all possible worlds, Liberal Democracy and Consumer Capitalism. All that remained was to export this model to the globe.

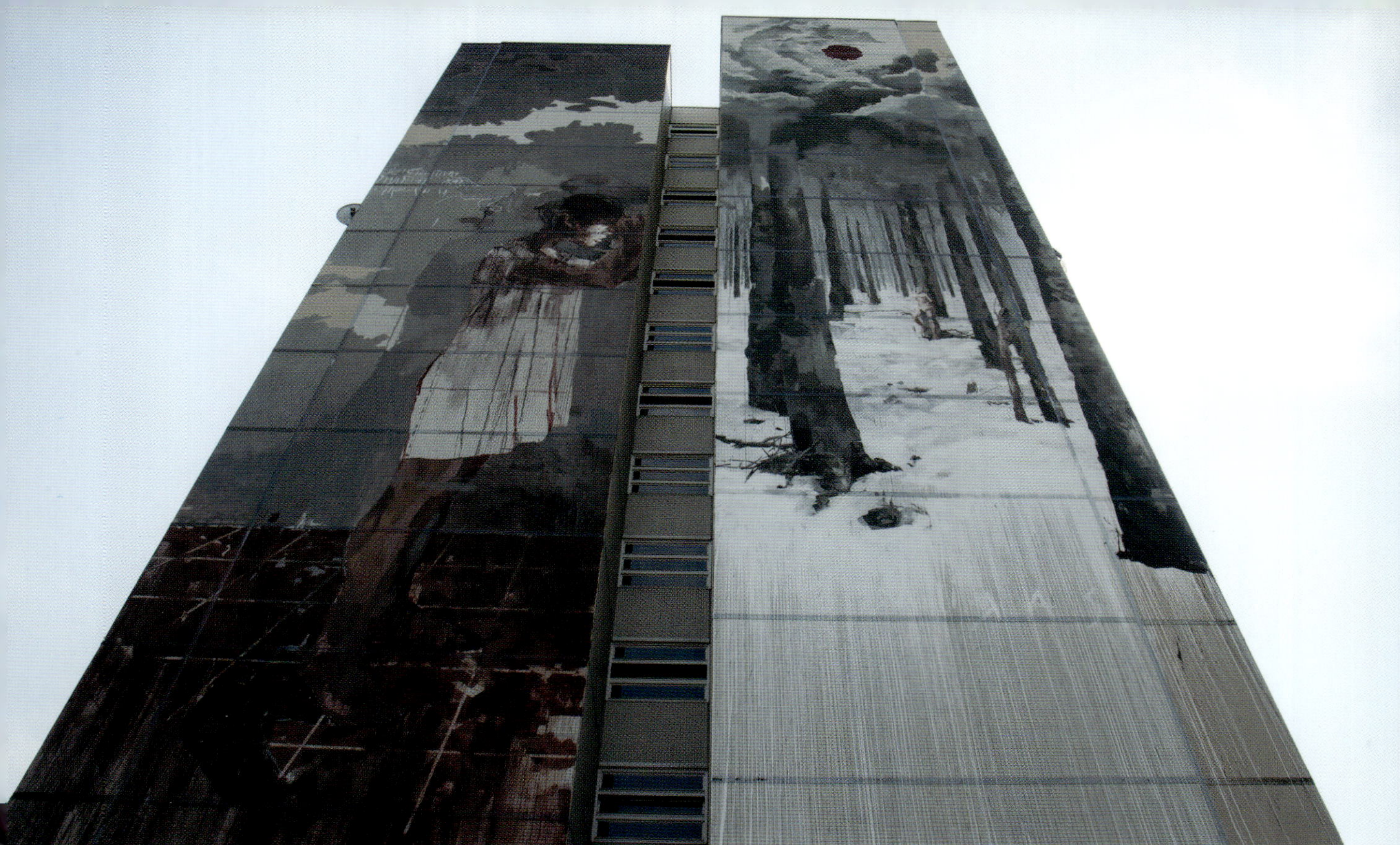

Post-modern art became a game of irony, with no longer any sense of an 'aura'. Art was part of commerce, commerce was art. Advertising guru Charles Saatchi buying up the YBAs was the epitome of this moment. It didn't even really matter who made art, and ideas of craftsmanship and representation were a laughable anachronism. But some people didn't want to get on board with that.

Lowbrow Art, Stuckists like Billy Childish and many Graffiti and Street Artists never bought into the Postmodern ideology that Art is Dead. And now Street Artists continue to use representational painting as part of a wide range of cut and paste aesthetics and techniques. Skill is still as highly valued as concept in much of the muralism seen in this book, and painting itself is still awarded a sense of aura, a touch of magic. Low-Brow and Punk influences allow for the more playful aspects of PoMo to come through - cut and paste, quotation, self-expression and a freedom to follow your individual obsessions.

This populist, urban art movement resurrects some of the psychedelic tone of late 1960's modernism, this is art after hip-hop, and hip hop includes in its sources funkadelic roots, and a tradition of psychedelic drug use. With or without the aid of narcotics, many of these mural artists are allowing themselves flights into the psychedelic realms of unfettered visual imagination, art as an expression of joy.

And we hope that this art is something more than just another commodity. We hope that it is a moment of truth in our hyperalienated lives.

"Reality erupts within the spectacle, and the spectacle is real." - Guy Debord

In other words, rebel art really does rebel, even as it simultaneously pushes up the rent.

BUDAPEST

HUNGARY

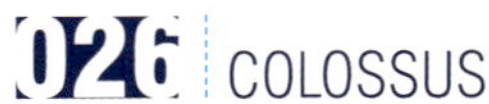

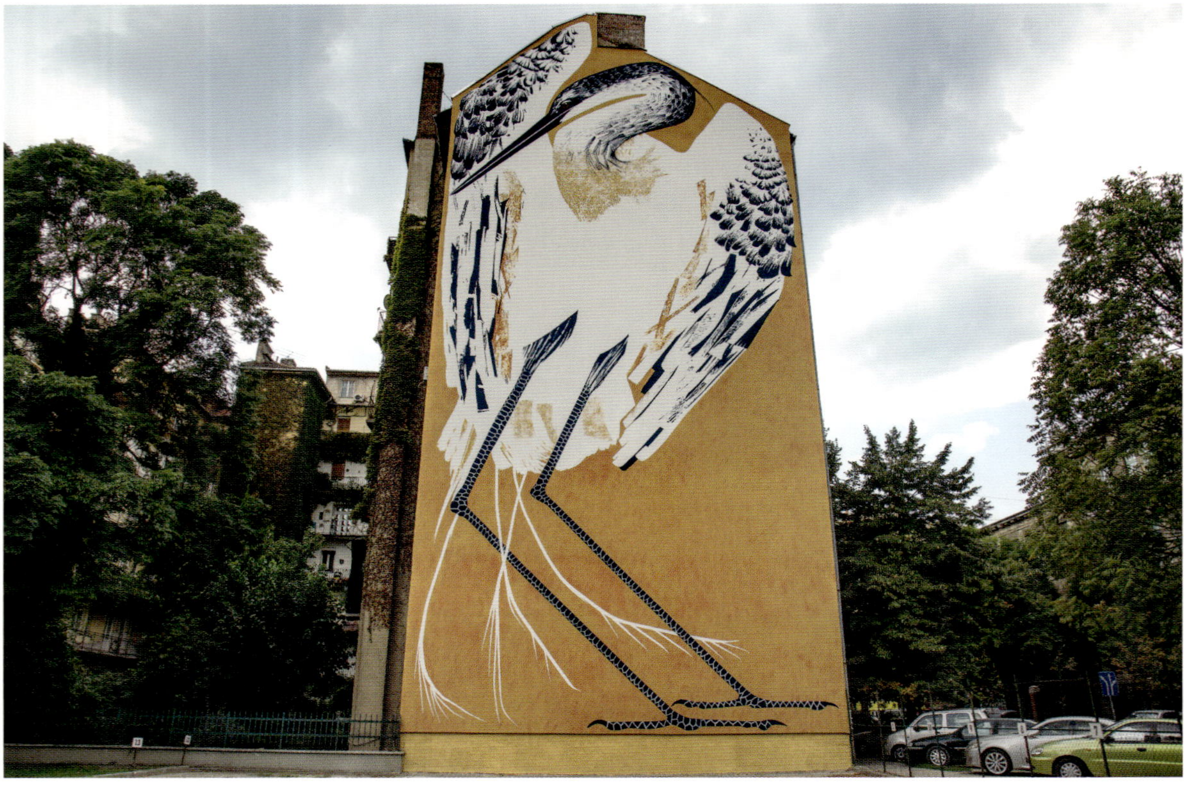

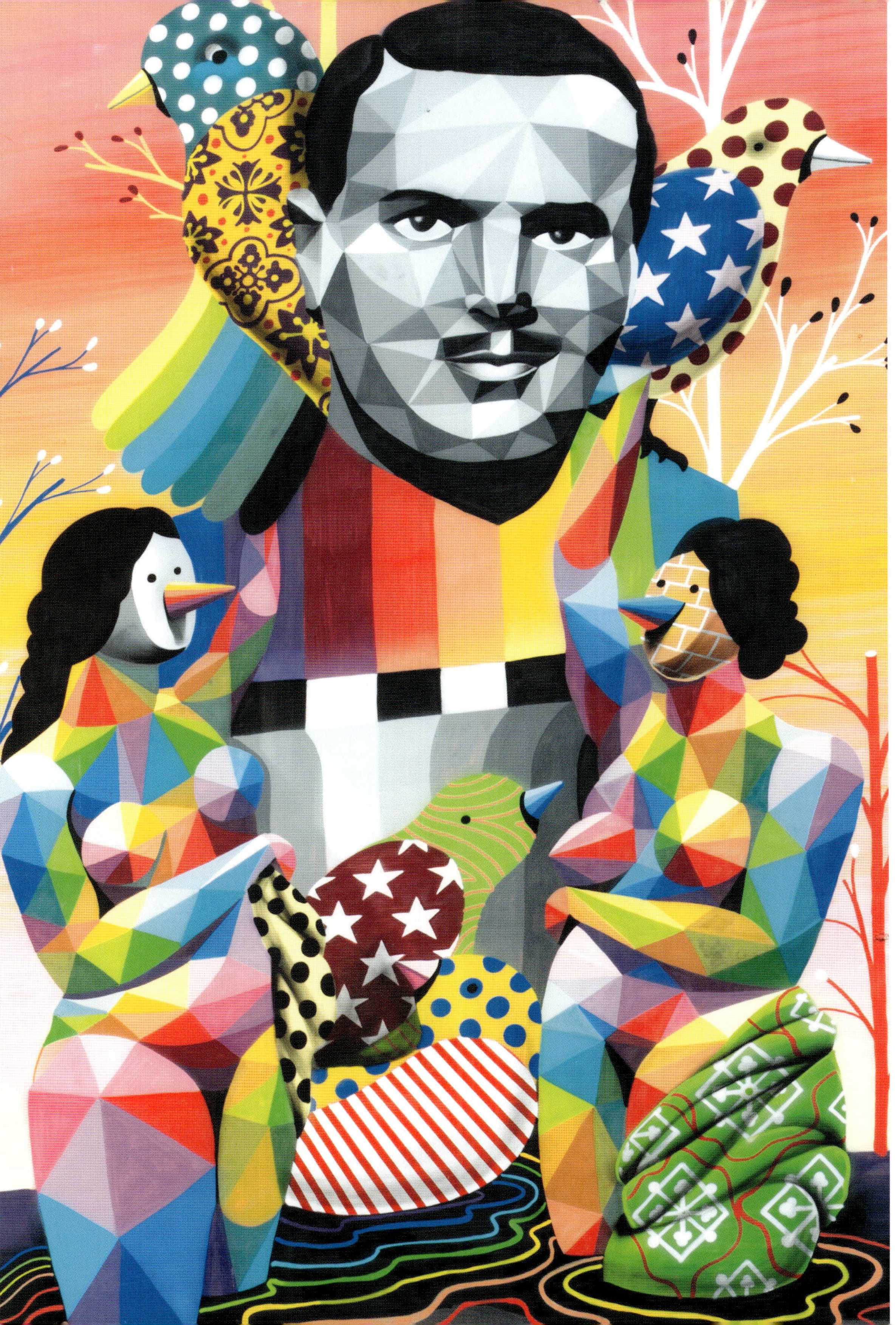

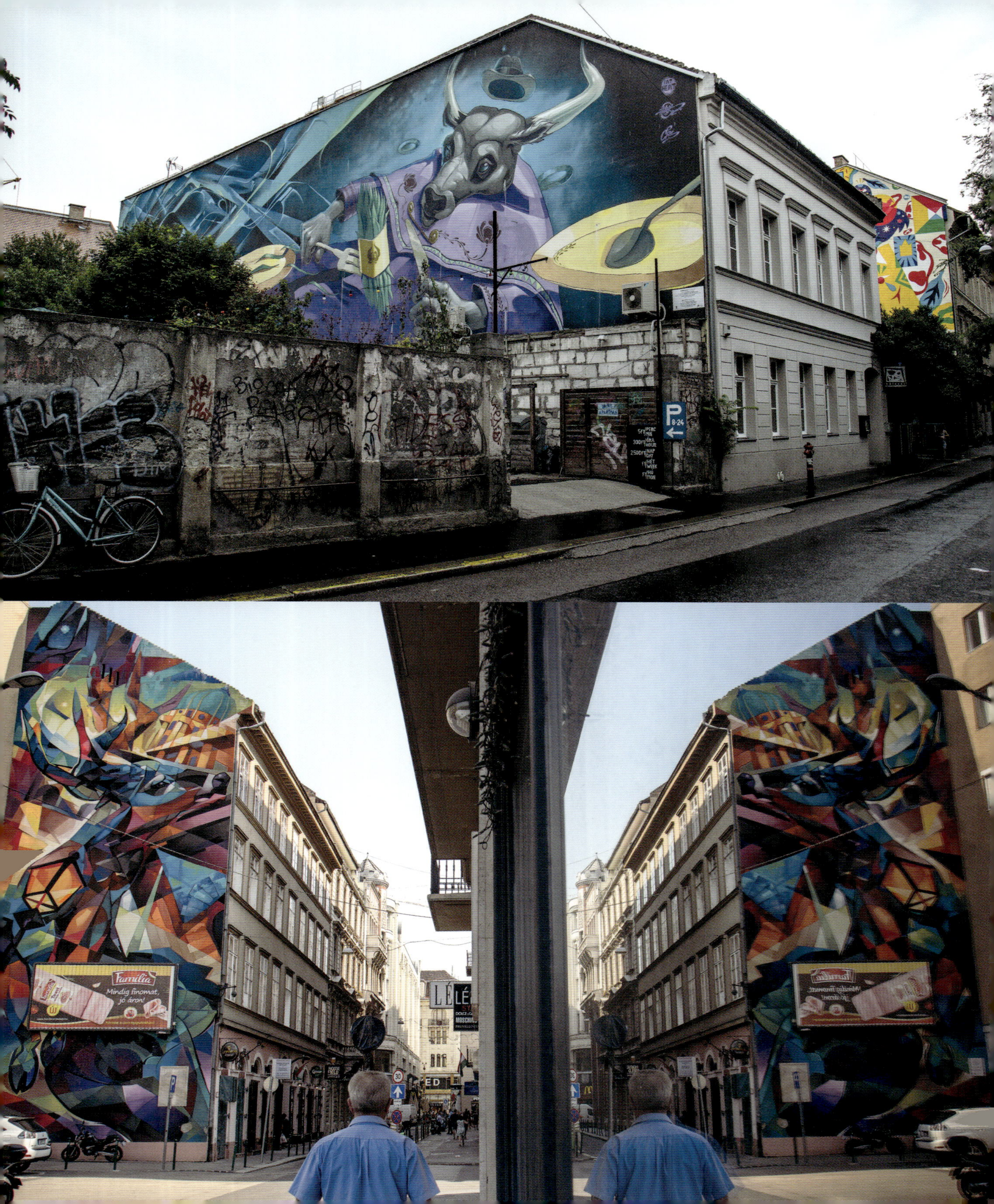

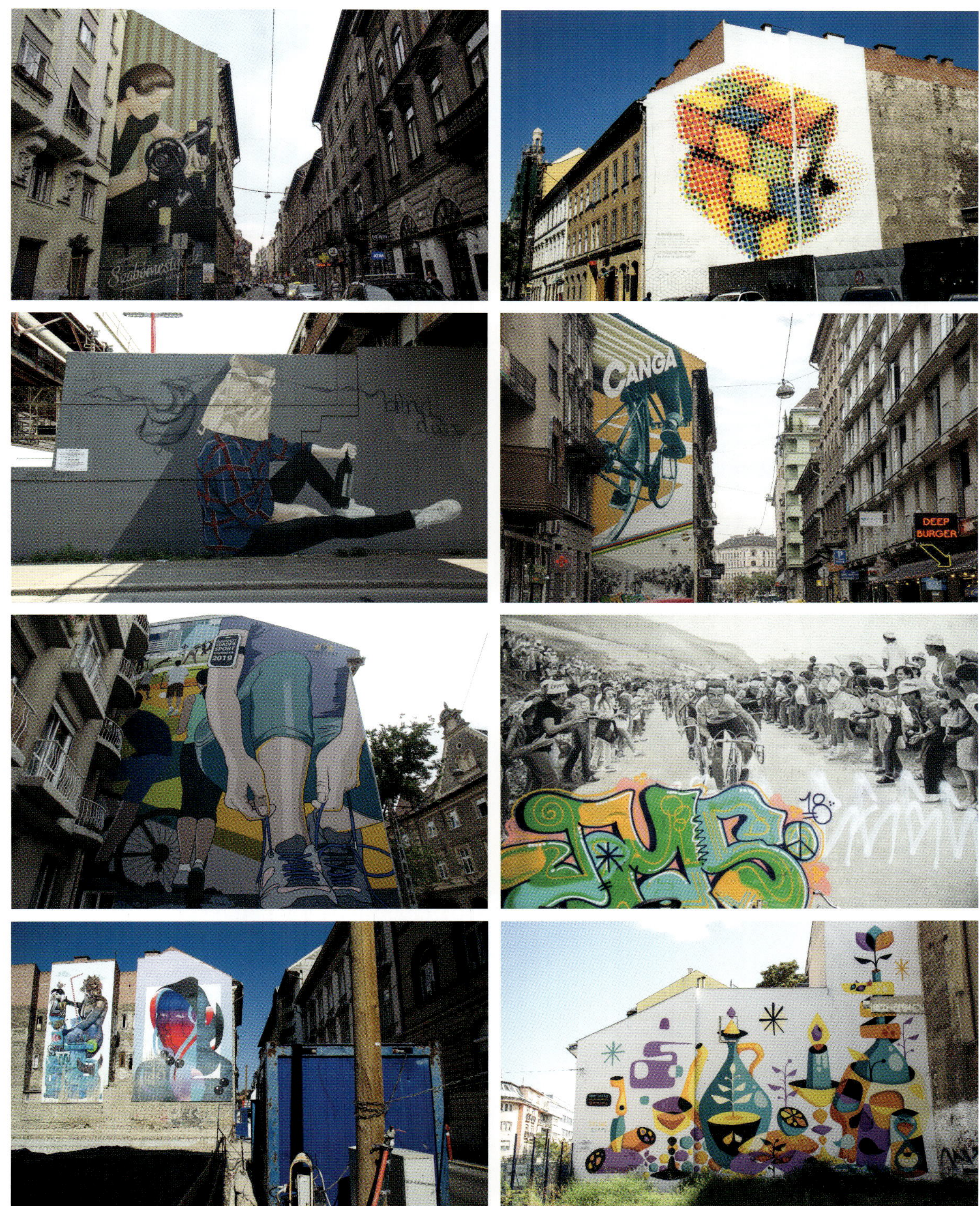

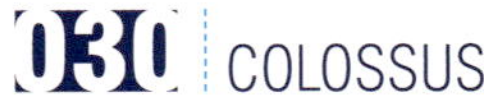

GDANSK ZASPA

POLAND

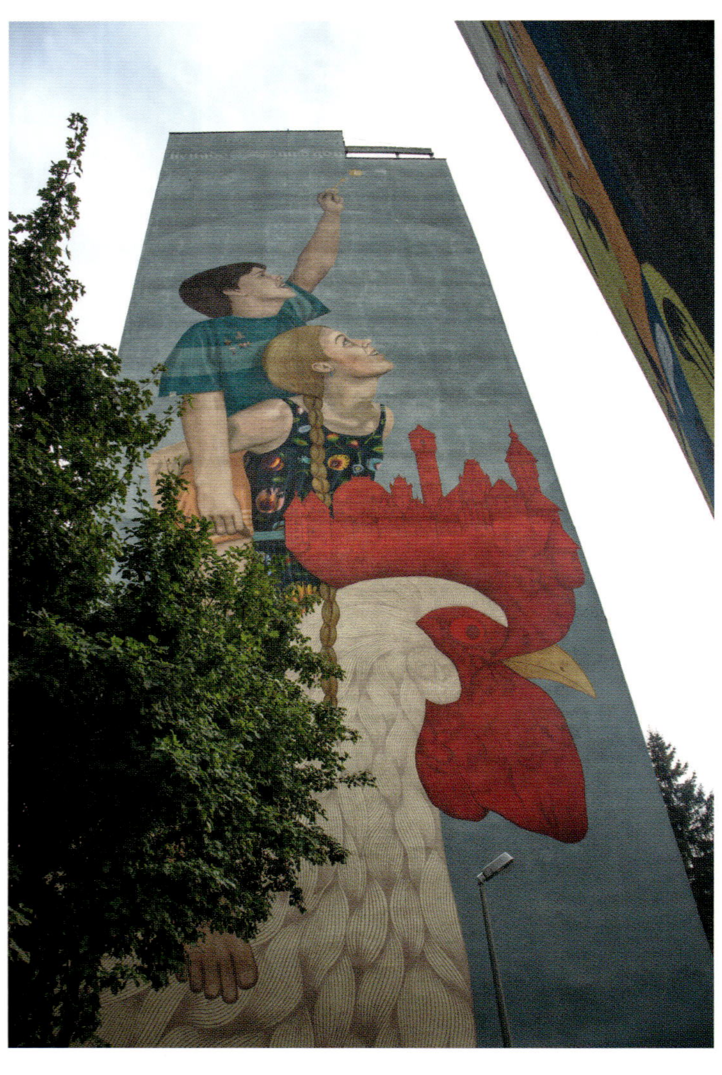

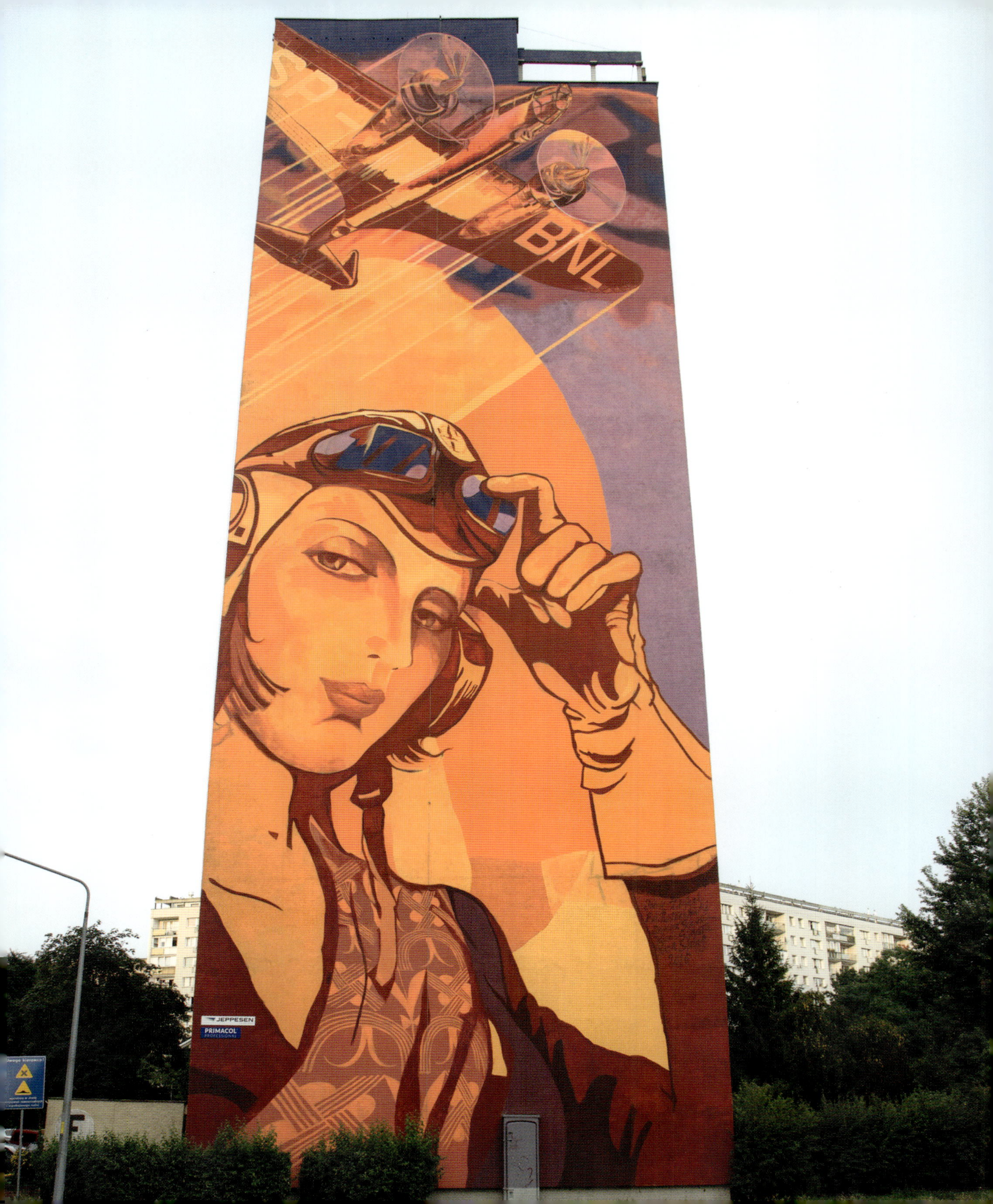
BNL
JEPPESEN
PRIMACOL
PROFESSIONAL

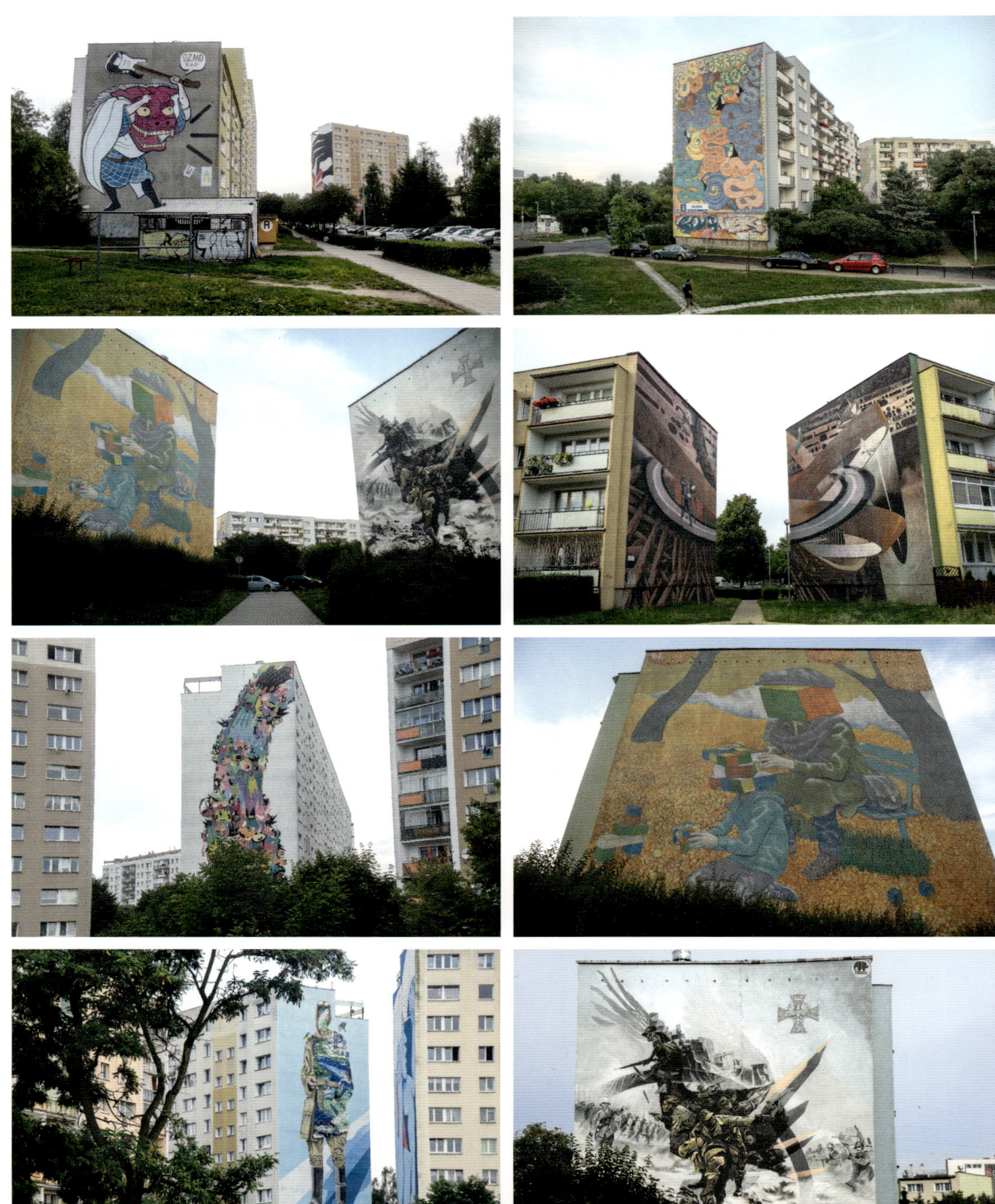

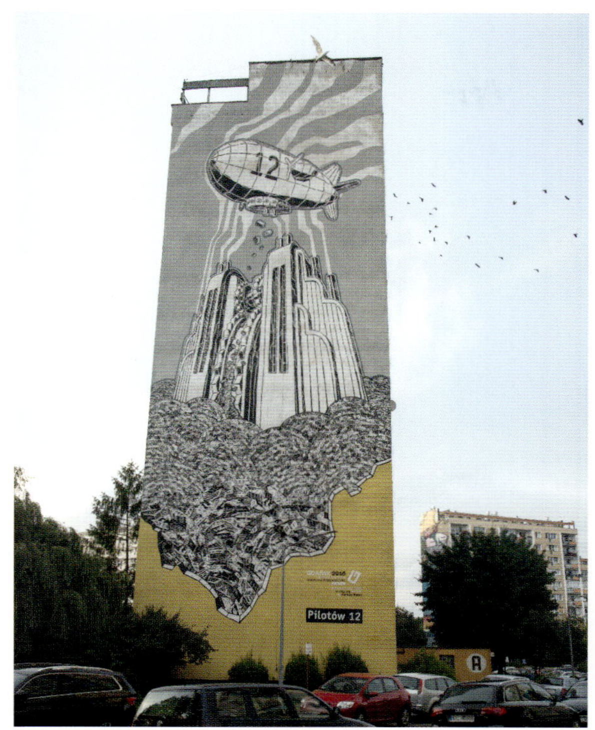
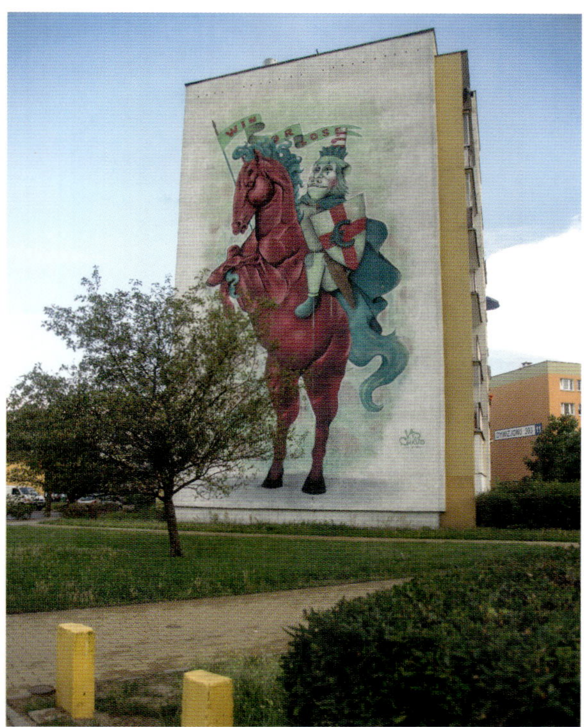
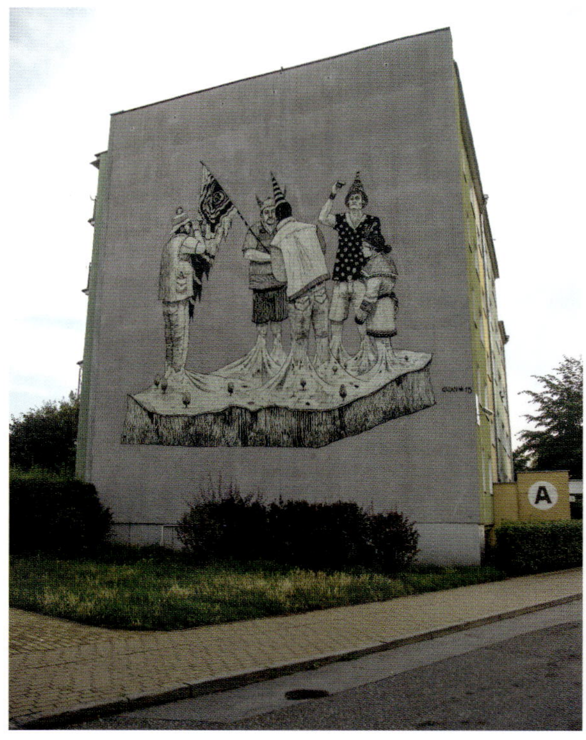
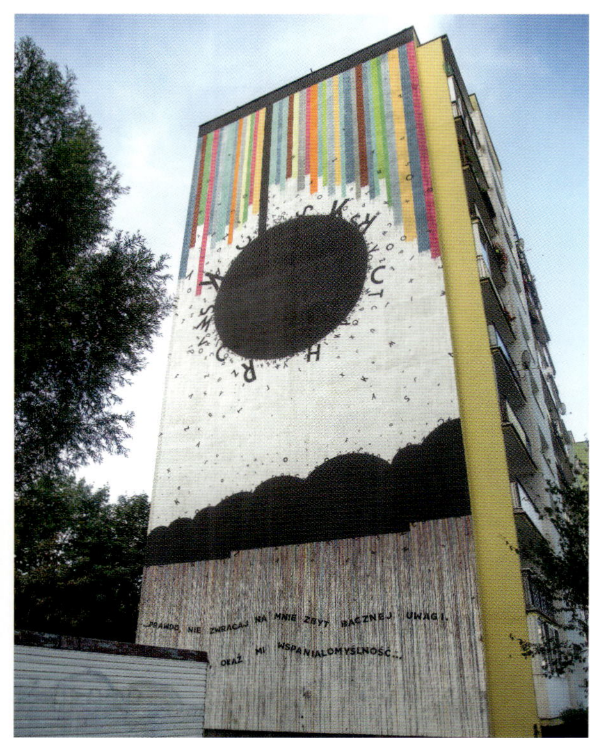

GDYNIA

POLAND

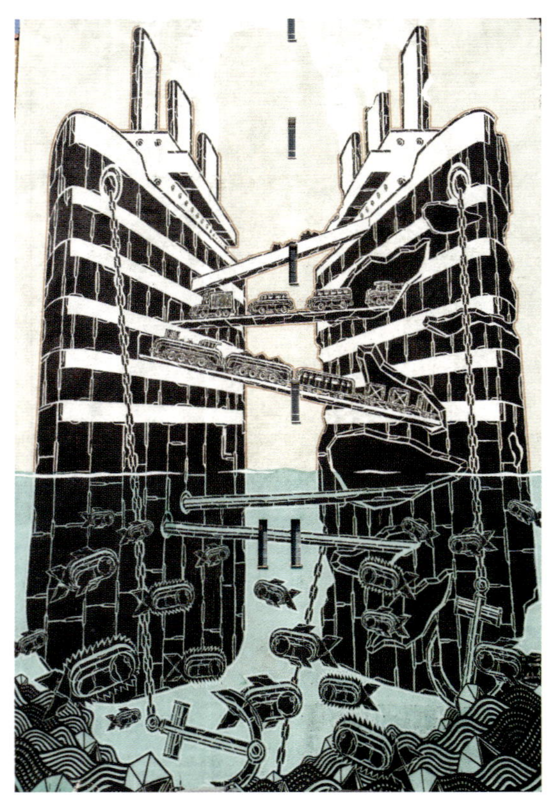

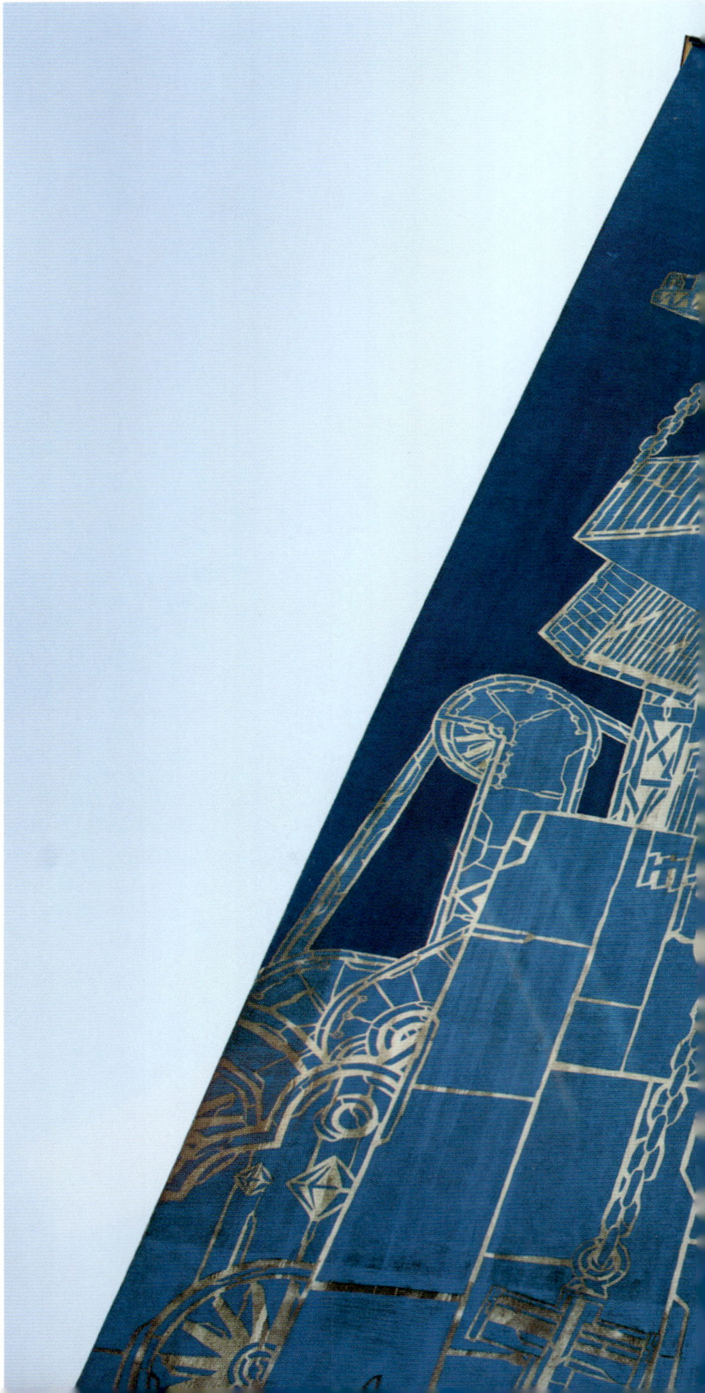

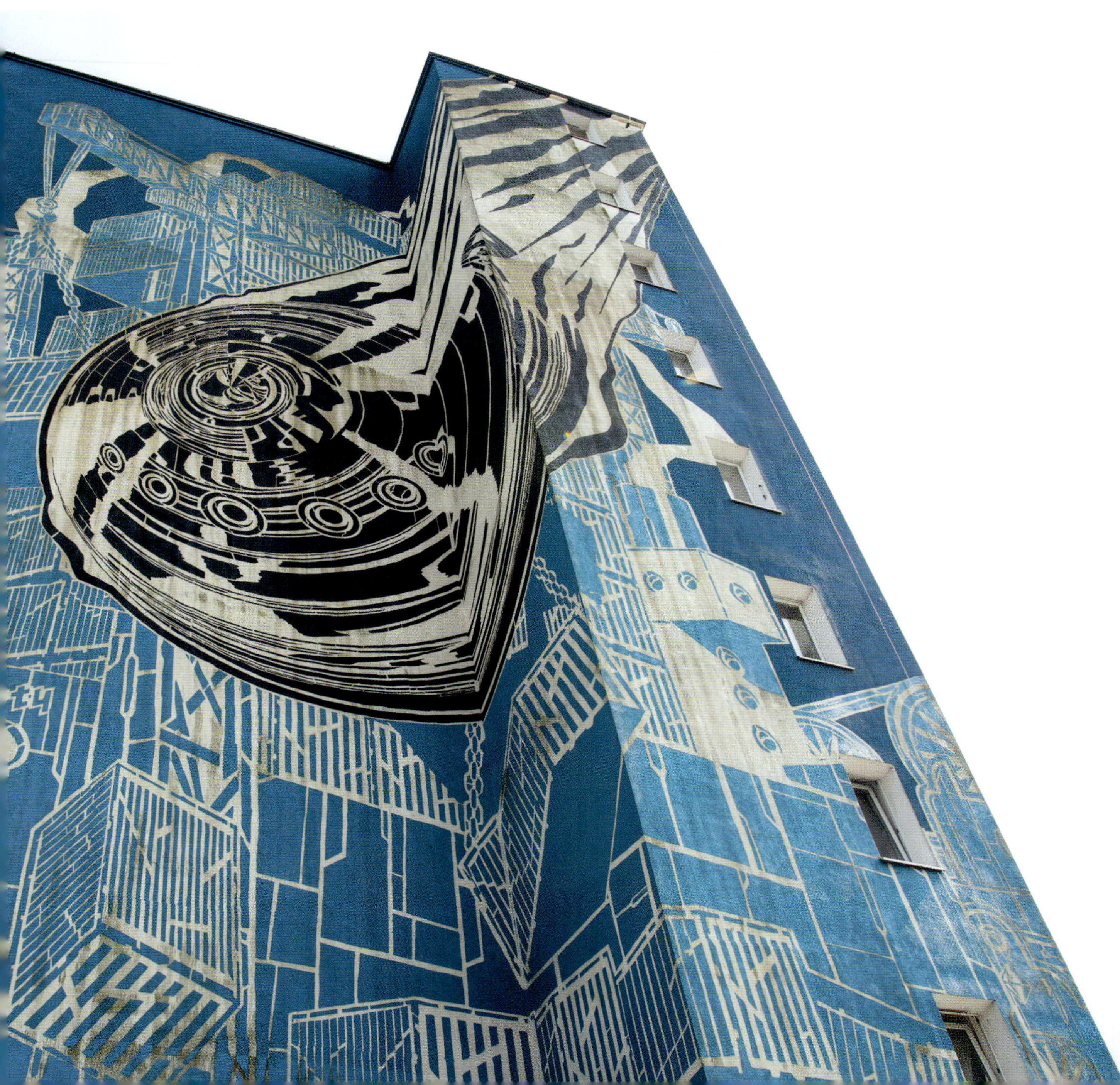

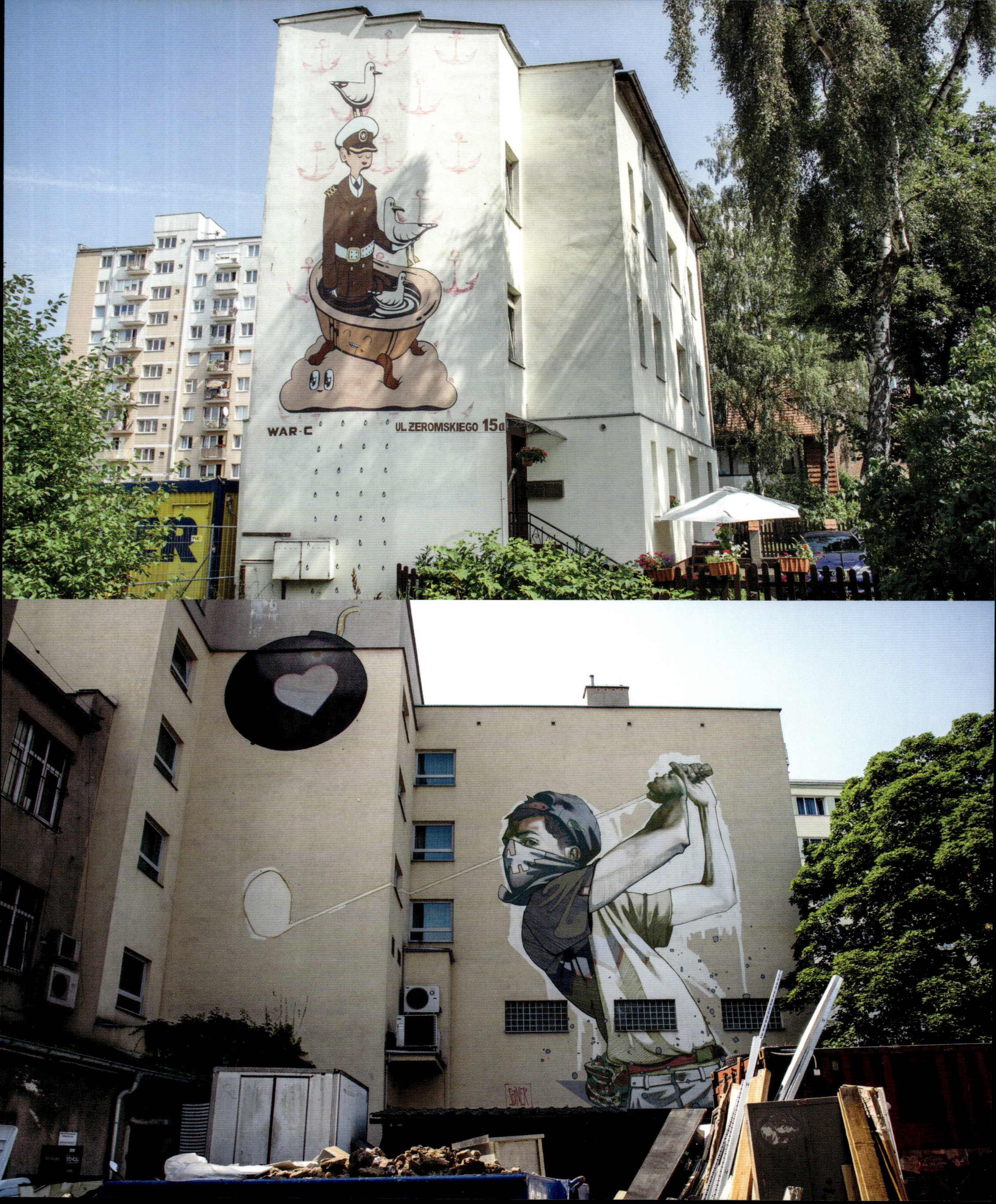

WAR-C
UL. ŻEROMSKIEGO 15a

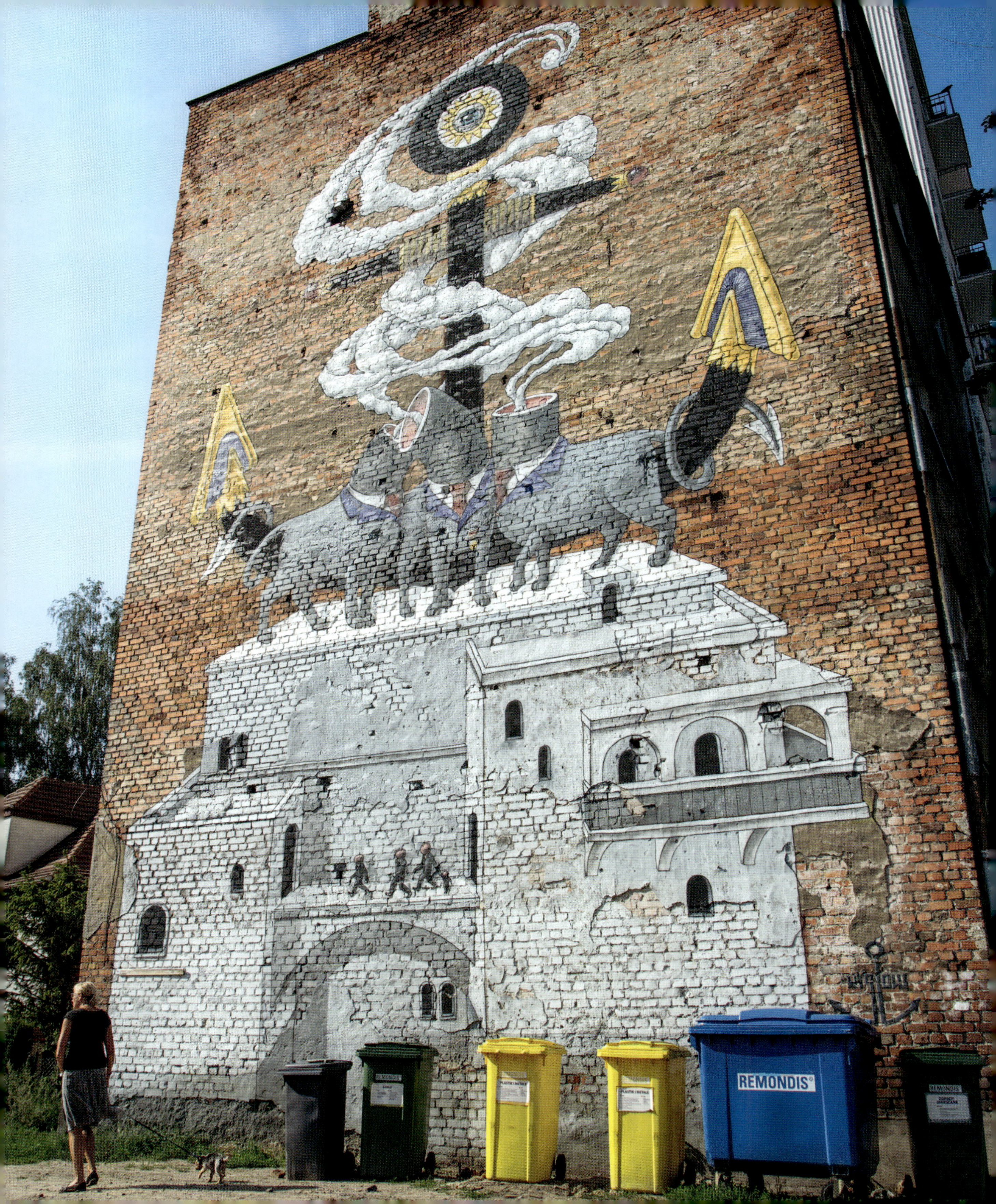

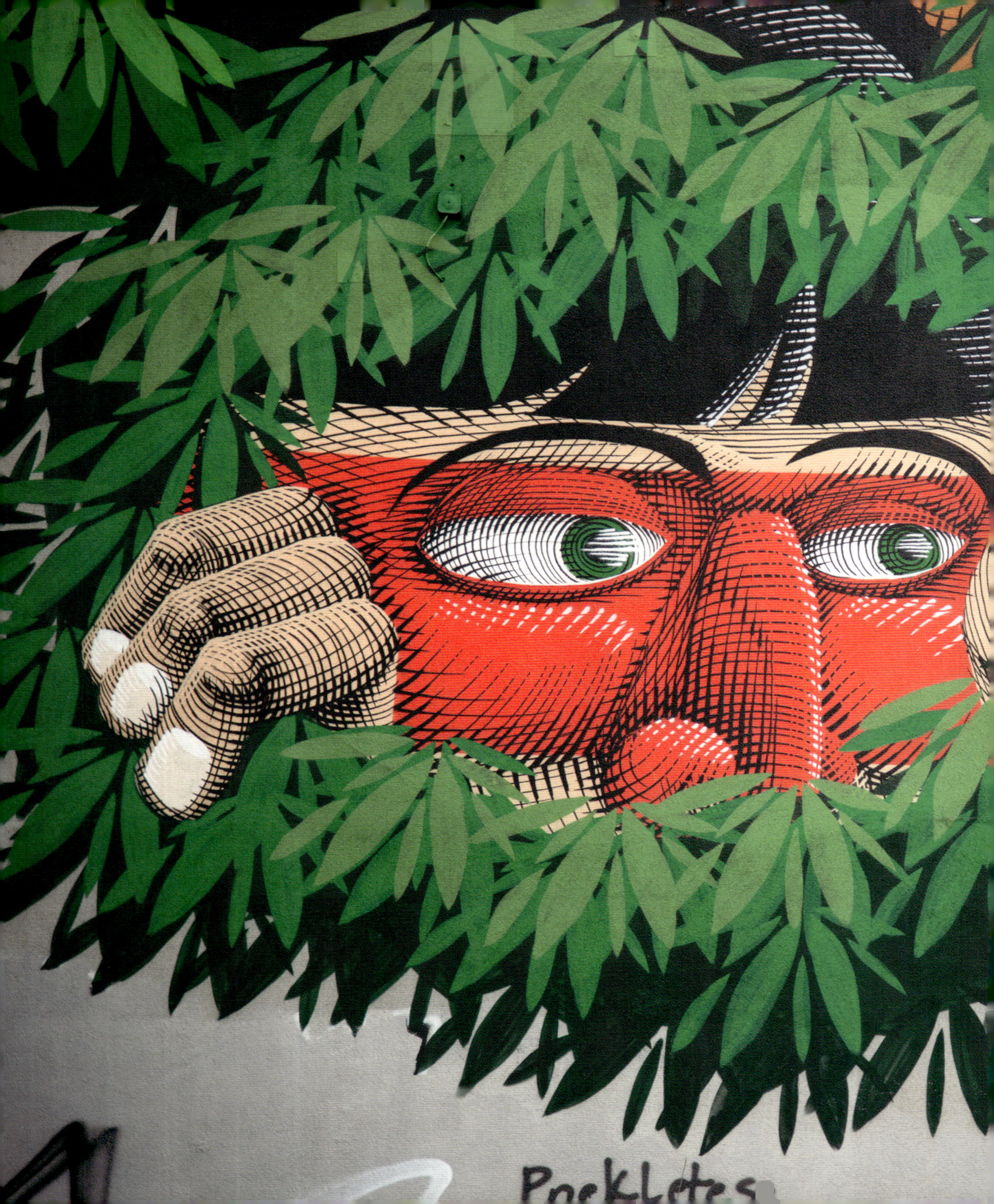

PoekLetes

Mural powstał w ramach projektu
GALERIA URBAN FORMS
autor: NUNCA (Brazylia)
2014
www.galeriaurbanforms.org

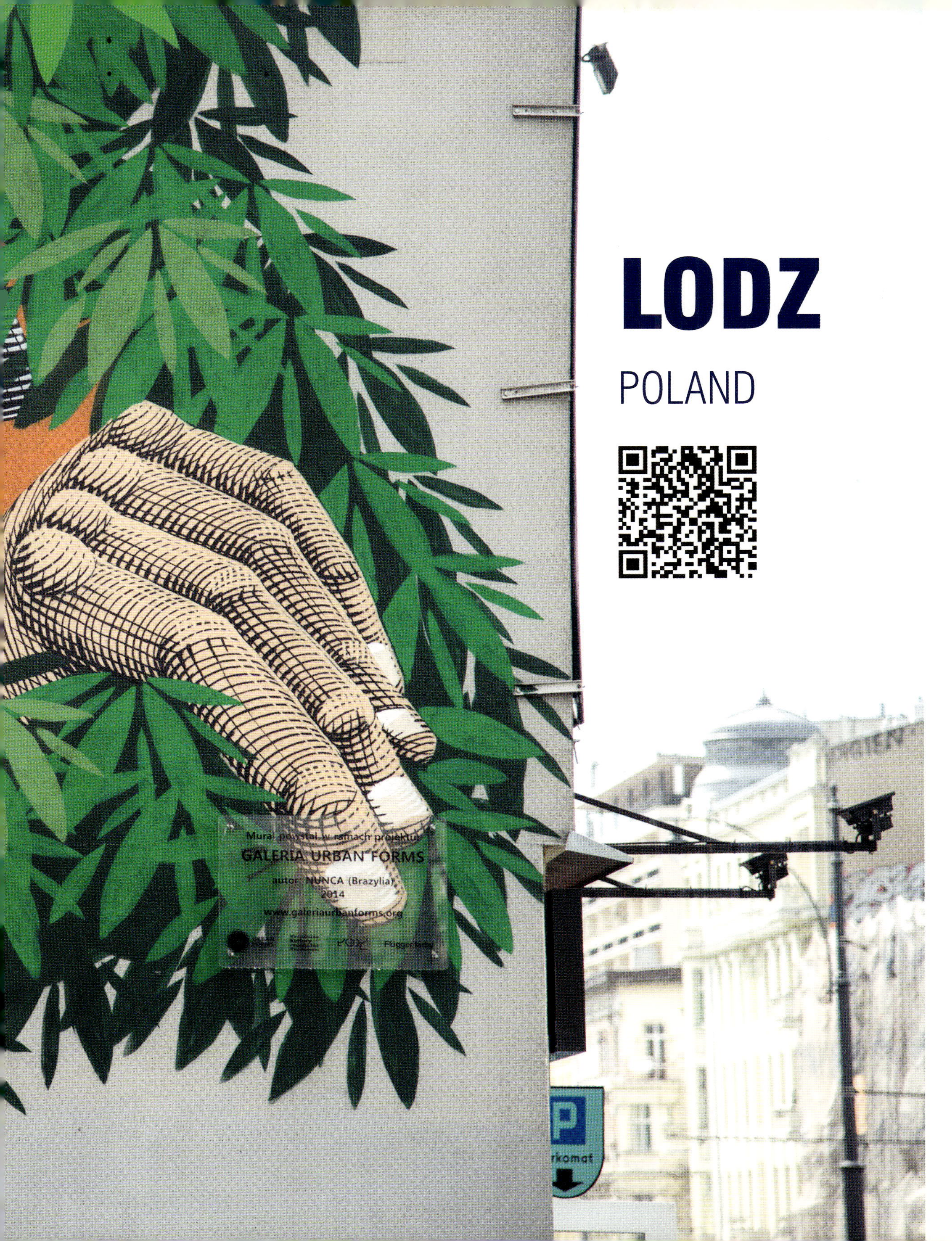

LODZ

POLAND

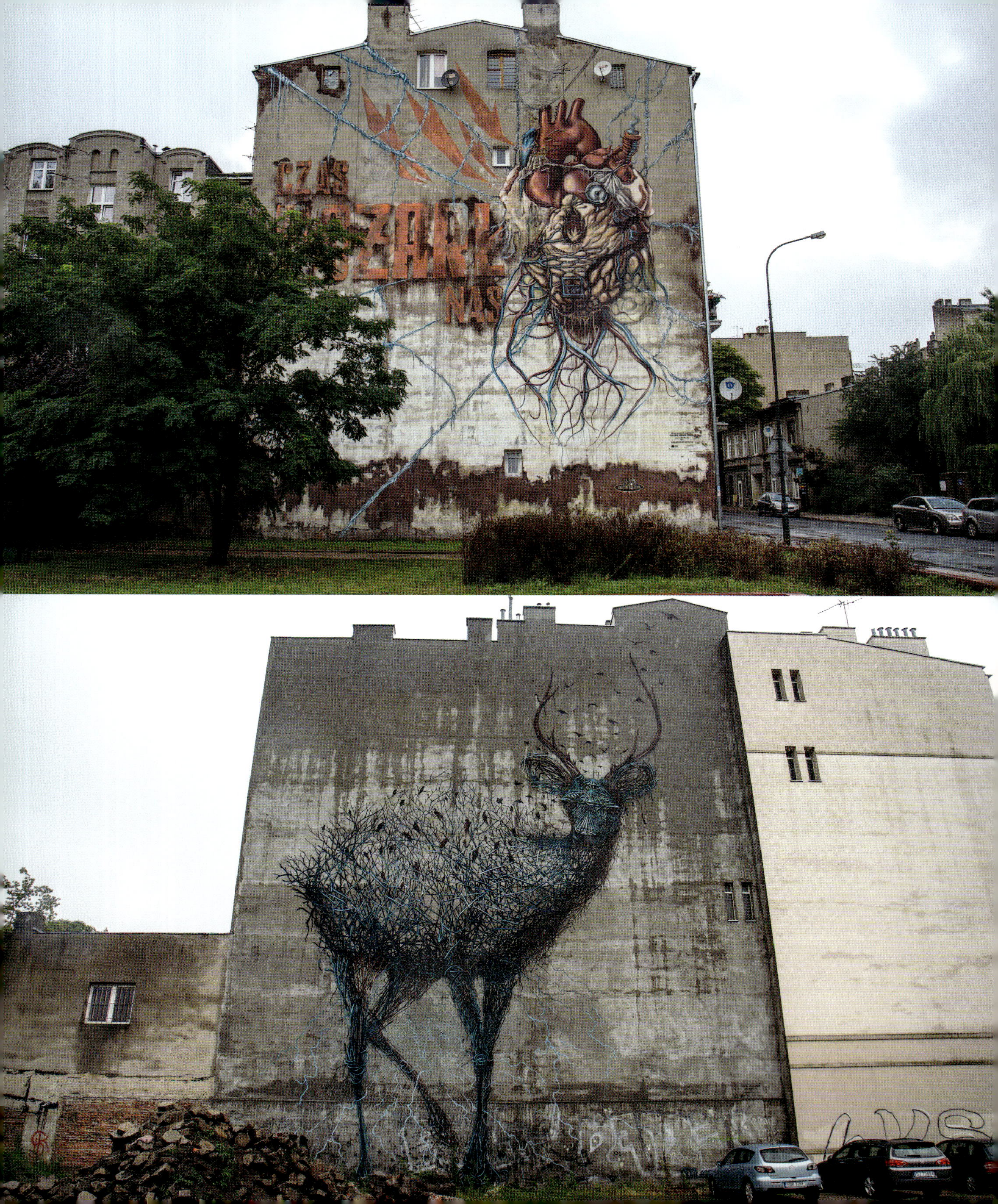
CZAS
ZARE
NAS

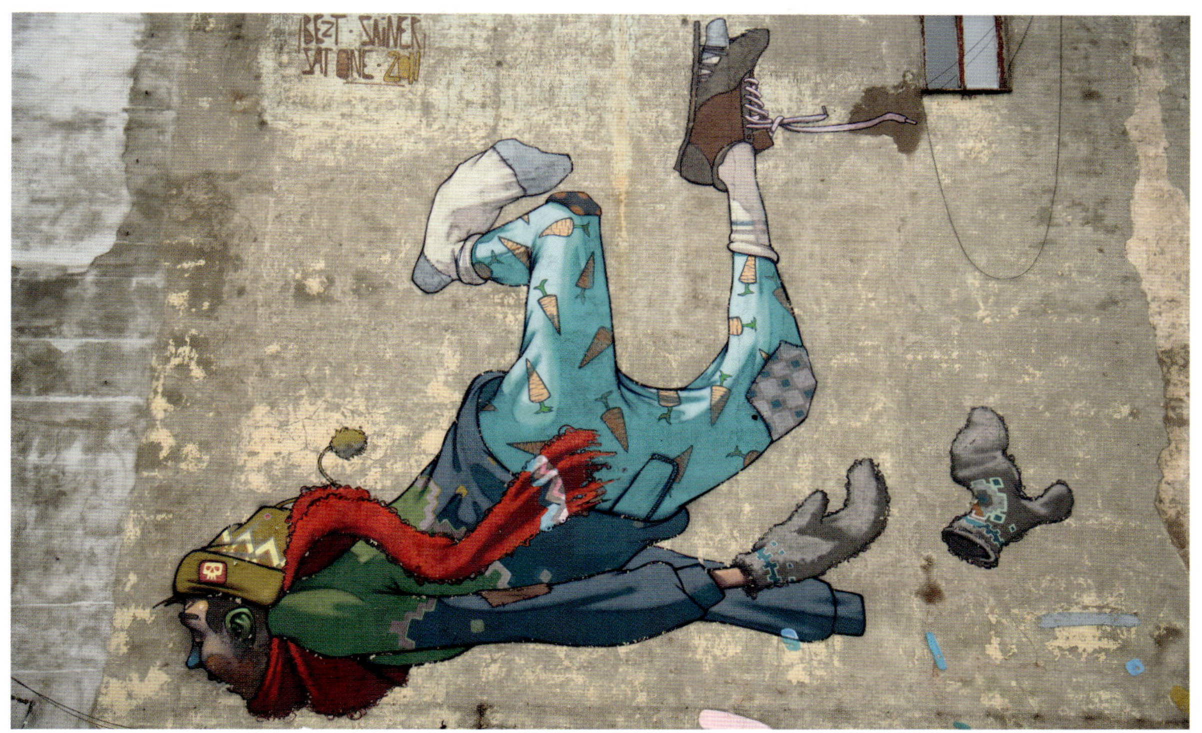

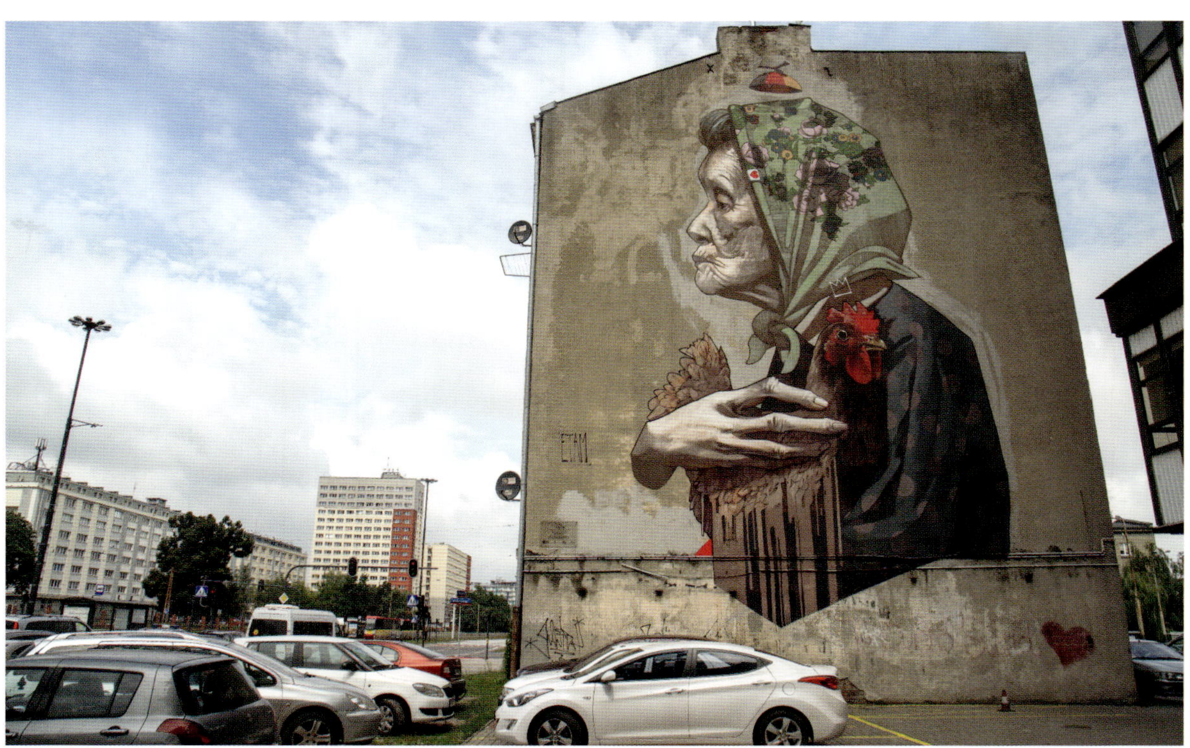

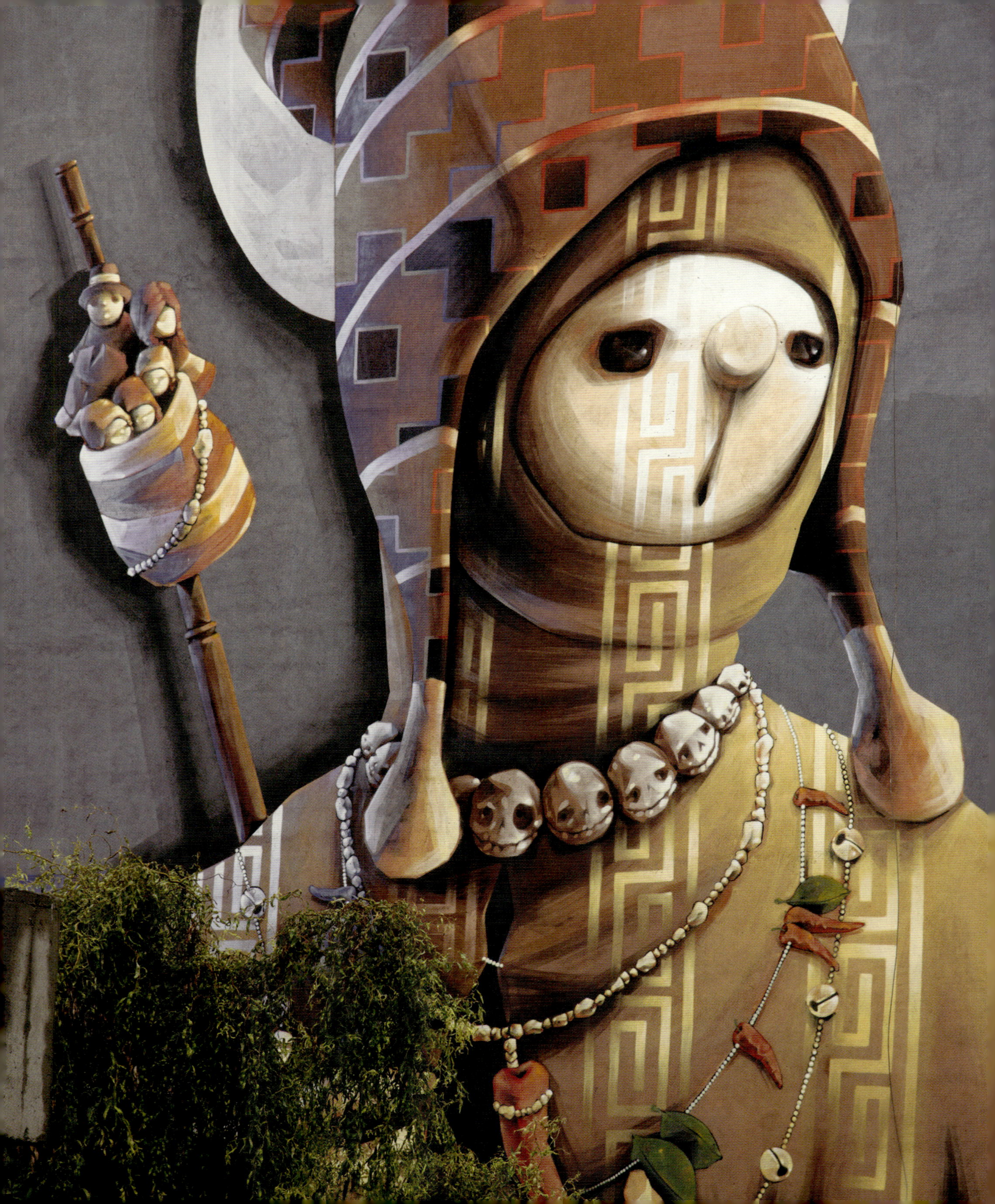

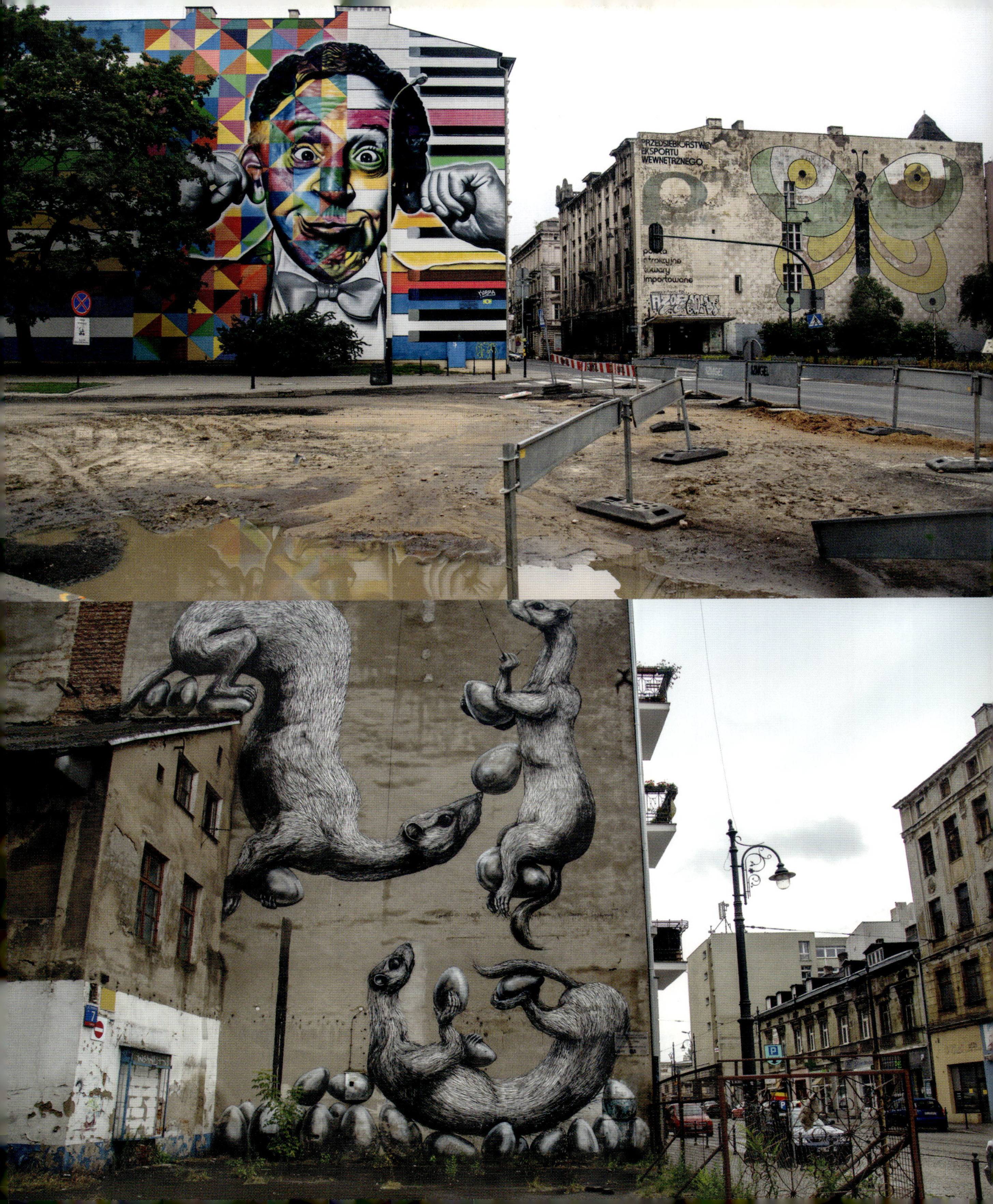

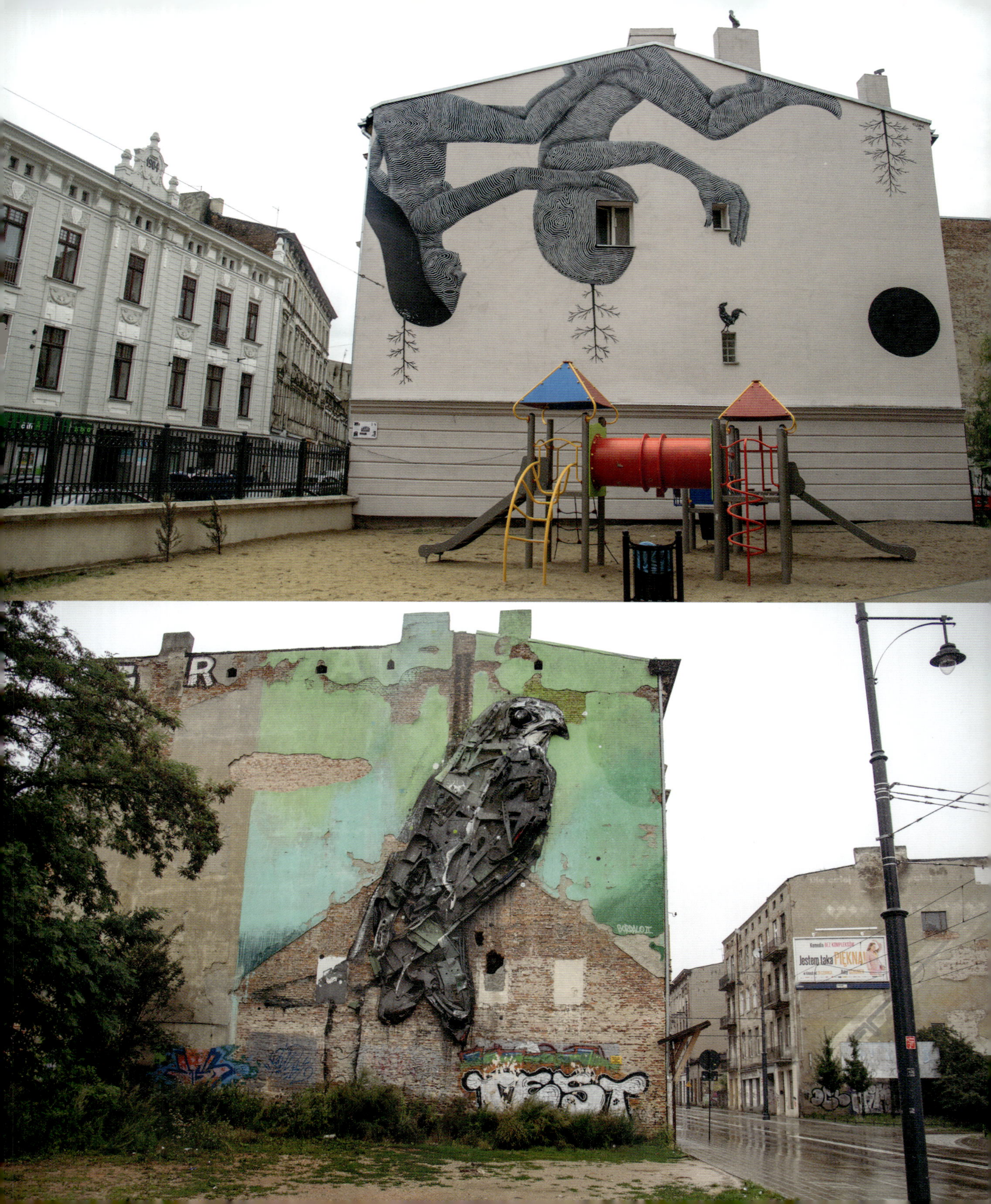

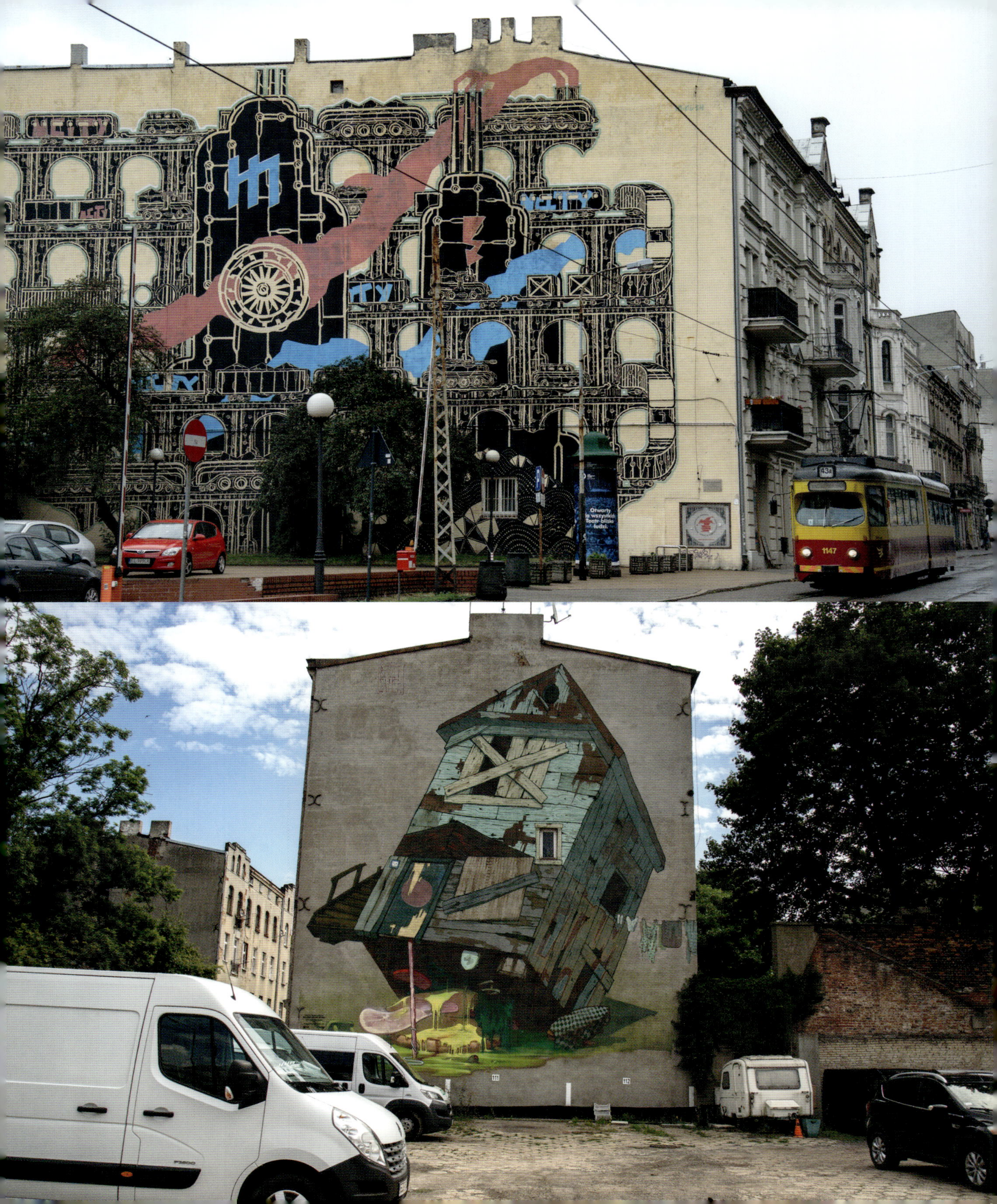

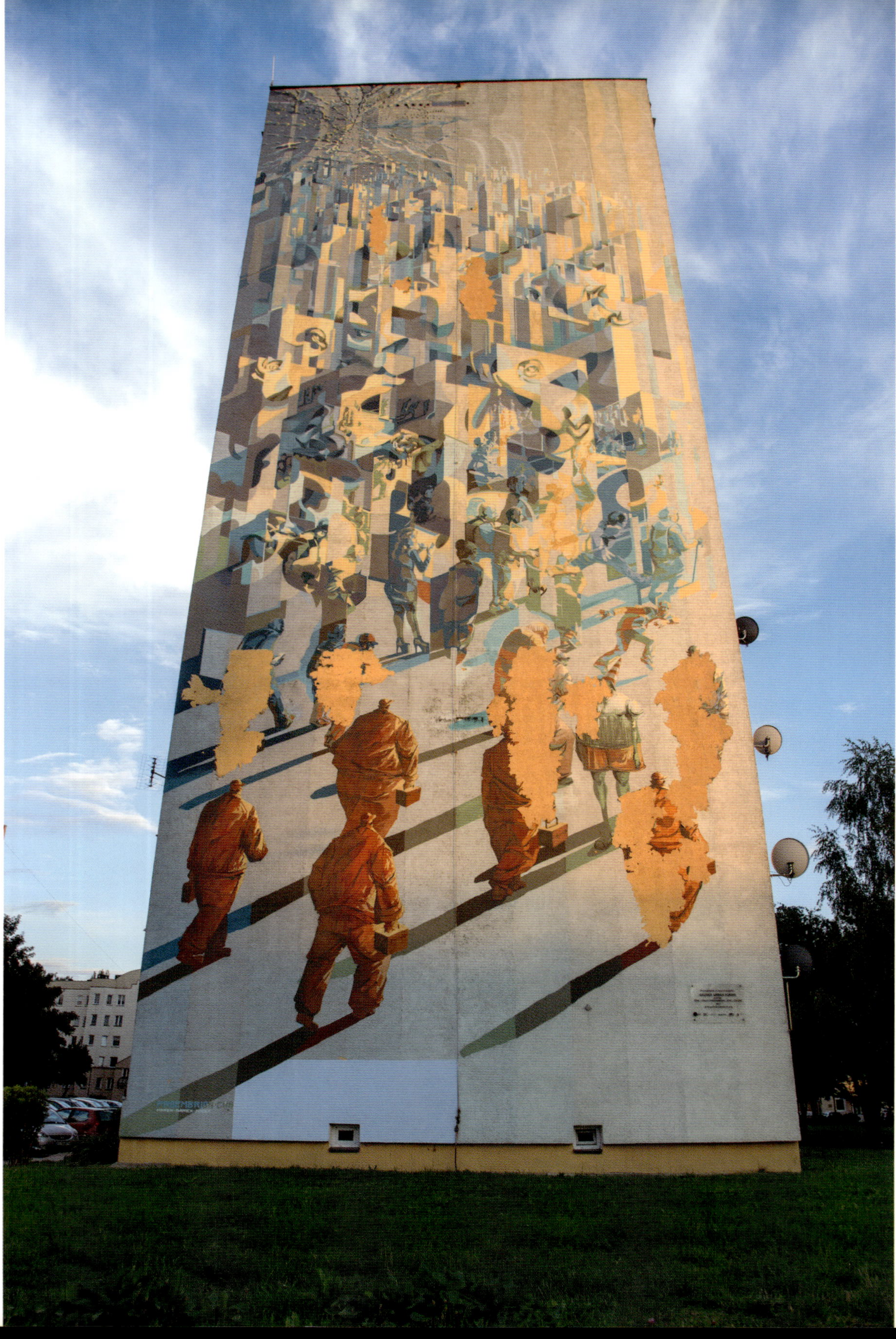

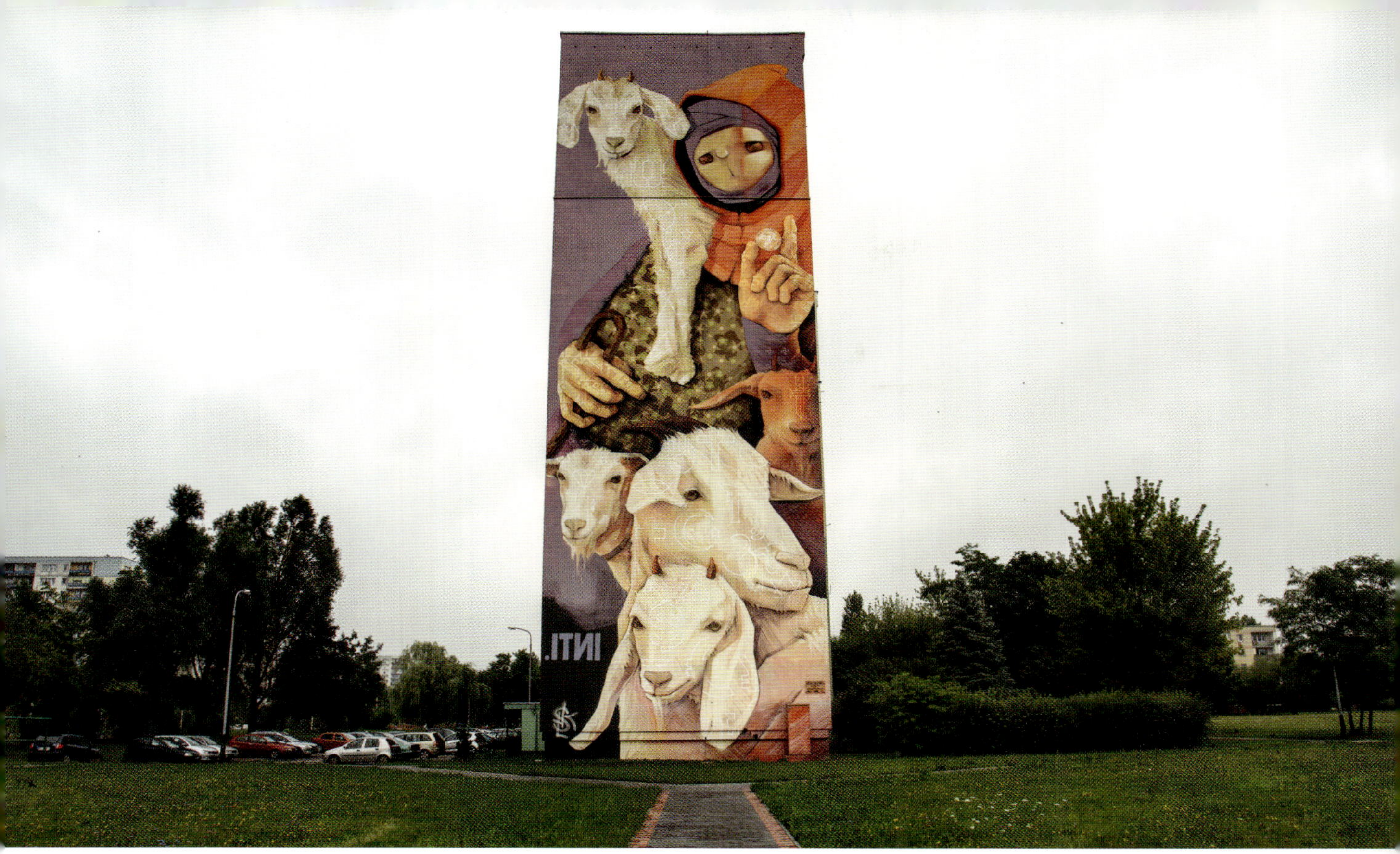

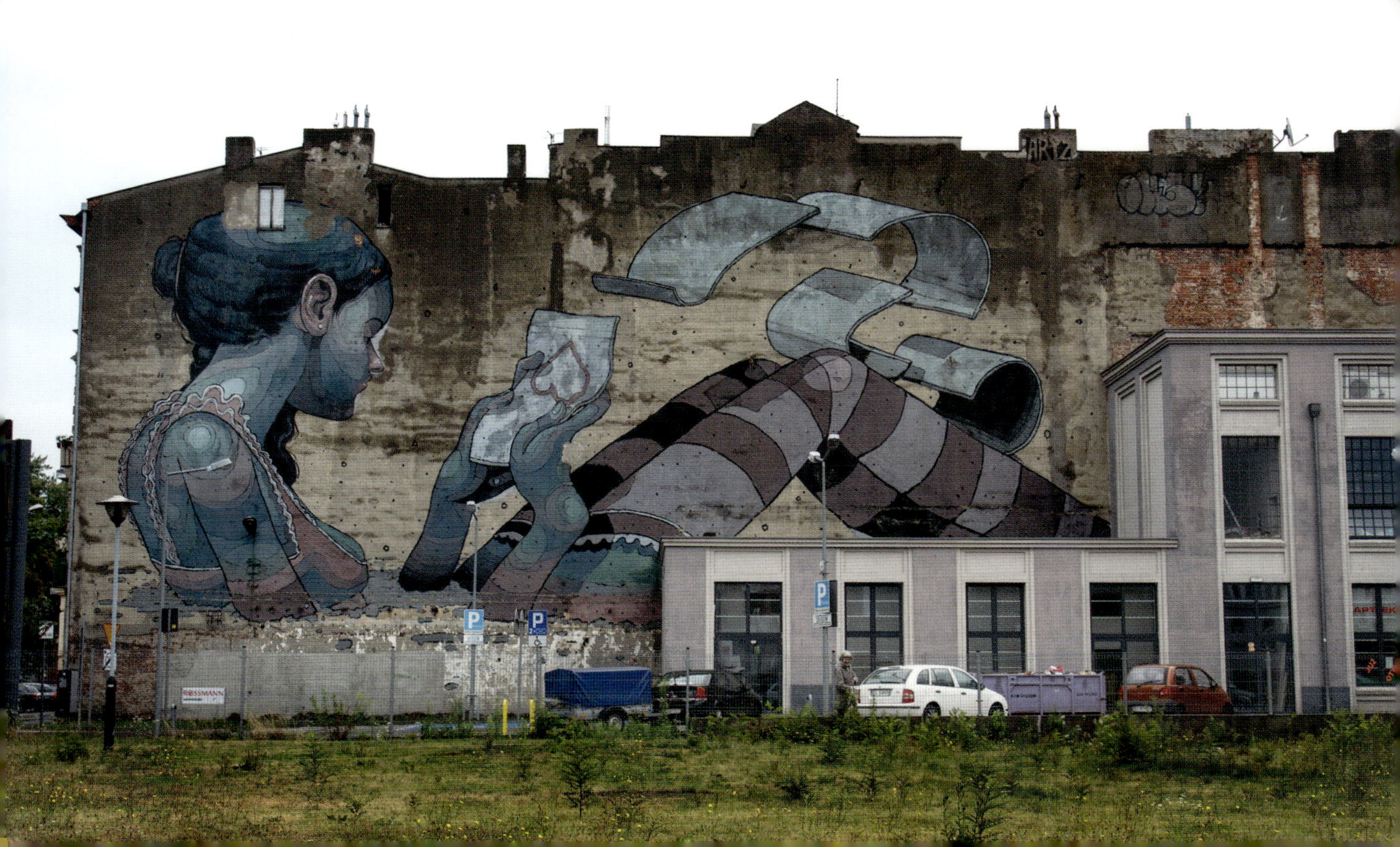

INTI.

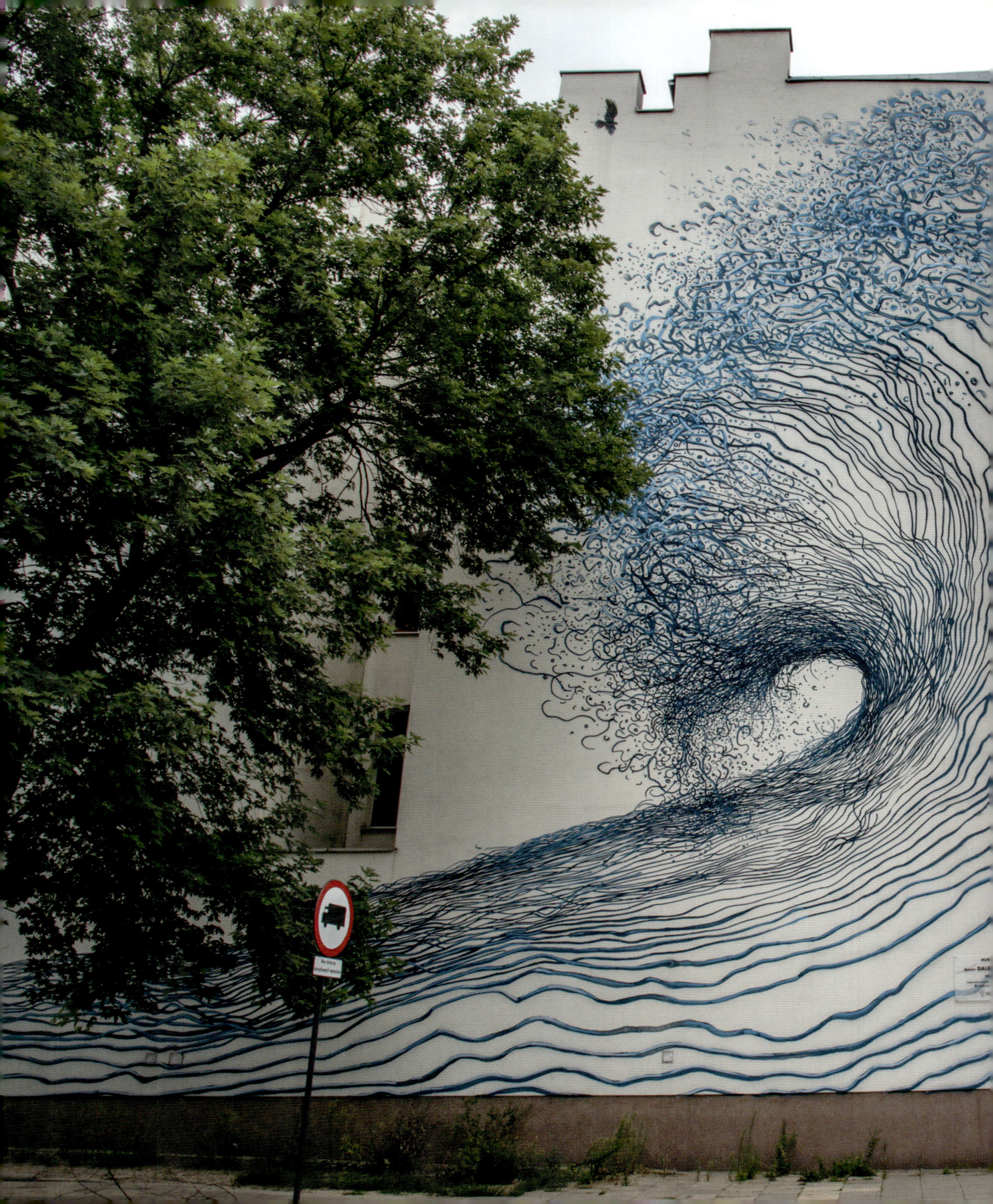

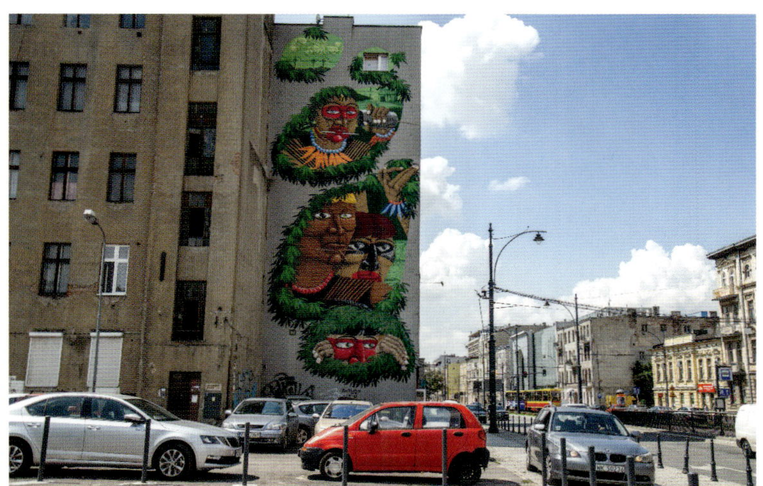

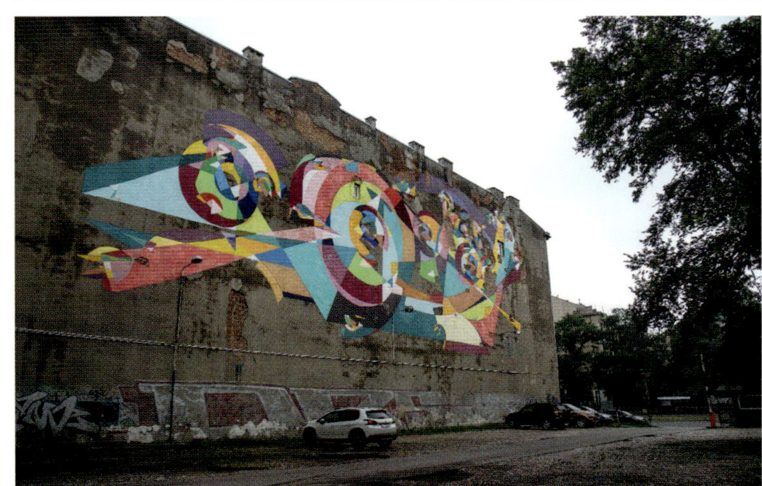

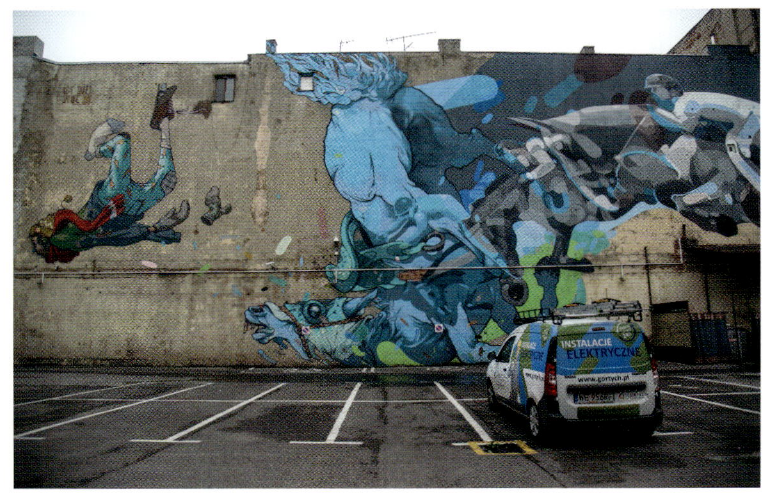

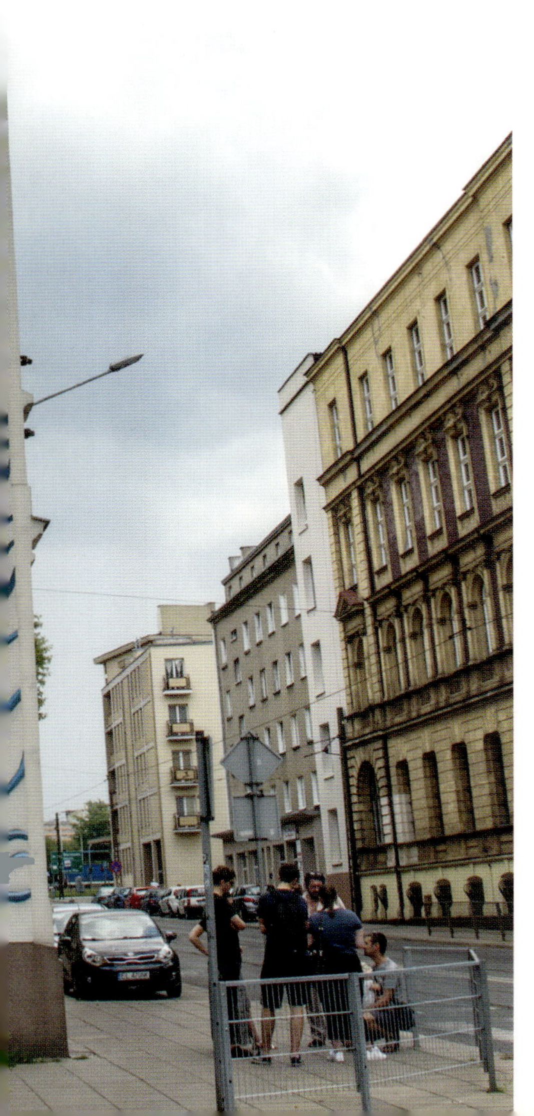

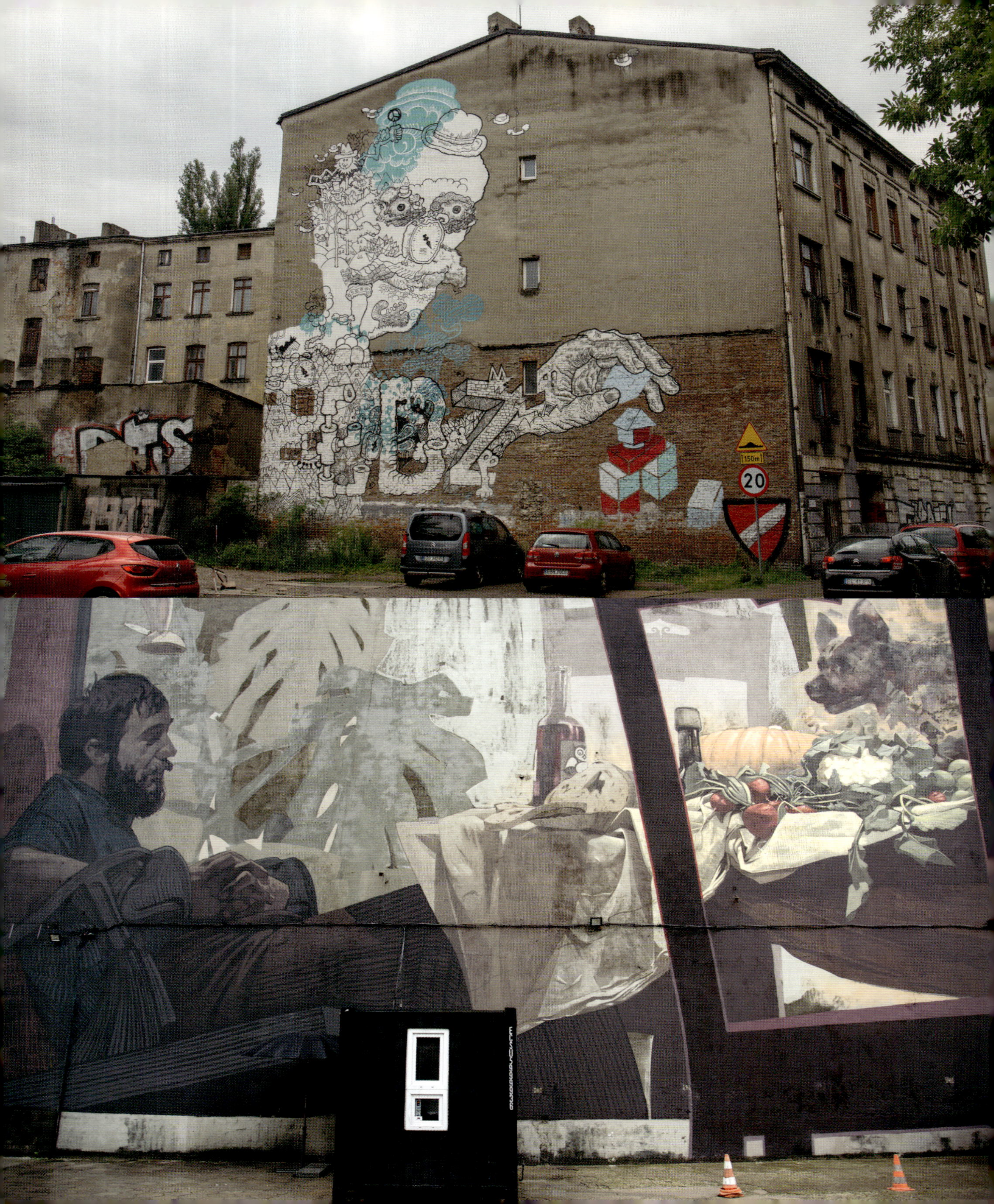

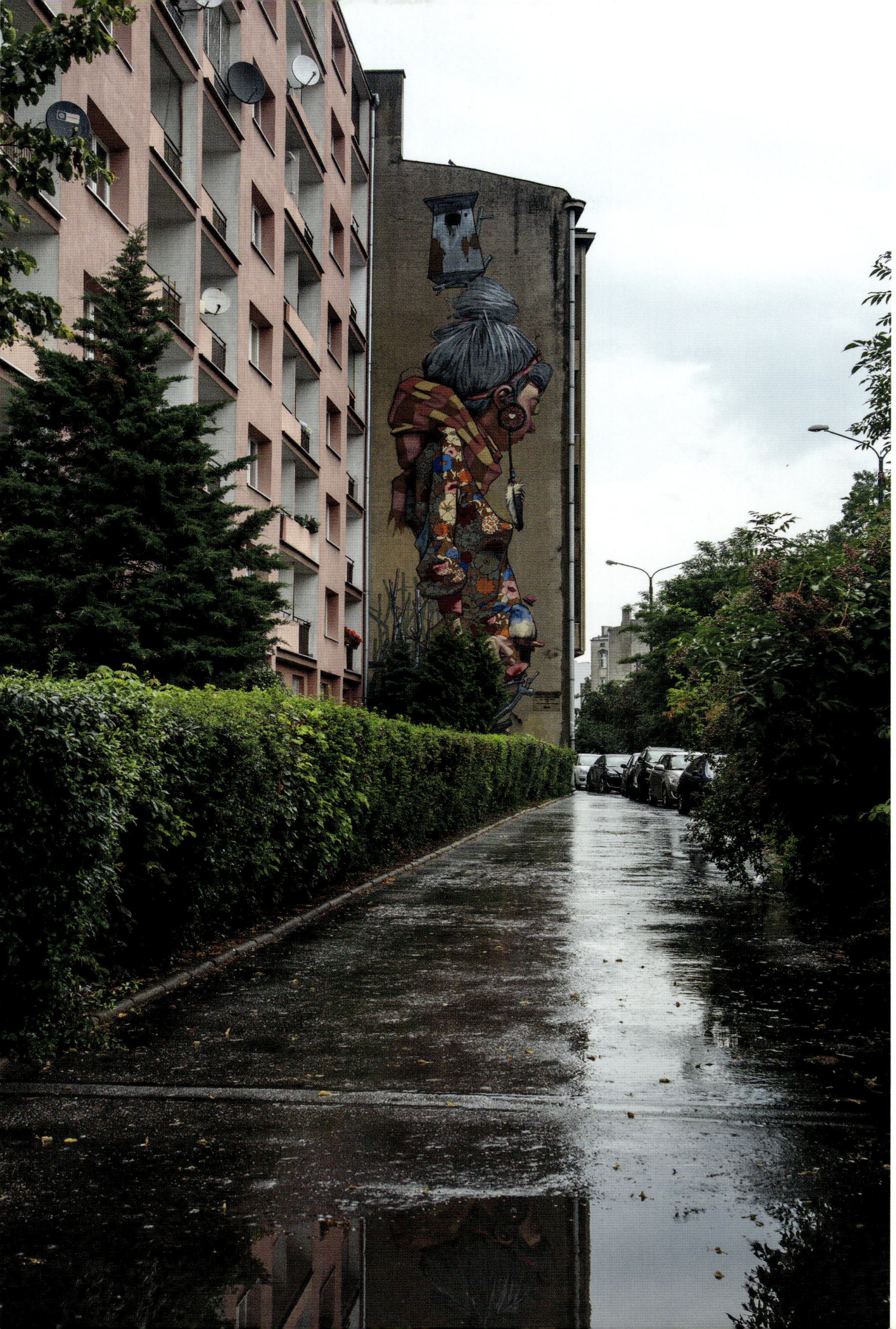

POZNAN

POLAND

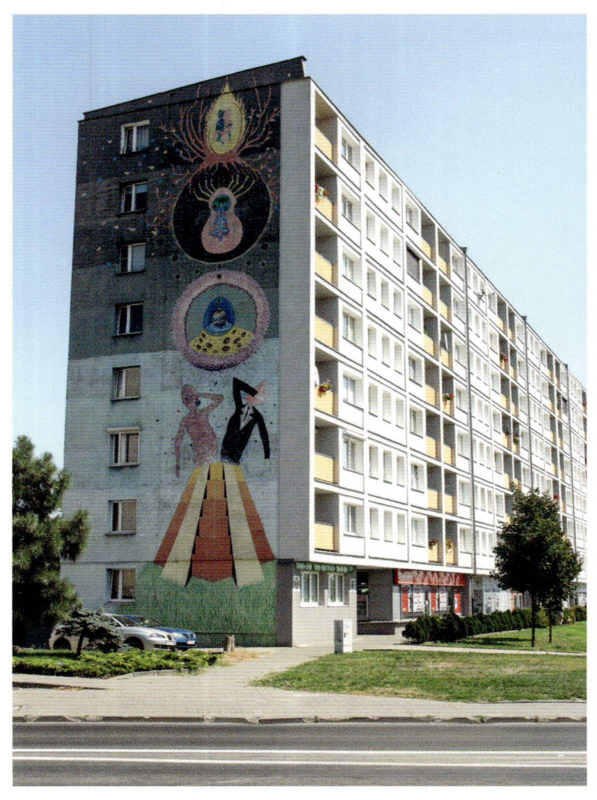

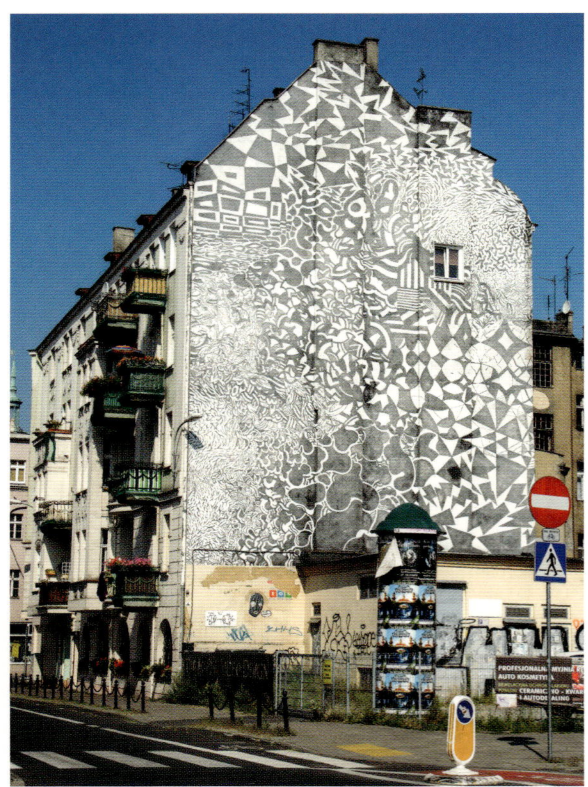

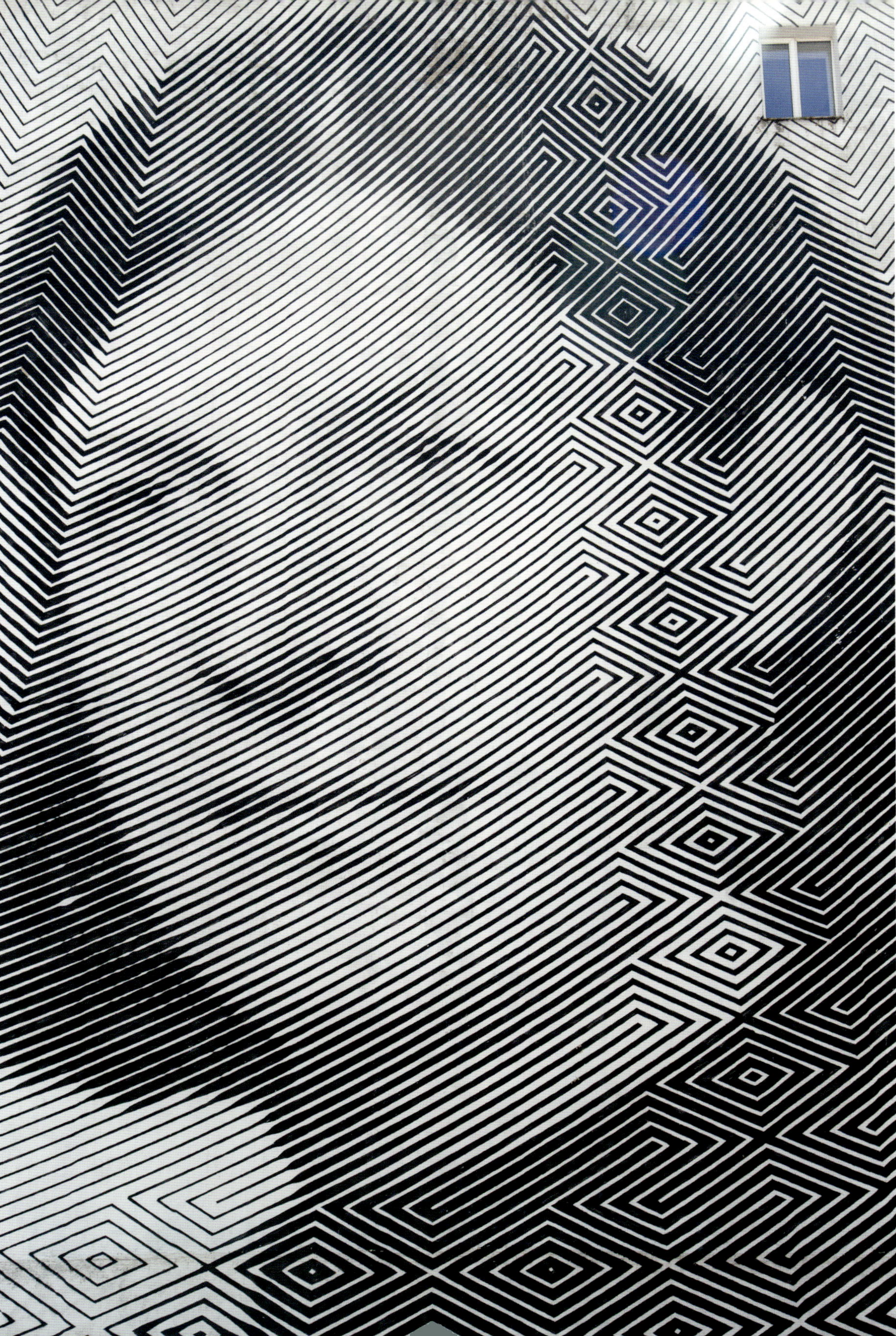

WARSAW

POLAND

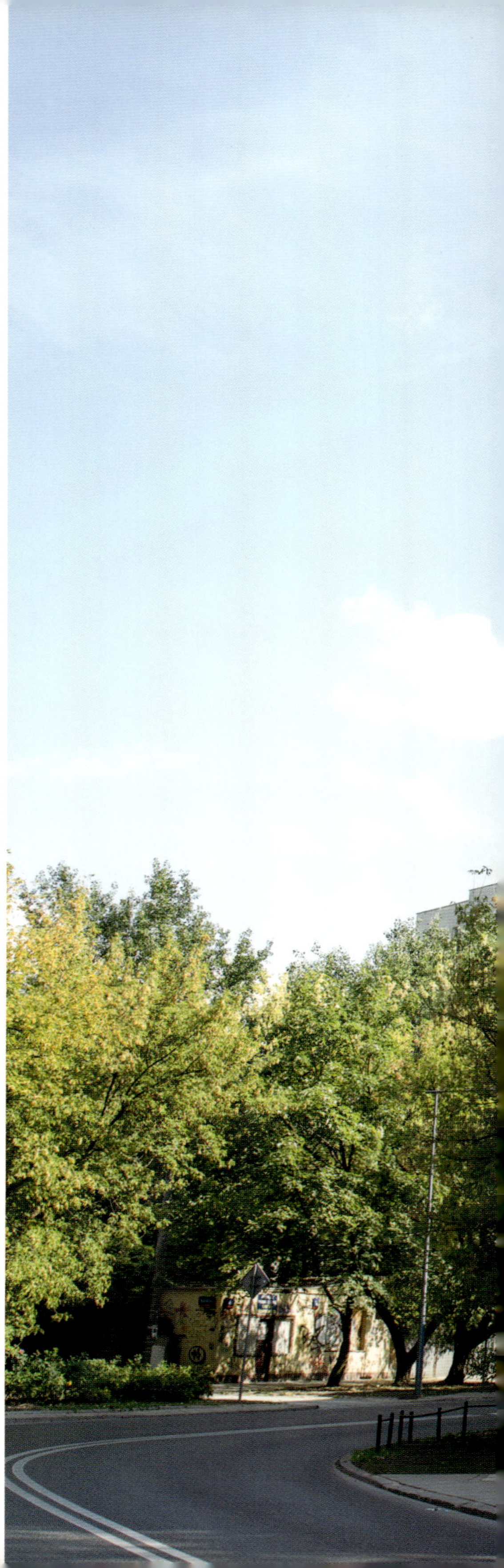

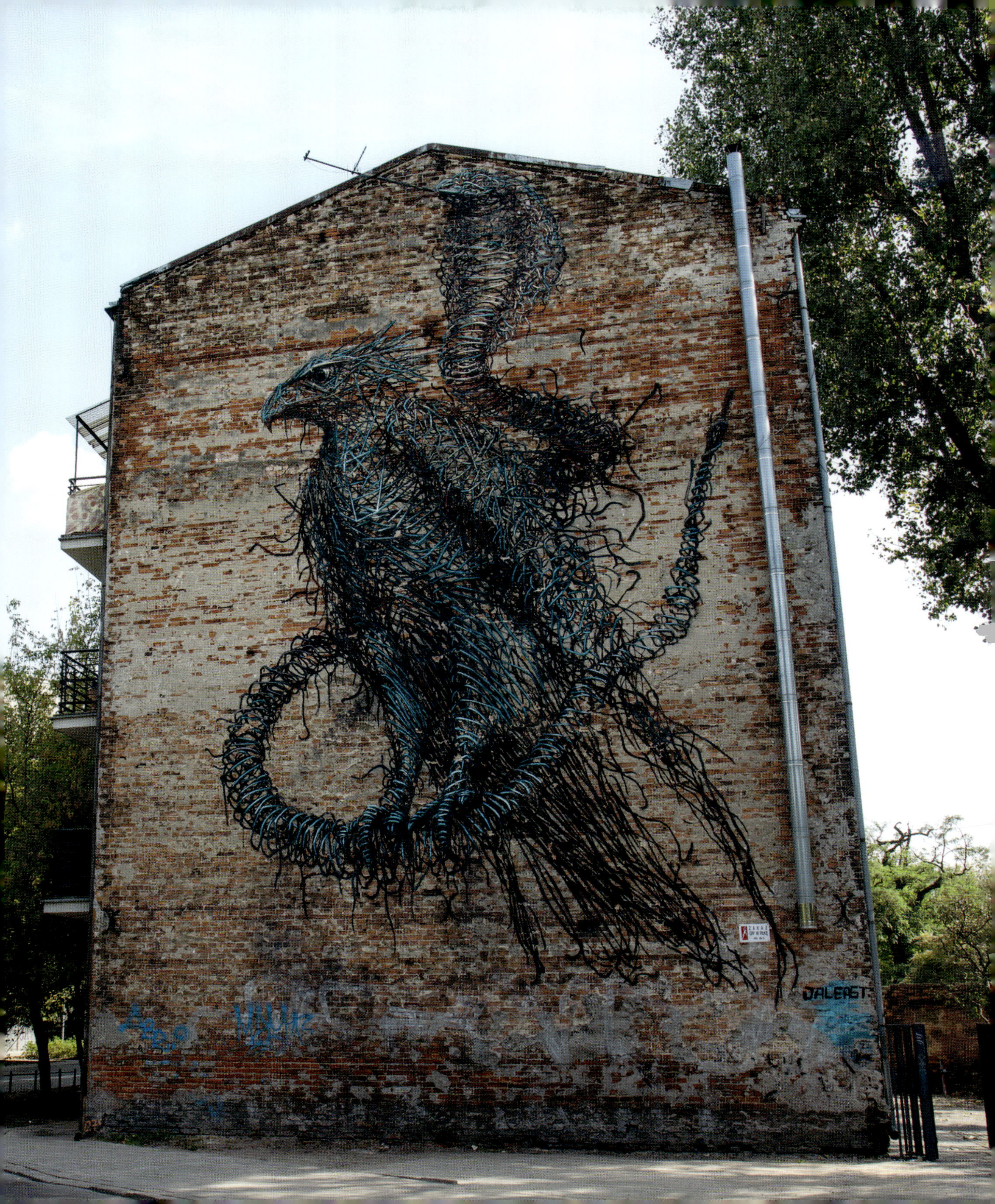

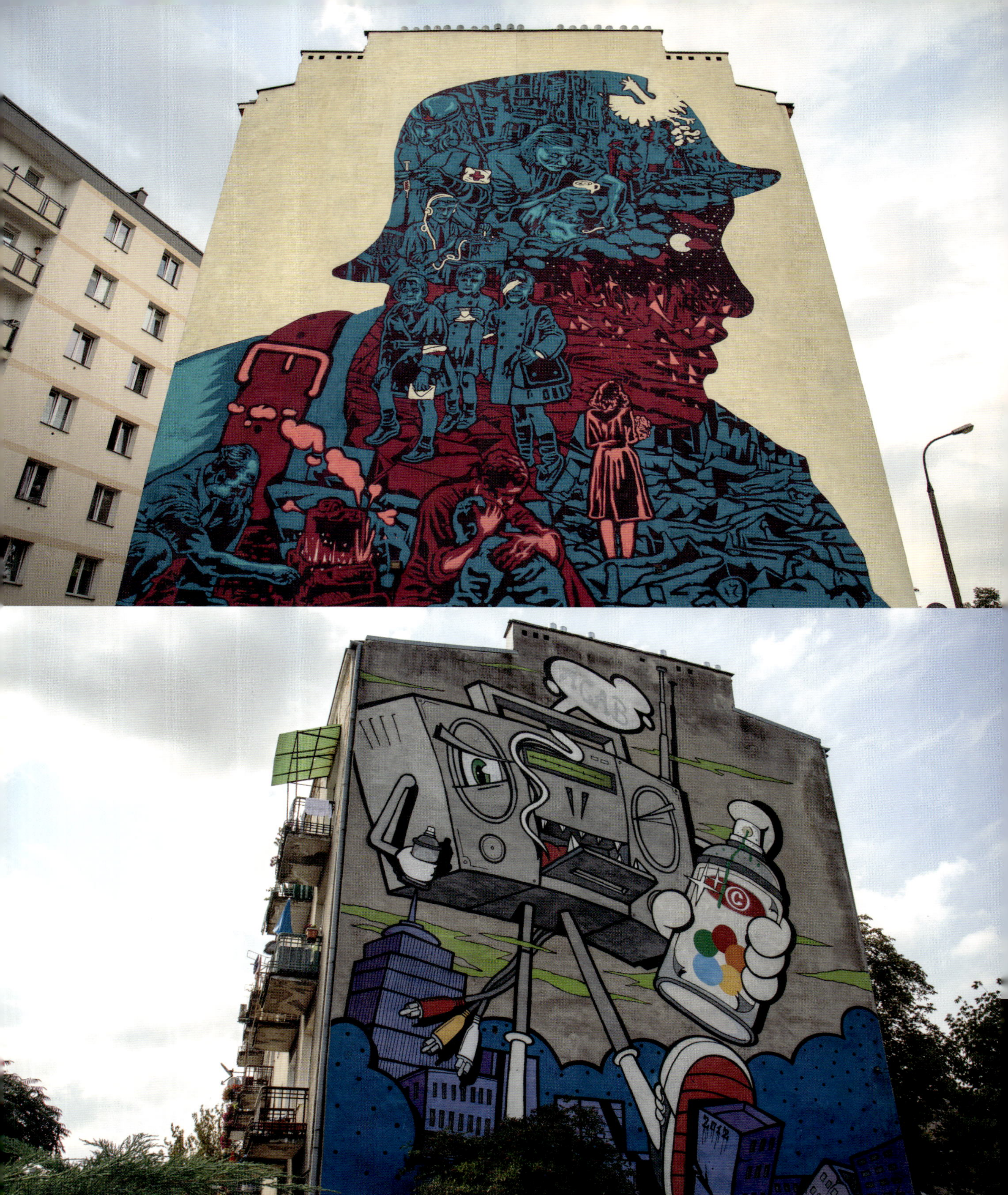

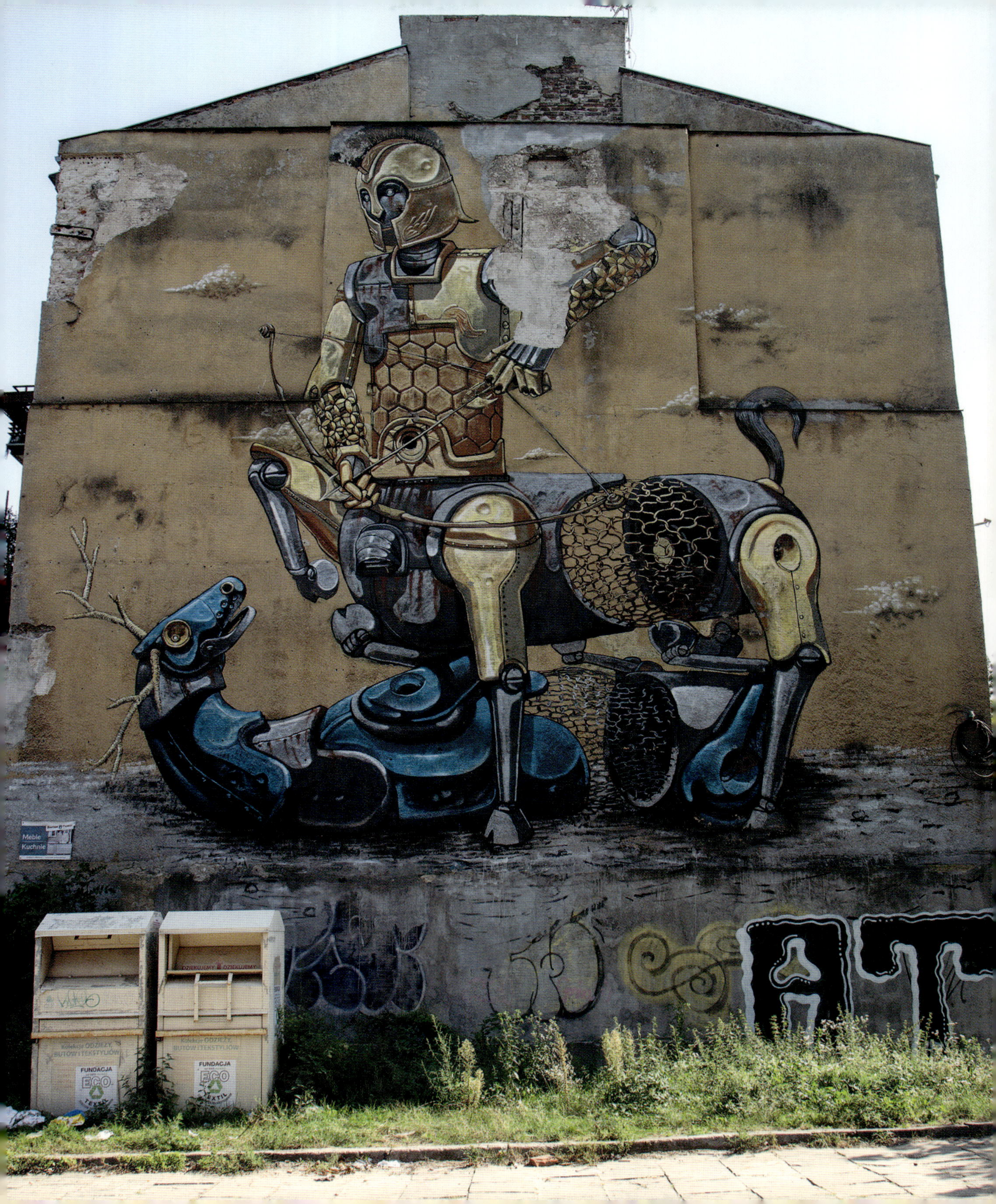

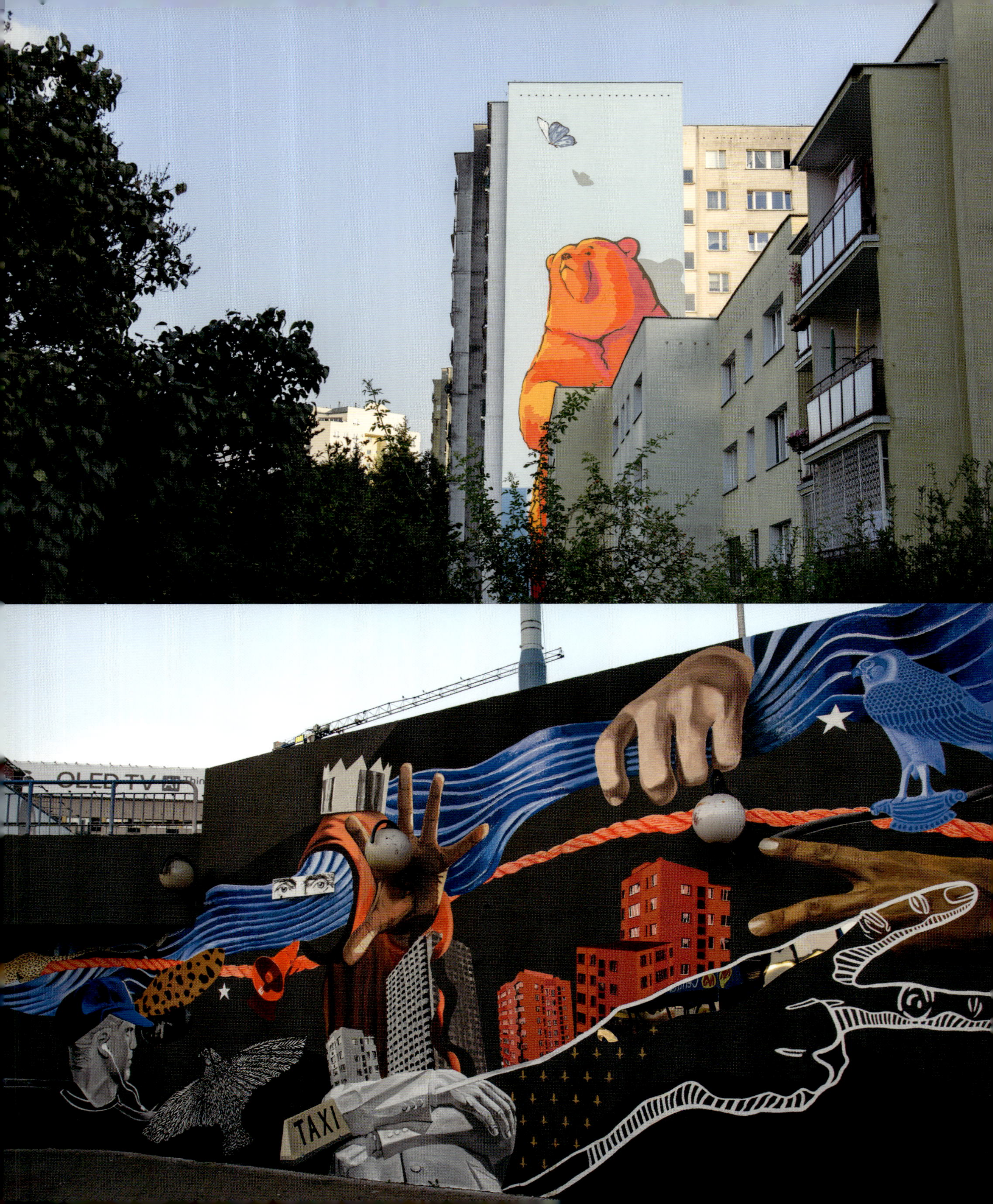

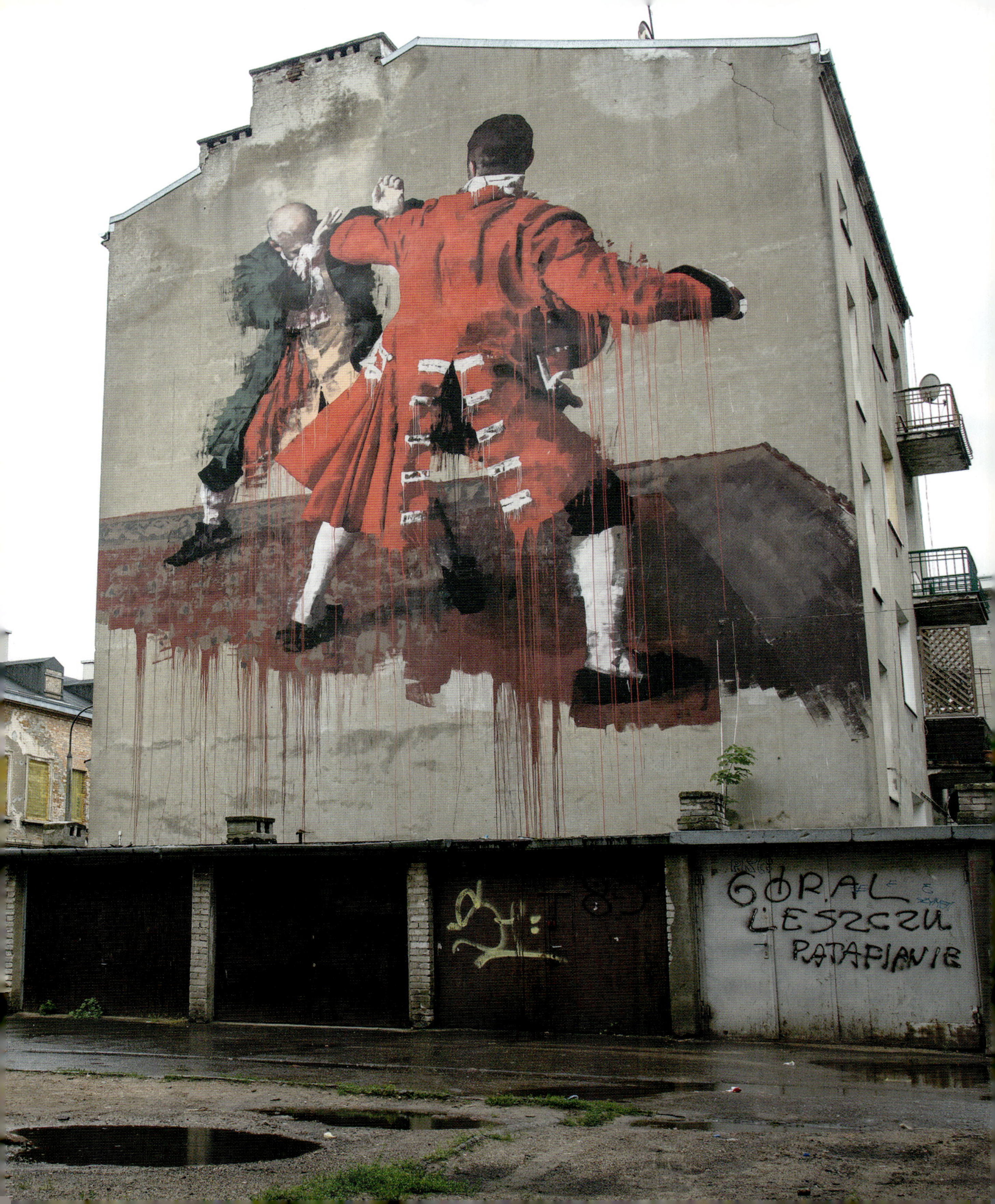

GORAL
LESZCZU
PATAFIANIE

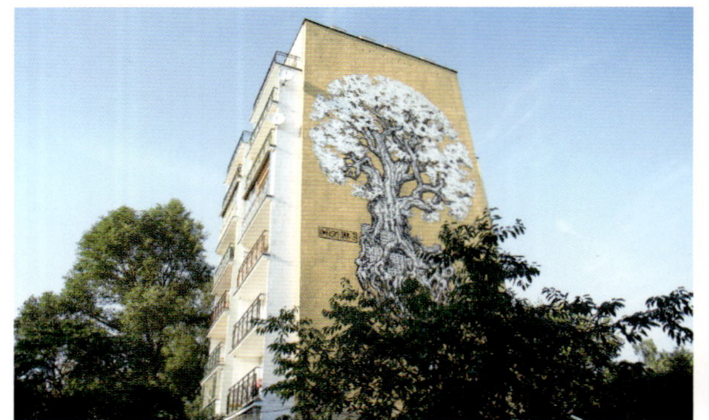
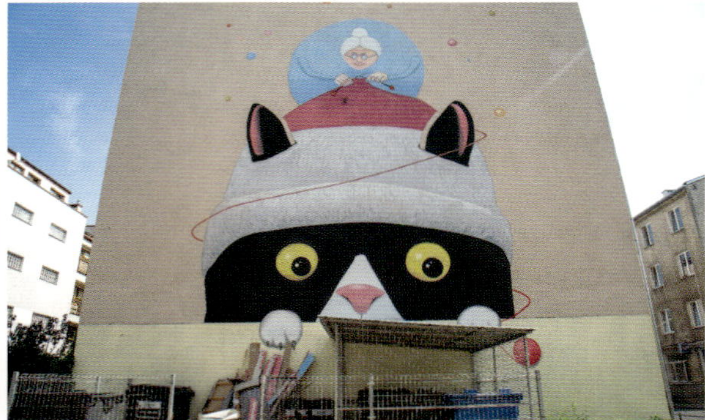
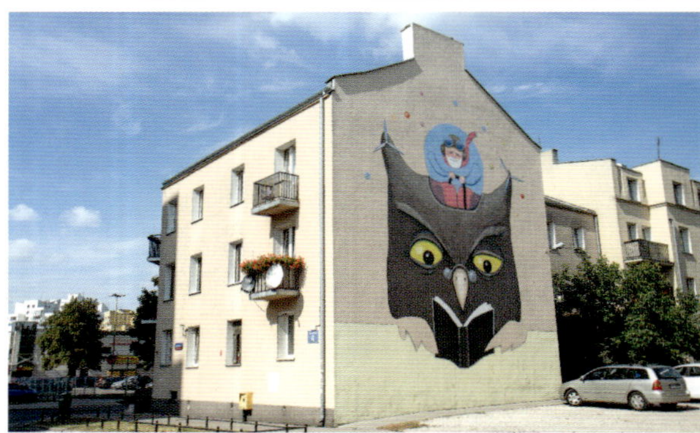
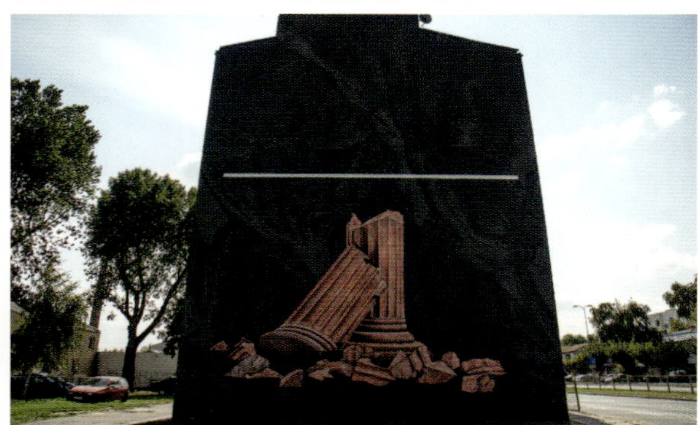
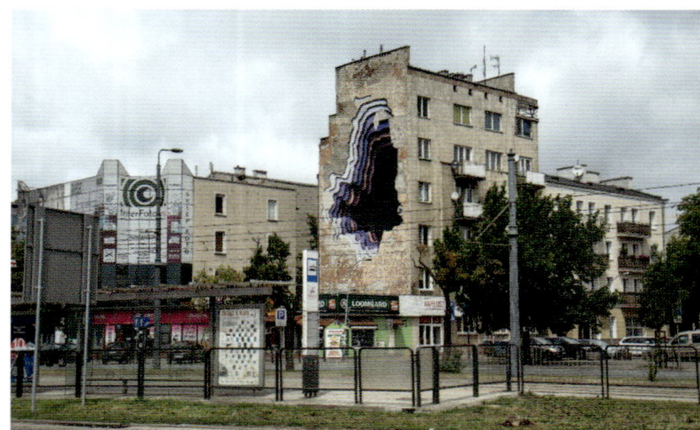
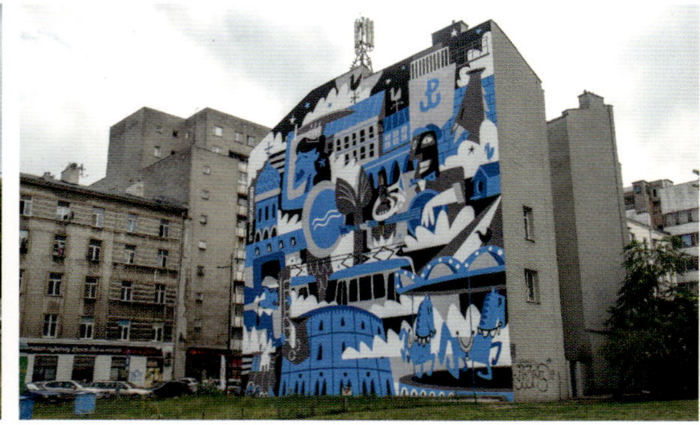
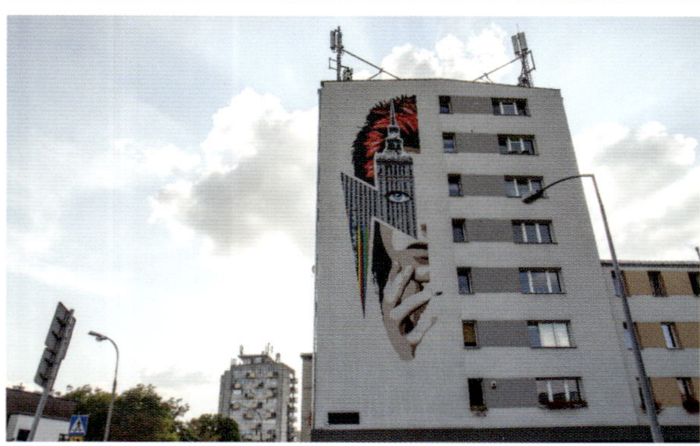
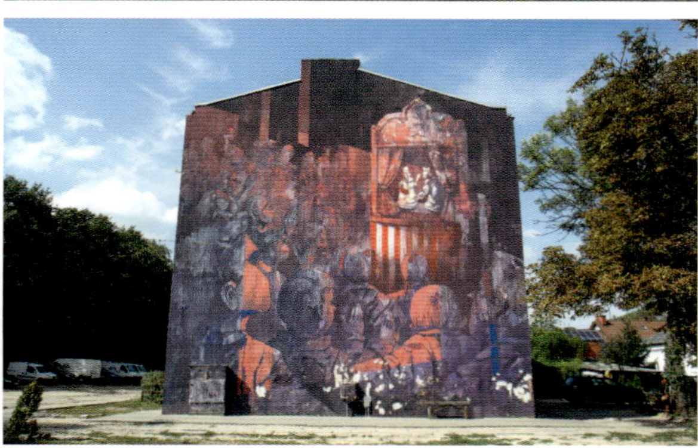

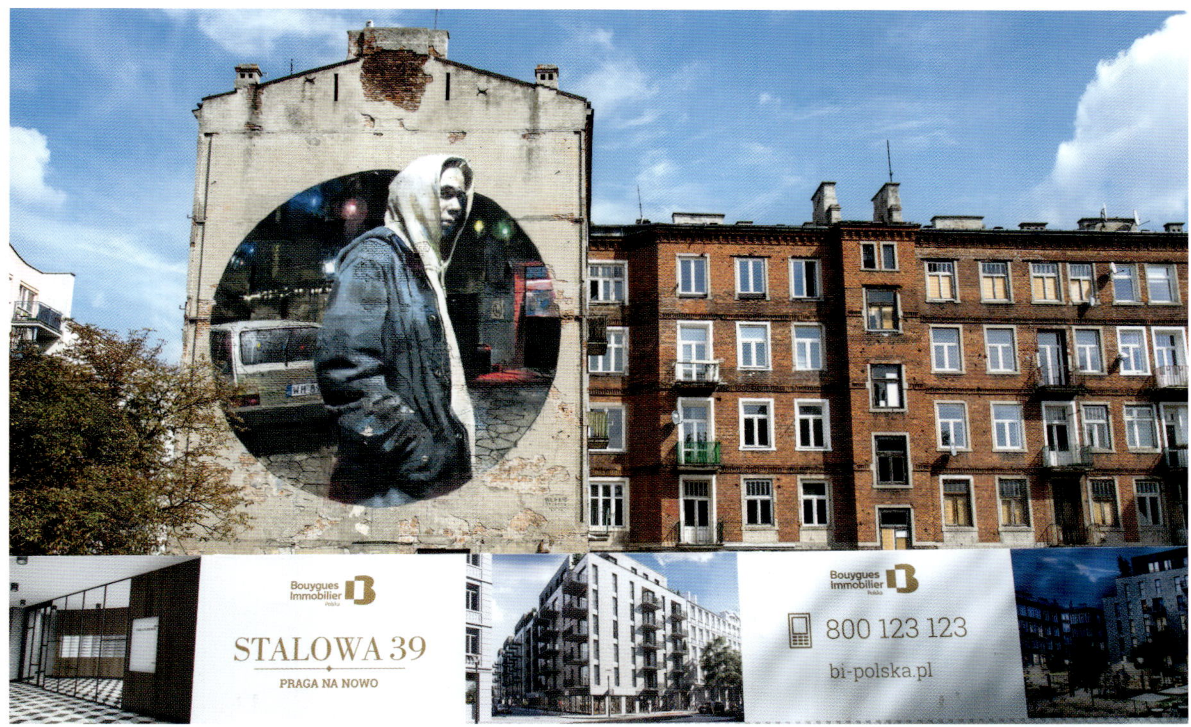
Bouygues
Immobilier
Polska
STALOWA 39
PRAGA NA NOWO
Bouygues
Immobilier
Polska
800 123 123
bi-polska.pl

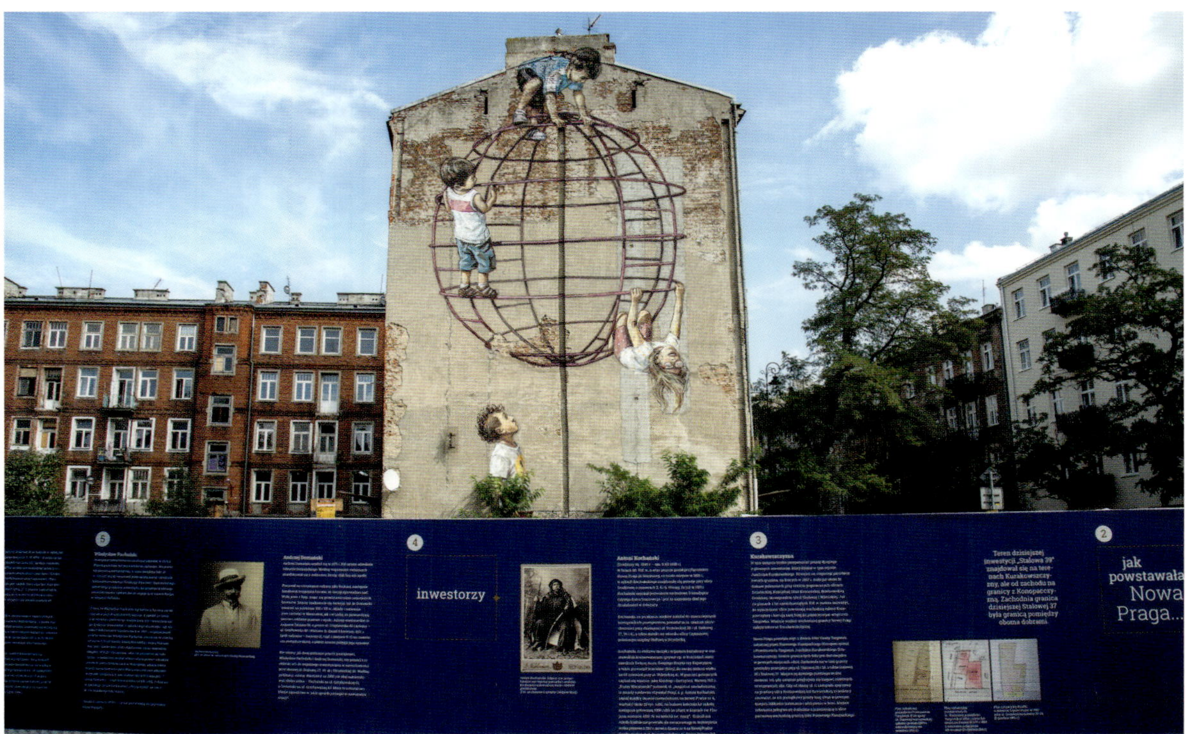

WROCLAW

POLAND

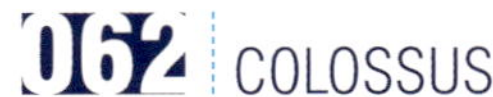

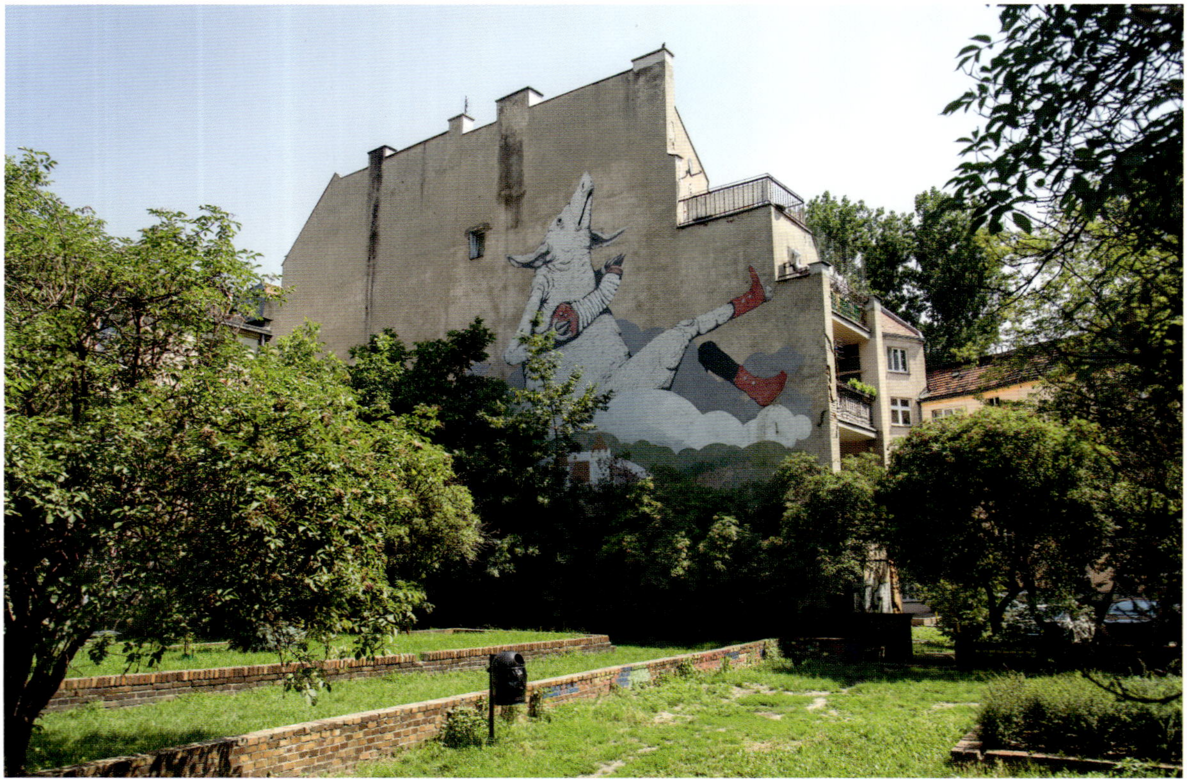

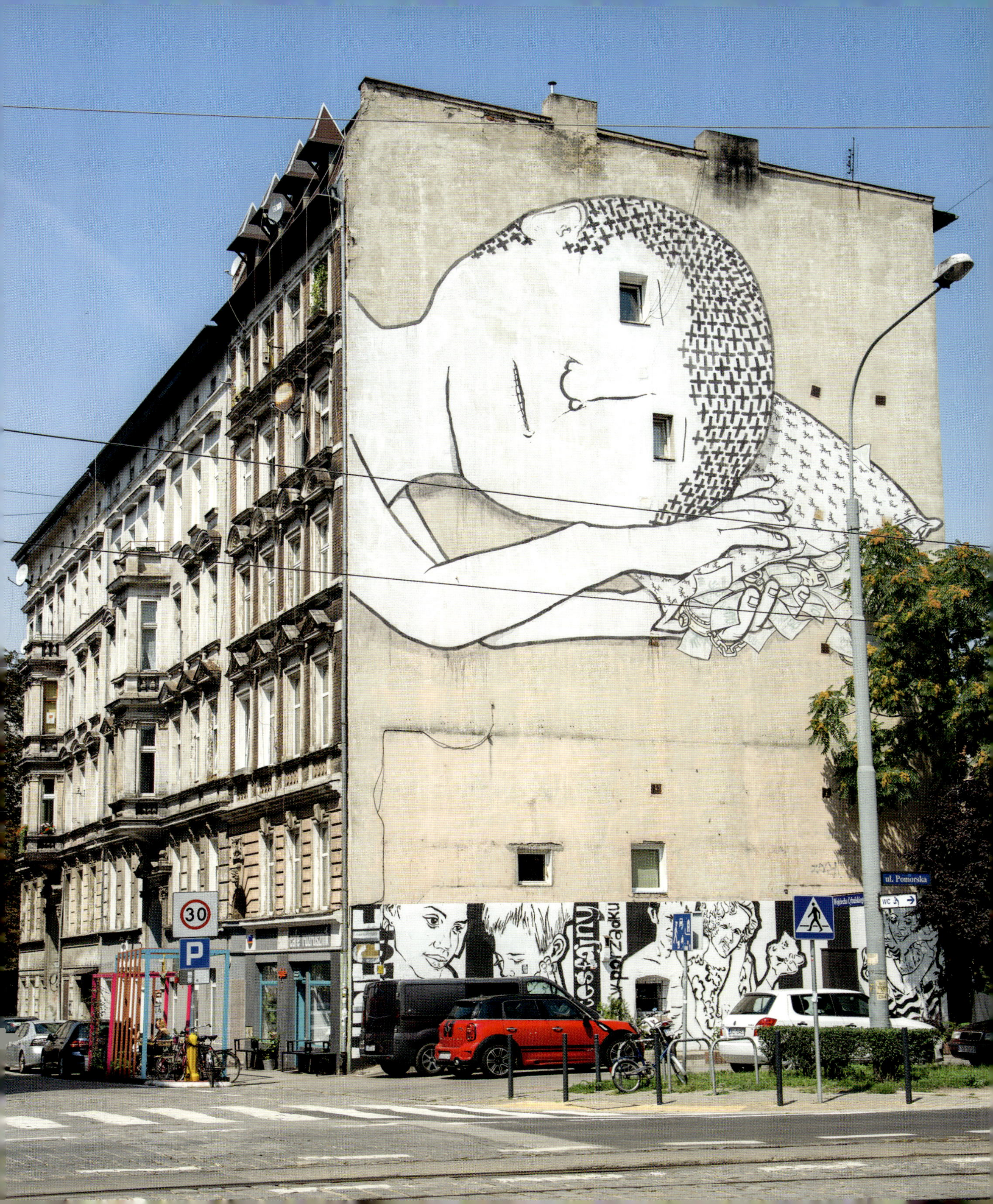

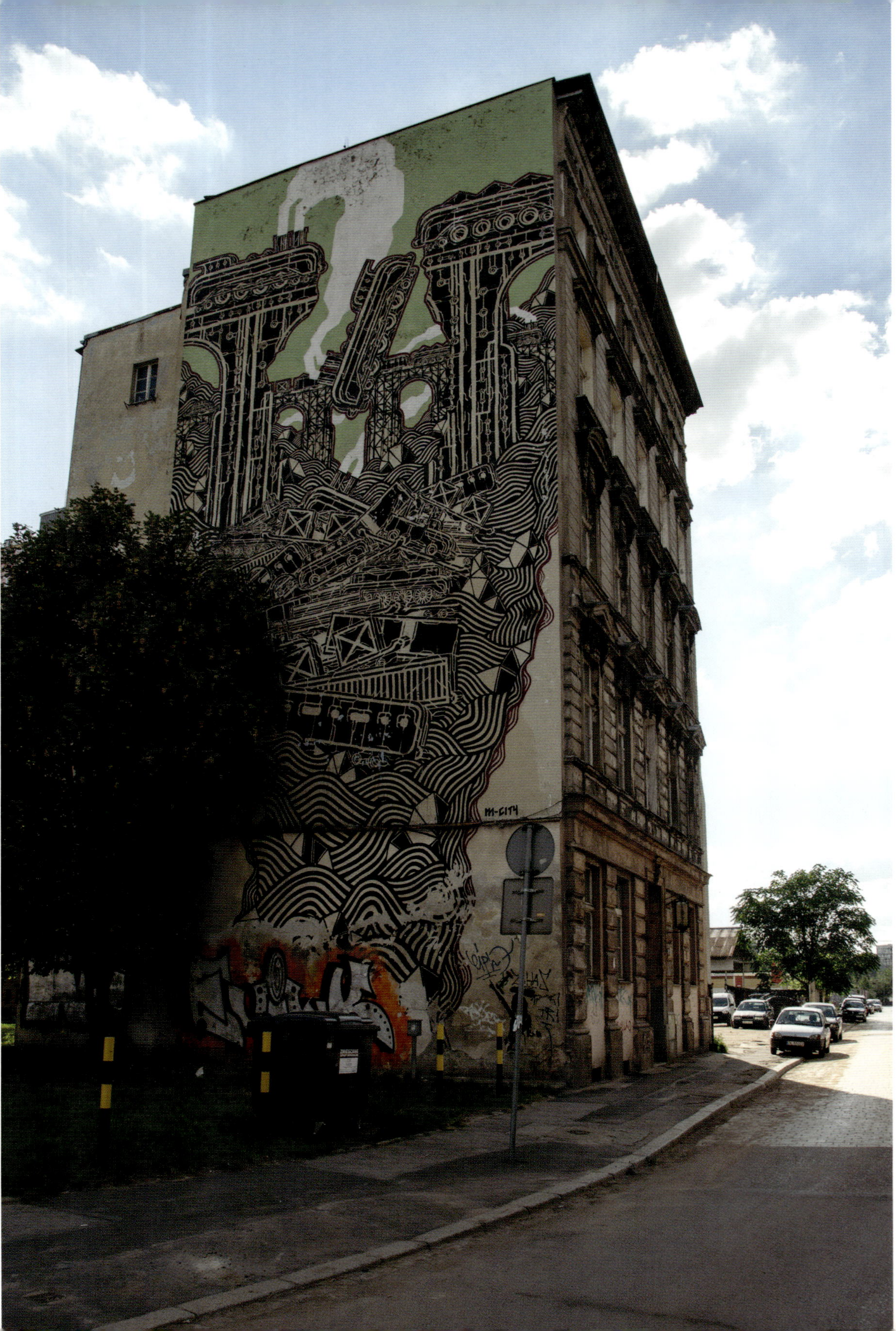

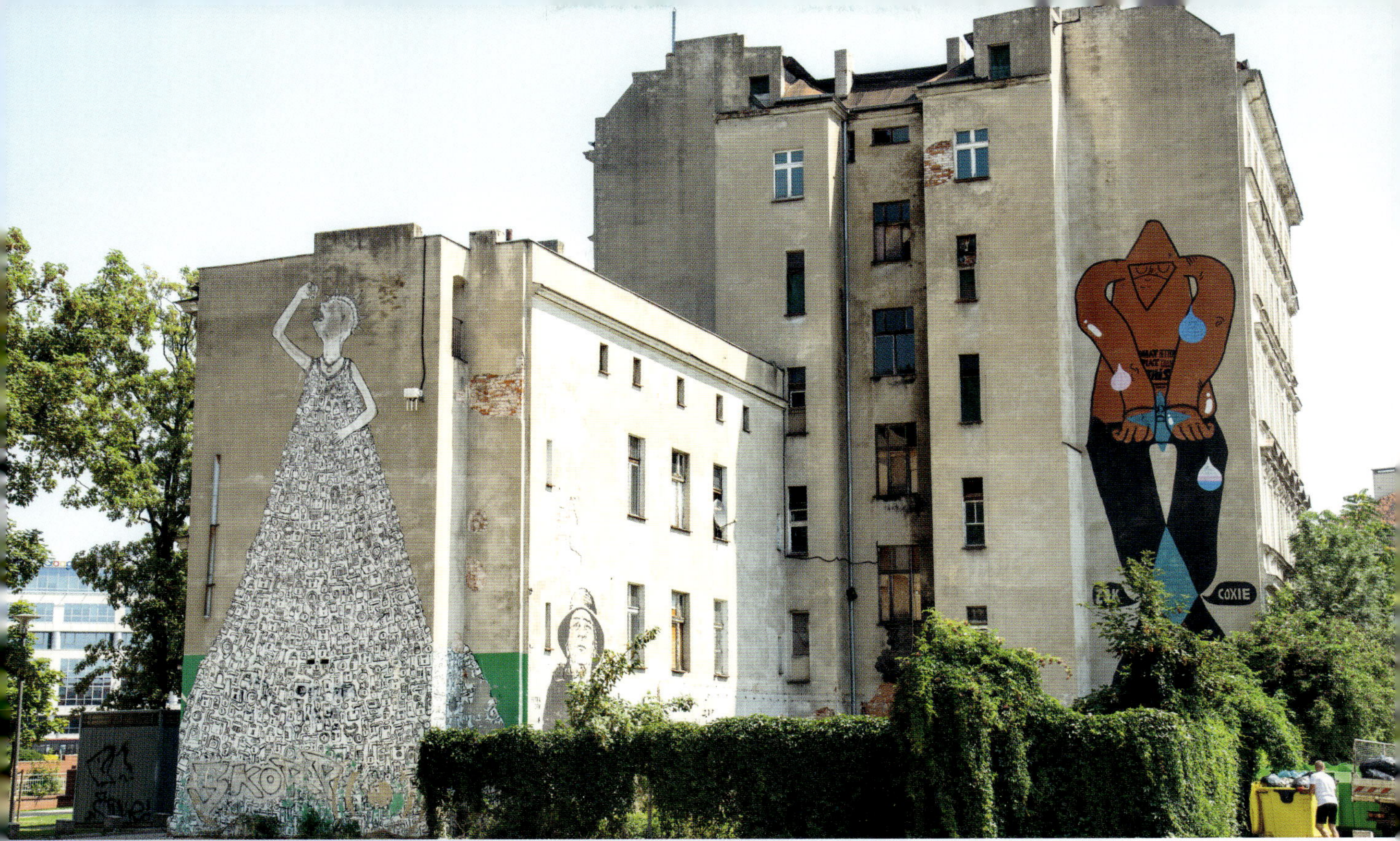

COXIE

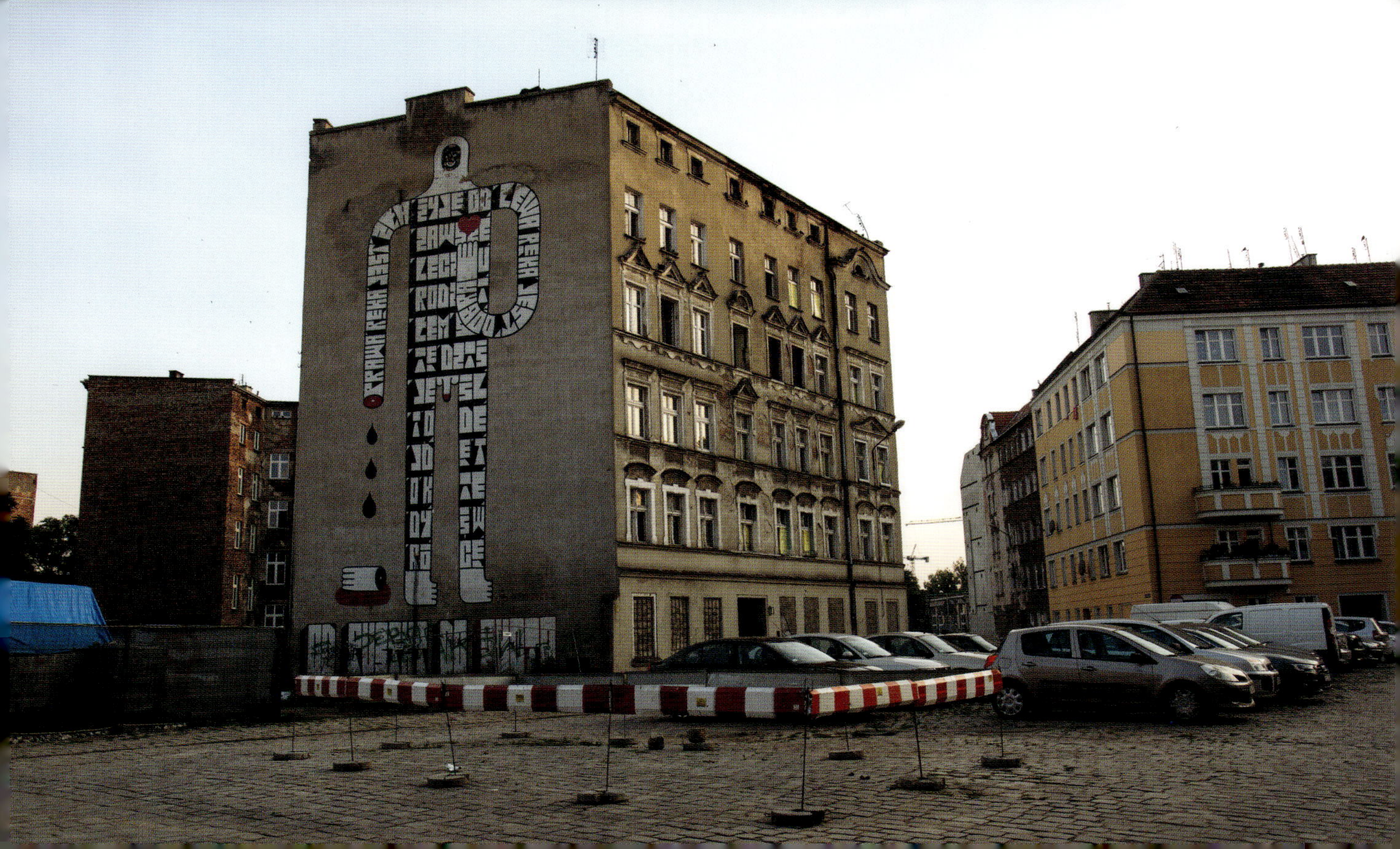

BRATISLAVA

SLOVAKIA

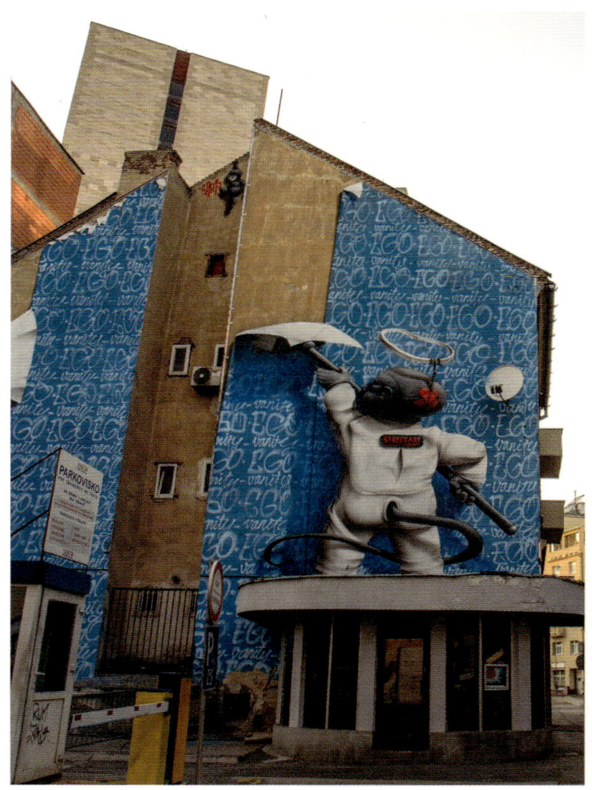

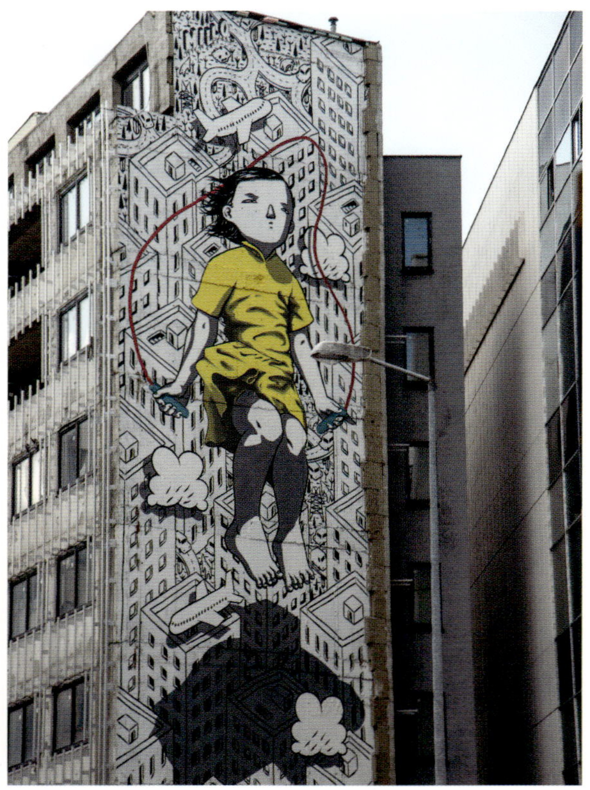

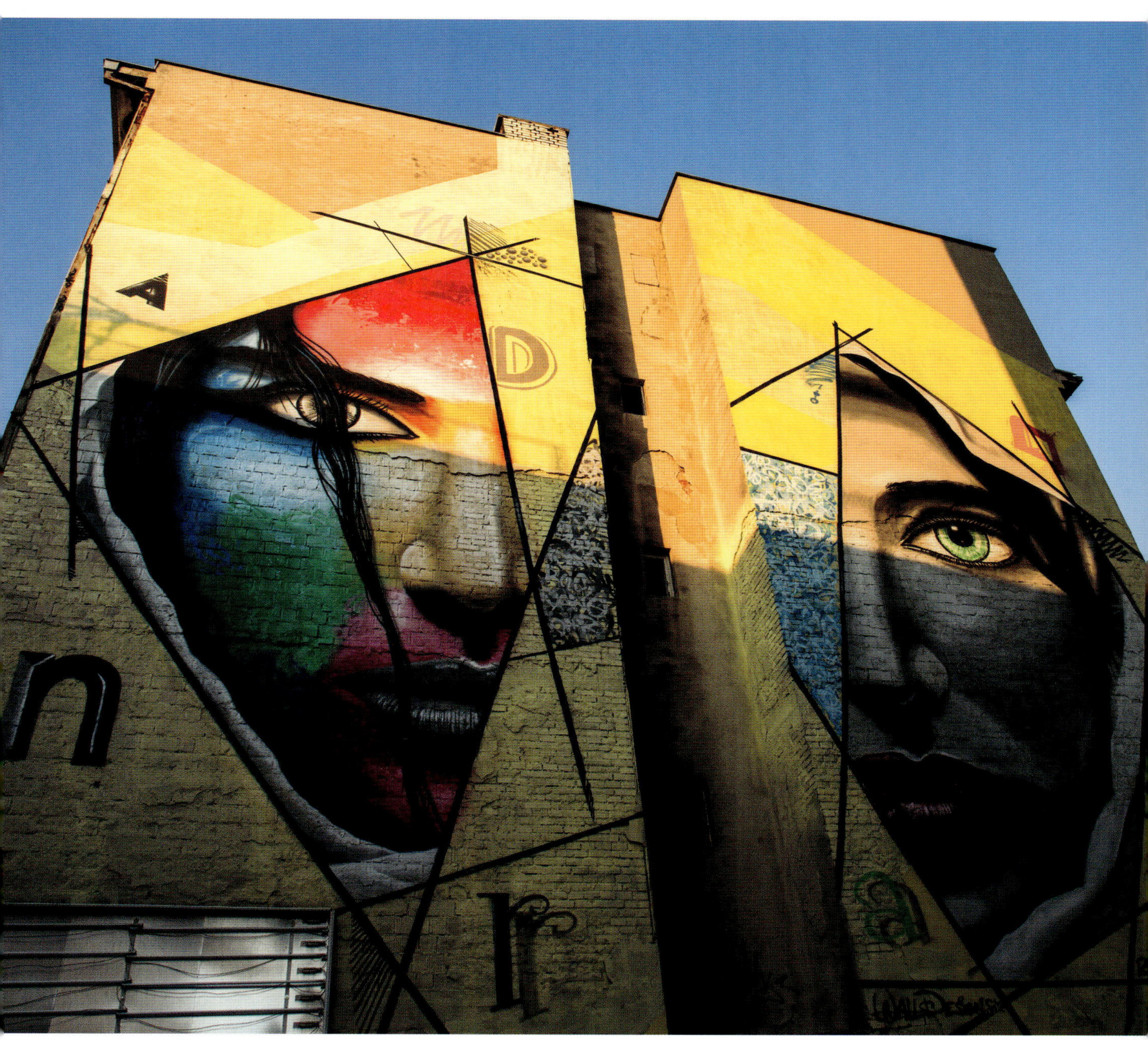

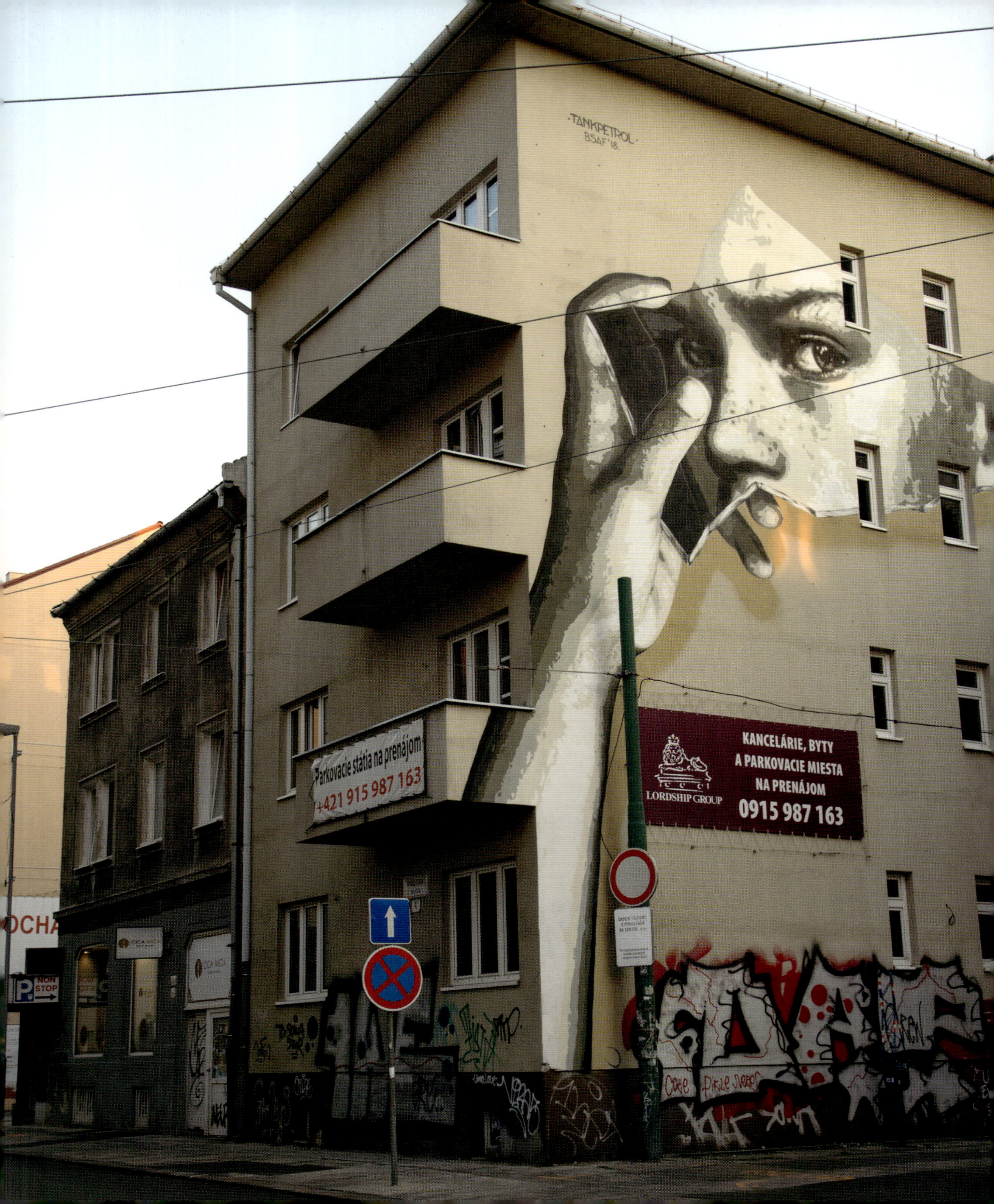

TANKPETROL
BSAF '18
Parkovacie státia na prenájom
+421 915 987 163
LORDSHIP GROUP
KANCELÁRIE, BYTY
A PARKOVACIE MIESTA
NA PRENÁJOM
0915 987 163
CICA MICA
NON STOP

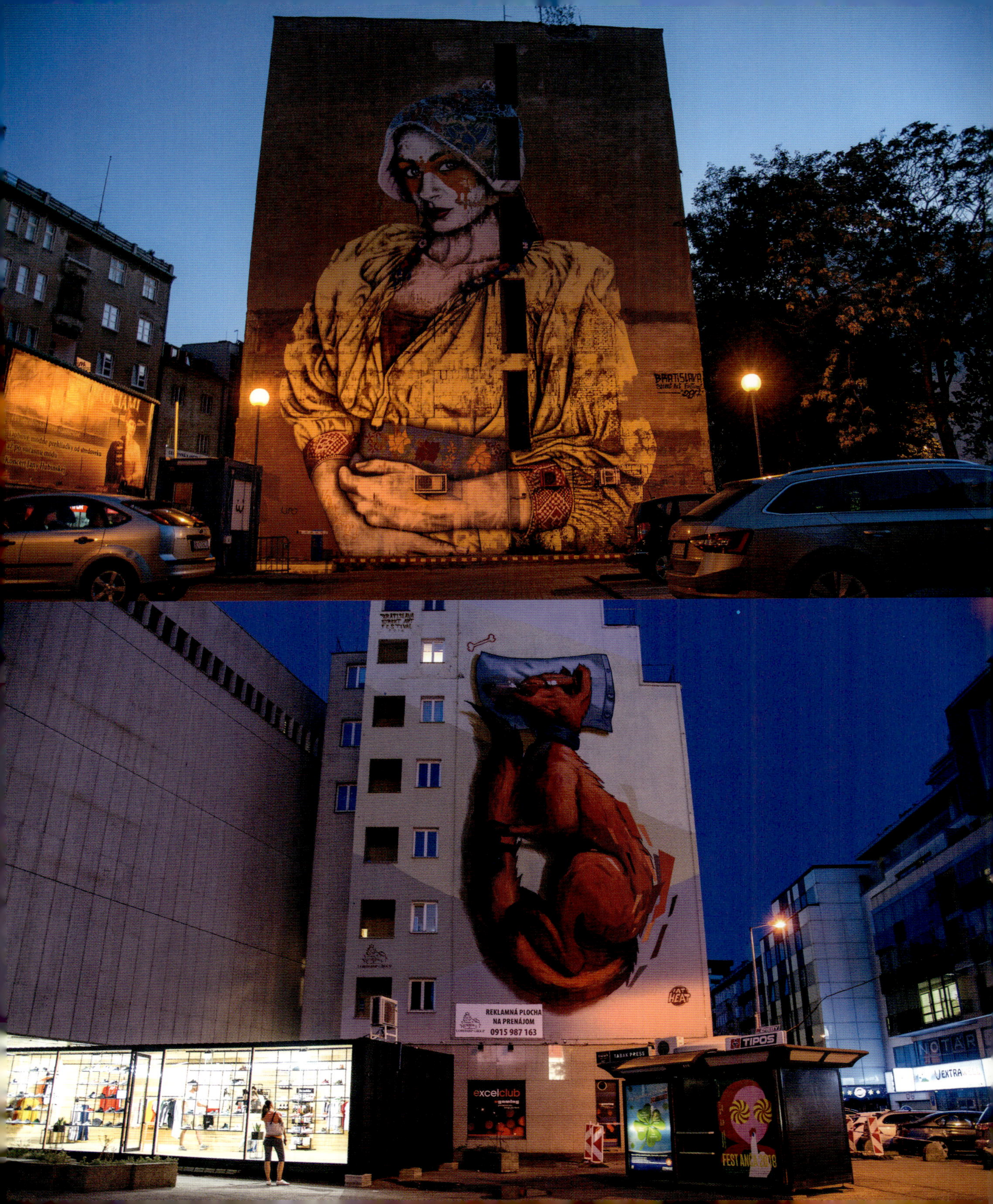

BRATISLAVA
Street Art Festival
2017

REKLAMNÁ PLOCHA
NA PRENÁJOM
0915 987 163

excelclub

TIPOS
TABAK PRESS
NOTAR
EXTRA
FEST ANCA 2018

KOSICE

SLOVAKIA

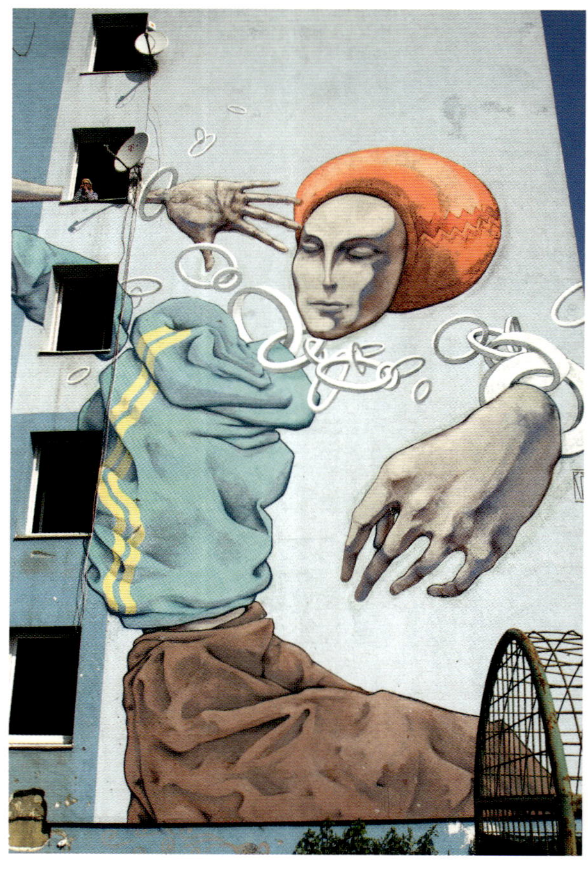

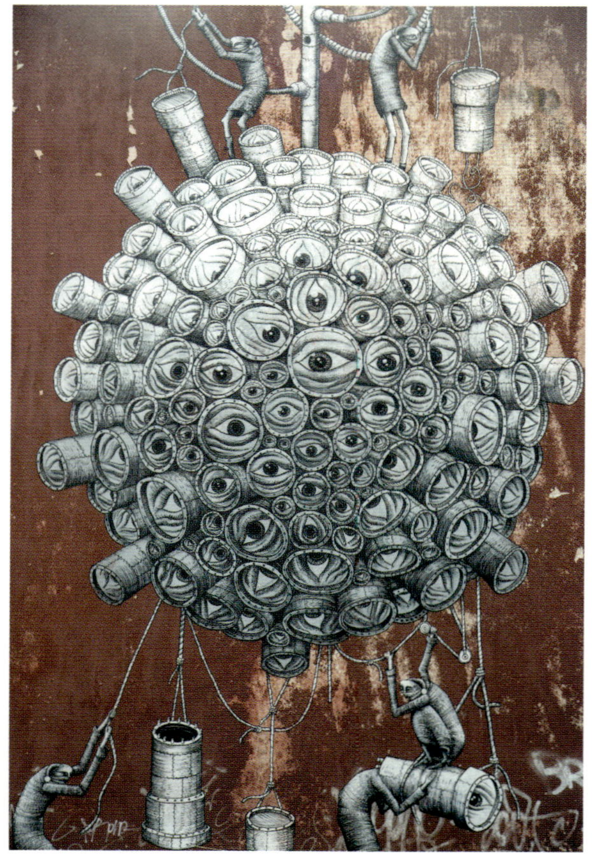

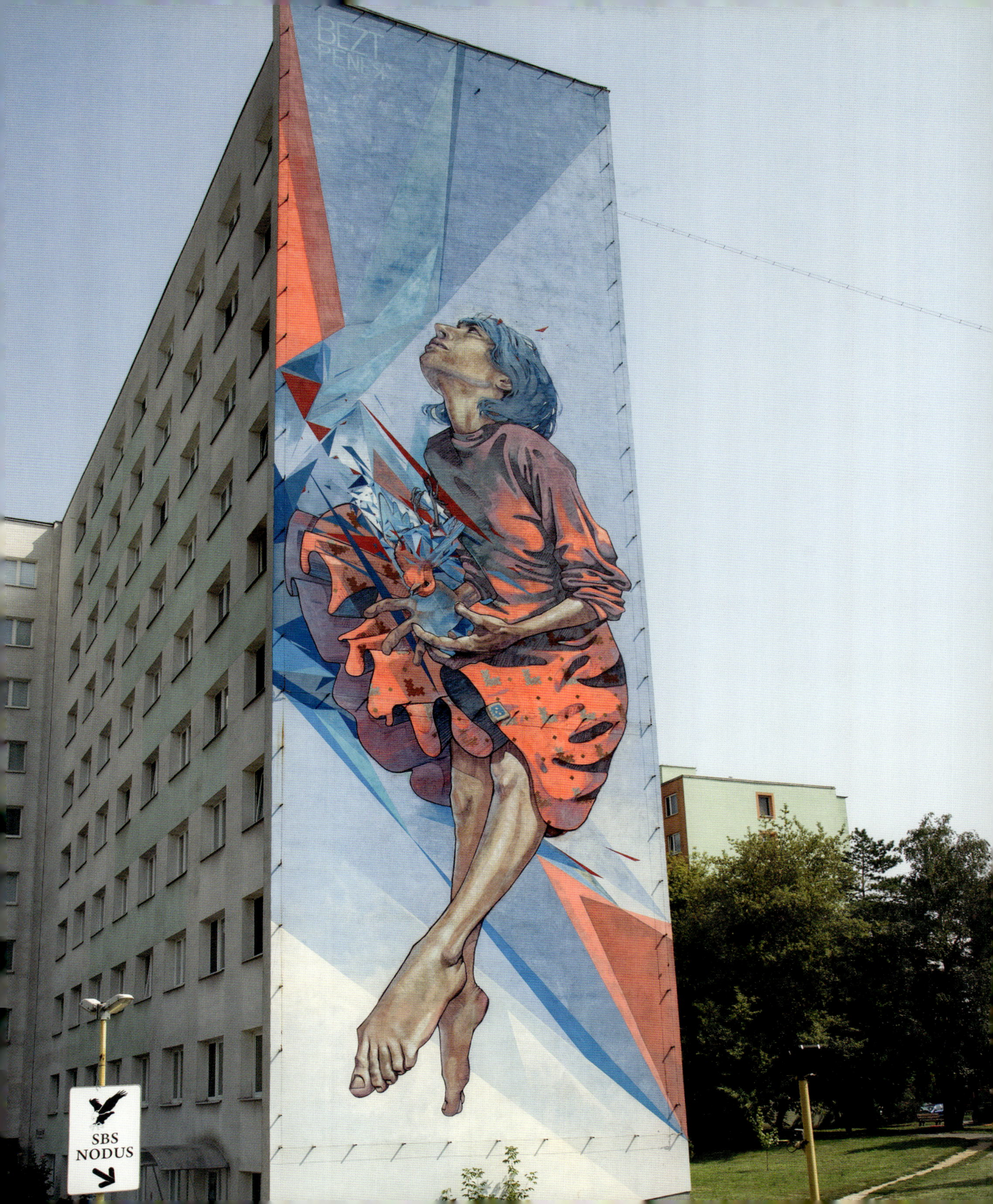

BEZT
PENER
SBS
NODUS

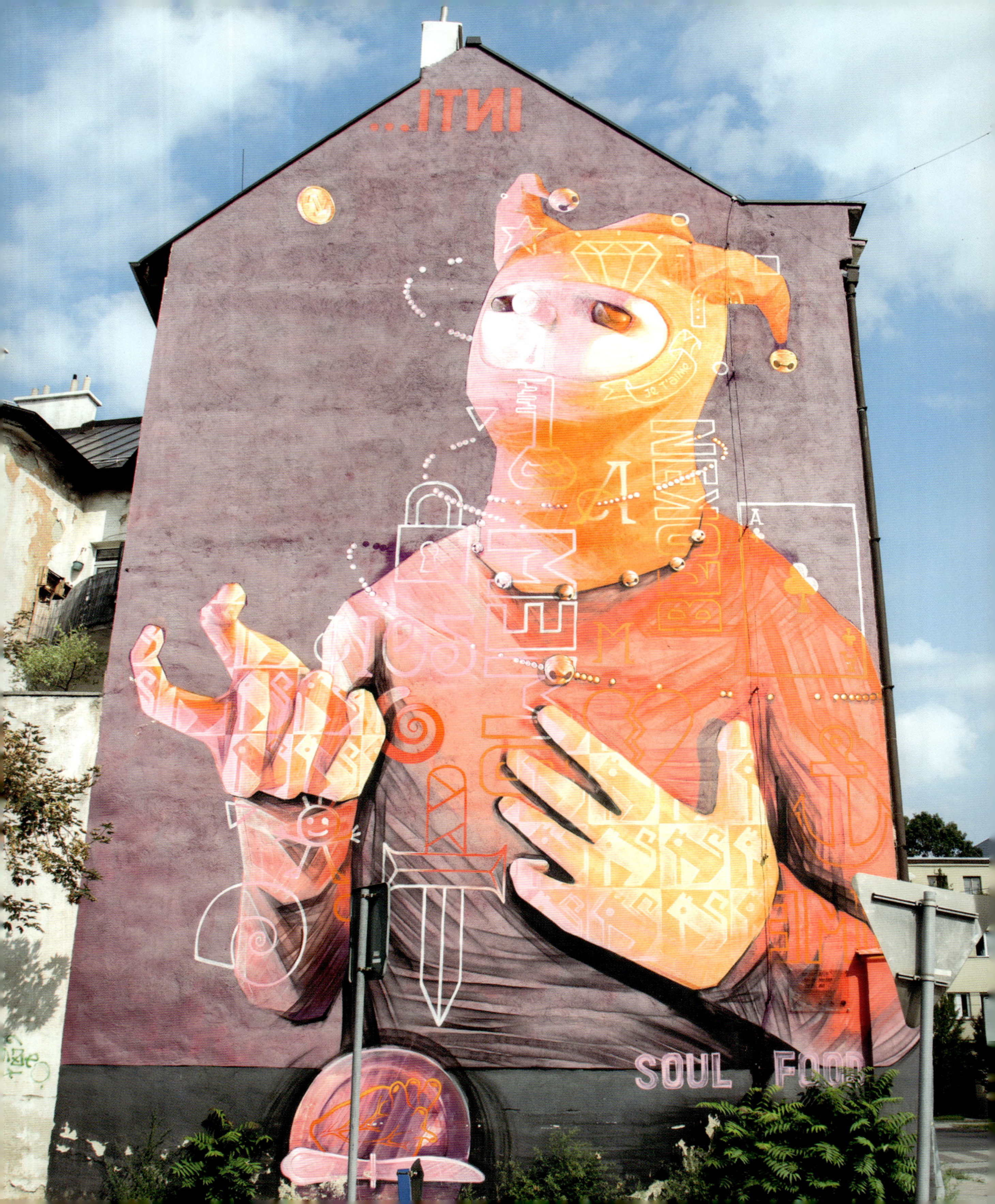
INTL...
SOUL FOOD

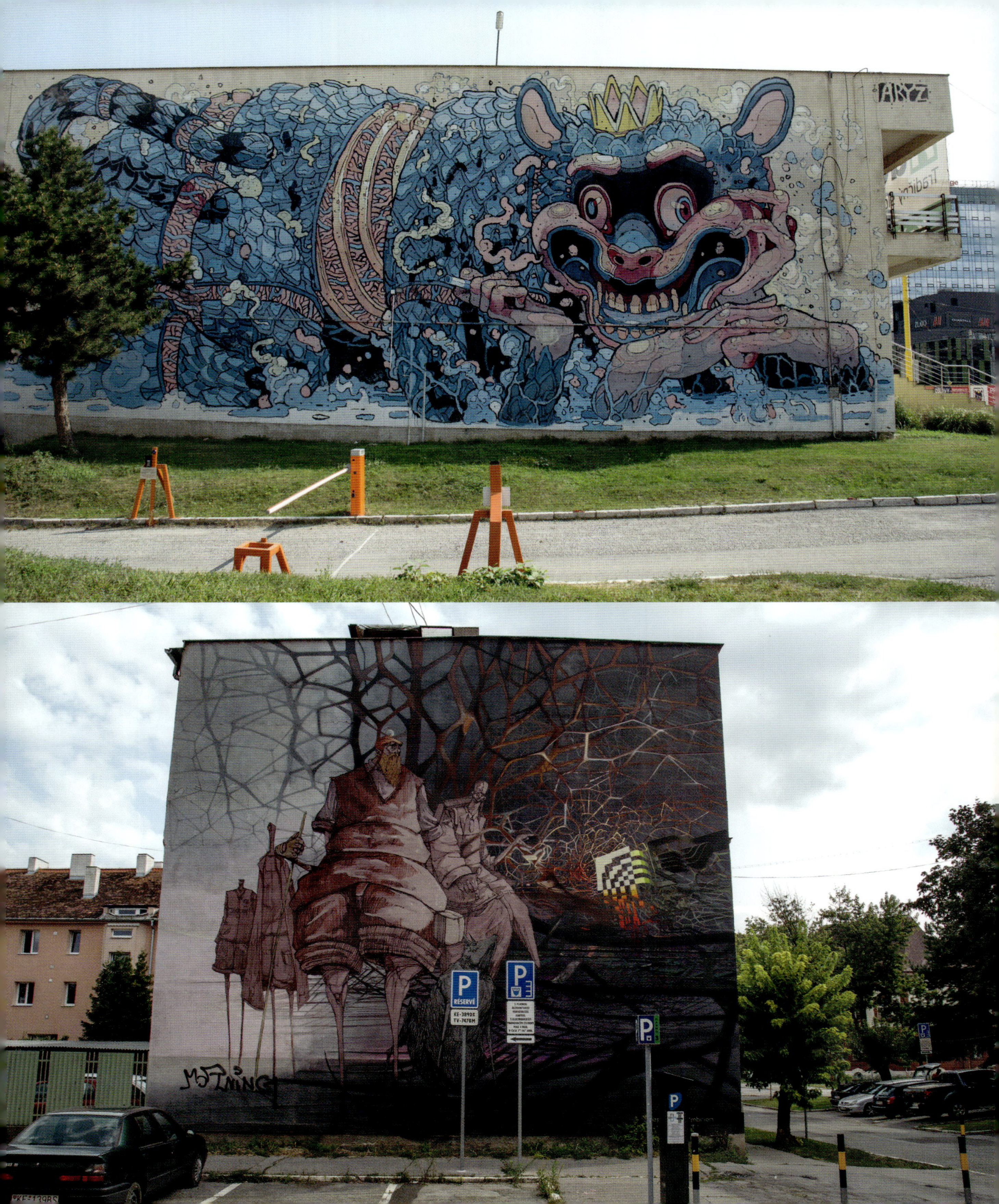

MINSK

BELARUS

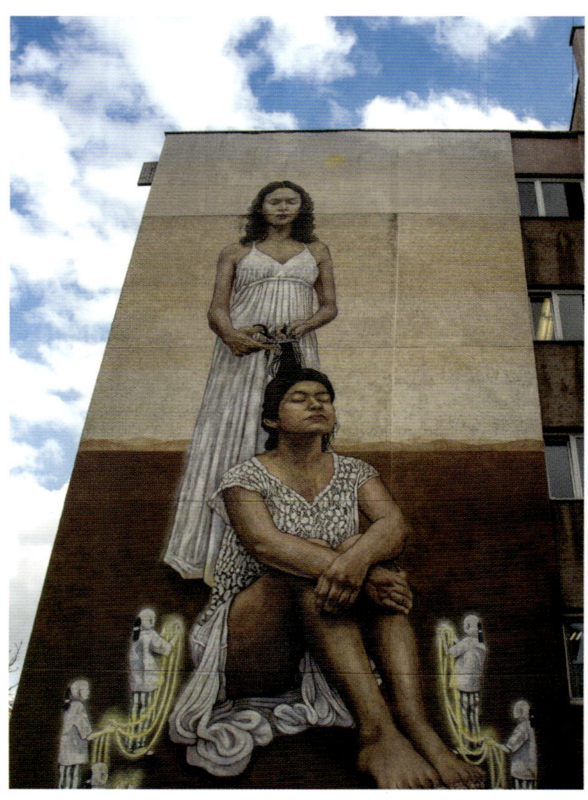

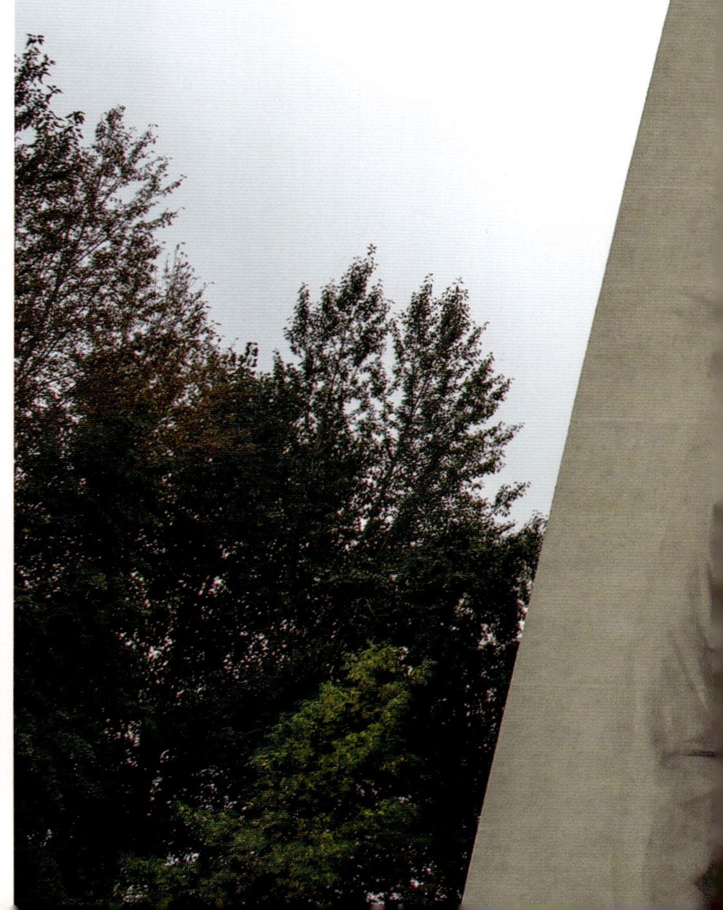

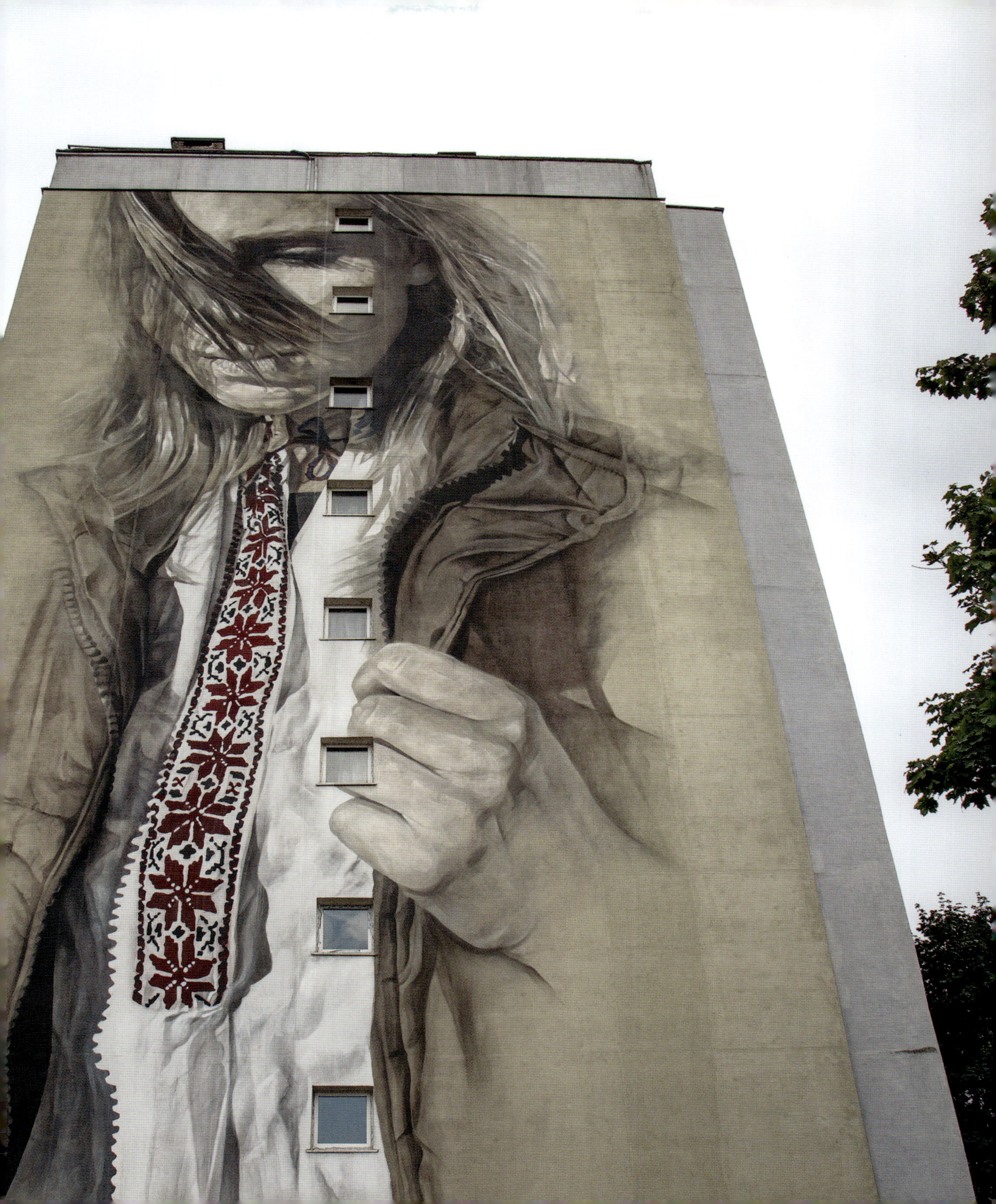

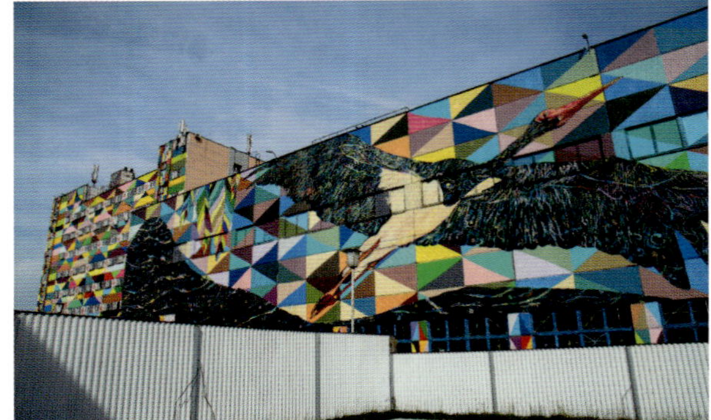

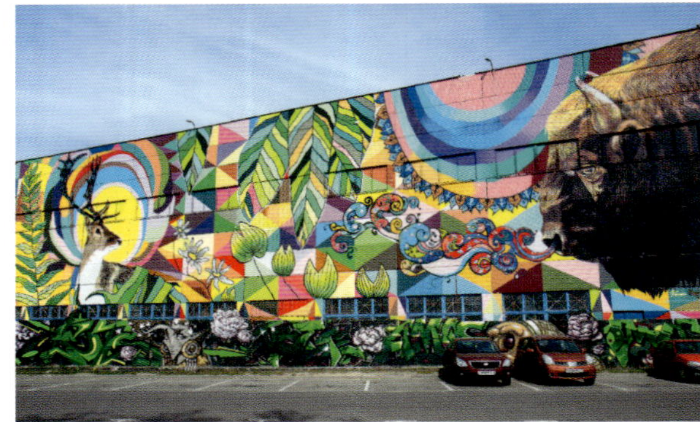

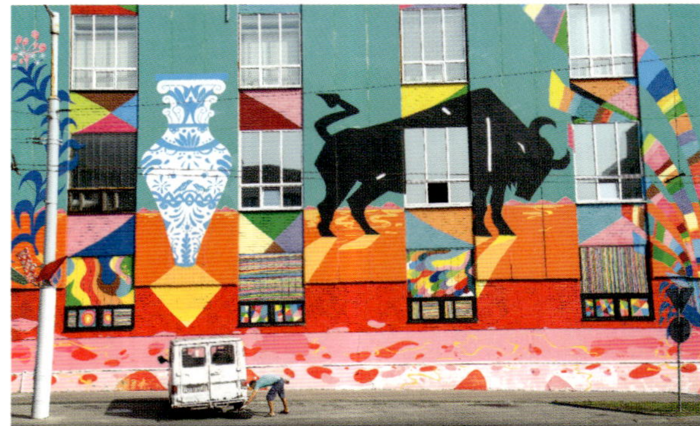

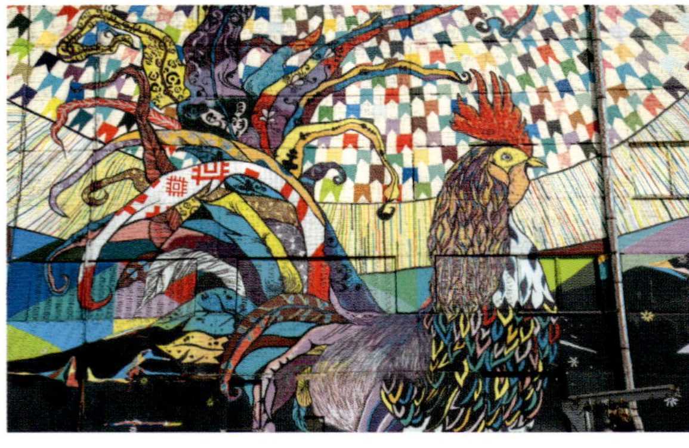

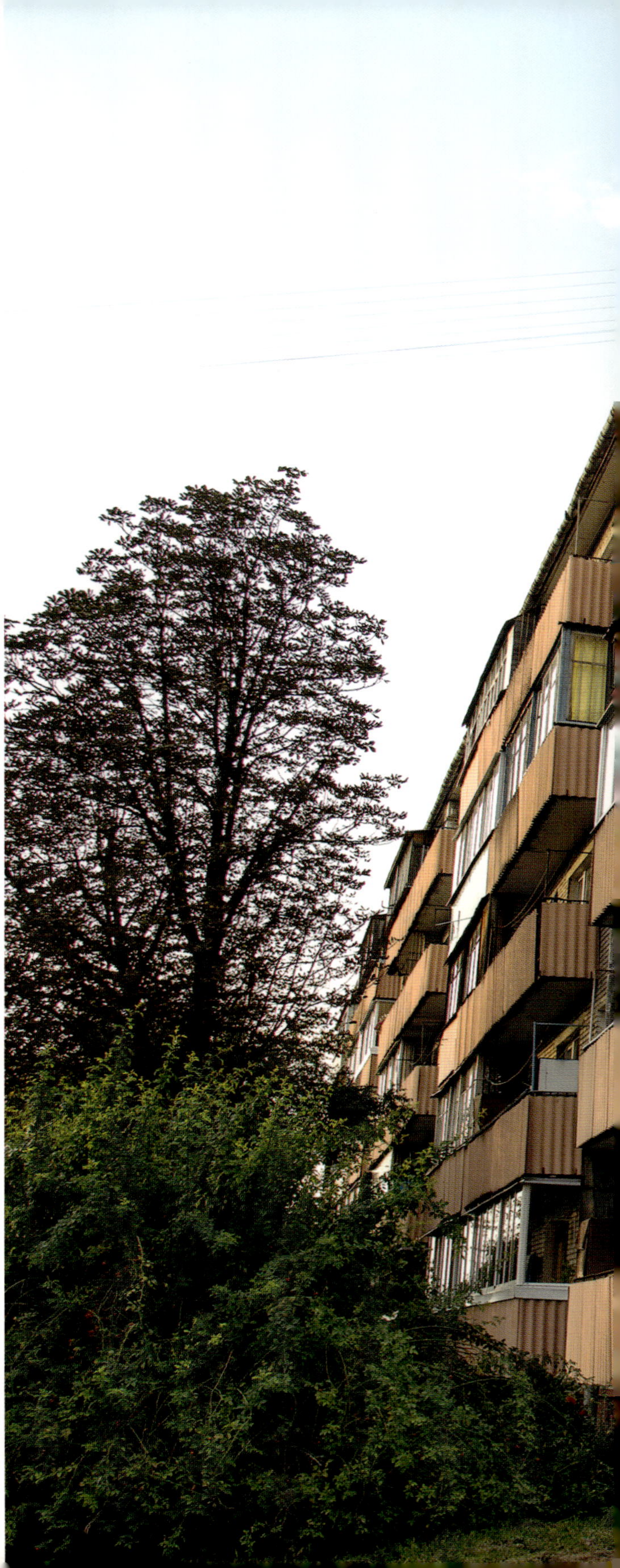

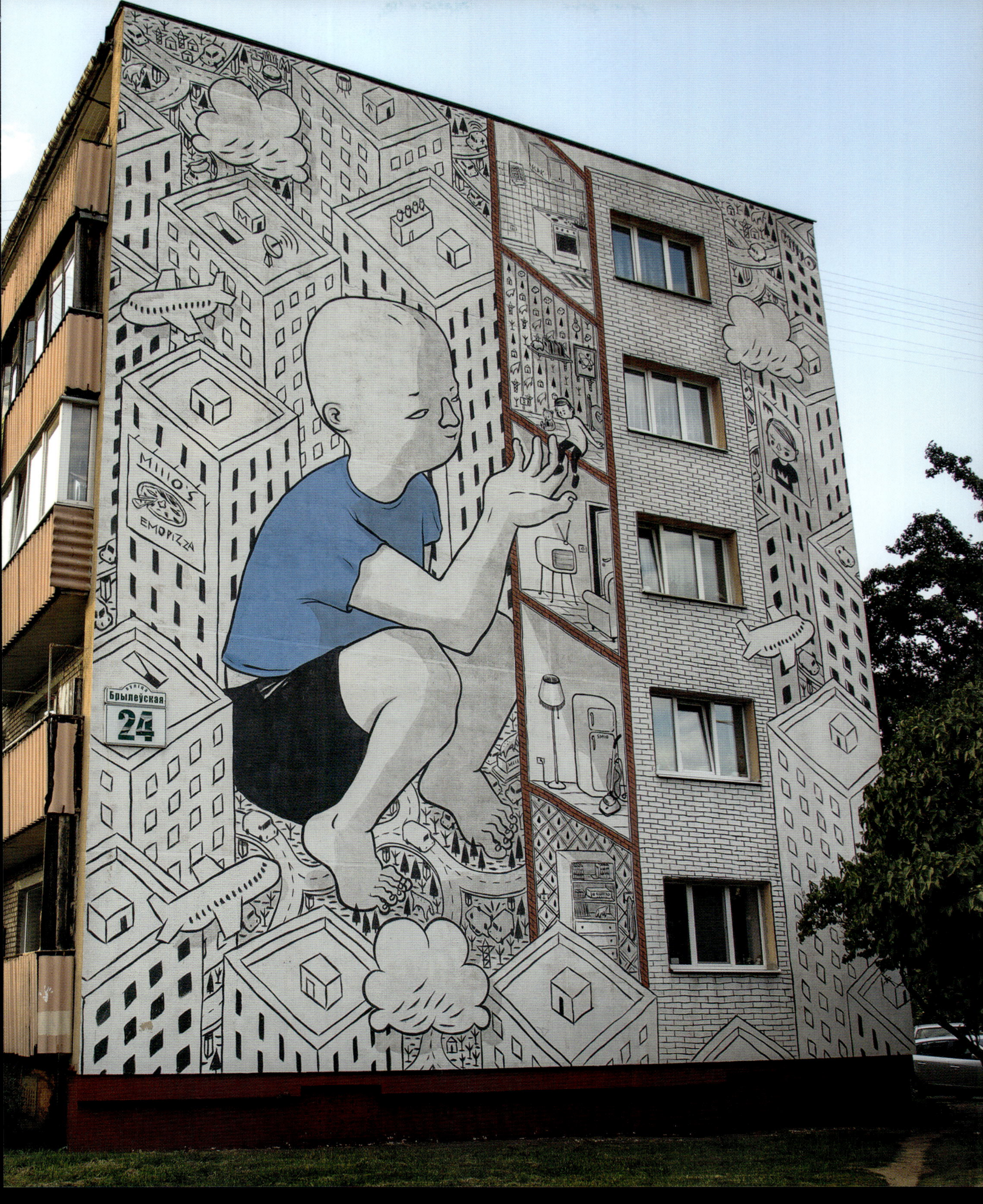
MILO'S
EMOPIZZA
Брылеўская
24

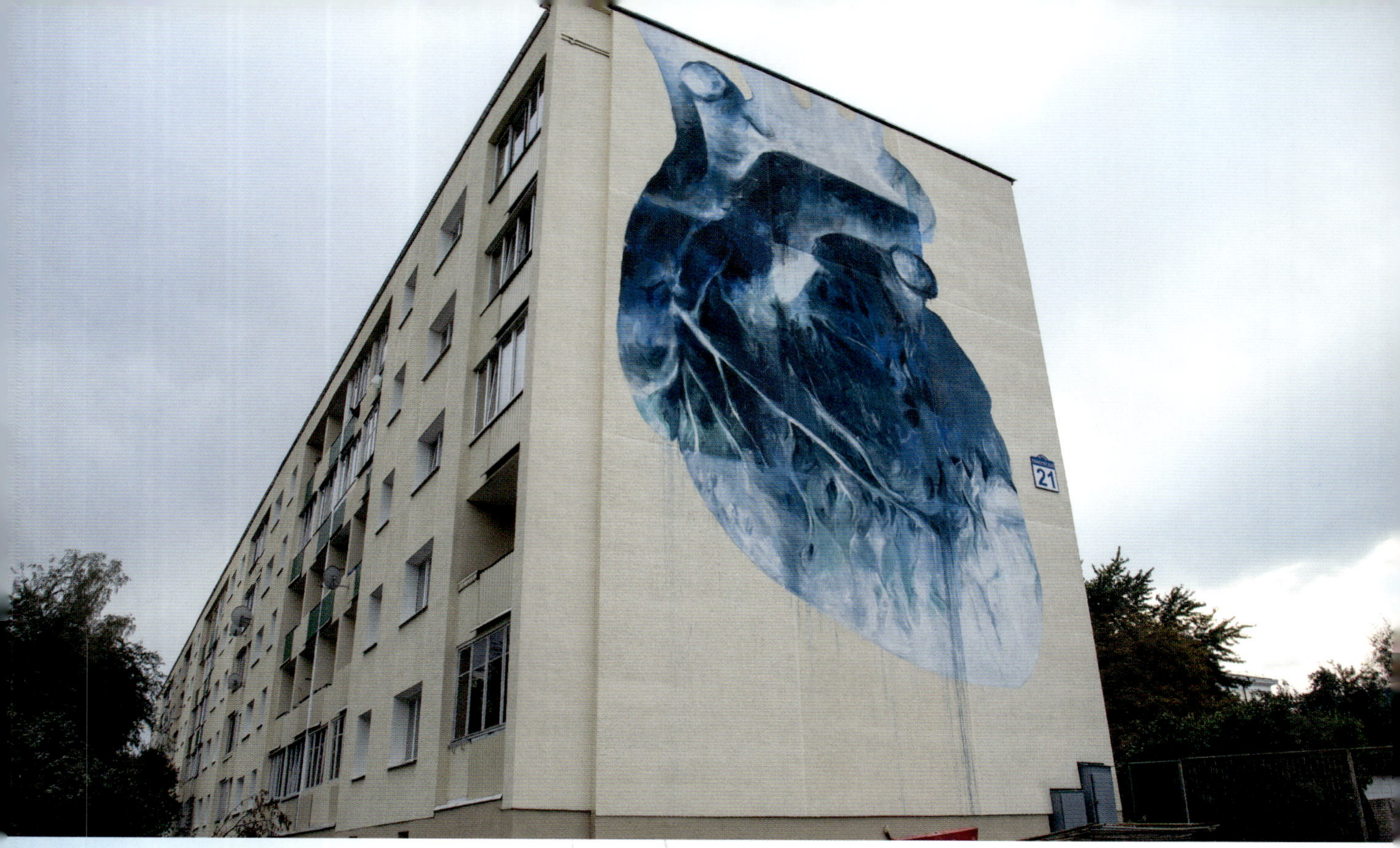

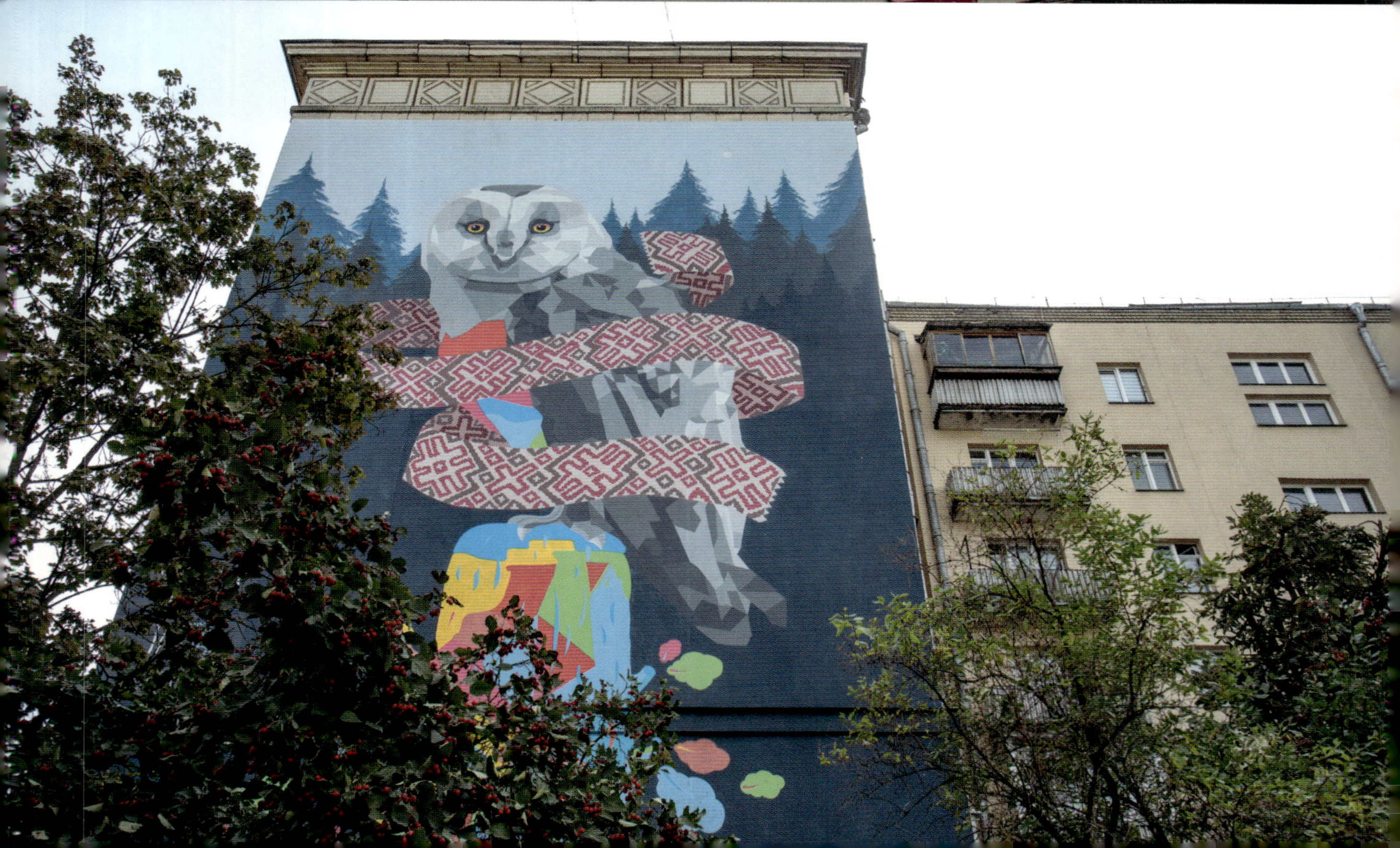

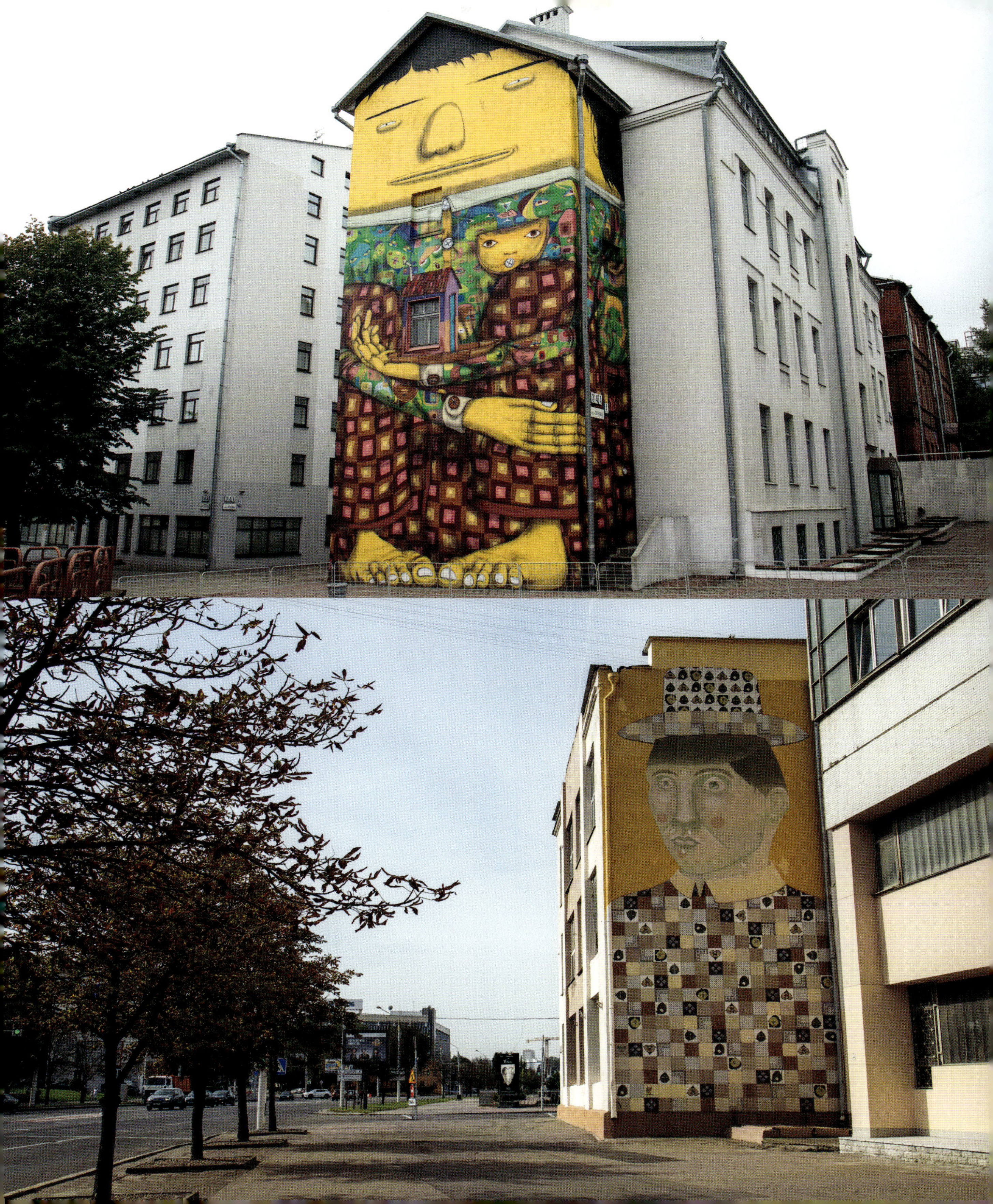

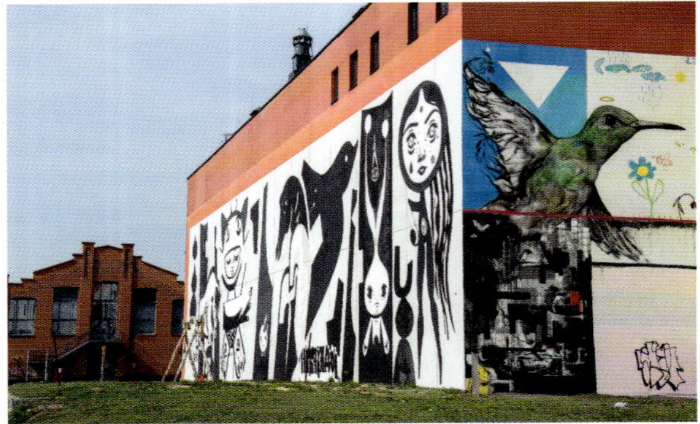

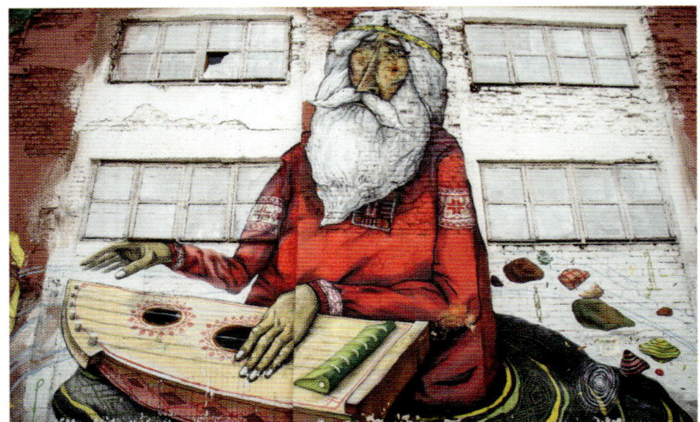

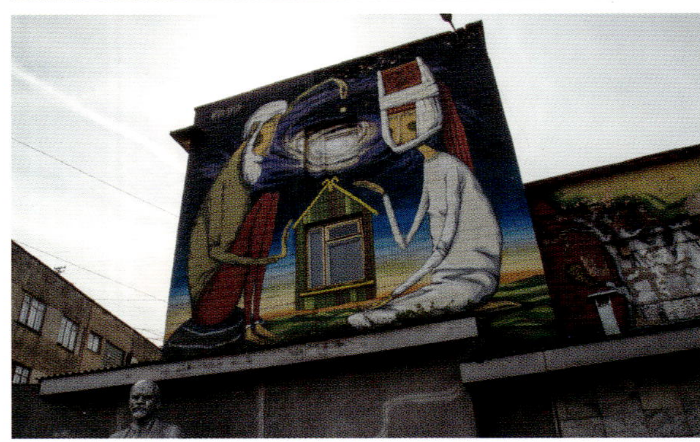

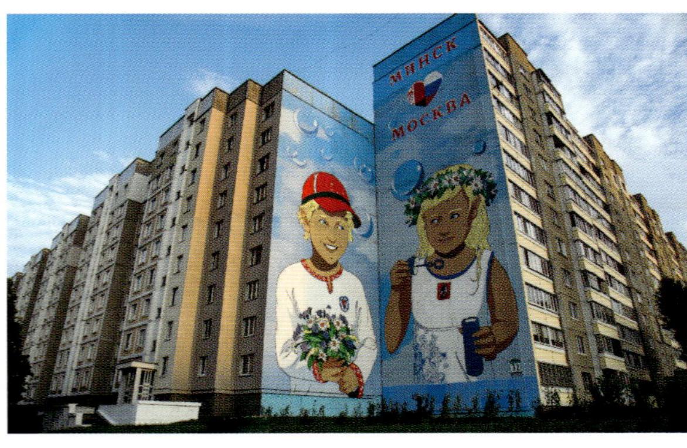

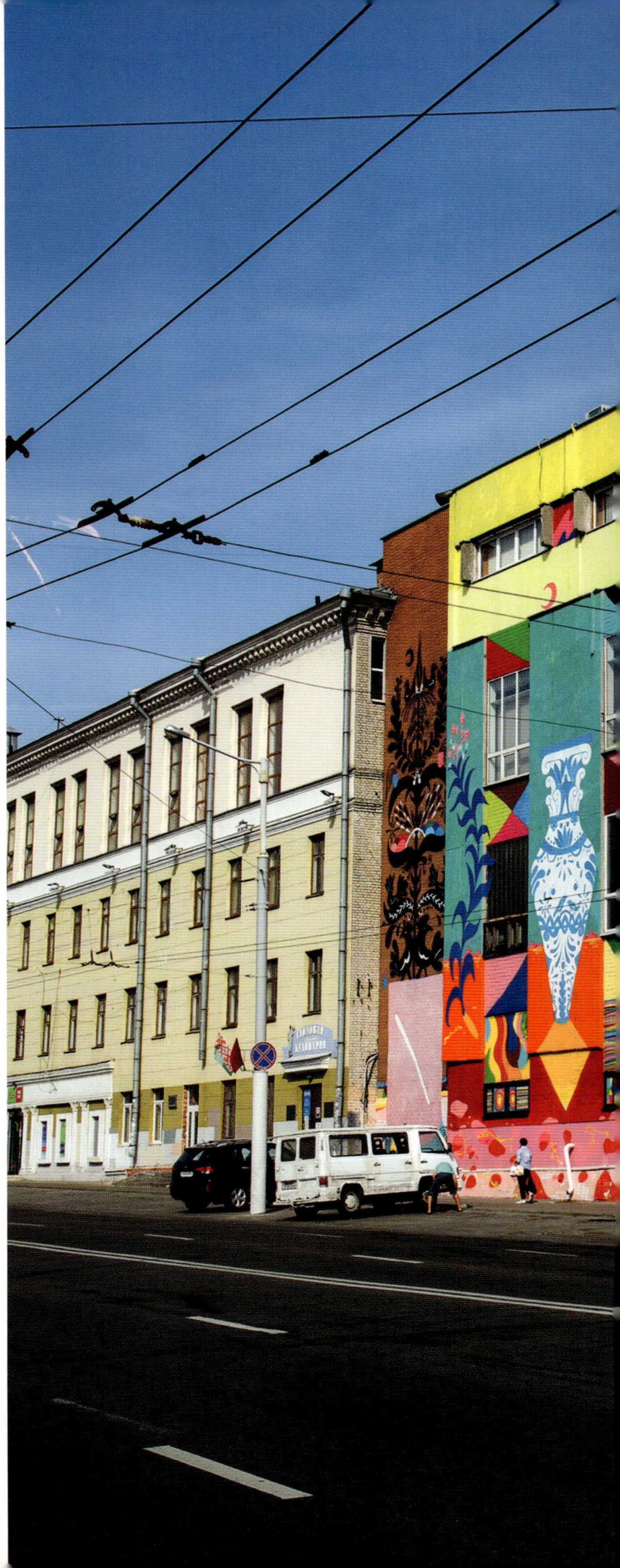

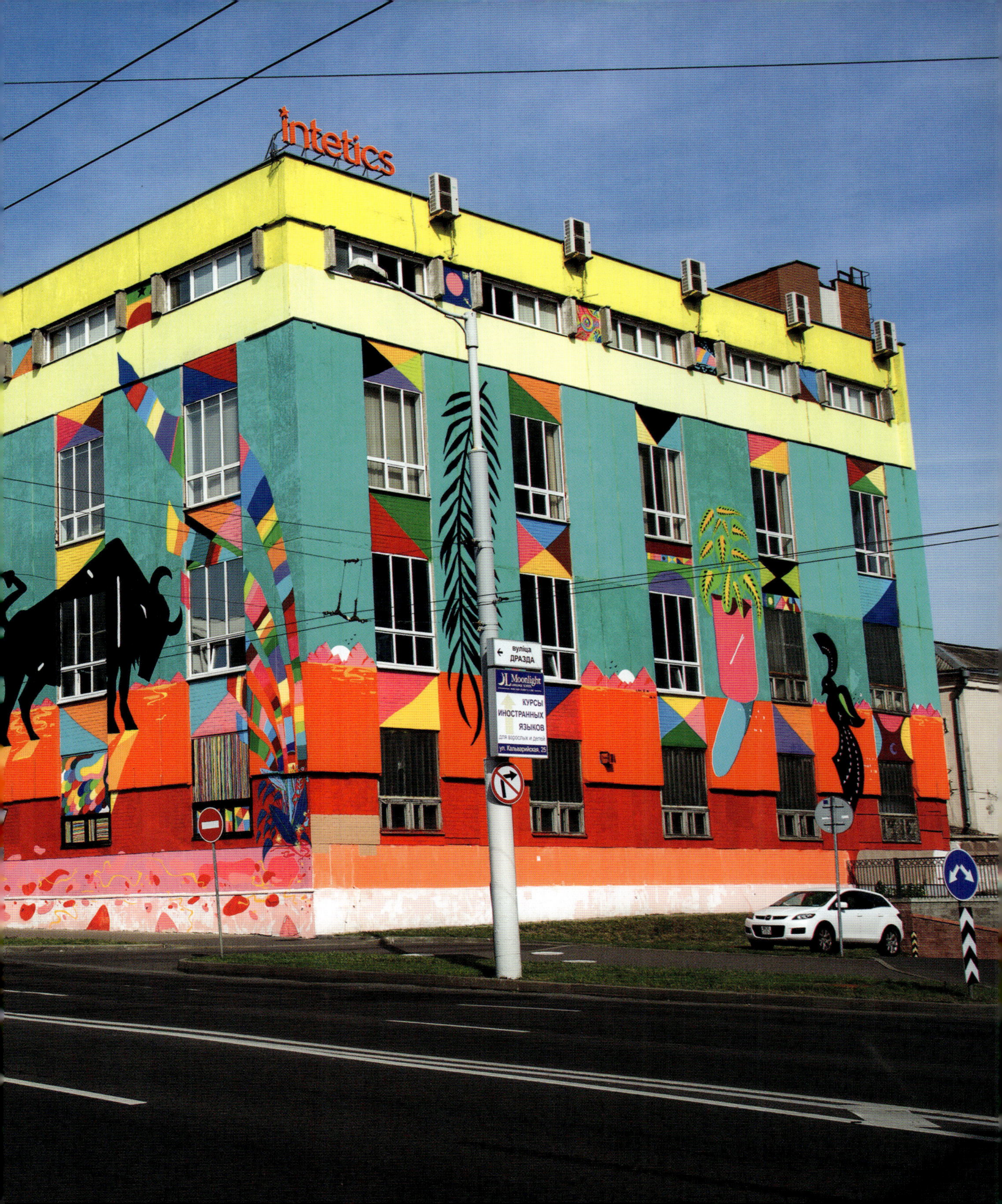

intetics
вуліца
ДРАЗДА
Moonlight
КУРСЫ
ИНОСТРАННЫХ
ЯЗЫКОВ
для взрослых и детей
ул. Кальварийская, 25

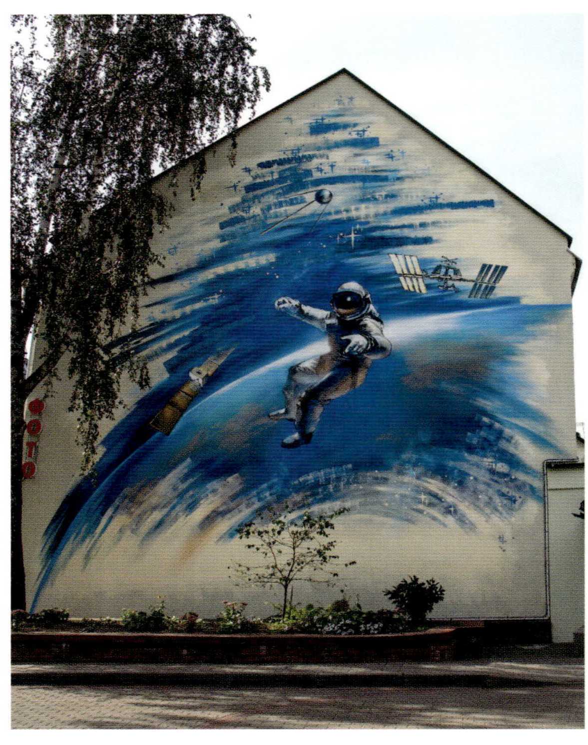

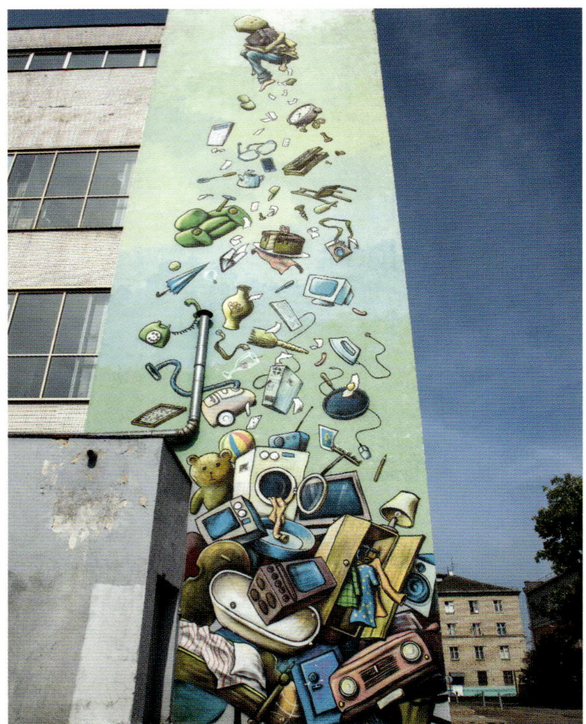

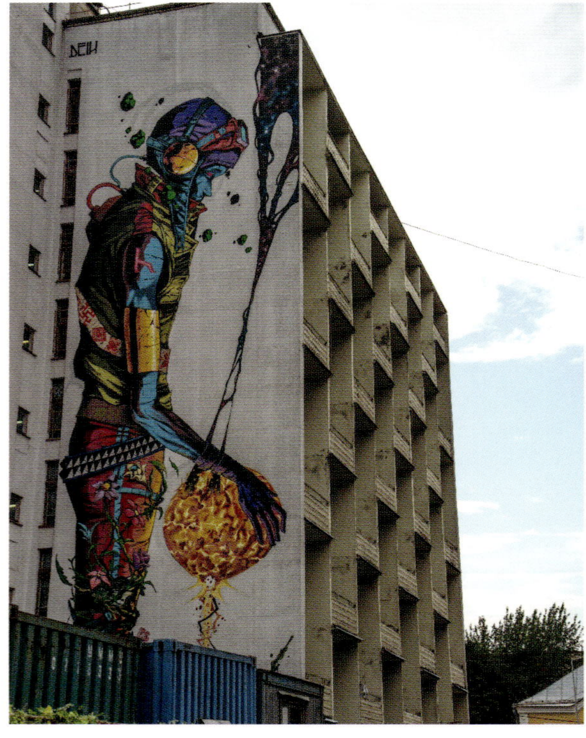

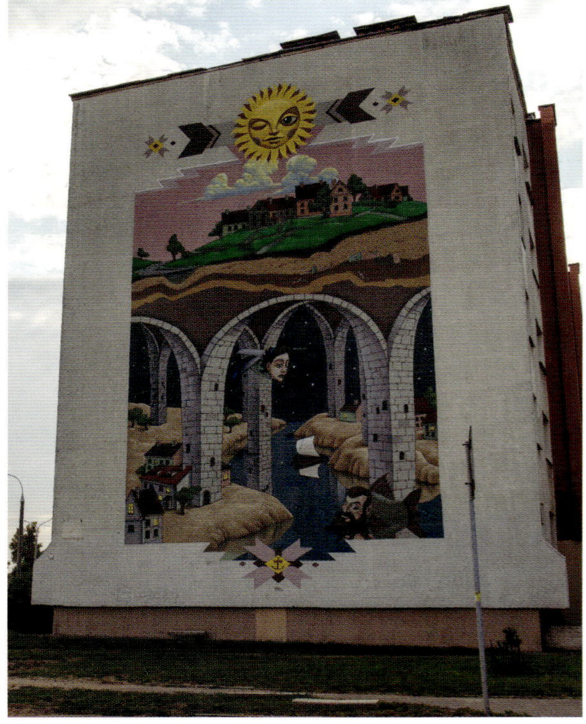

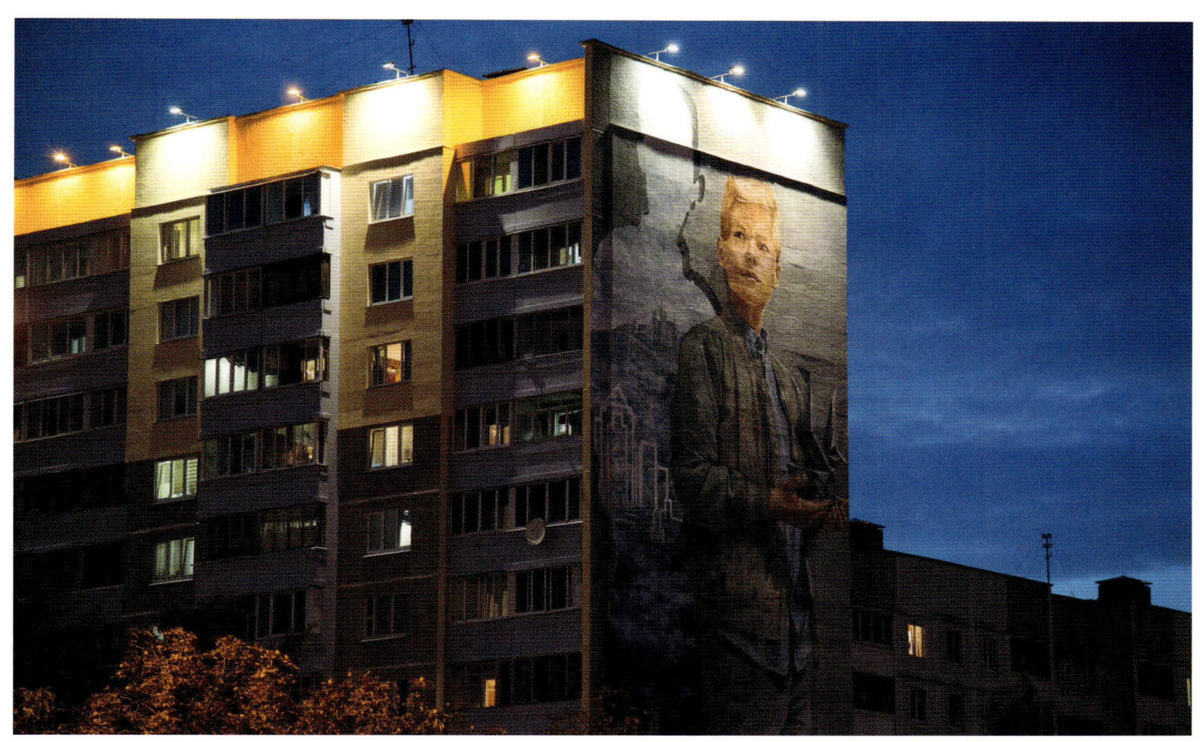

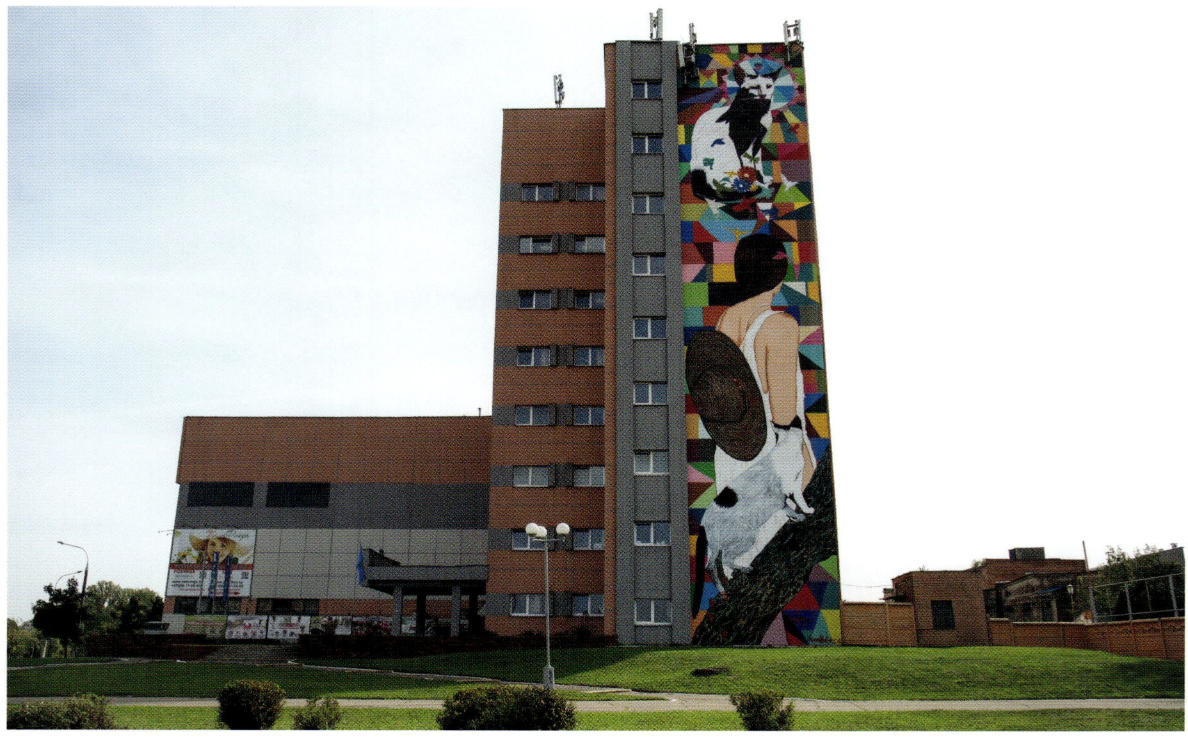

MOSCOW

RUSSIA

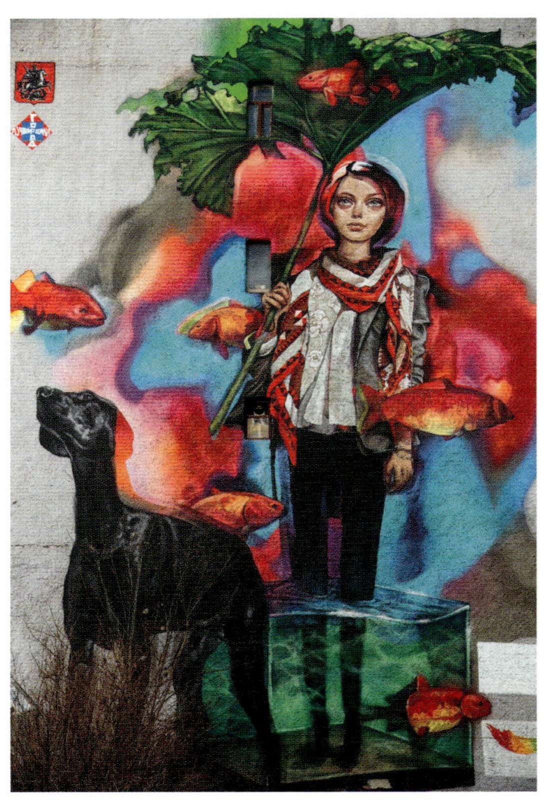

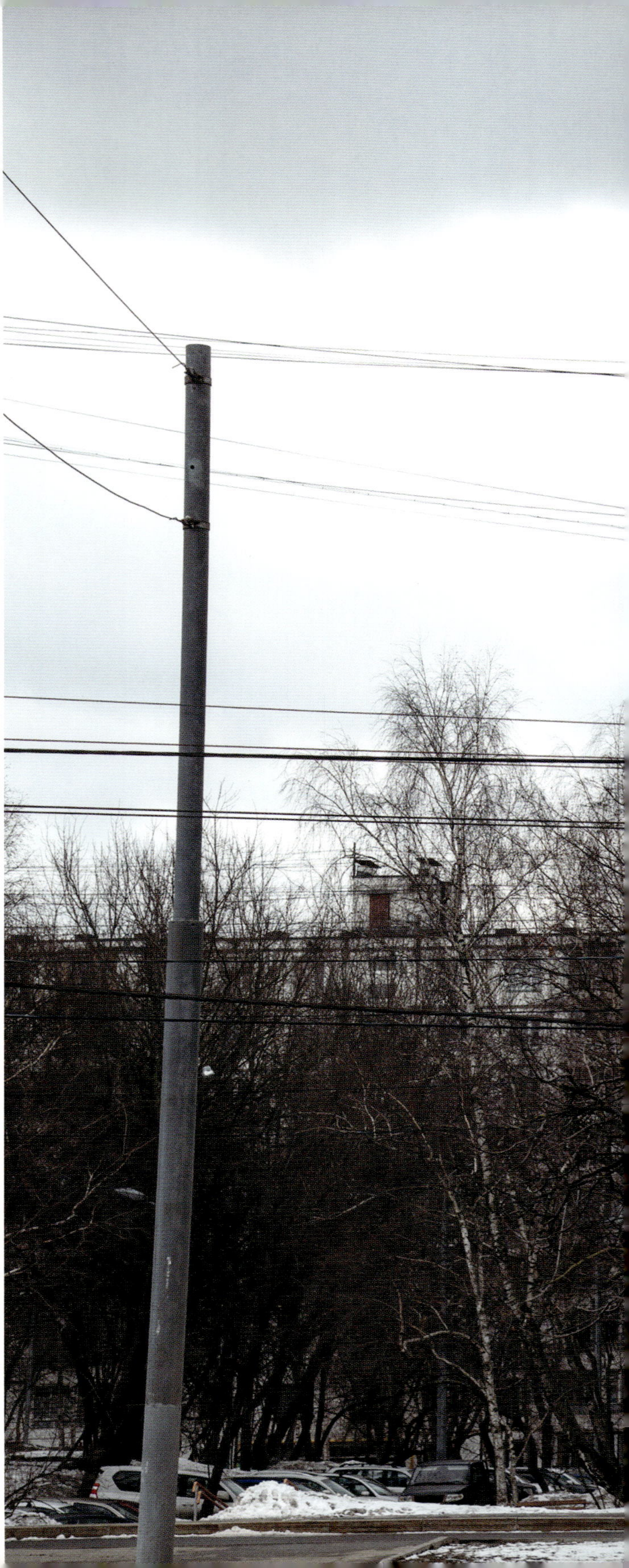

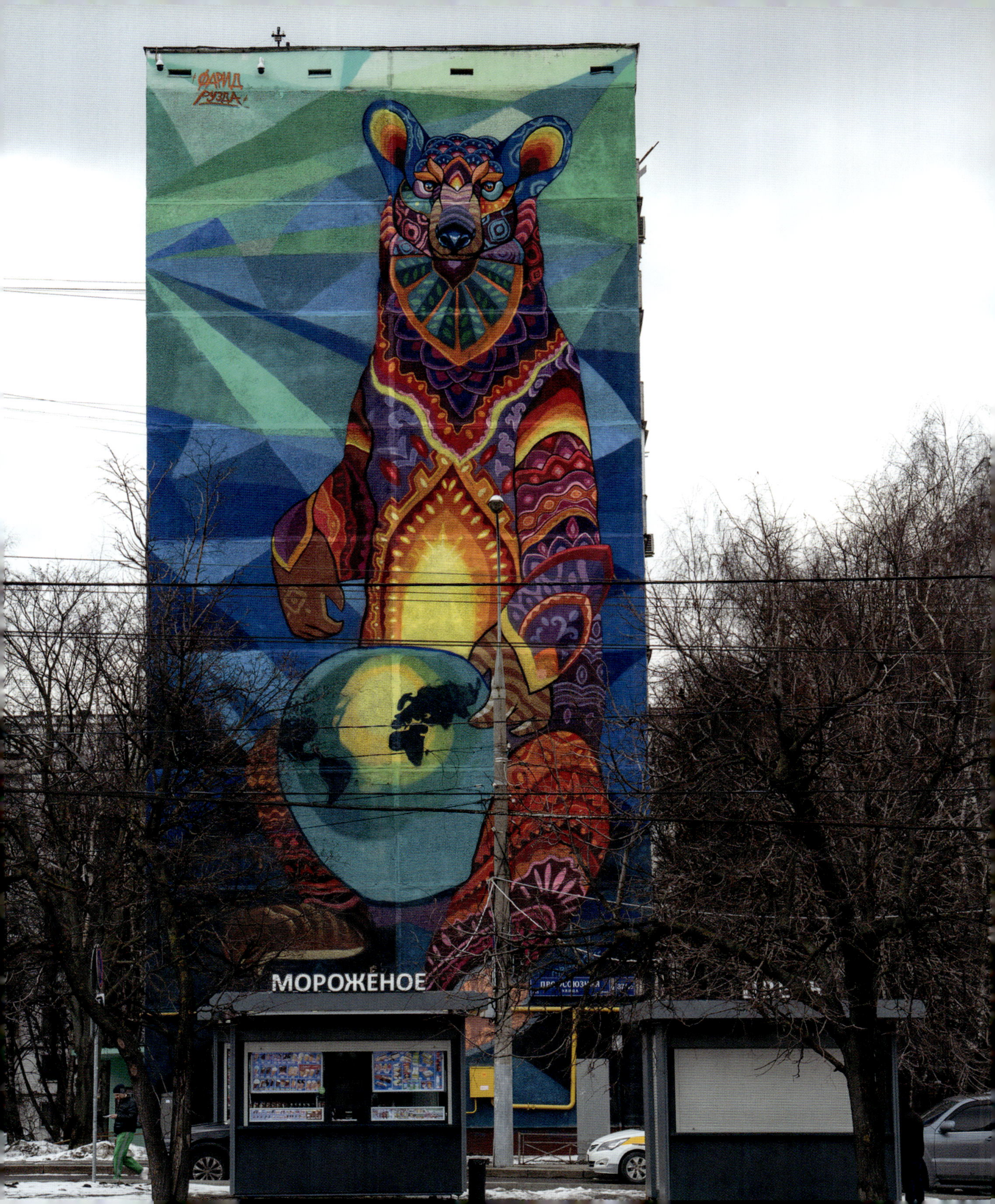
ФАРИД
РУЭДА
МОРОЖЕНОЕ

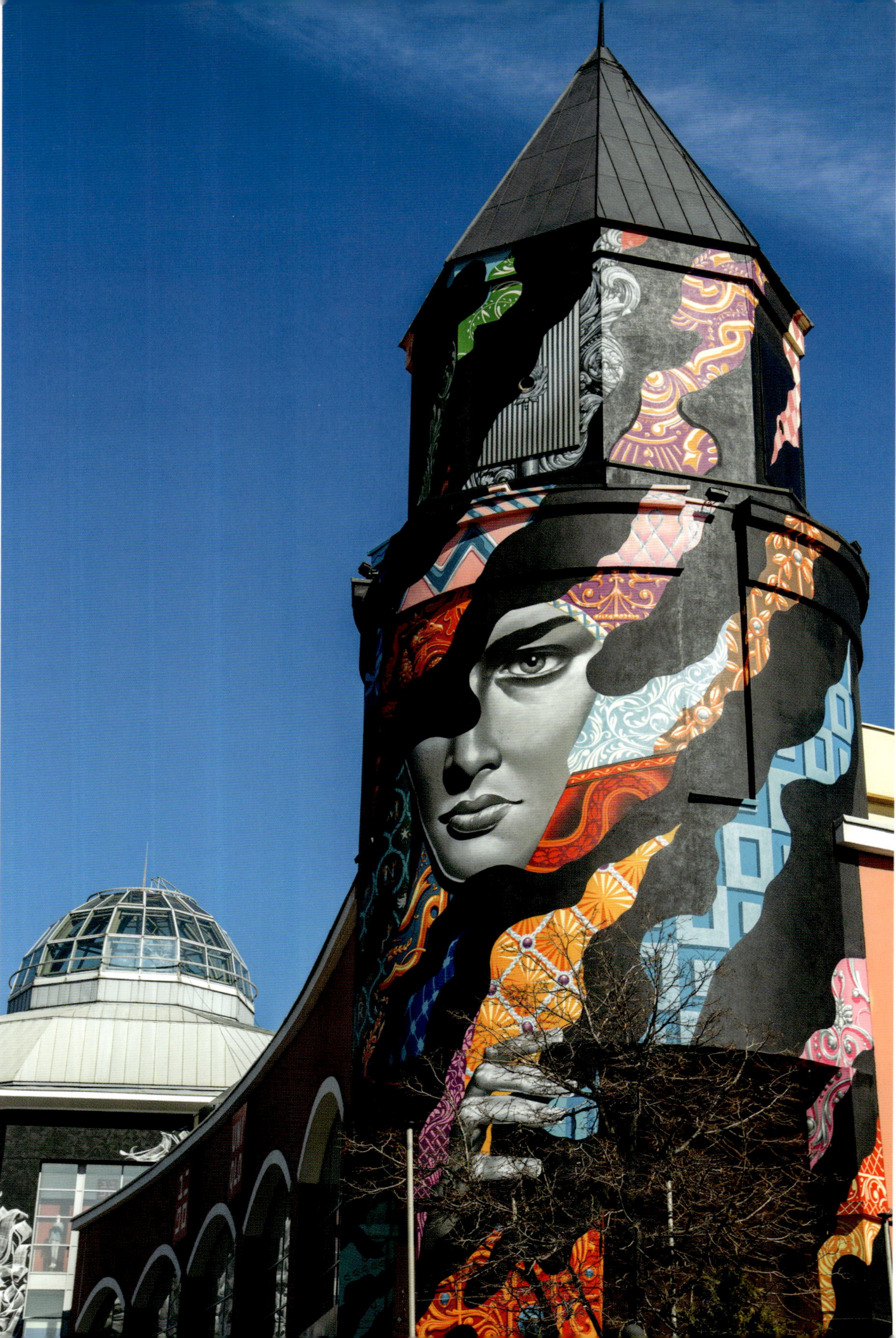

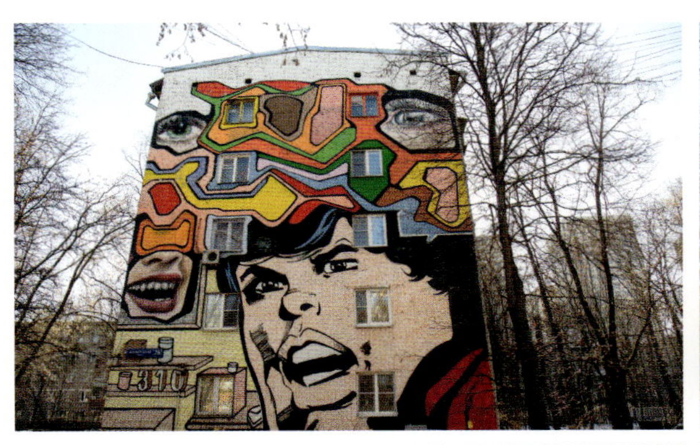
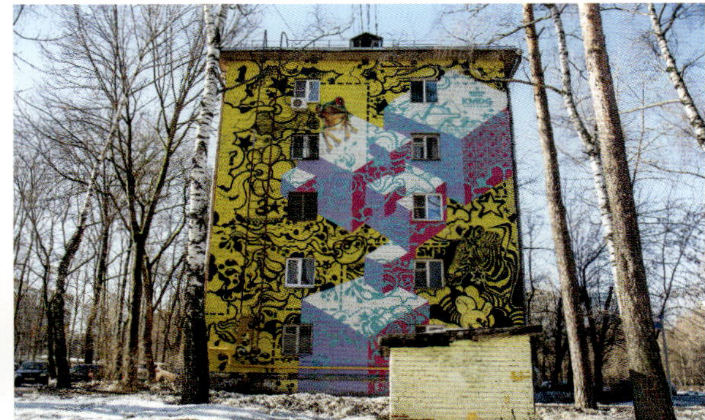
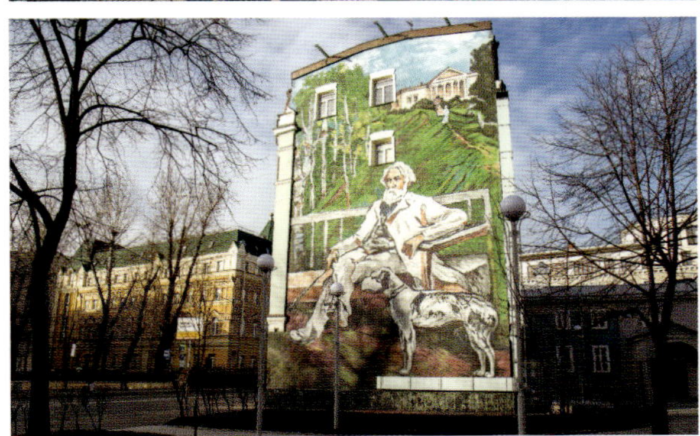
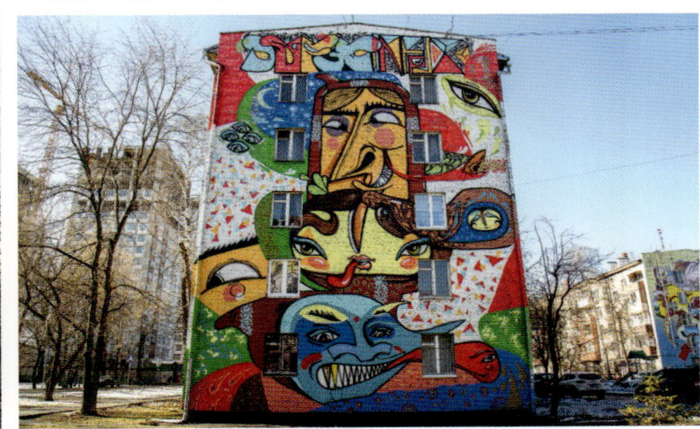
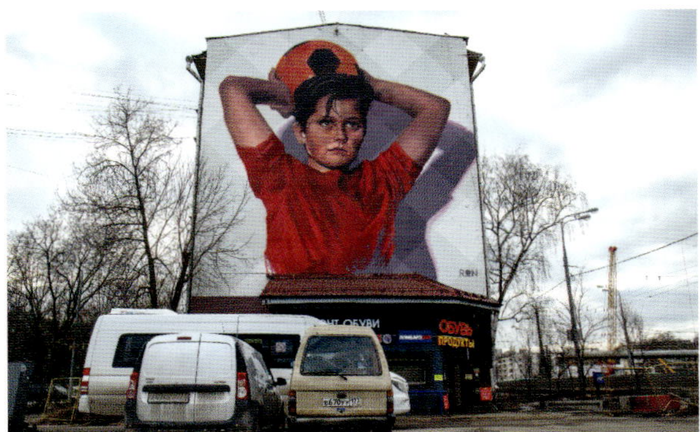
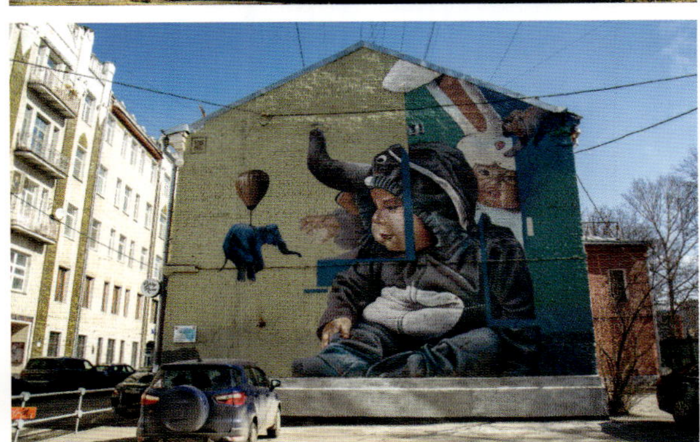
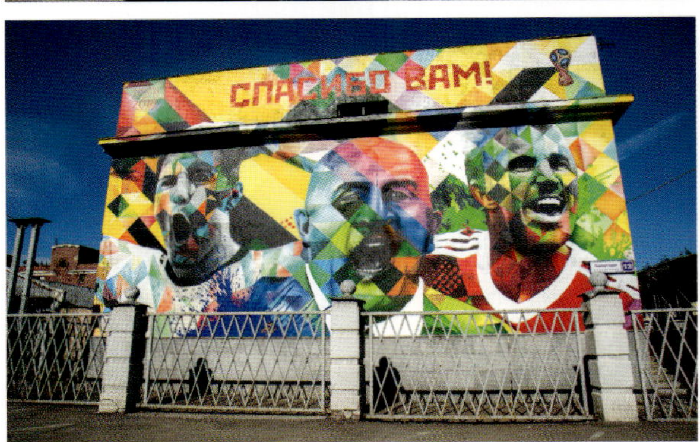

СПАСИБО ВАМ!

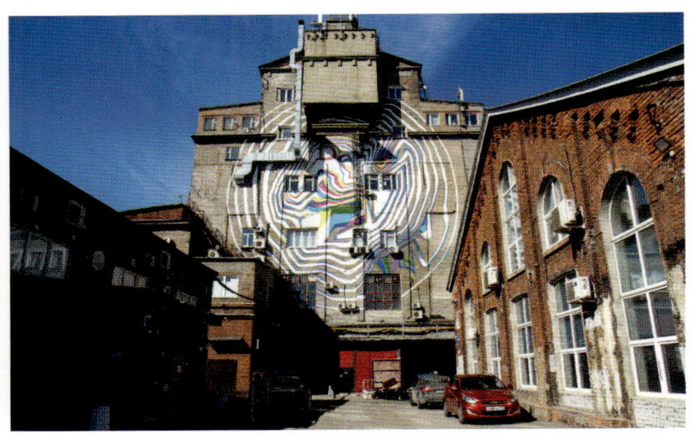

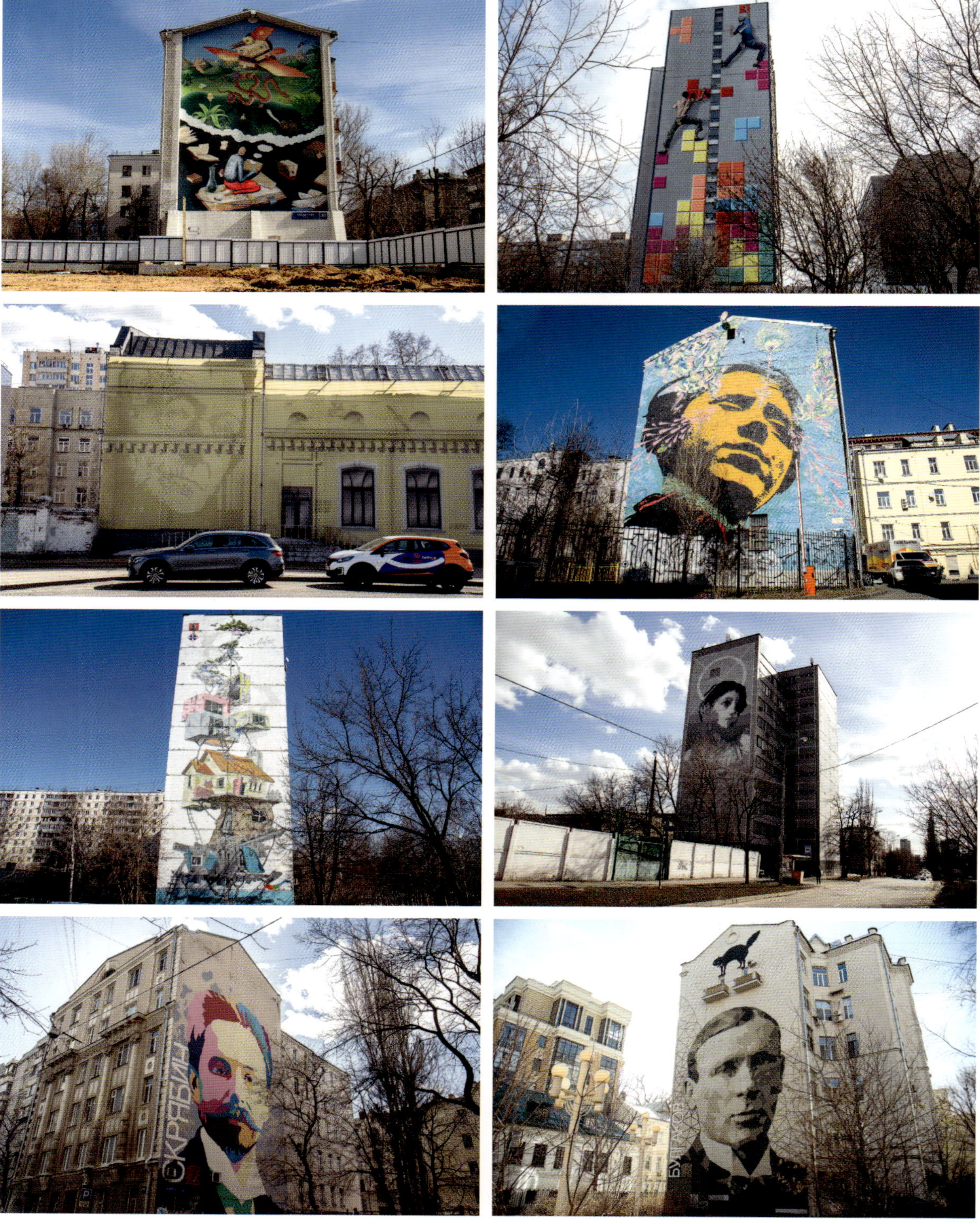

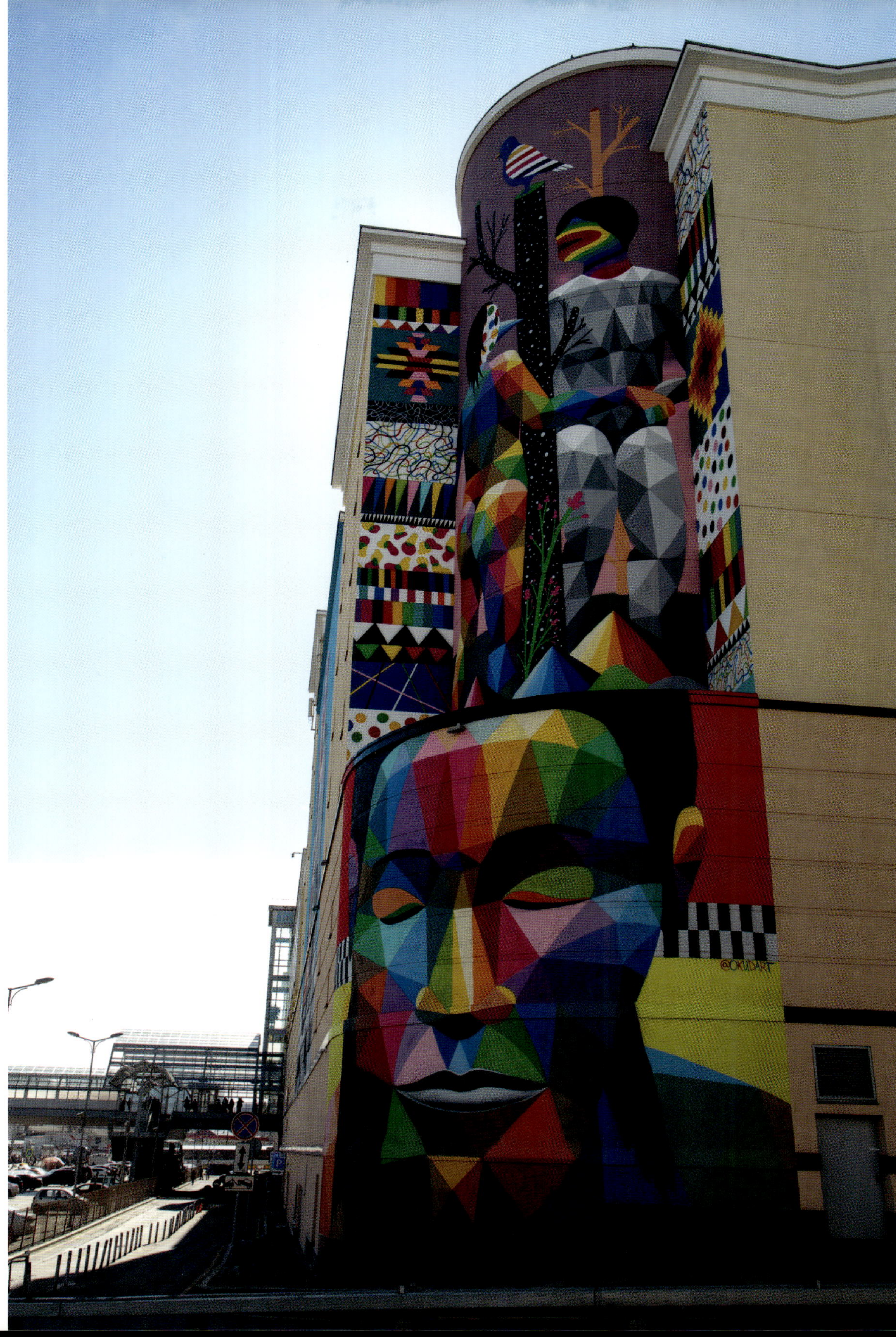

KIEV

UKRAINE

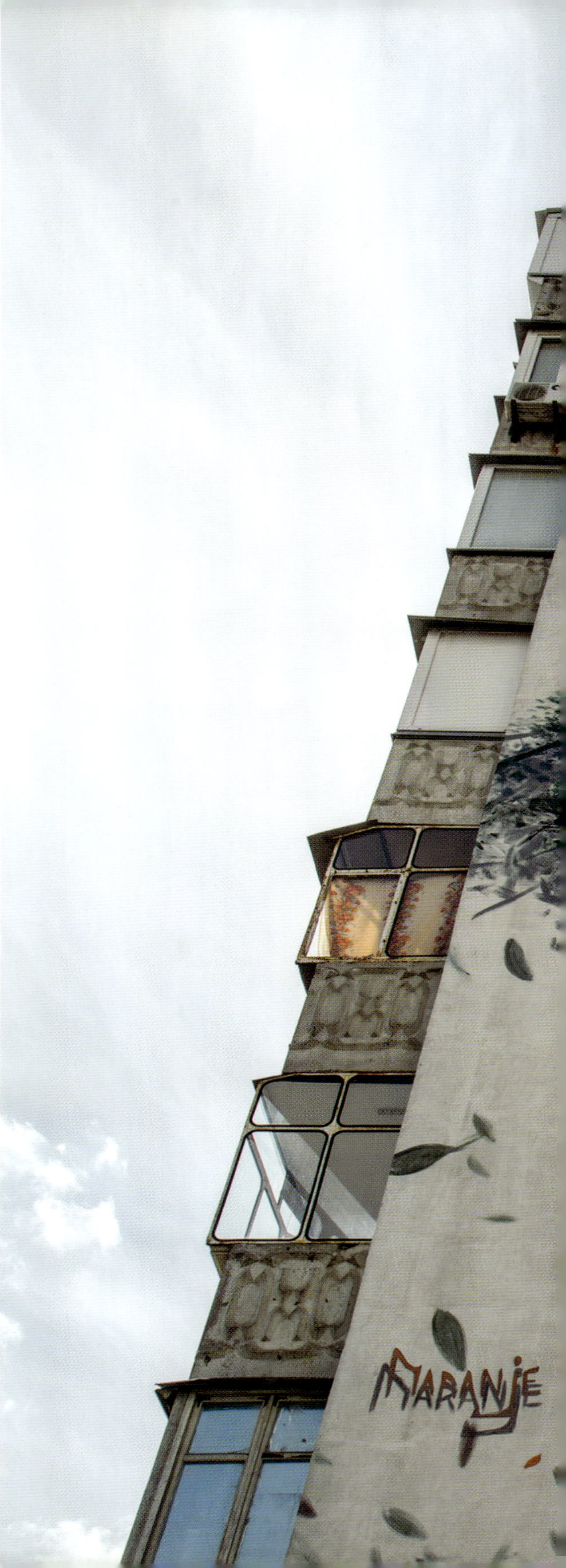

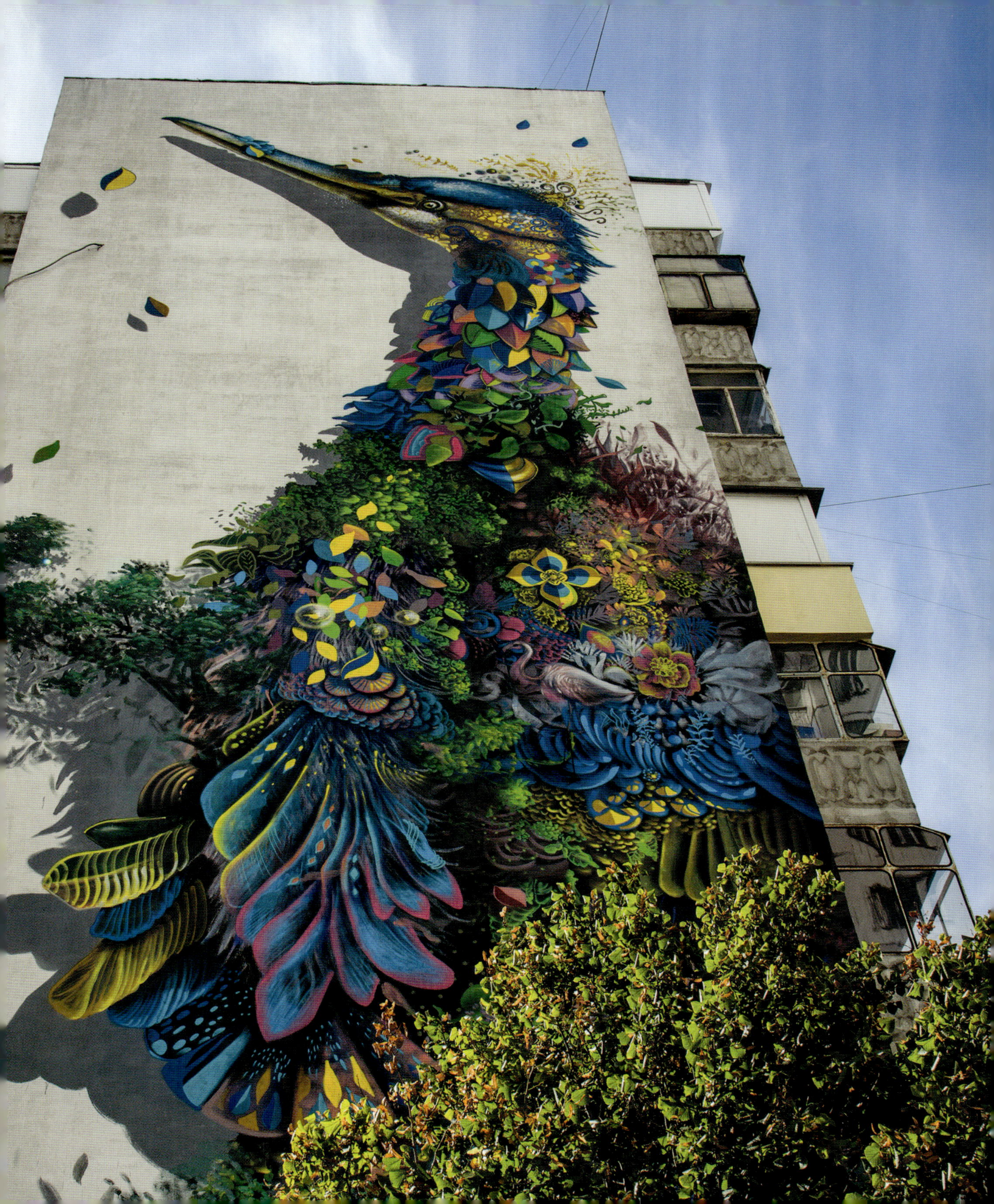

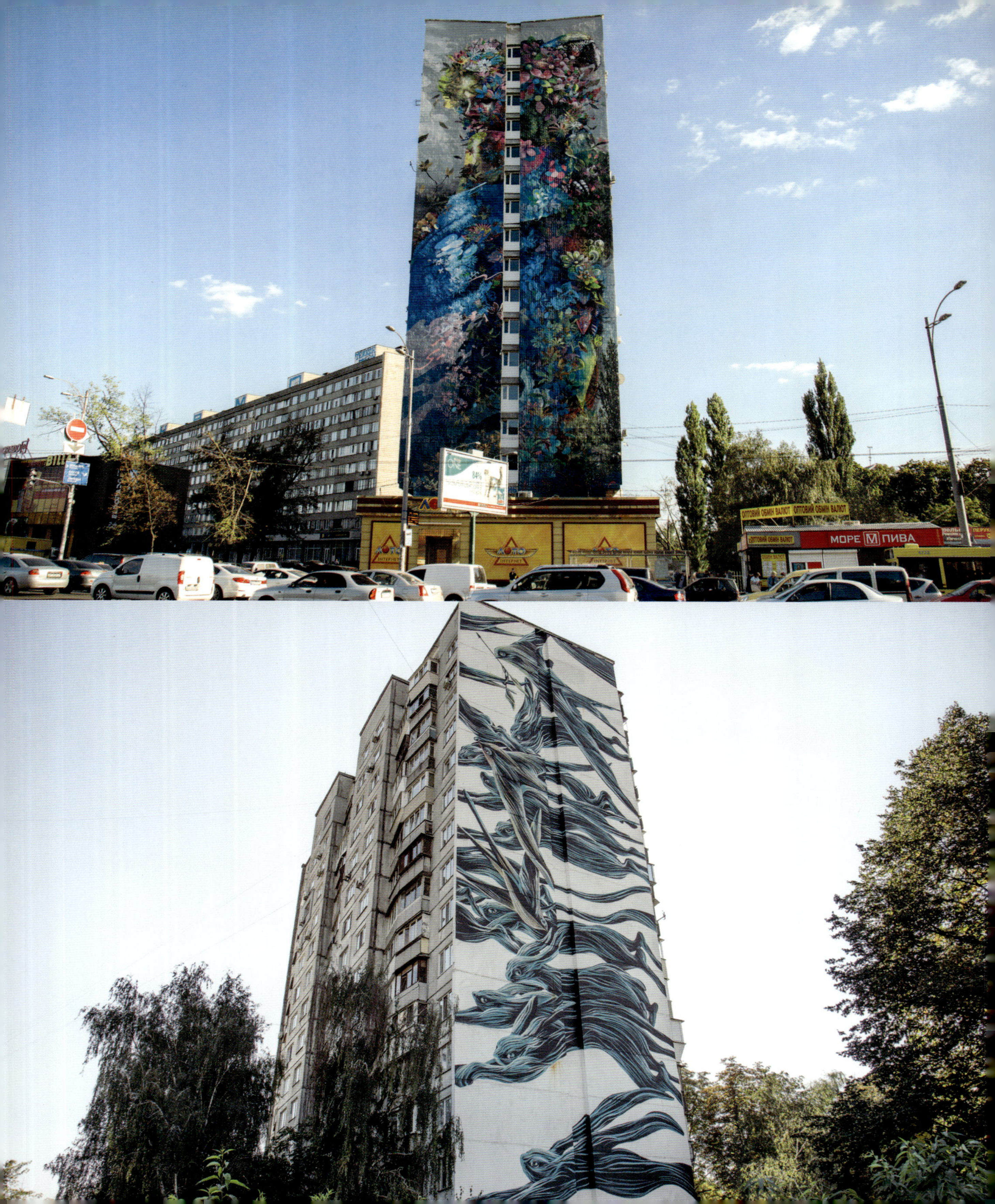

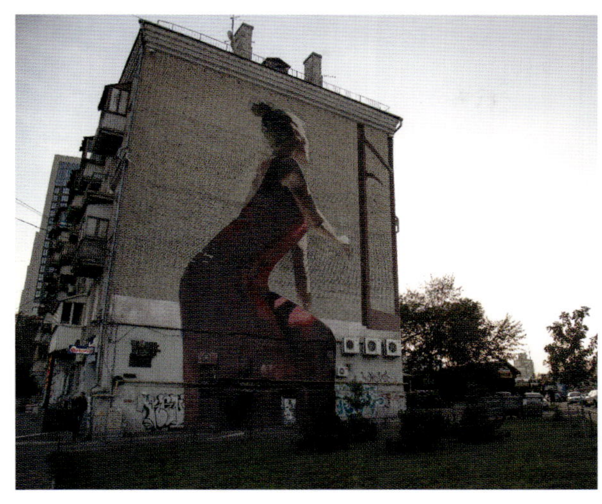

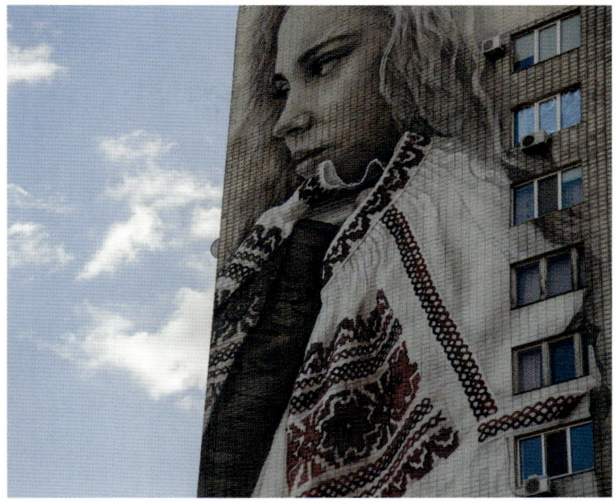

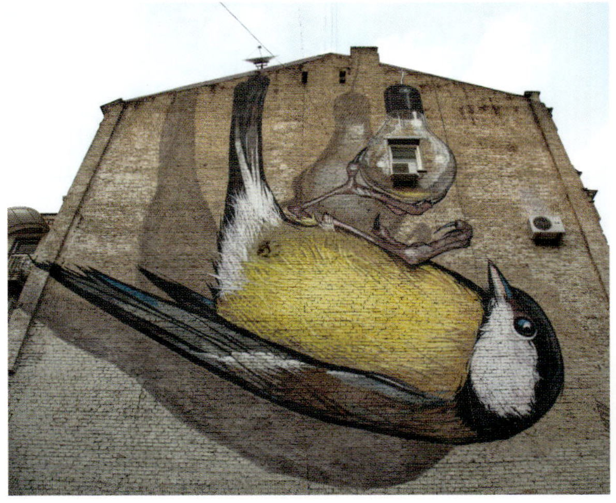

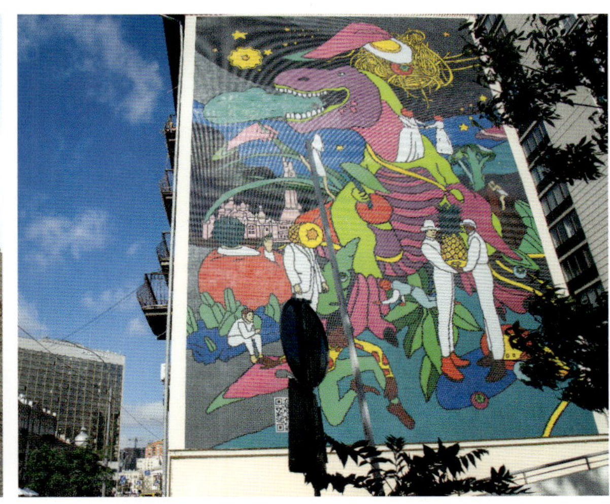

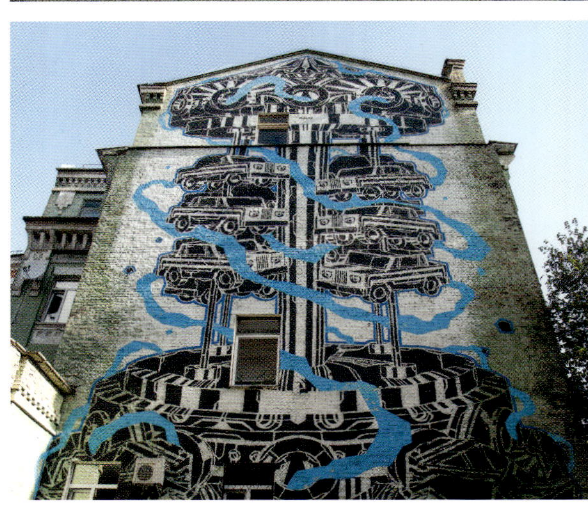

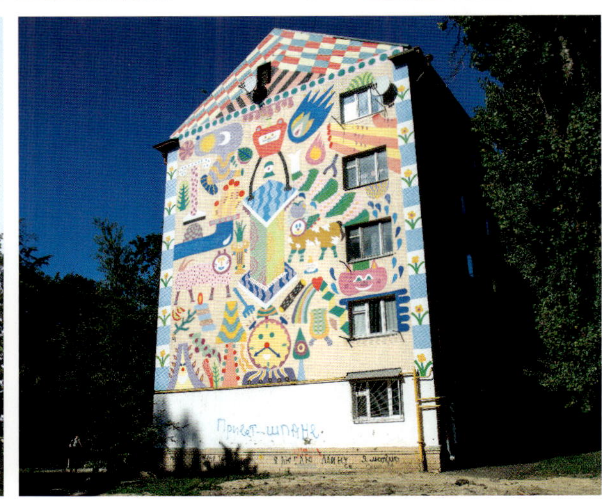

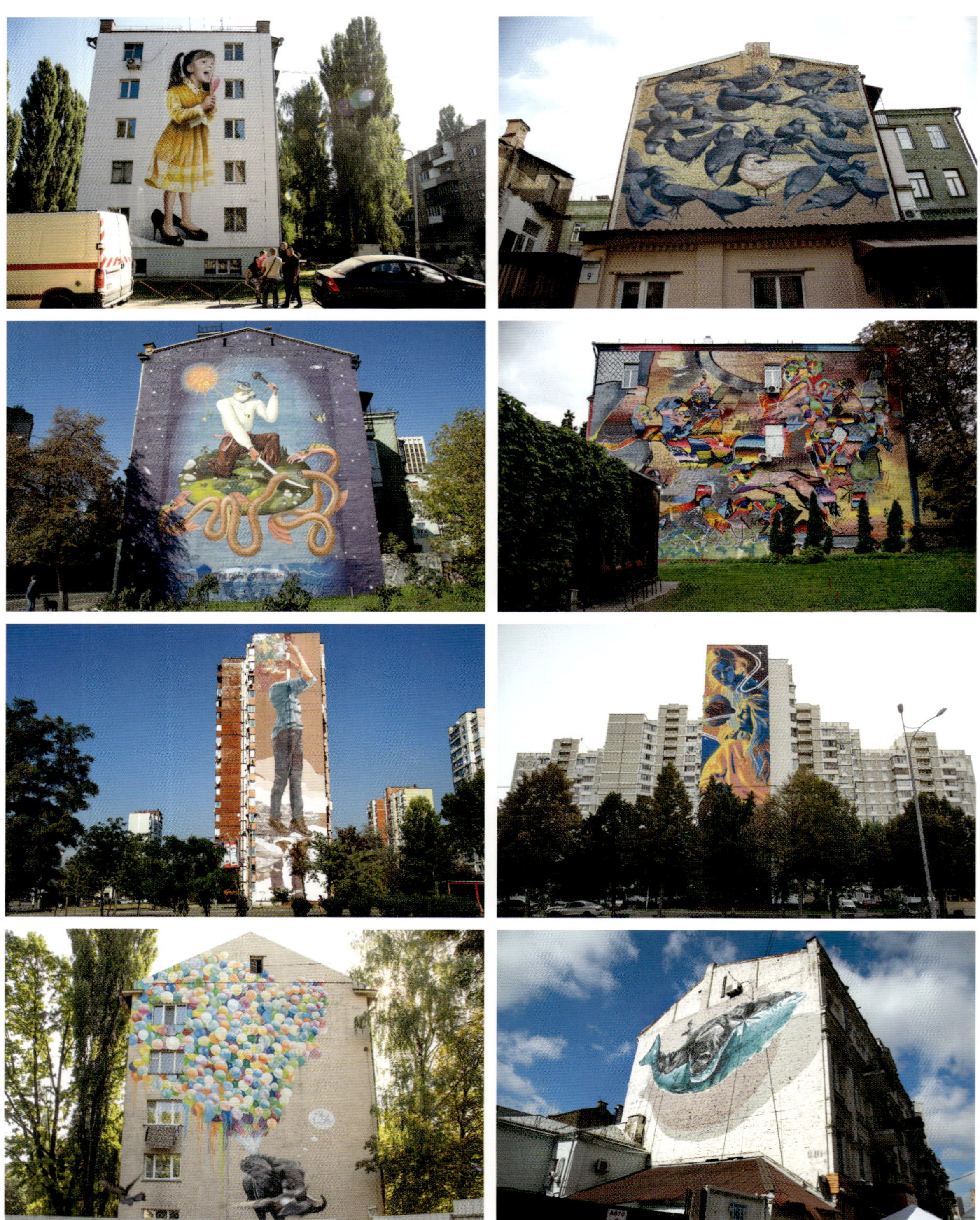

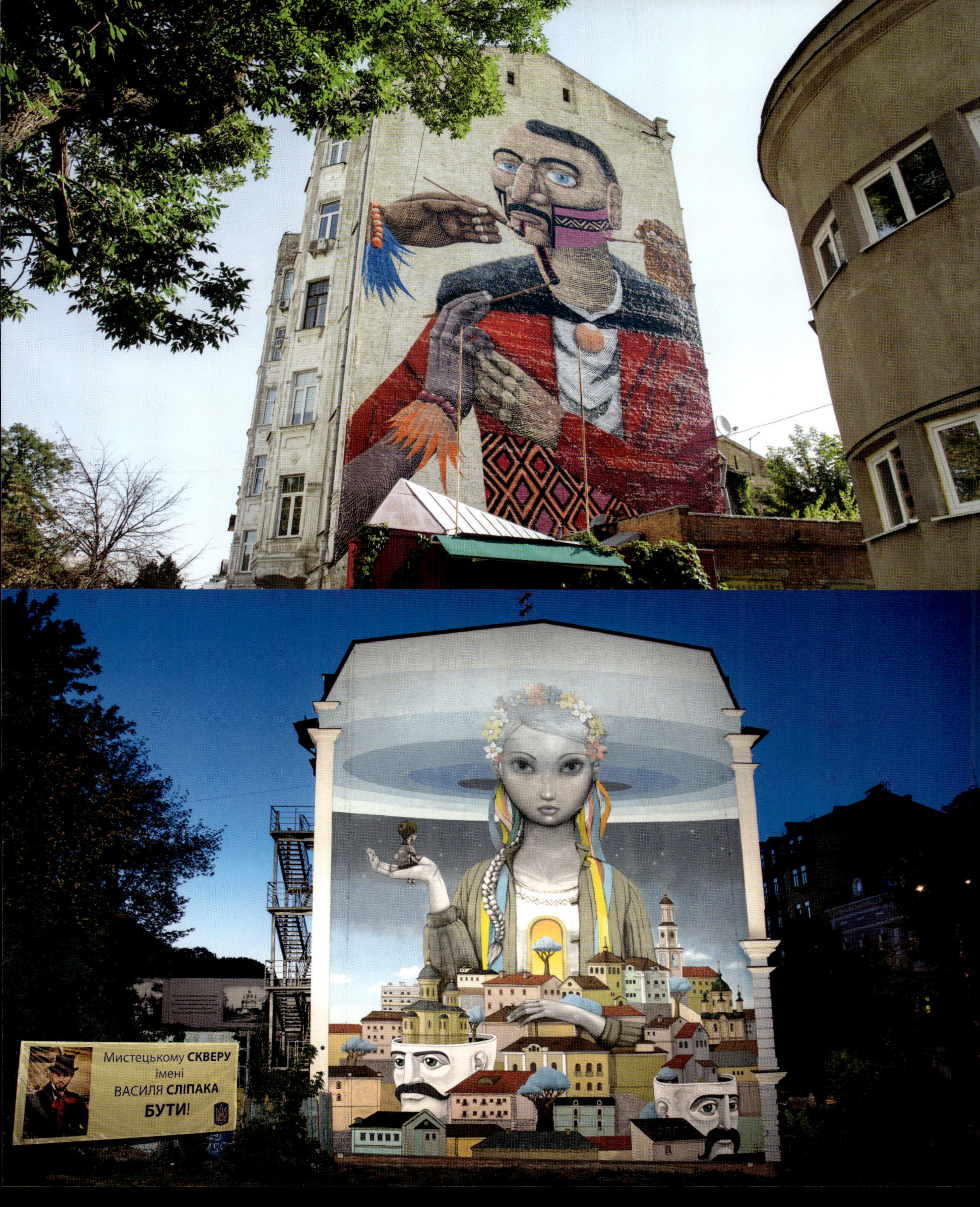

Мистецькому СКВЕРУ
імені
ВАСИЛЯ СЛІПАКА
БУТИ!

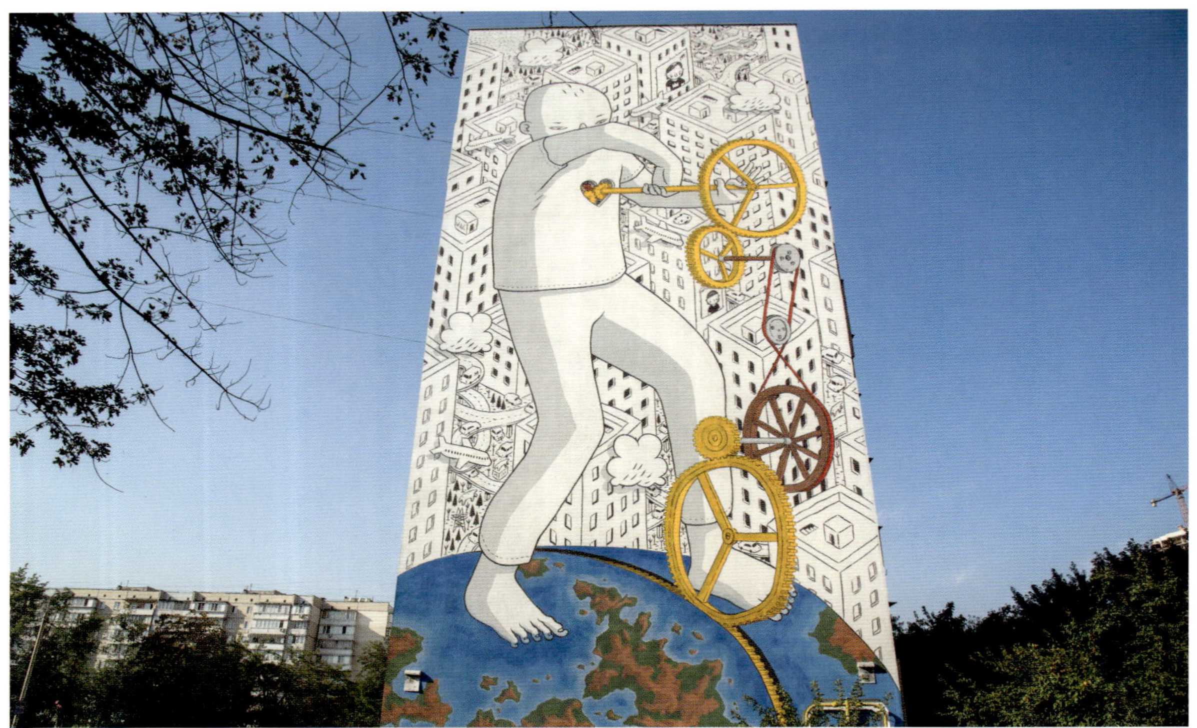

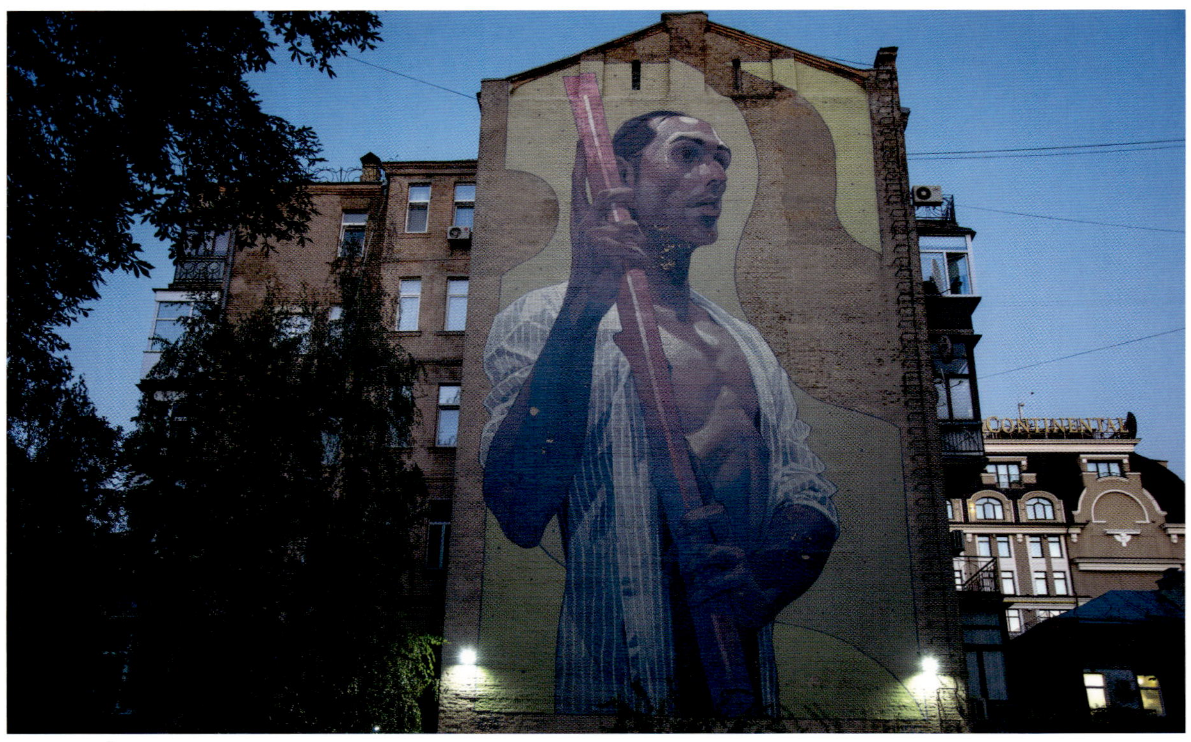

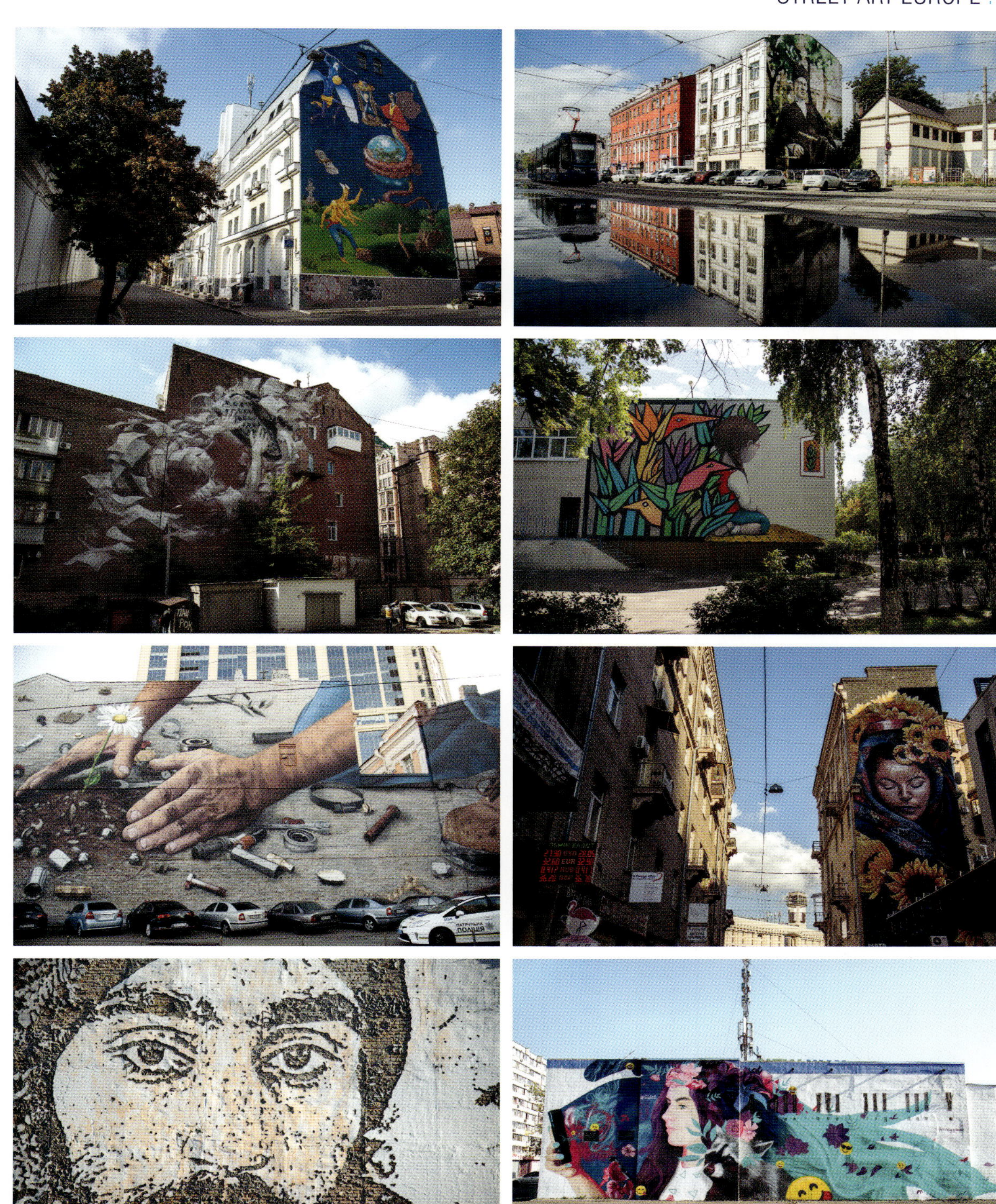

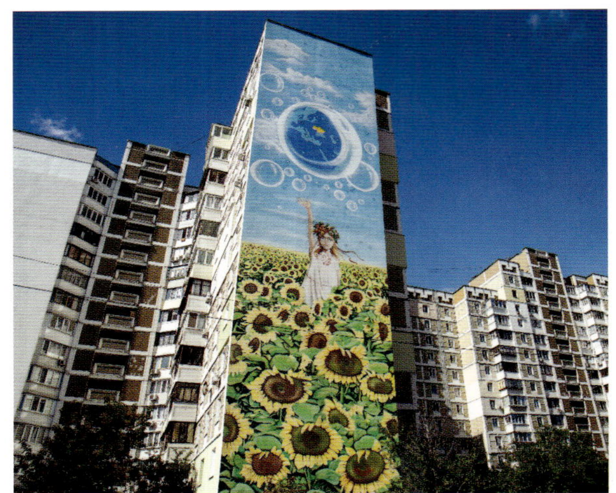

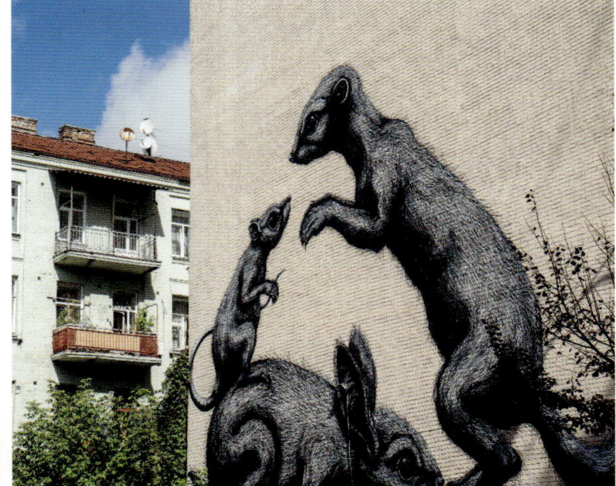

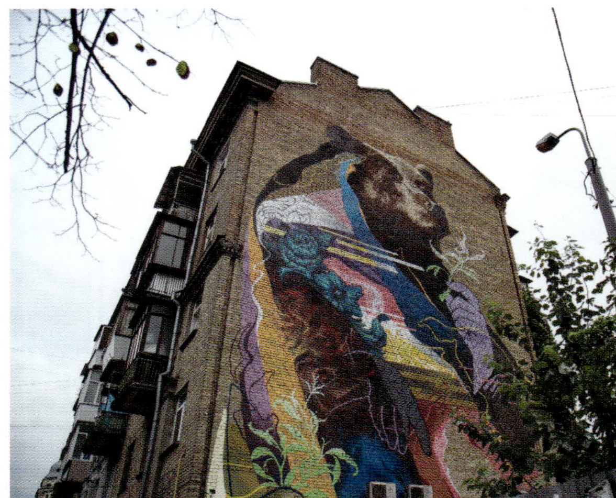

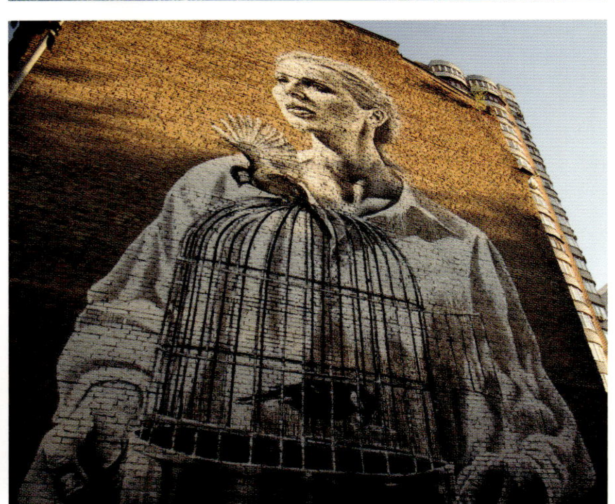

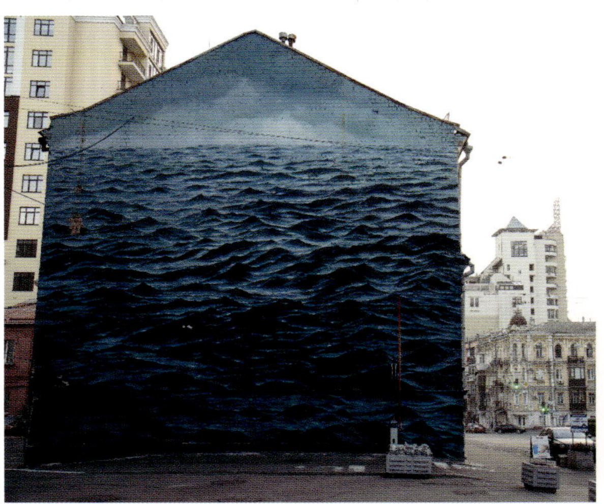

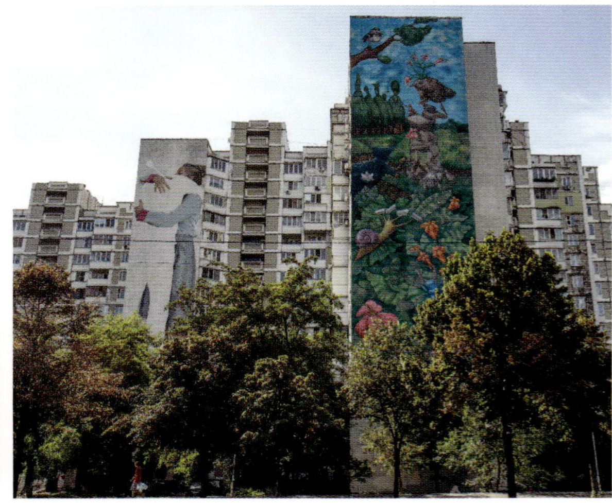

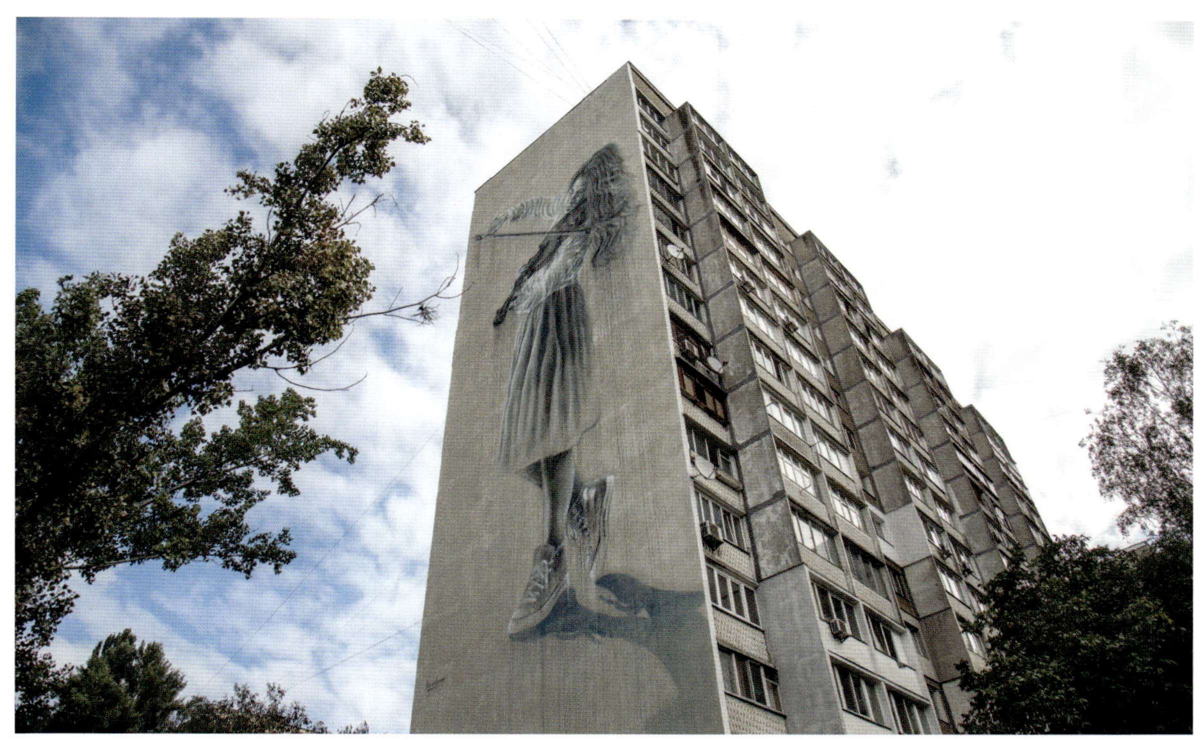

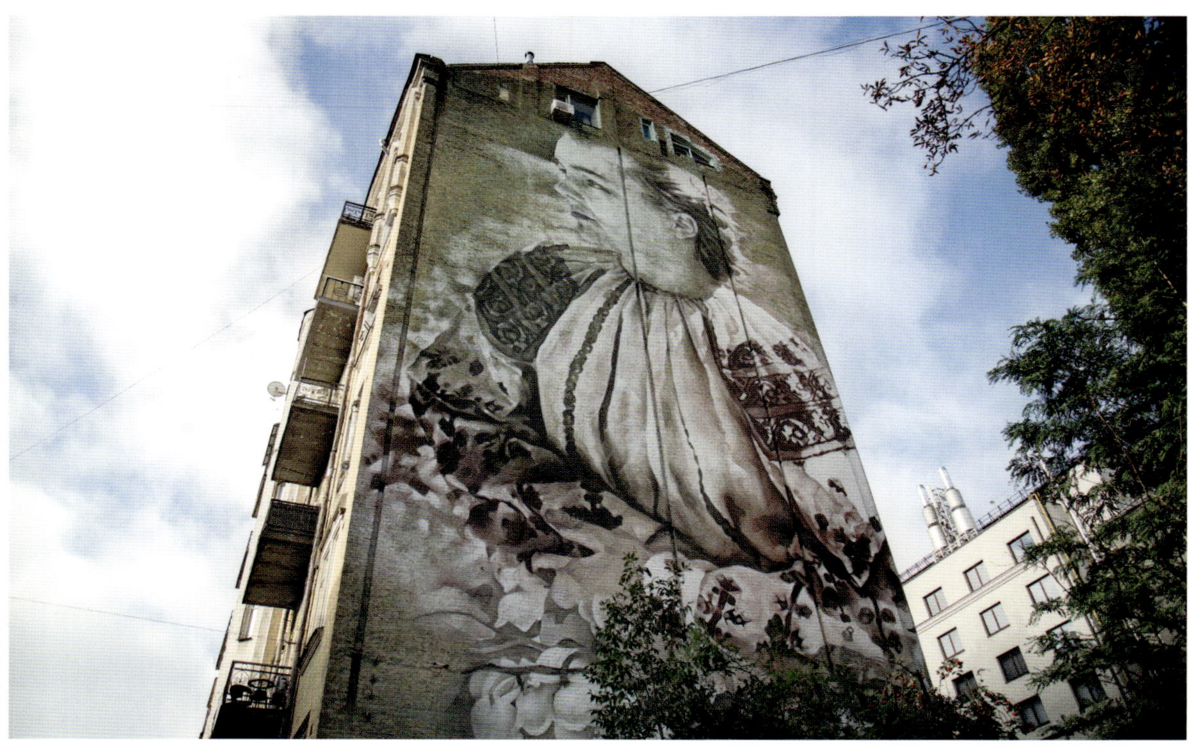

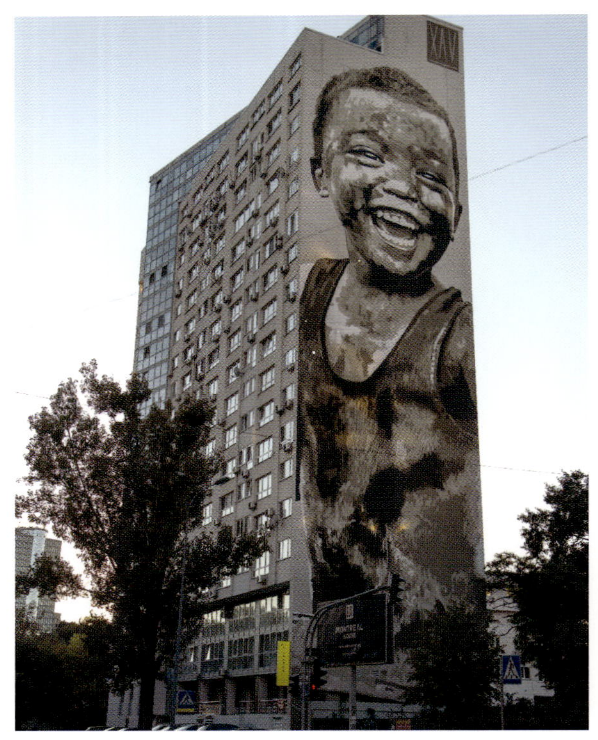

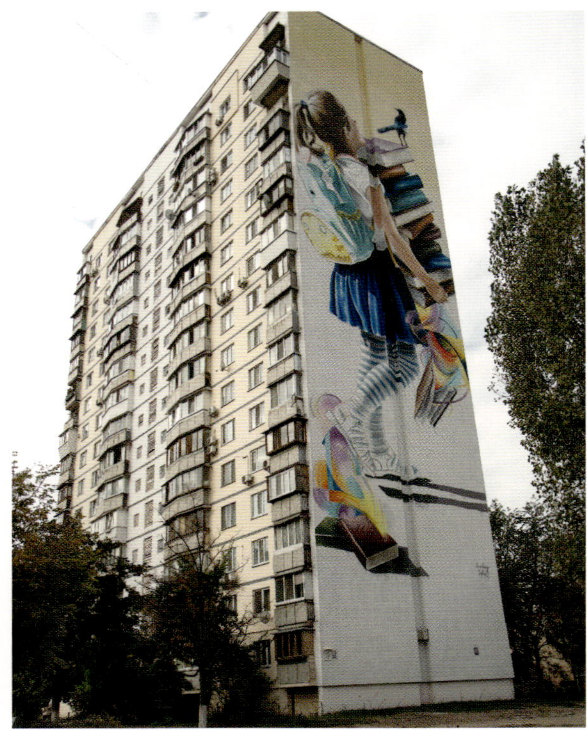

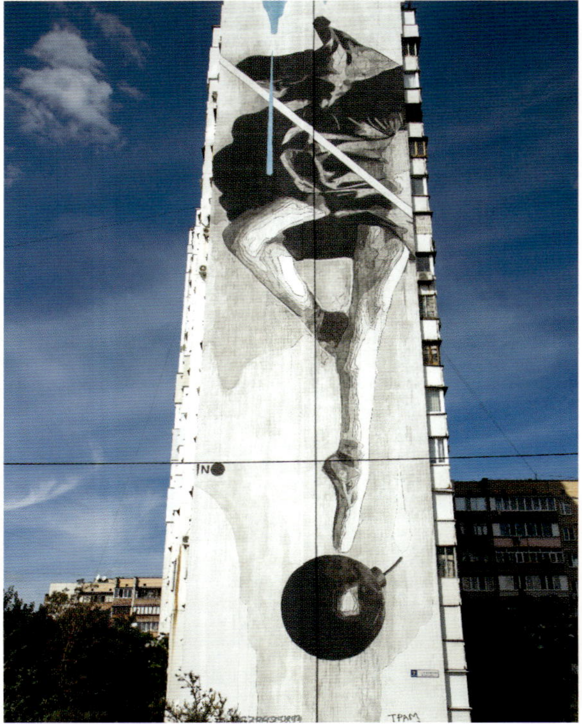

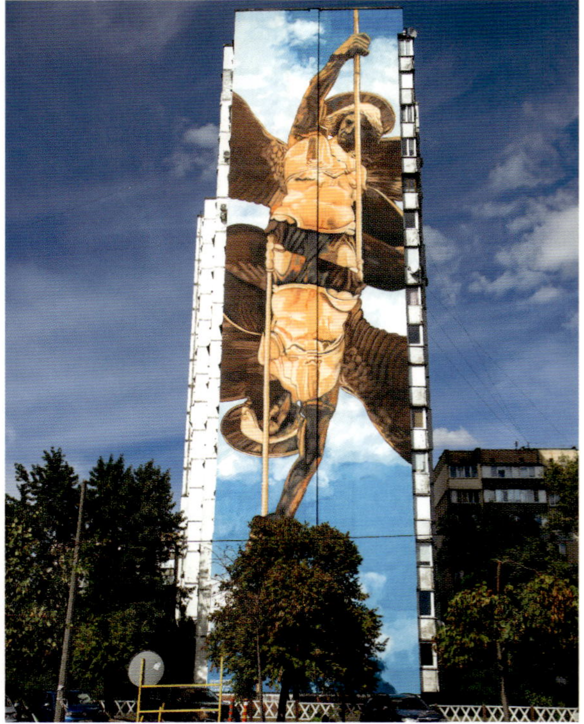

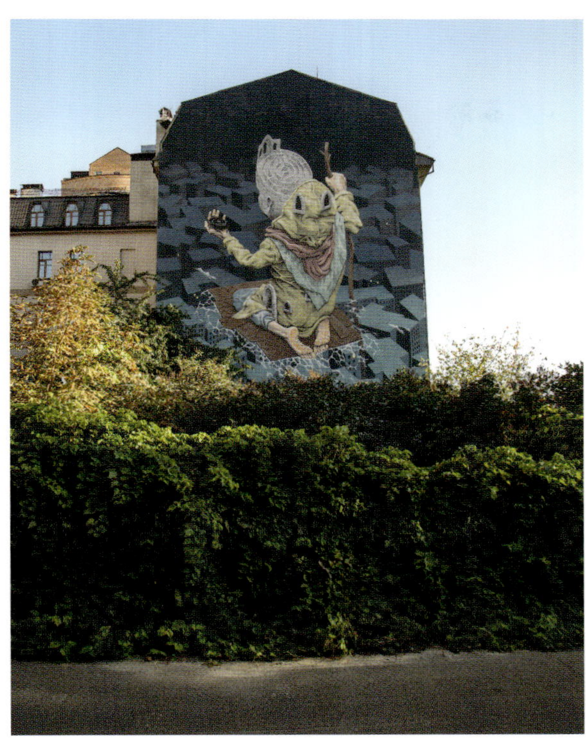

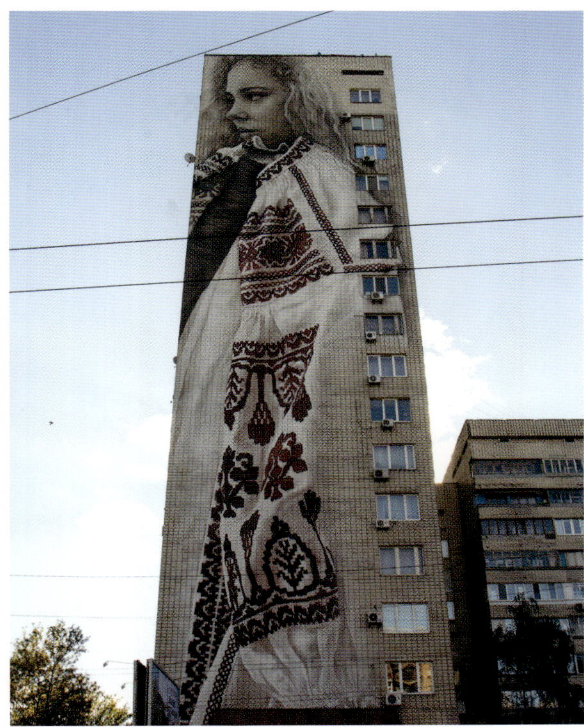

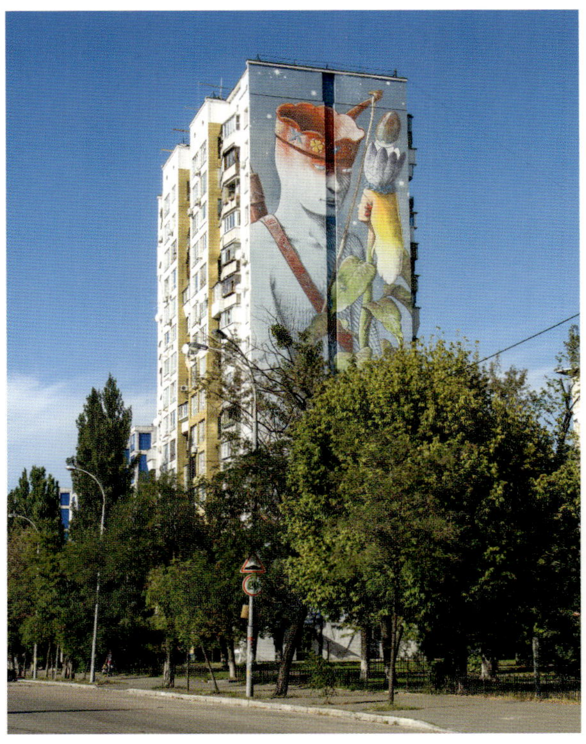

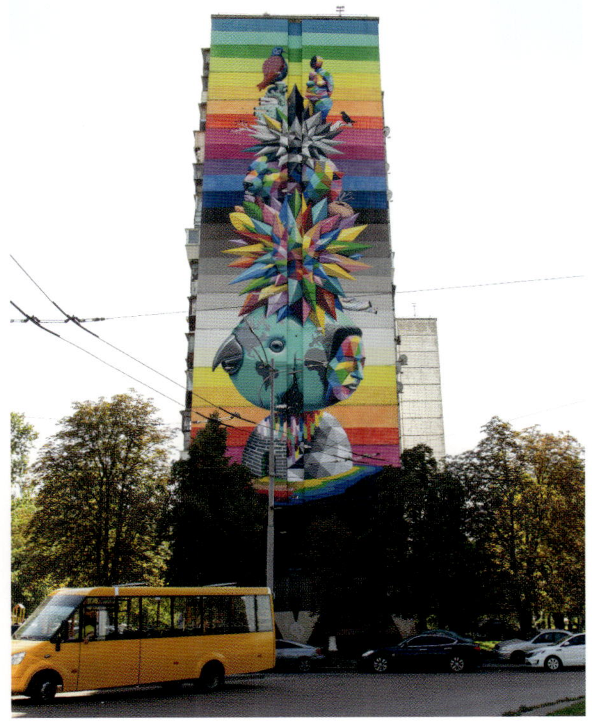

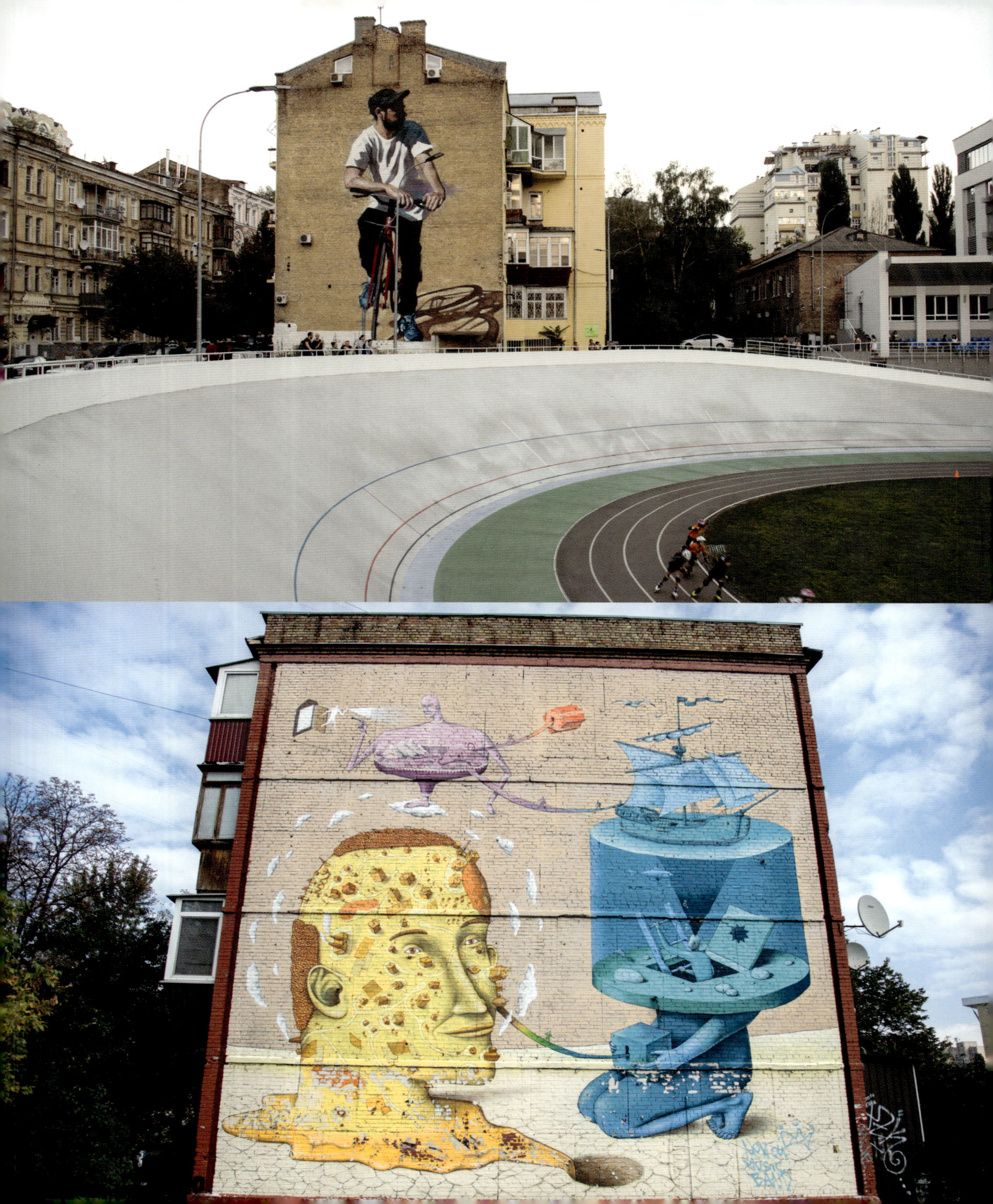

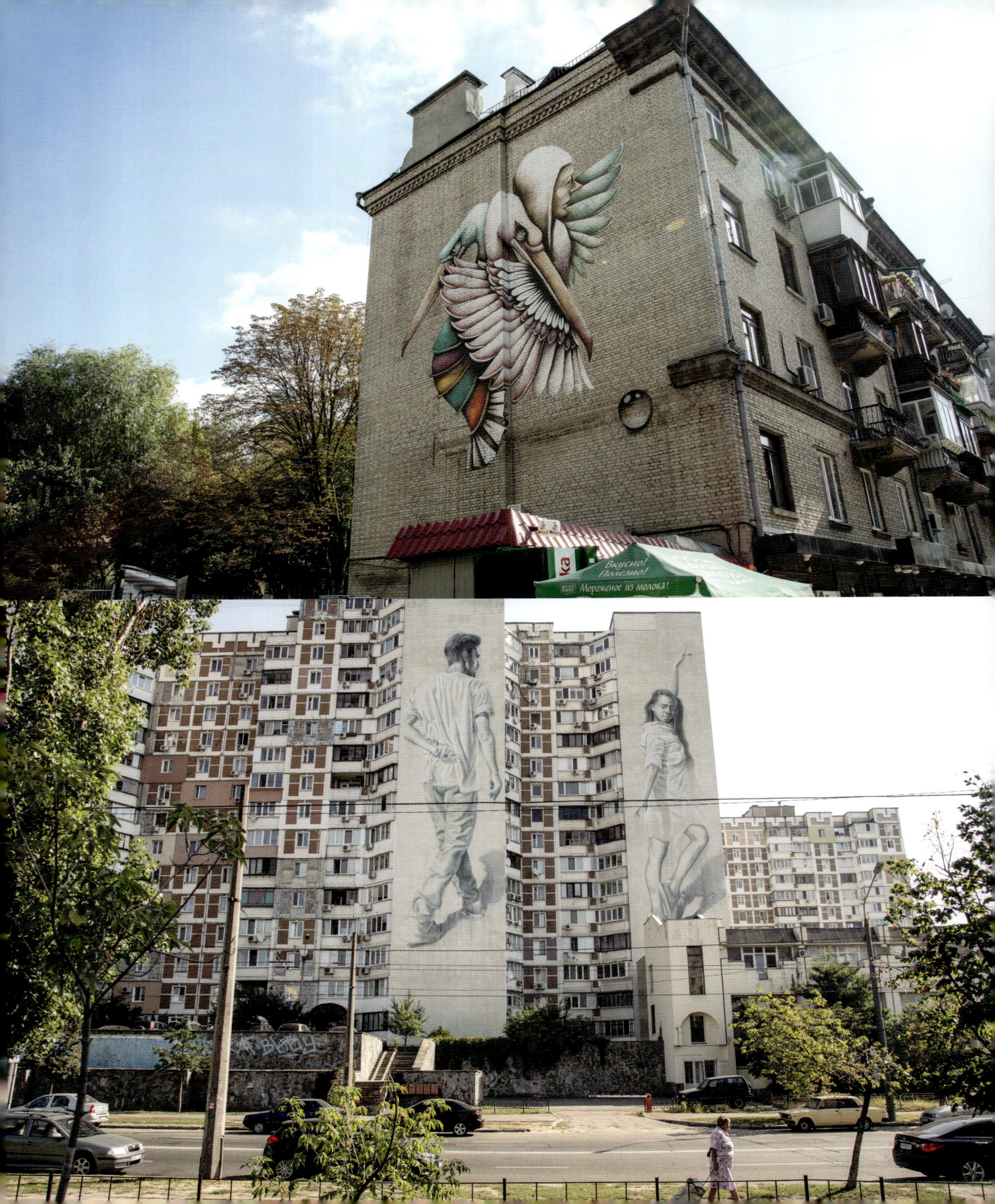

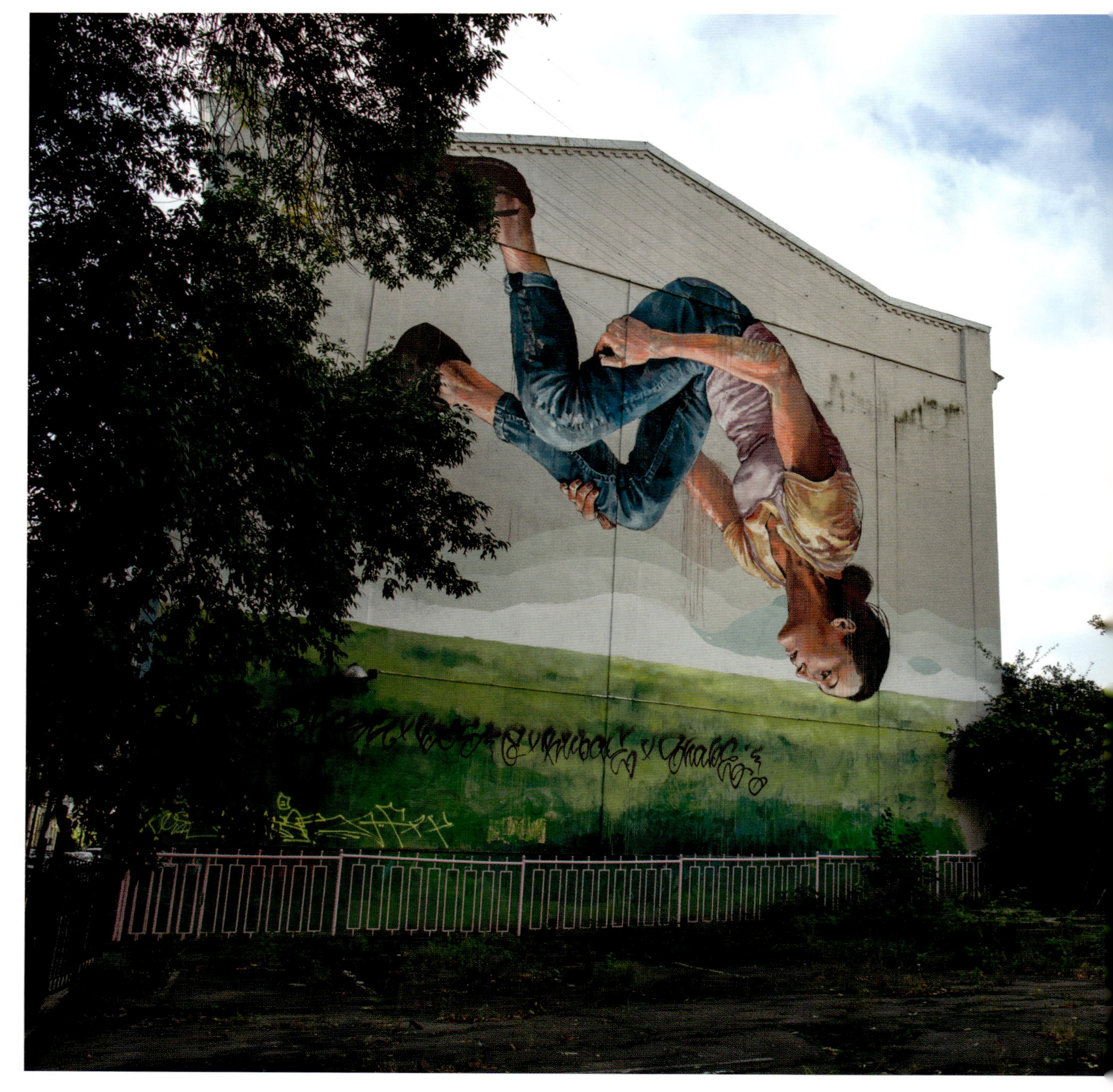

Art in the Streets

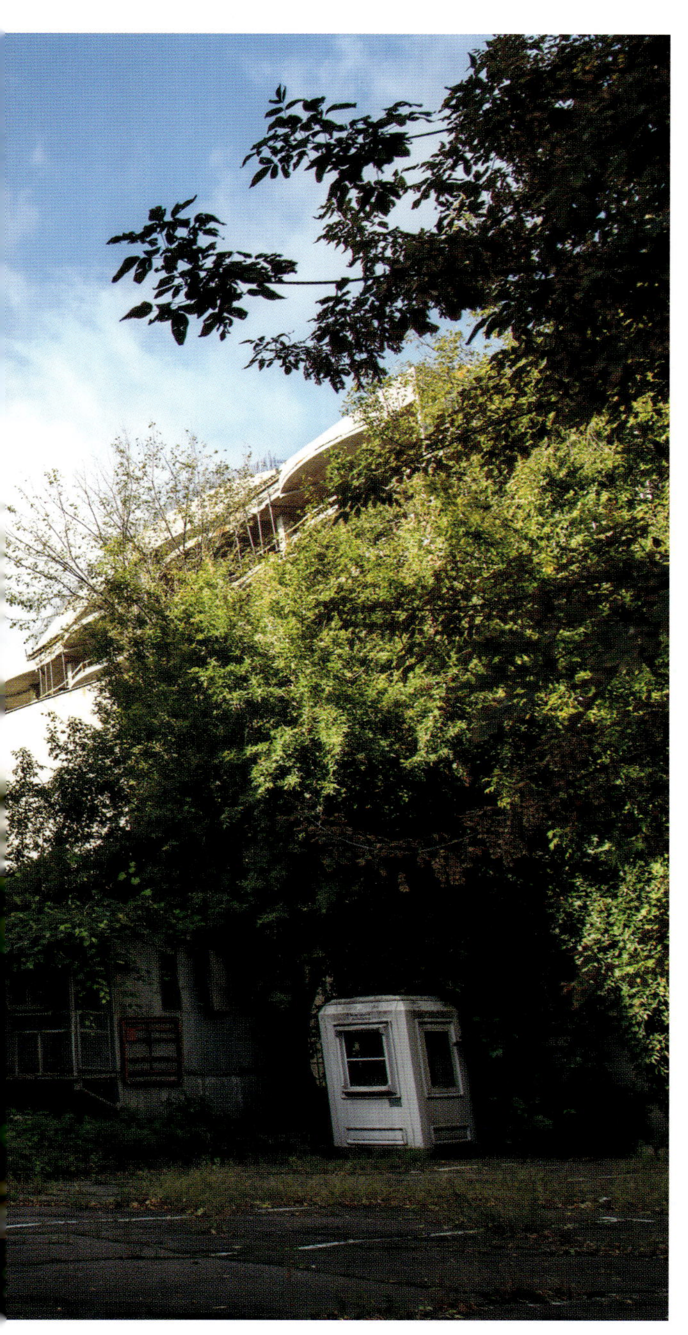

Public art is a theatre of the war for control of modern life. The partisan forces involved struggle both for mindshare and wall space, hearts and mortar. The free market uses weaponised art to further the glorious goals of commerce, The nexus of corporate power and state results in corporate public art, often abstract sculpture, of the kind ridiculed in 'Fight Club'.

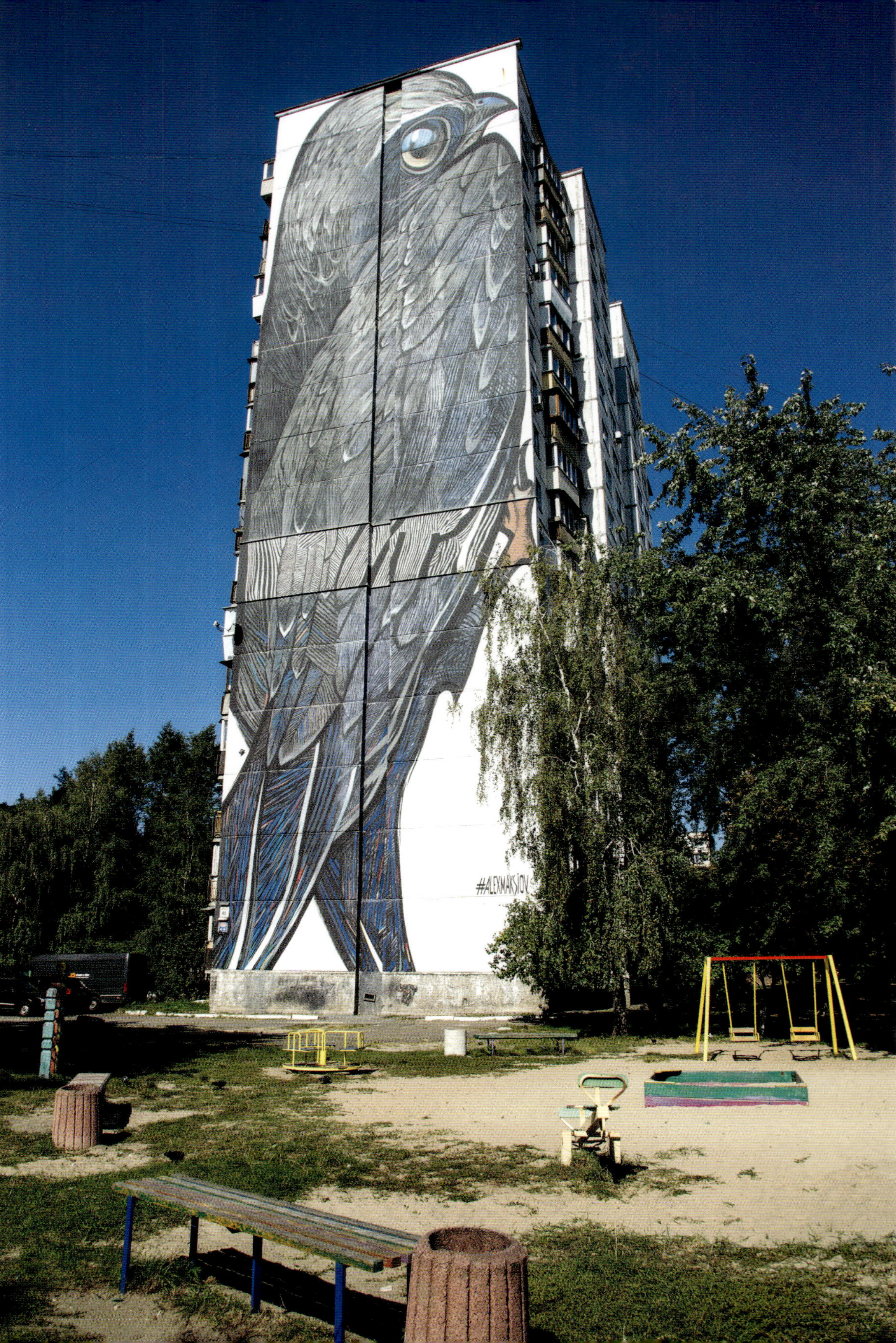

Then again, sometimes the state plays a more paternal and didactic role, educating the masses in the value of contemporary fine art, commissioning fine art mega stars like Anish Kapoor to do their thing. This again can be weaponised, witness the USA pressuring Paris to accept a gigantic Jeff Koons as a gesture of 'solidarity' after the Terror Attacks. It's a gift, but you have to place it where we tell you to place it, or else.

Then there are the guerrilla factions in this multi-sided conflict, the graffiti writers, the street artists, the fly posters and guerilla marketers. Not forgetting the good old fashioned delinquent youth, still scratching, burning, scribbling and smashing their own aesthetic contributions into the urban environment, as they have since classical Greece.

And now something mutates out of that guerrilla scene, looking at Brick Lane and Shoreditch in London, downtown Barcelona or Kreuzberg in Berlin - Street Art becomes the advance guard of property development and rocketing rents, a driver of hipster capitalism. It is a war like any civil war, lines are blurred, nothing is ever quite about what it is about.

But still the images are there, glimpses of our 'plague of fantasies', the unreal that is more real than real. We are half real creatures, and art has always been the forum in which we can see our unreality reflected back at us, easing our alienation, reminding us that it is not weird to be weird, we are all wandering around, going through the motions, living in cloud of fantasies. Urban space is Corbusier's machine for living in, but we wouldn't be able to cope with such hard functionalism. We soften the edges by our arts. We learn to see the world by looking at its reflection.

"Whenever the intensity of looking reaches a certain degree, one becomes aware of an equally intense energy coming towards one through the appearance of whatever it is one is scrutinizing." - John Berger

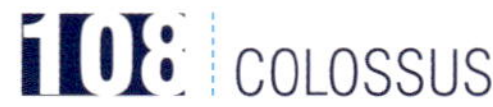

AALBORG

DENMARK

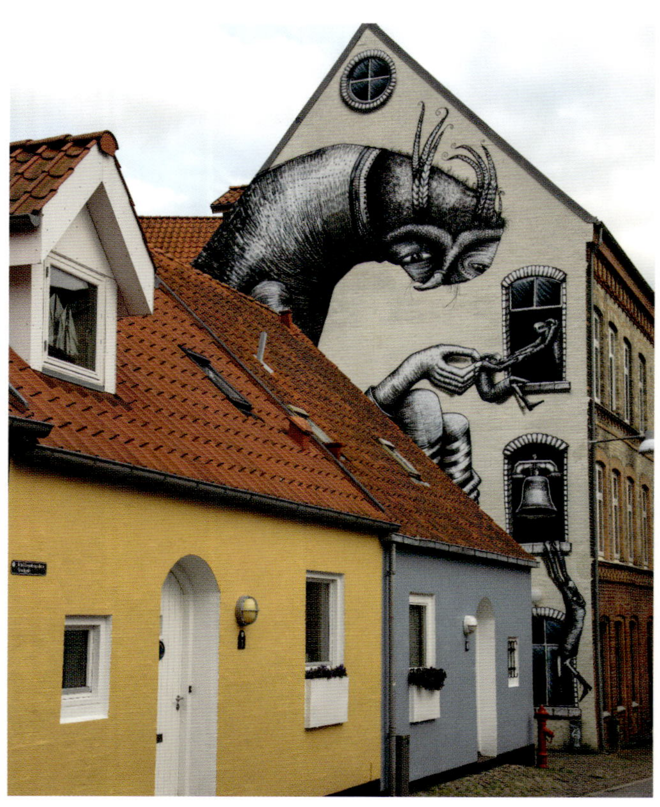

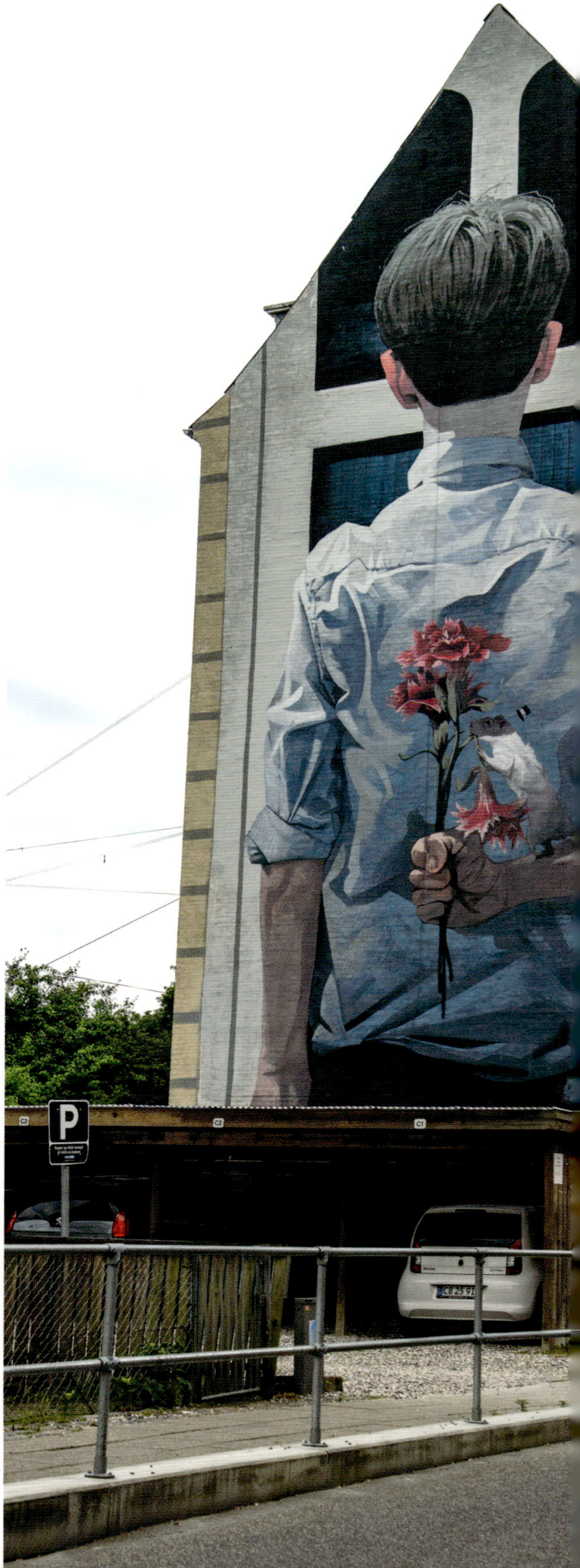

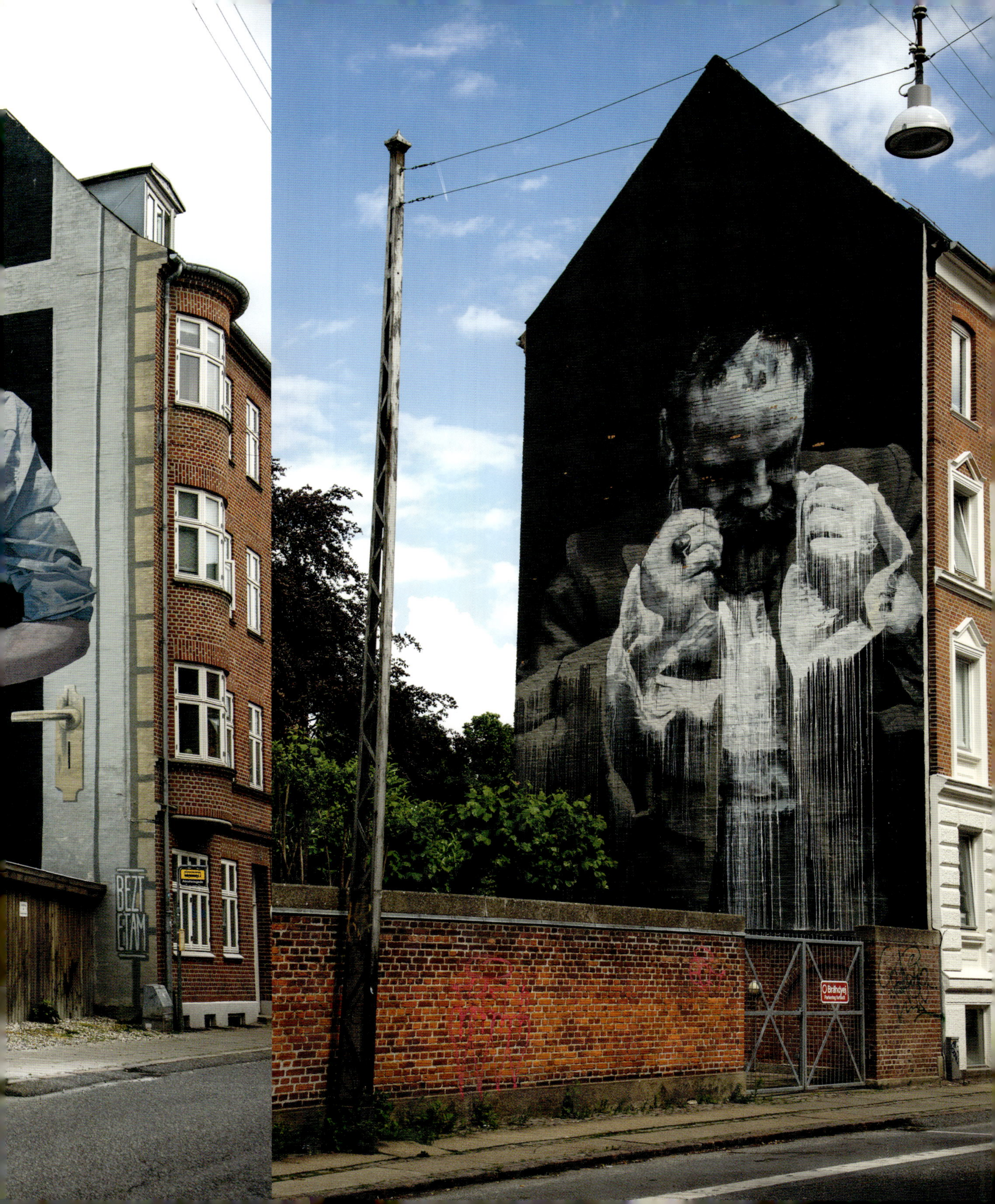

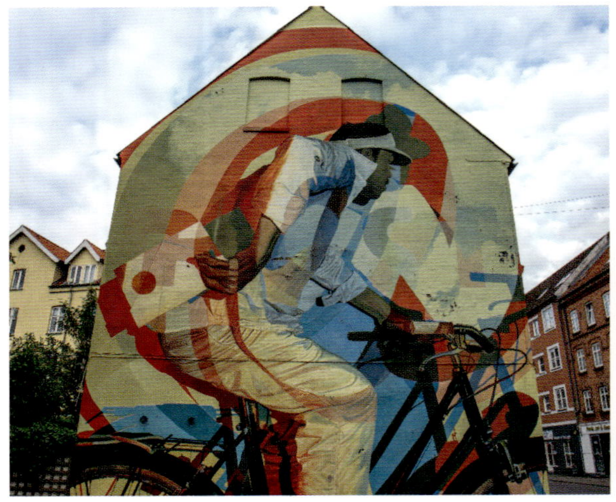
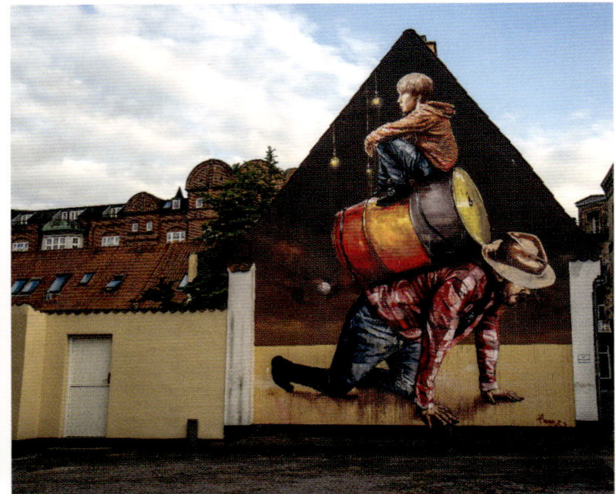
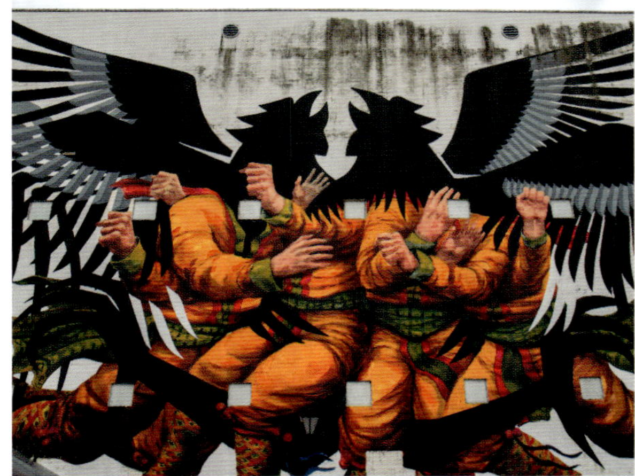
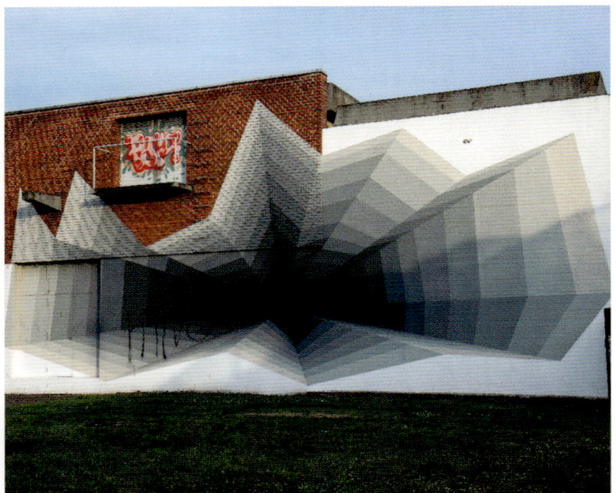
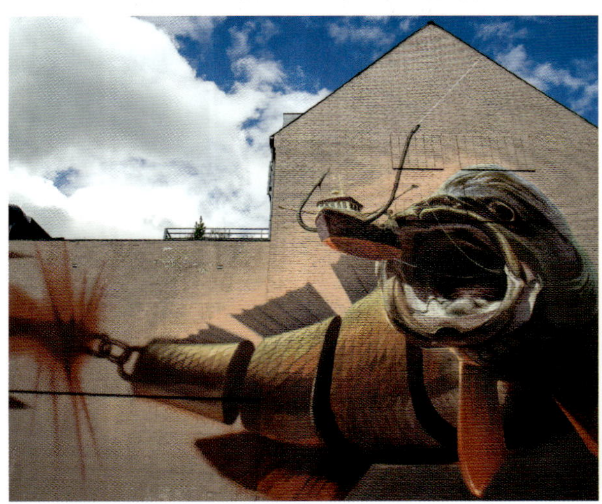
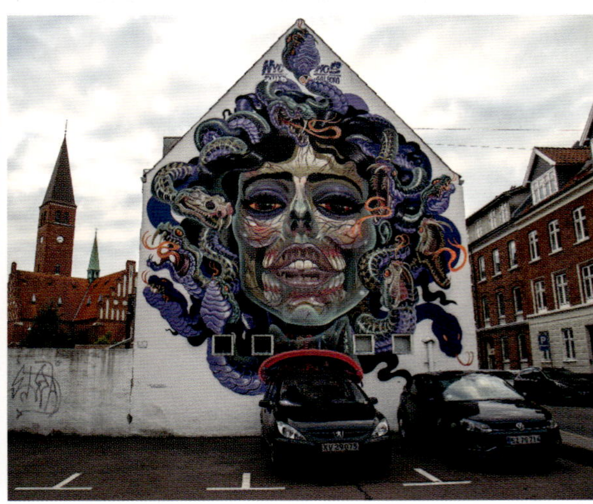

 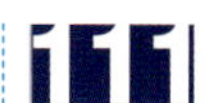

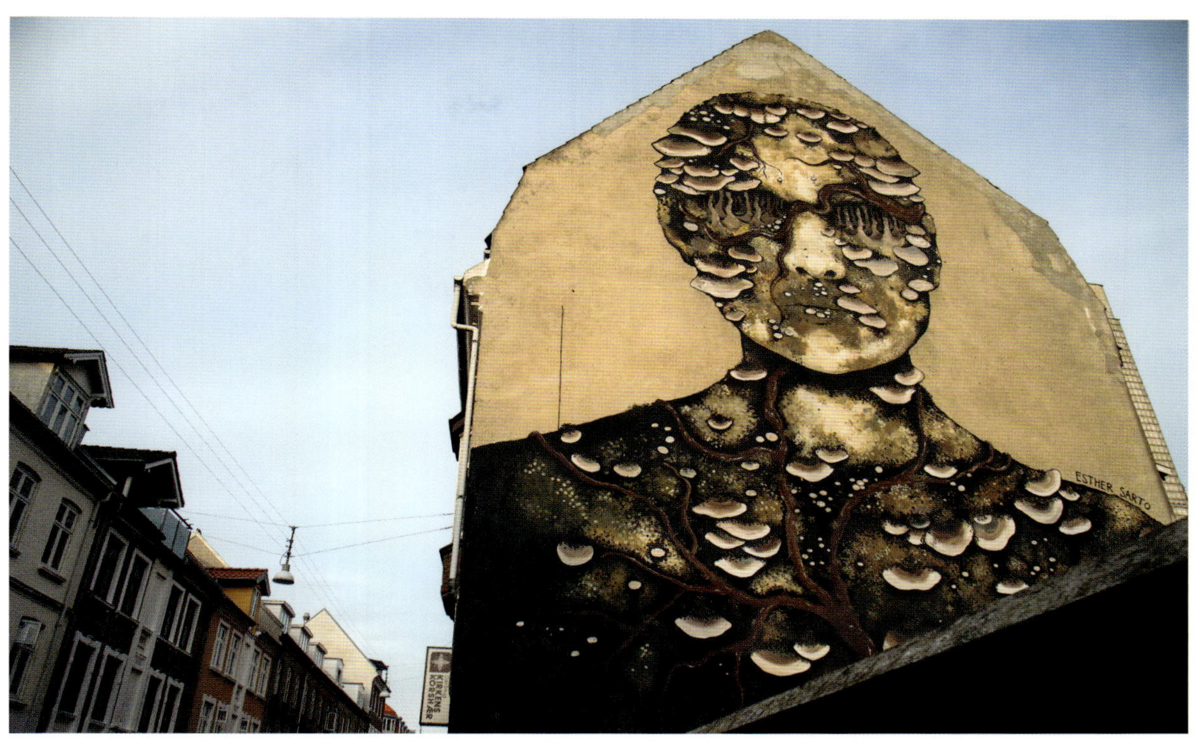
ESTHER SARTO

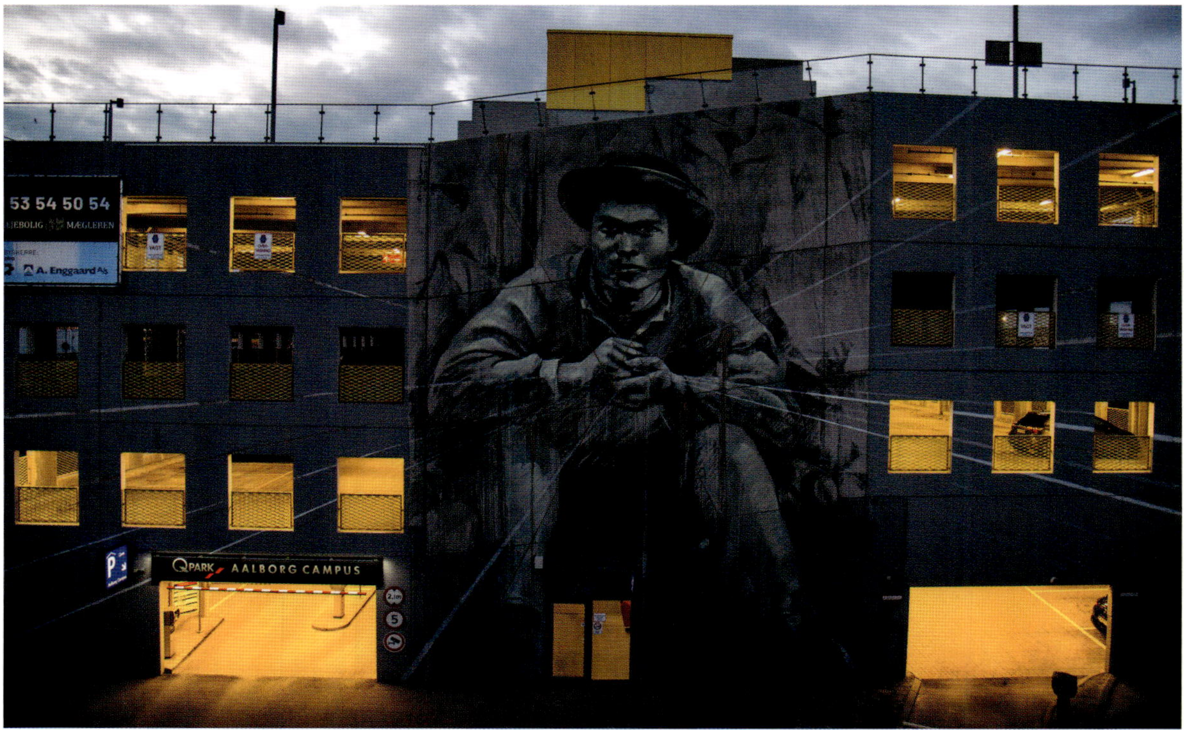
53 54 50 54
A. Enggaard A/S
QPARK AALBORG CAMPUS

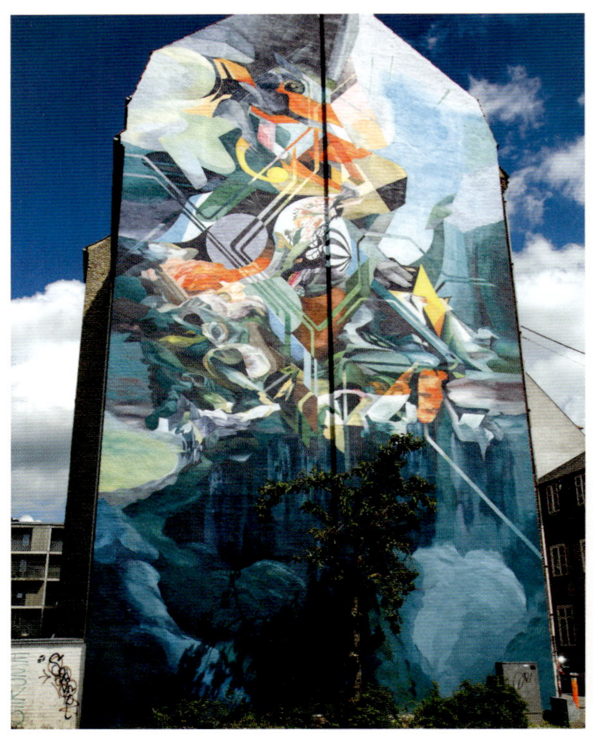
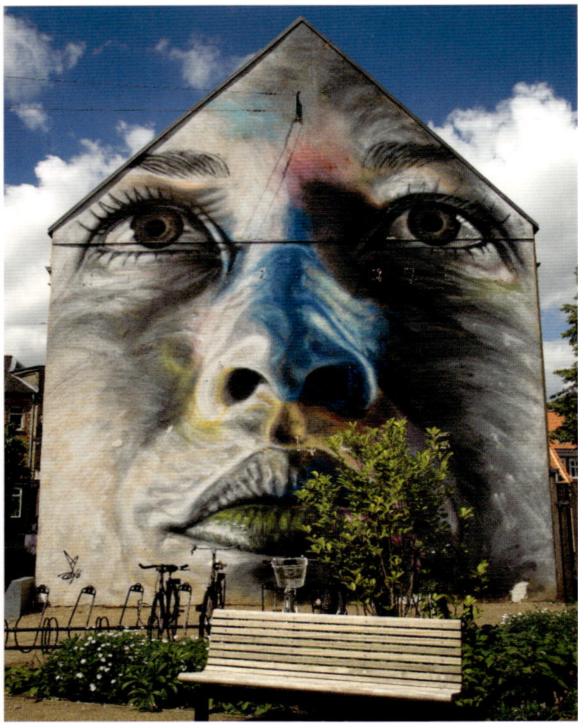
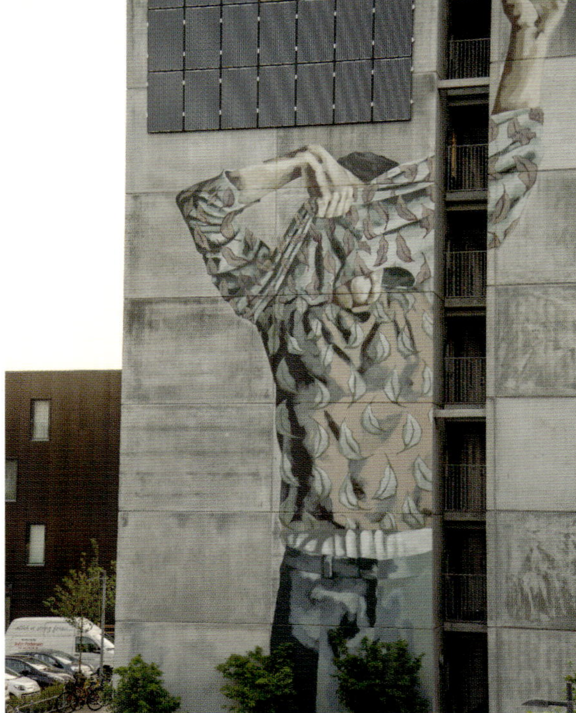
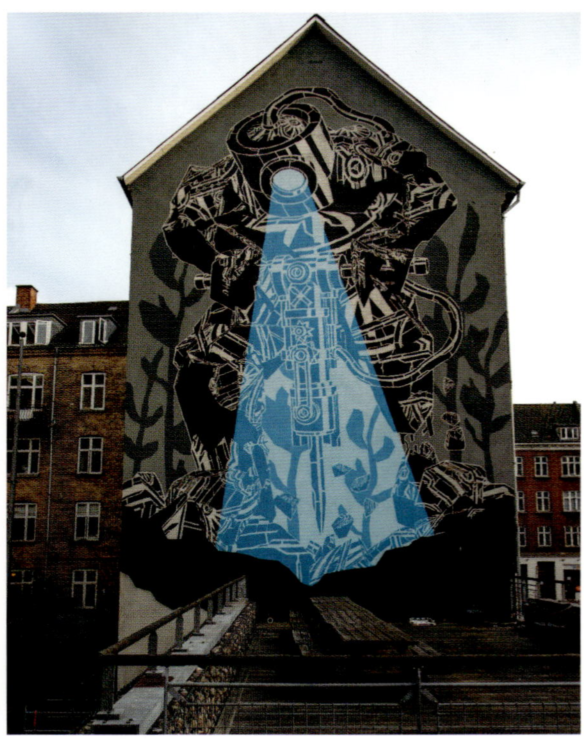

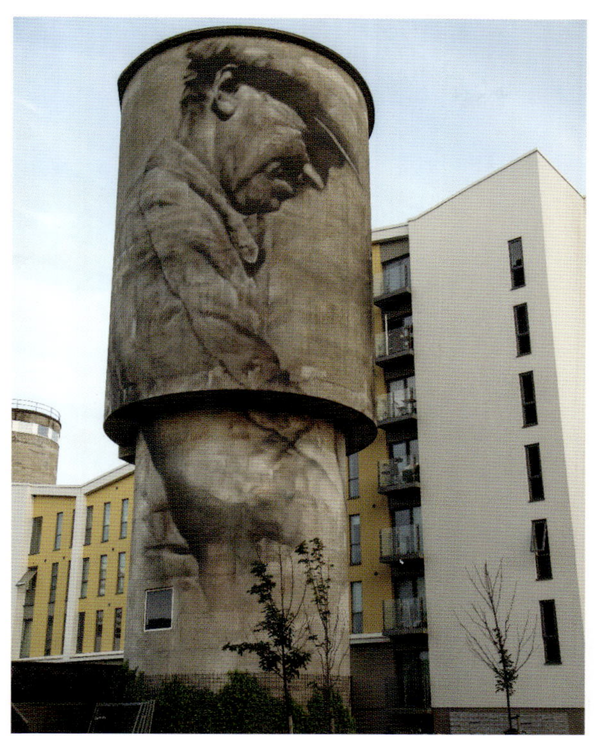

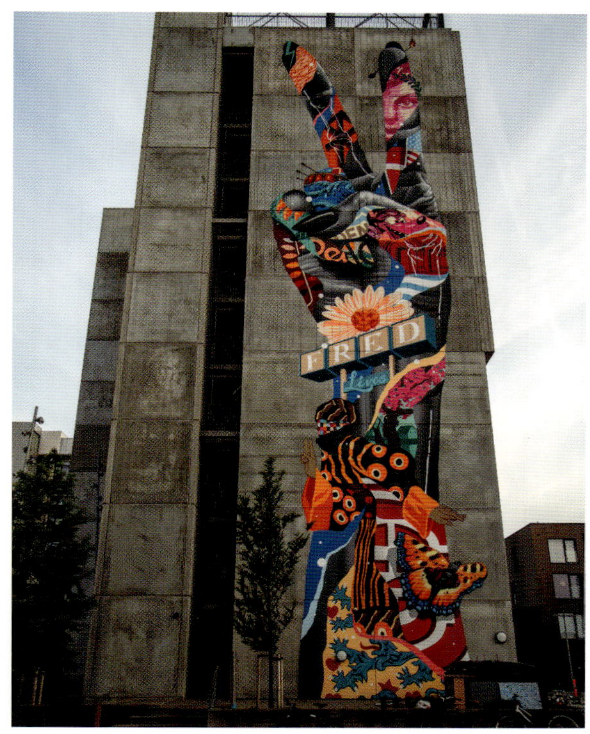

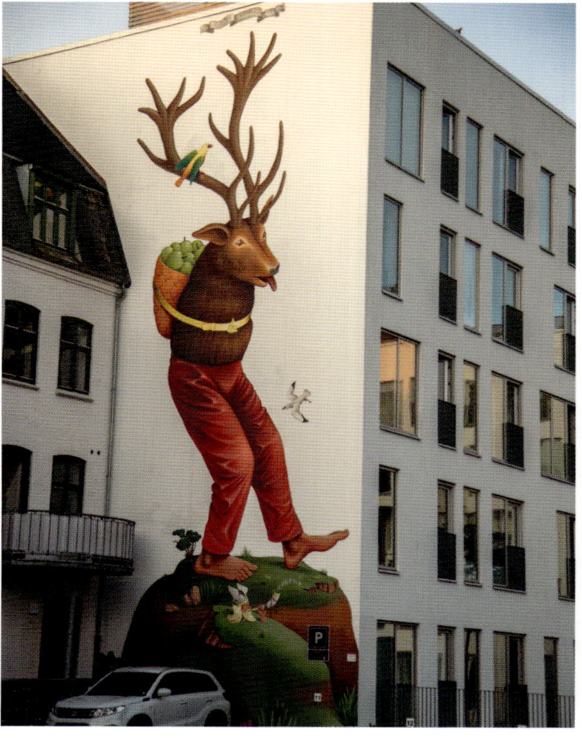

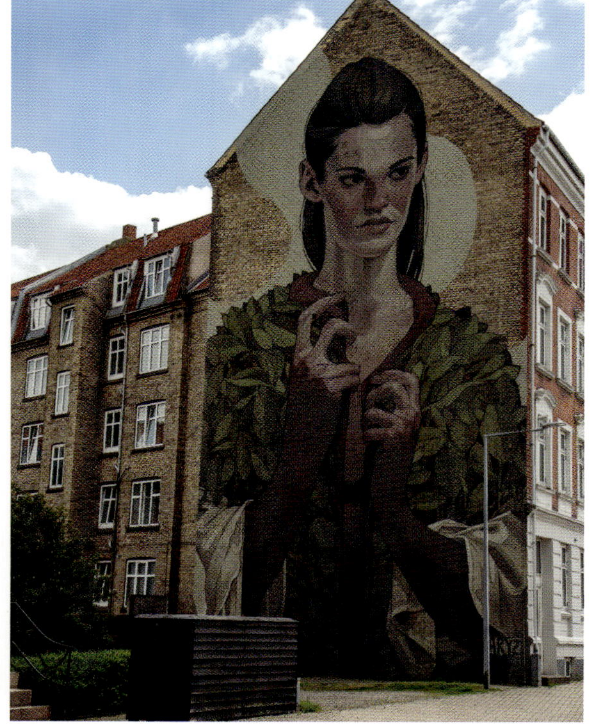

COPENHAGEN

DENMARK

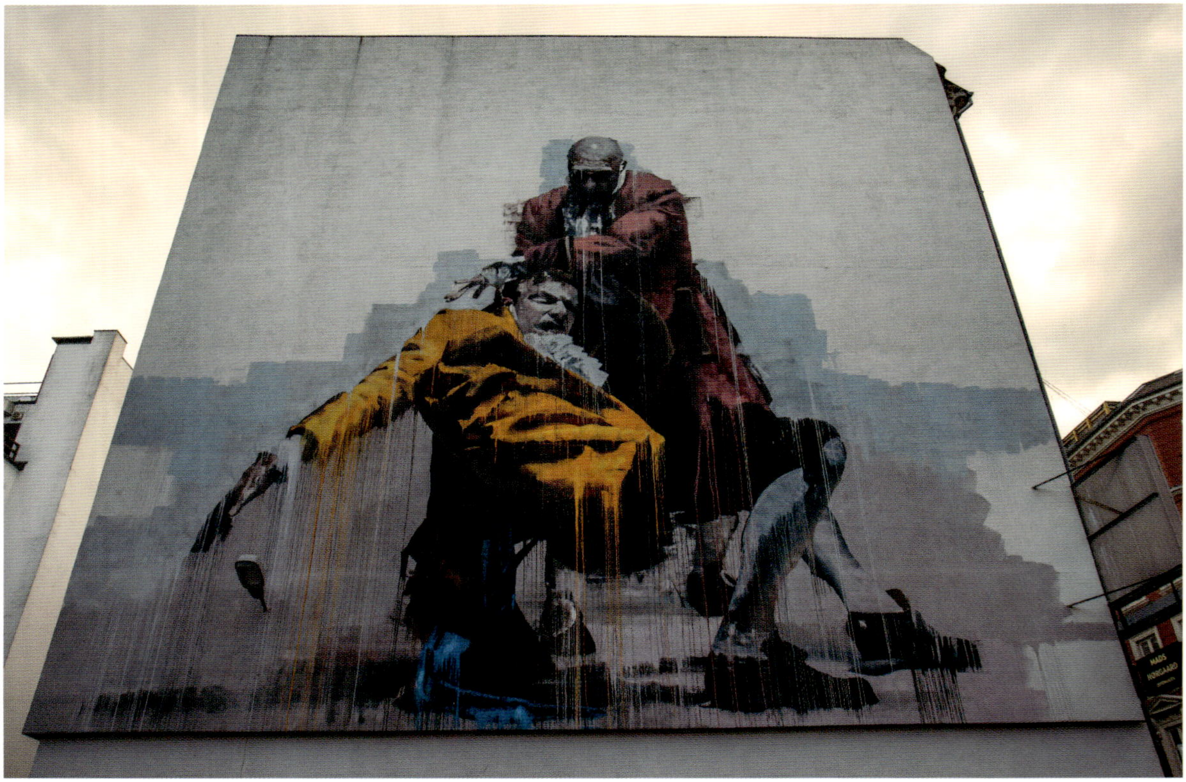

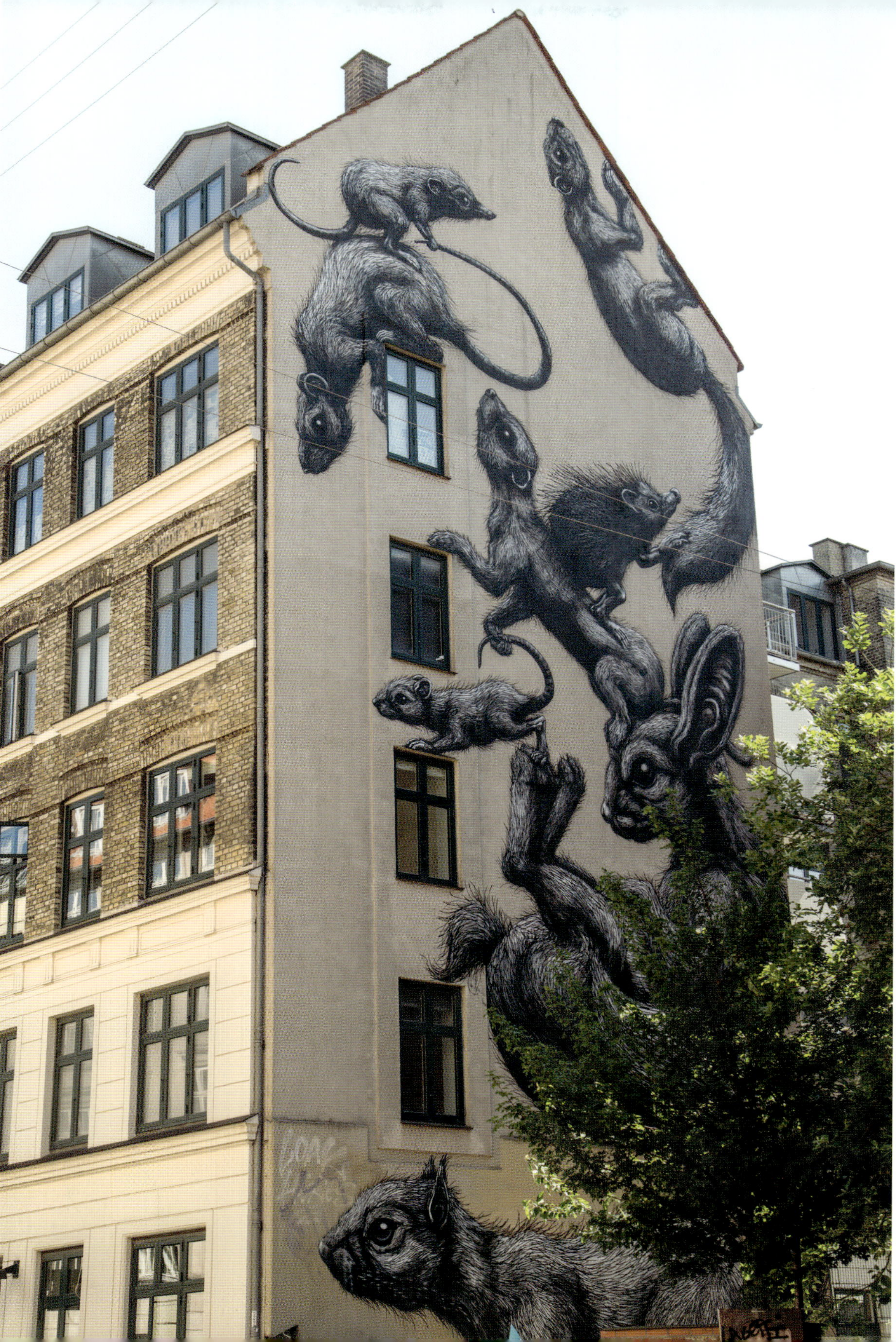

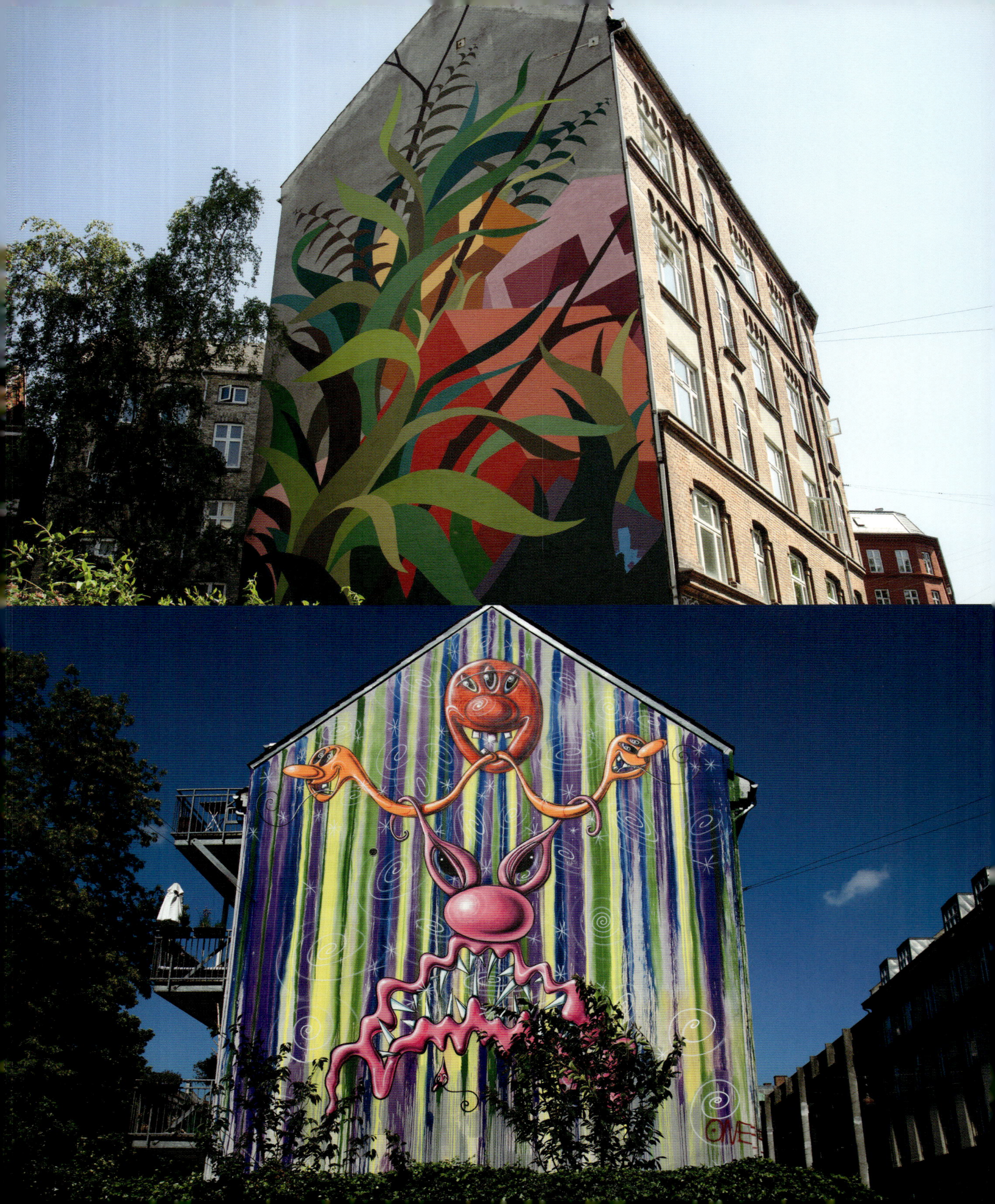

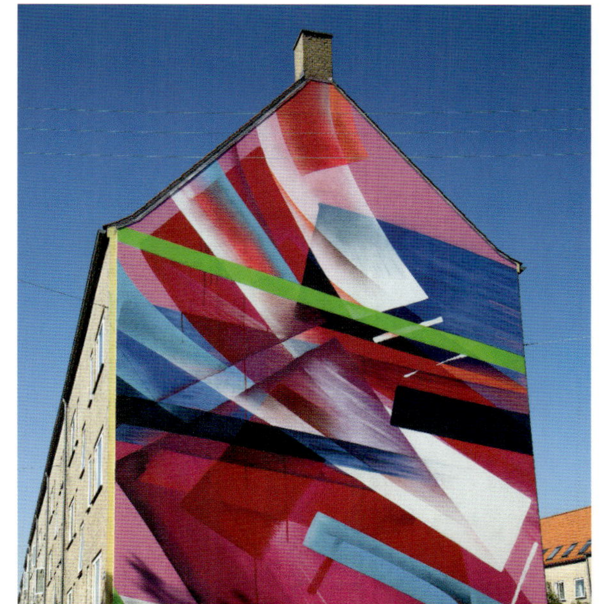
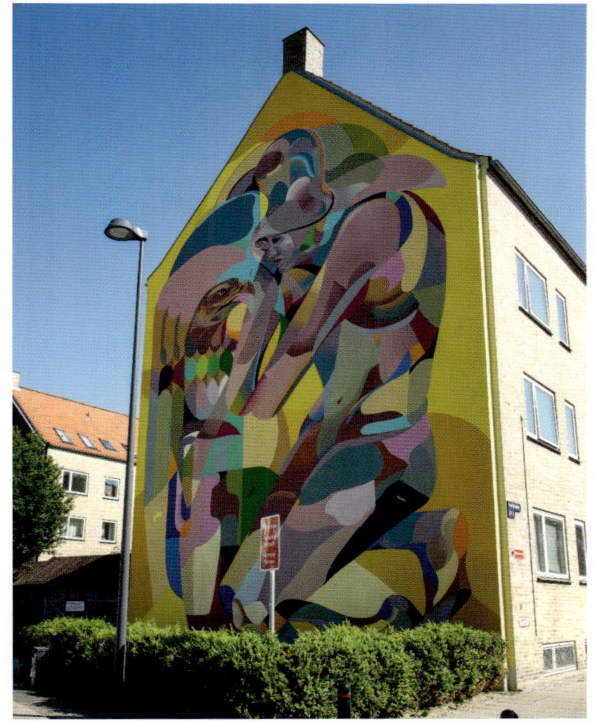
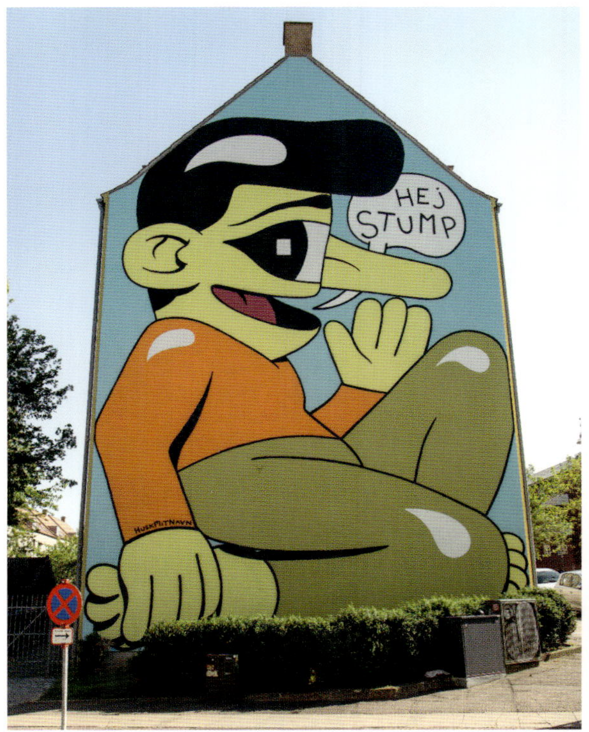
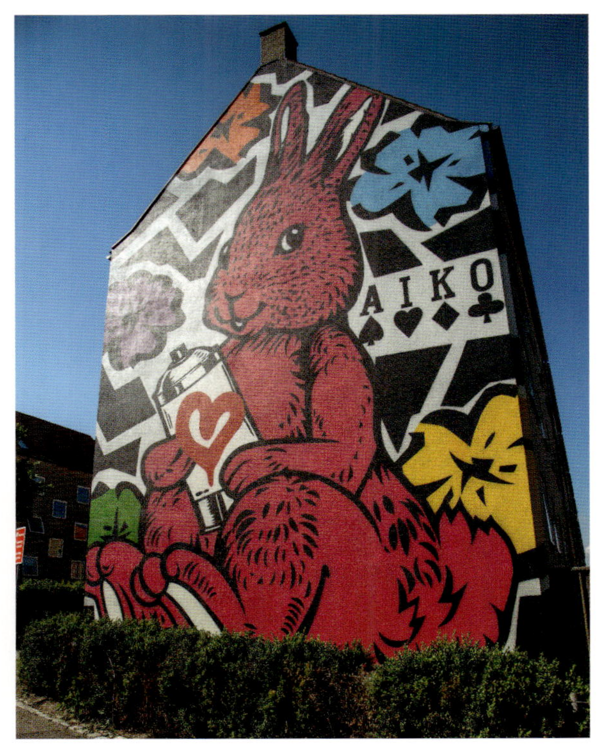
HEJ
STUMP
AIKO

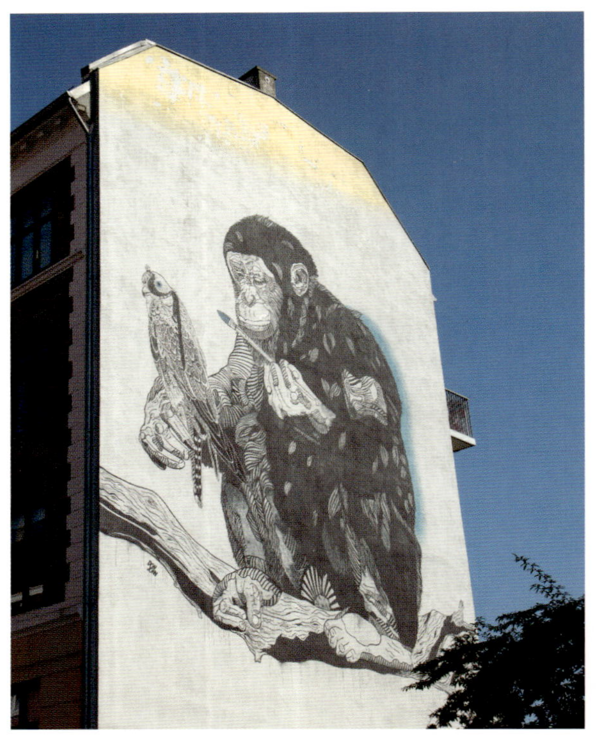
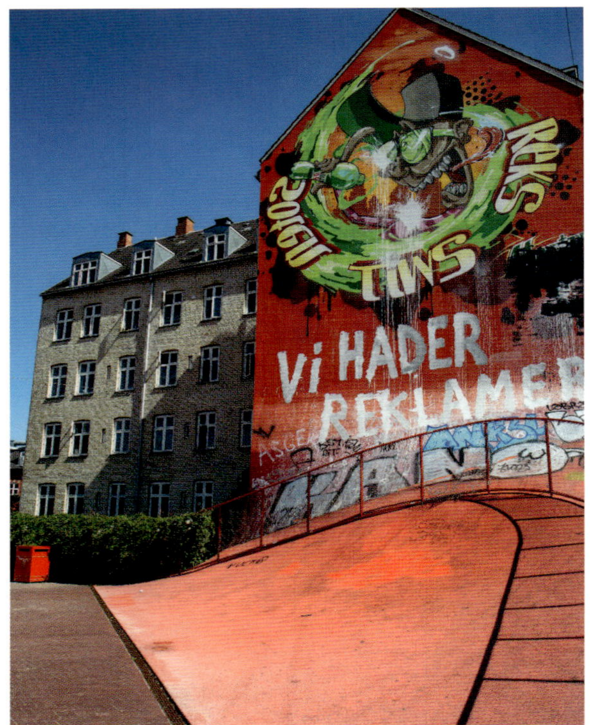

SORGU
TINS
RCKS
VI HADER
REKLAMER

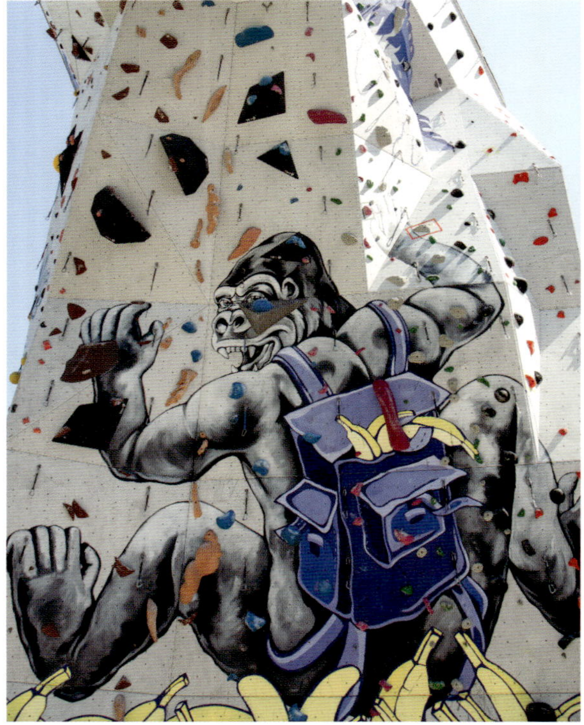
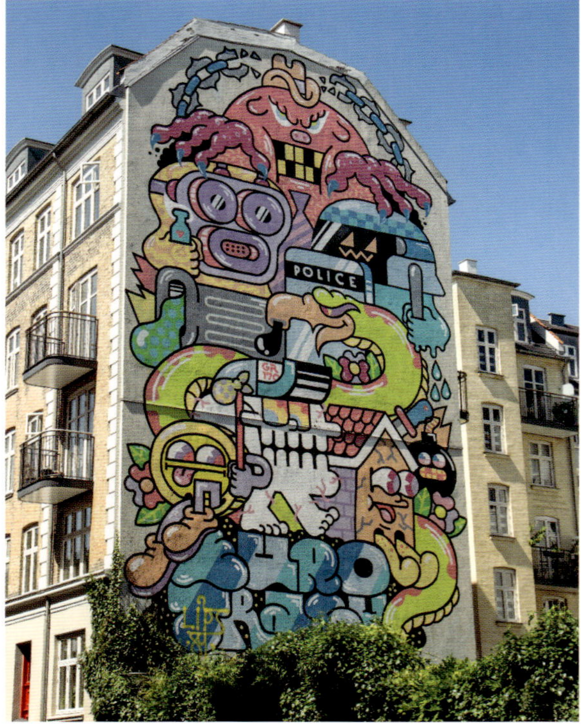

POLICE

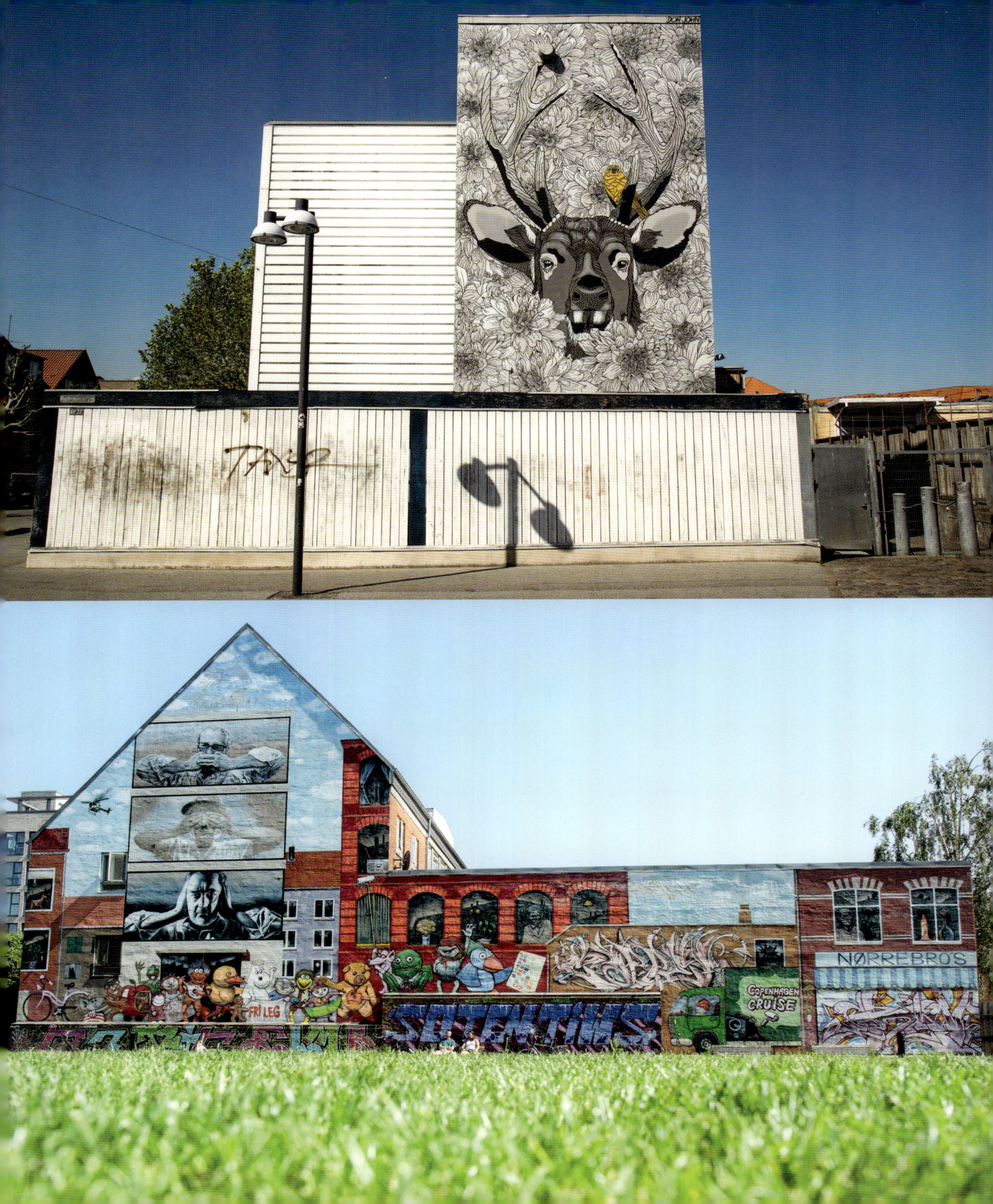

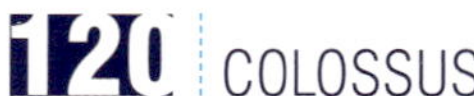

TIRANA

ALBANIA

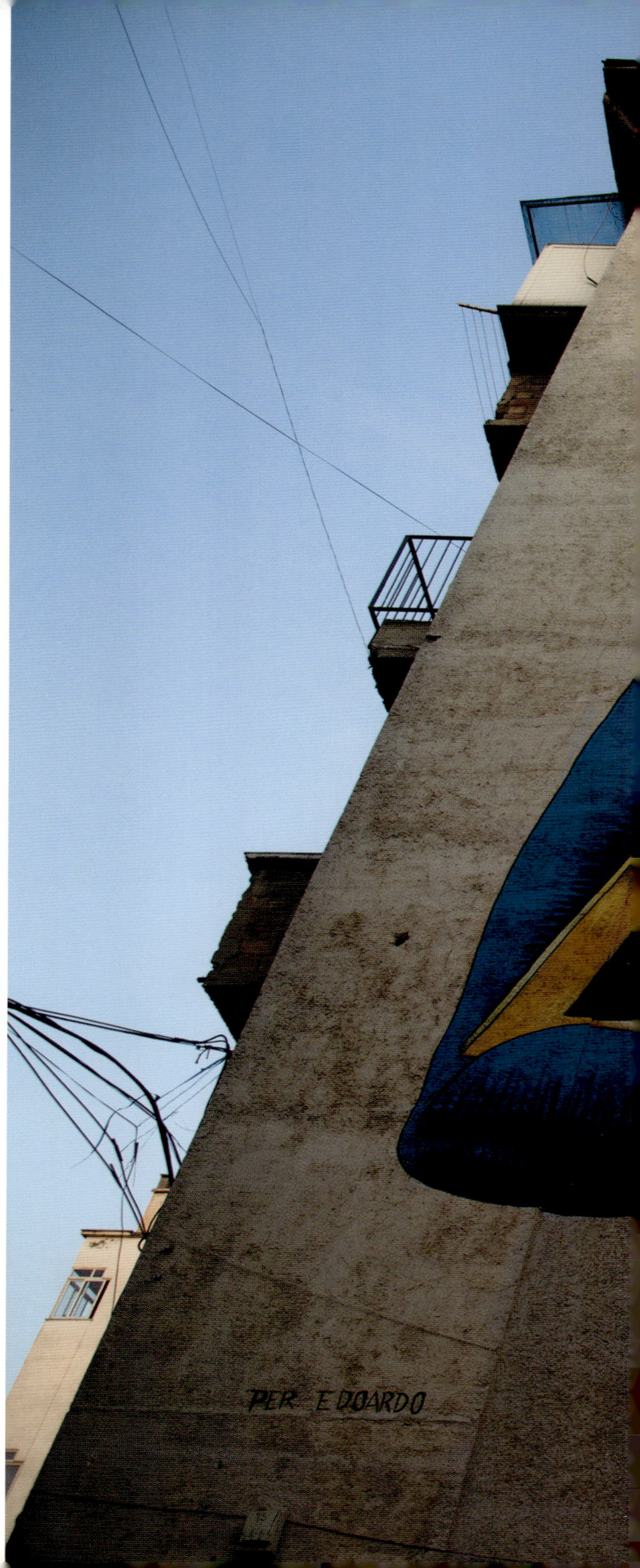

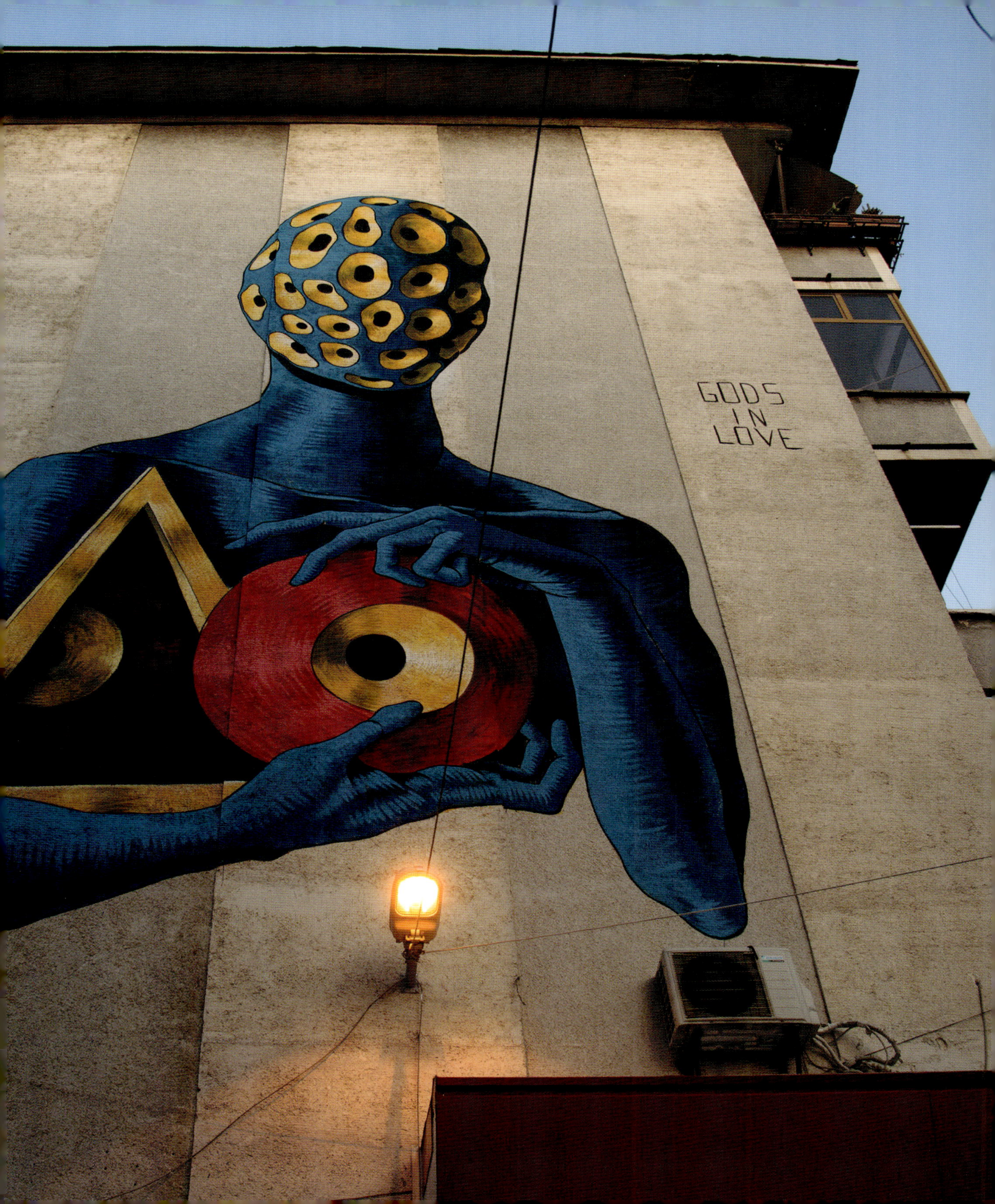

GODS
IN
LOVE

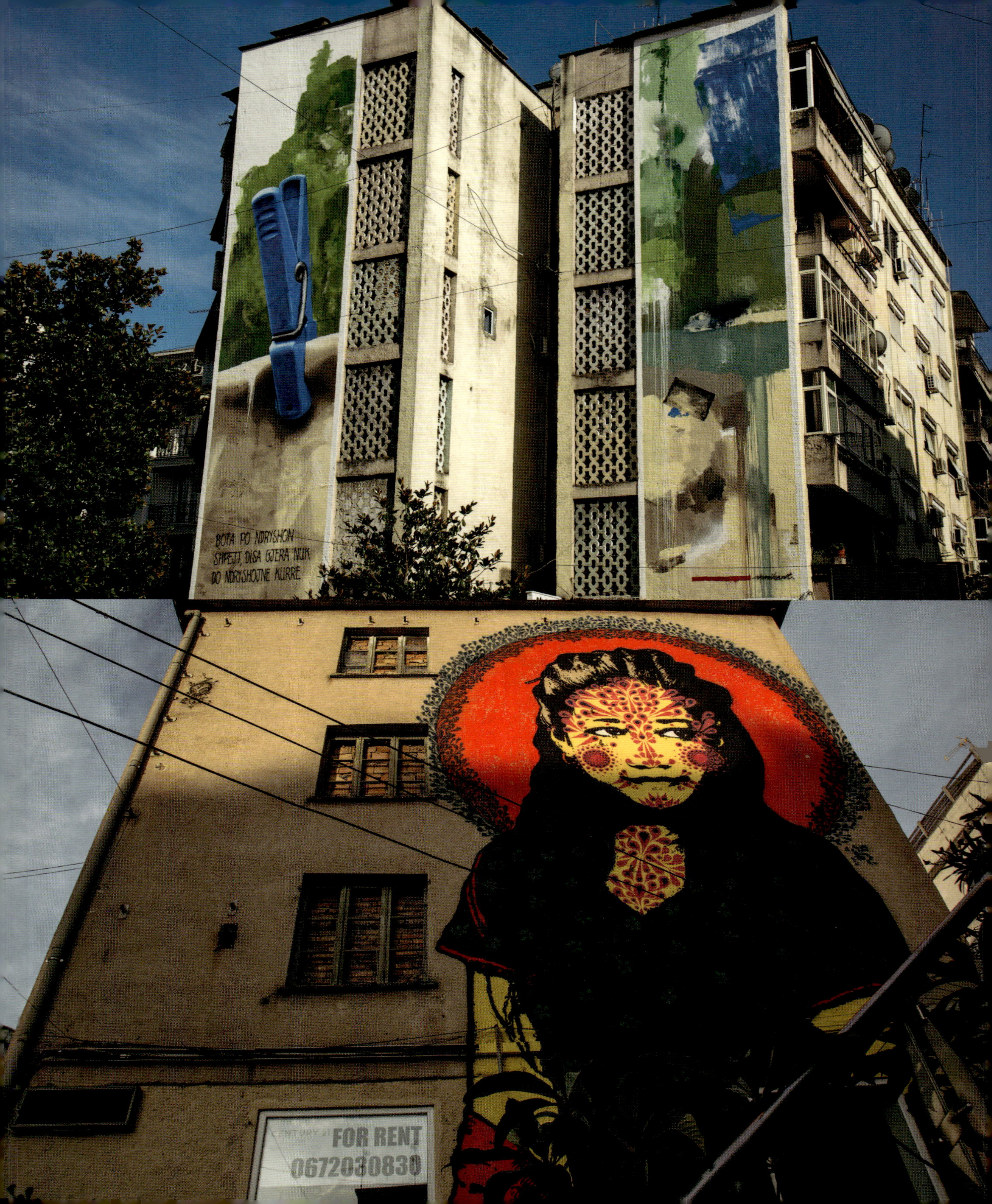

BOTA PO NDRYSHON
SHPEJT, DISA GJERA NUK
DO NDRYSHOJNE KURRE

CENTURY 21
FOR RENT
0672030830

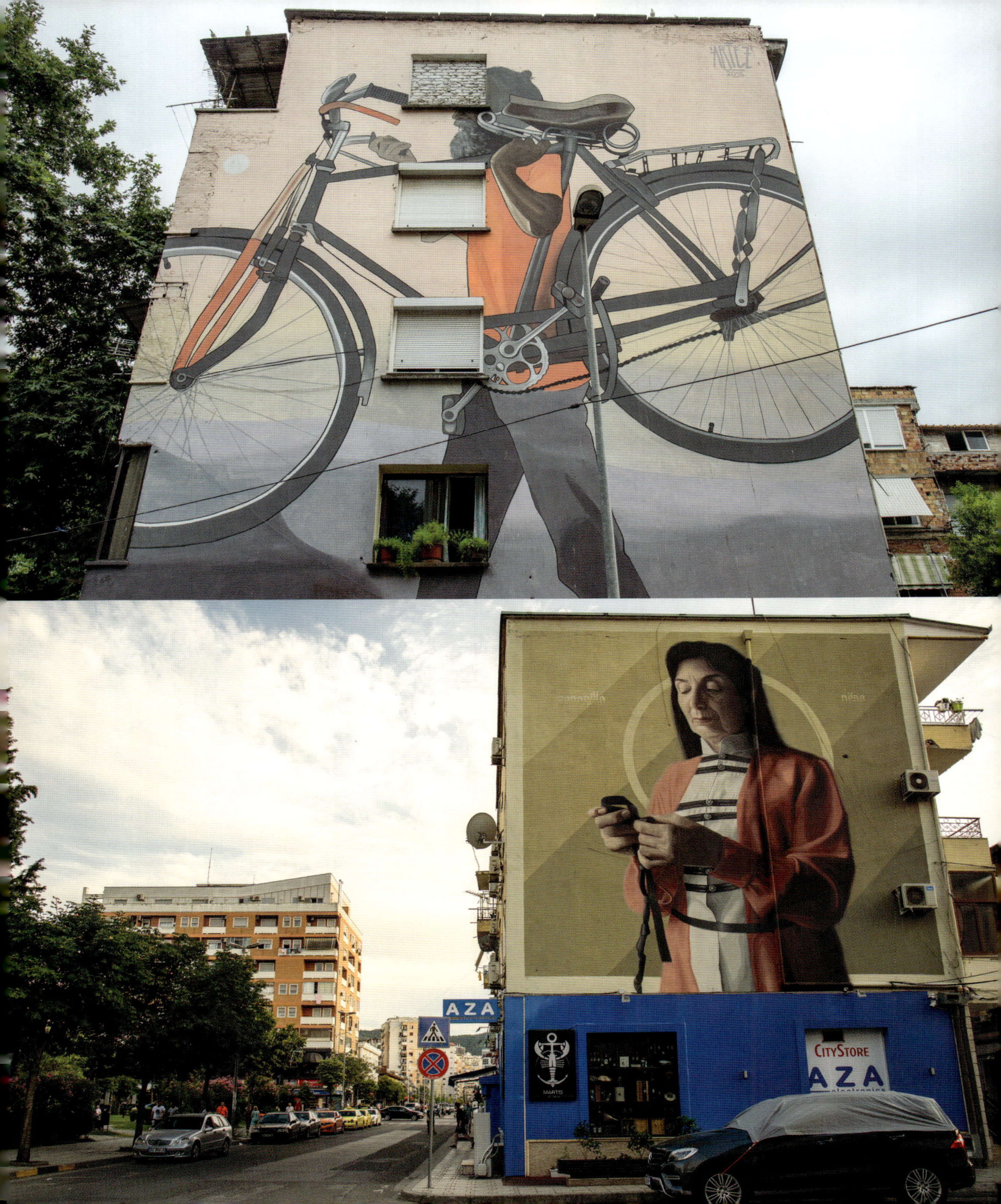

ARTEZ
2020
AZA
electronics
CityStore
AZA
electronics
MARTIS

ATHENS

GREECE

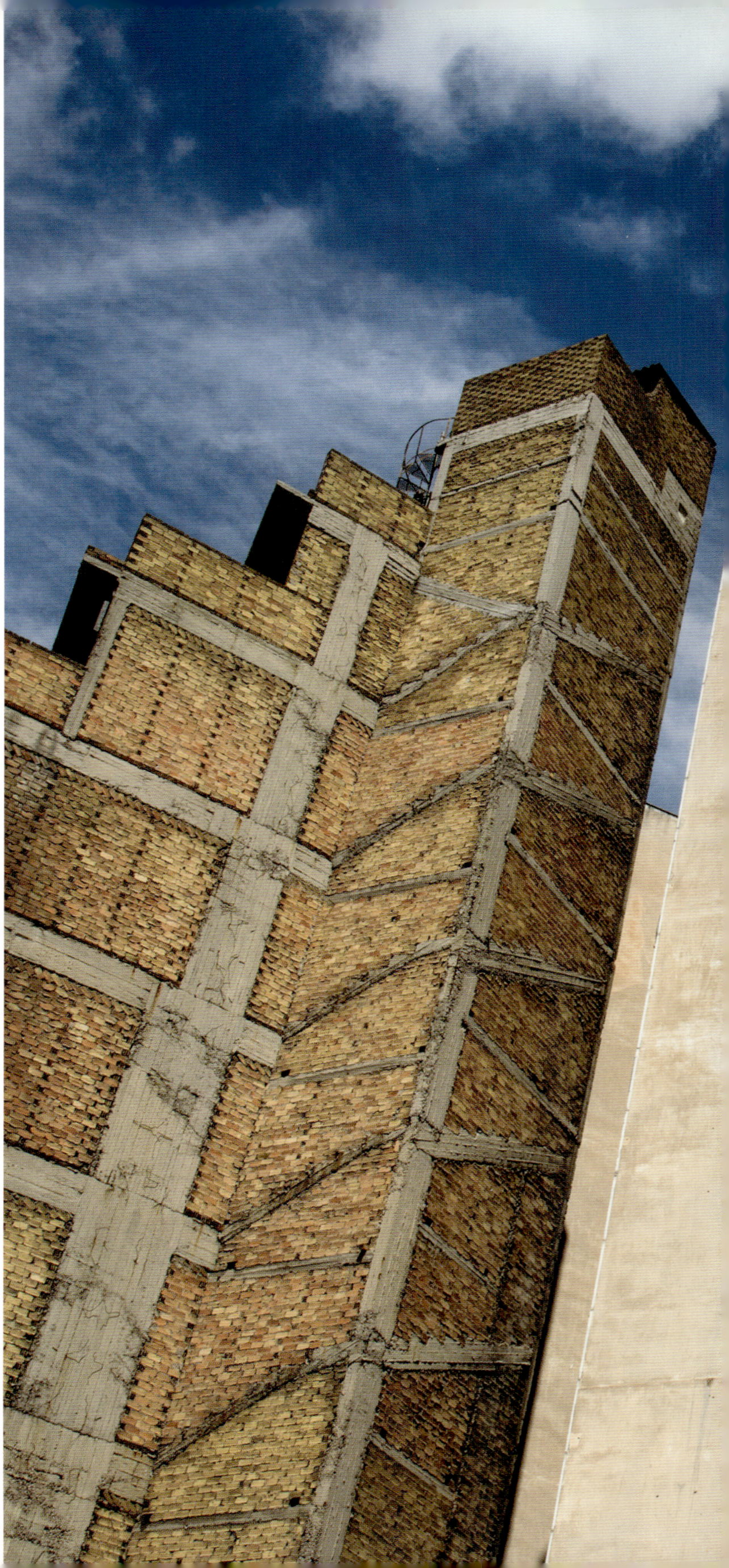

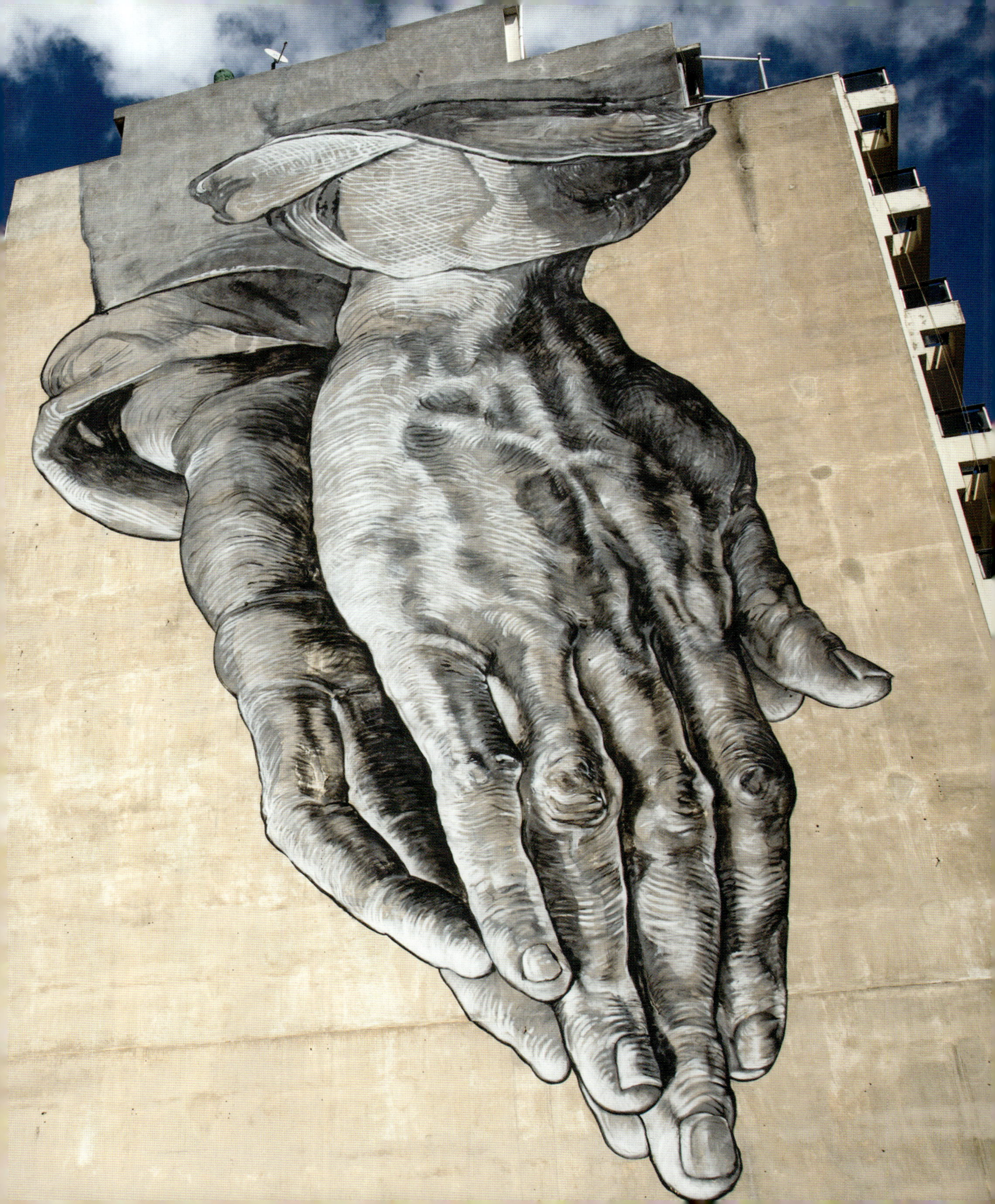

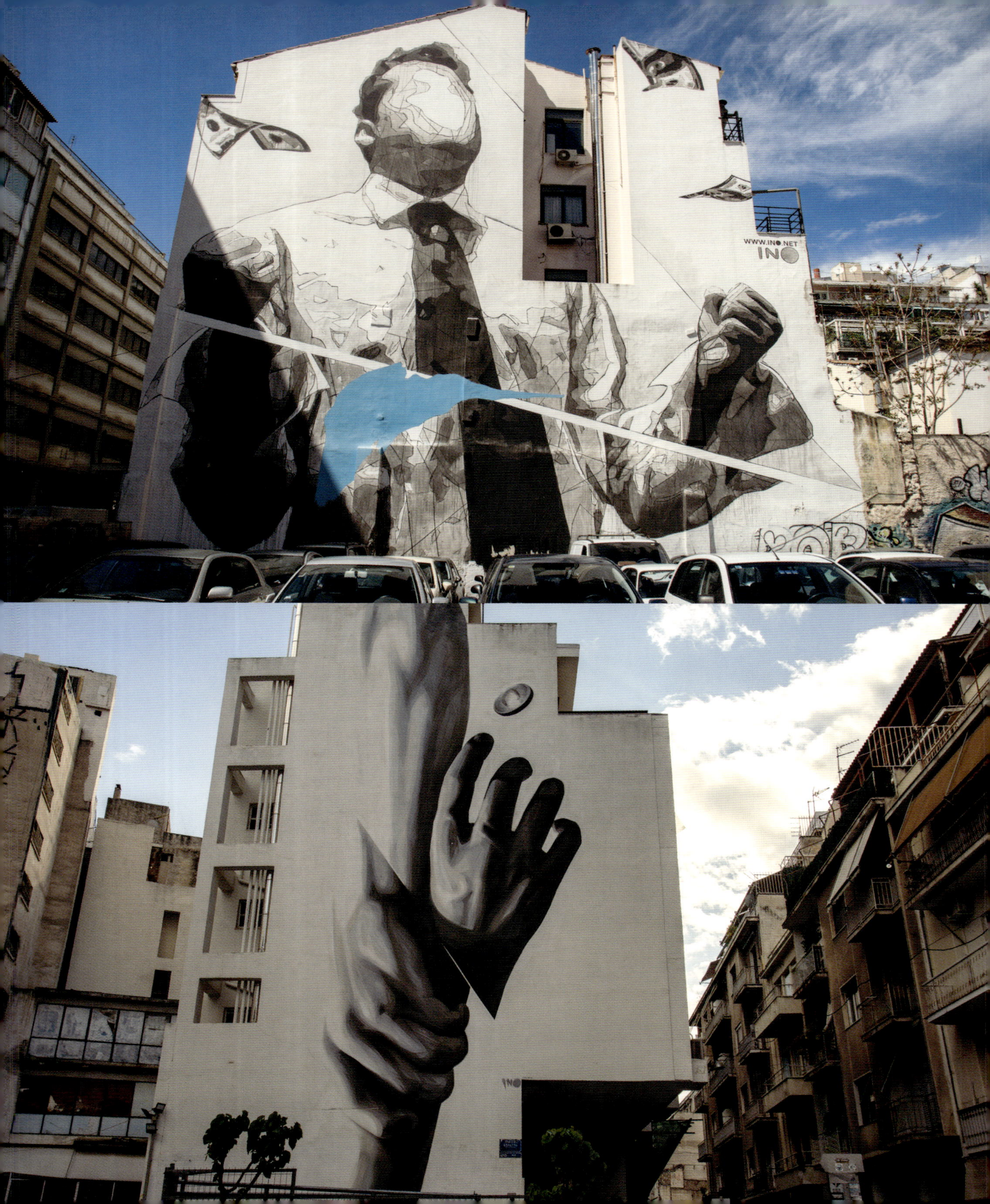

WWW.INO.NET
INO

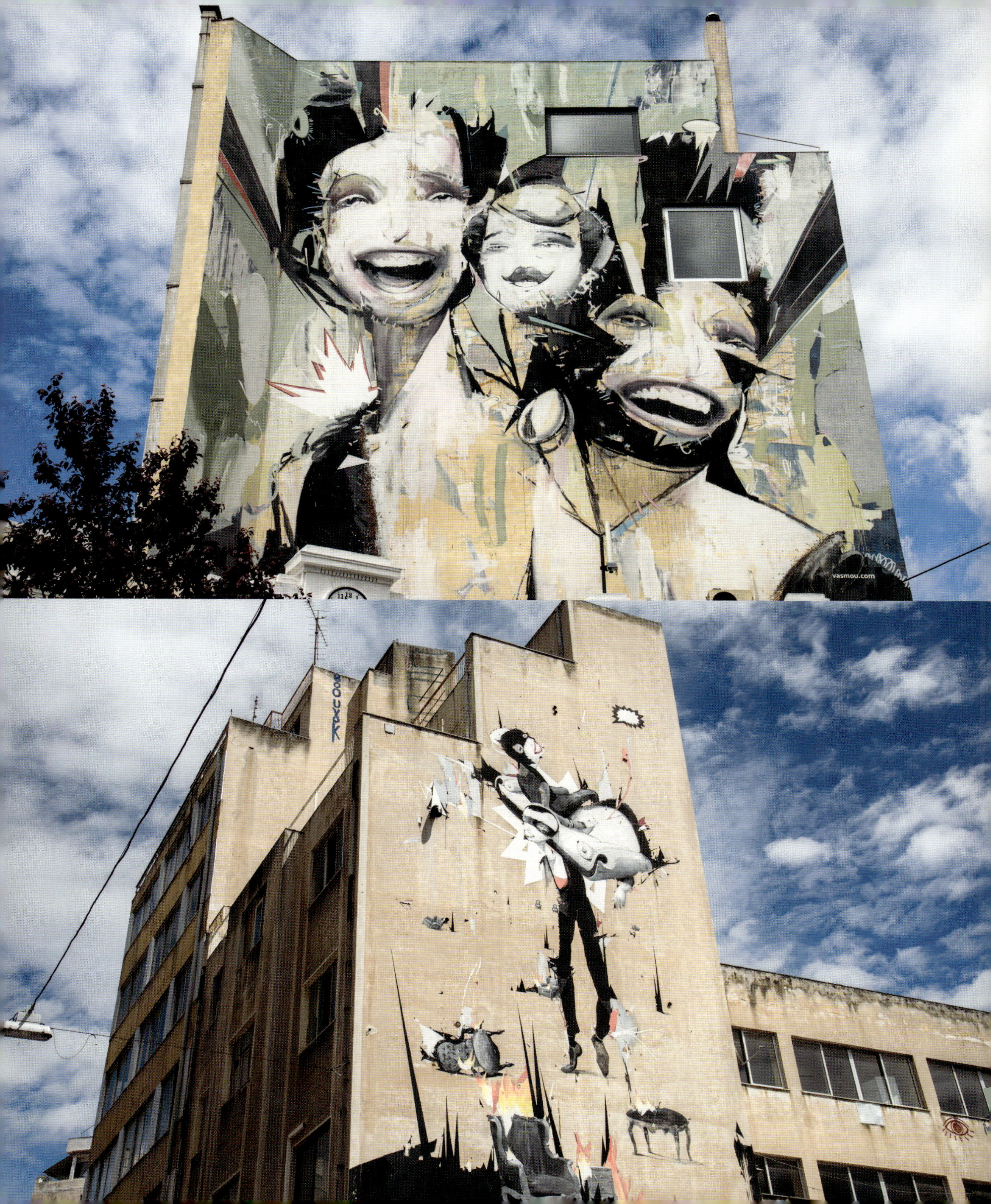
vasmou.com

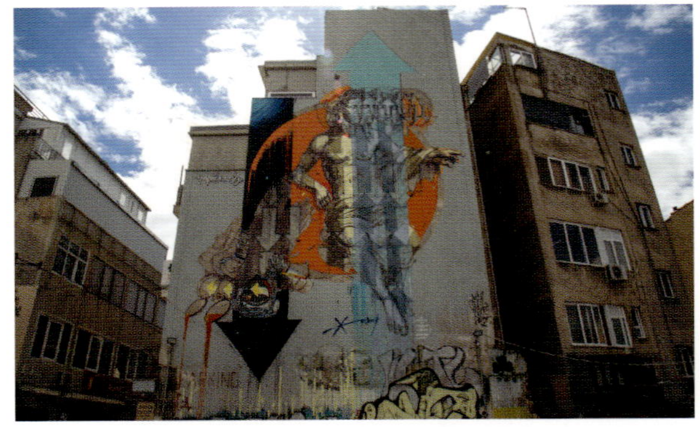

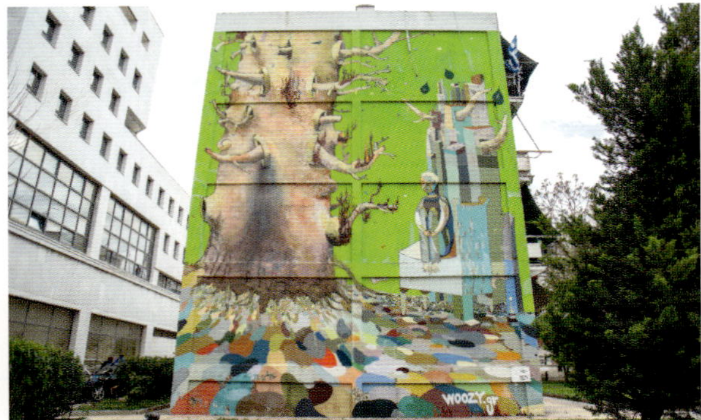

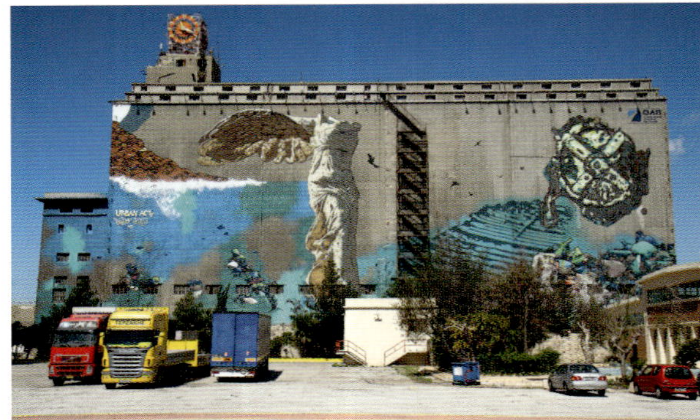

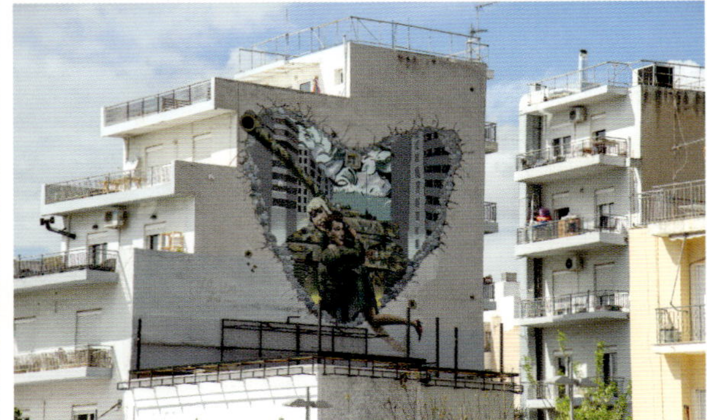

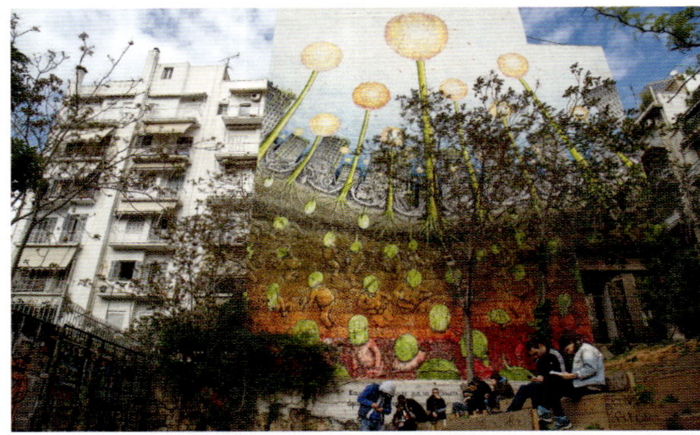

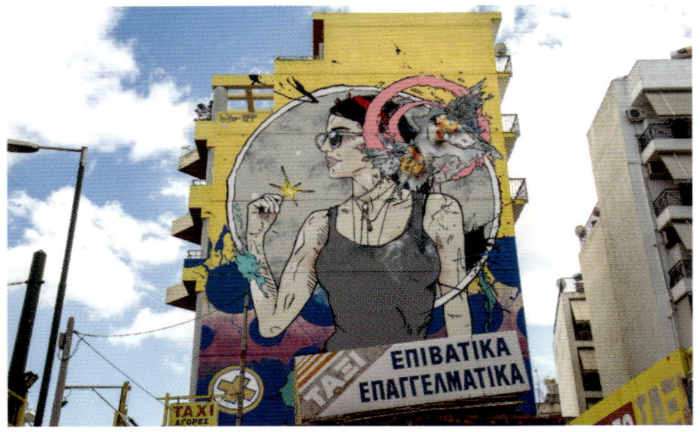
ΕΠΙΒΑΤΙΚΑ
ΕΠΑΓΓΕΛΜΑΤΙΚΑ
ΤΑΞΙ

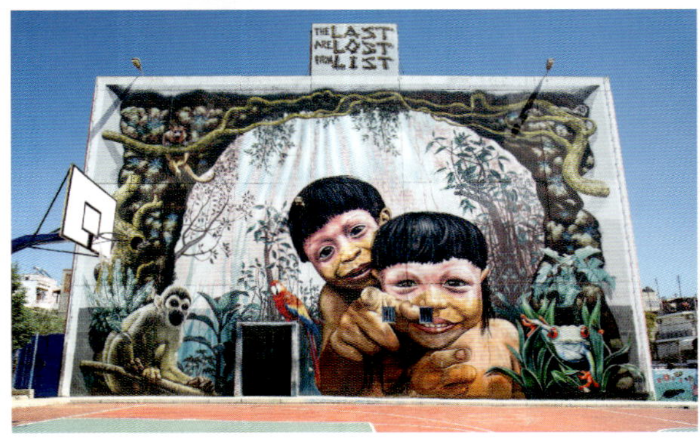
THE LAST
ARE LOST
FROM LIST

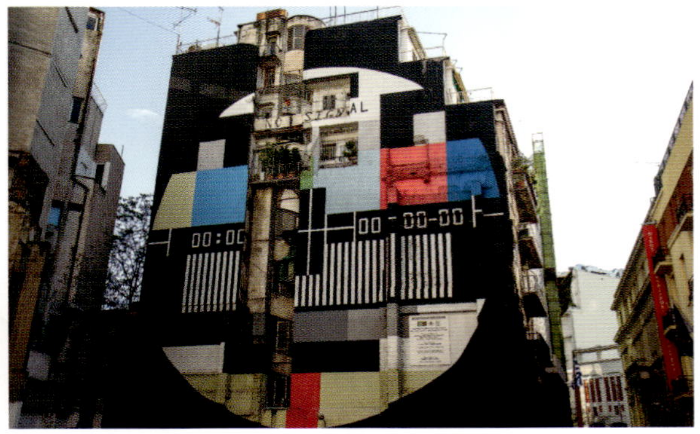
00:00   00-00-00

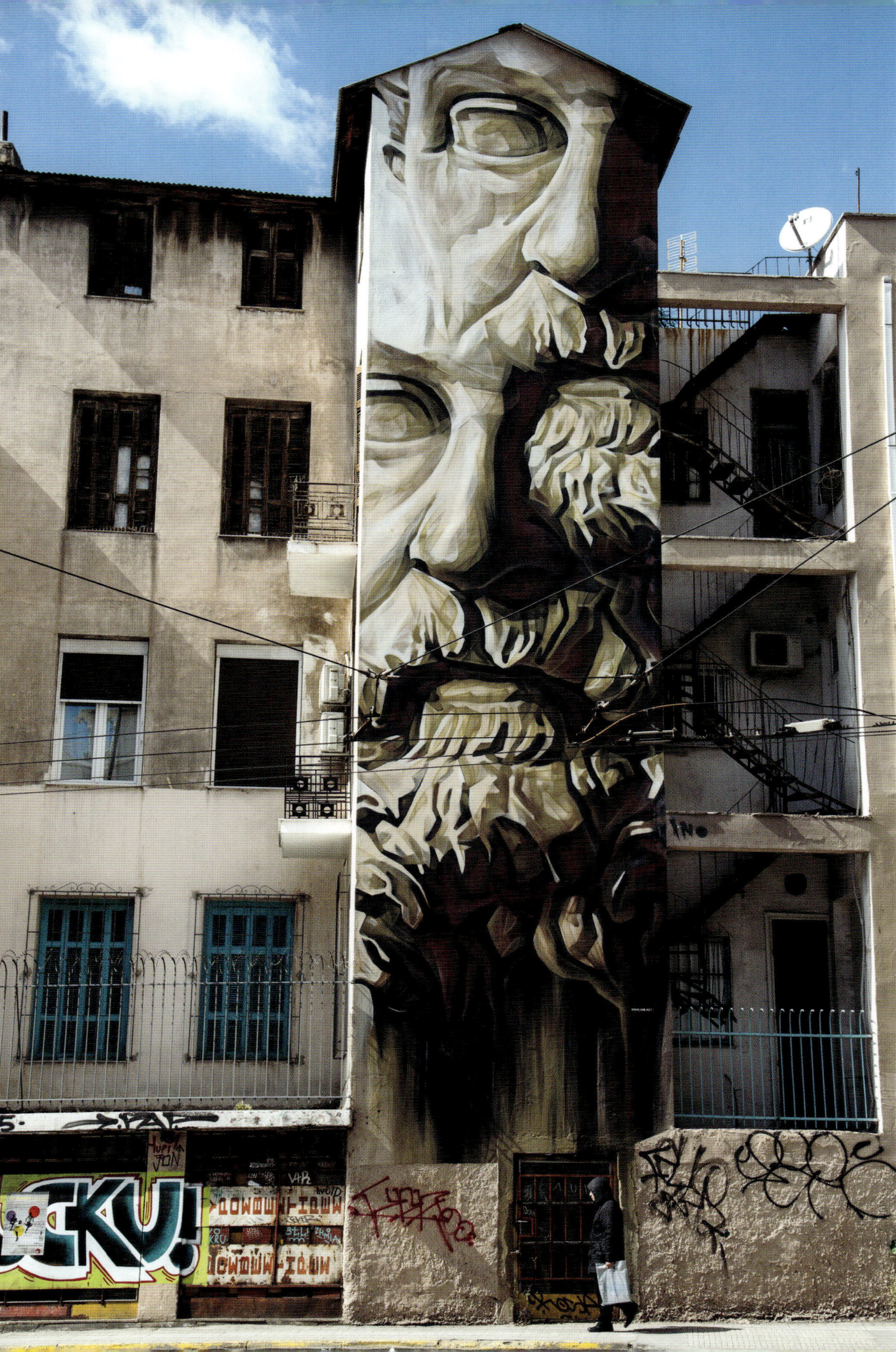

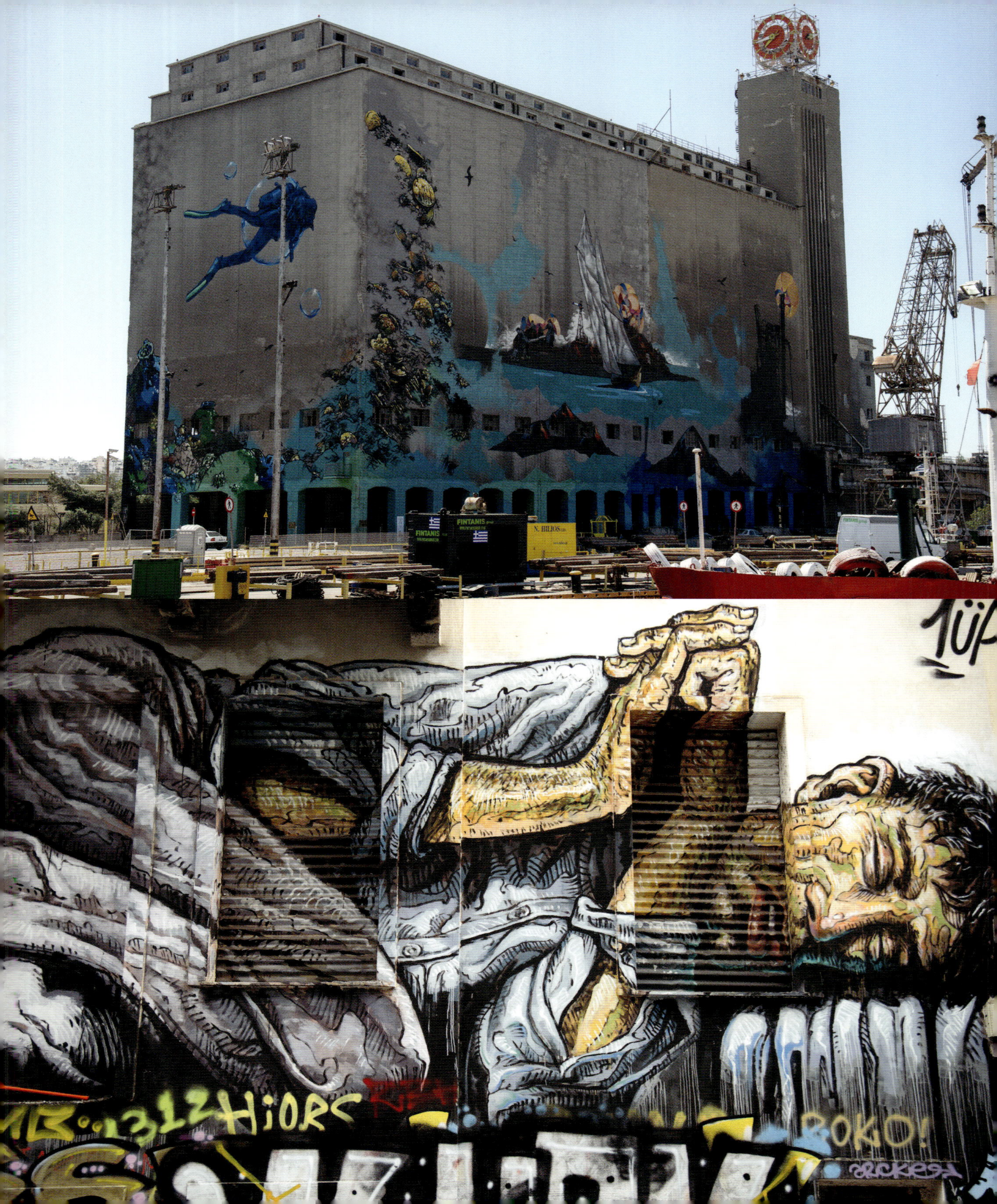

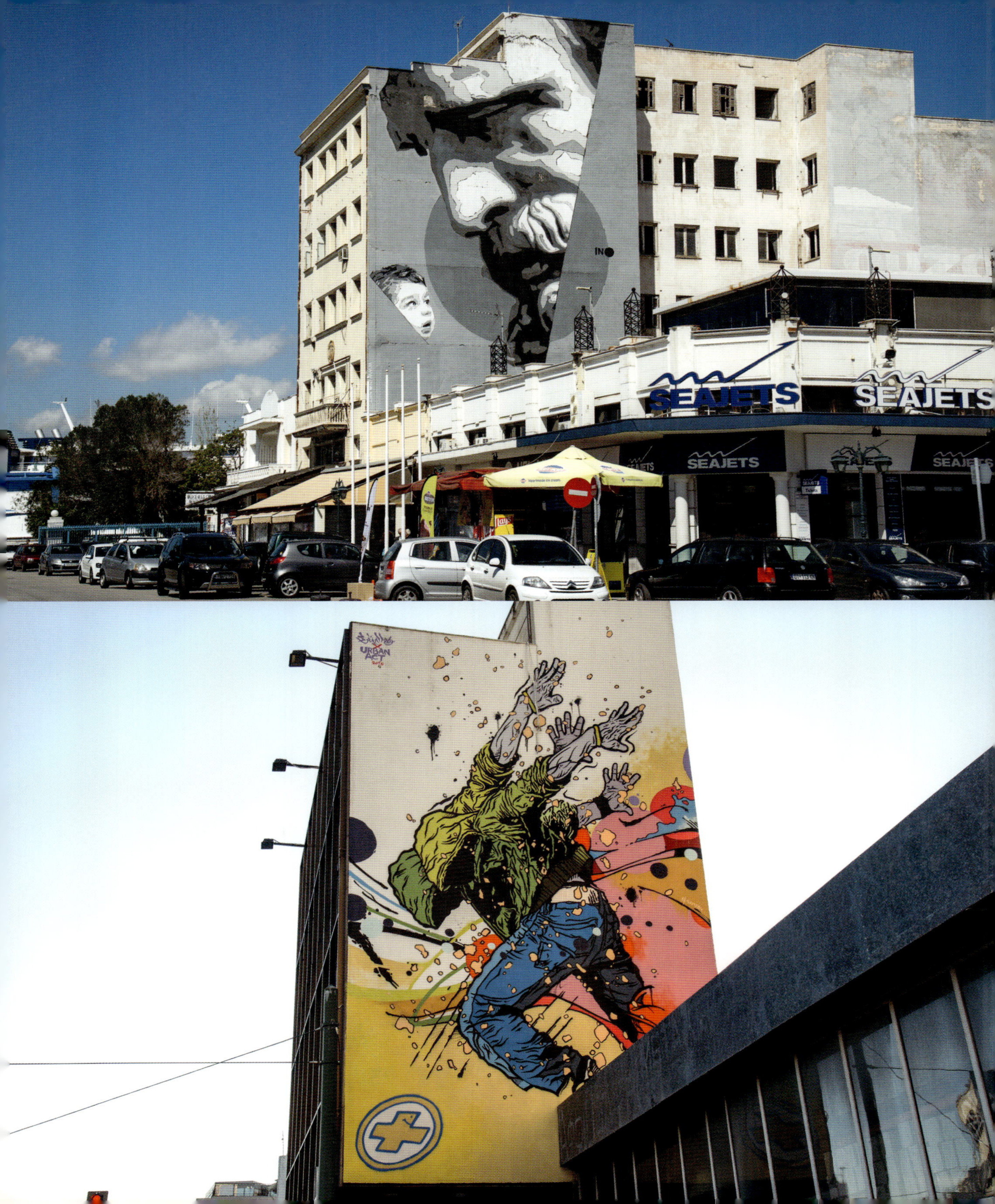

SEAJETS
SEAJETS
SEAJETS
SEAJETS

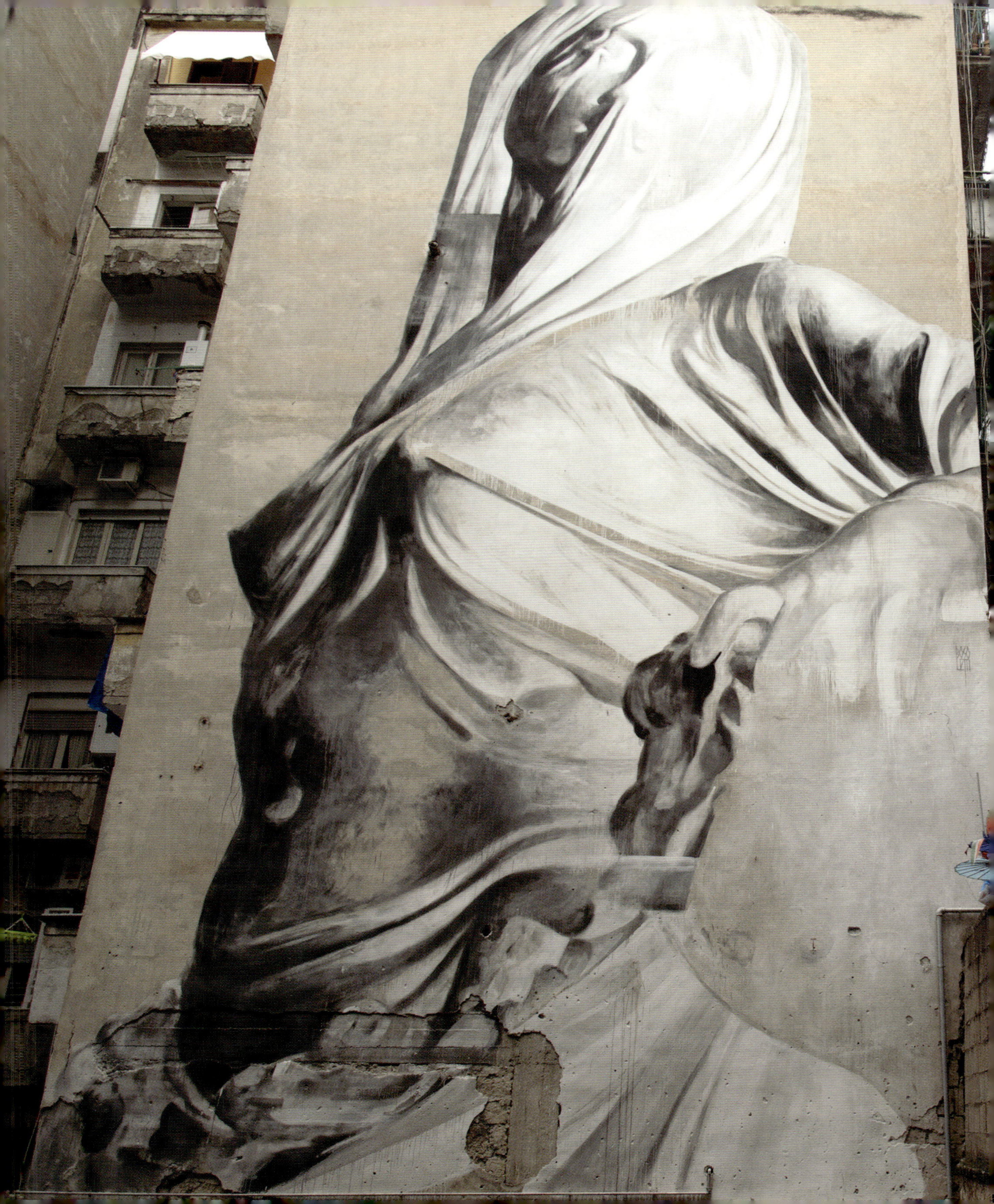

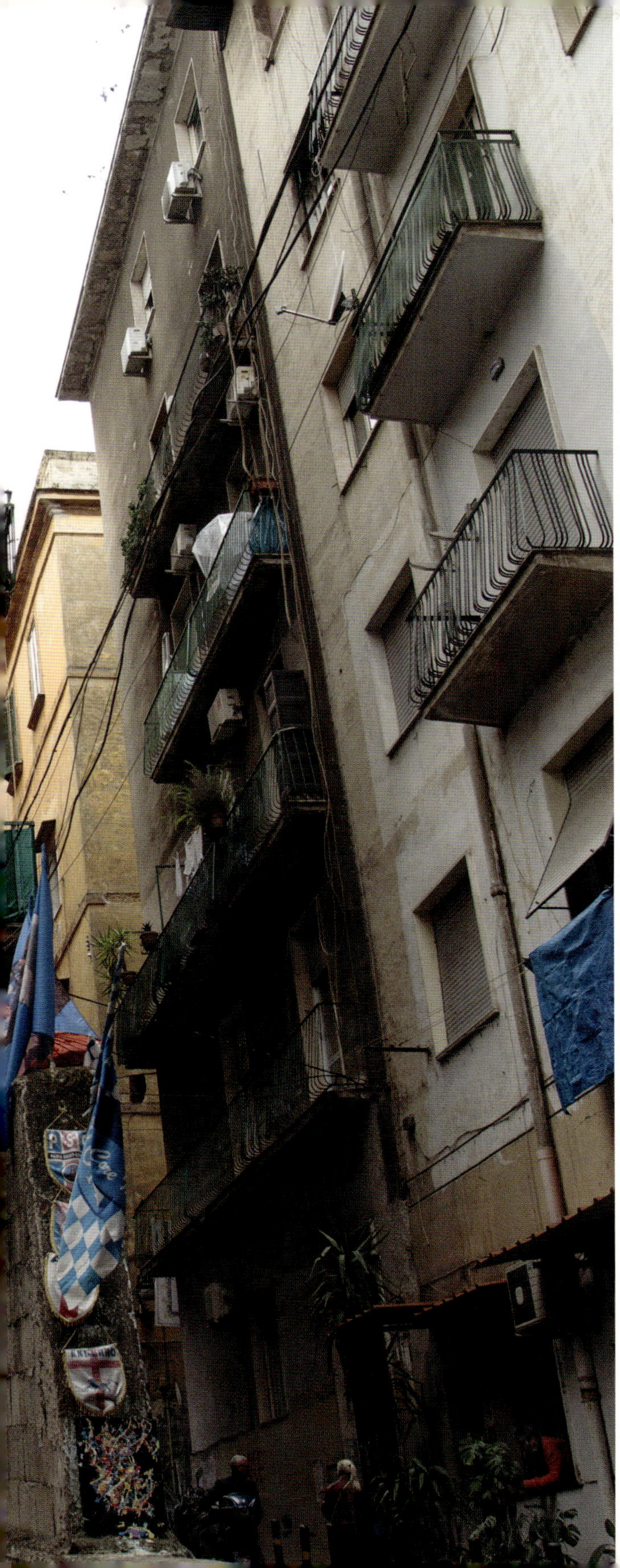

NAPLES

ITALY

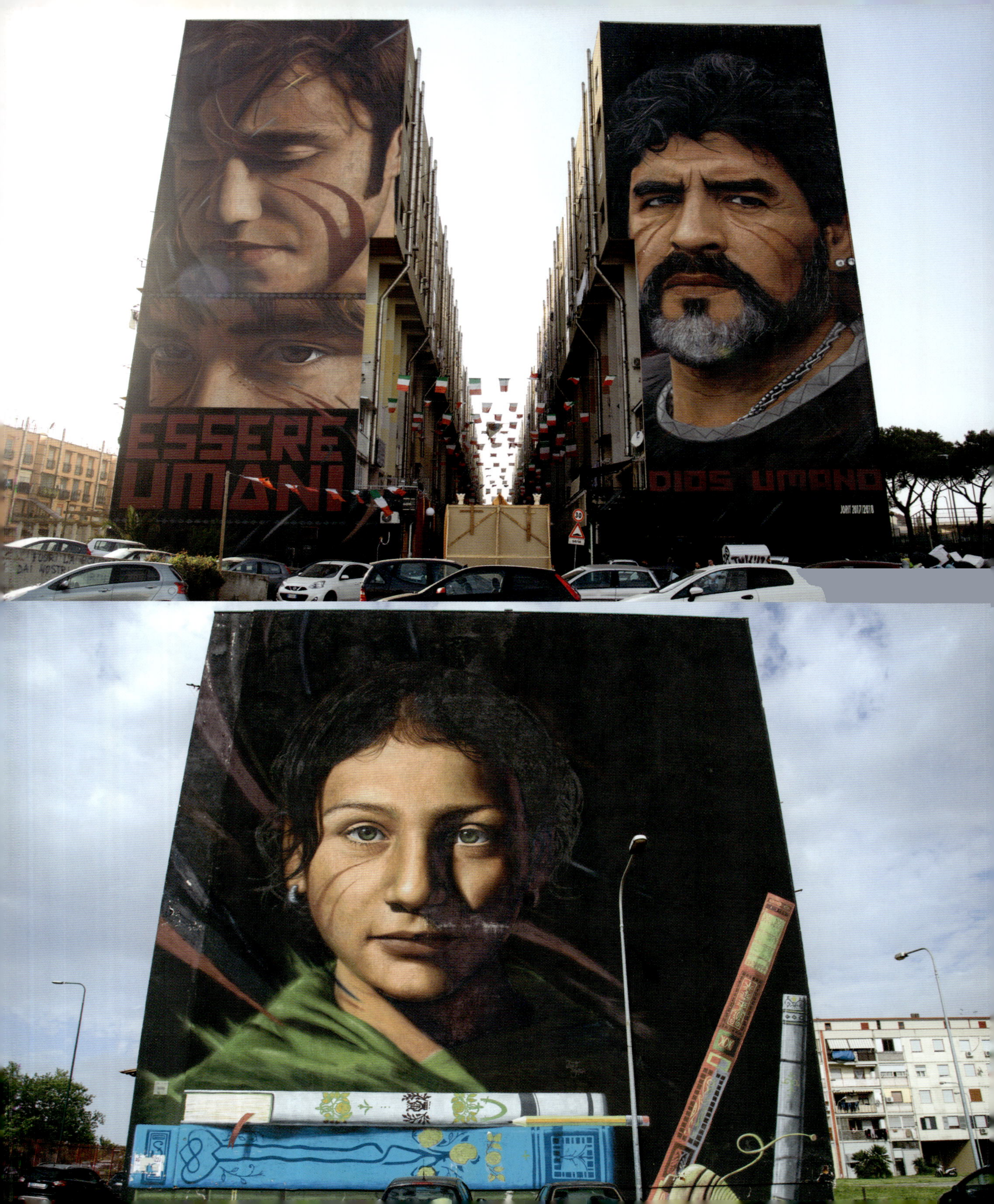

ESSERE
UMANI
DIOS UMANO
JORT 2017/2018

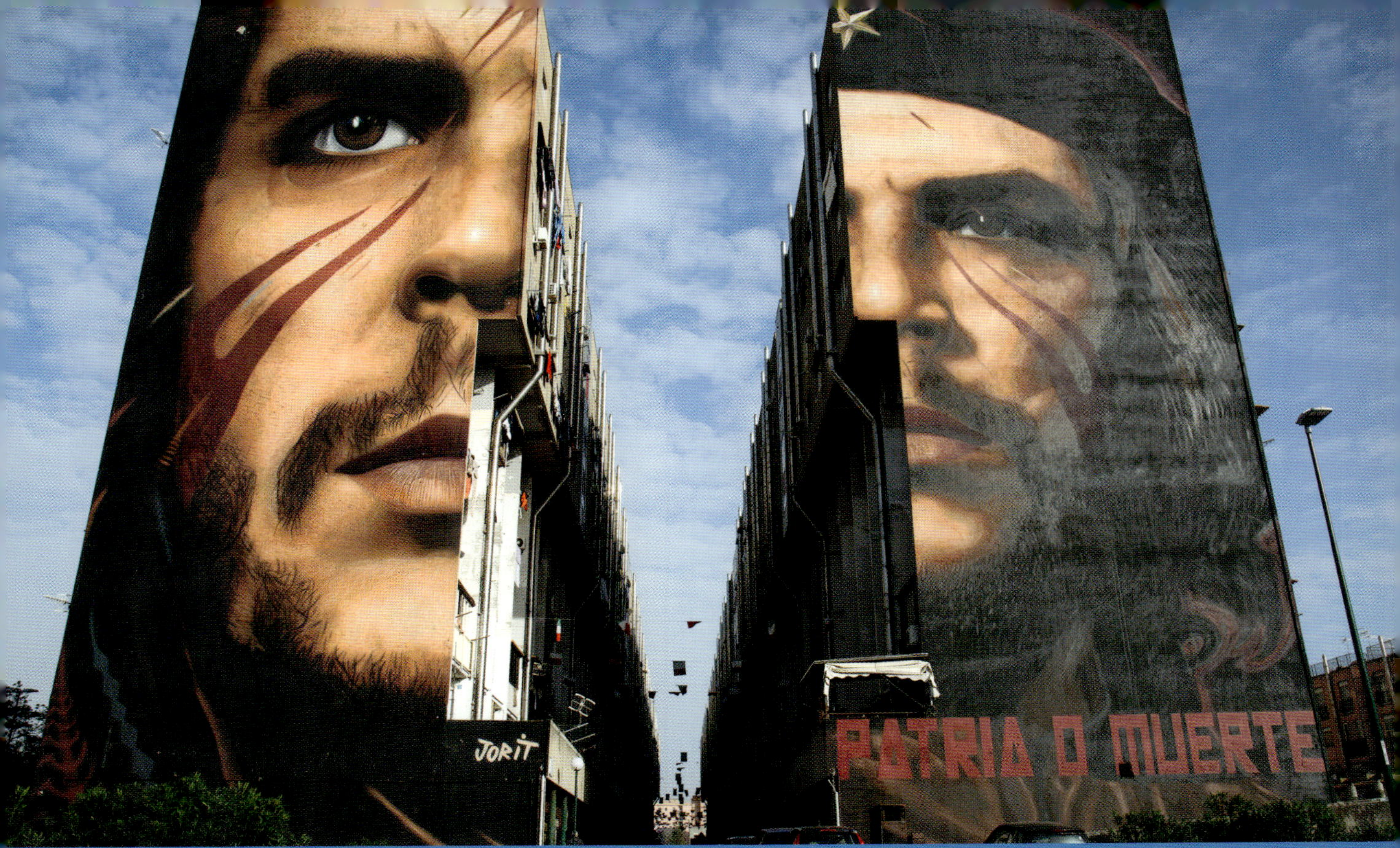

JORIT
PATRIA O MUERTE

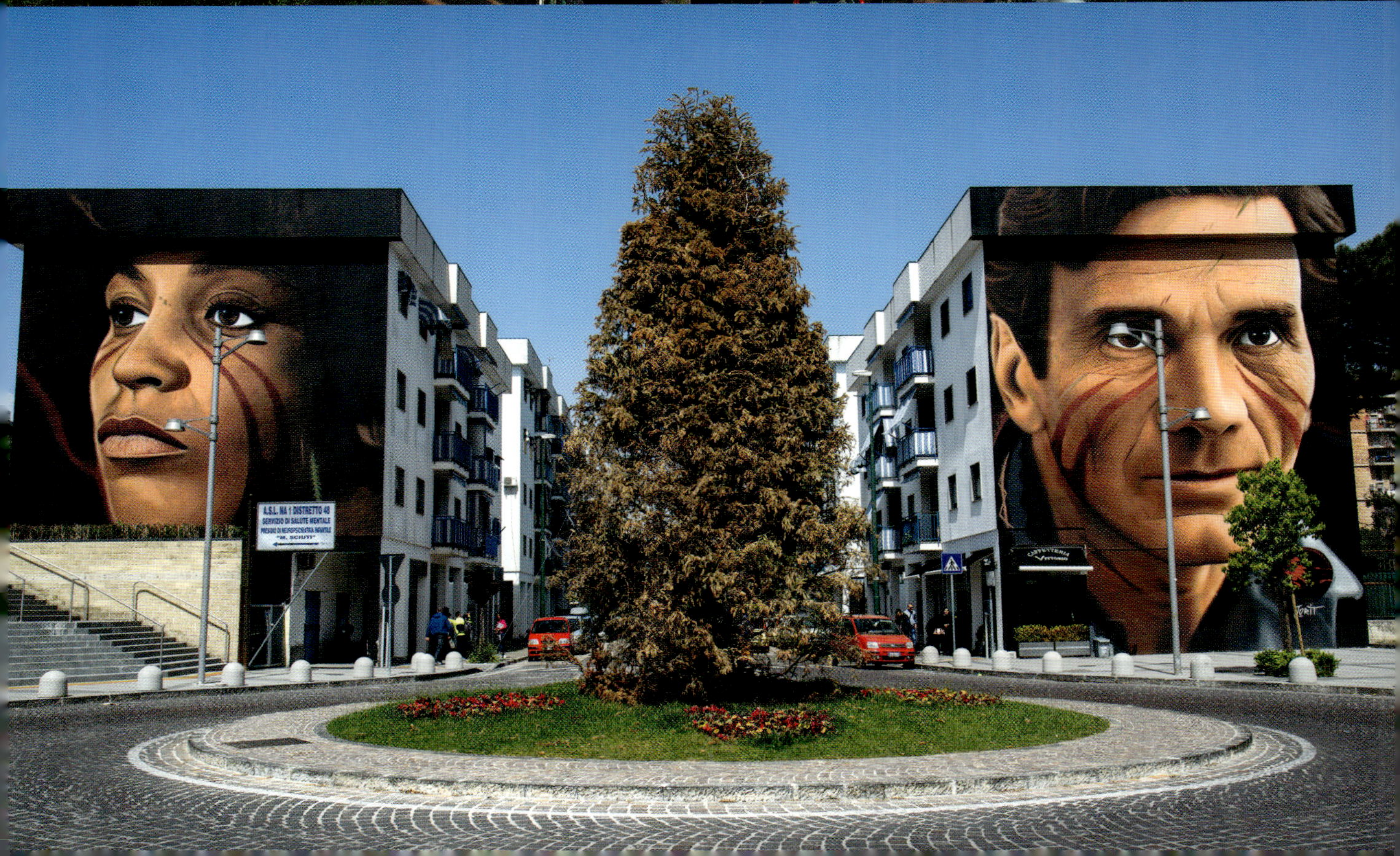

A.S.L. NA 1 DISTRETTO 48
SERVIZIO DI SALUTE MENTALE
"M. SCOTT"
JORiT

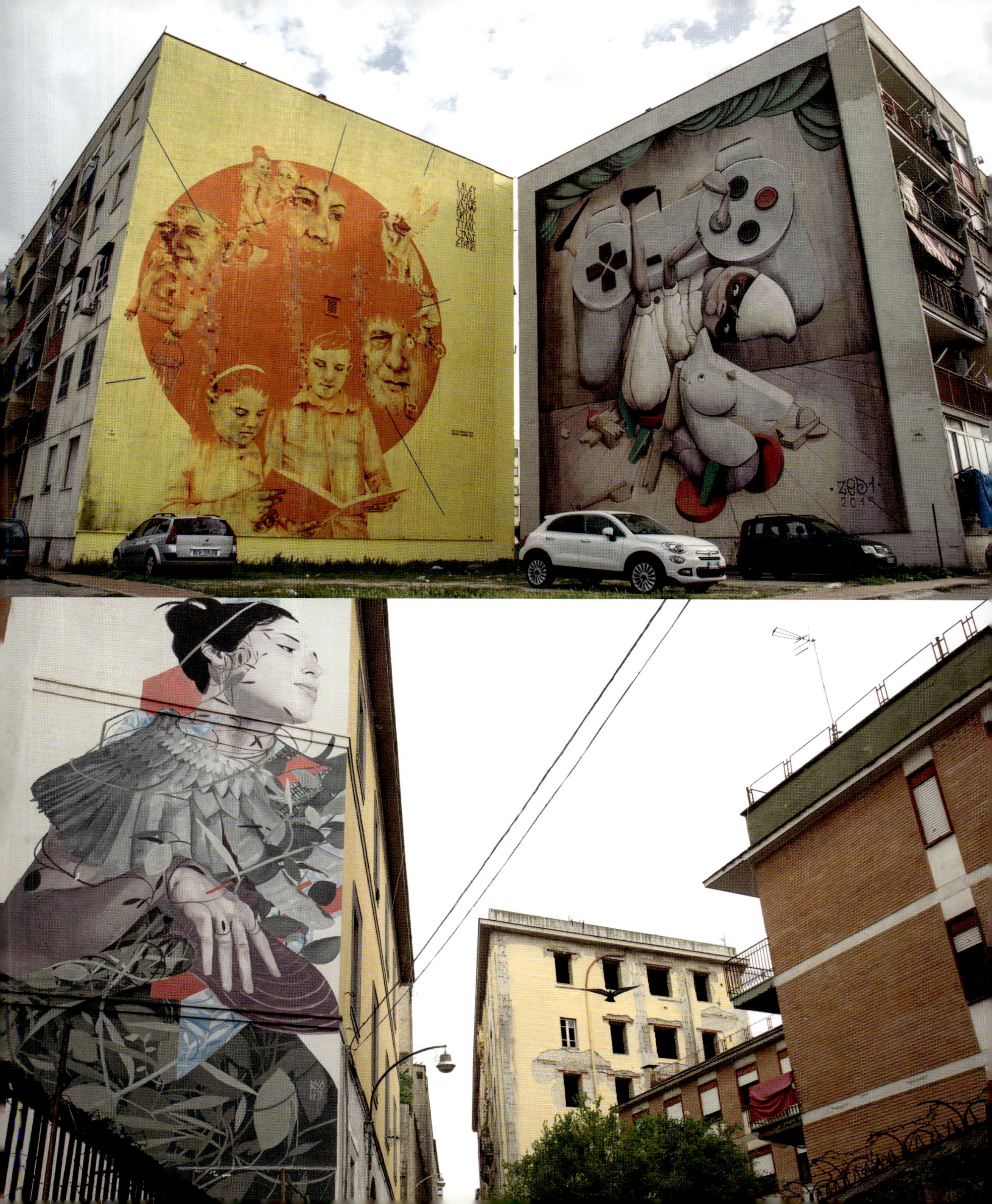

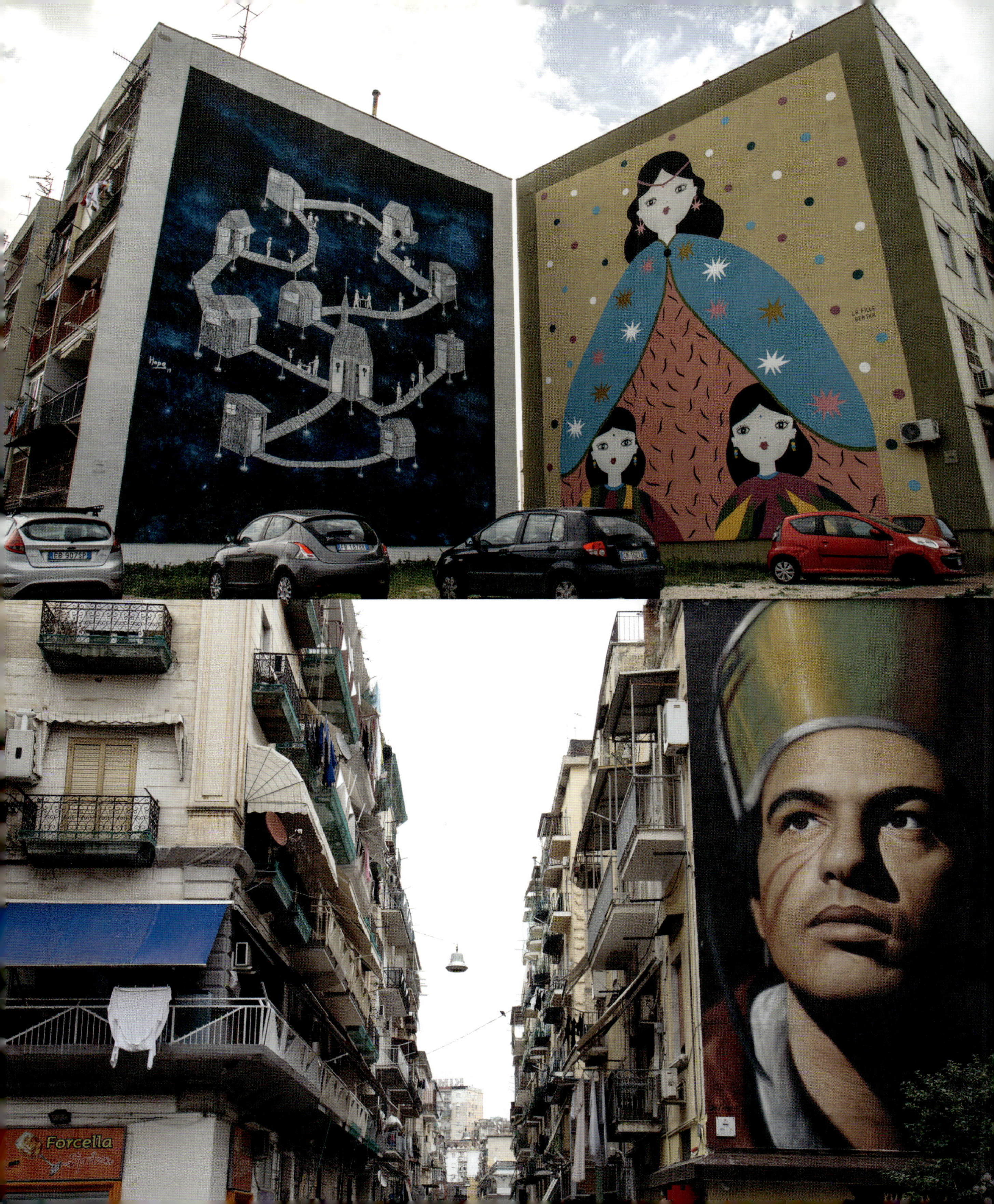

LA FILLE
BERTHA
Forcella

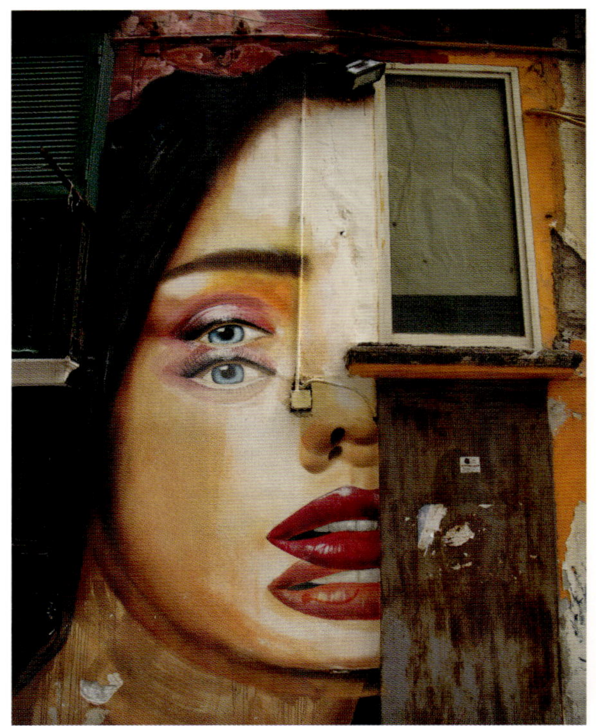

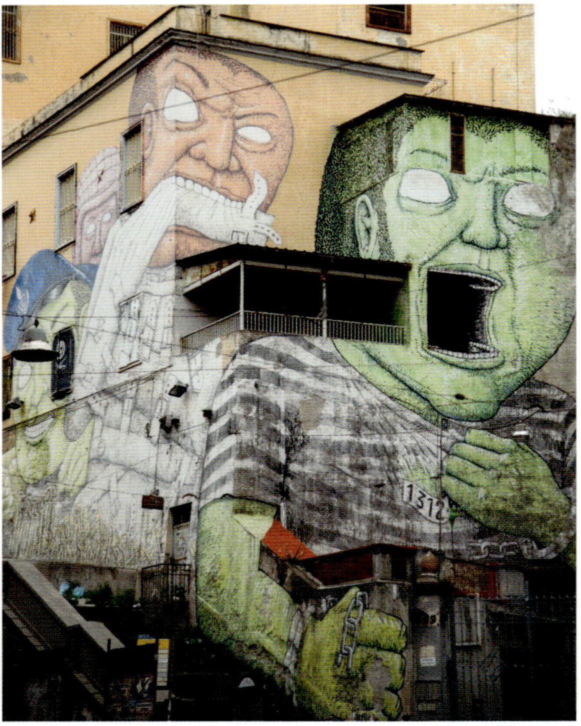

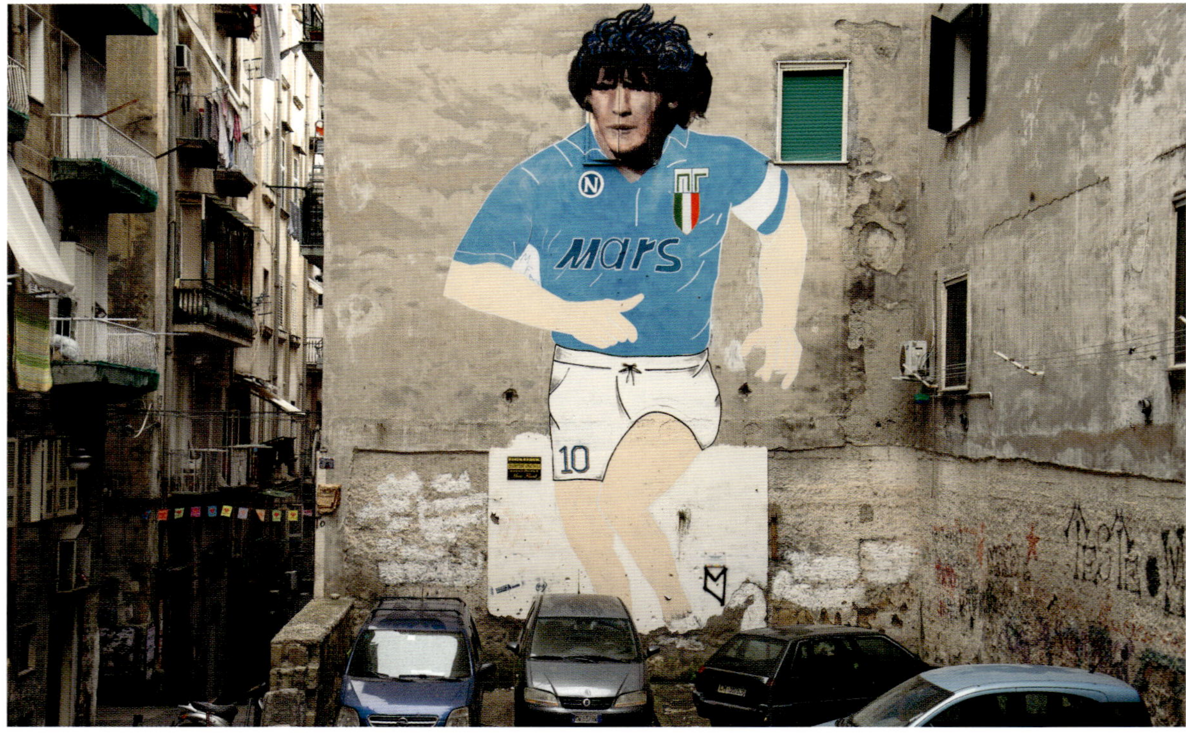

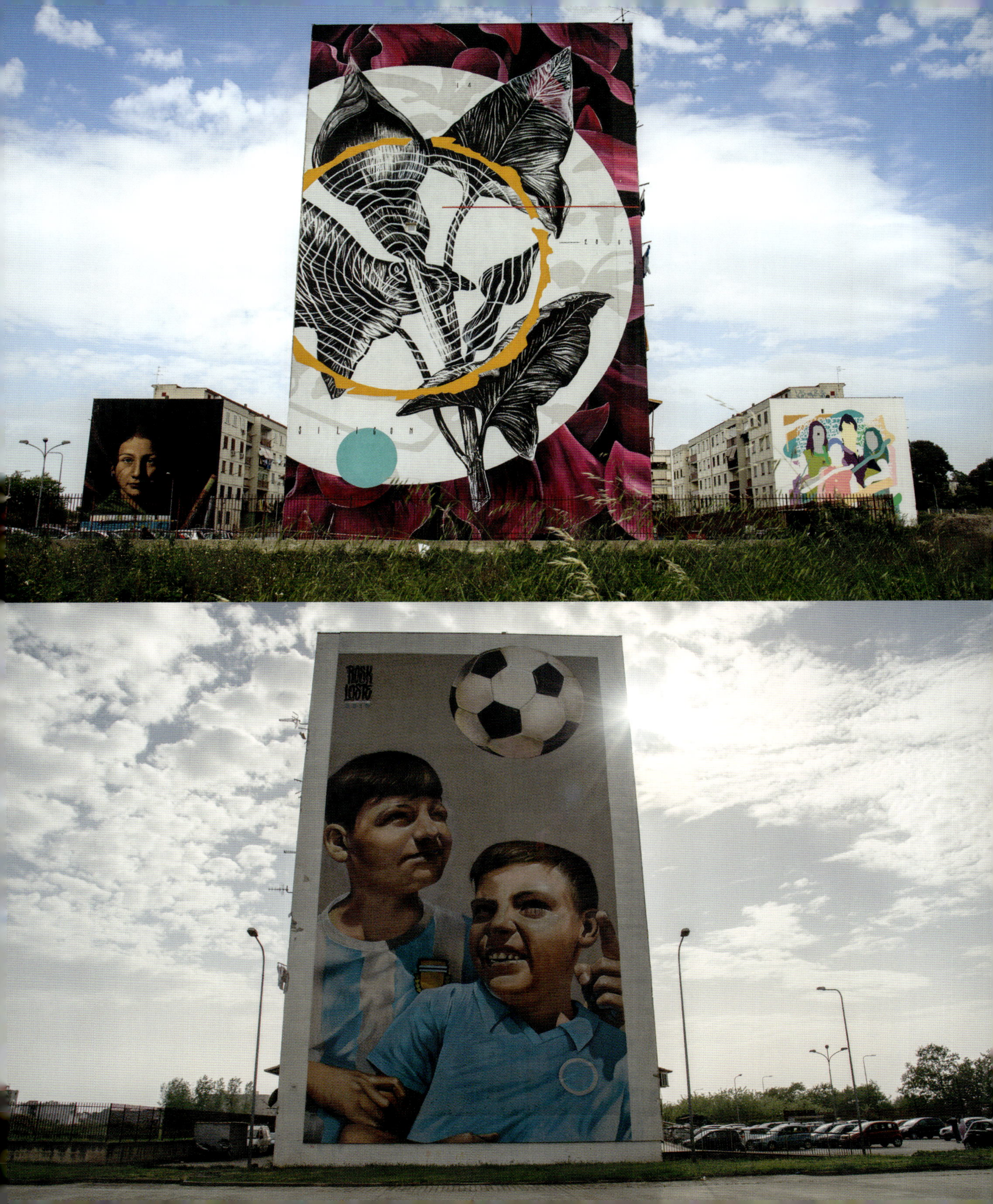

ROME

ITALY

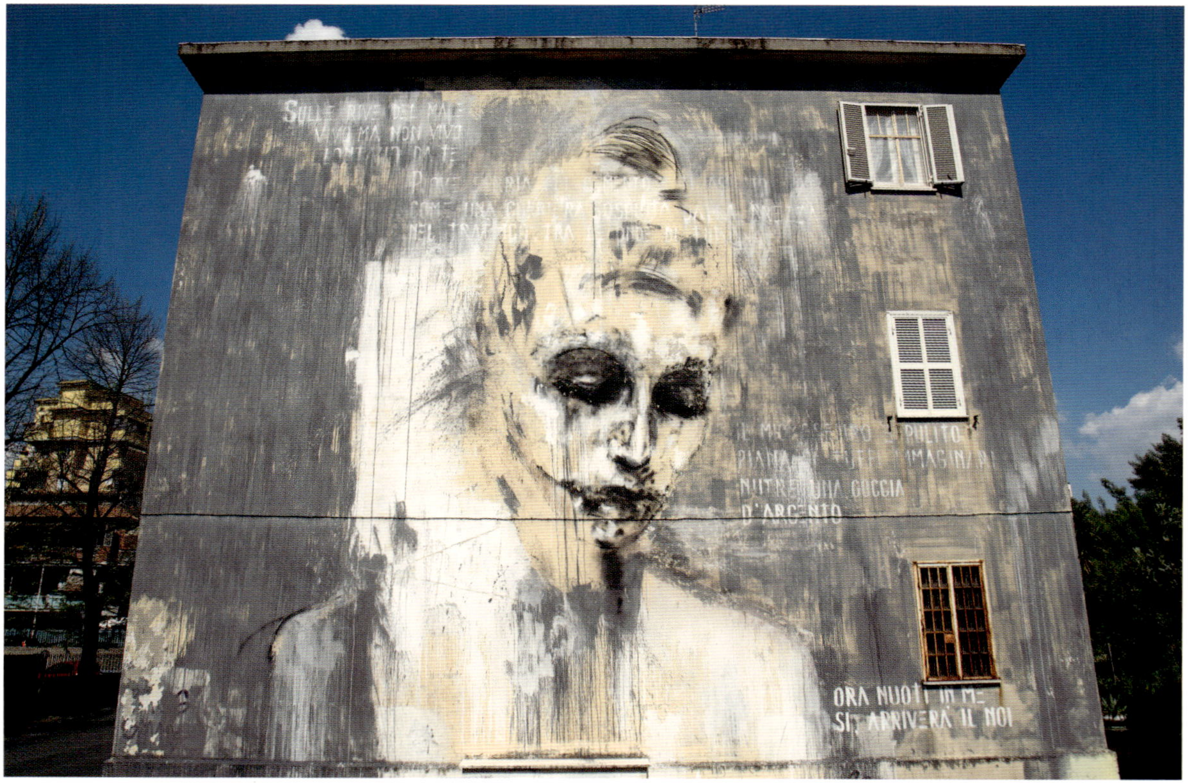

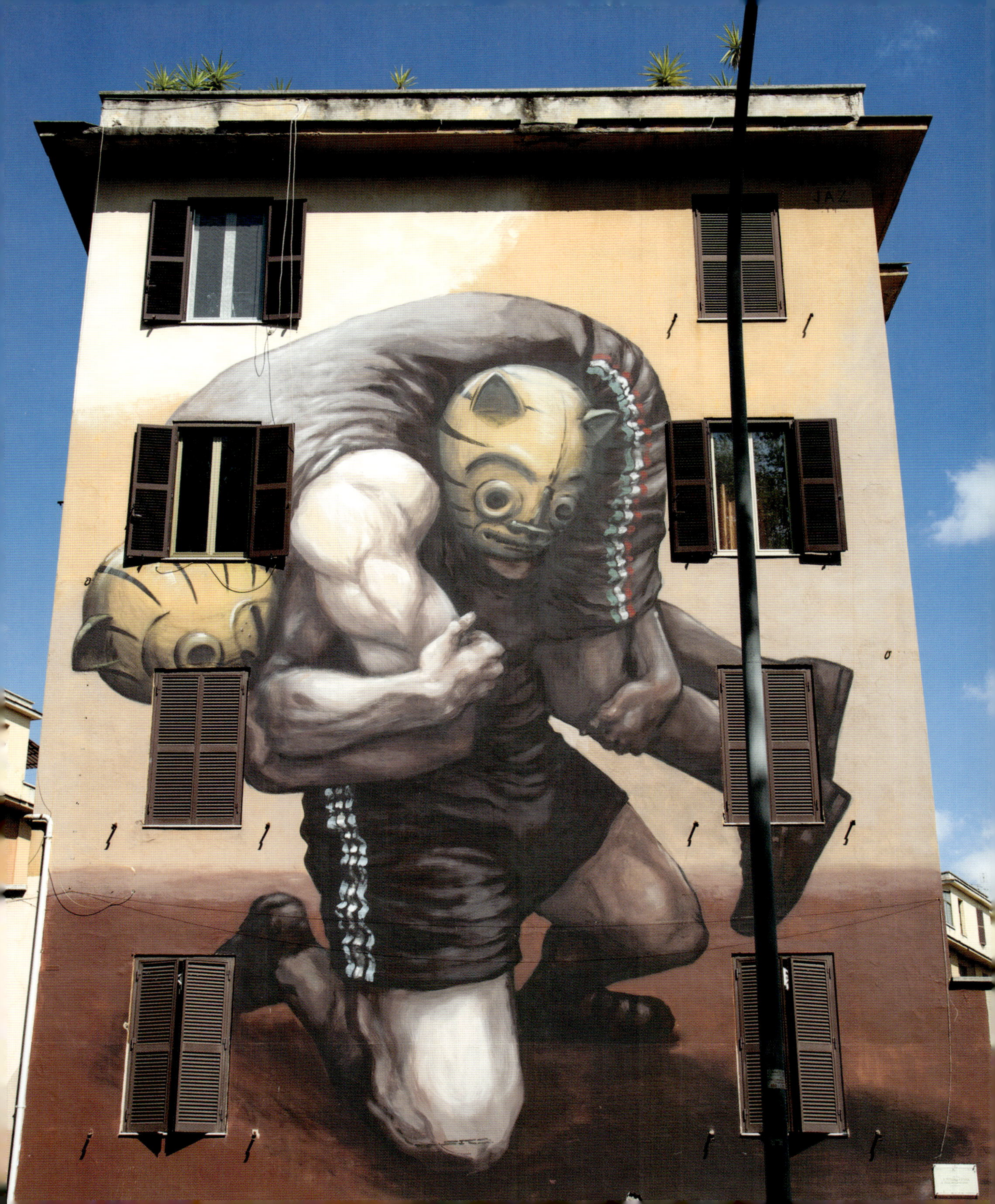
JAZ

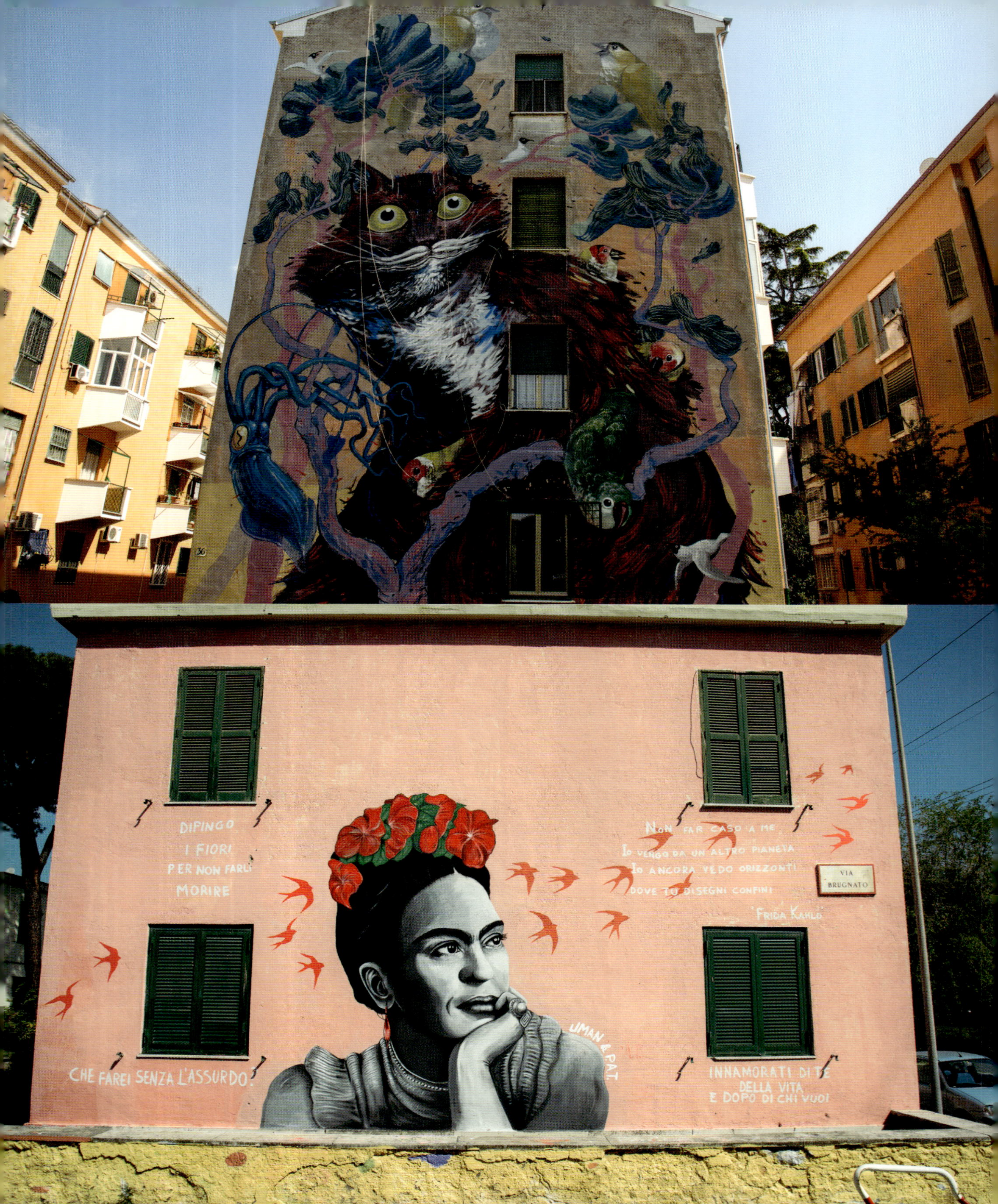
DIPINGO
I FIORI
PER NON FARLI
MORIRE

NON FAR CASO A ME
Io VENGO DA UN ALTRO PIANETA
Io ANCORA VEDO ORIZZONTI
DOVE TU DISEGNI CONFINI

'FRIDA KAHLO

VIA
BRUGNATO

UMAN & PAT

CHE FAREI SENZA L'ASSURDO?

INNAMORATI DI TE
DELLA VITA
E DOPO DI CHI VUOI

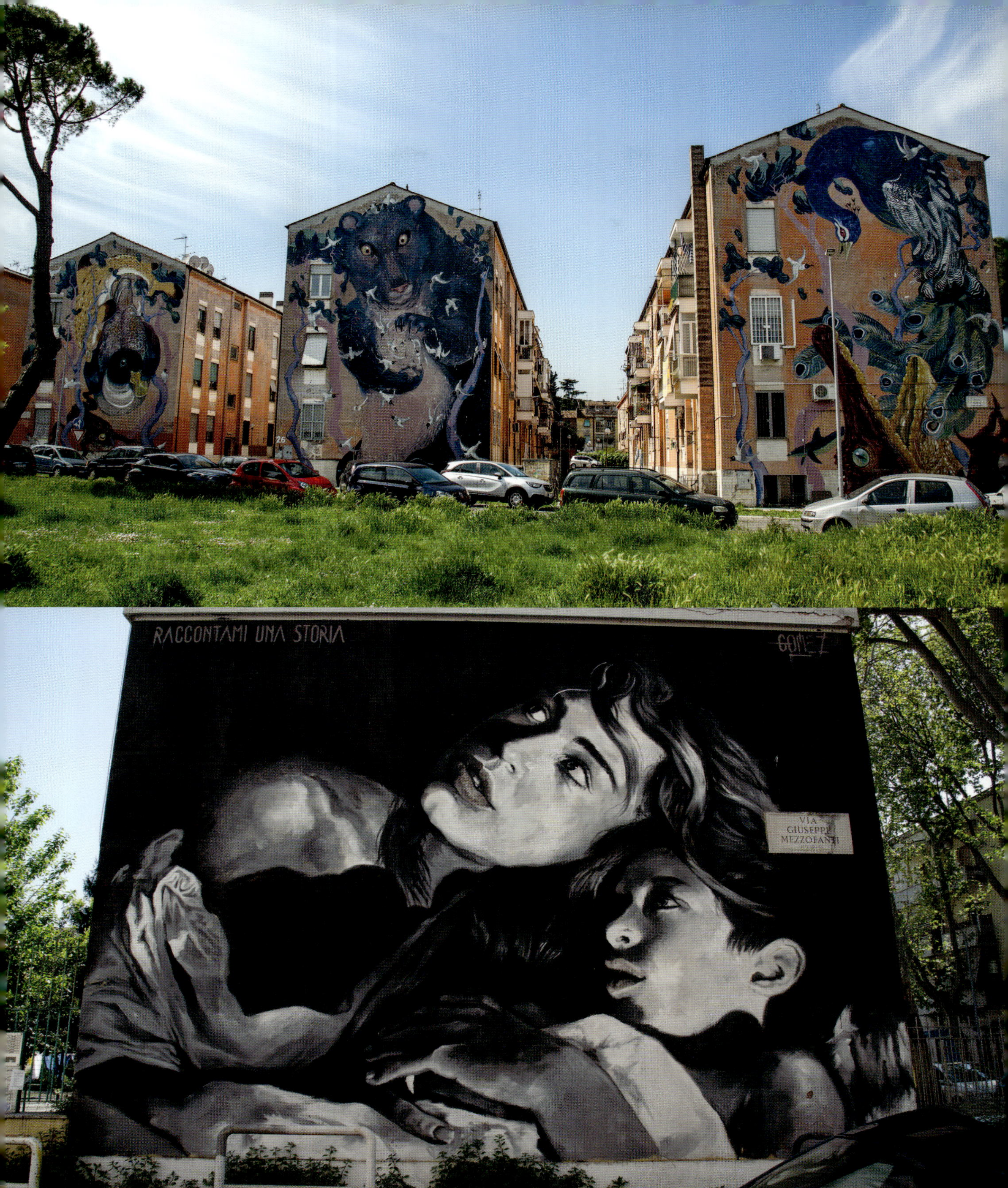
RACCONTAMI UNA STORIA
GOMEZ
VIA
GIUSEPPE
MEZZOFANTI

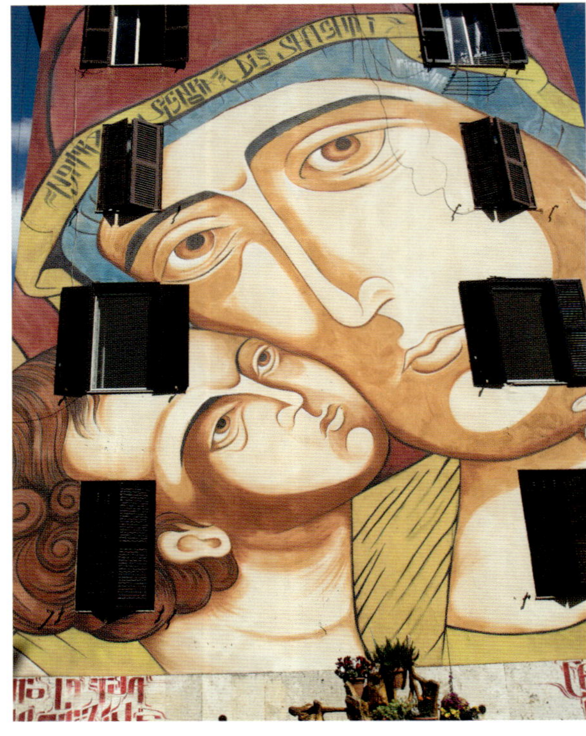
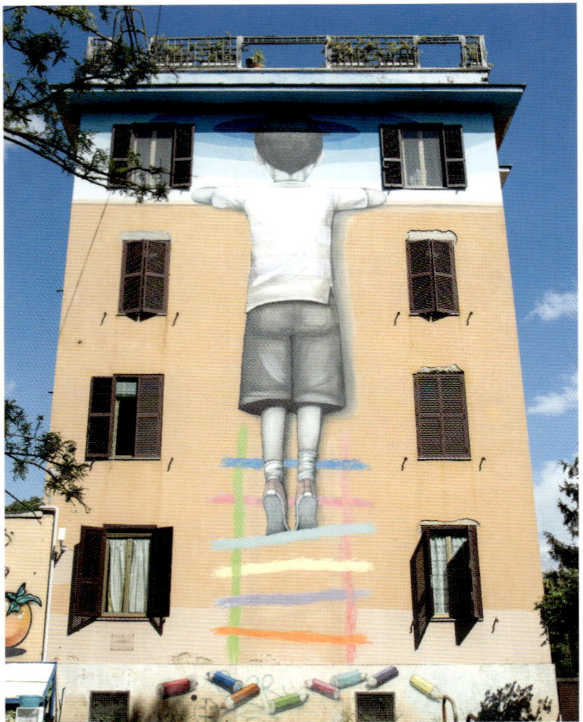
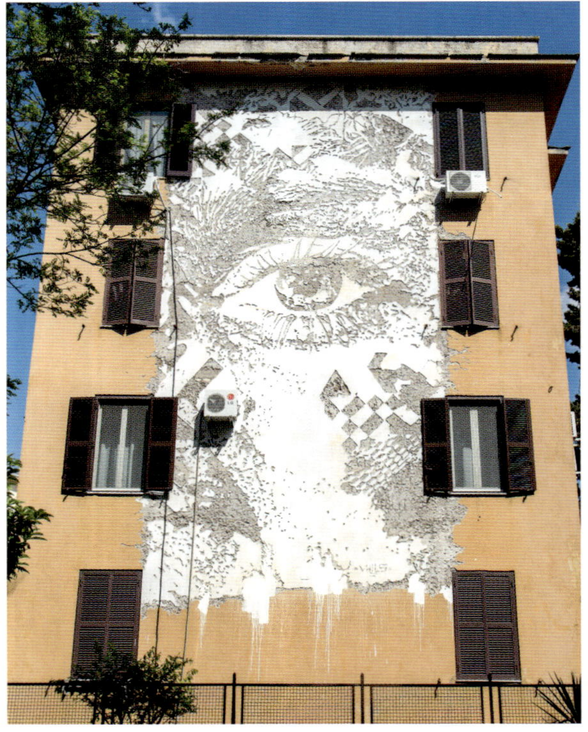
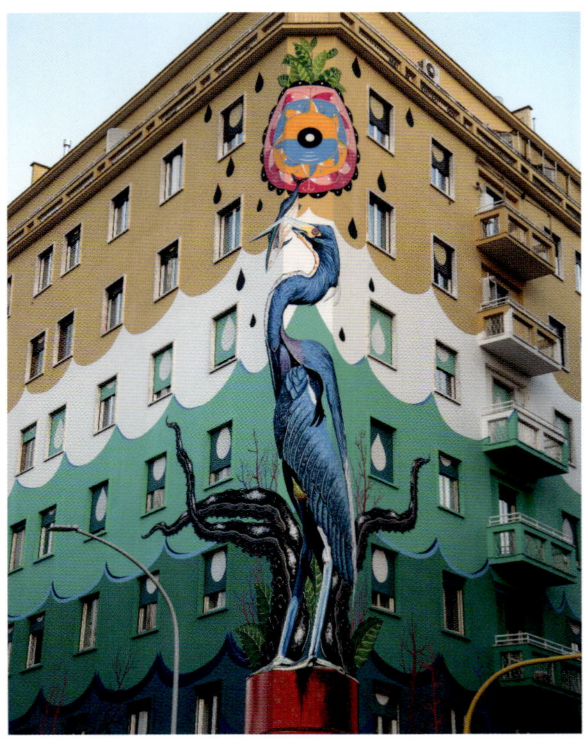

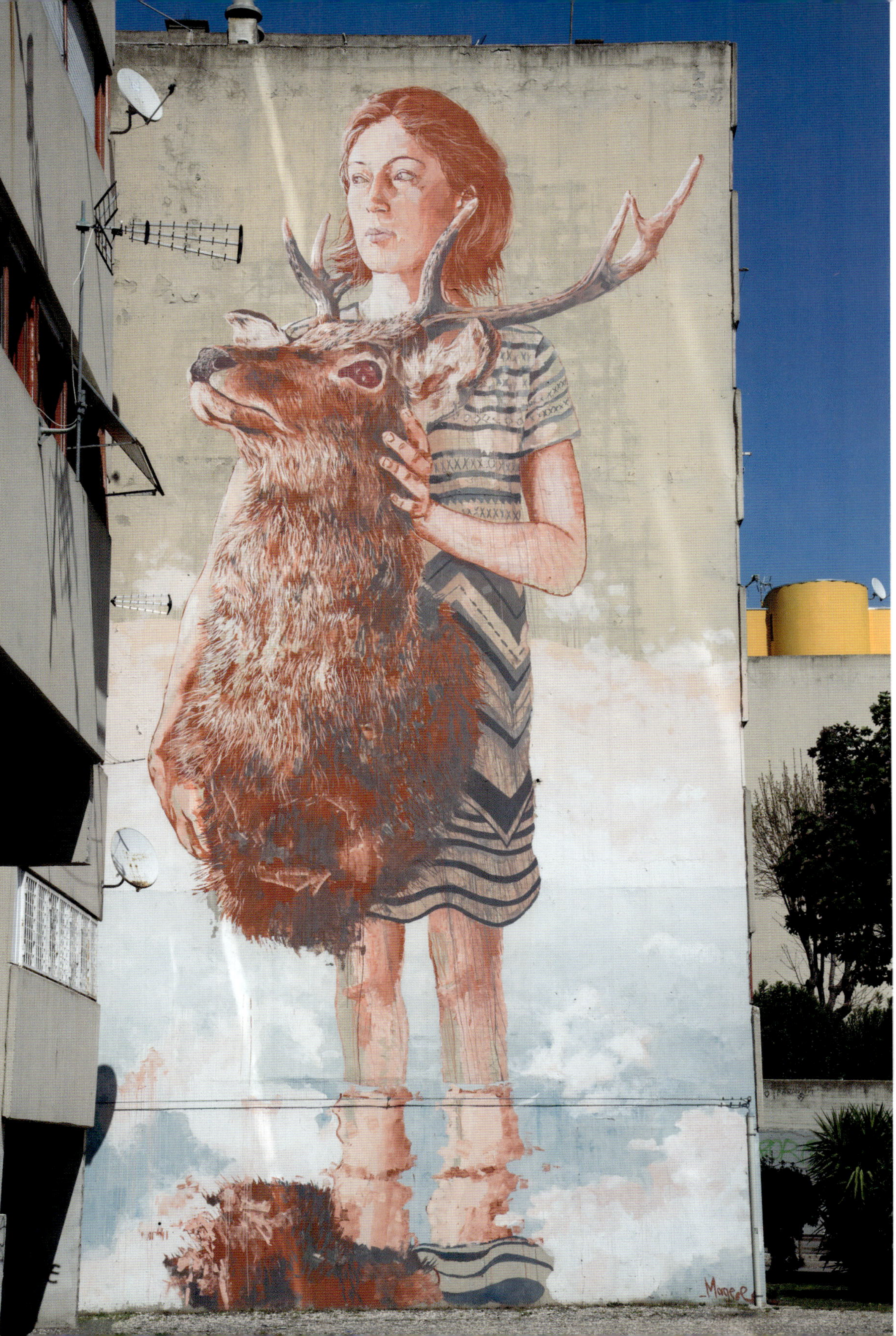

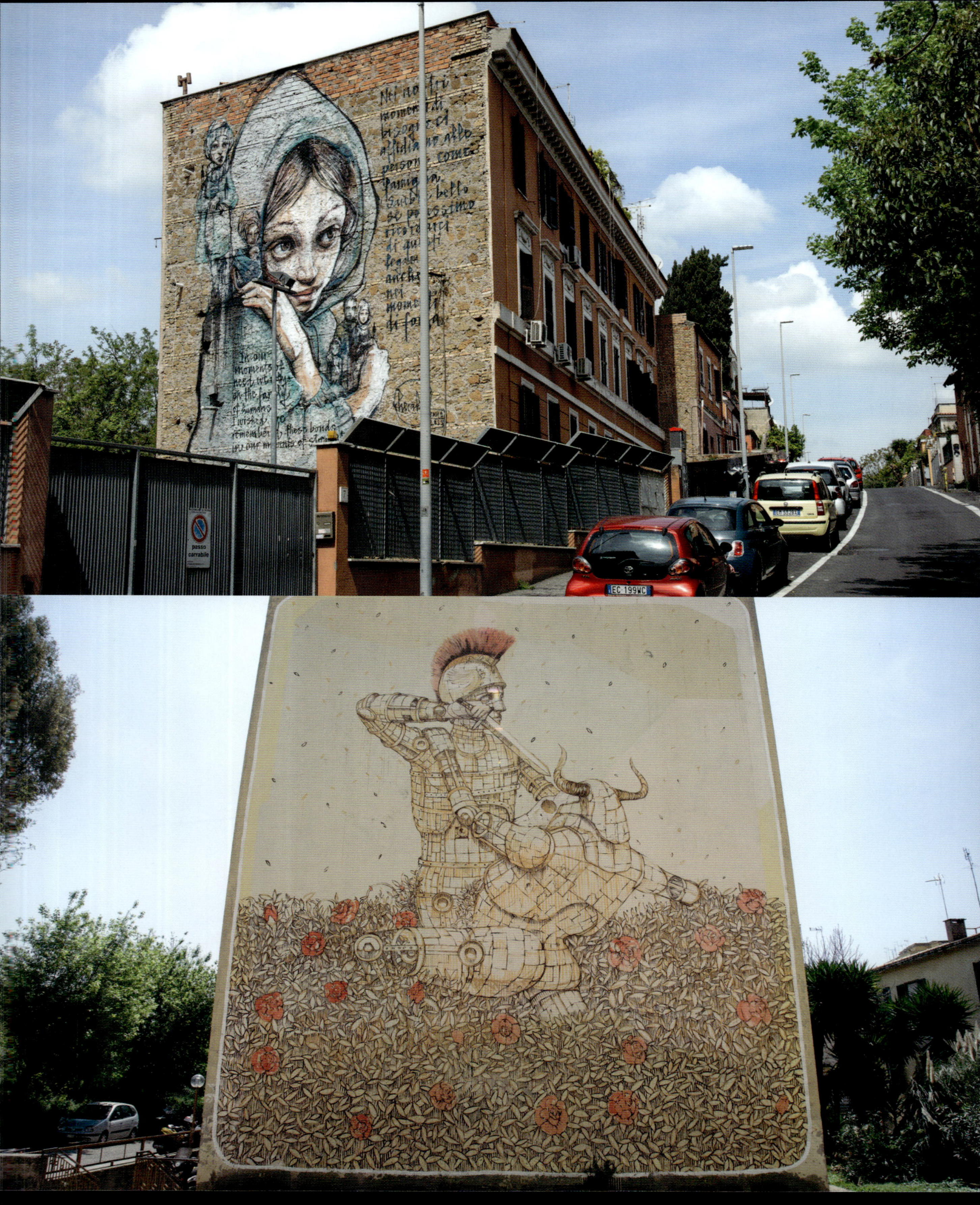

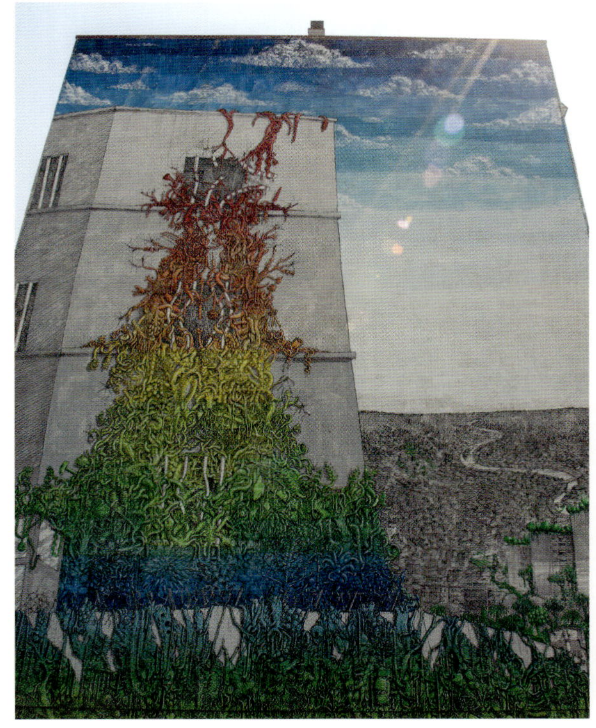

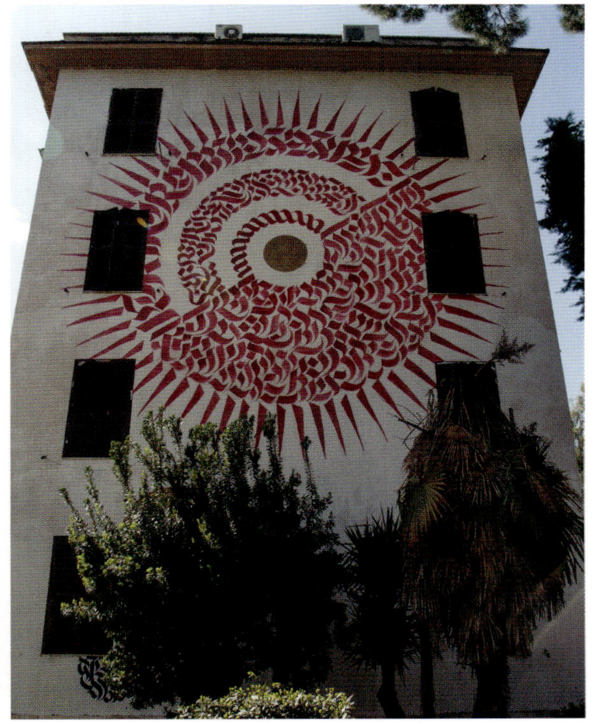

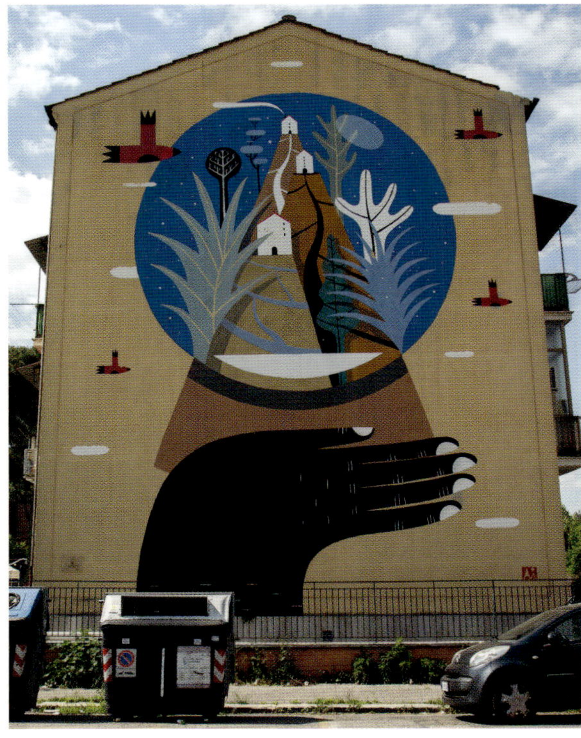

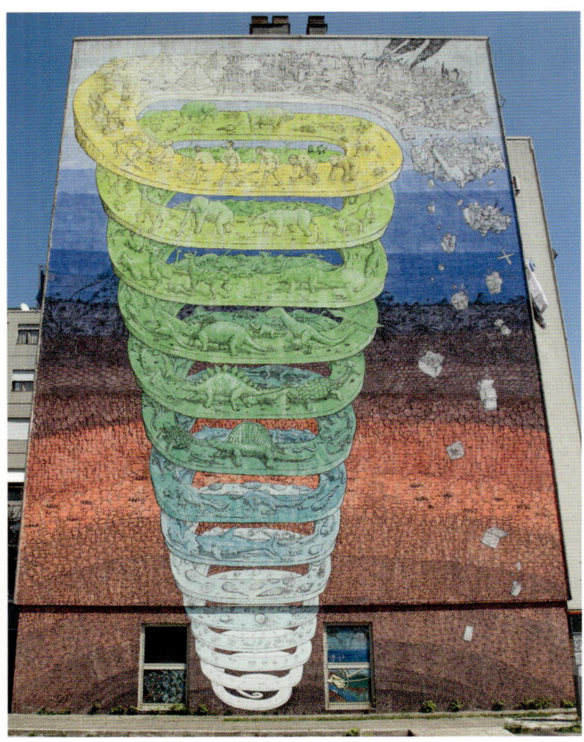

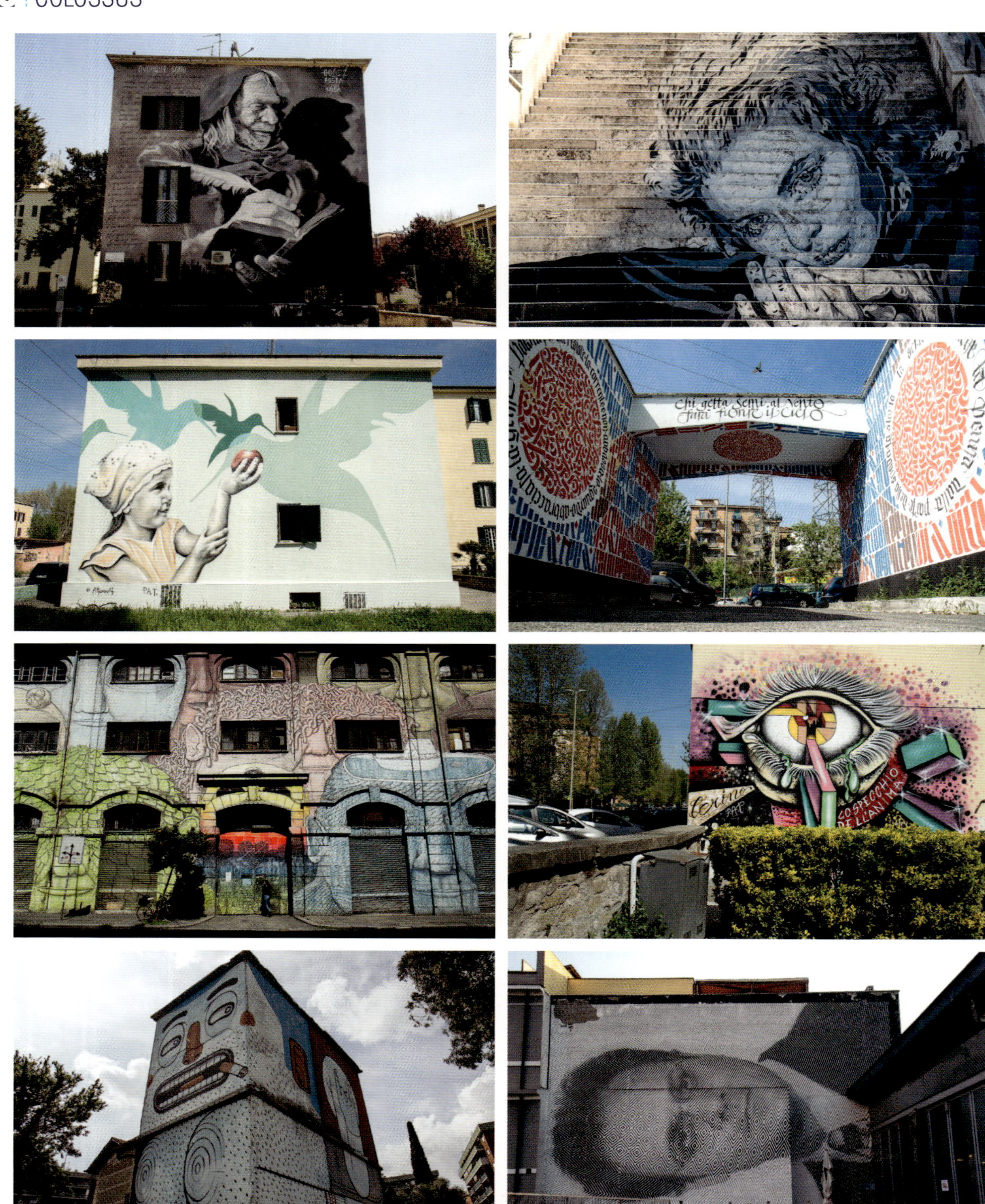

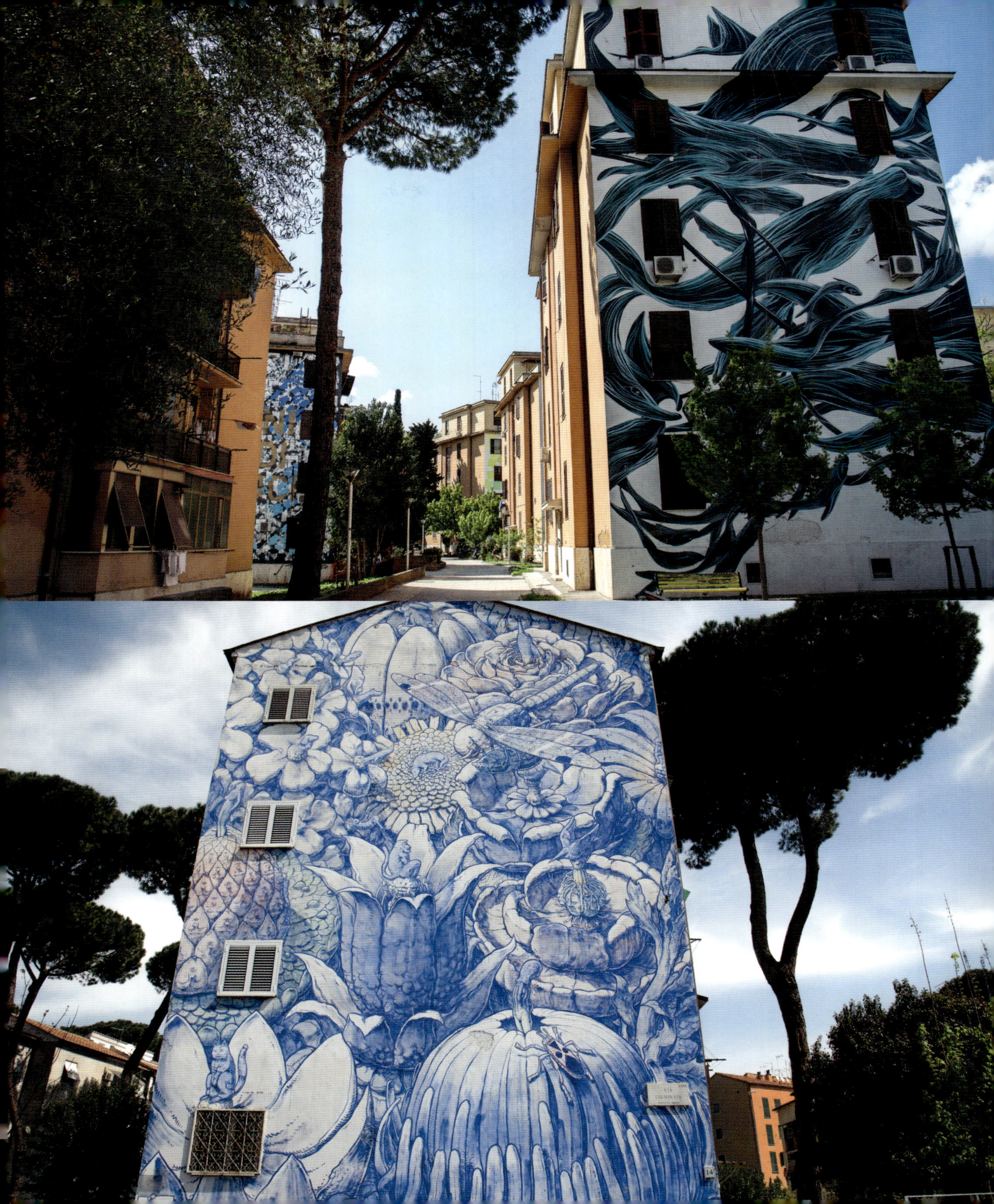

BAIRRO PADRE CRUZ

PORTUGAL

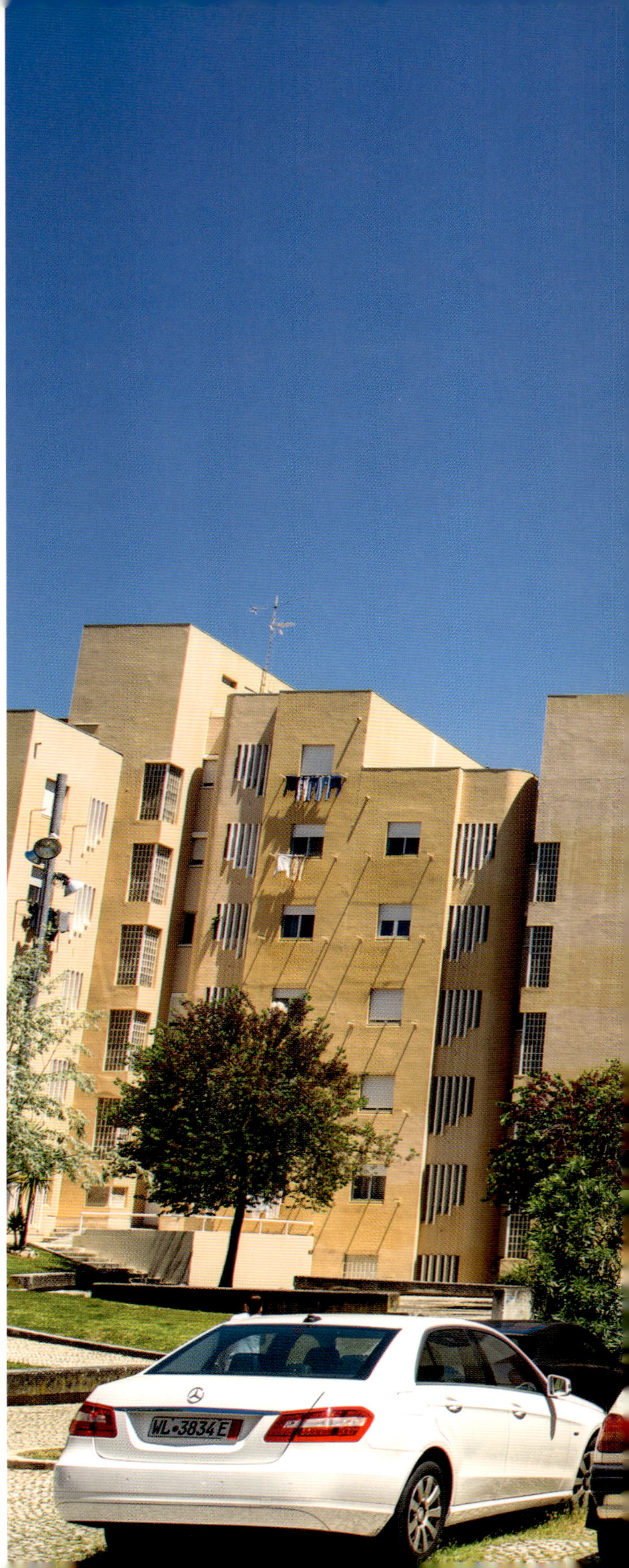

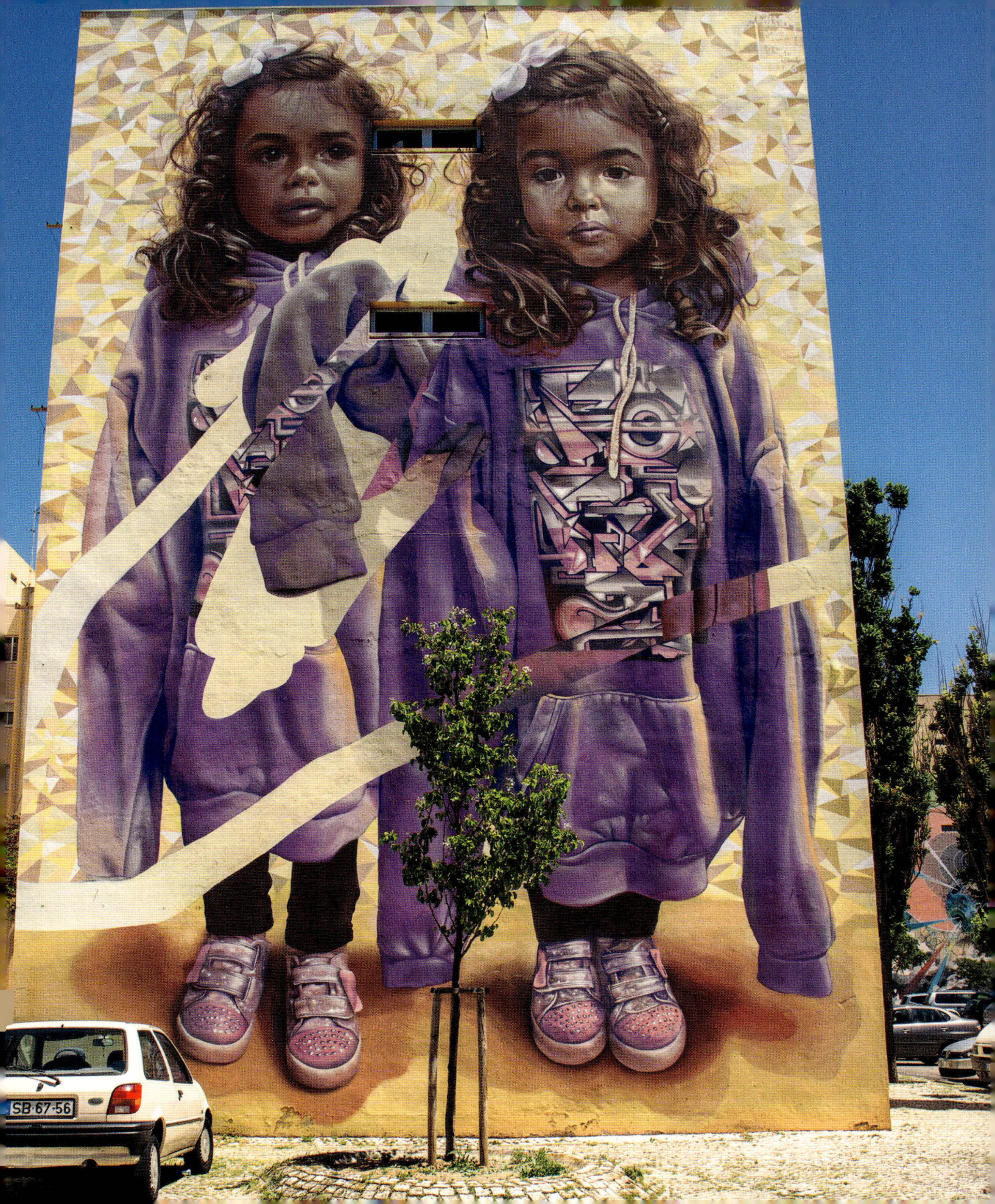

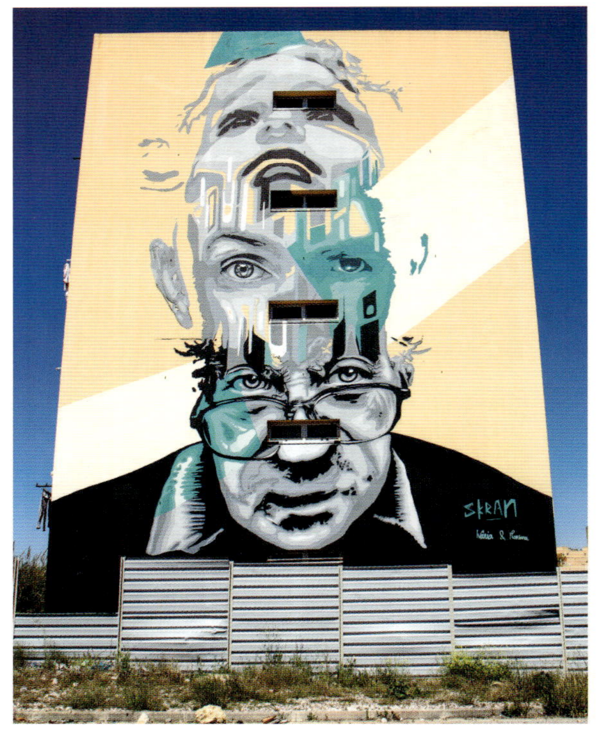

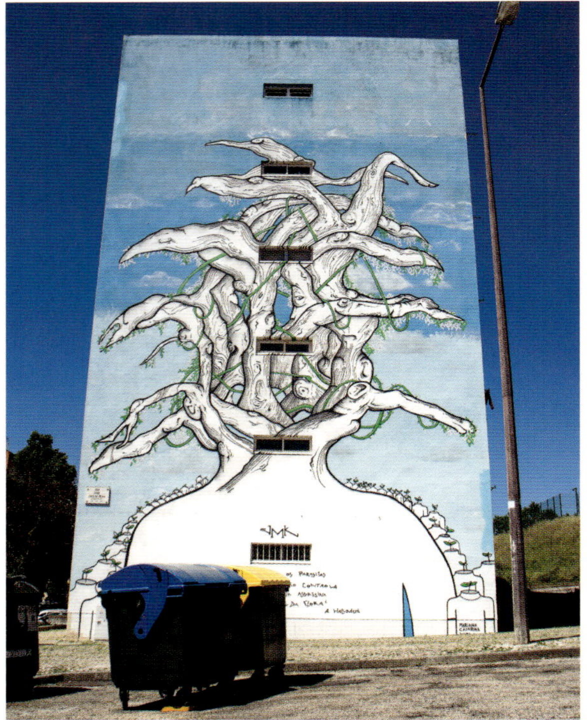

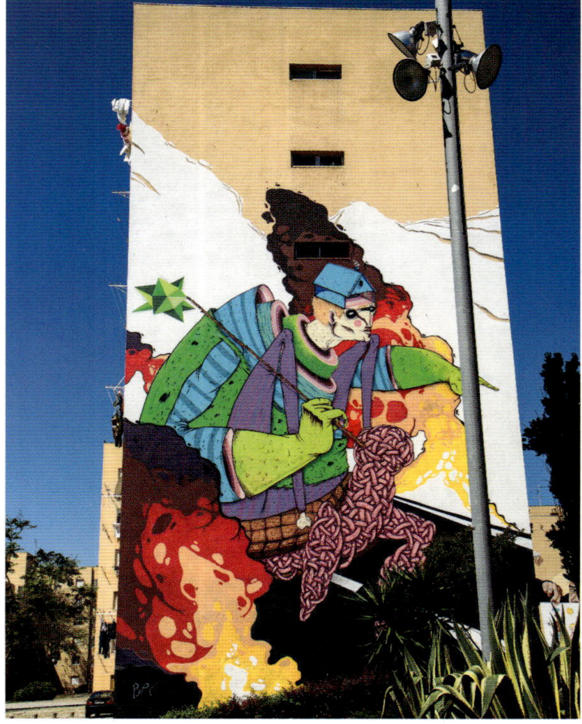

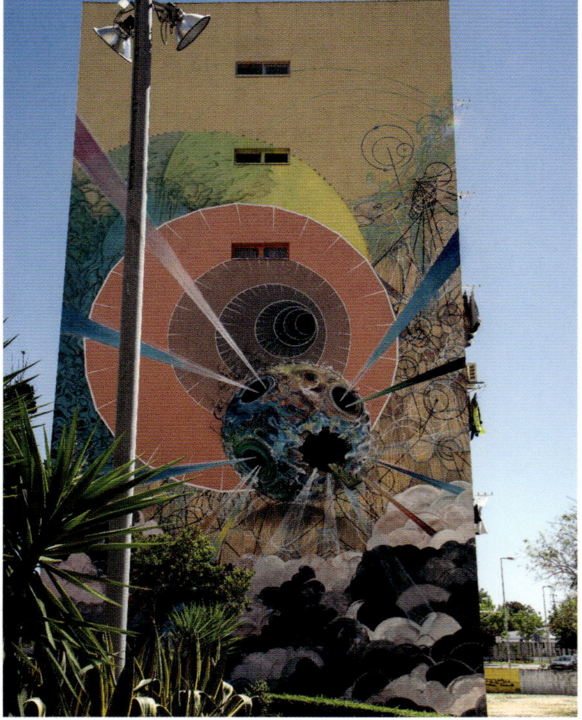

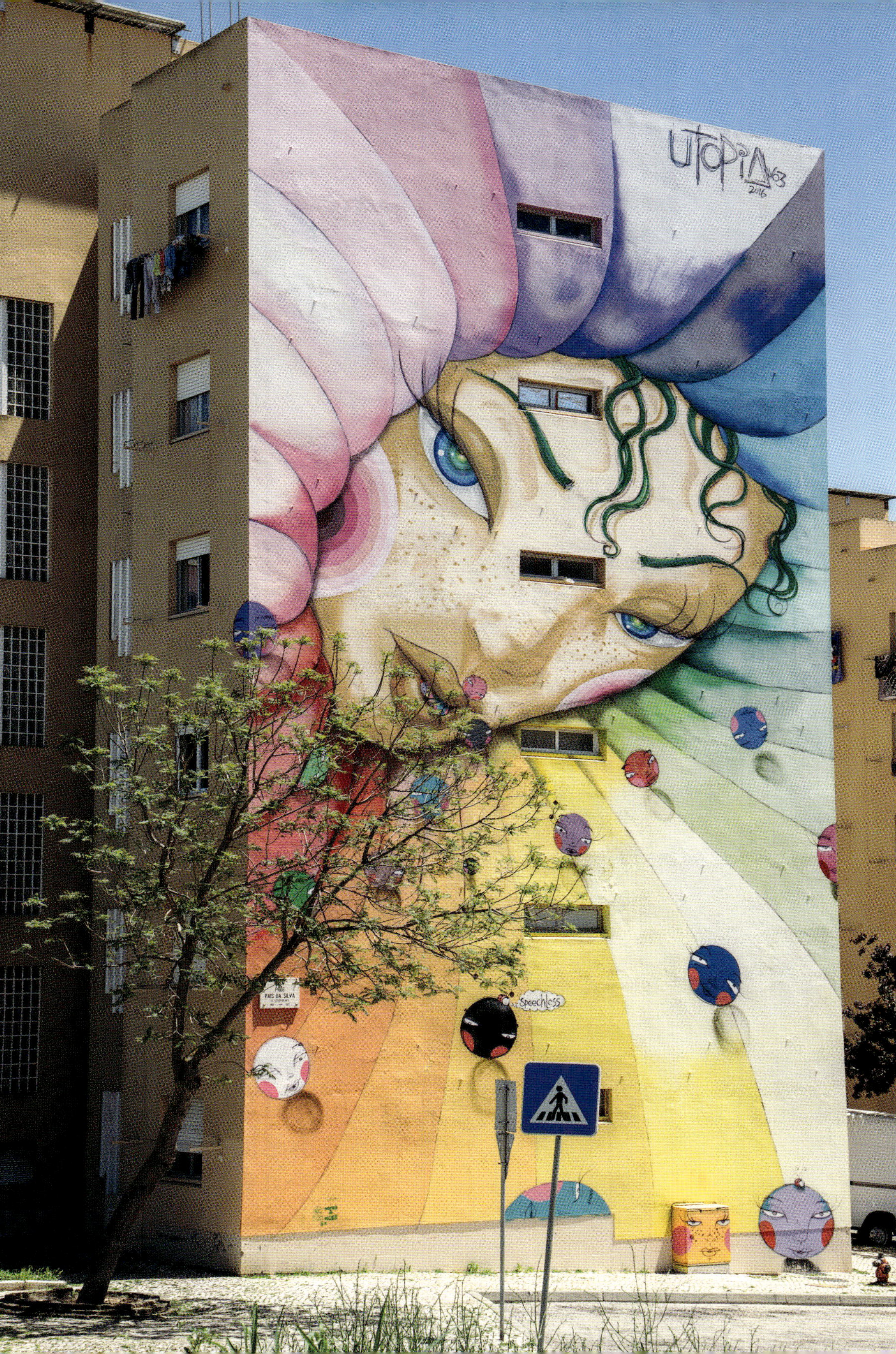
UTOPiA 63
2016
Speechless
PAIS DA SILVA

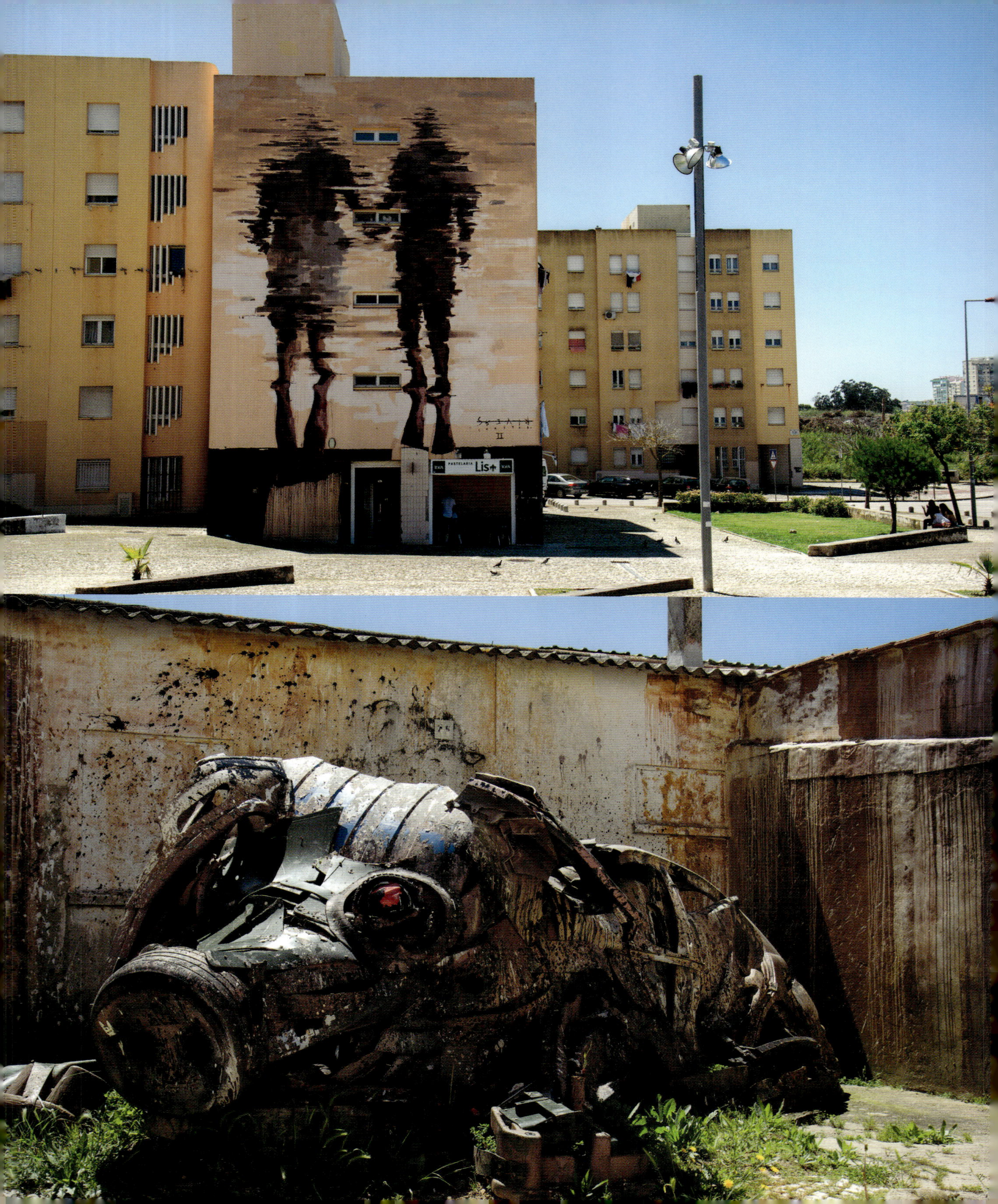

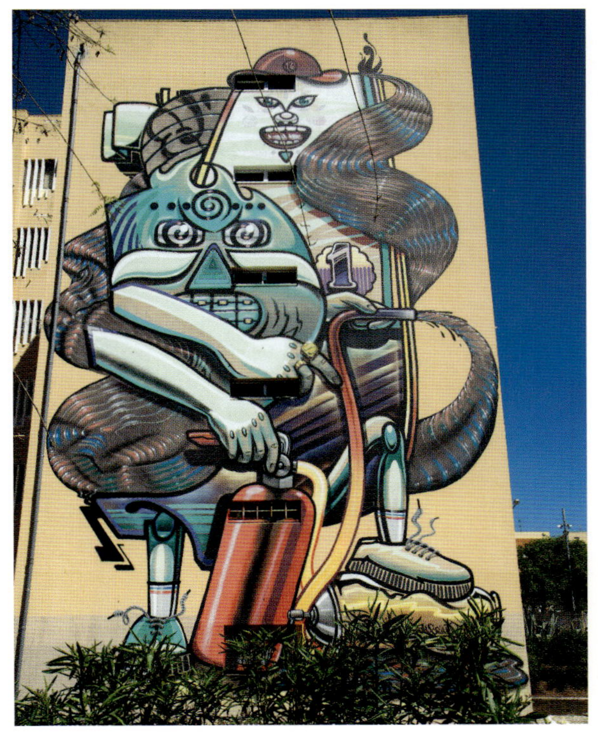

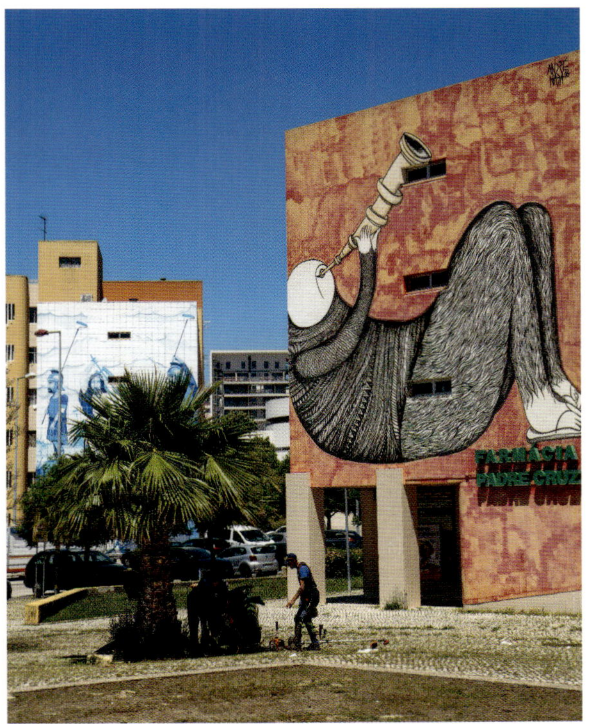
FARMACIA
PADRE CRUZ

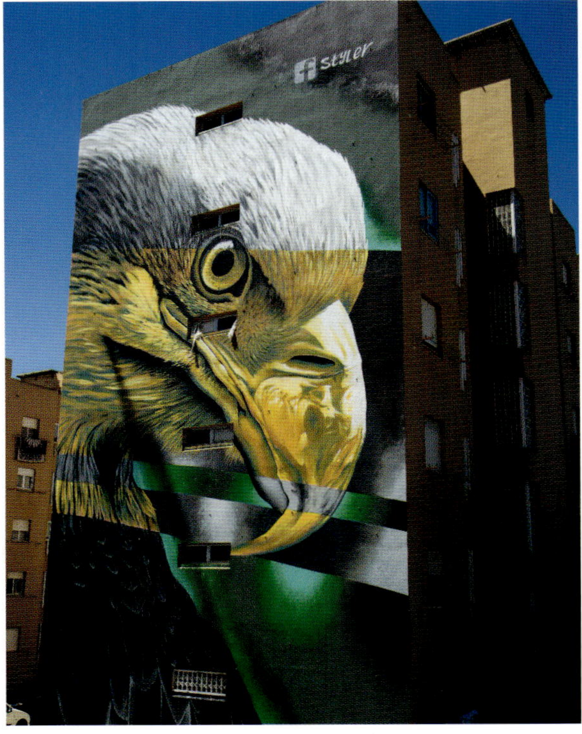
styler

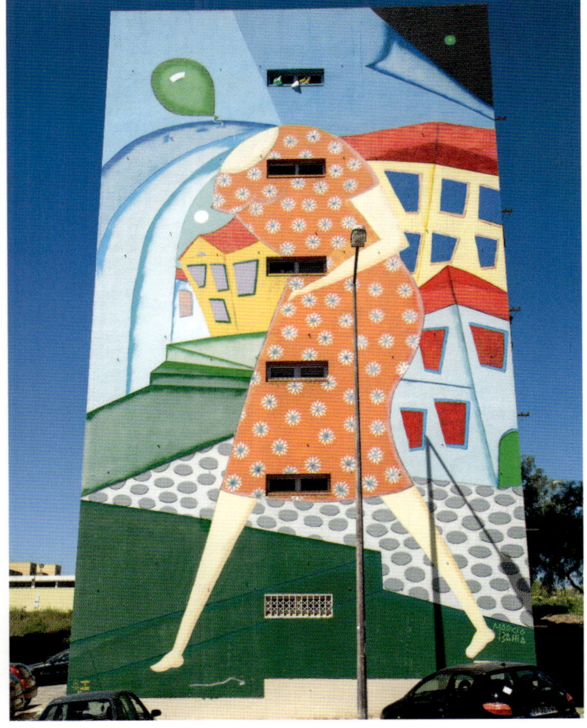

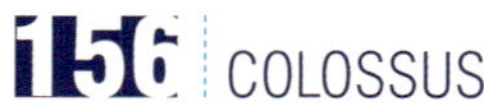 COLOSSUS

QUINTA DO MOCHO

PORTUGAL

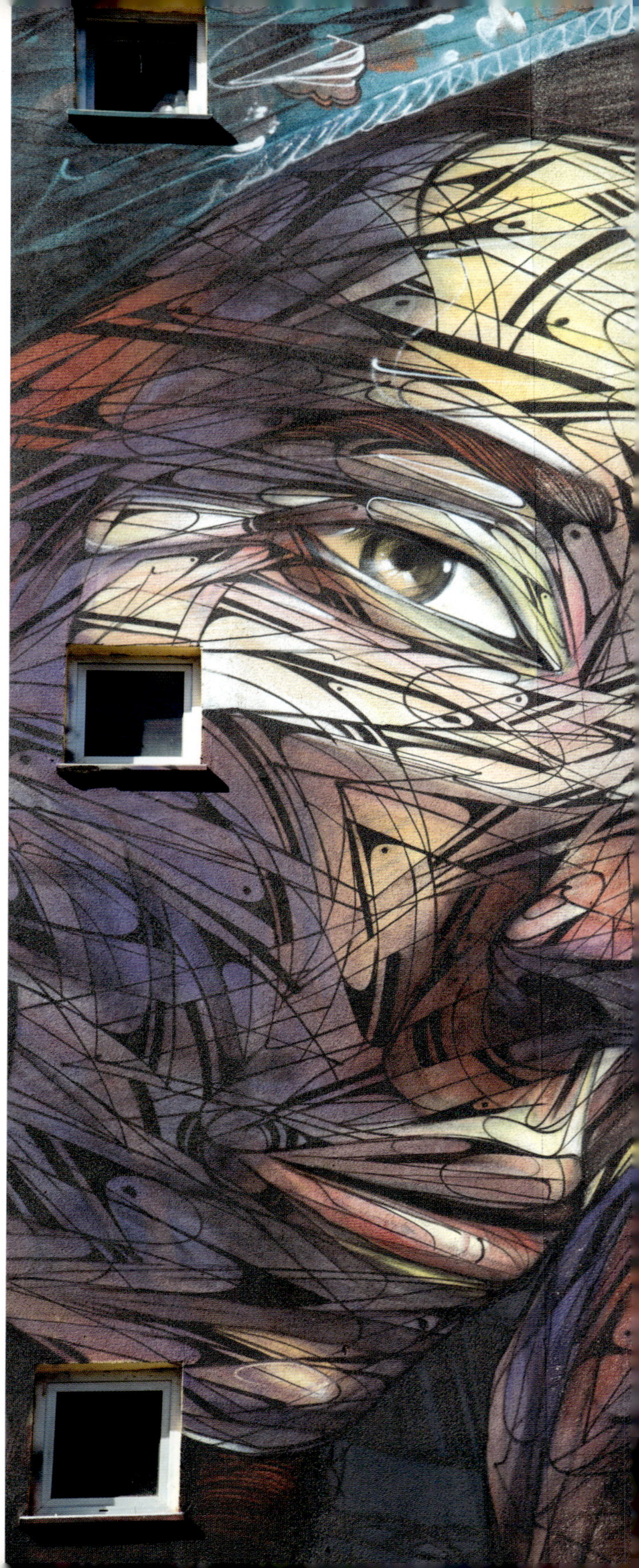

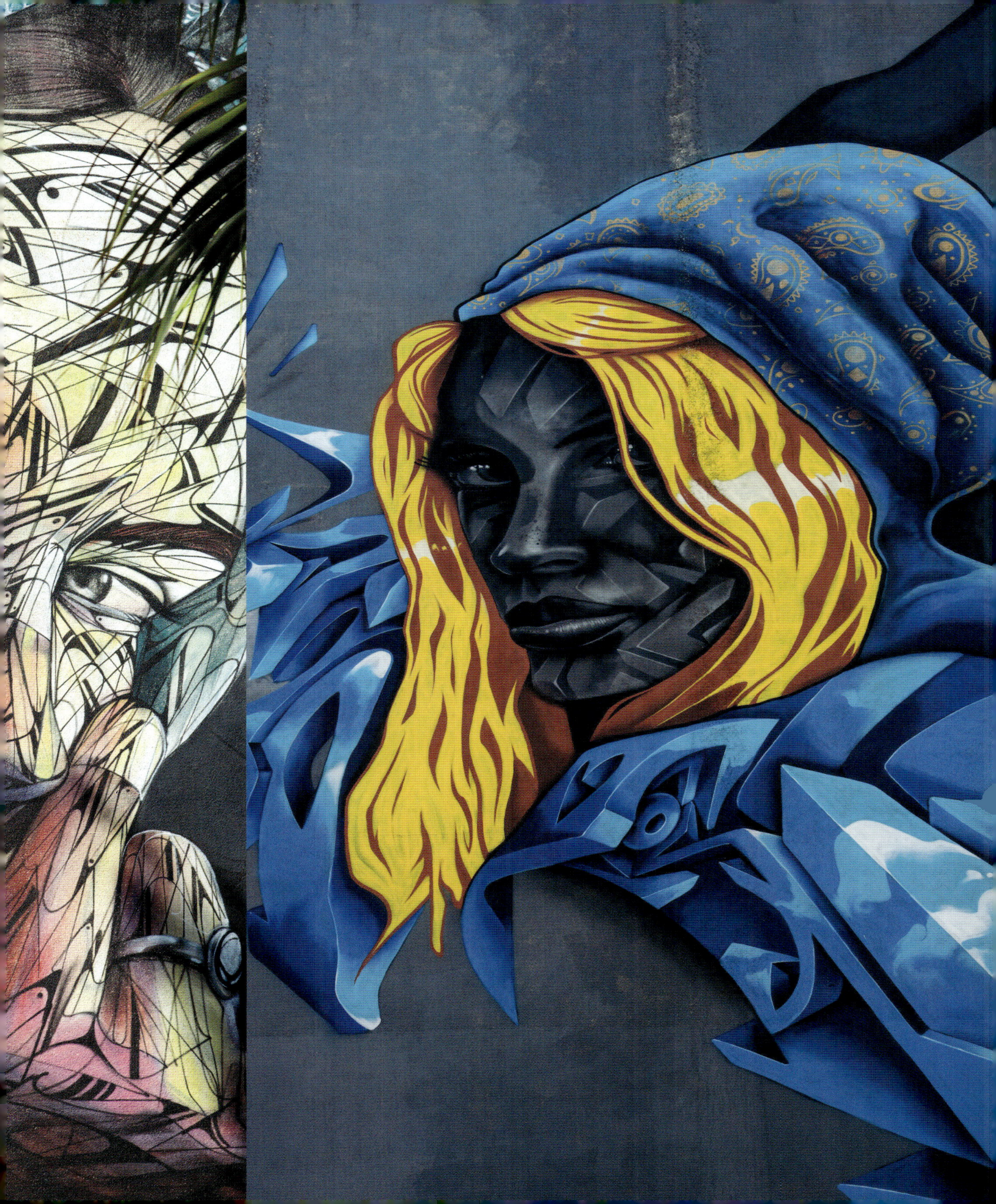

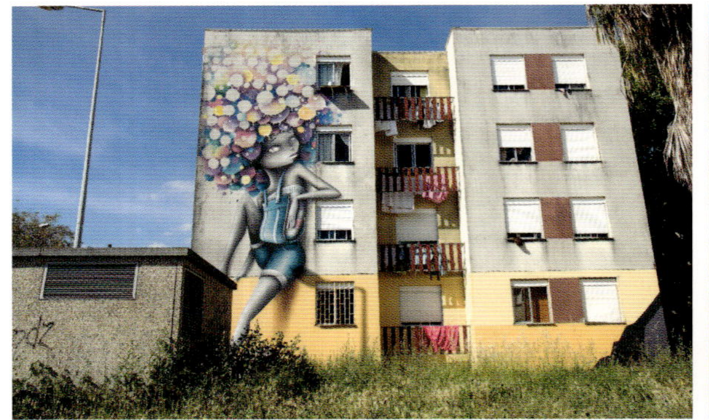
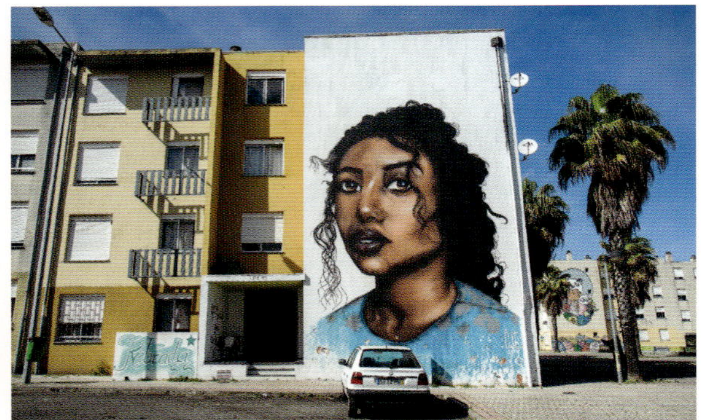
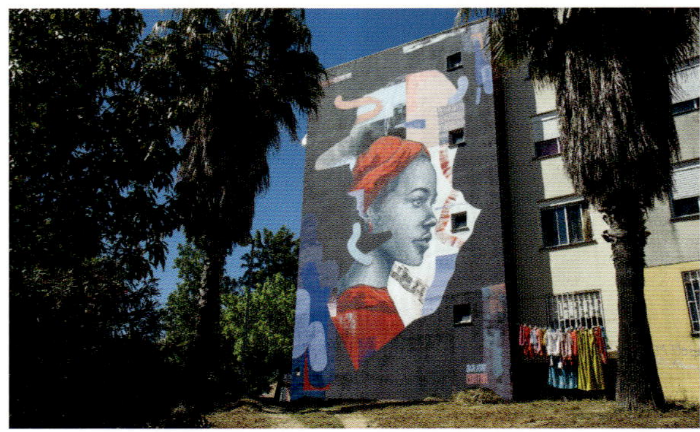
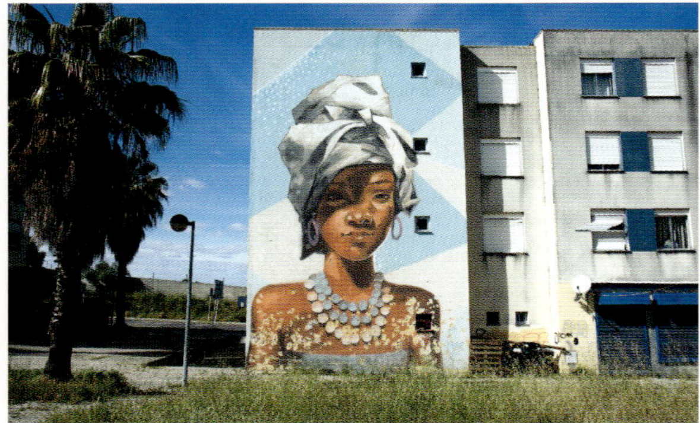
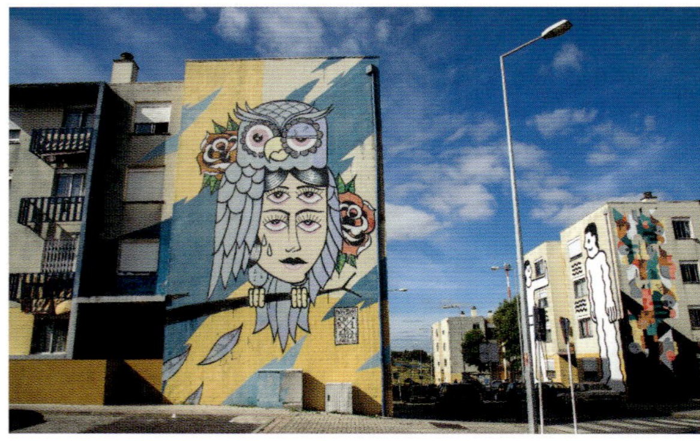
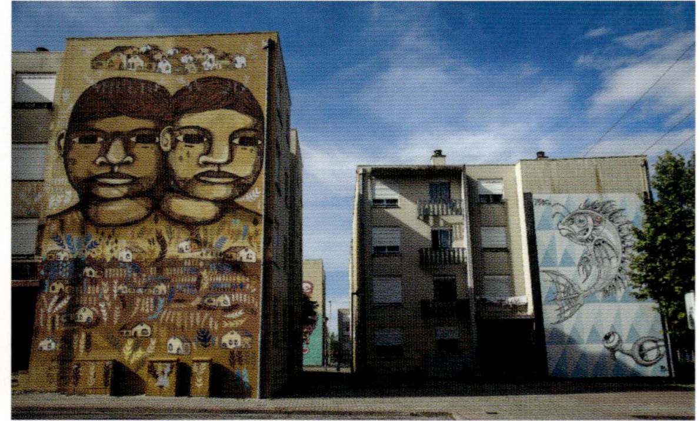
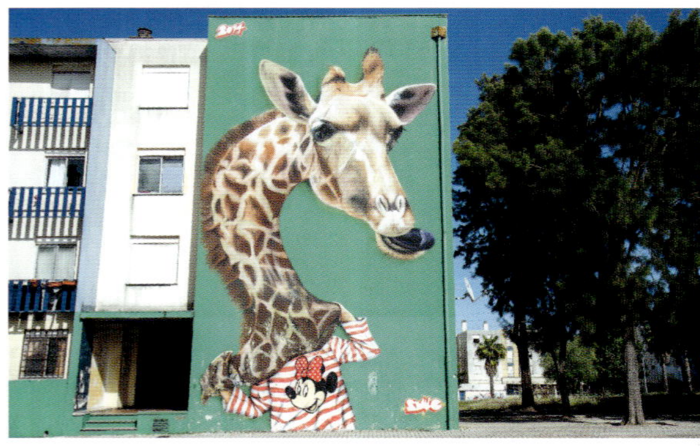
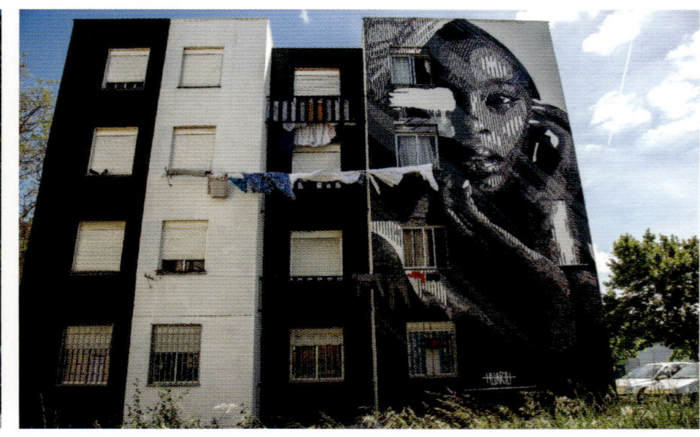

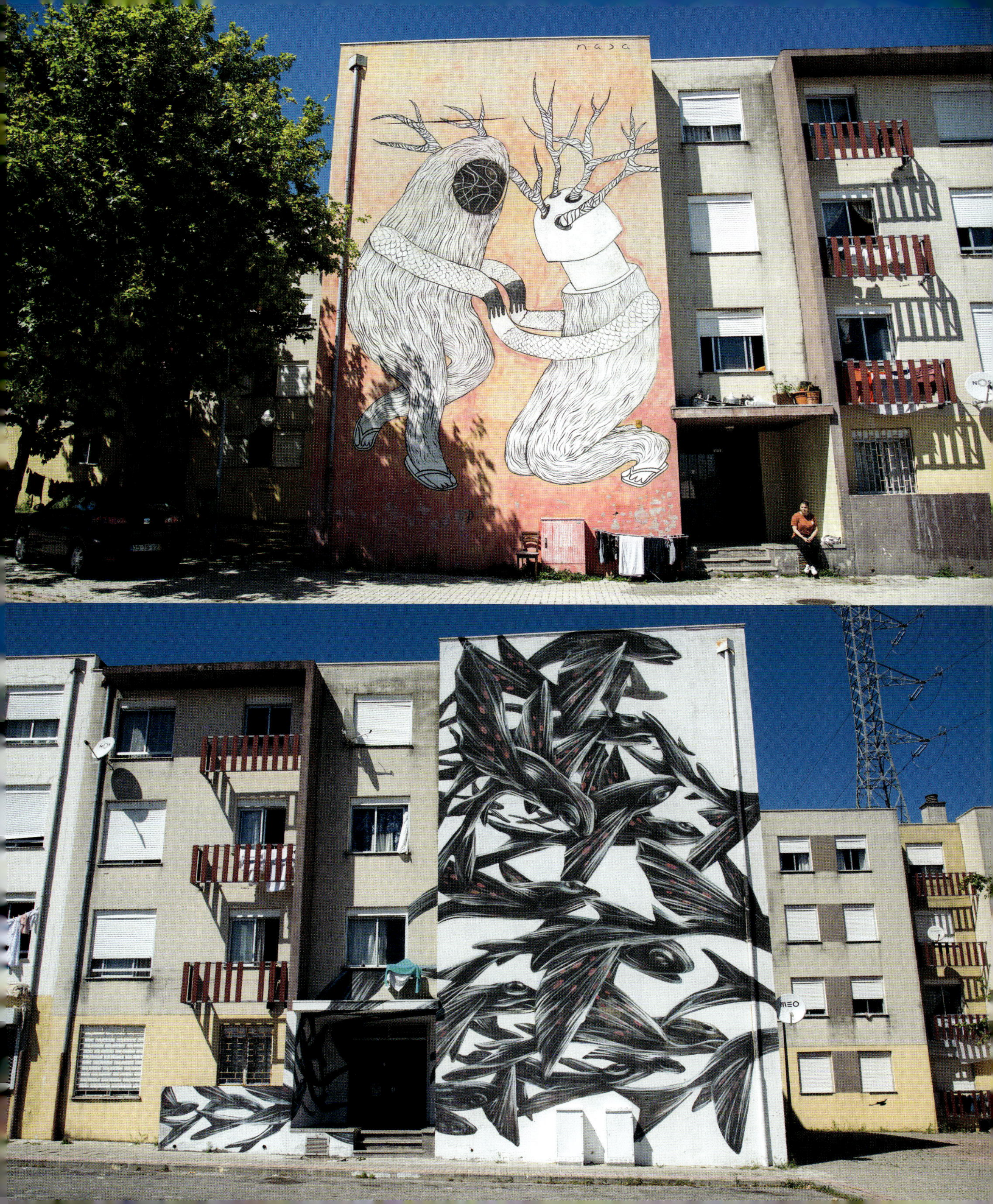

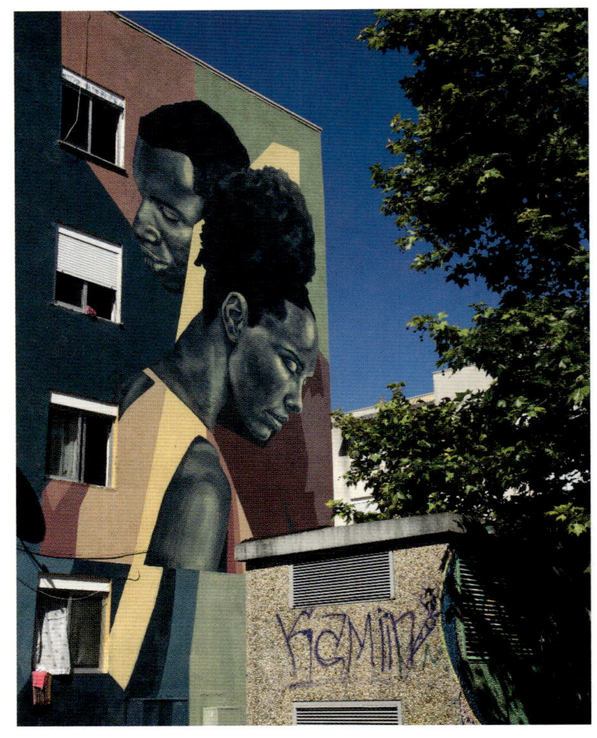

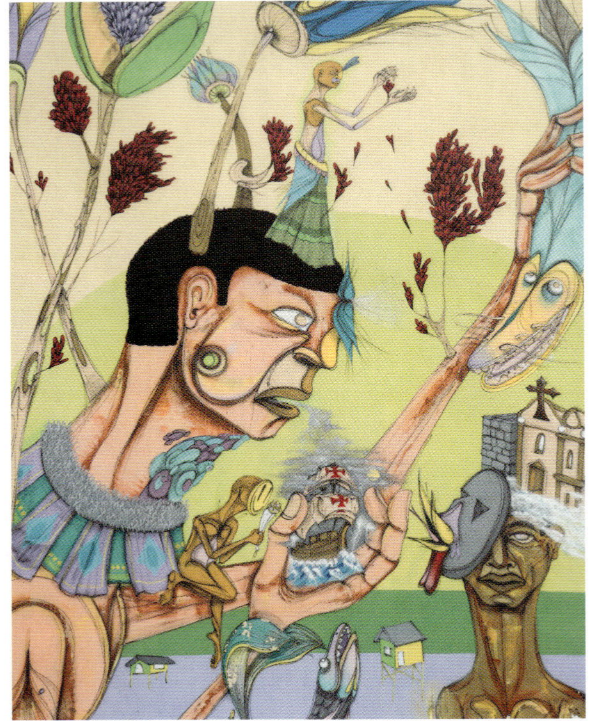

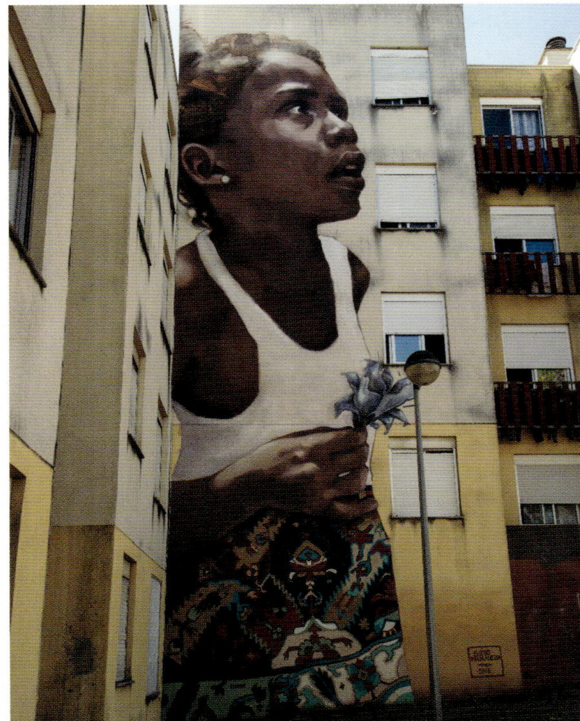

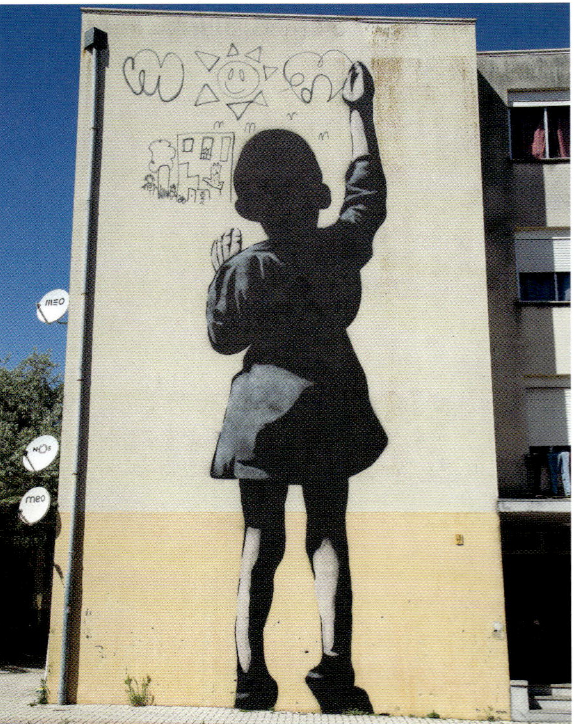

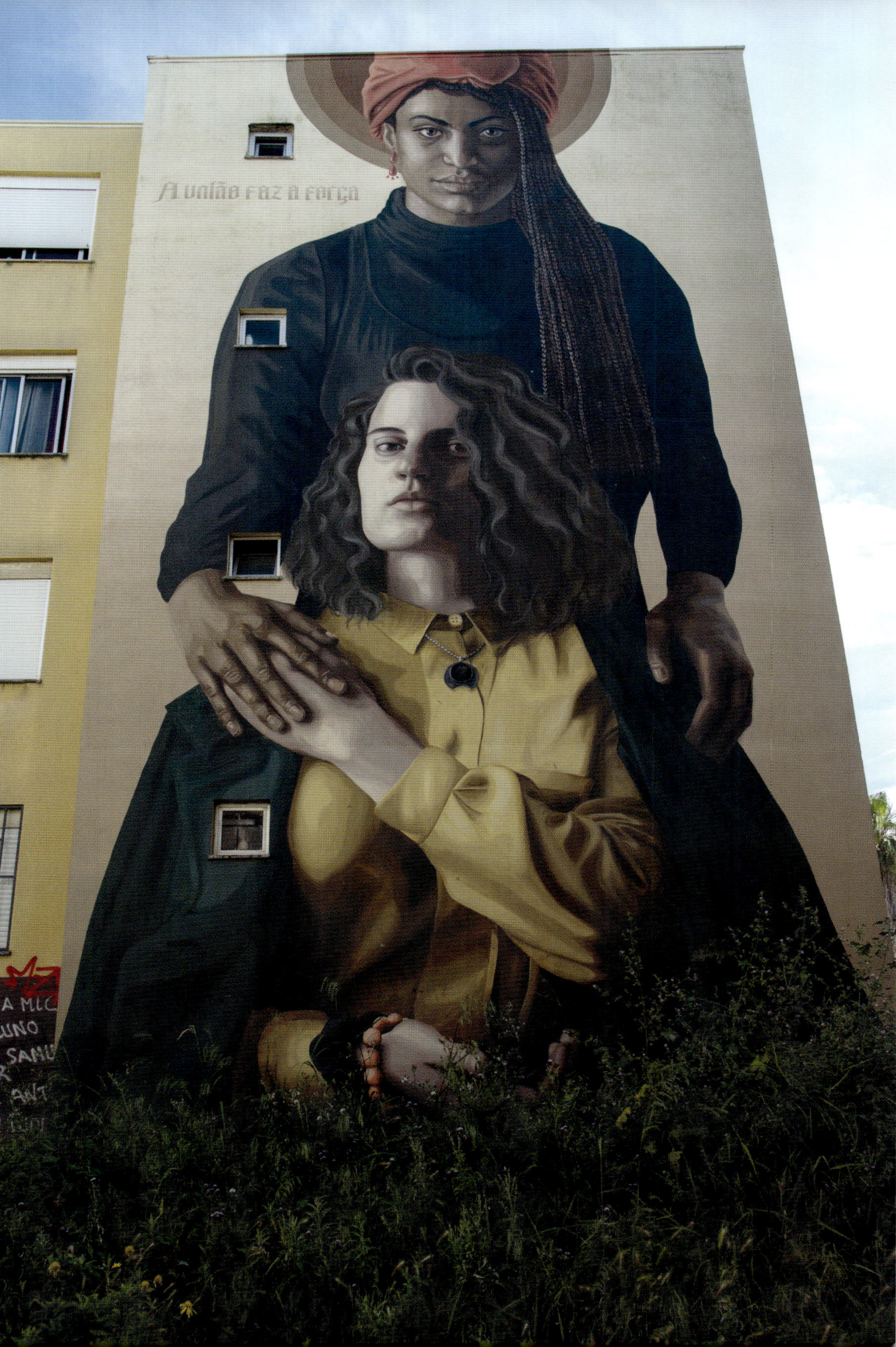
A UNIÃO FAZ A FORÇA

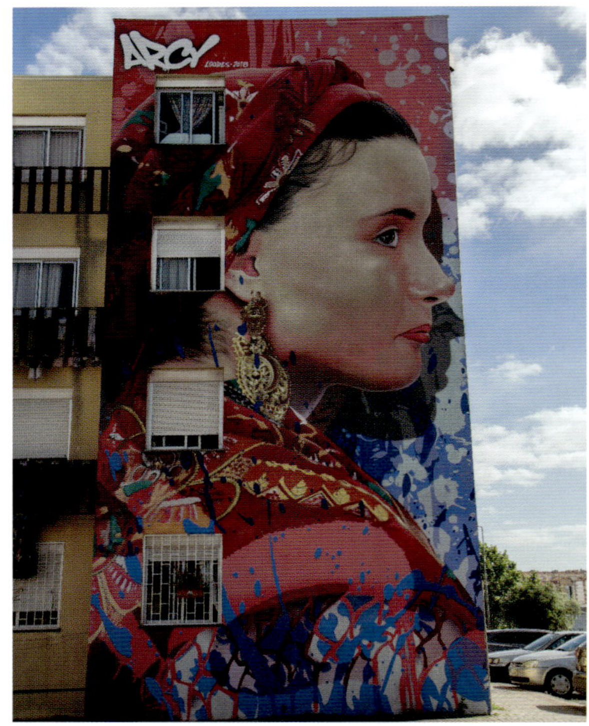
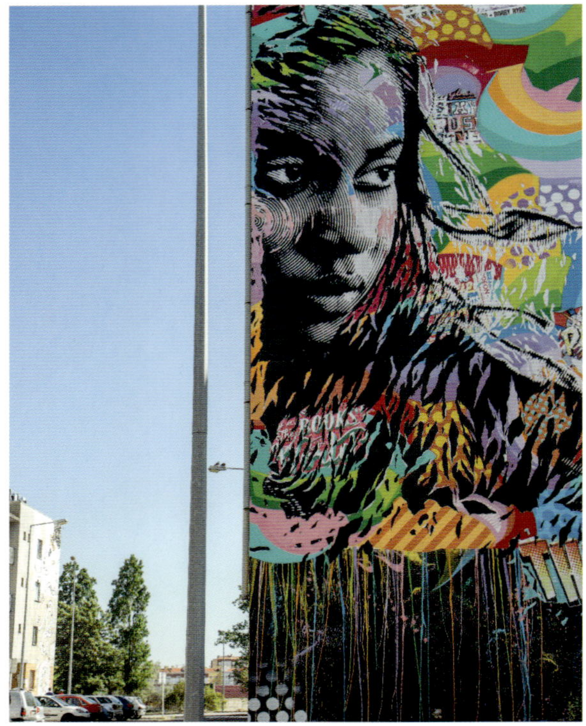
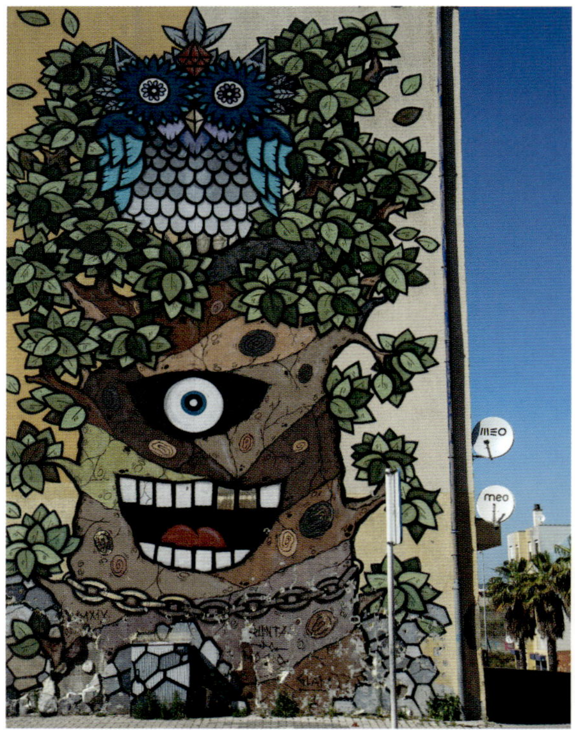
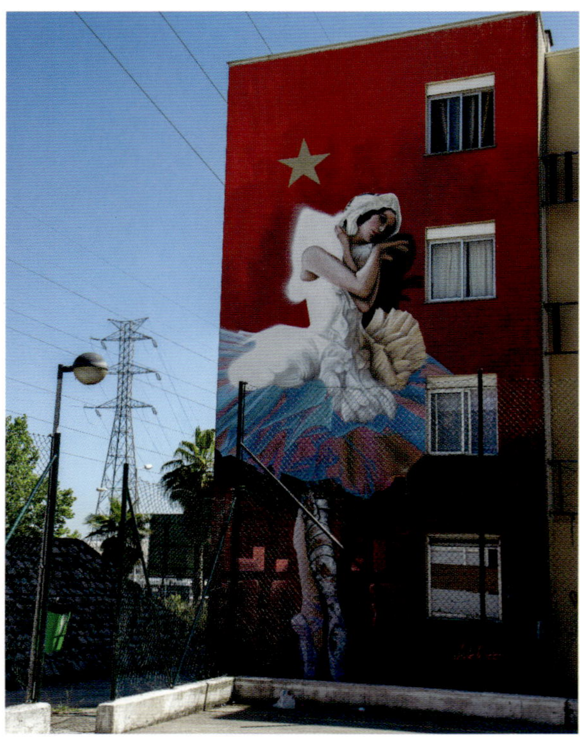

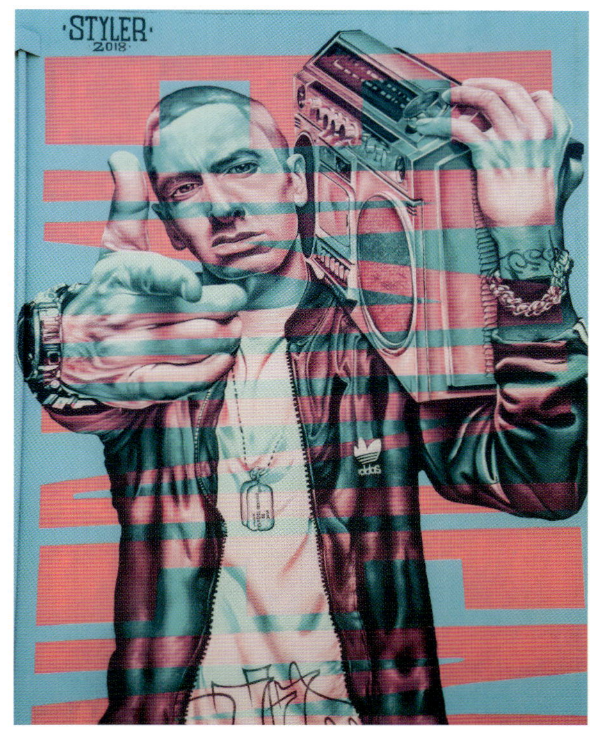
·STYLER·
·2018·

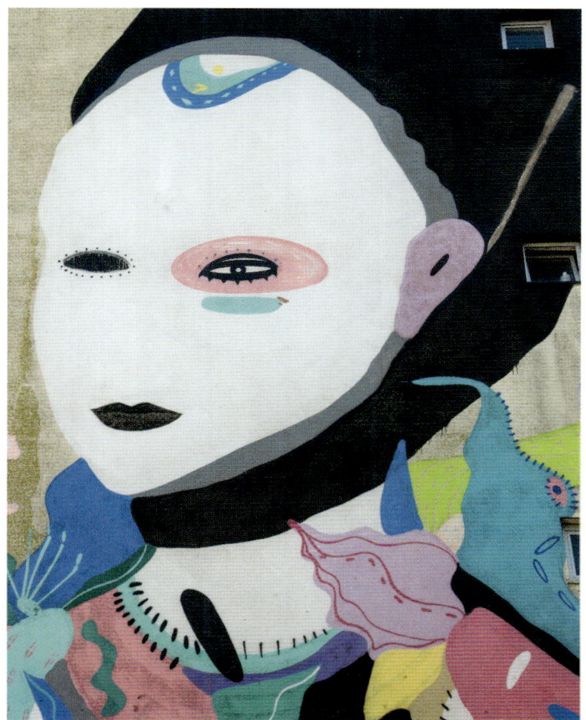

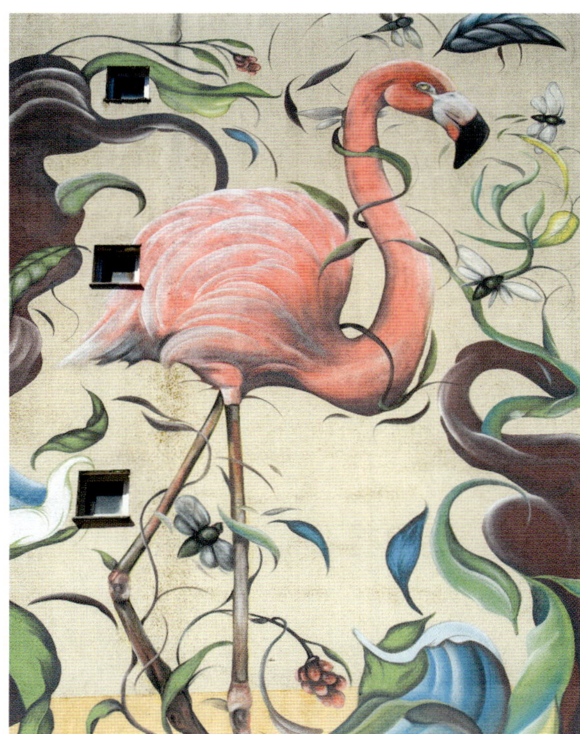

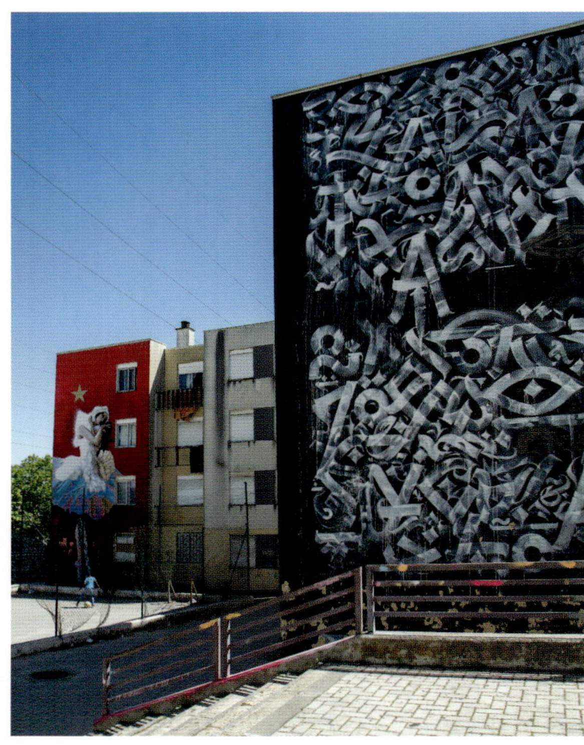

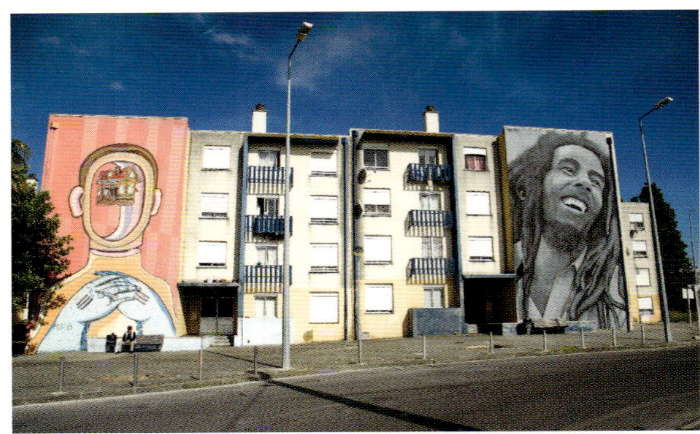
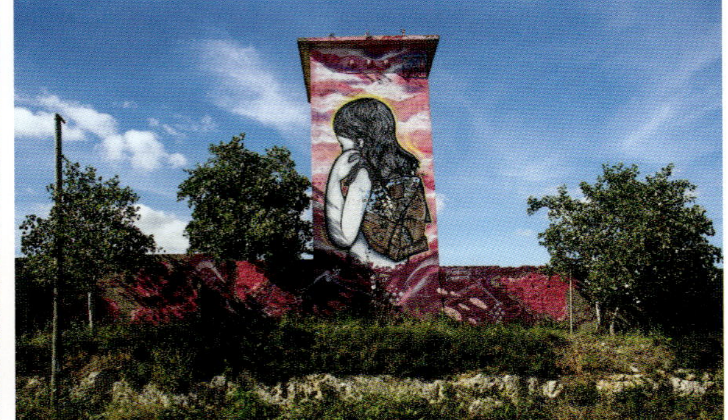
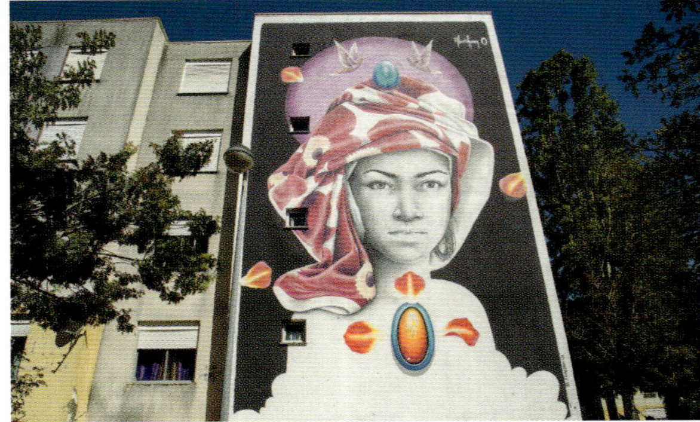
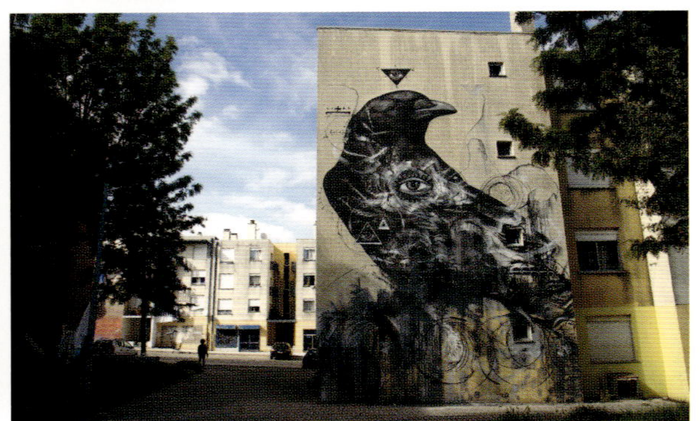
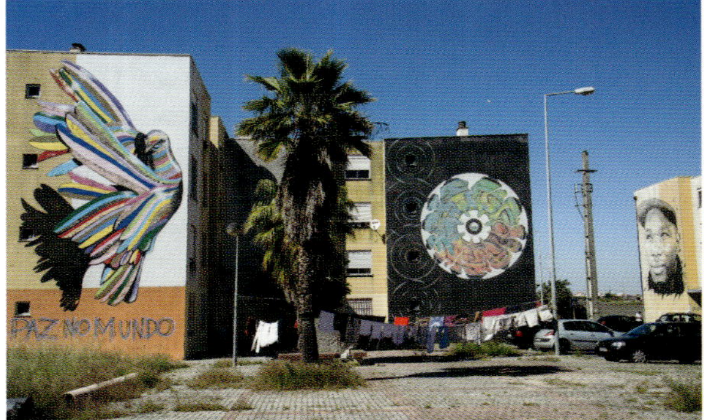
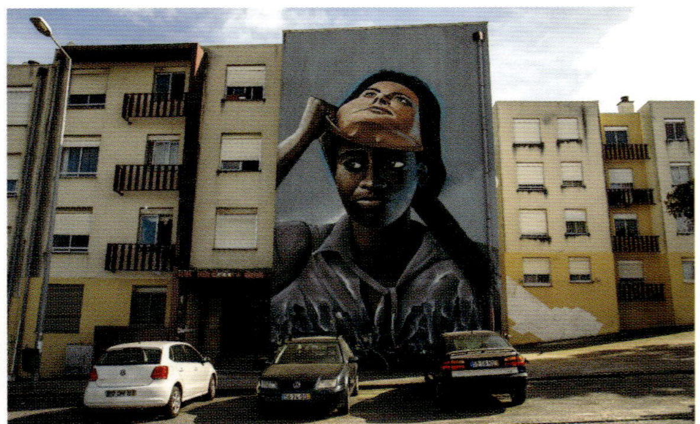
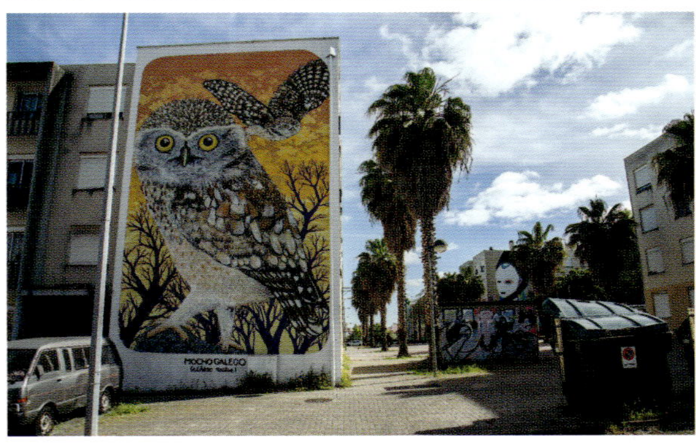
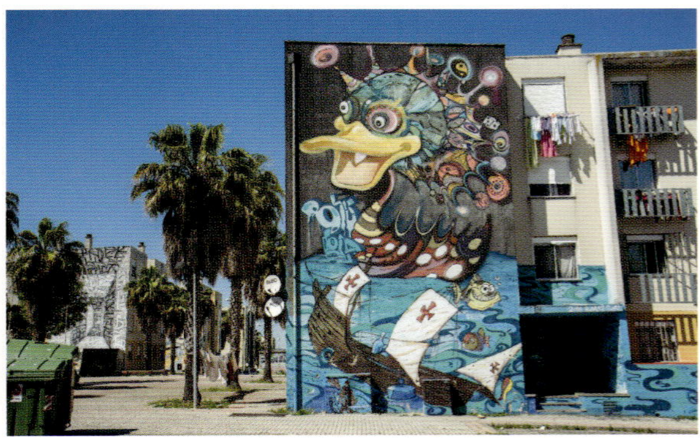

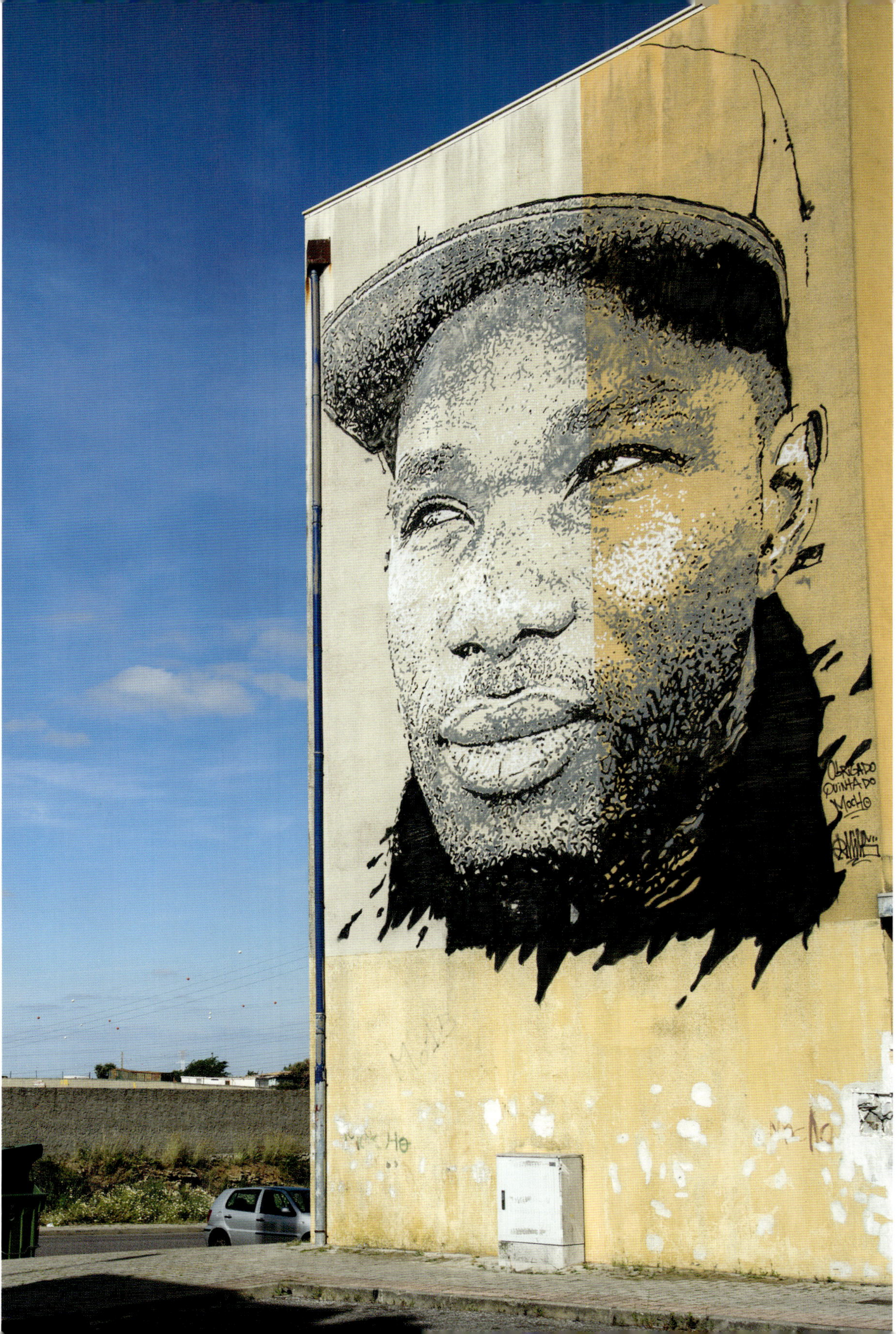

OBRIGADO
QUINTA DO
MOCHO

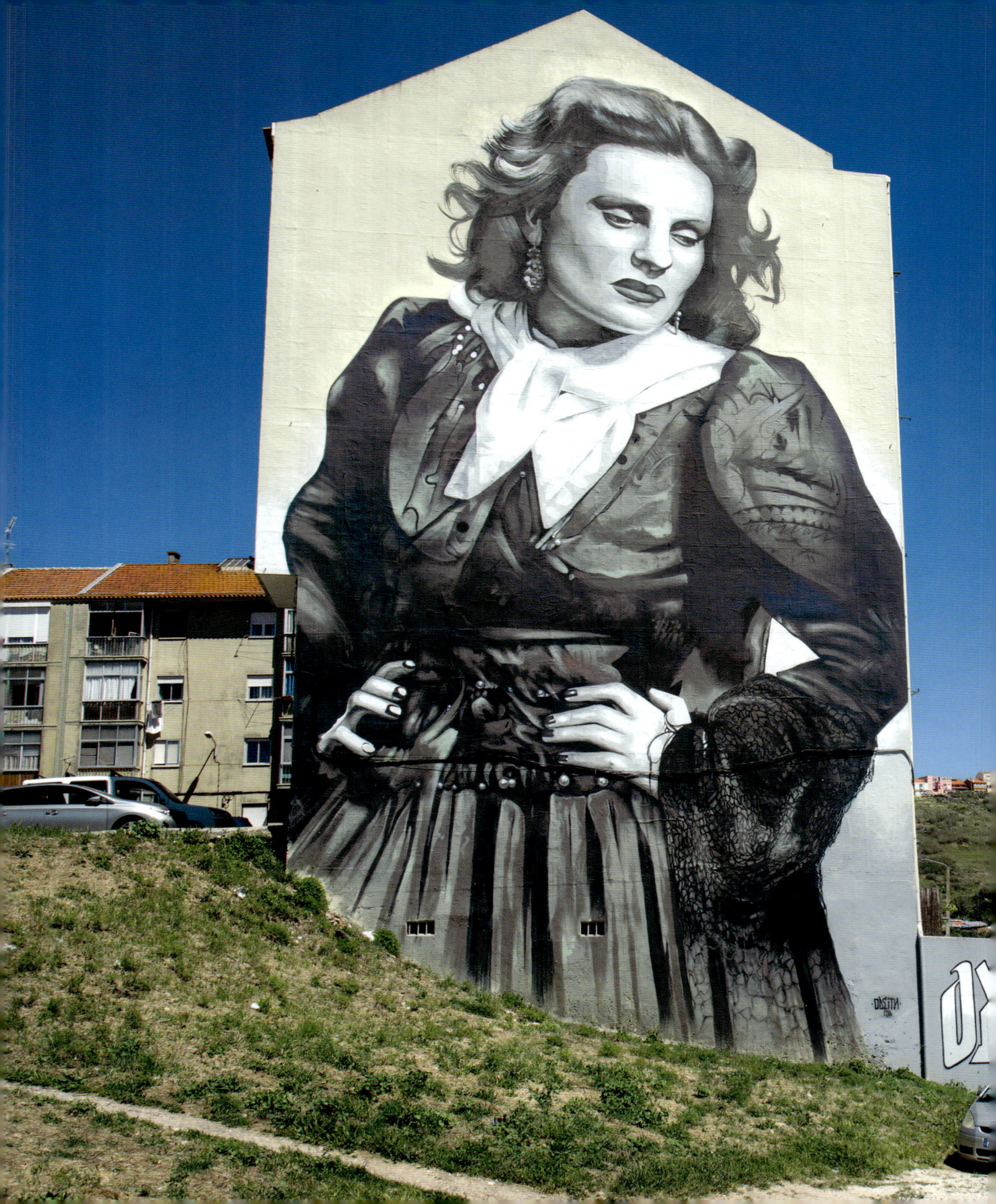
DASTTN

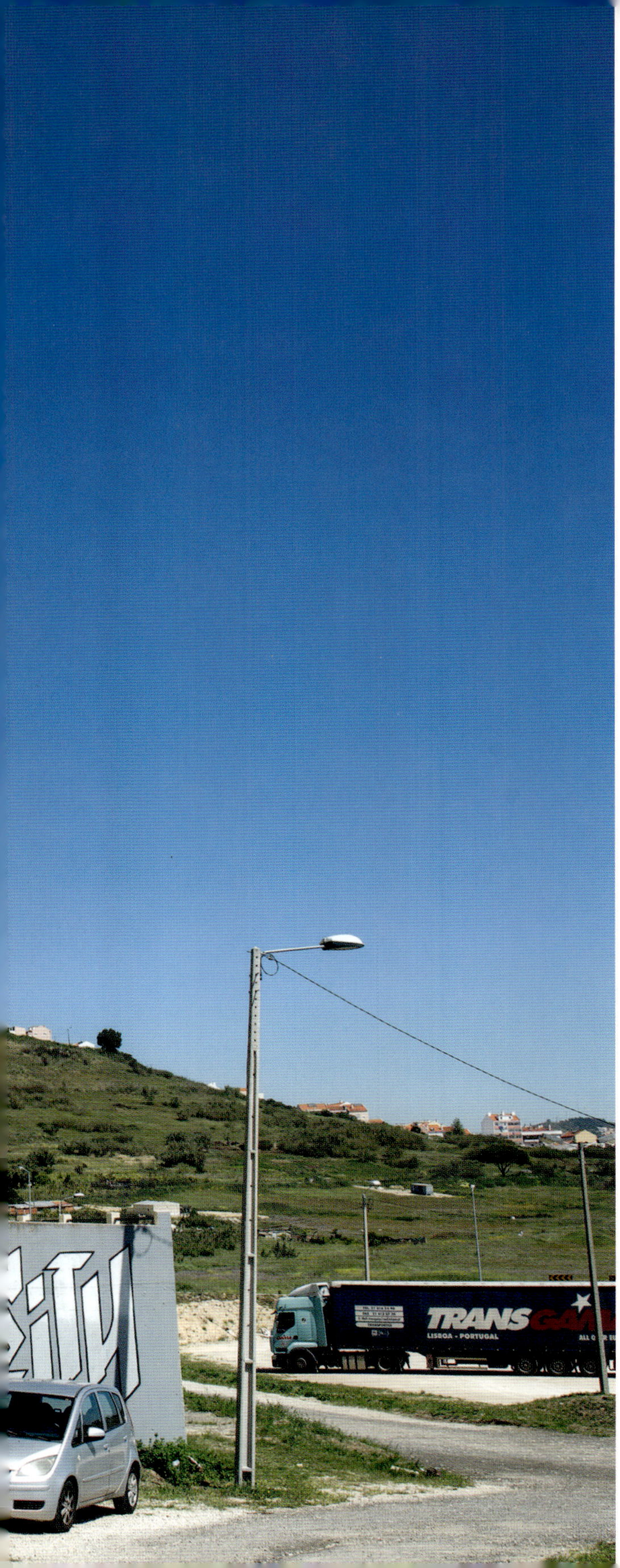

LISBON

PORTUGAL

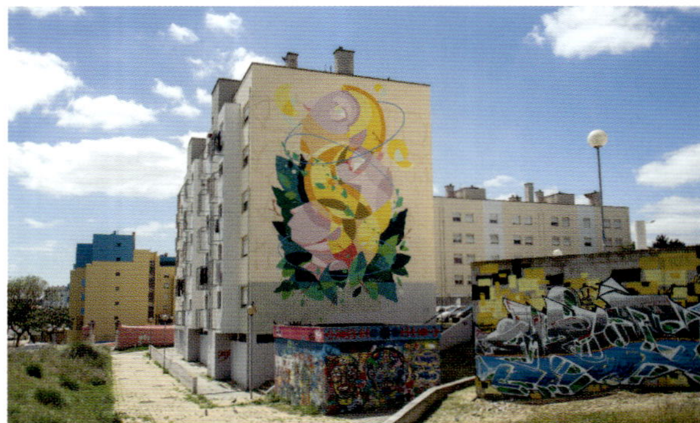

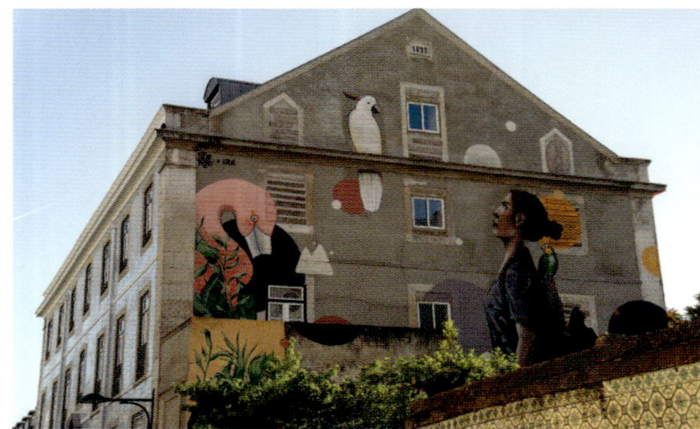

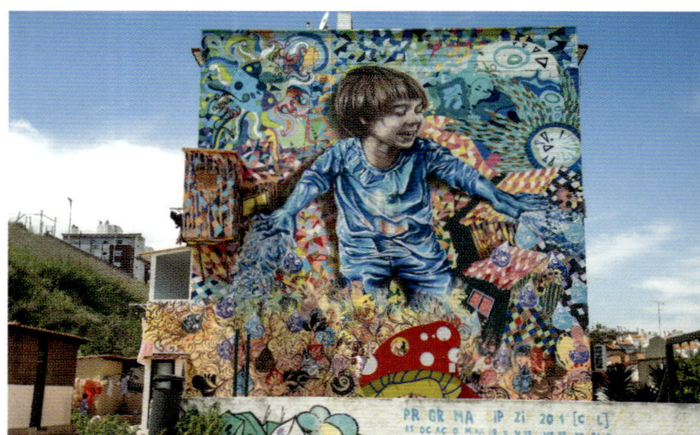

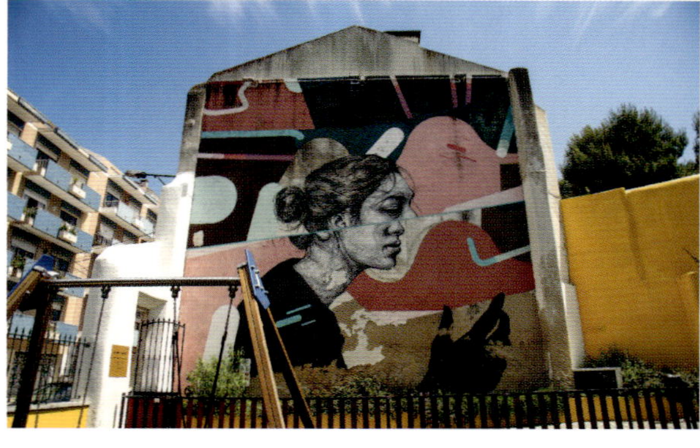

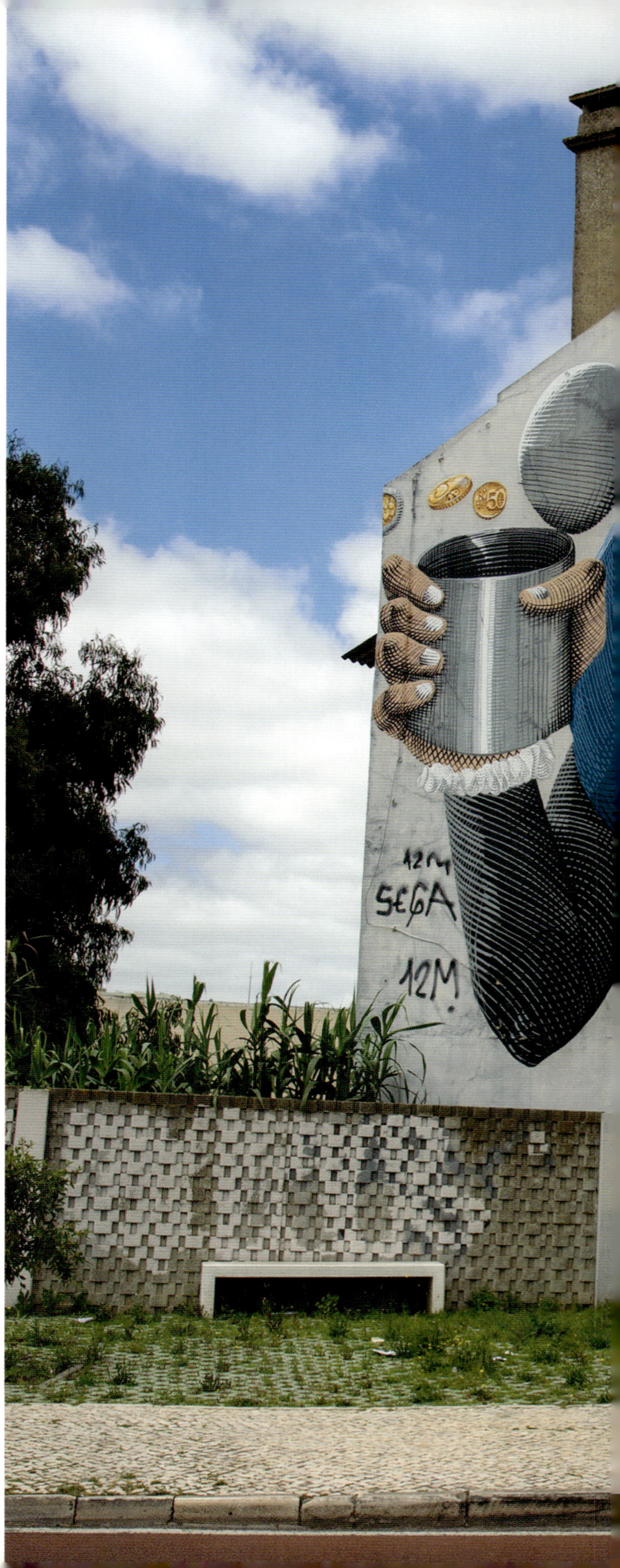

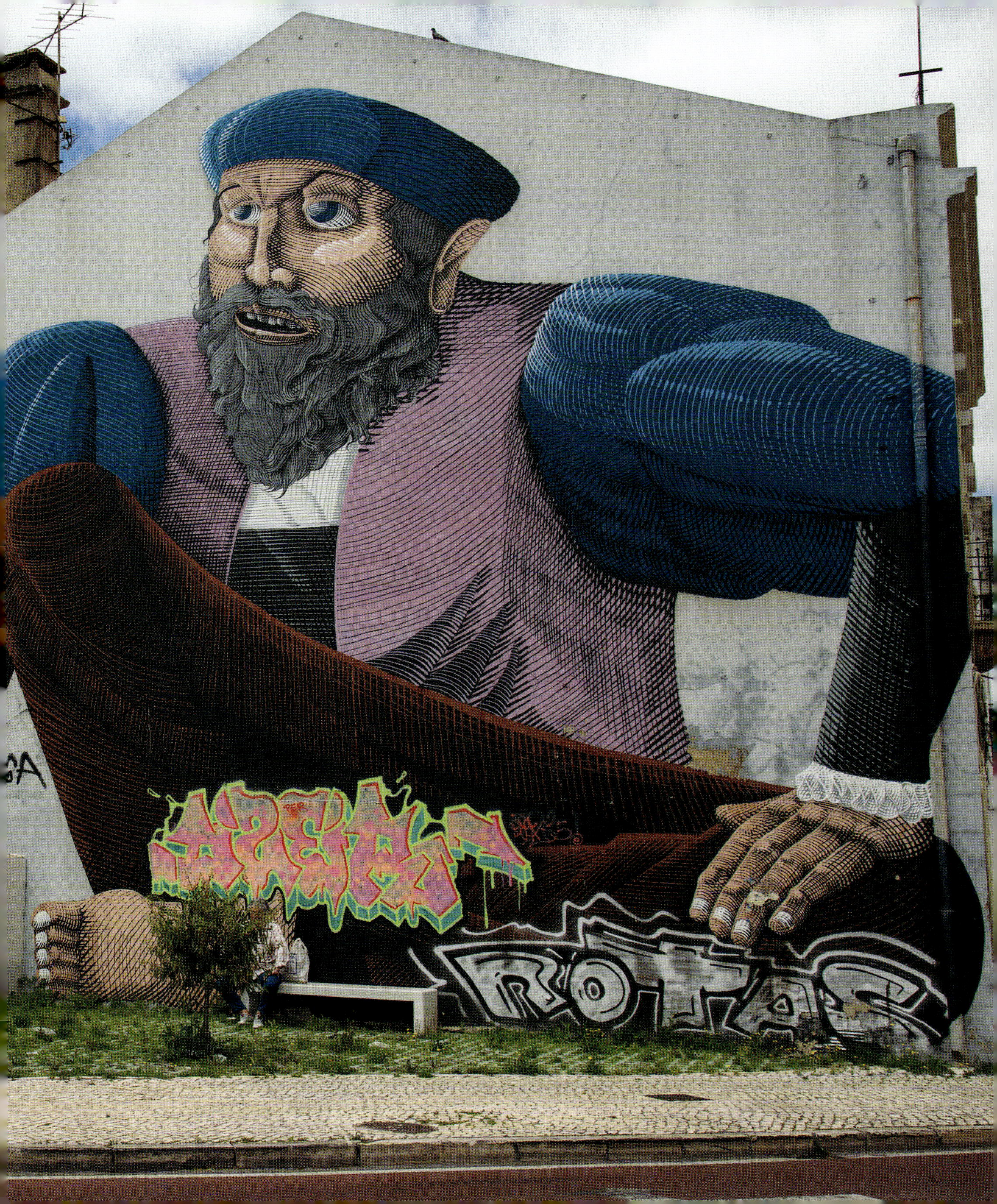

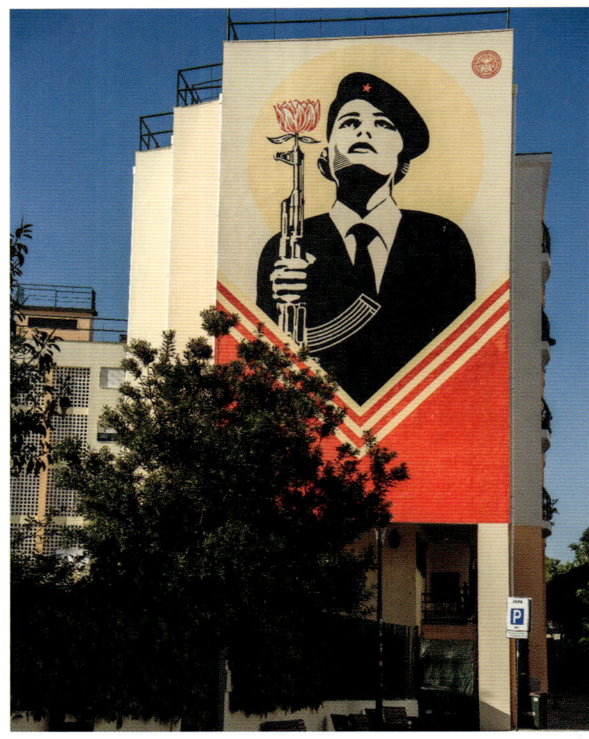

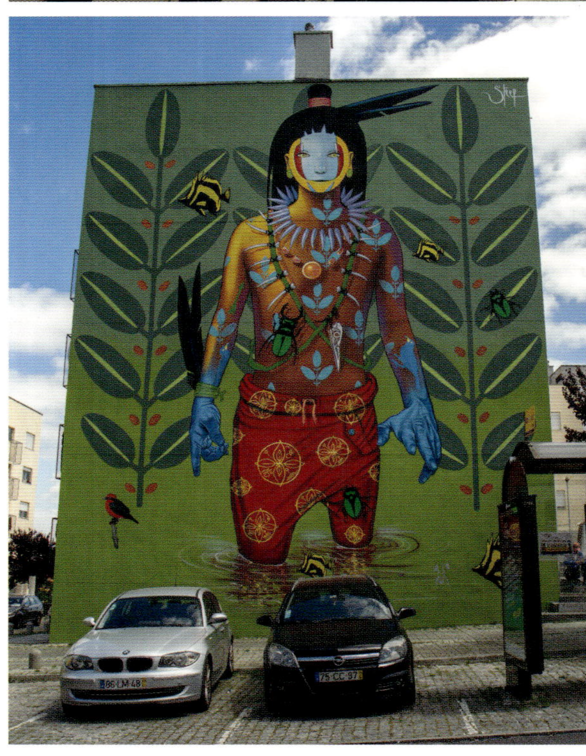

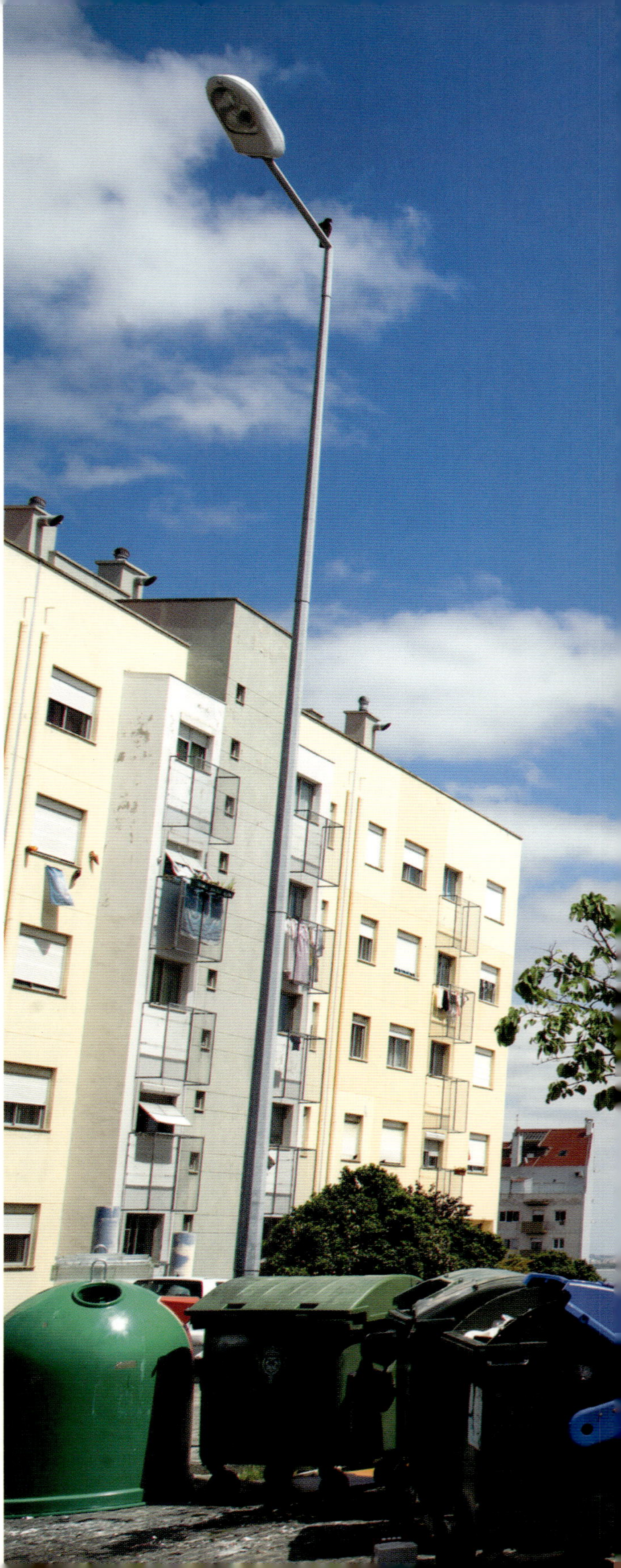

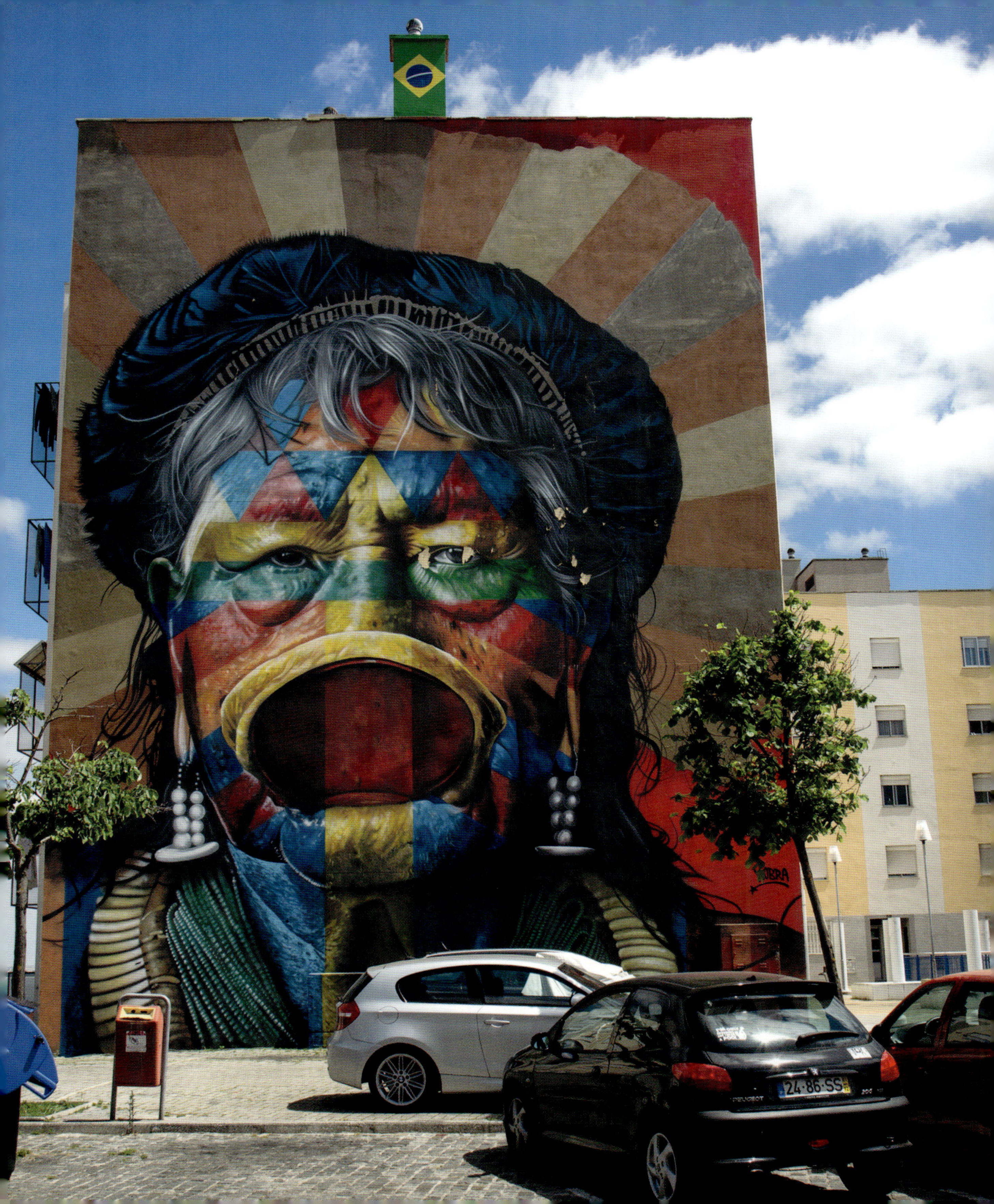

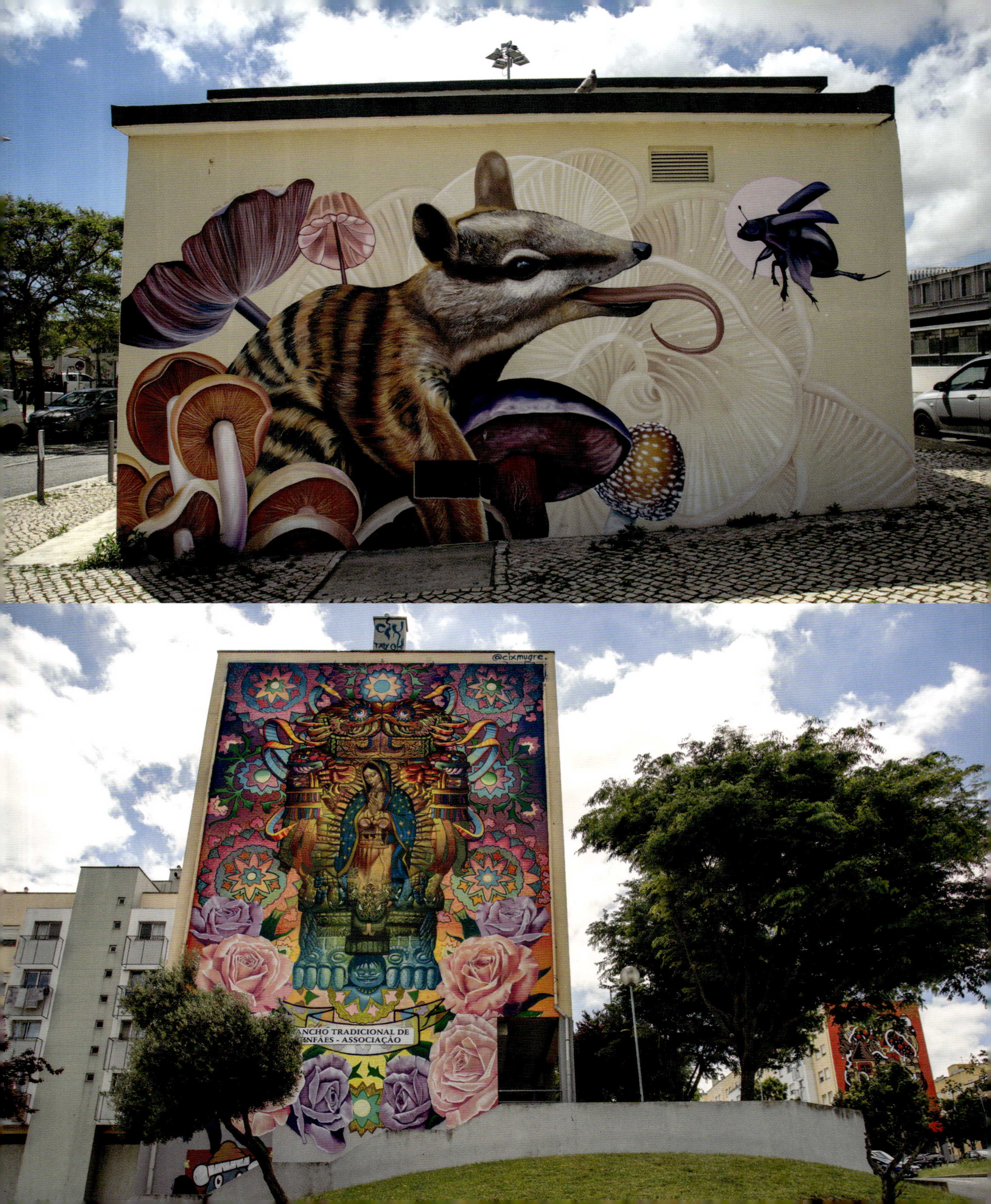

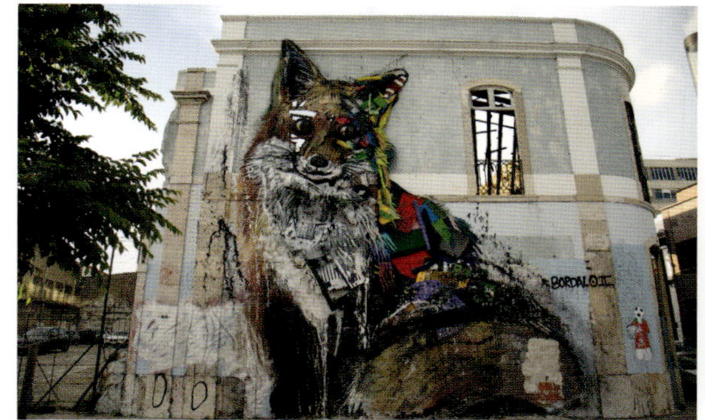

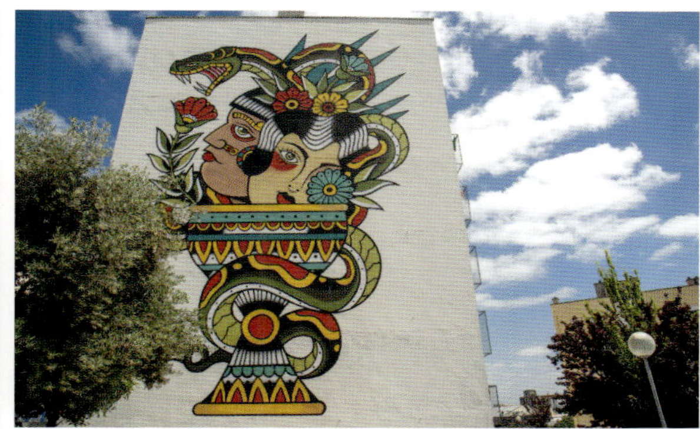

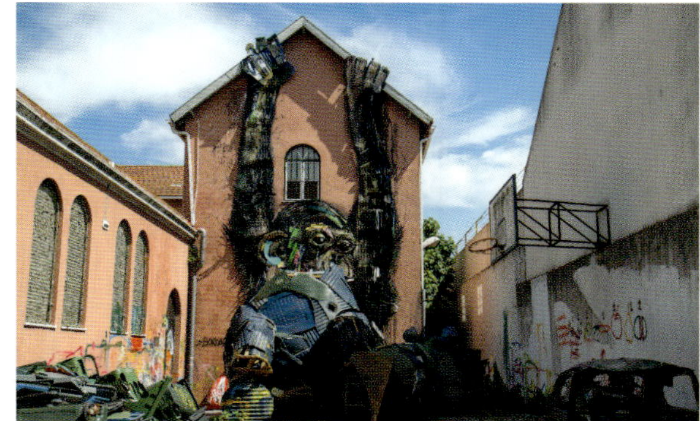

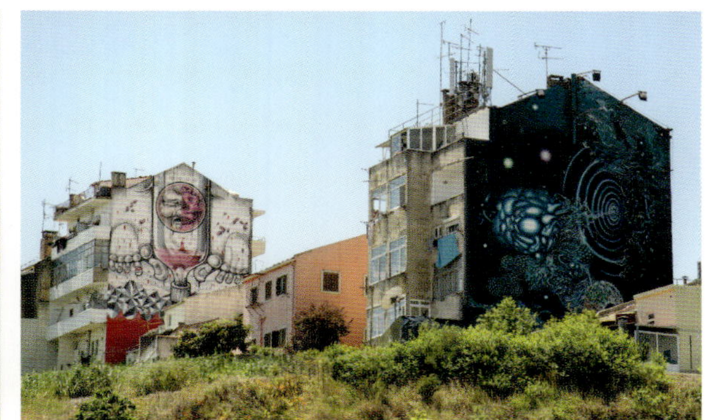

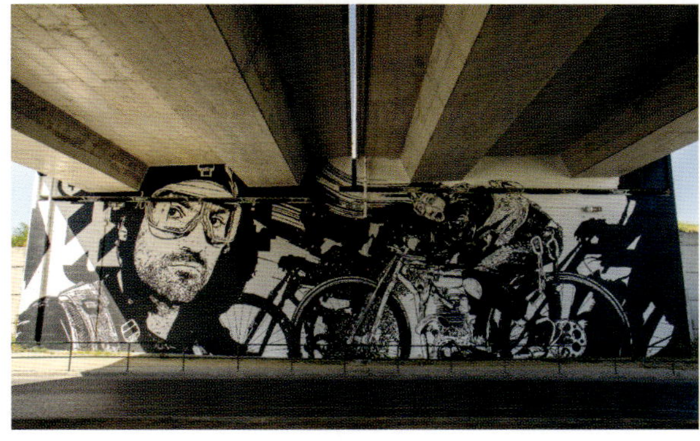

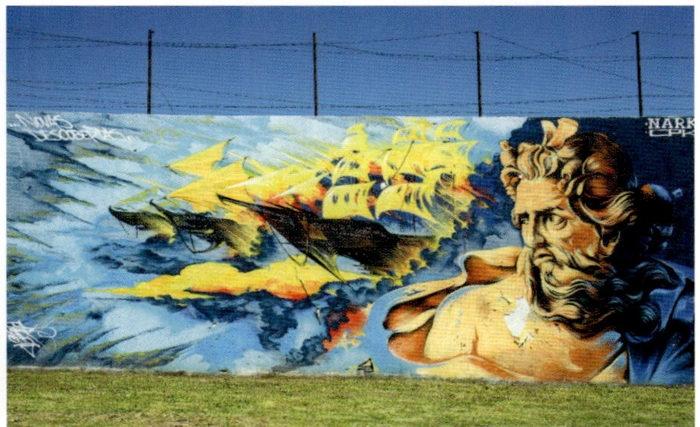

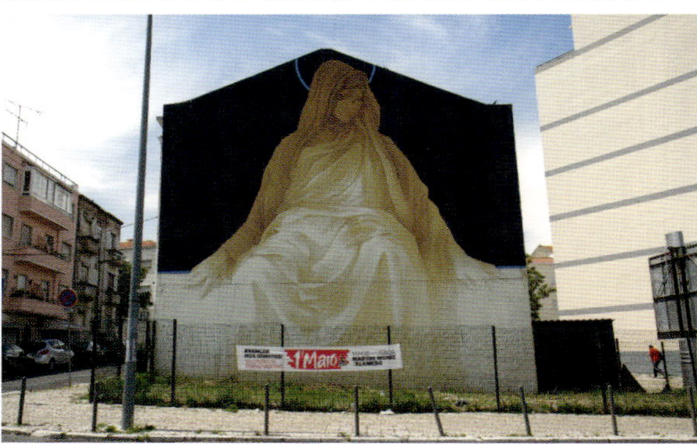

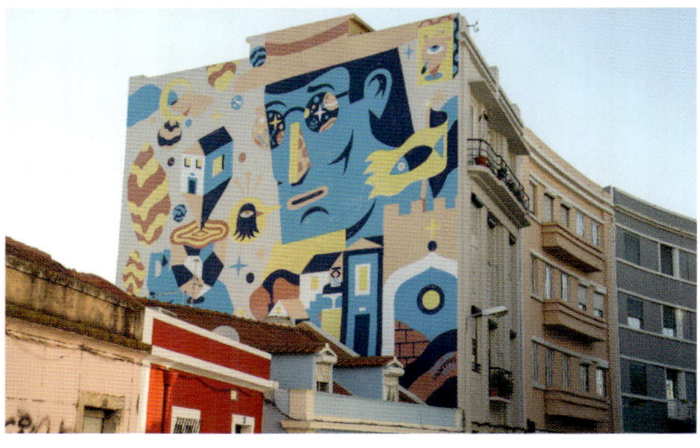

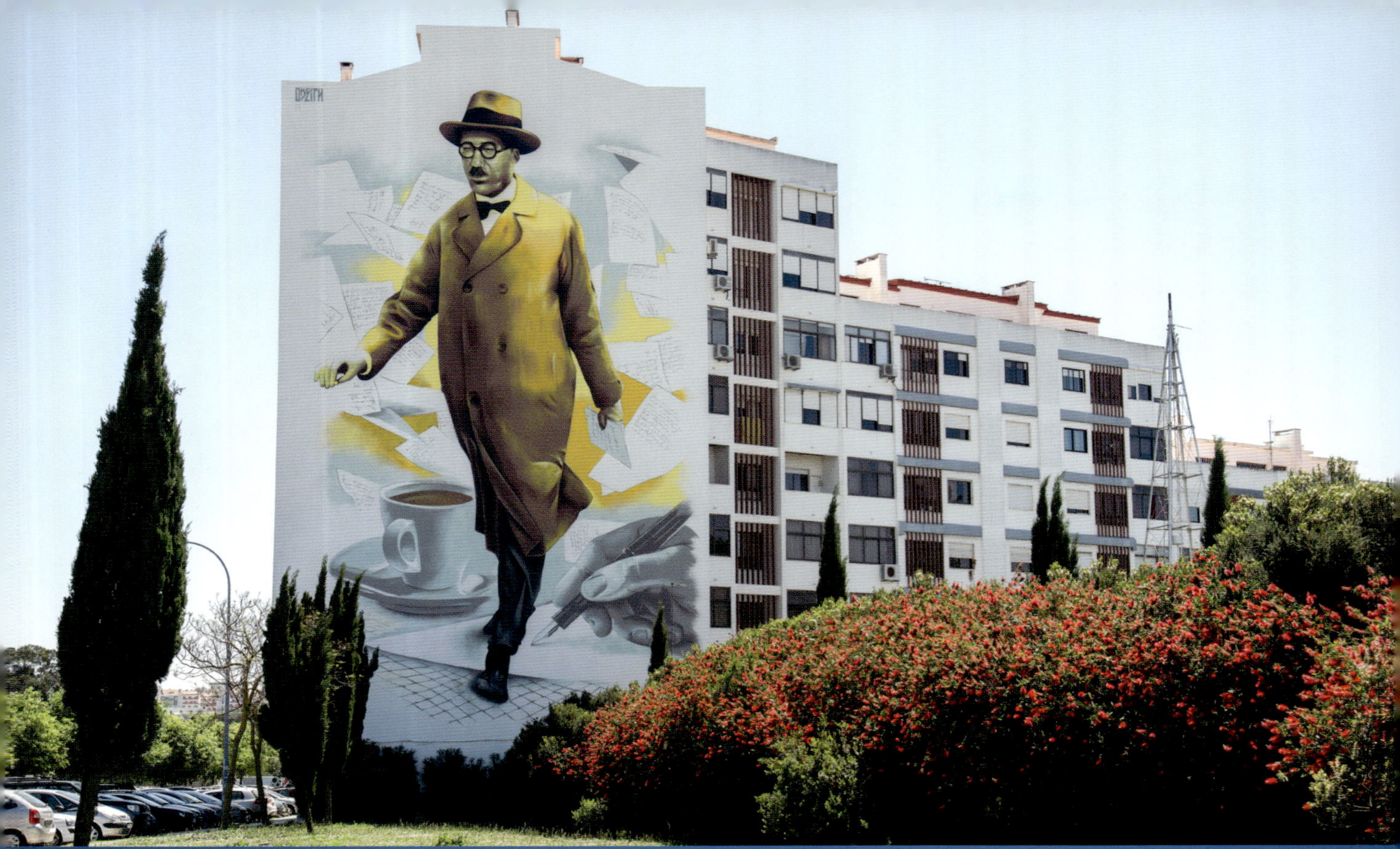

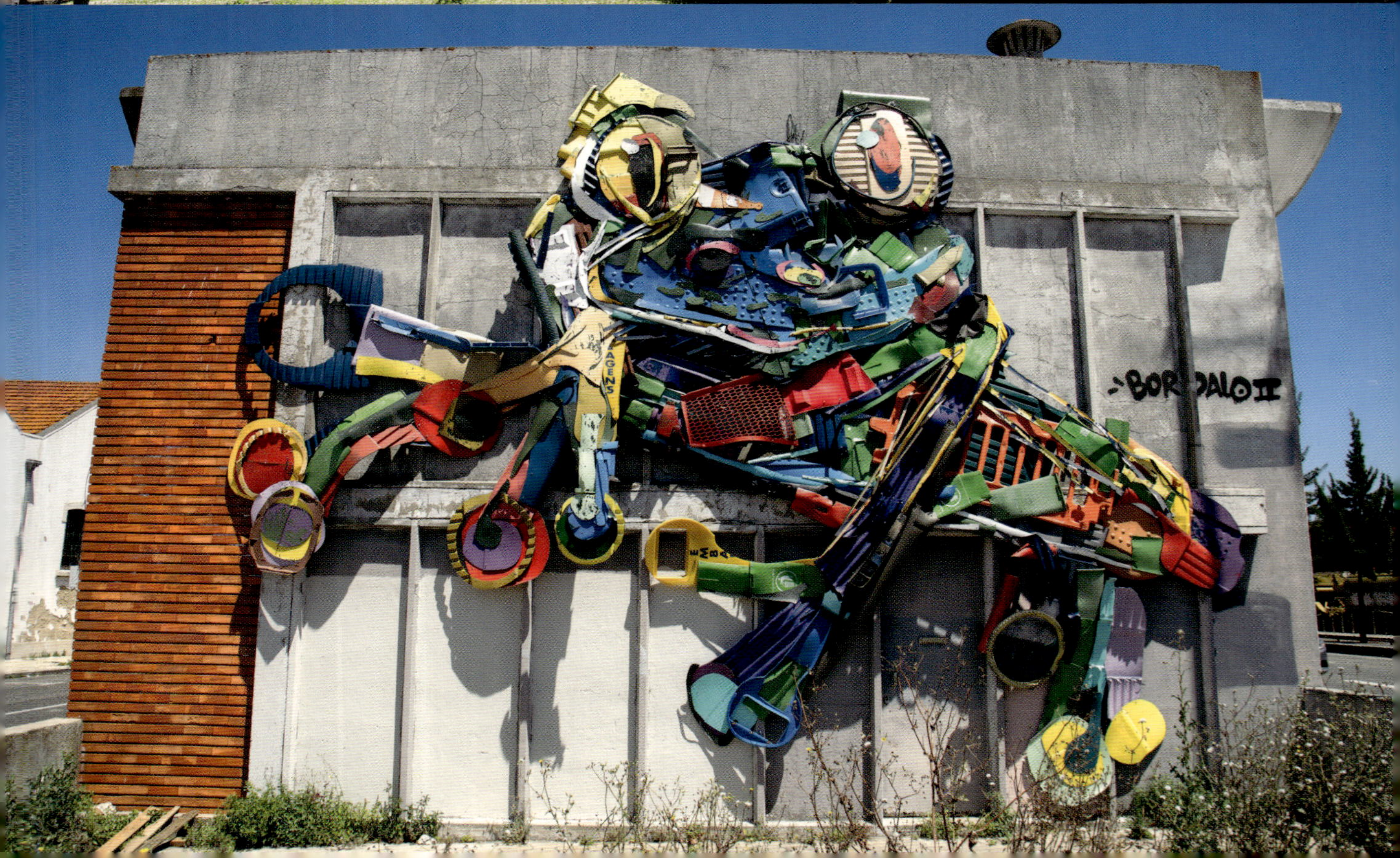

ODEITH

BORDALO II

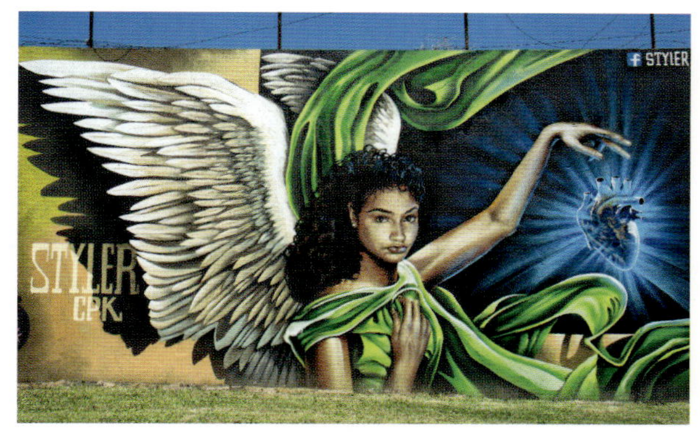
STYLER
CPK.
f STYLER

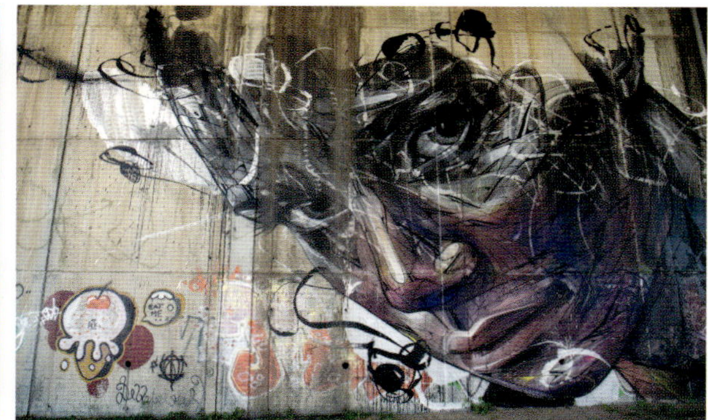

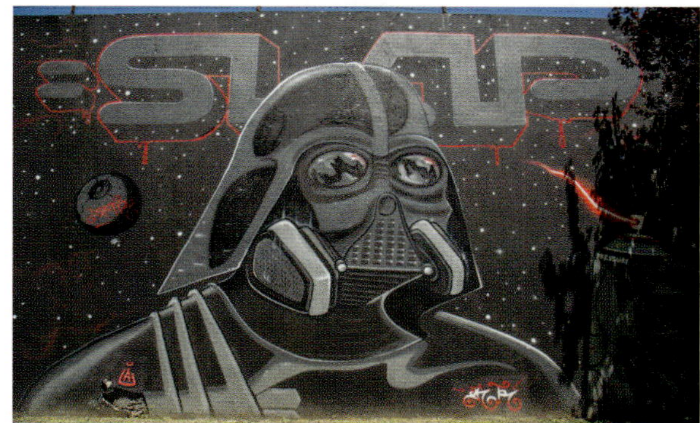

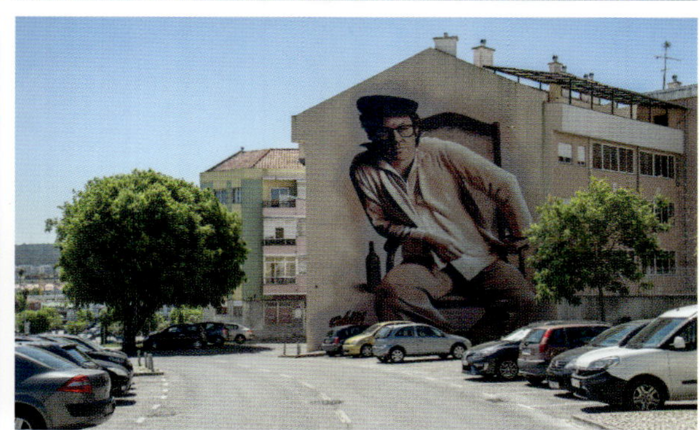

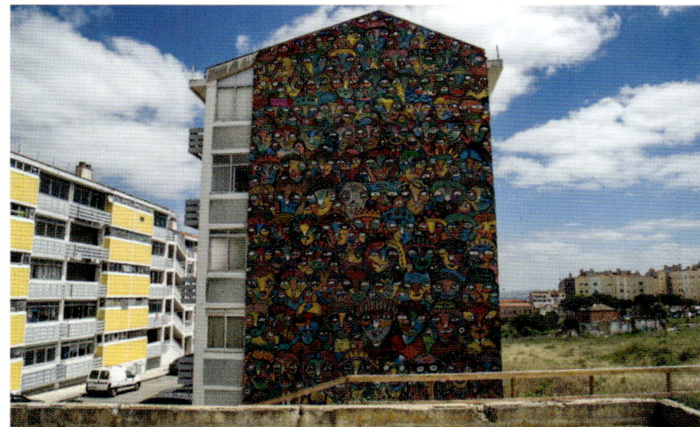

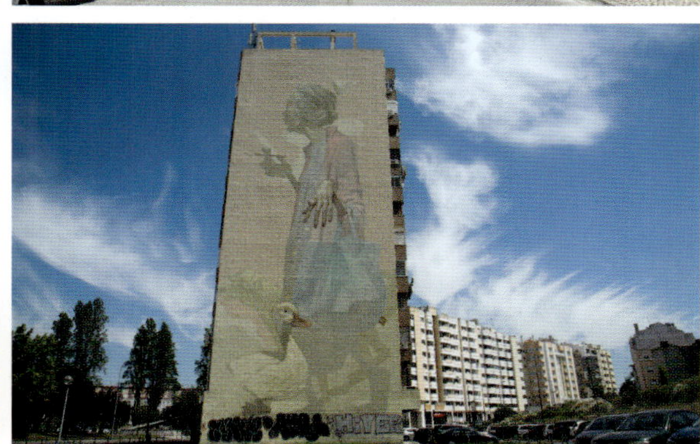

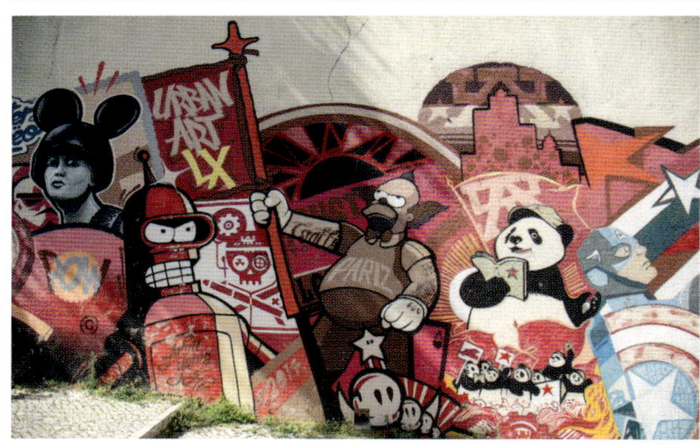
URBAN
ART
LX

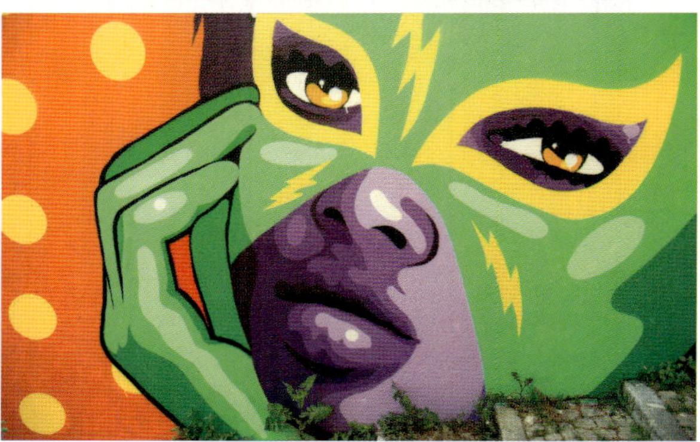

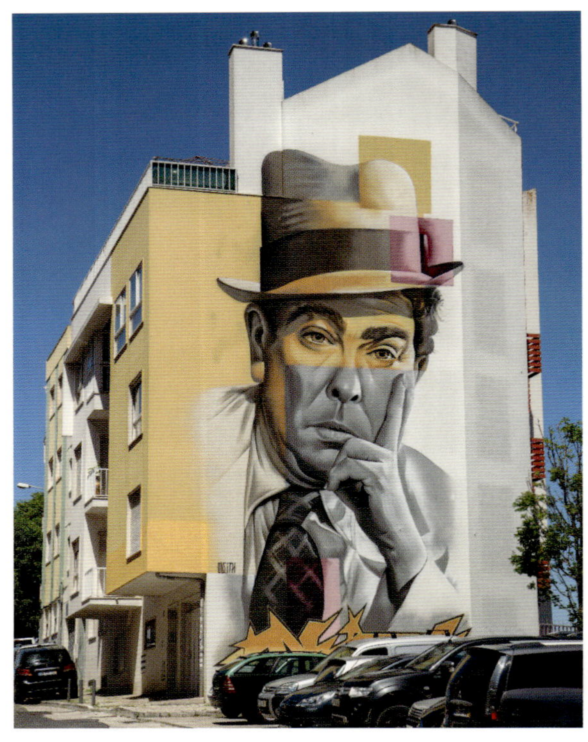

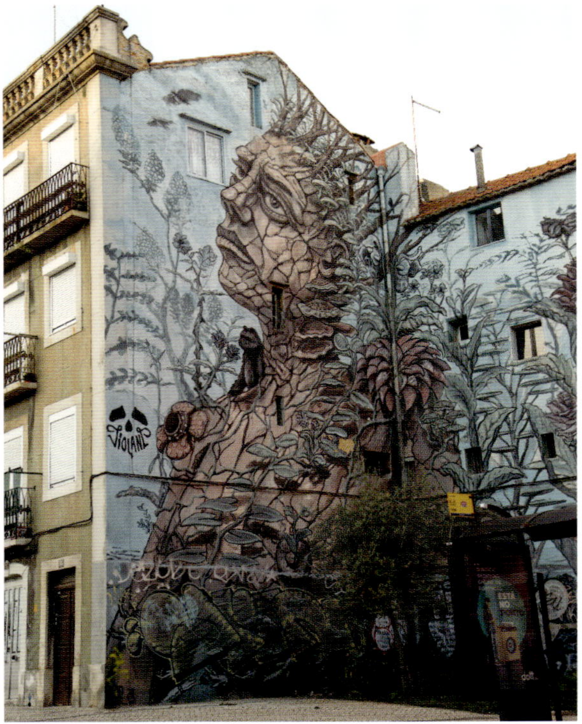

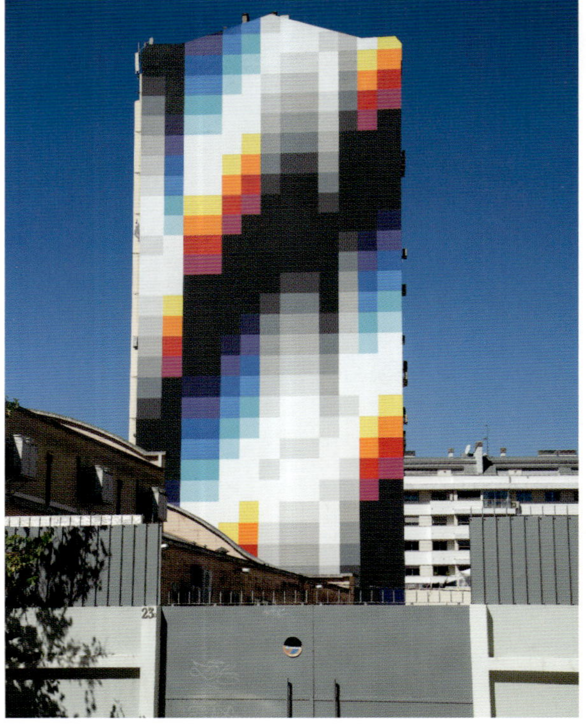

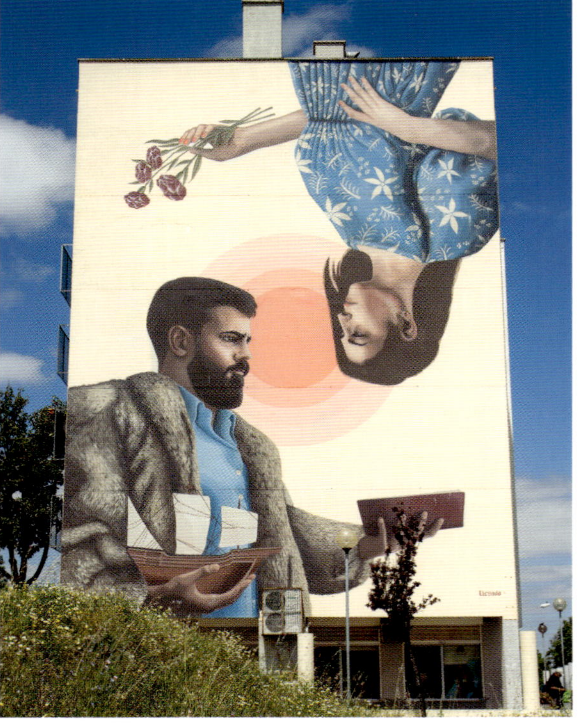

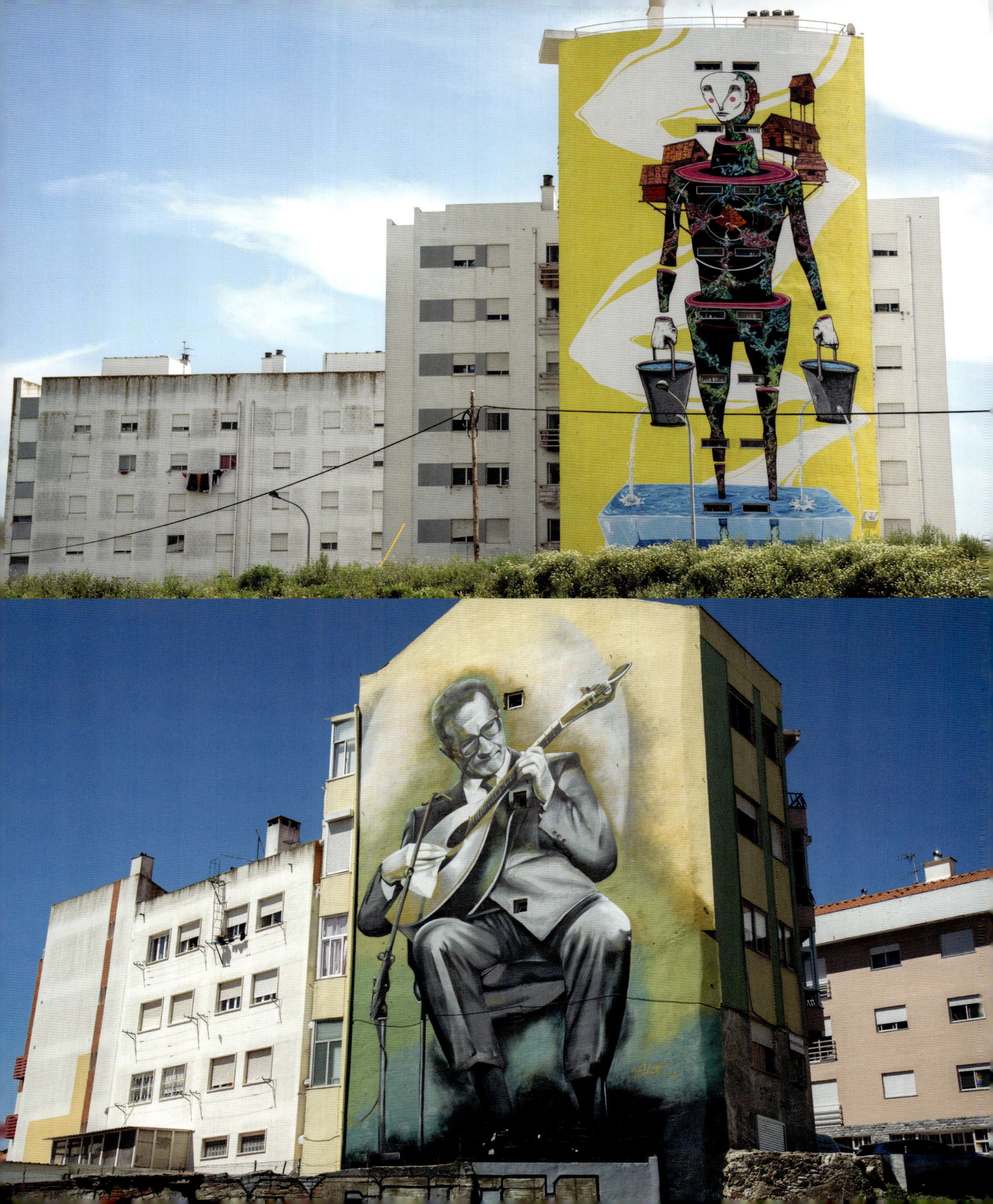

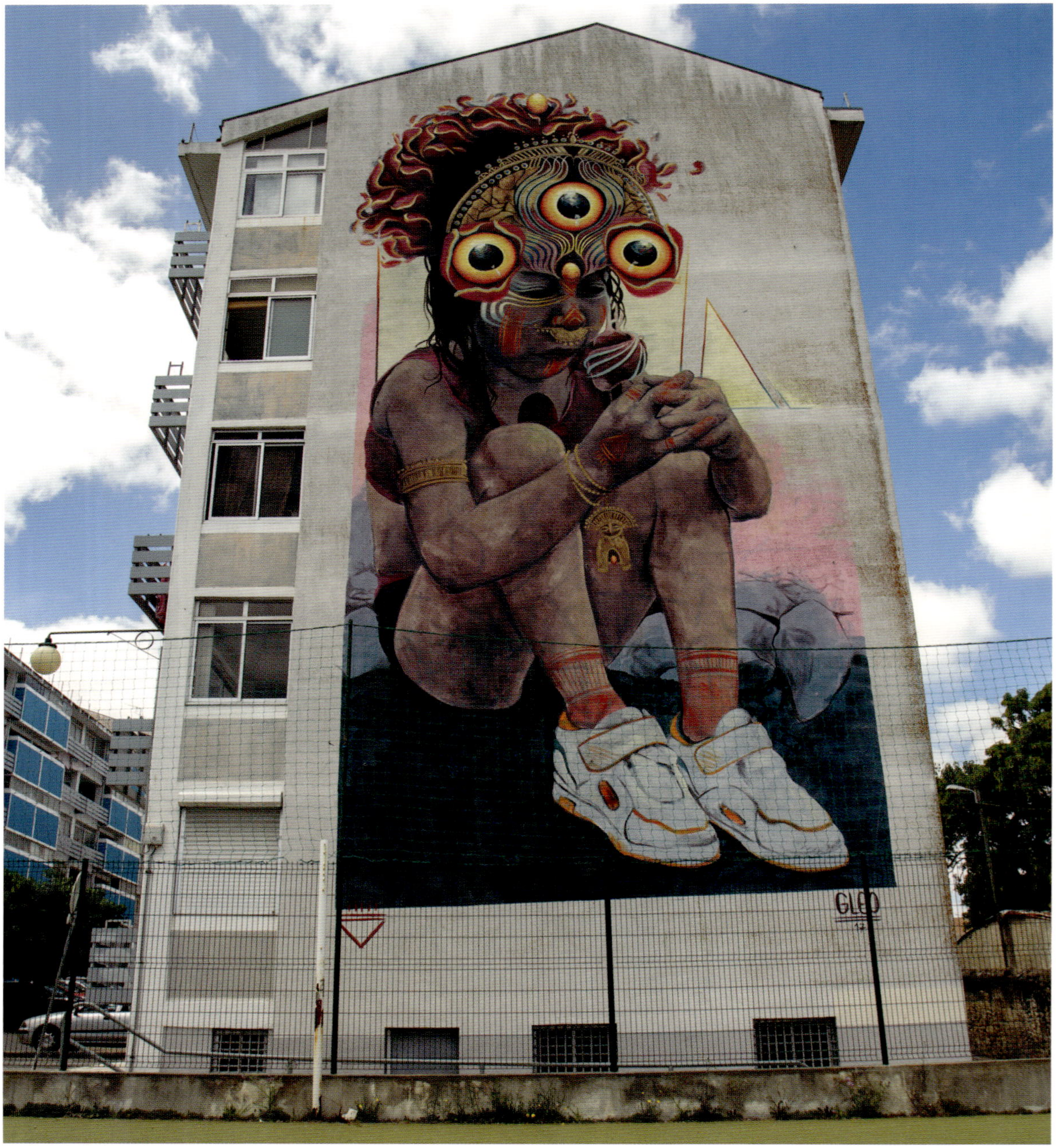

From Modern Graffiti to Street Art

The distinction between graffiti and muralism is surely a fine one. There are perfectly preserved murals on the walls of the preserved city of Pompeii. But there is also graffiti saying things like 'the girls here are well fit.' and other such classics. There are probably penises scratched into ancient Sumerian bus stops. The powerful scribe class of ancient Egypt did their officially sanctioned writing on walls, but there must have been Egyptian peasants called Dave who, not being able to write, drew the odd knob on the back of a mud hut.

If the original sense of Graffiti is any writing on a wall that is not legitimised, then Modern Graffiti is something else, a movement that has become synonymous with hip hop culture. It began in the late 1970's, and there are arguments over where exactly. Most agree it was New York or Philadelphia, perhaps it happened at the same time in Paris and Chicago. But it was a time when the city was becoming the mega urban sprawl of modernity, and the extreme inequality, the slums, the lawlessness of the city centres all gave rise to this flowering of rebel cultures, and graffiti was one of these accessible ways that kids who had nothing could respond to the culture of fame and conspicuous consumption that characterised the popular culture of the time.

And so it was that Taki 183 wrote his name and post code all over the city with a stolen marker pen. And this became a kind of fame for those who could not have real fame, success for those who were excluded from success. It spread across the modern world like a plague. Today it remains an essential part of the aesthetic of the modern city. No city is without it.

Graffiti rapidly evolved from tagging to something much closer to muralism - the 'piece' or masterpiece, an extensive work of art featuring advanced lettering styles and characters often taking up one or more whole carriages of a New York subway train. The characters were often taken from the underground comics of the day, especially the work of Vaughn Bode. This was the peak of the hip hop graffiti culture - as Urban Centres began to experience gentrification, it became largely impossible to do work on such a scale unless it was legal.

The world of power responded to graffiti in two distinct but linked ways. It co-opted urban culture and the desire for five minutes of fame to refine and re-invent consumer capitalism. How long before graffiti was first used in an advertising campaign?

But there was also a repression. Eventually the city secured the train yards that had been such an easy target. The 1980's saw the proliferation of CCTV, a normalisation of video surveillance in public spaces. In 1993 Mayor Giuliani introduced Zero Tolerance policing in New York. By the mid 1990's it was so difficult to operate as a spray can graffiti artist in the UK that one Bristolian switched to using stencils, because it was quicker. Banksy was his tag. Influenced by wheatpaste artist Blek le Rat in Paris, Banksy popularised a new type of graffiti that was dubbed 'Street Art' by the media.

Street Art enjoyed a brief but explosive moment on a worldwide scale from the late 1990's through to the late 2000's. An array of Street Art superstars emerged, mostly politically engaged, working in a punk and urban tradition, attacking the gentrification and commercialisation of urban life.

Artists like Banksy echoed a popular surge of dissent against capitalism that culminated in the Occupy movements and a year of unrest in 2011. But right from the beginning some voices called it a gentrification of graffiti culture - an art school hijack of a working class movement. The increasing move towards art gallery shows, critical acclaim from the fine art world, and the dizzying financial success of some of these artists suggested a move away from the streets where the style was born.

But Street Art continues to enjoy an afterlife as a new school of legal public art. Projects by JR and Os Gemeos among others traded the running battle with authority for the ability to push their art up to new levels of scale and impact. They brought into the language of muralism, their punk, countercultural heritage. They brought lowbrow influences from pop and underground cultures like comic books, computer games, movies, punk mashup, collage and themes; and a kind of postmodern romanticism - sad and beautiful faces, lost souls. It's a syntax that people like, it makes sense to people who live in the city. It's an art movement that isn't so aggressively avant garde that it alienates any potential audience, but it's also not so tame that it feels like corporate propaganda.

Banksy remains an outlaw, and he's not the only one, but 'Street Art' is no longer considered a menace to society. Maybe it can now become something else, perhaps an idea of what an alternative city space might look like, a world after corporate rule.

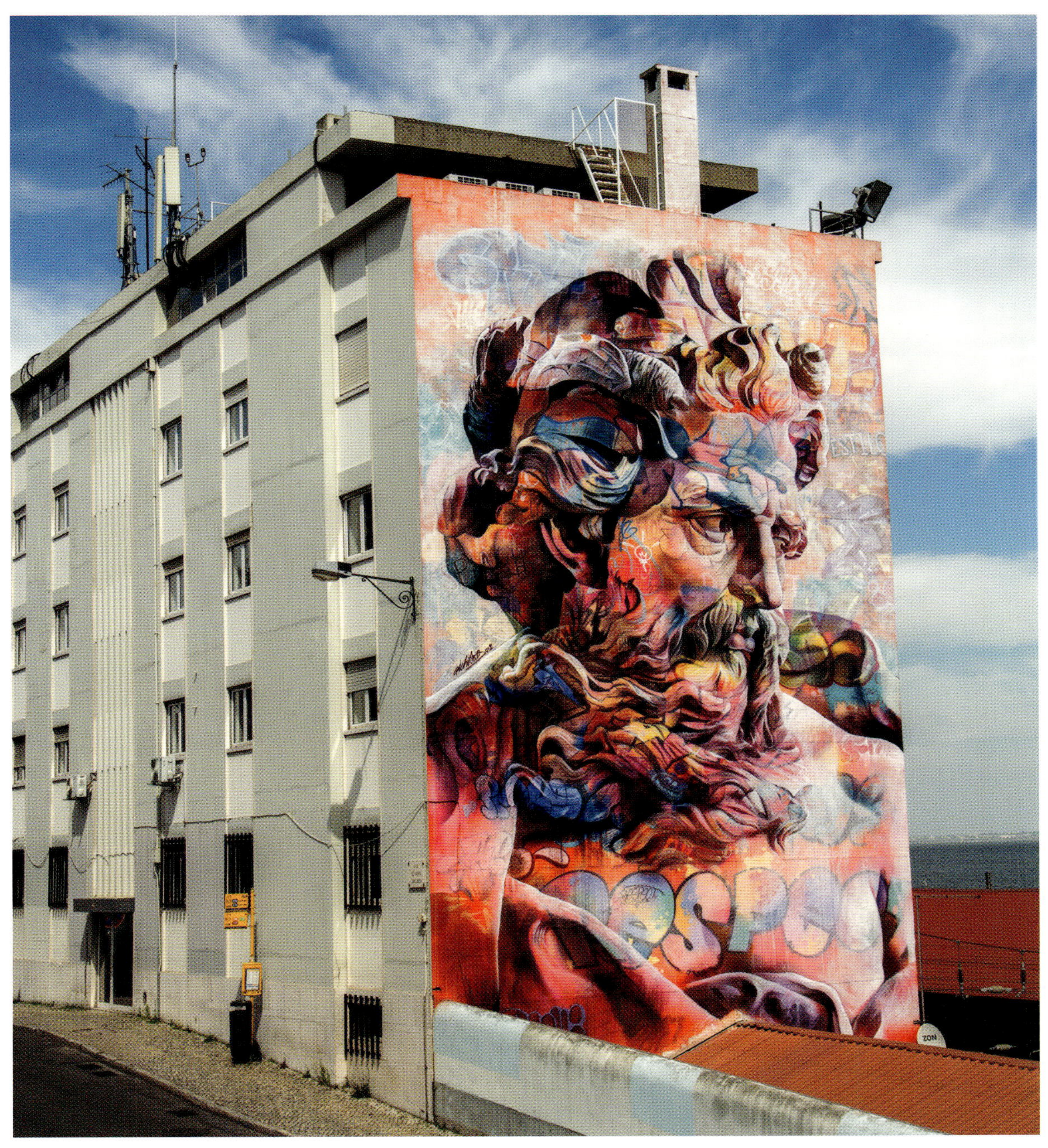

BADALONA

SPAIN

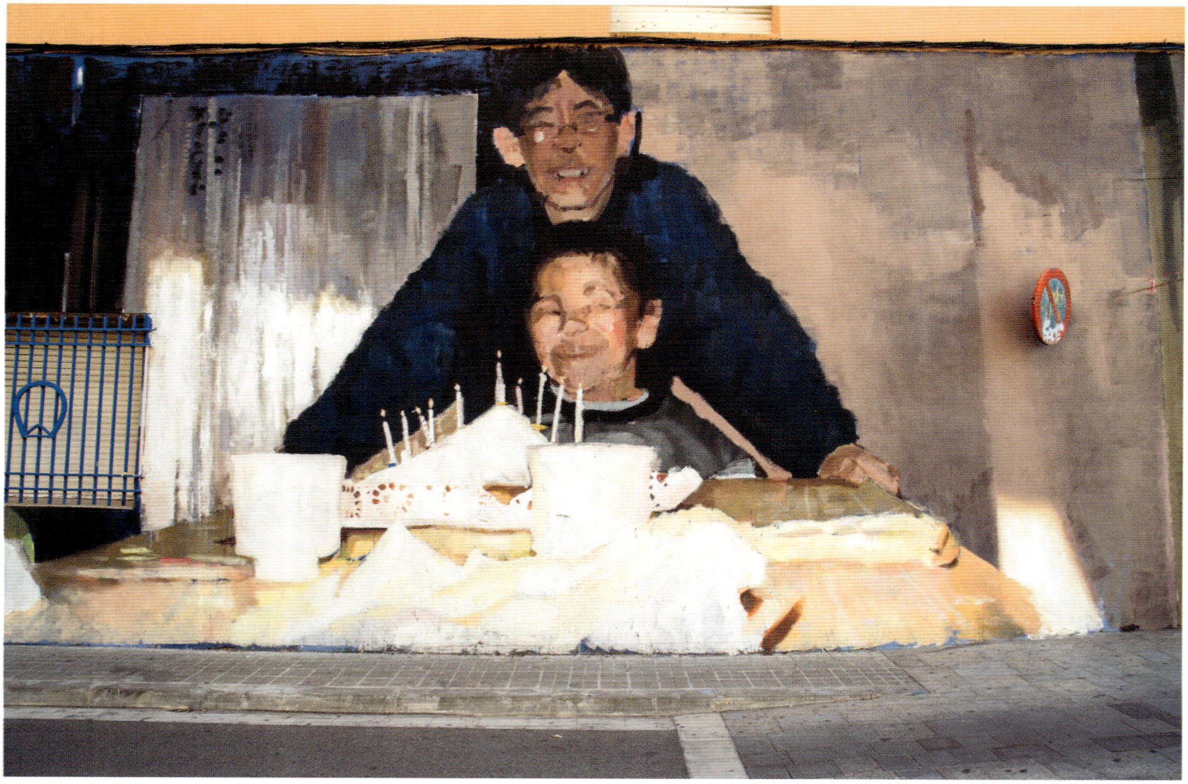

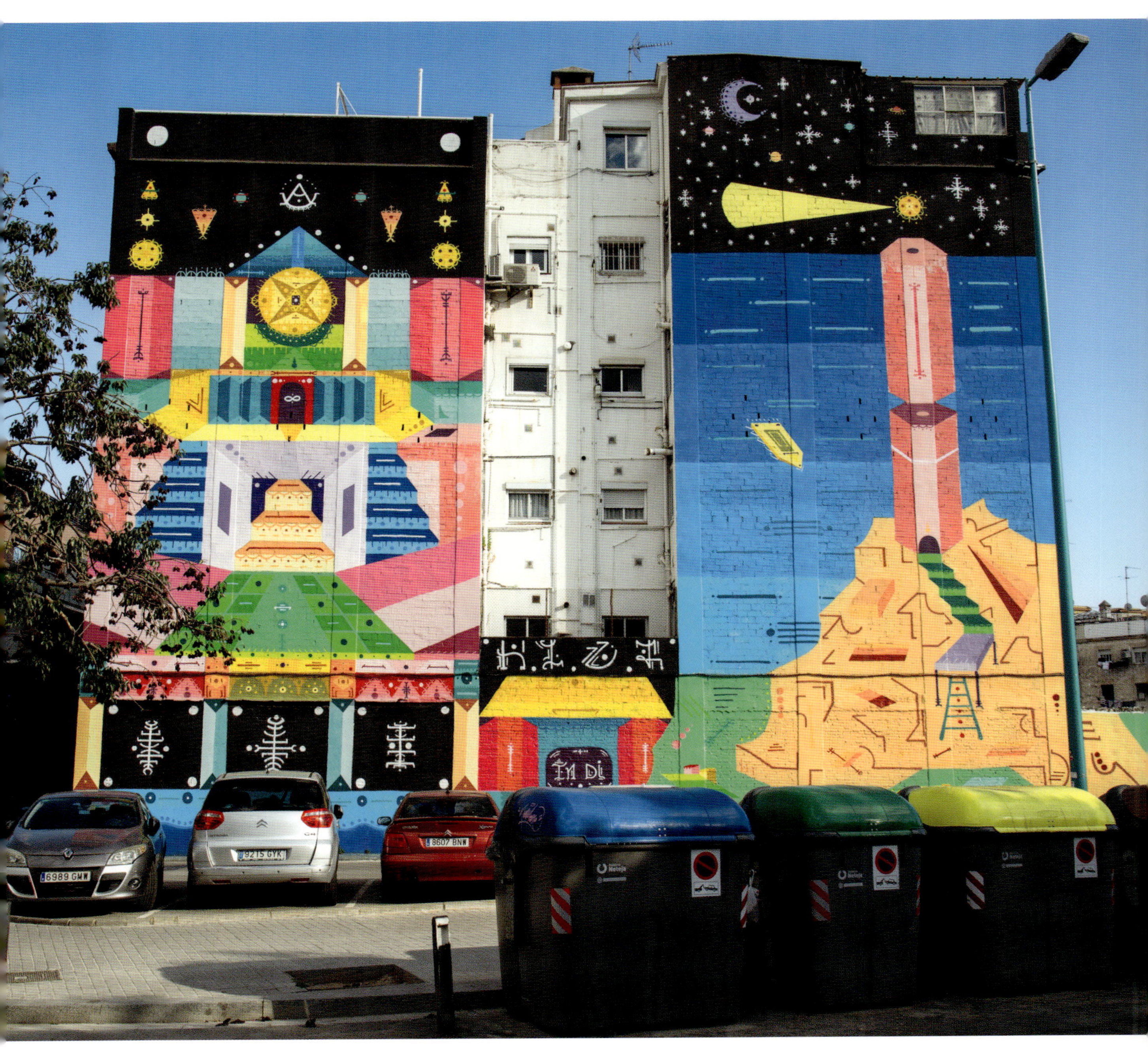

BARCELONA

SPAIN

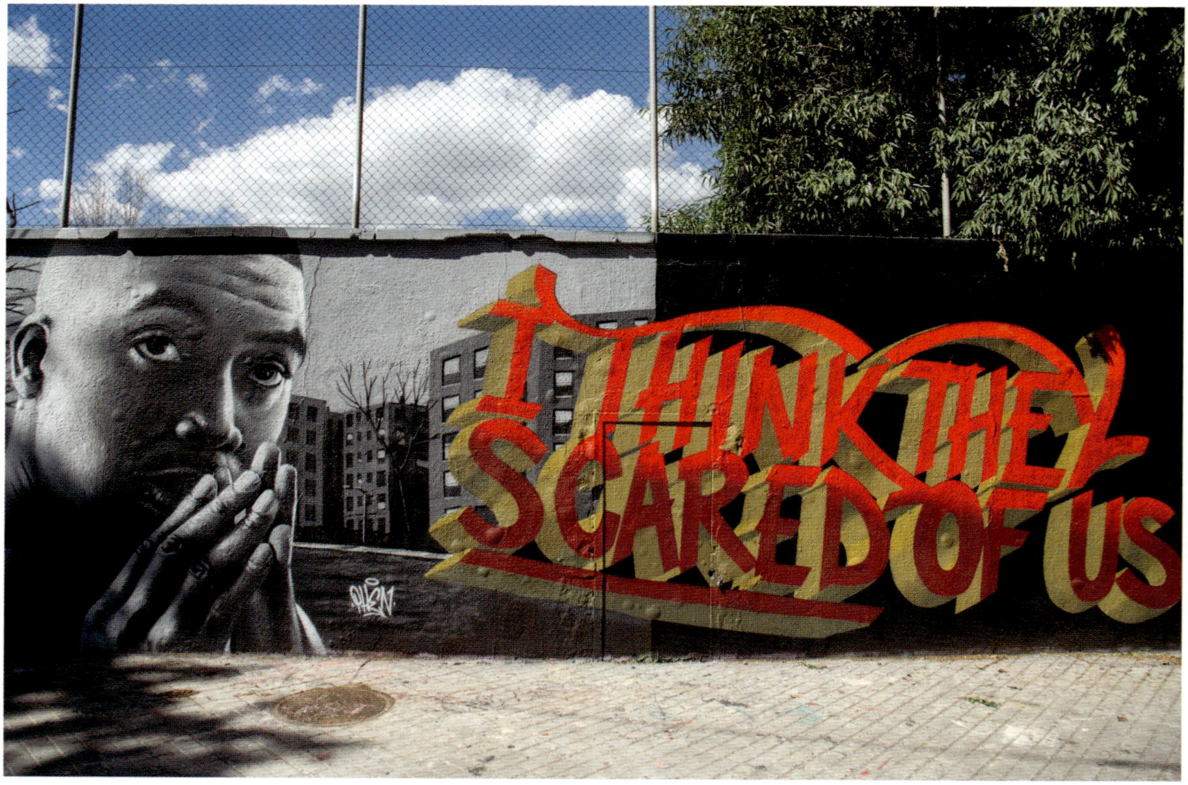

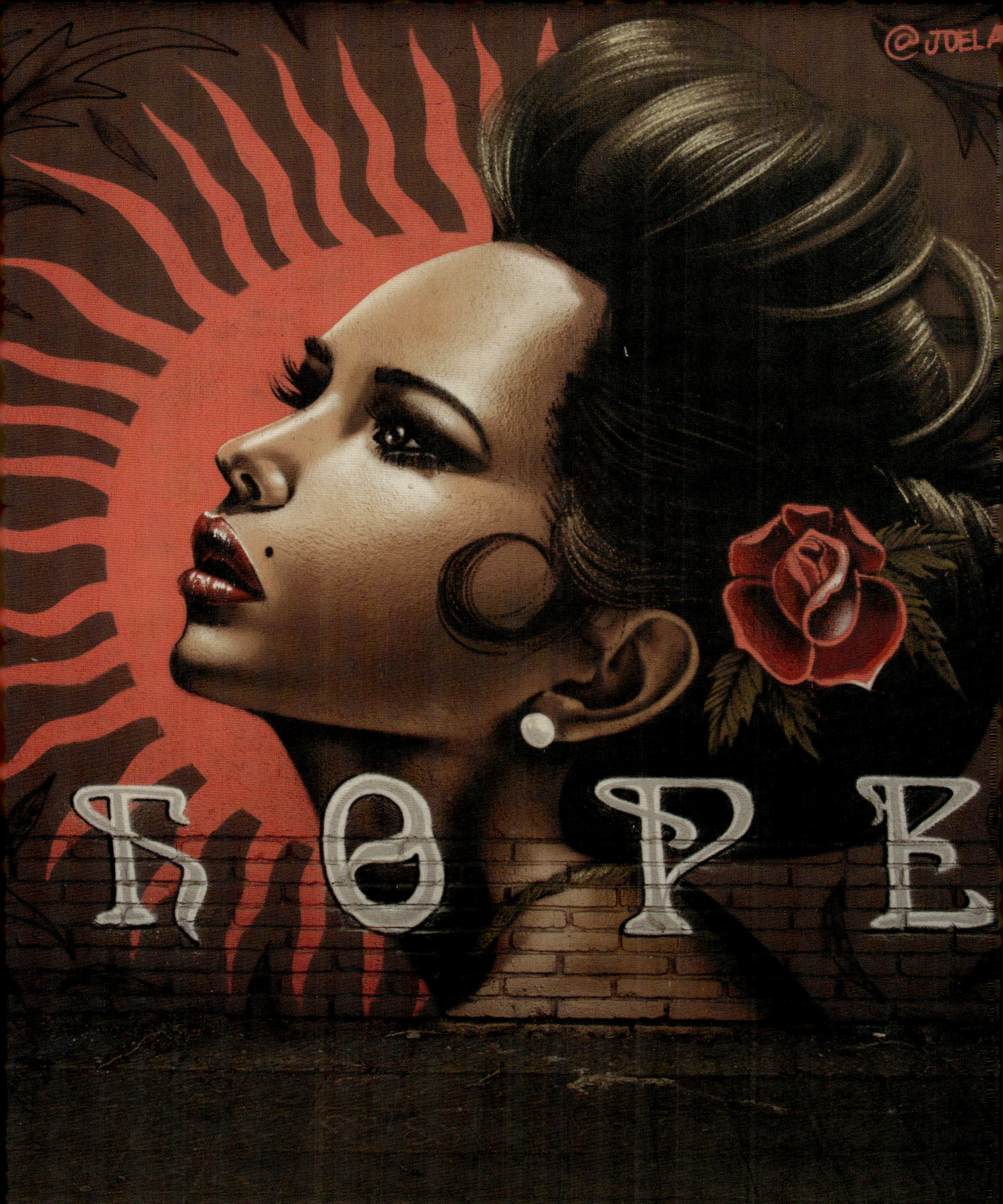

@JOELA
HOPE

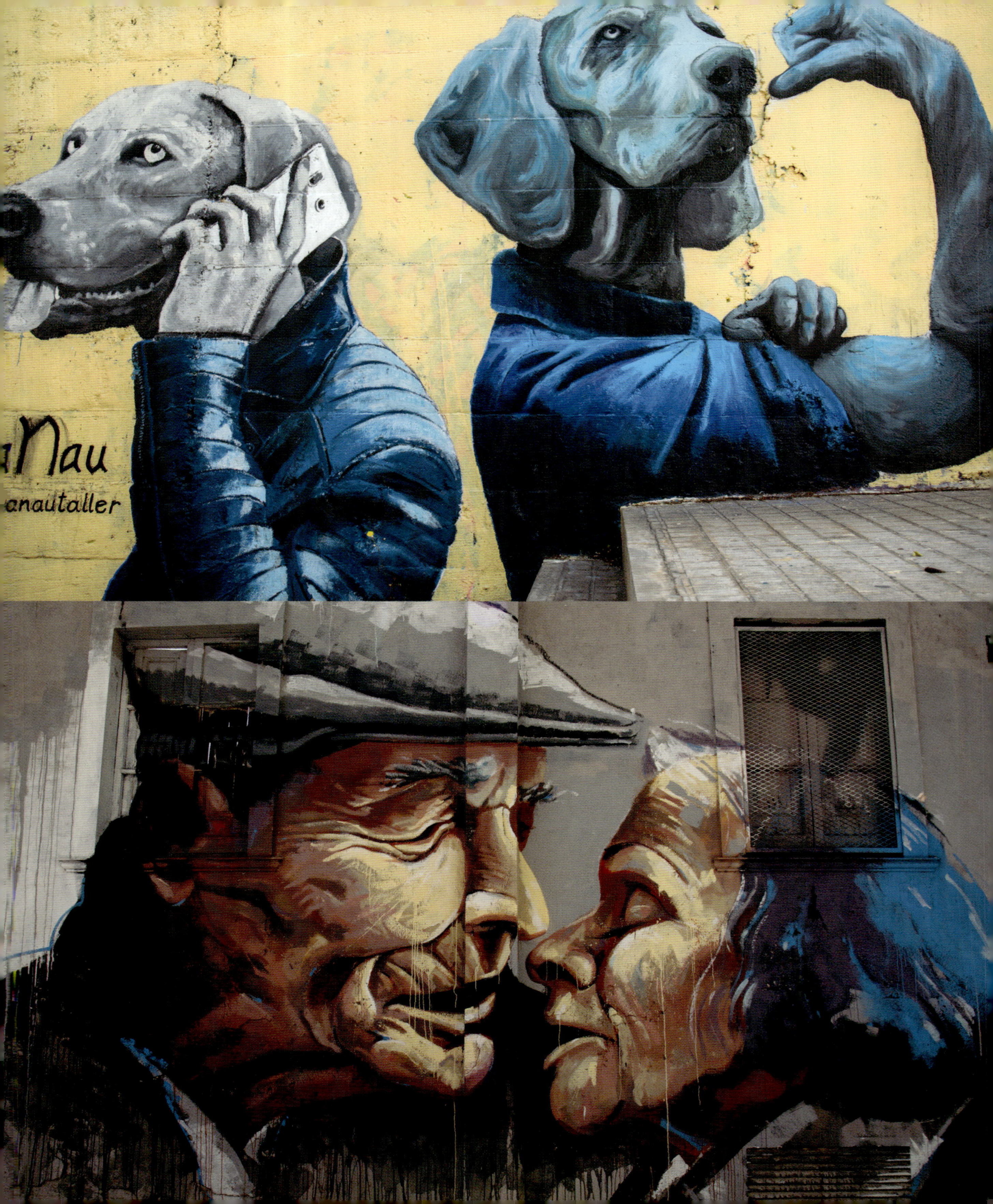
Nau
anautaller

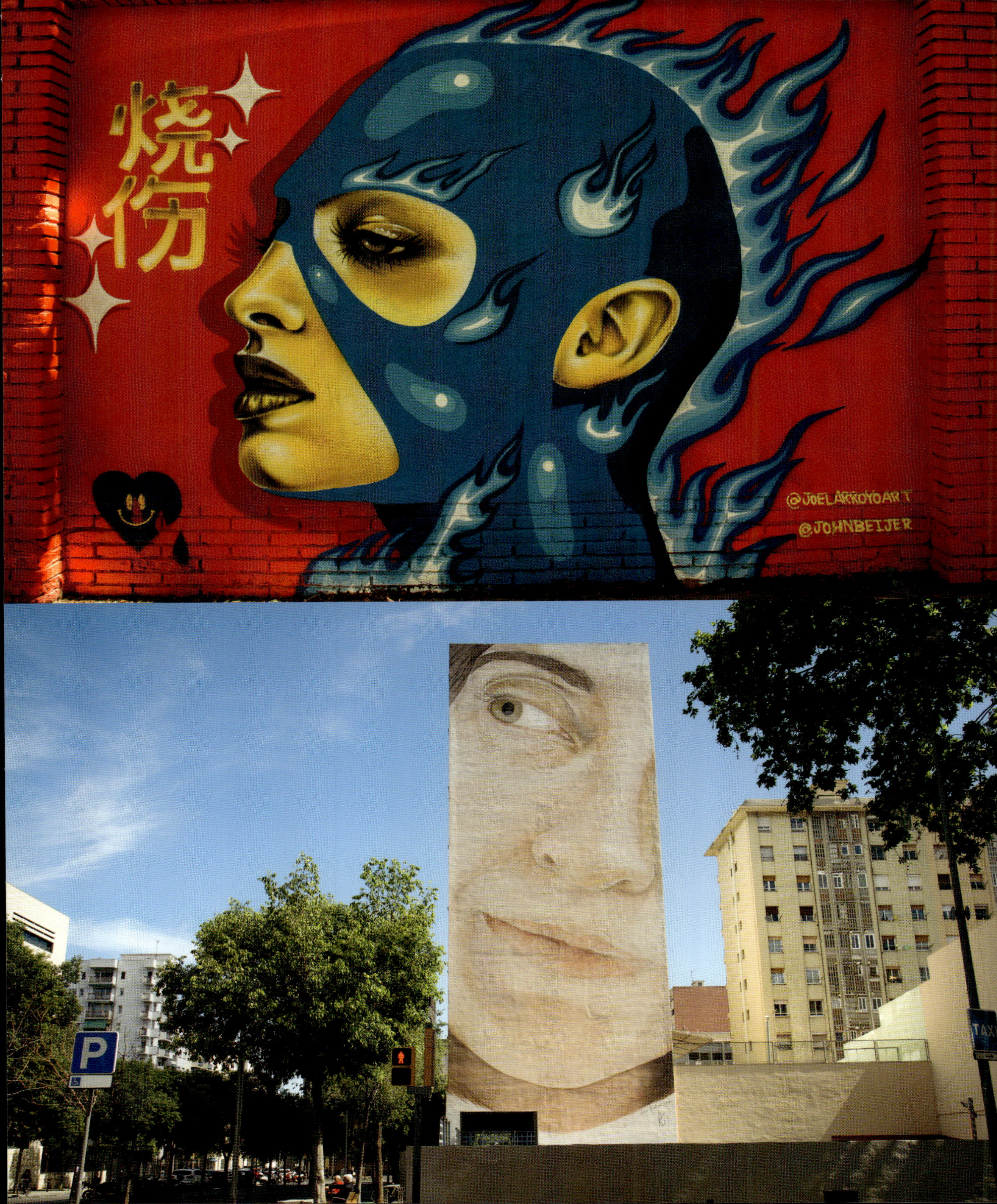

烧伤
@JOELARROYOART
@JOHNBEIJER

GRANOLLERS

SPAIN

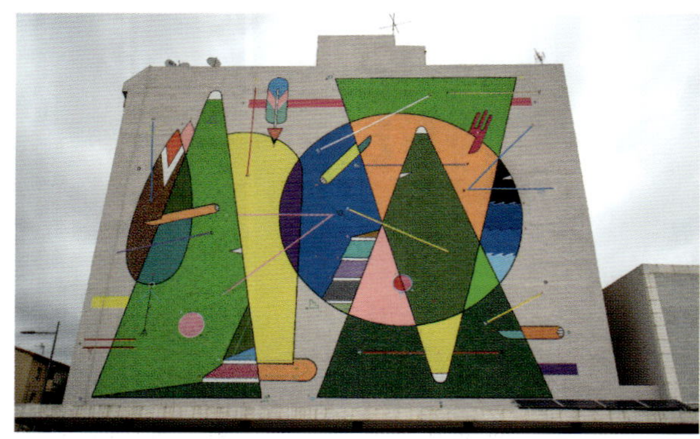

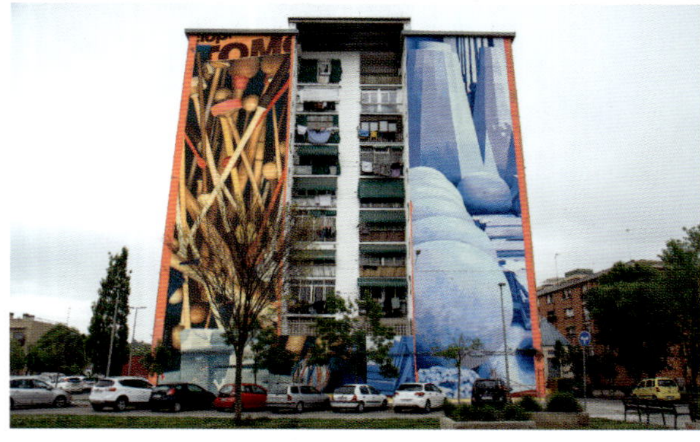

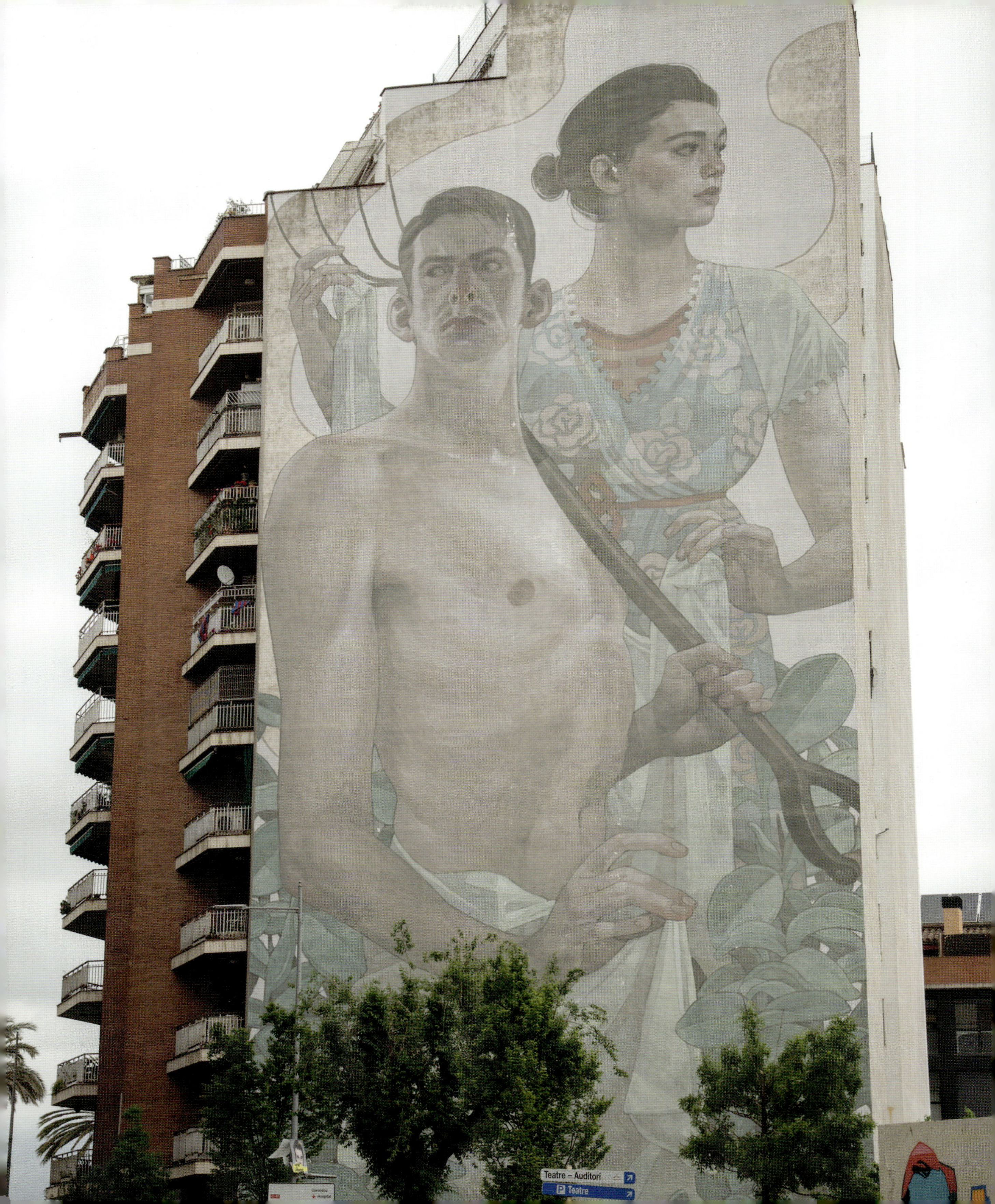
Teatre – Auditori
P Teatre

VIGO

SPAIN

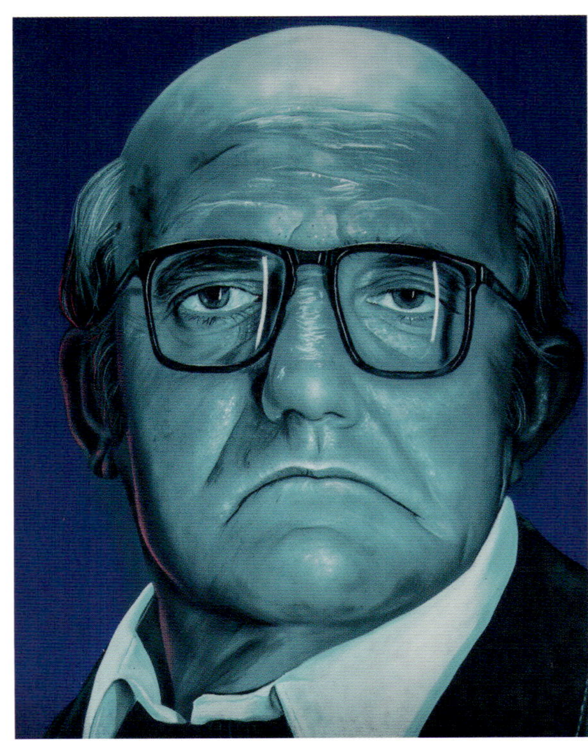

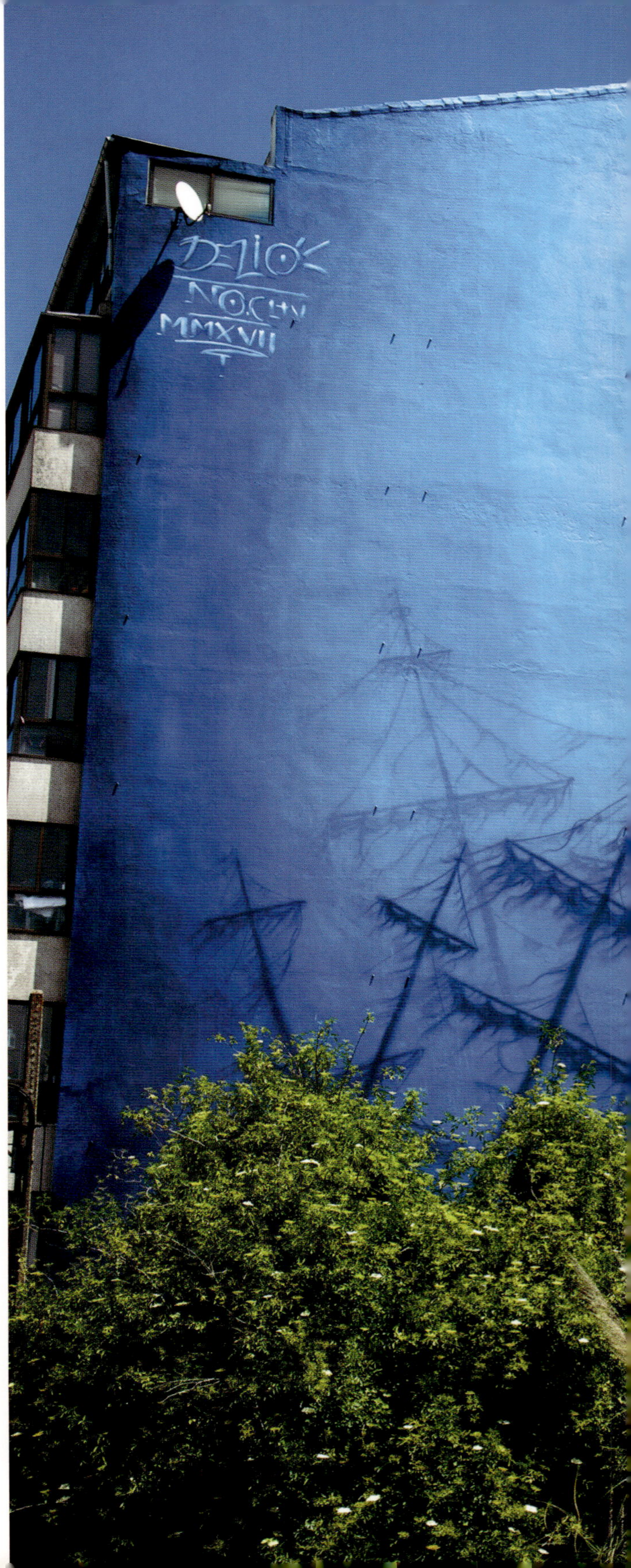

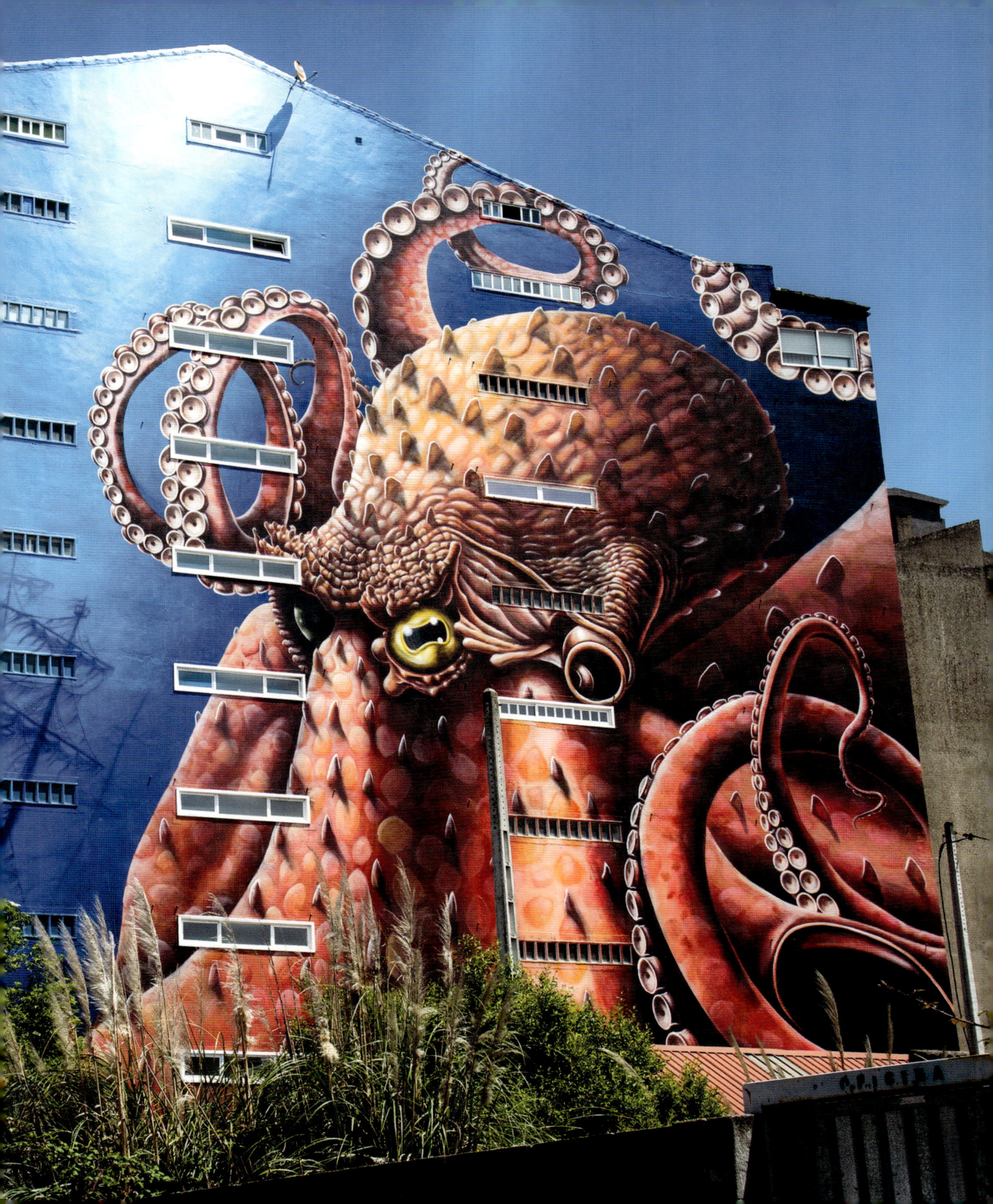

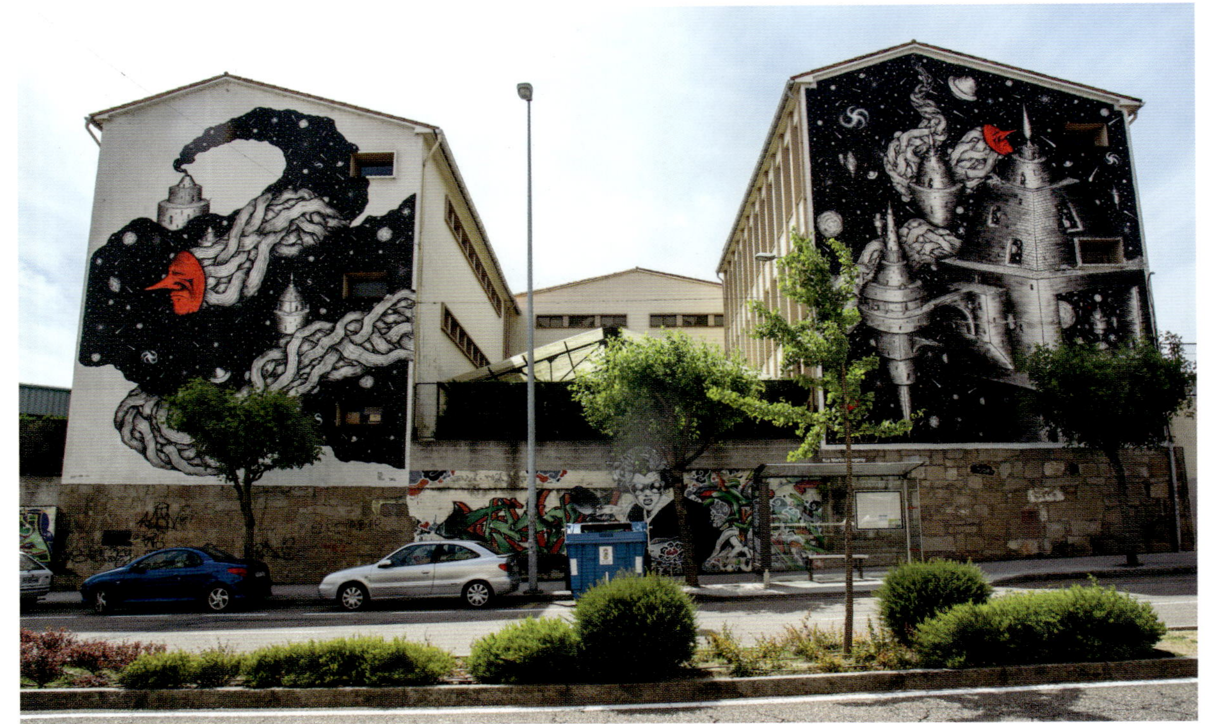

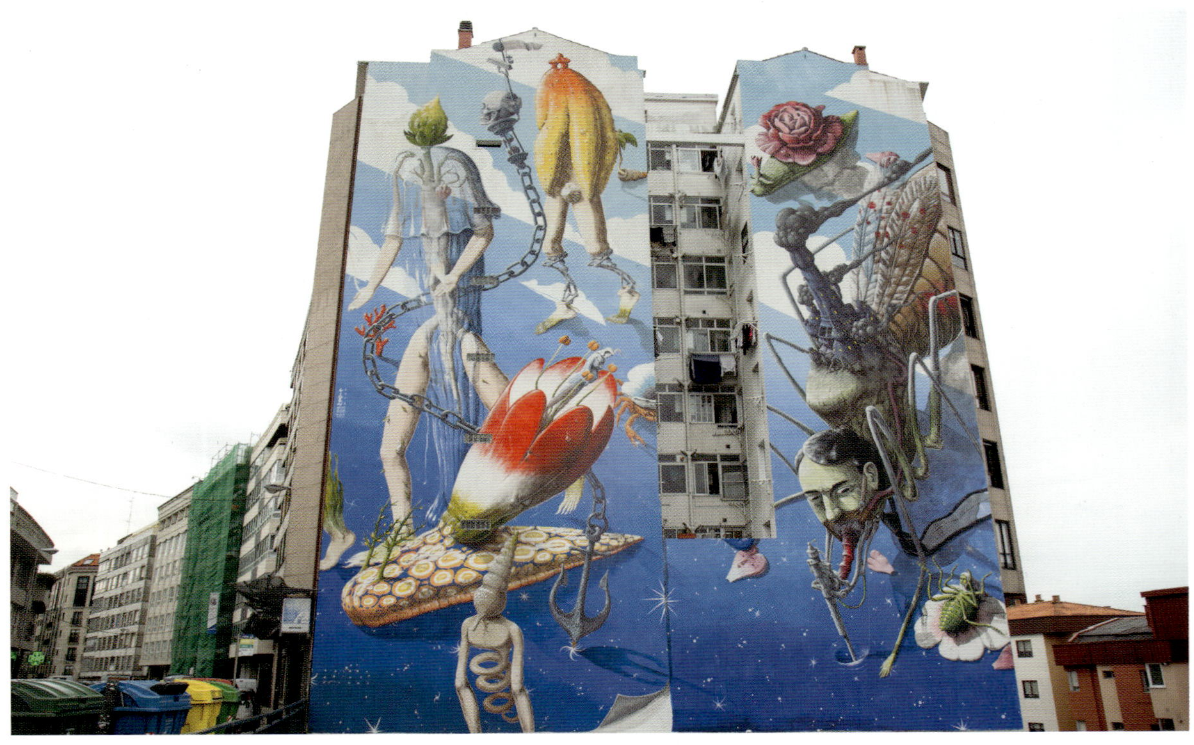

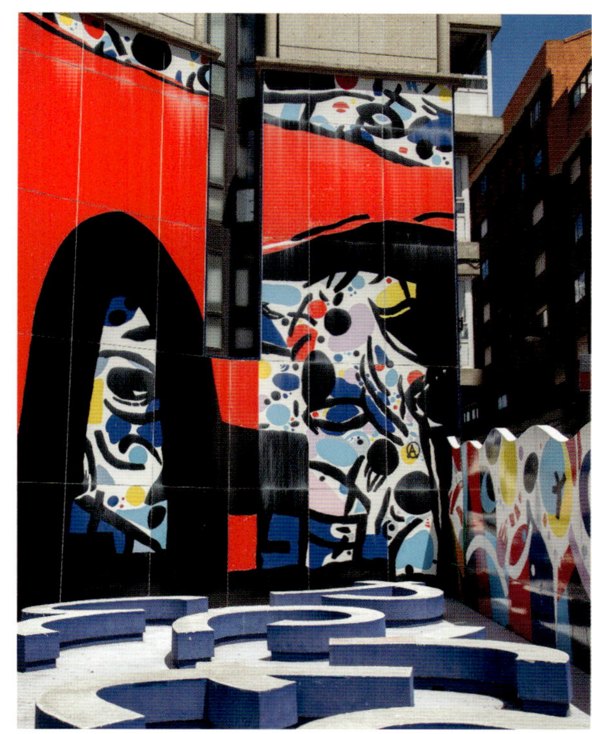

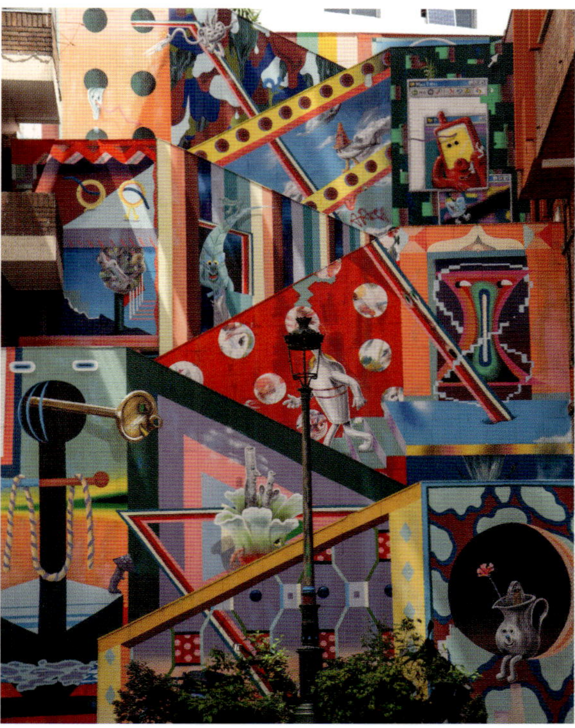

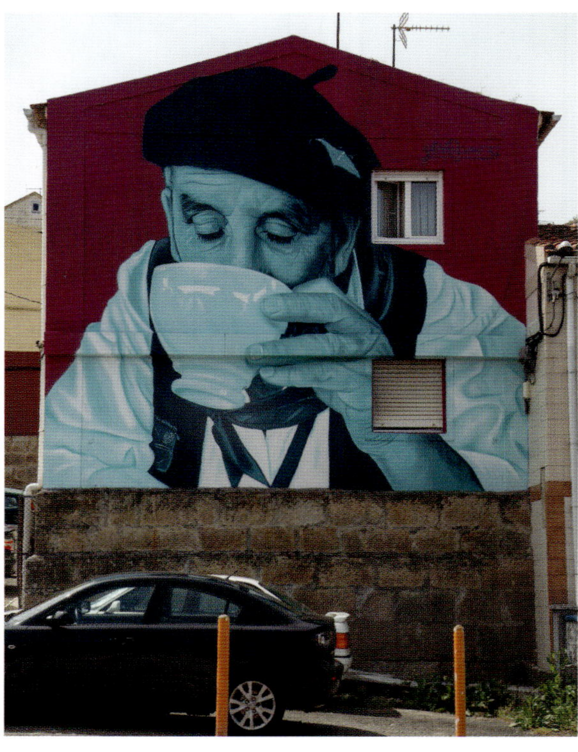

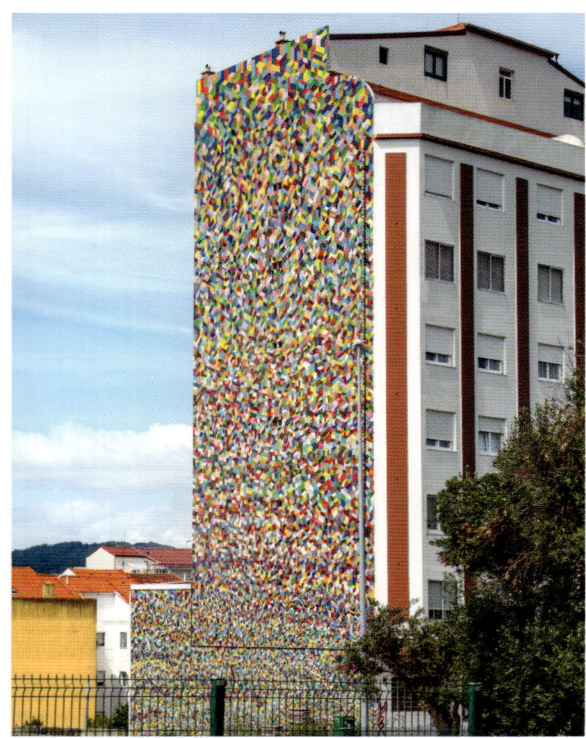

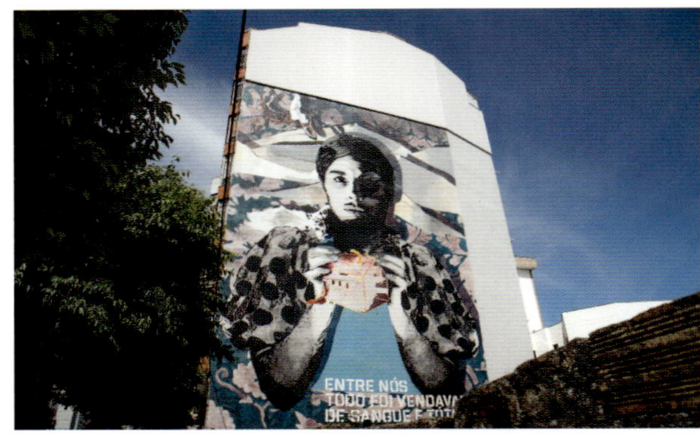
ENTRE NÓS
TODO FOI VENDAVAL
DE SANGUE E FOGO

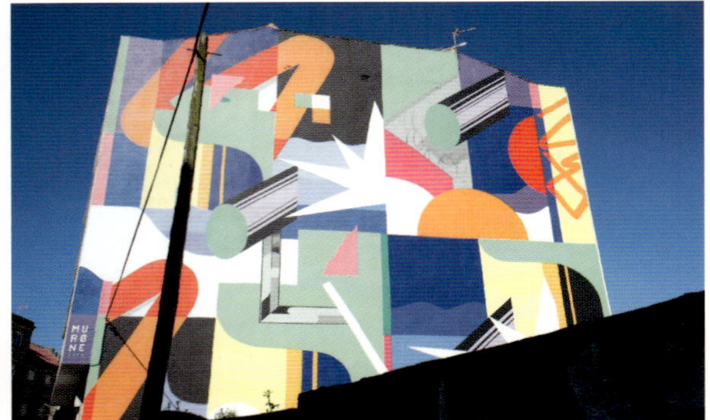

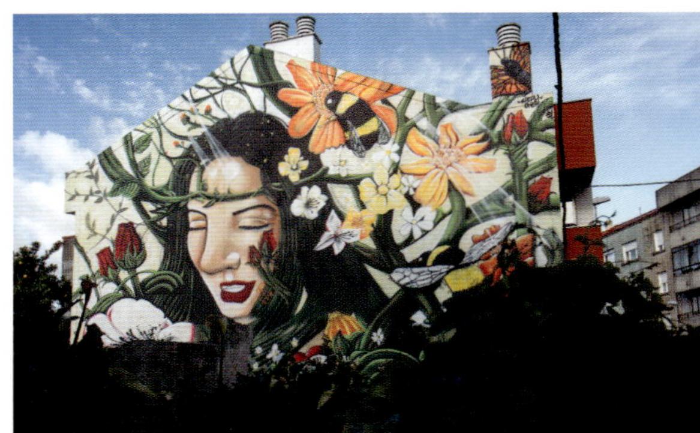

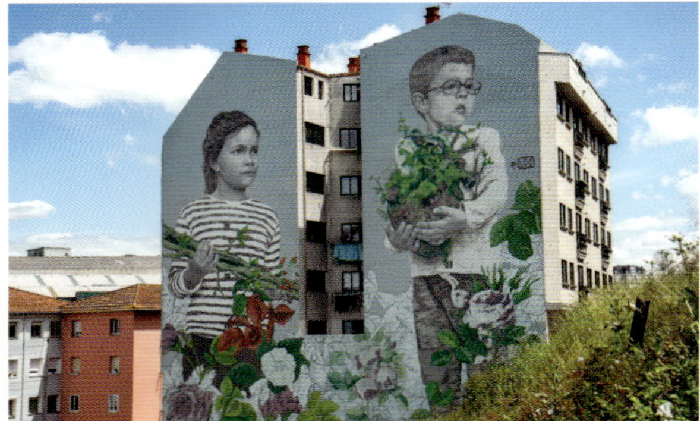

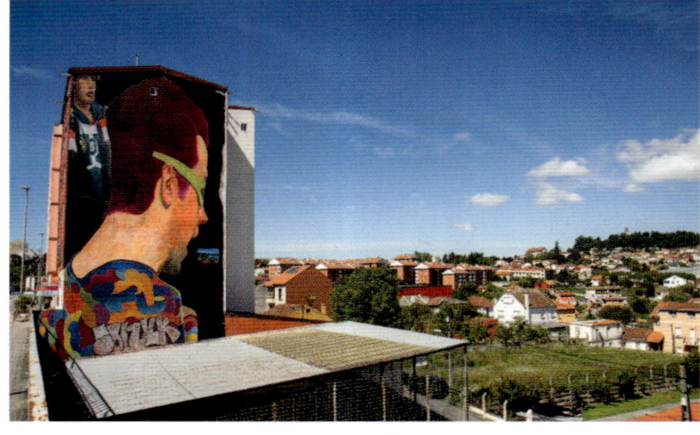

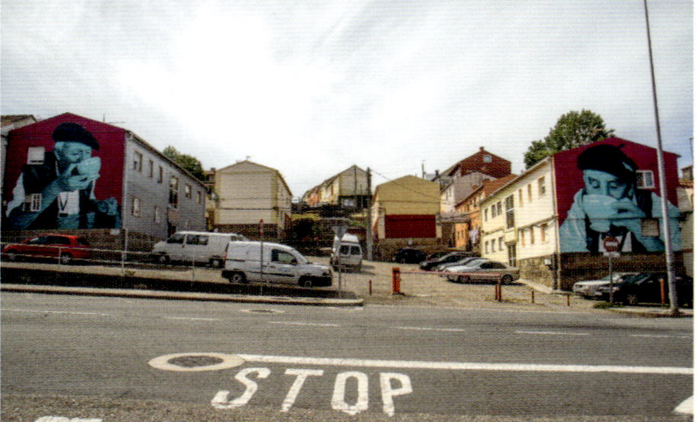
STOP

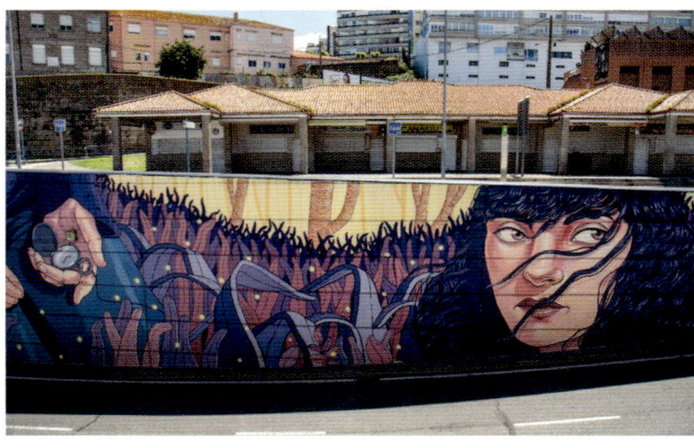

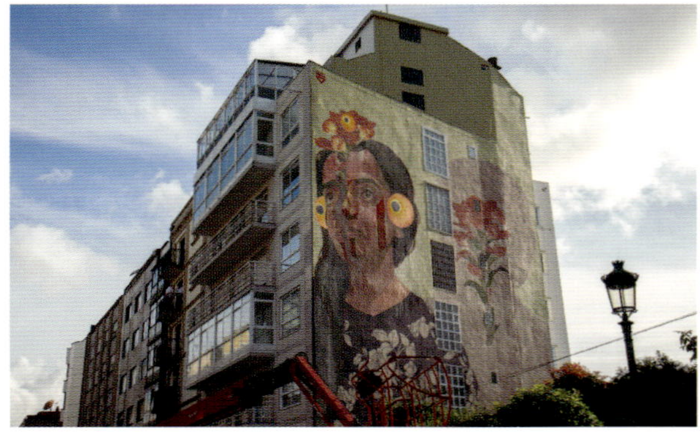

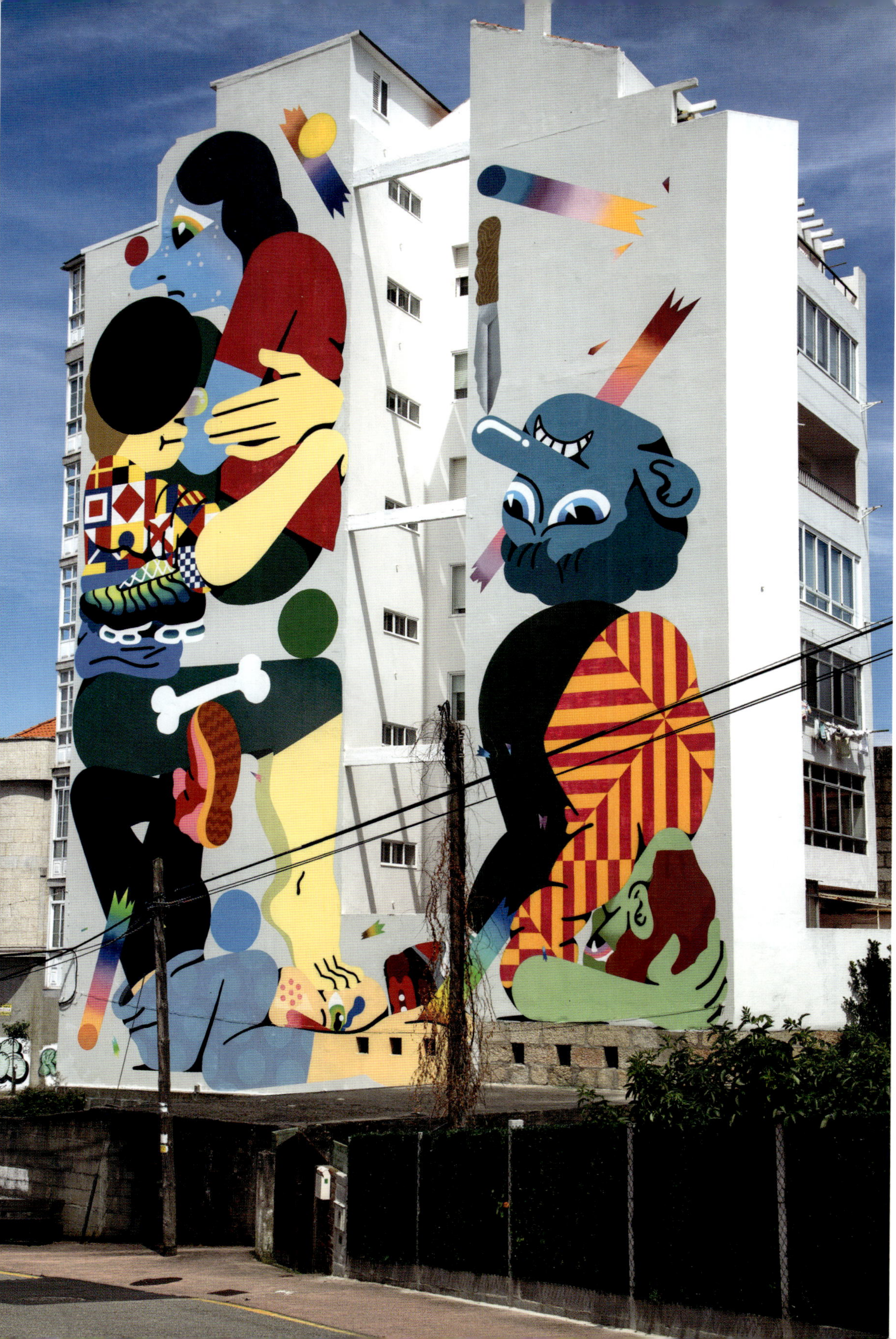

ZARAGOZA

SPAIN

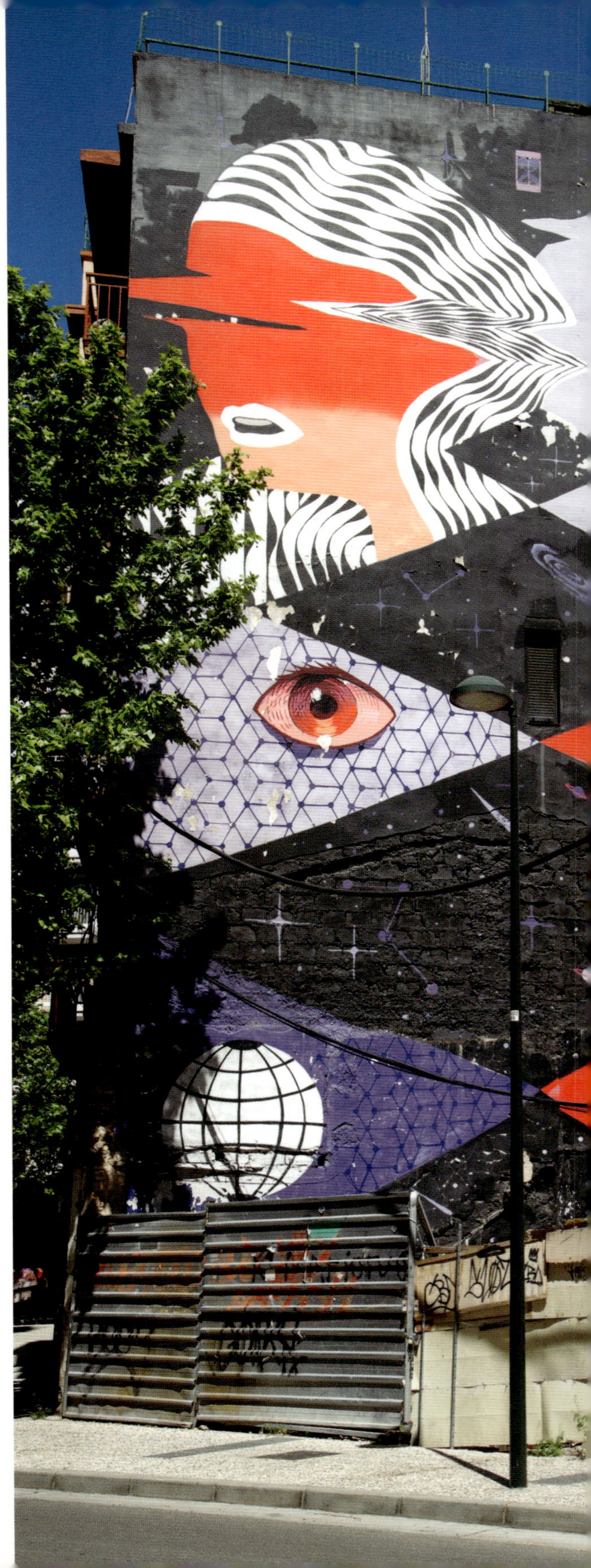

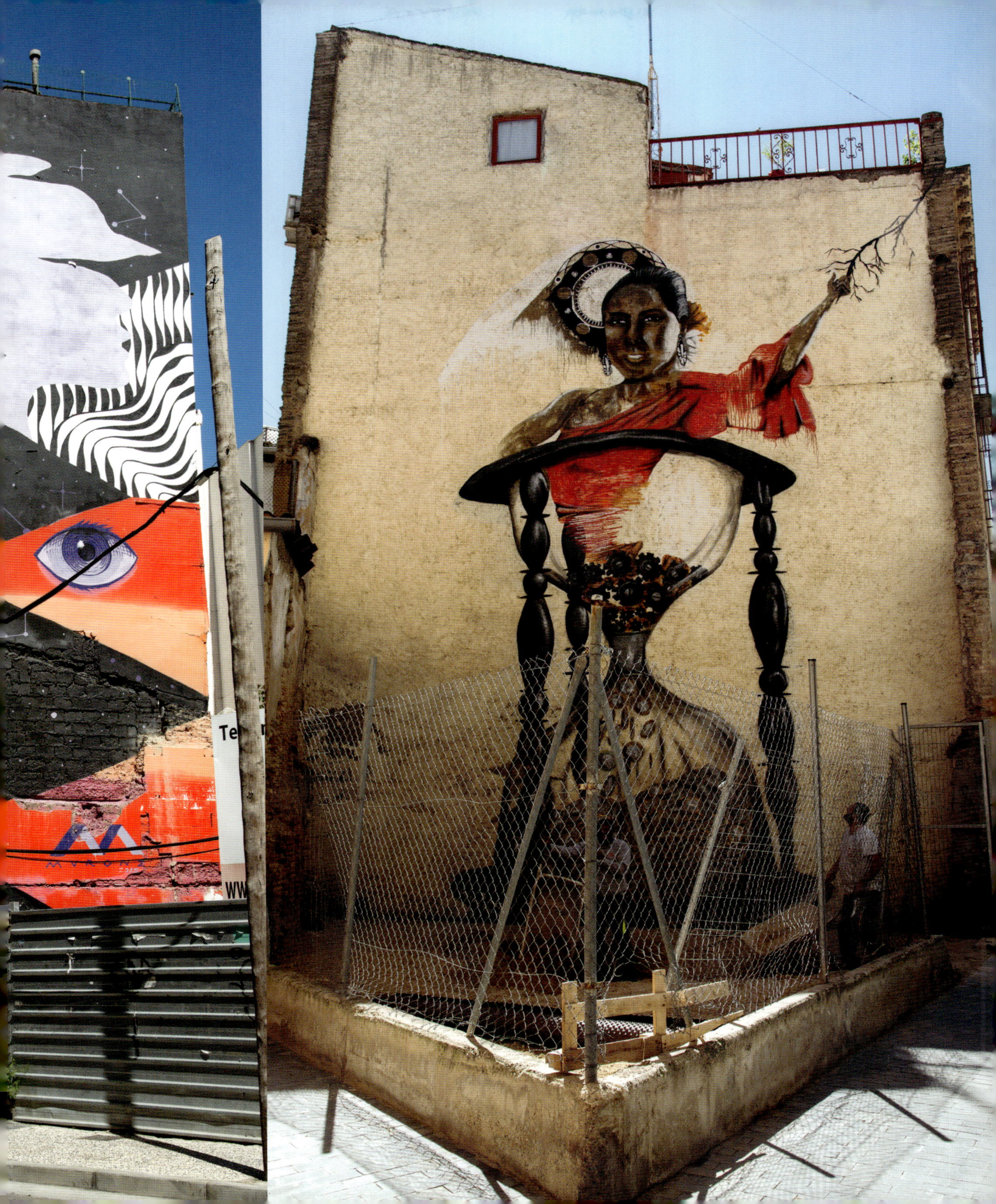

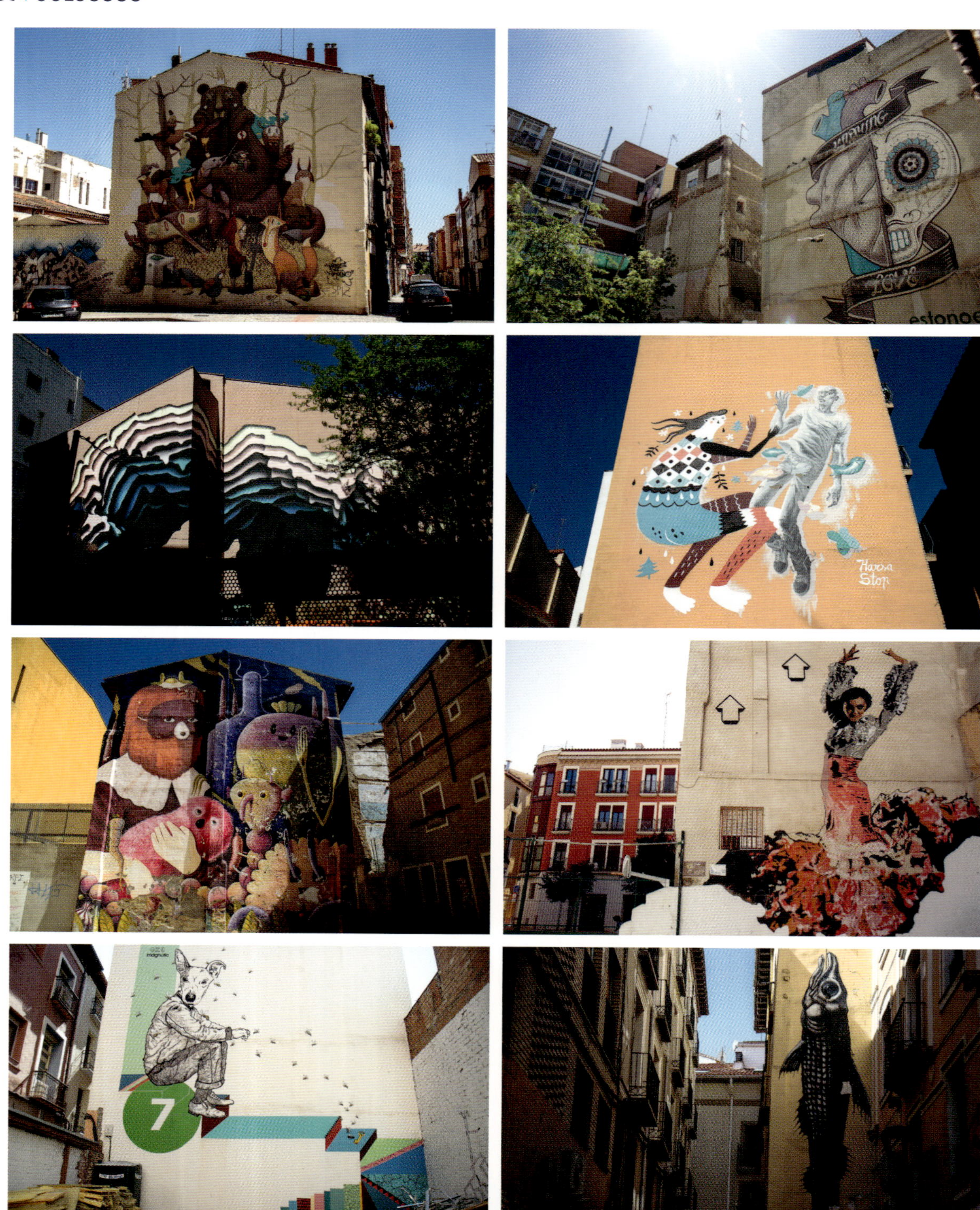

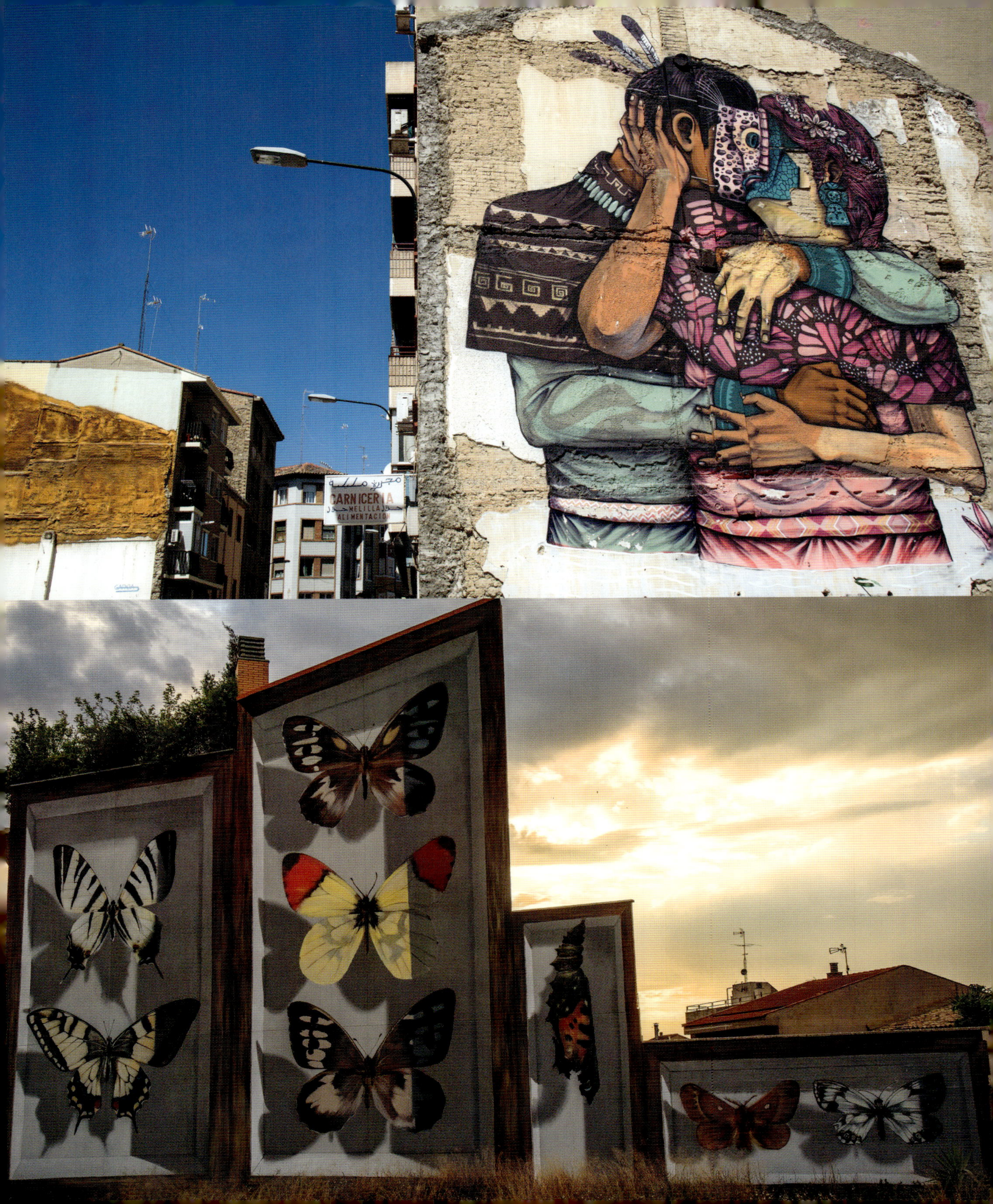
CARNICERIA
MELILLA
ALIMENTACION

ISTANBUL

TURKEY

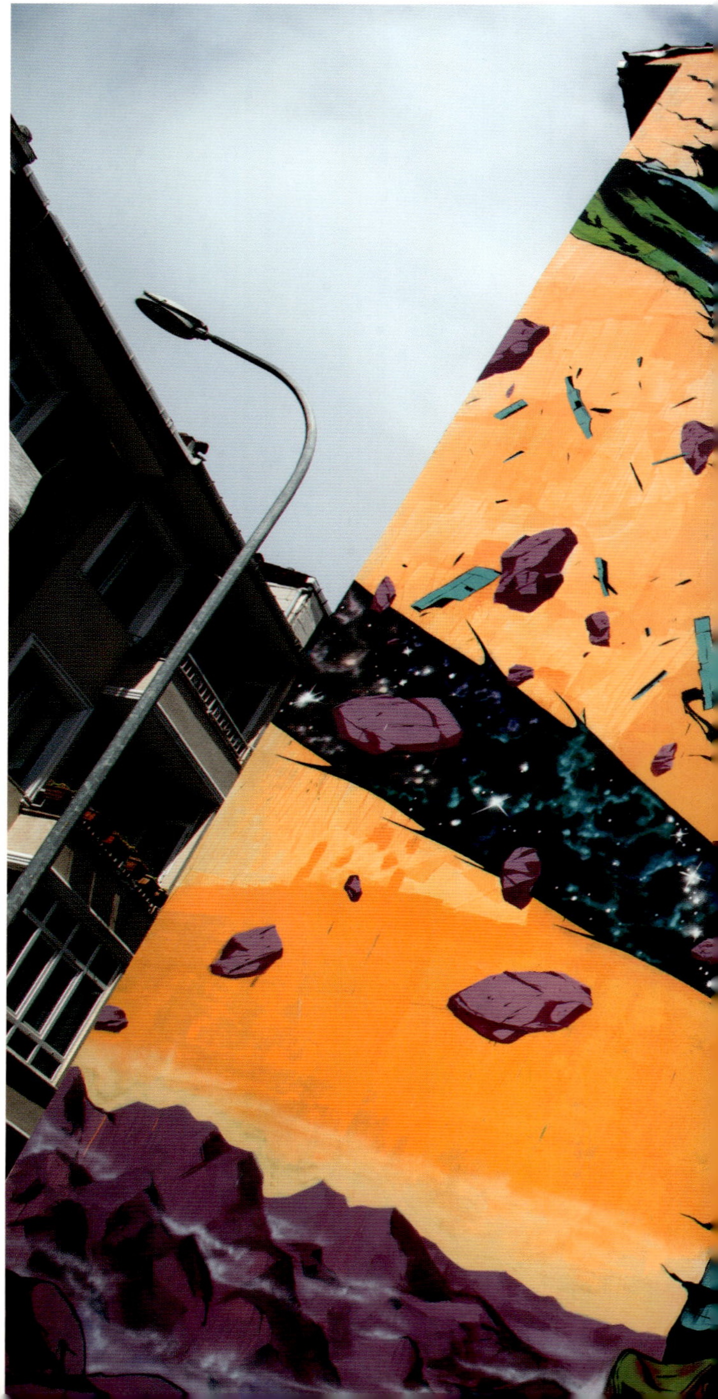

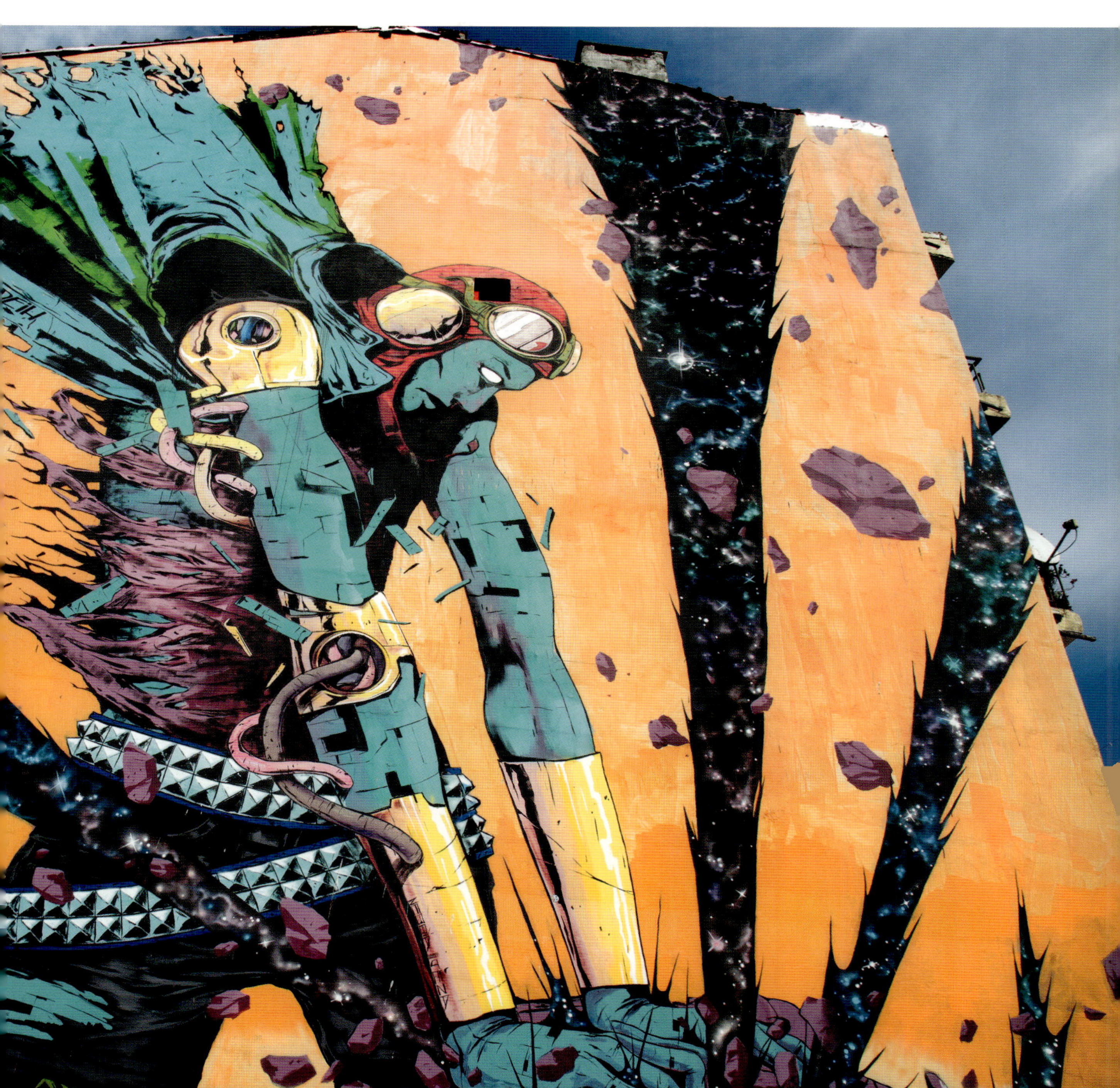

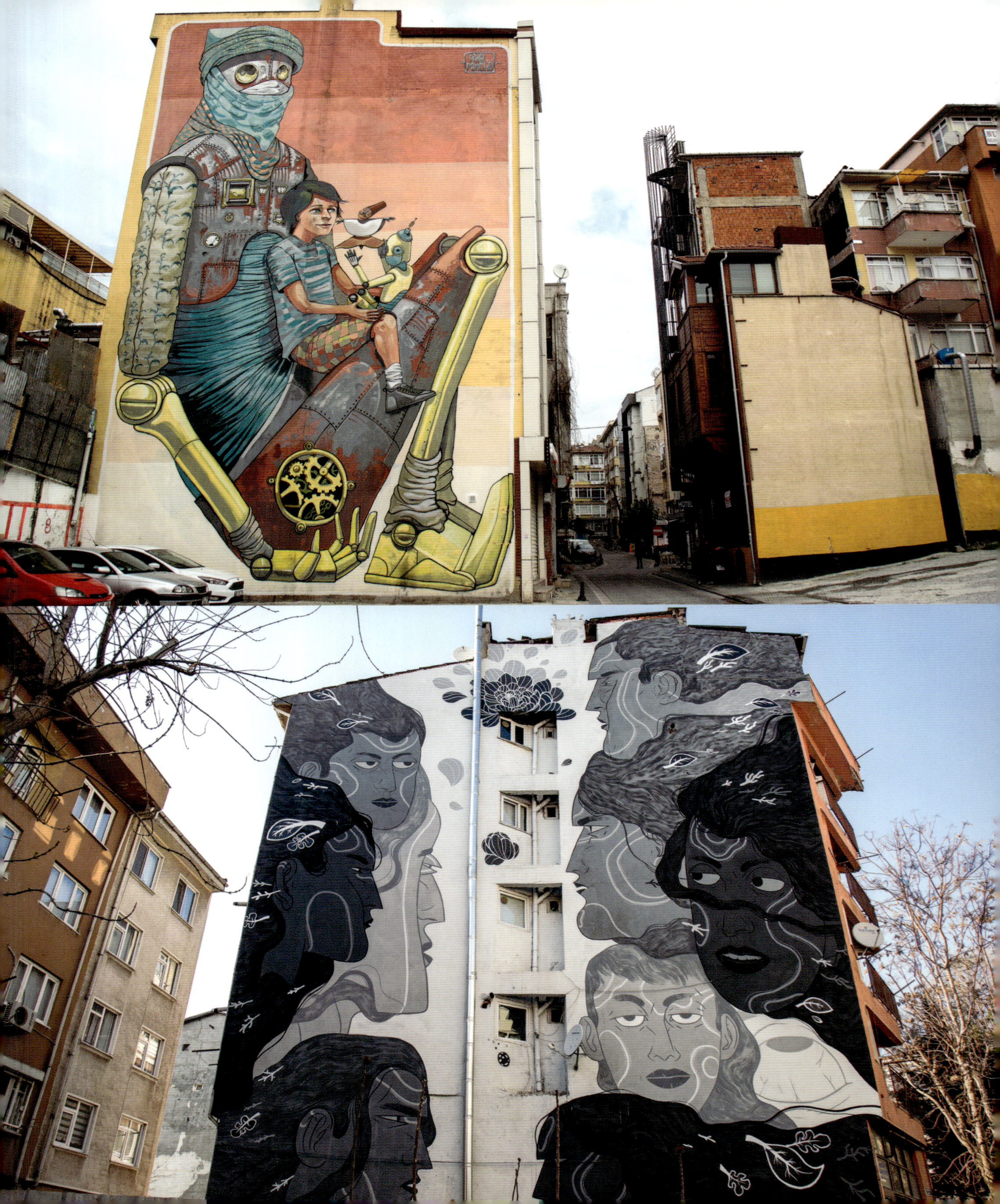

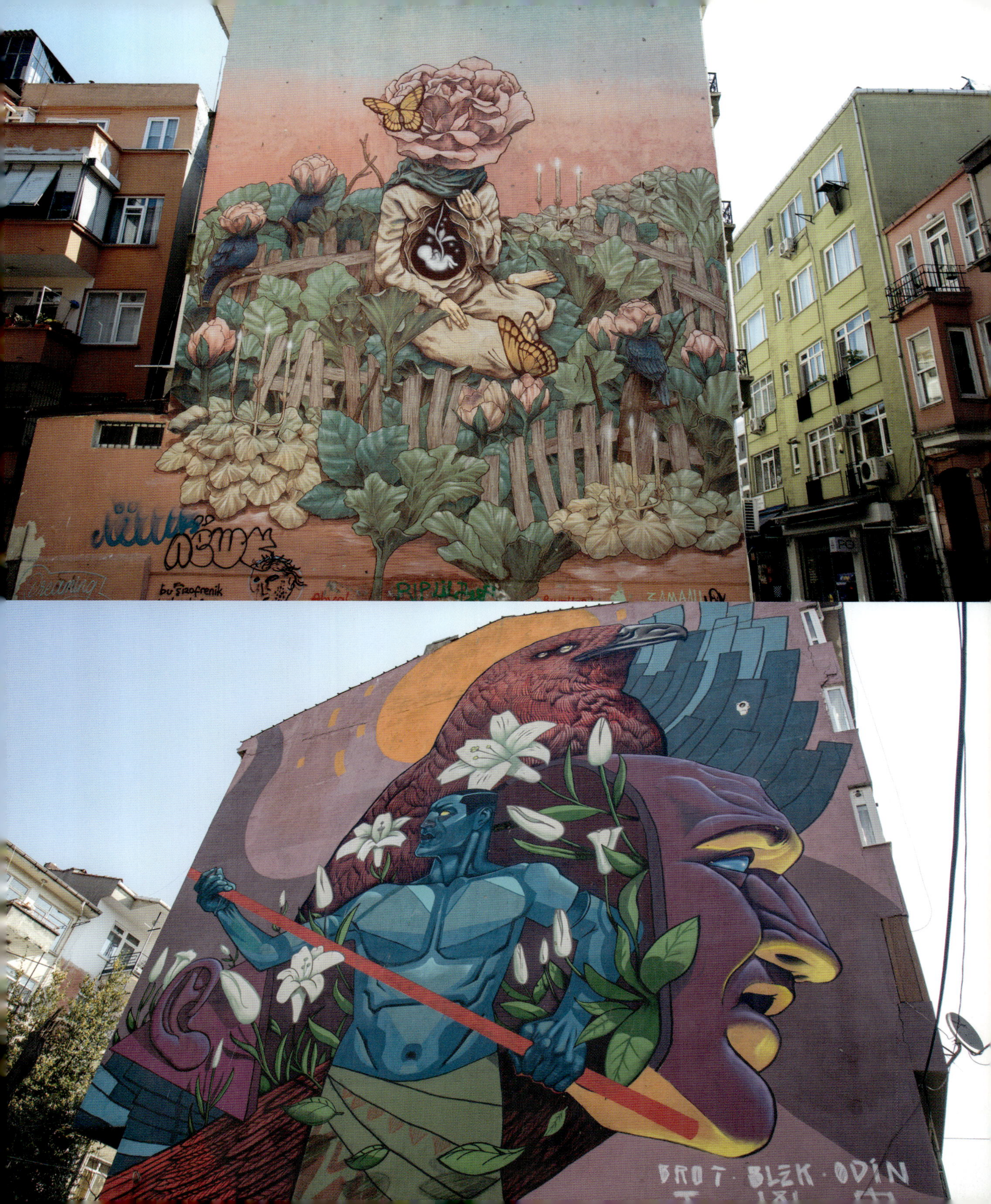
bu şizofrenik
RIP
ZAMANI
BROT · BLEK · ODIN

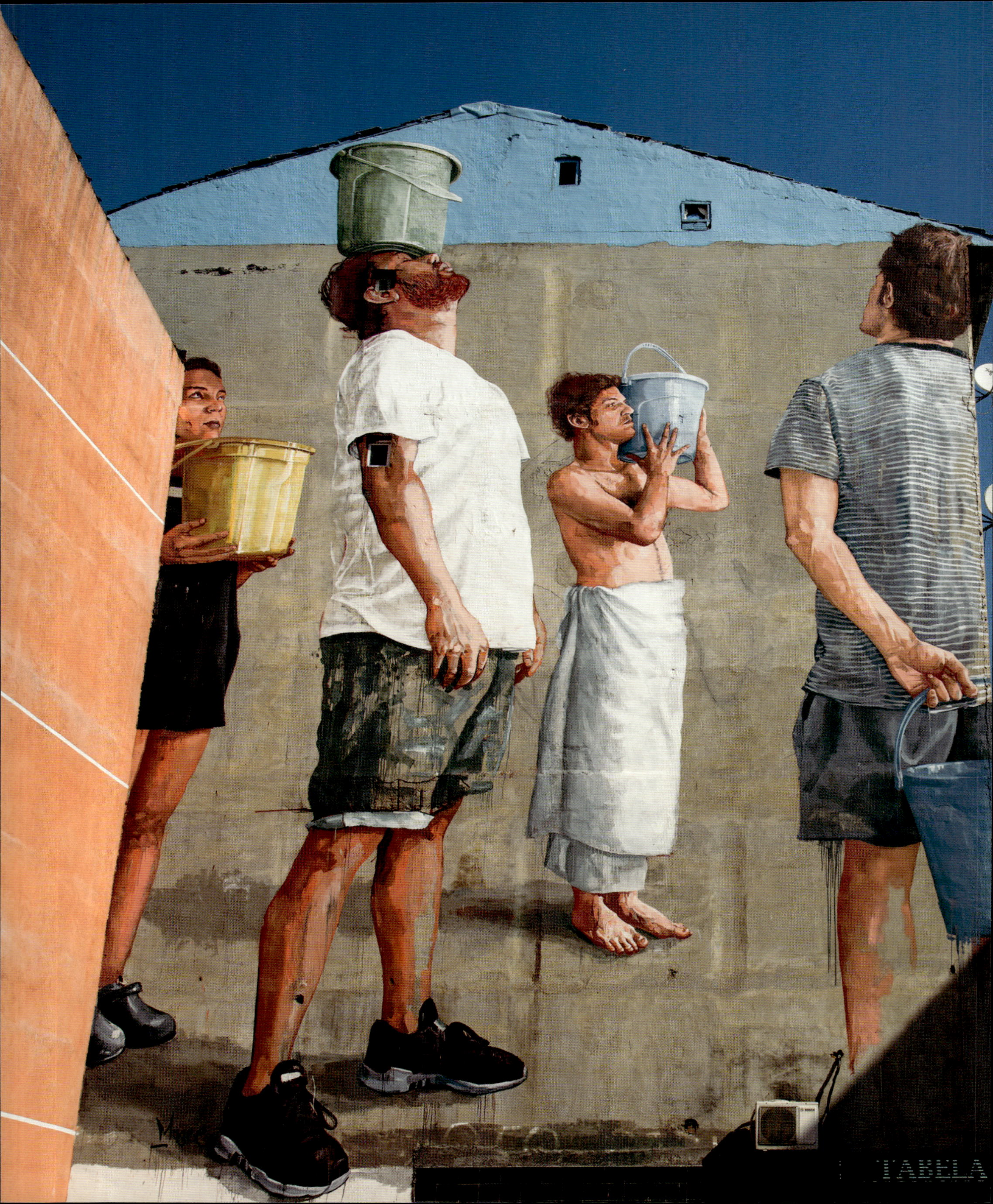

BOSCH
TABELA

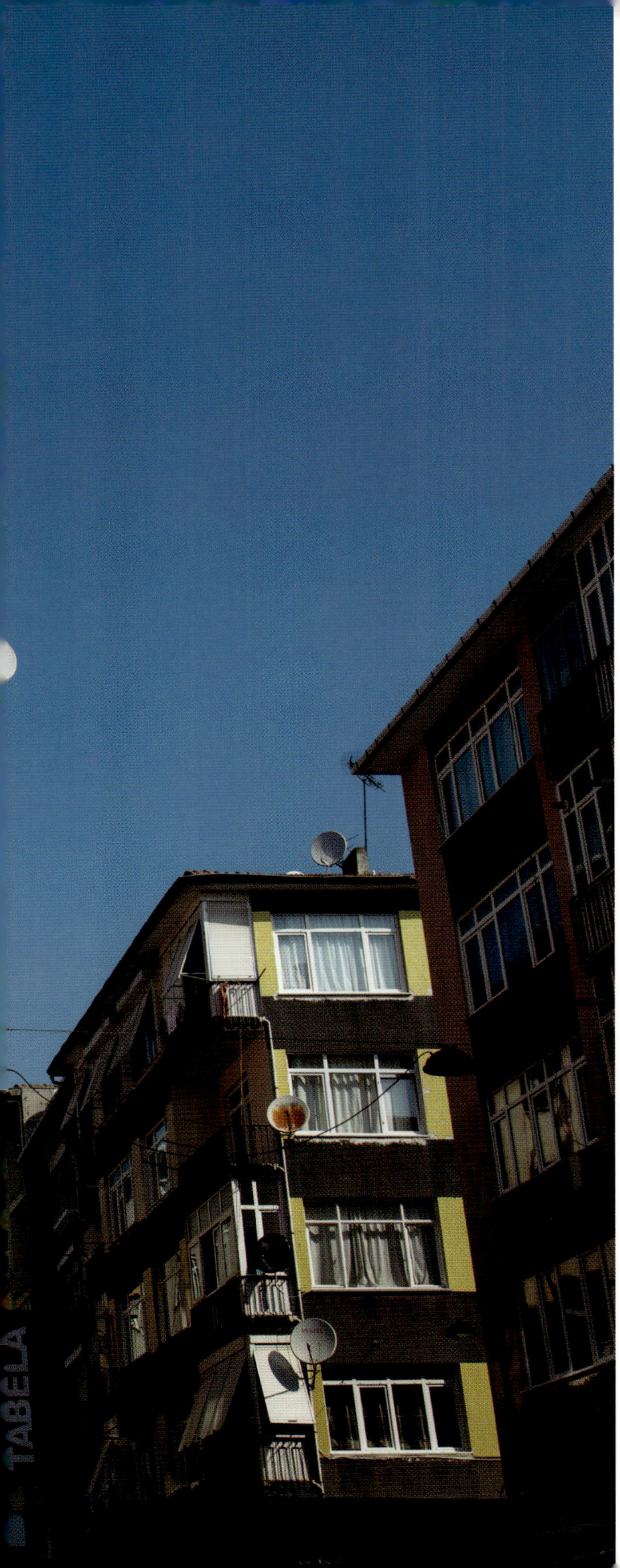

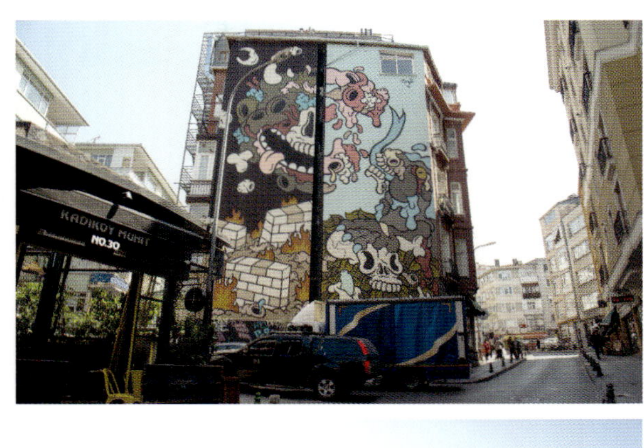

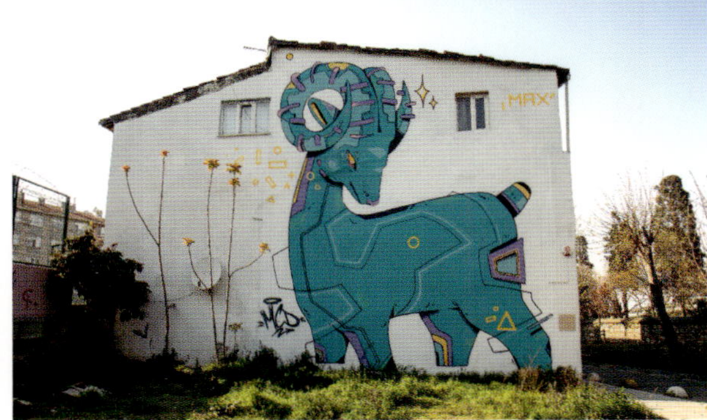

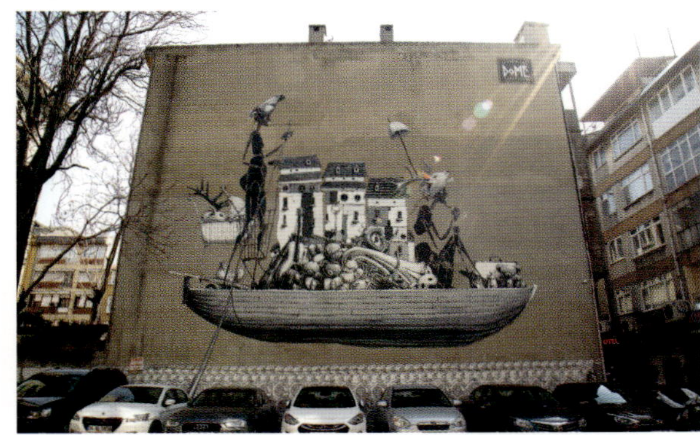

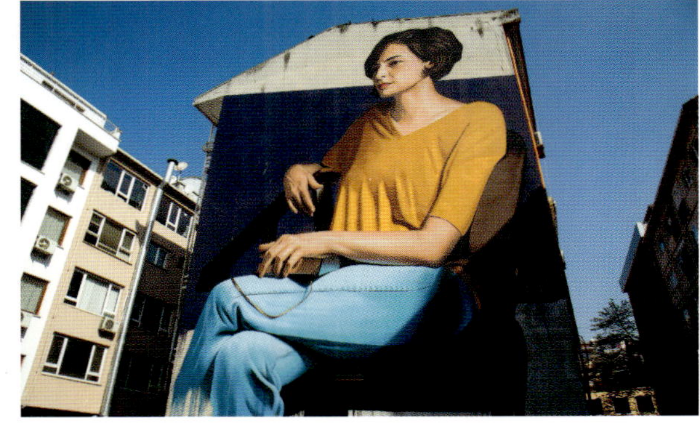

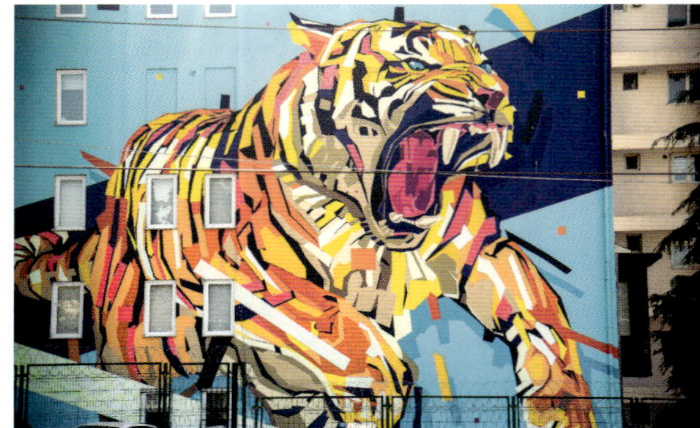
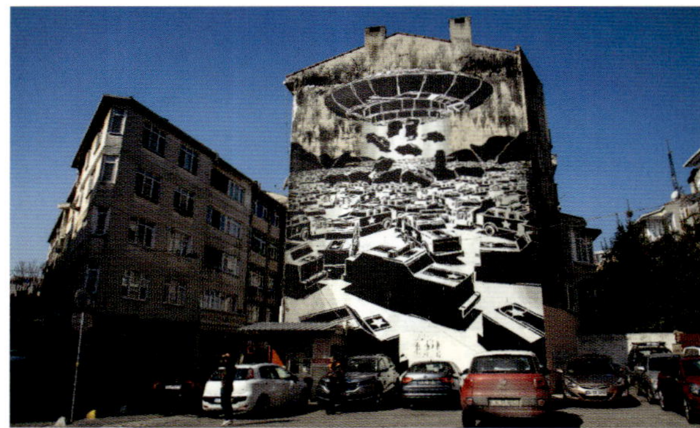
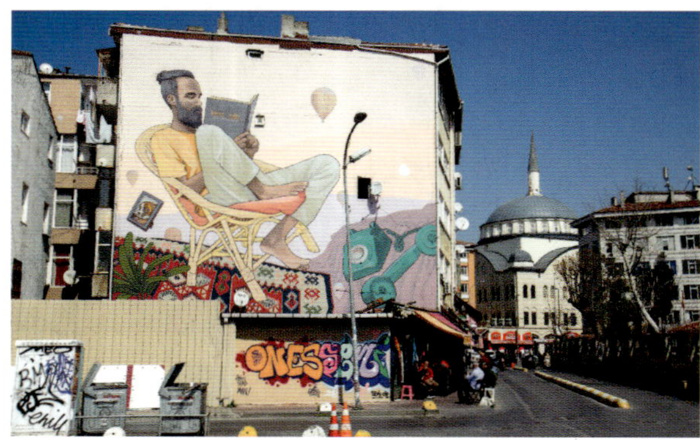
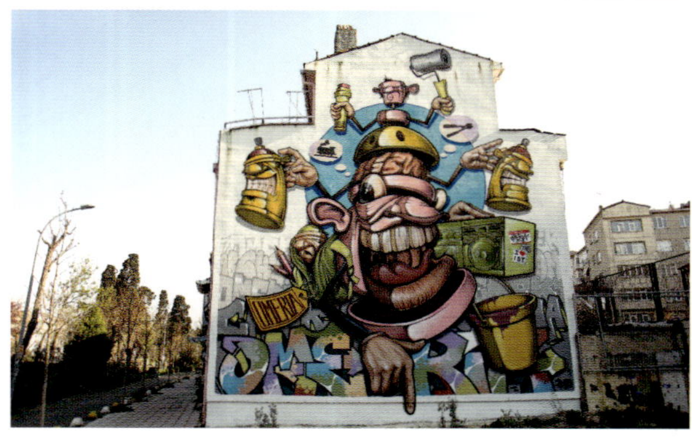

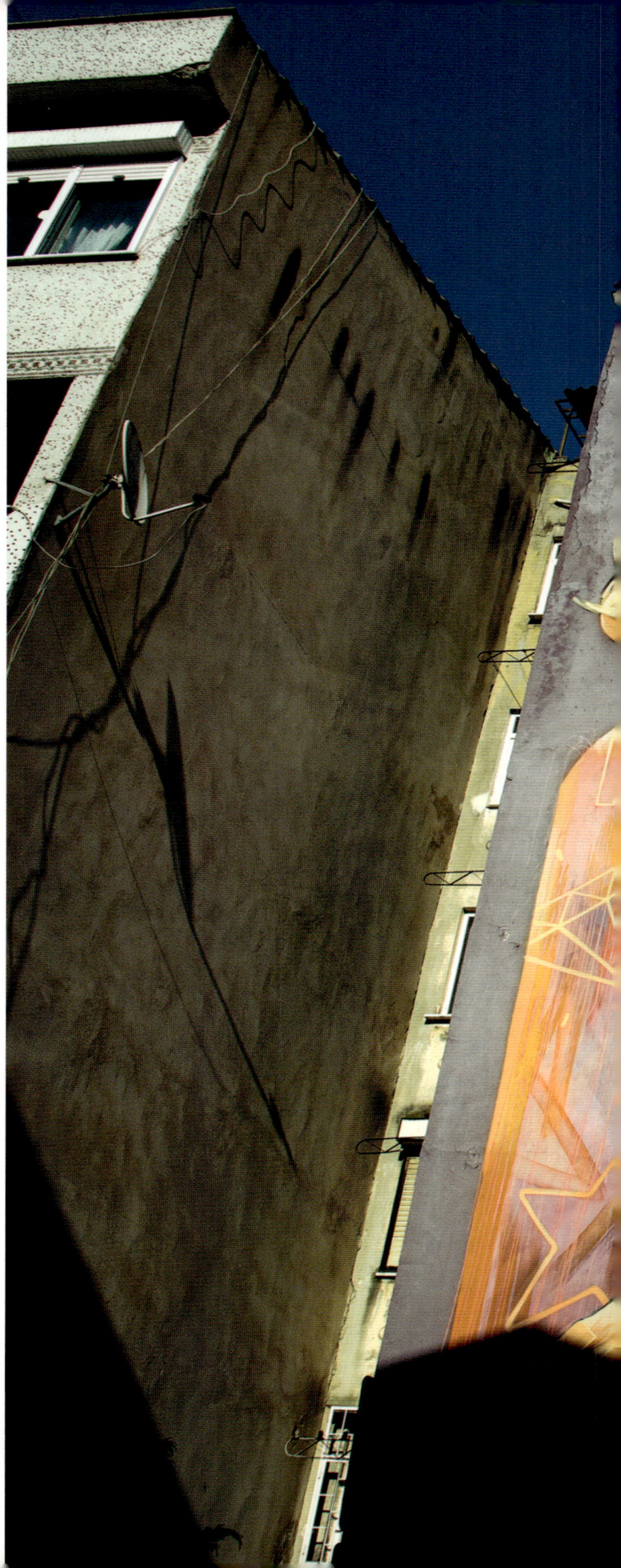

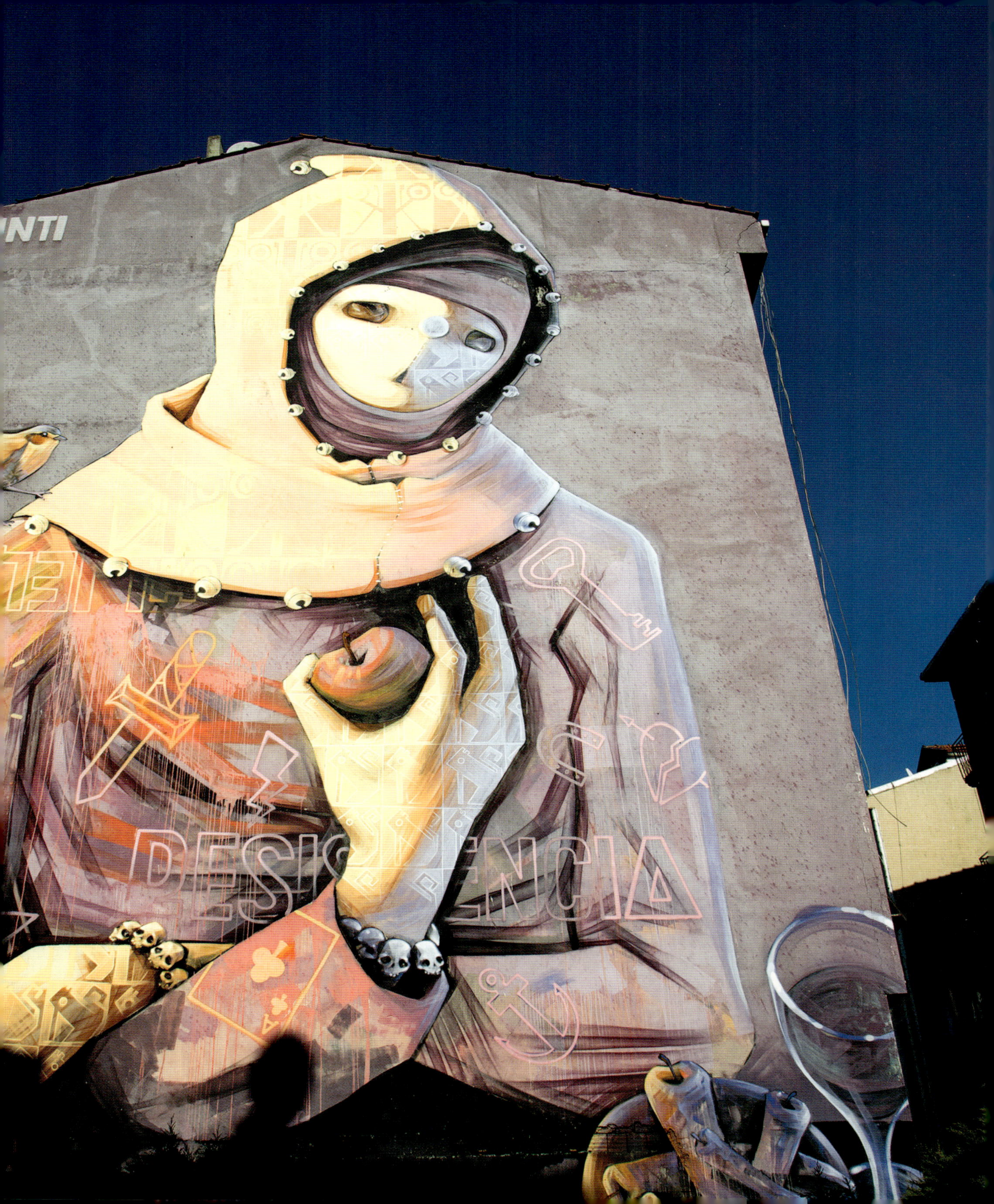
INTI
DESIDENCIA

ANTWERP

BELGIUM

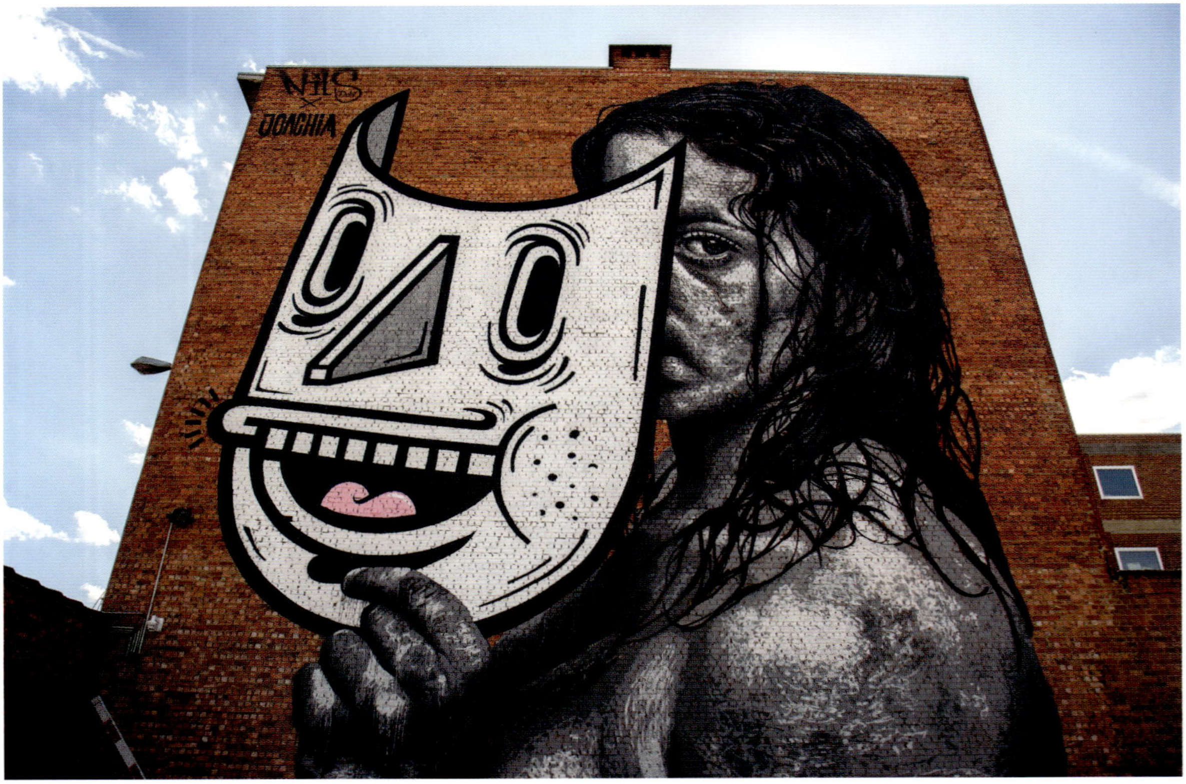

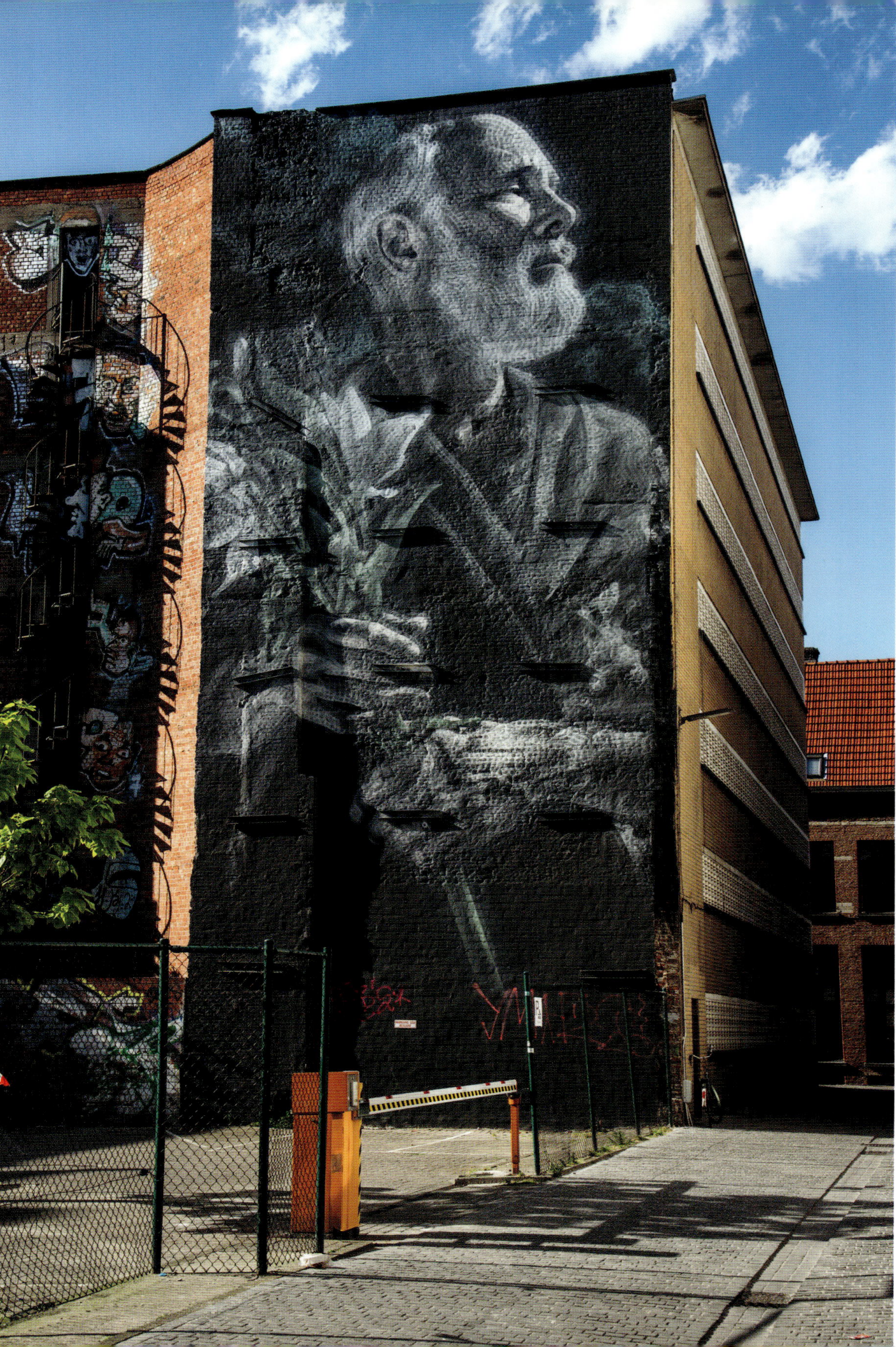

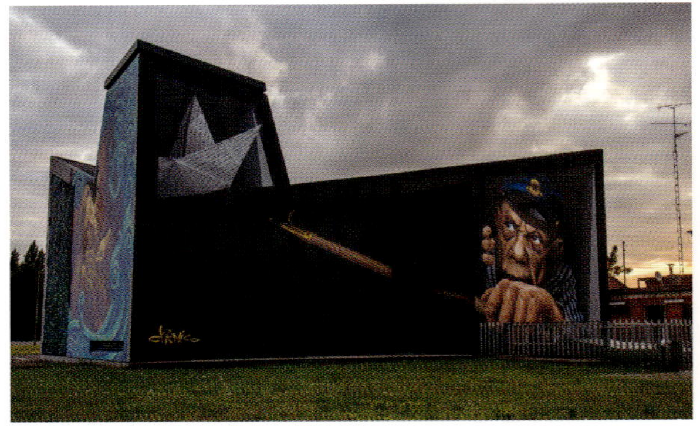

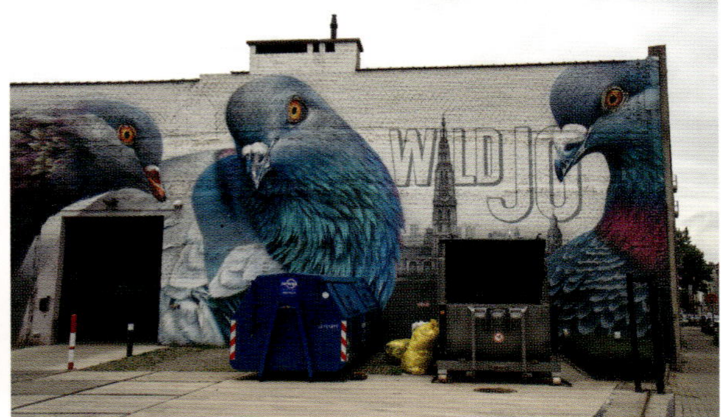

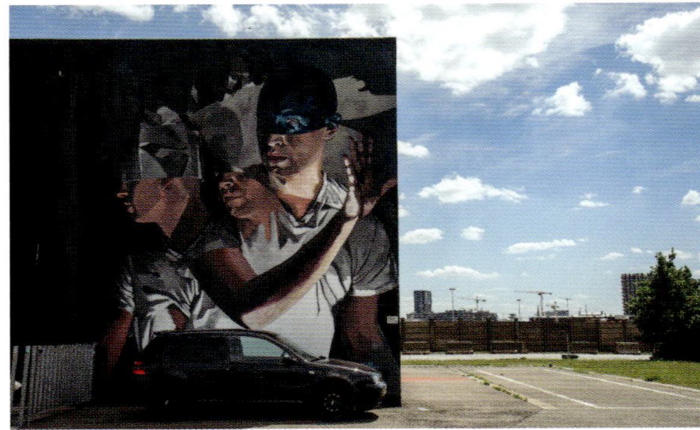

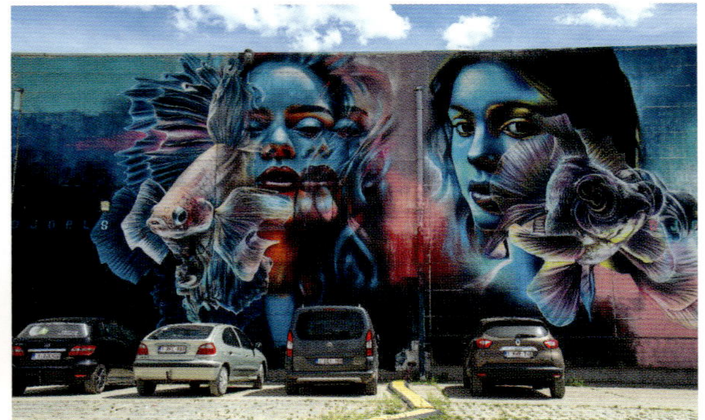

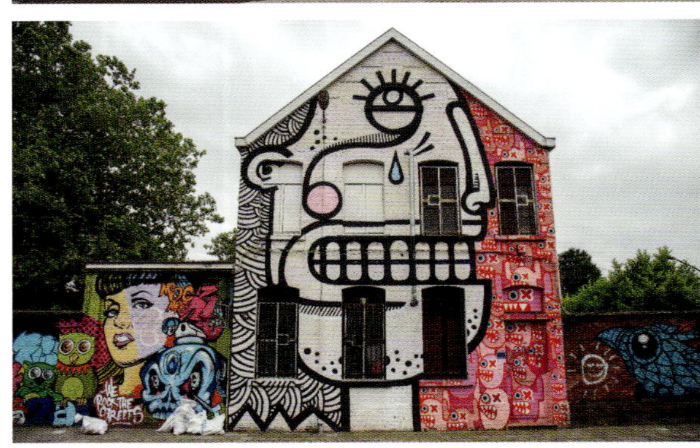

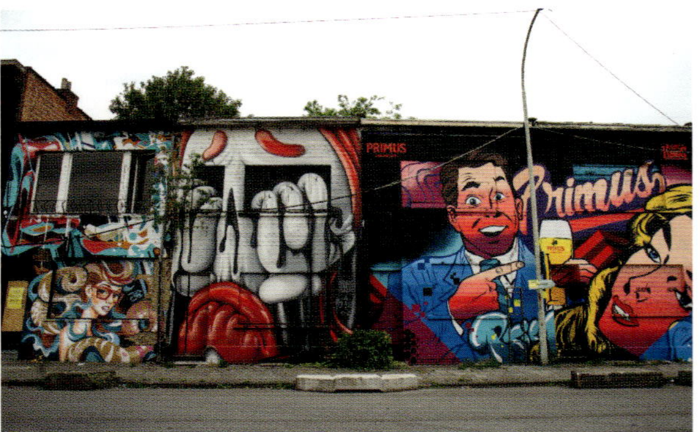

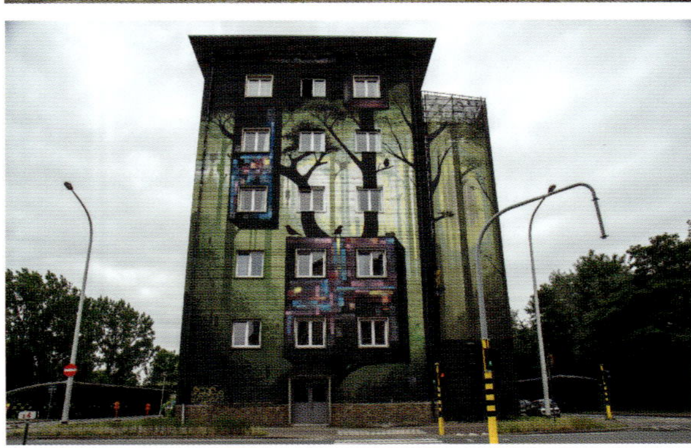

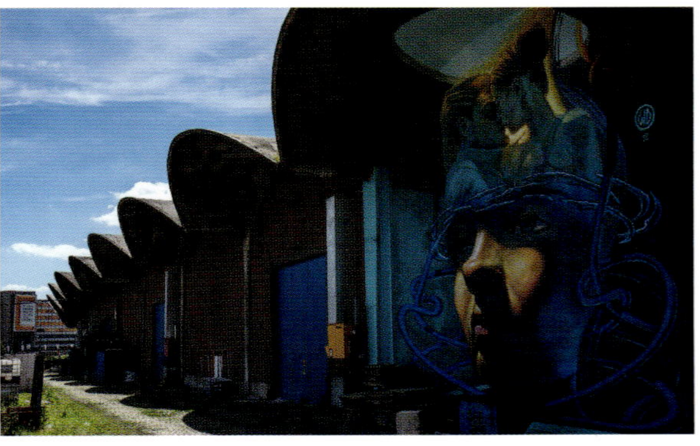

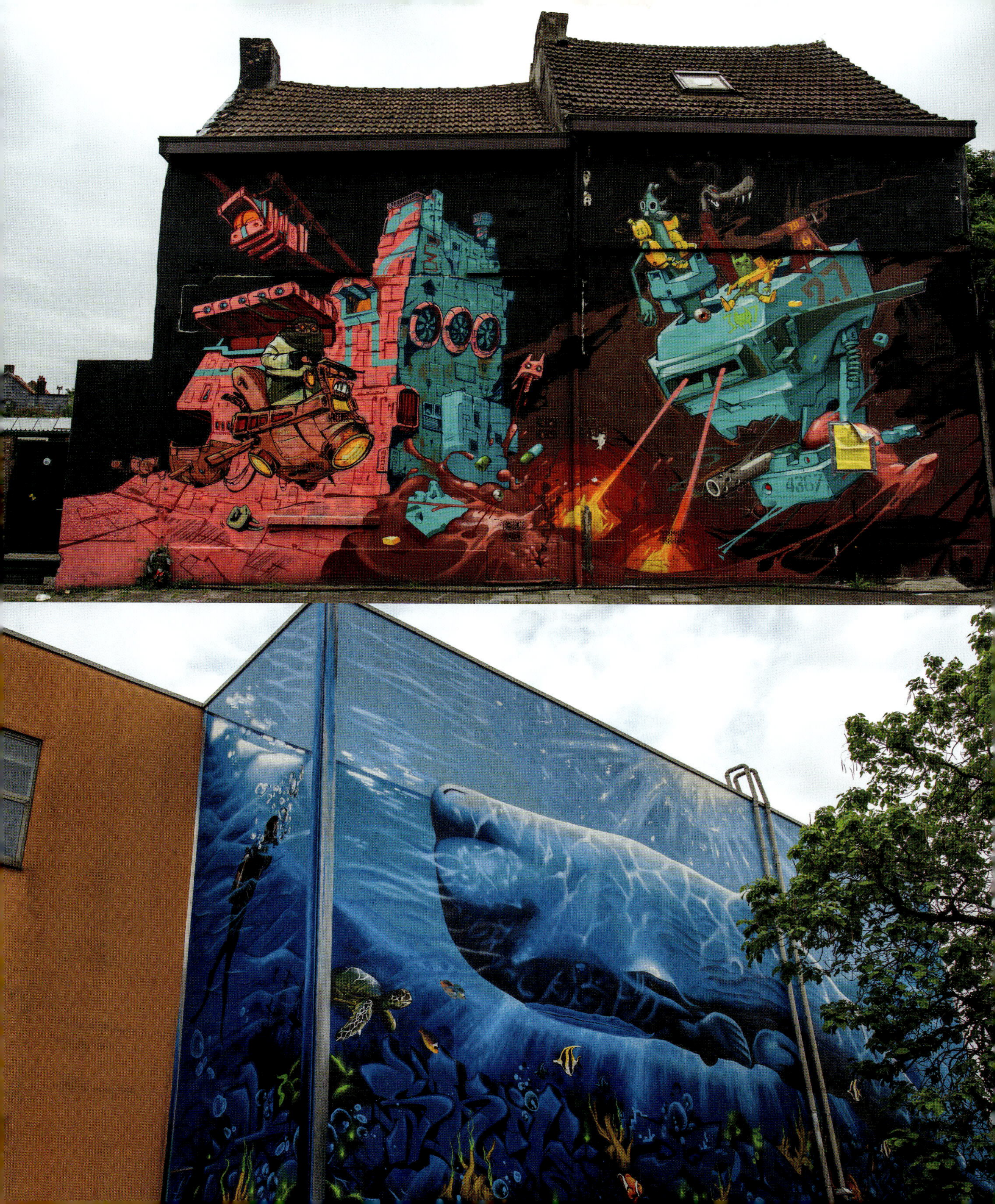

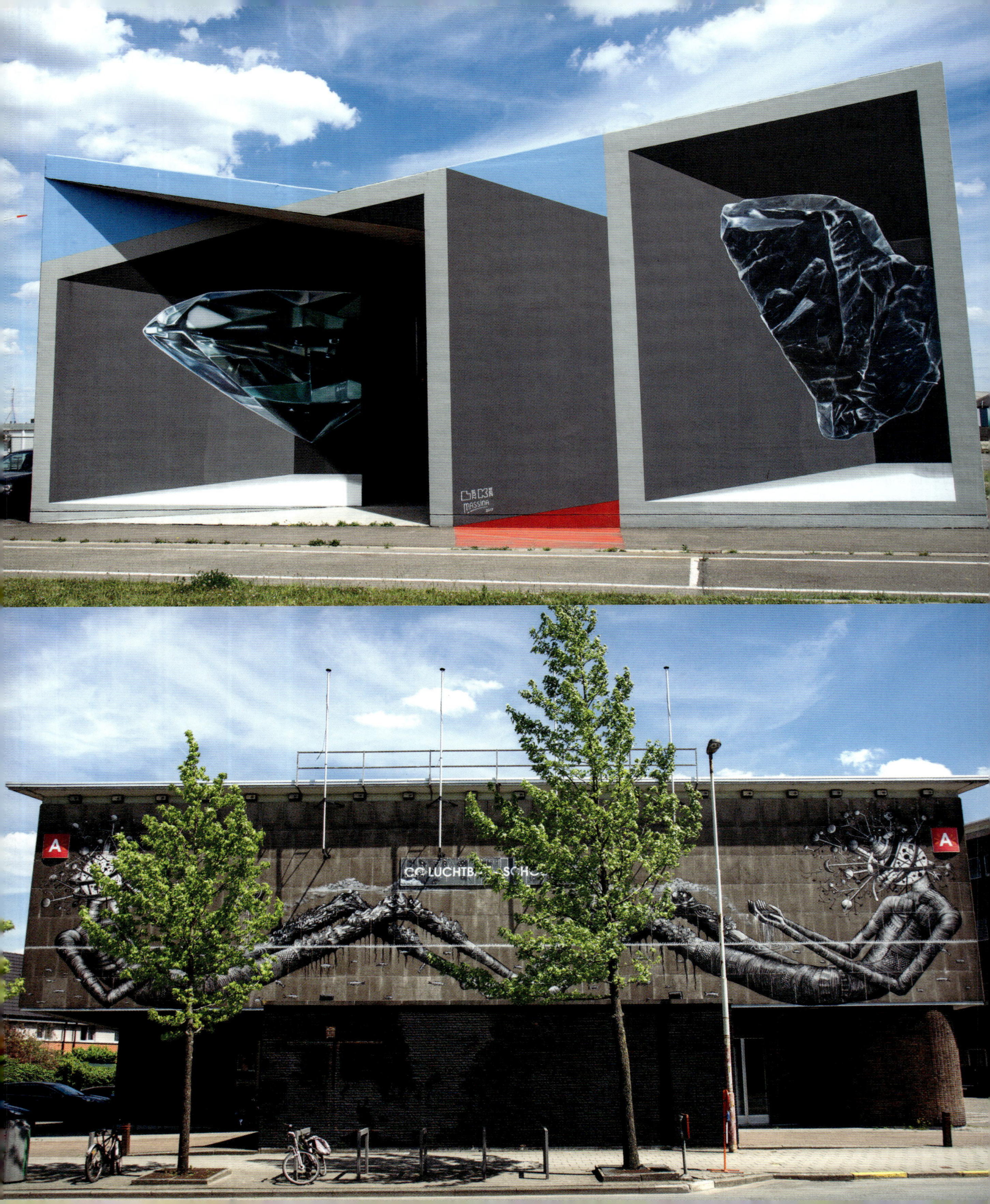

MASSINA
LUCHTB   SCH
A
A

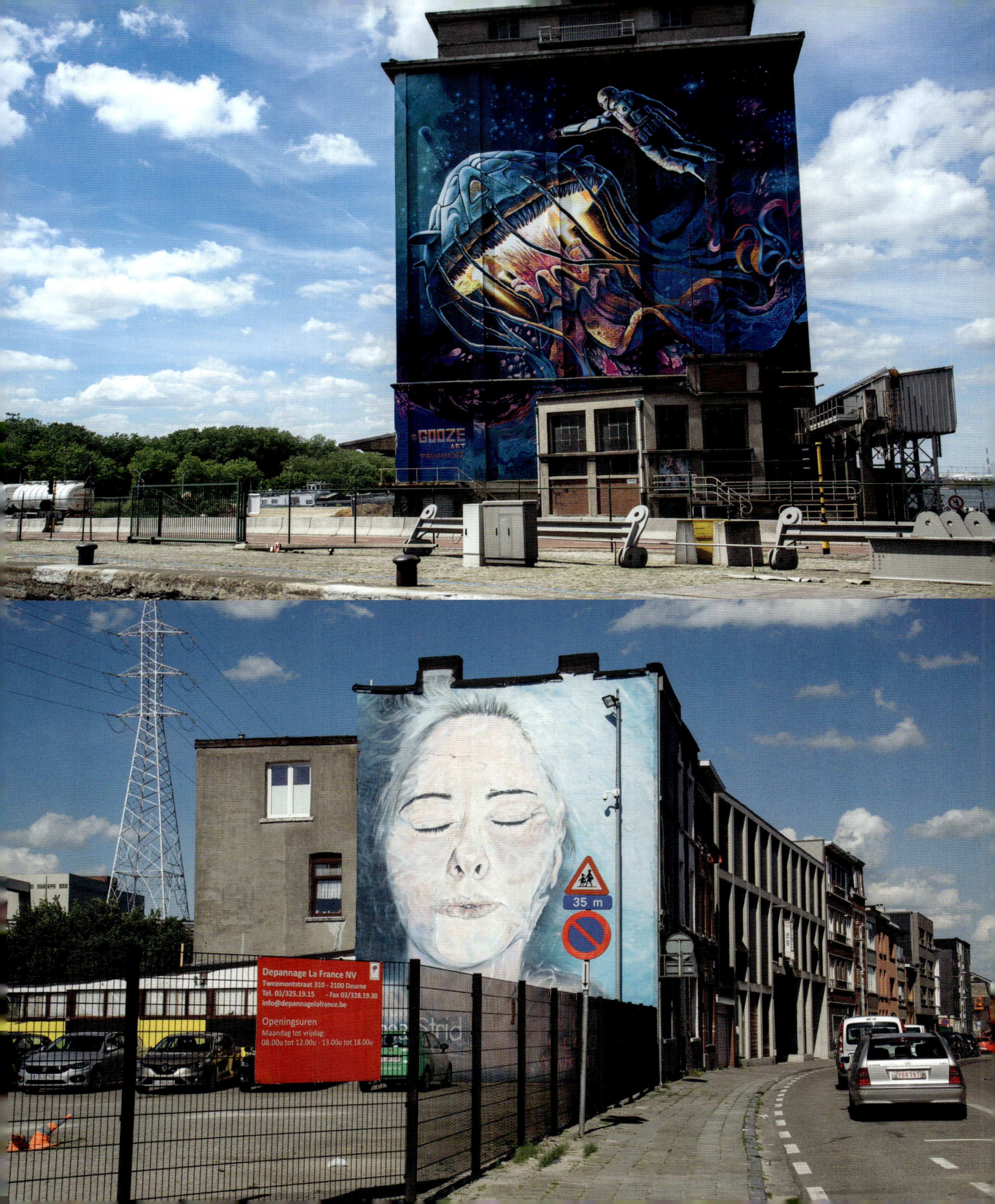
GOOZE
ART
Depannage La France NV
Tweemontstraat 310 - 2100 Deurne
Tel. 03/325.19.15   - Fax 03/328.19.30
info@depannagelafrance.be
Openingsuren
Maandag tot vrijdag:
08.00u tot 12.00u - 13.00u tot 18.00u
35 m

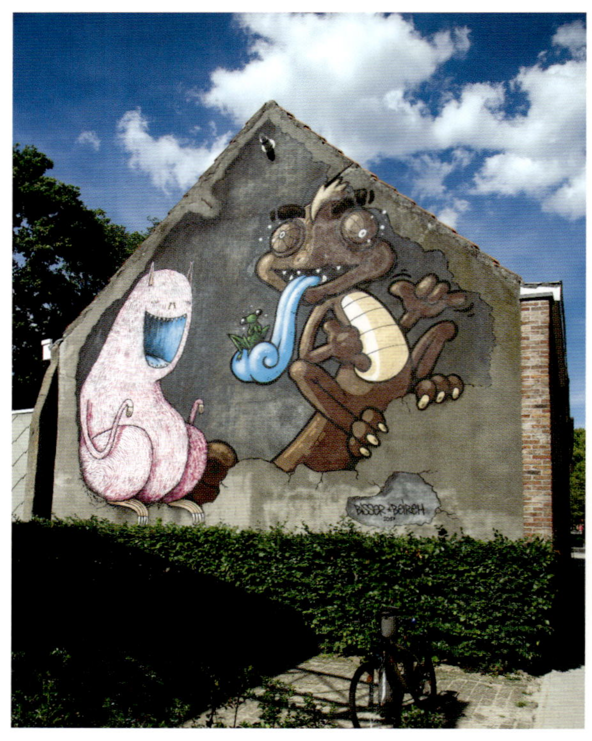

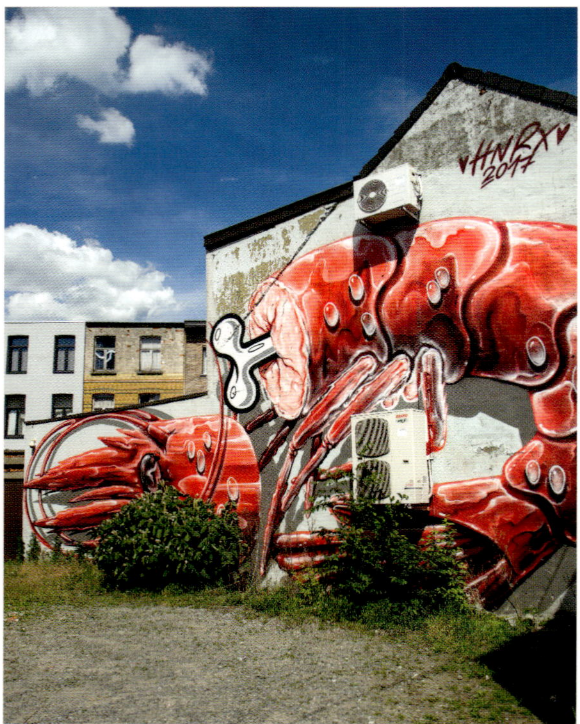

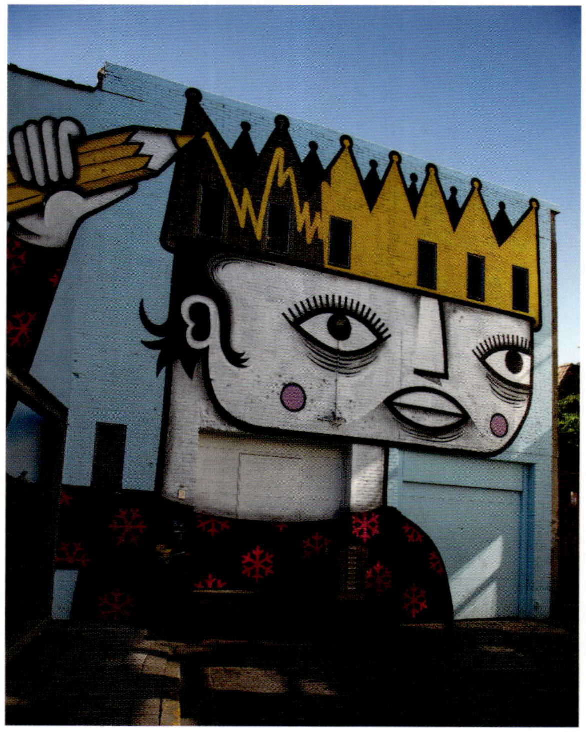

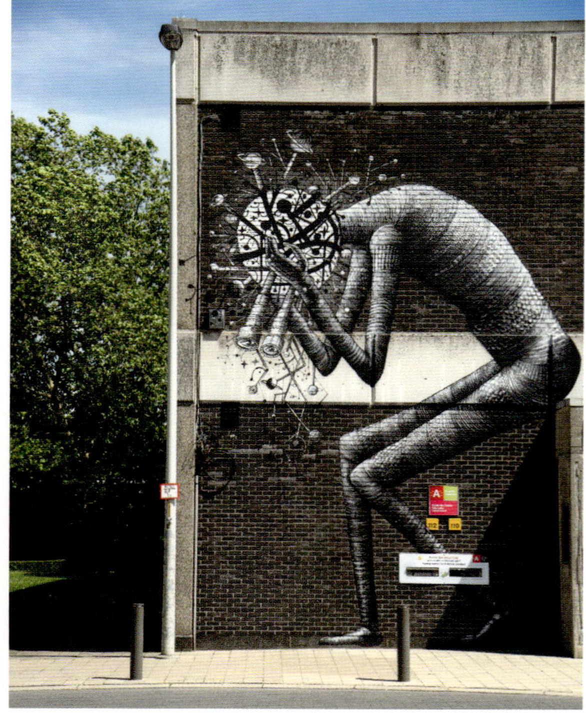

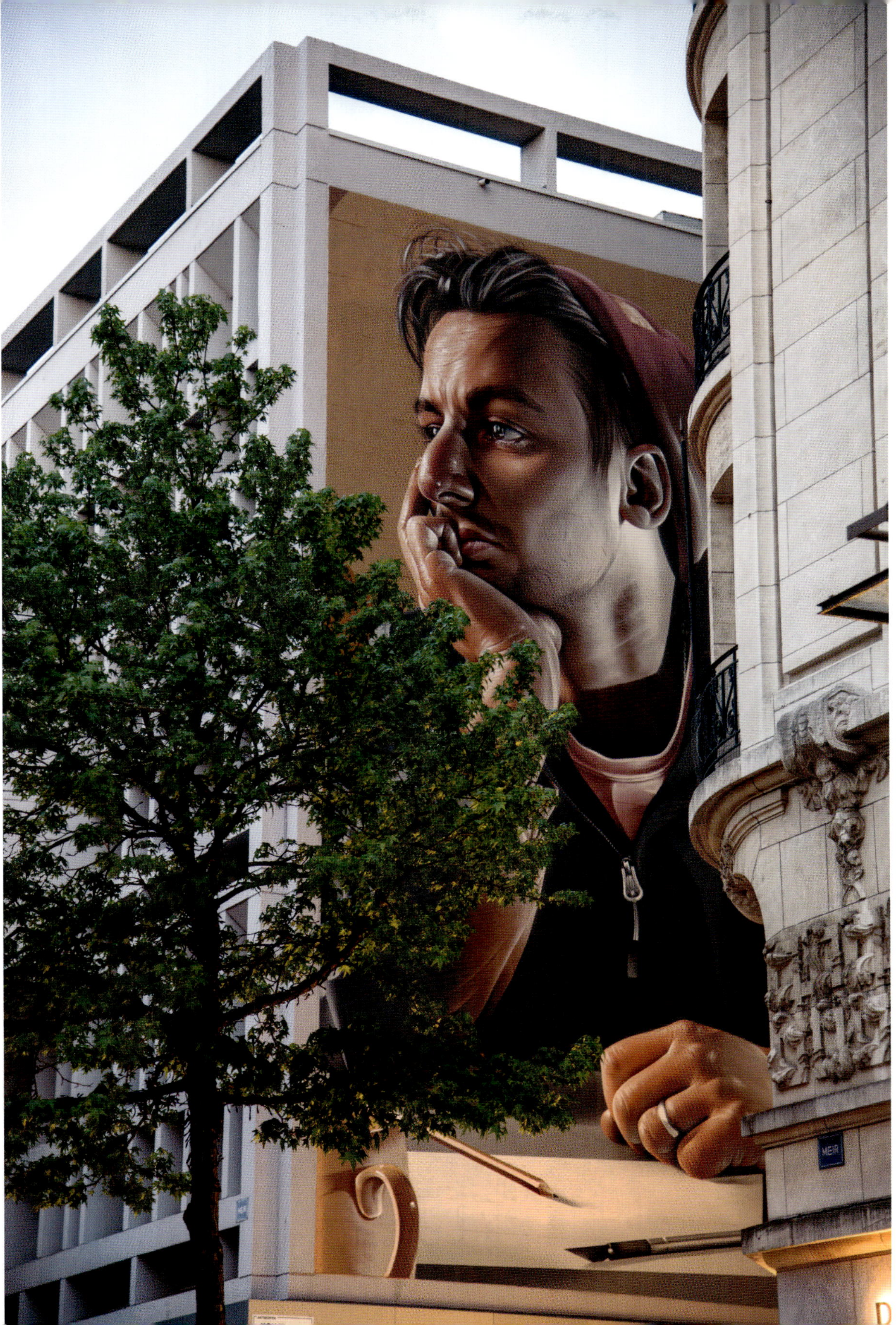

BRUSSELS

BELGIUM

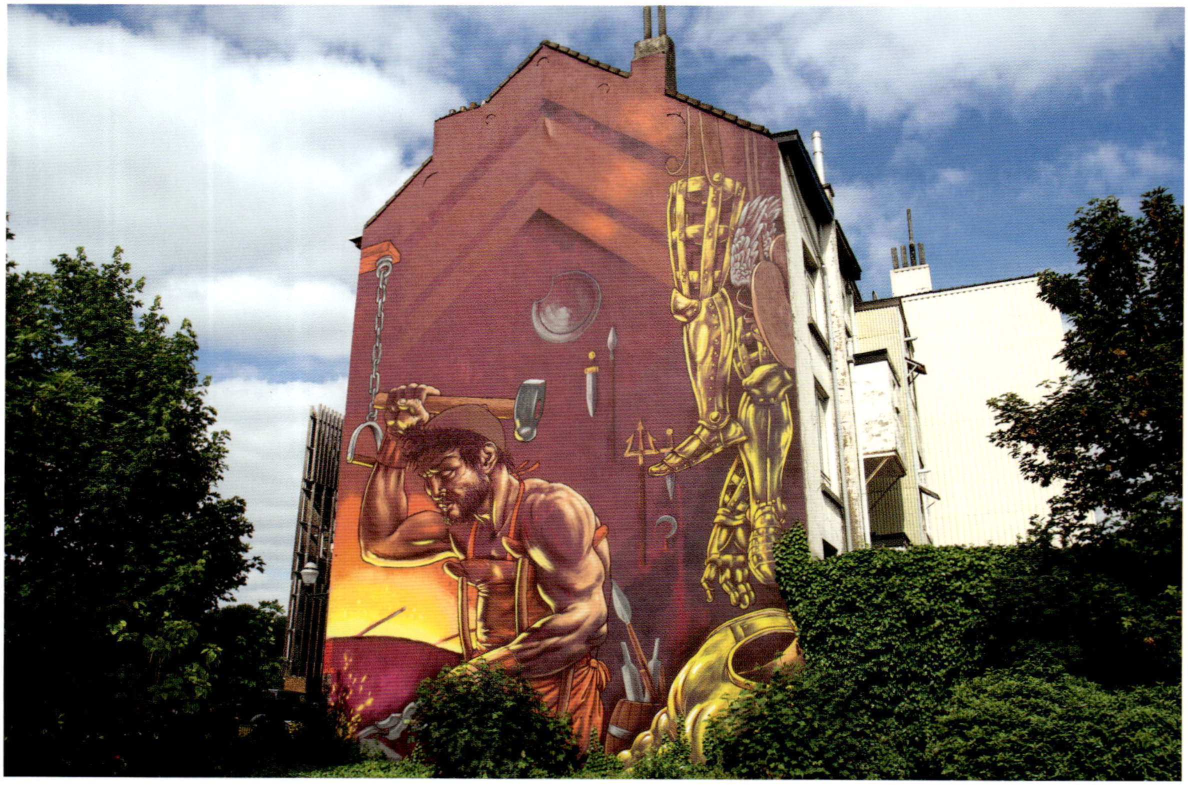

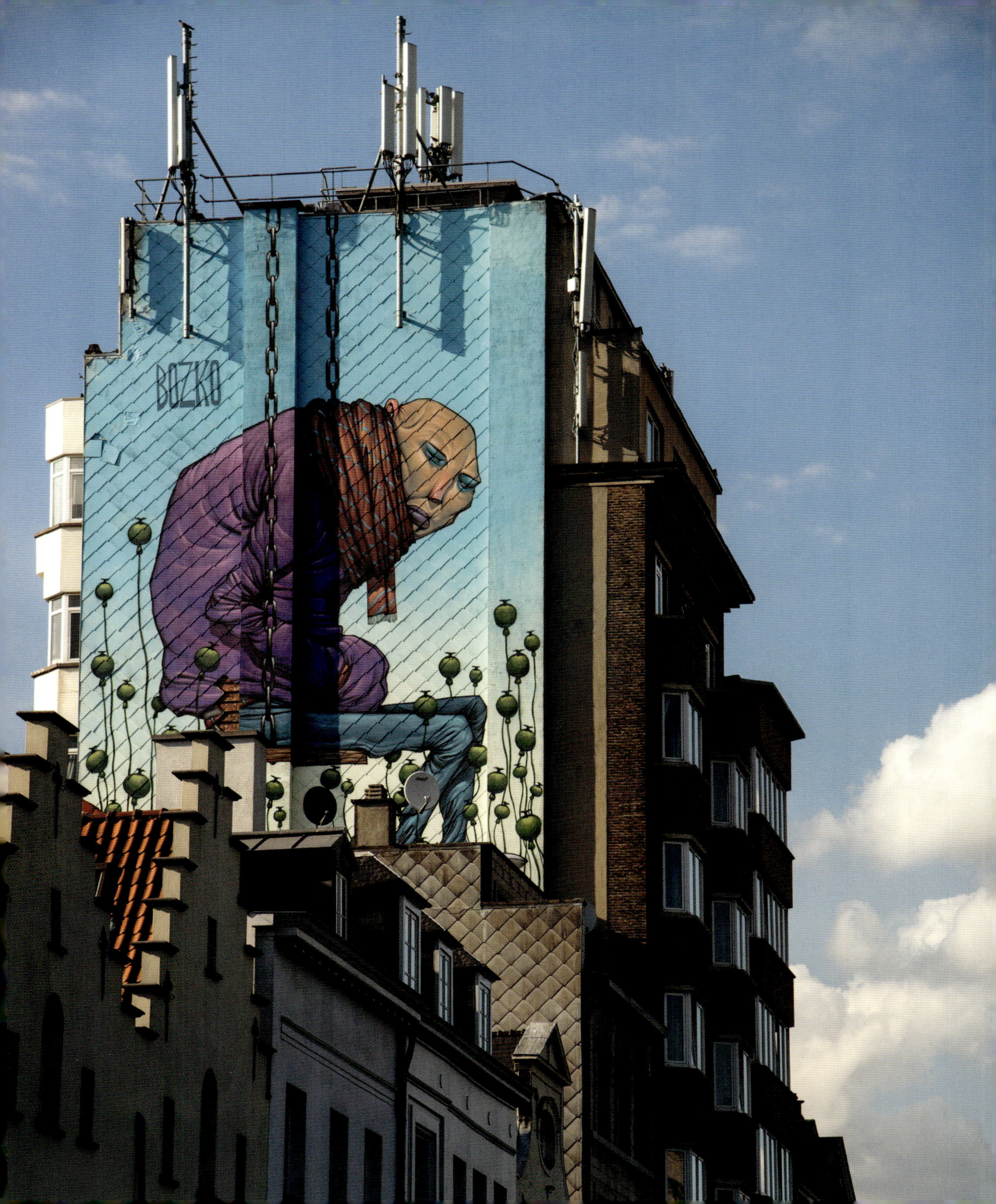
BOZKO

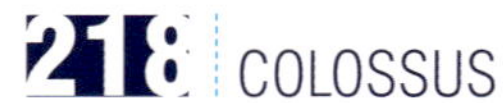

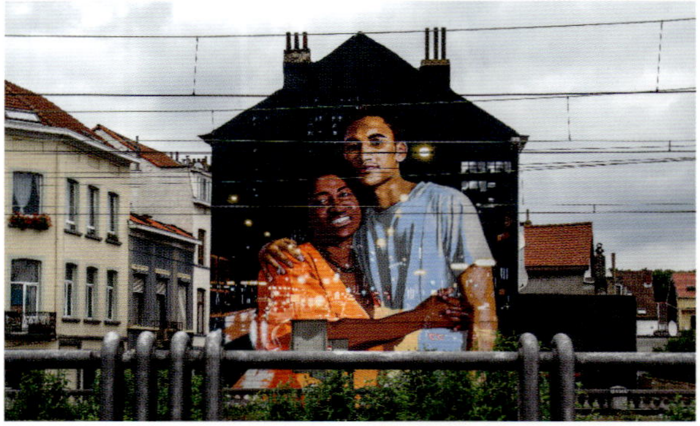

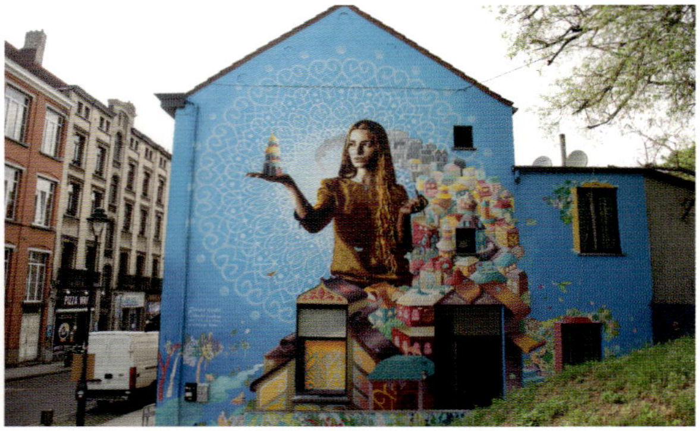

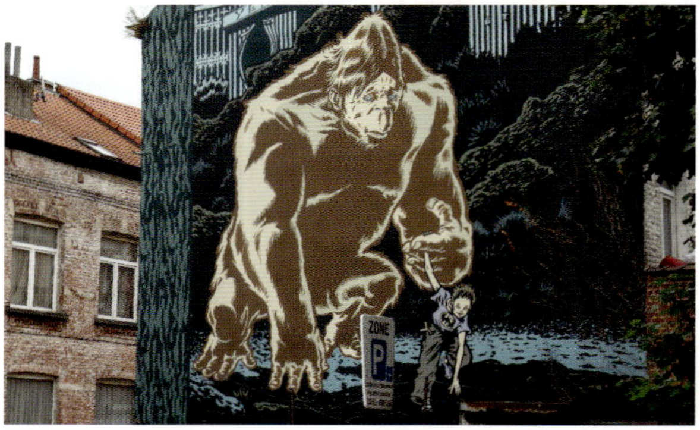

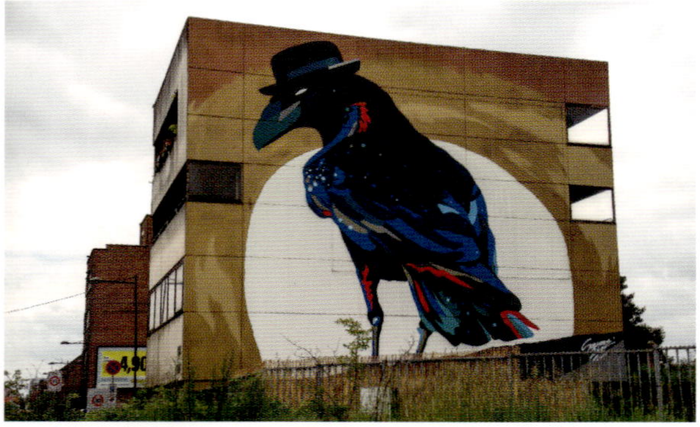

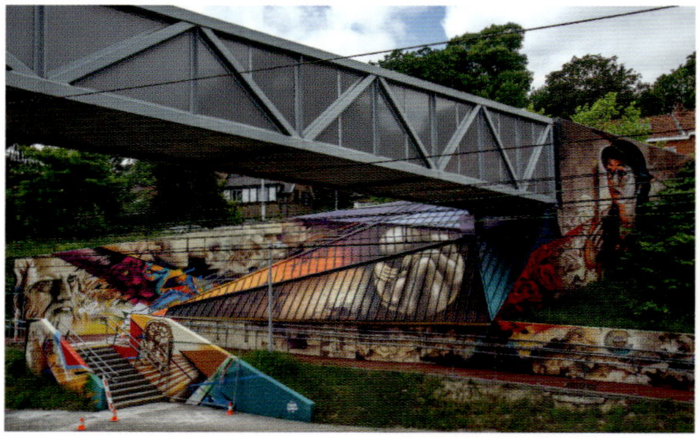

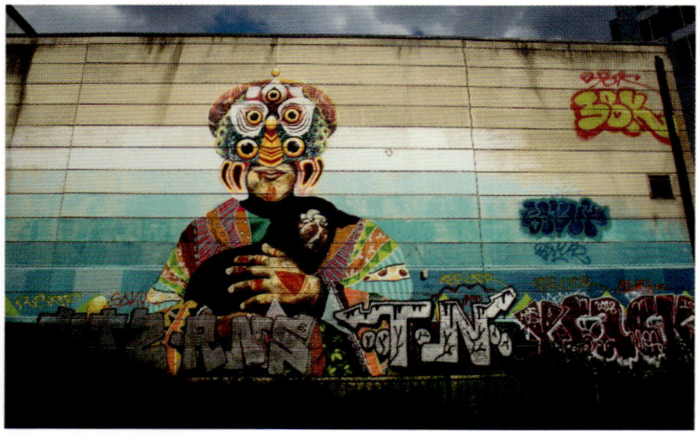

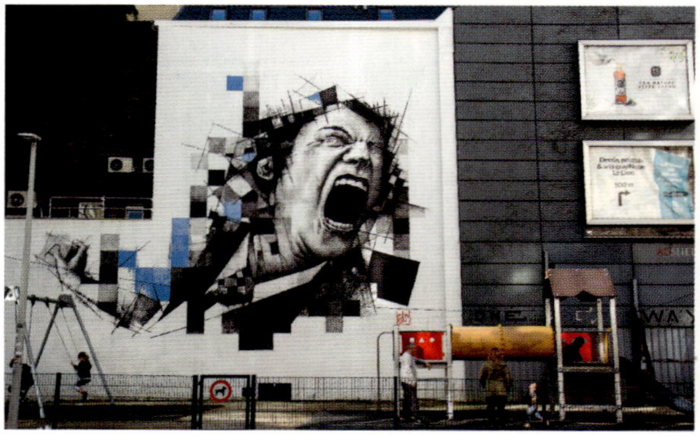

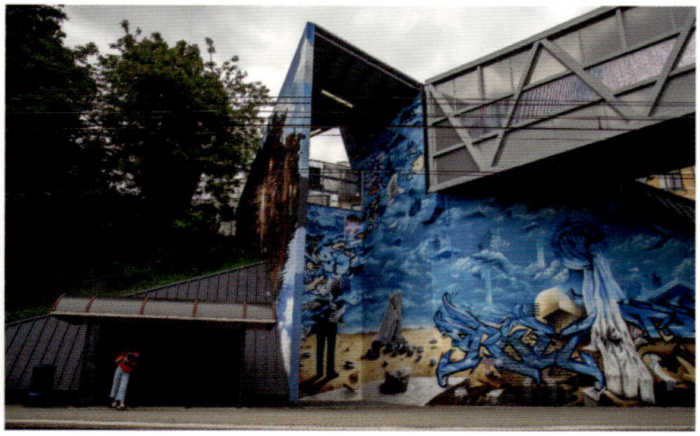

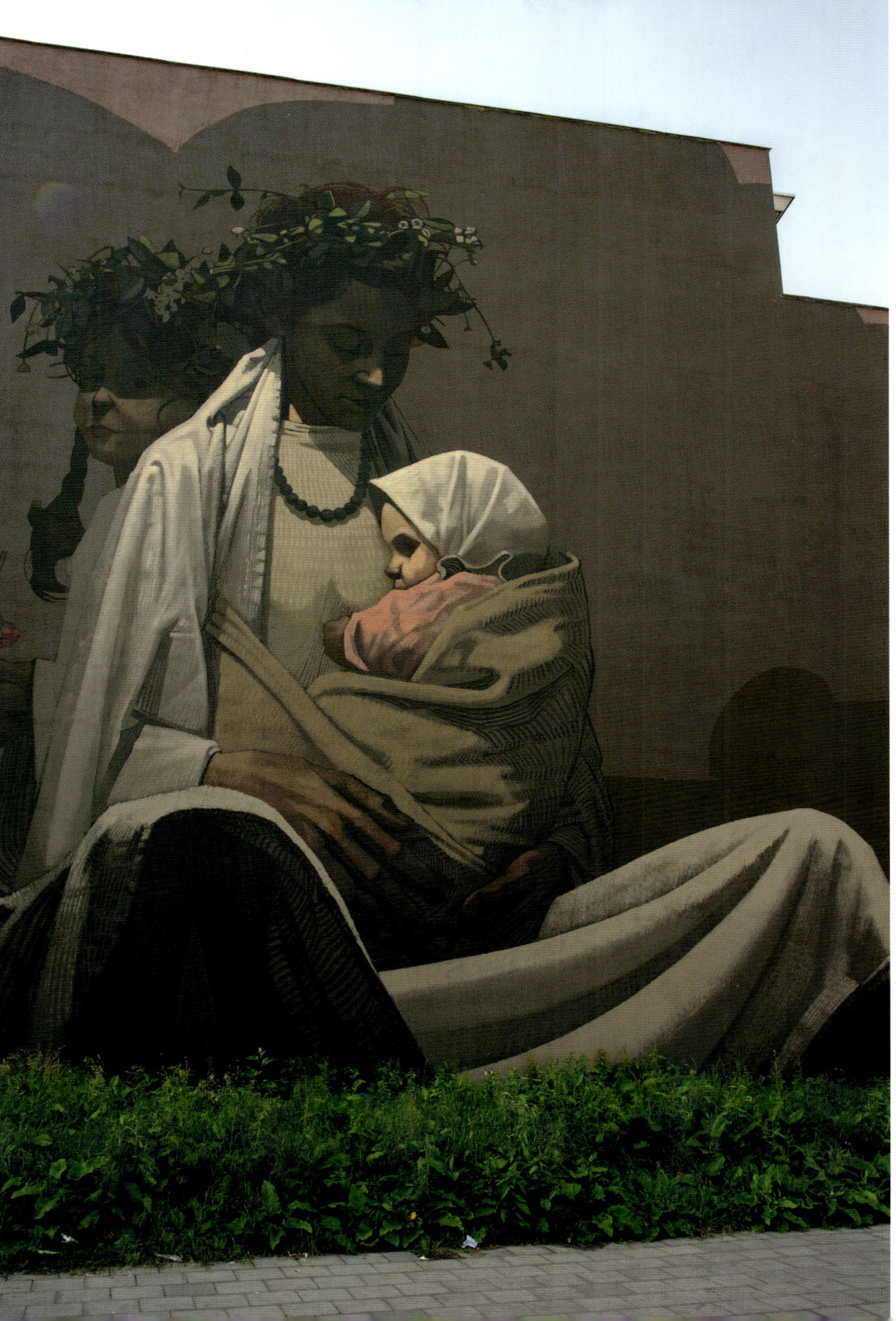

PARIS

FRANCE

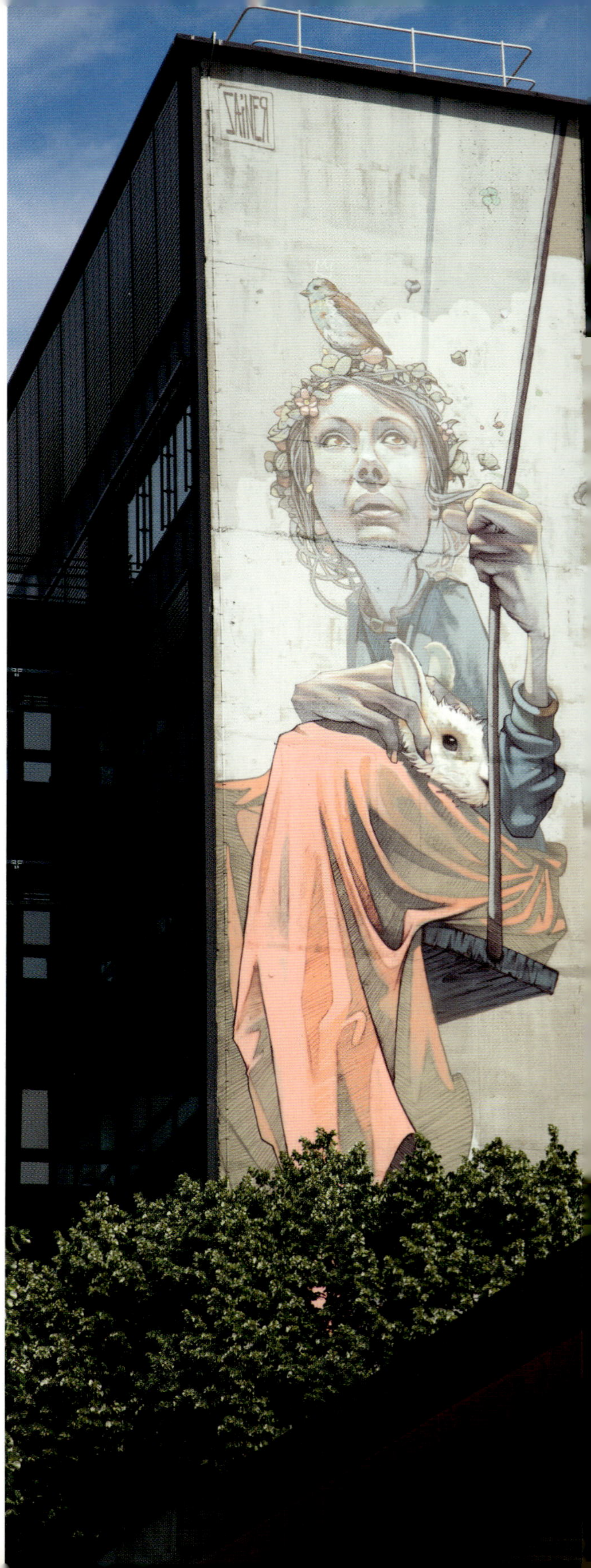

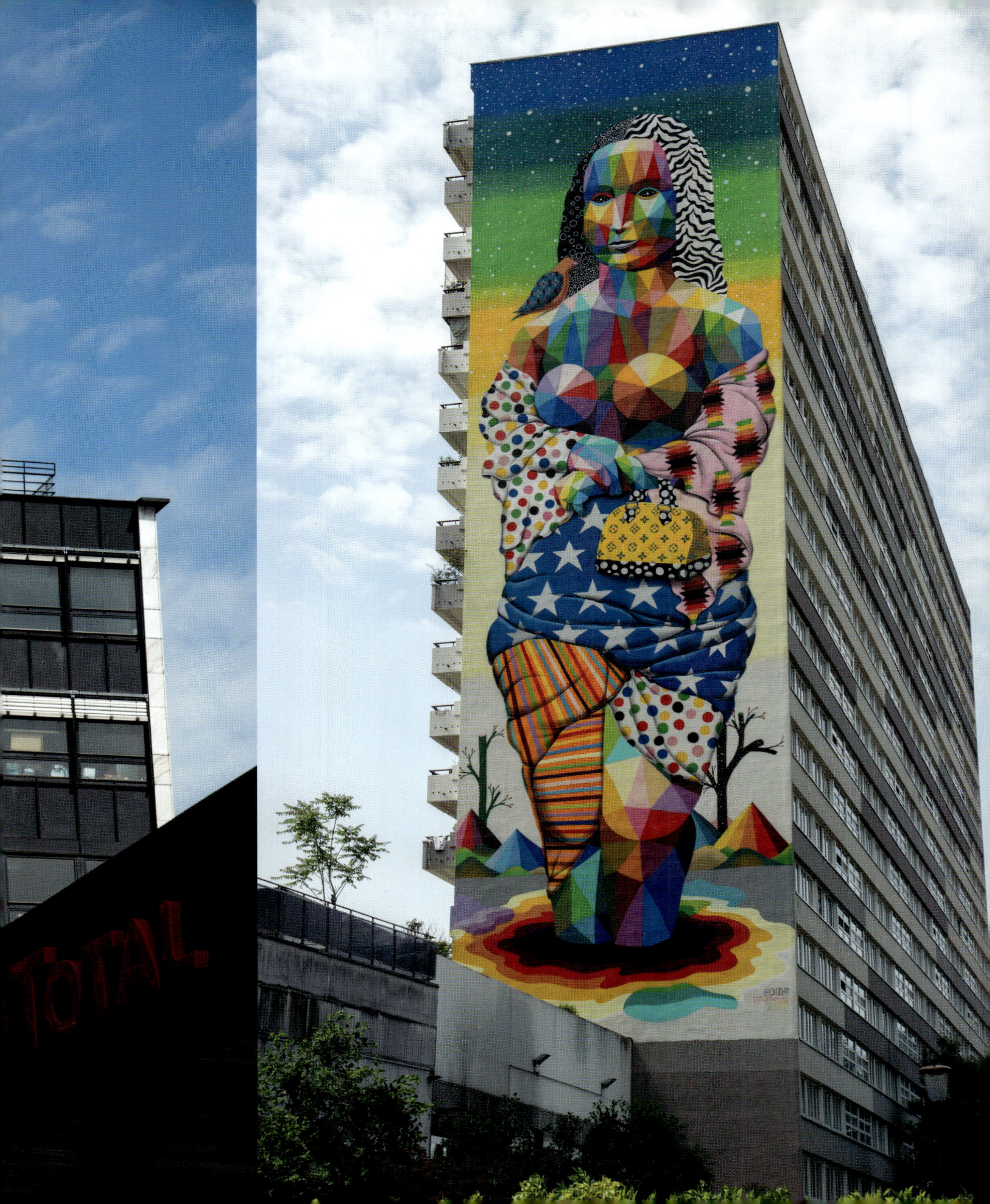

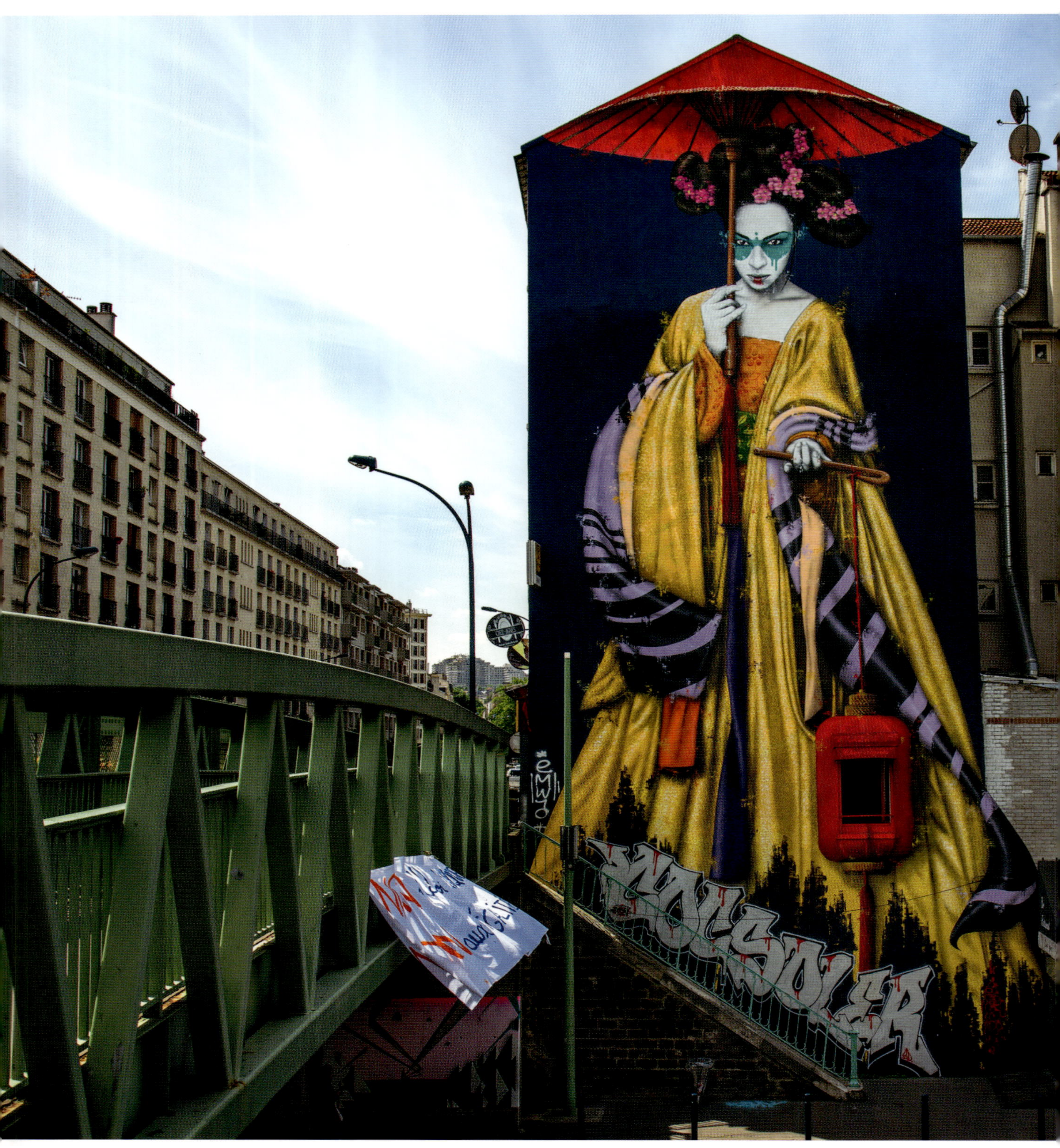

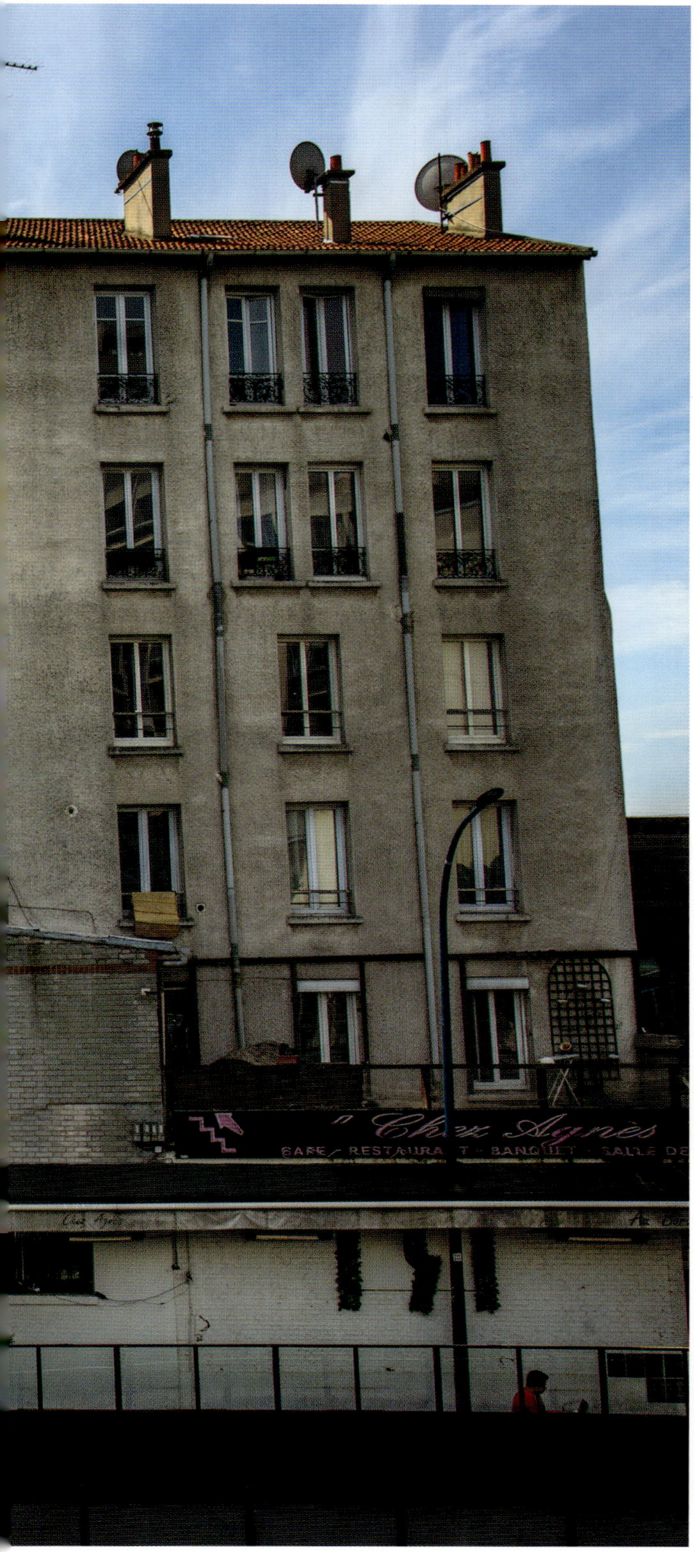

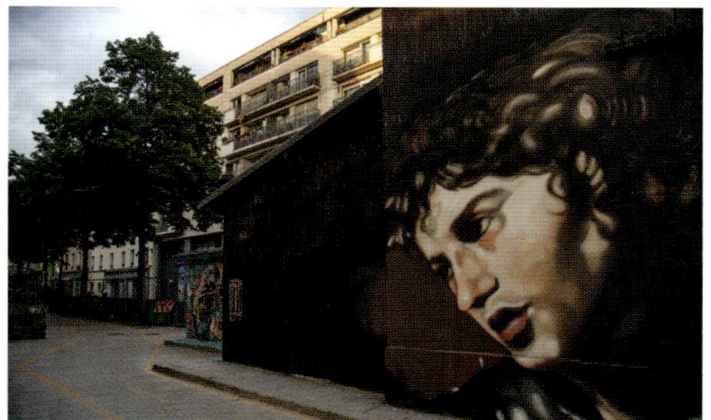

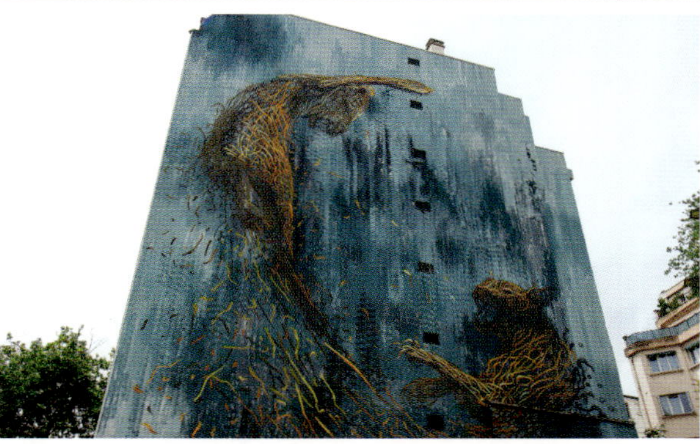

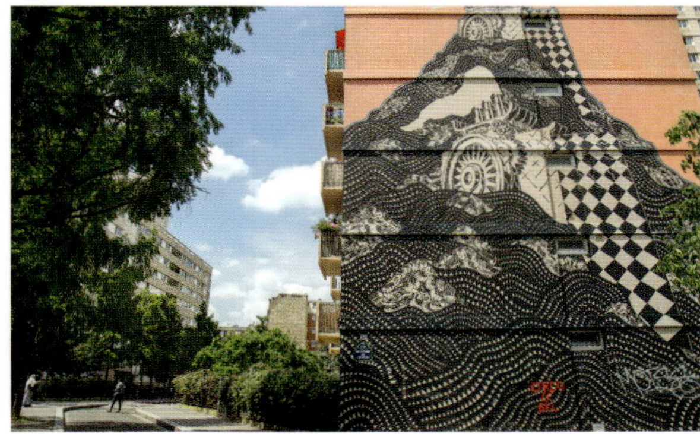

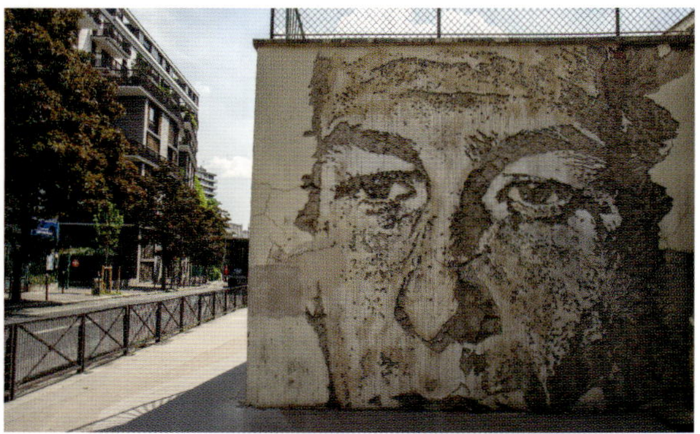

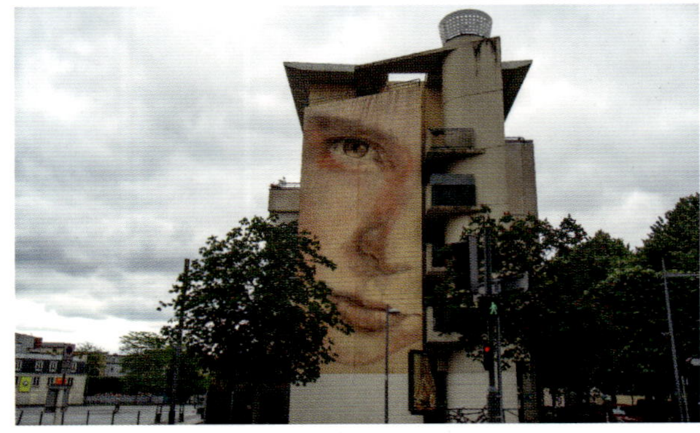
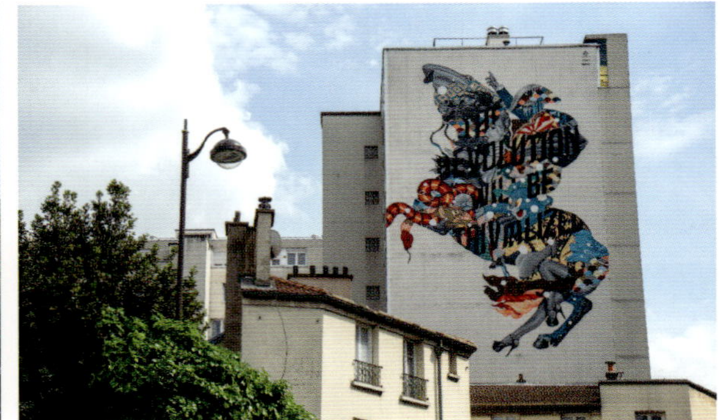
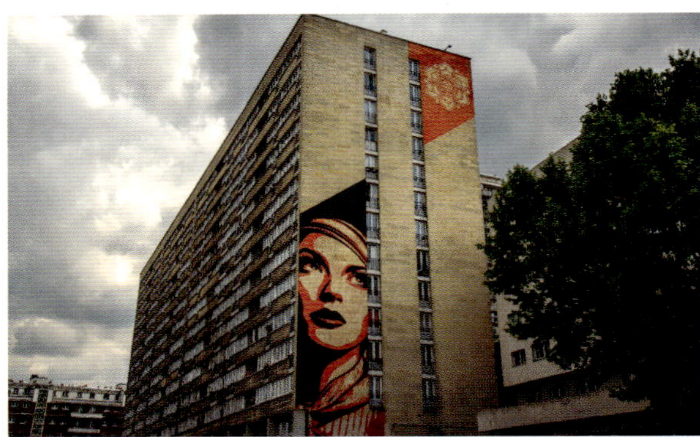
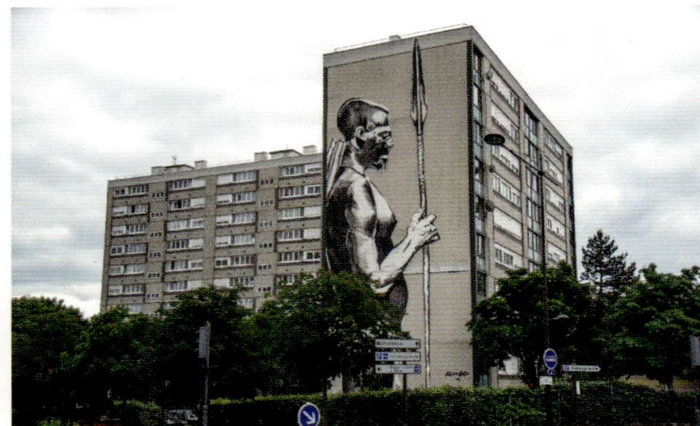
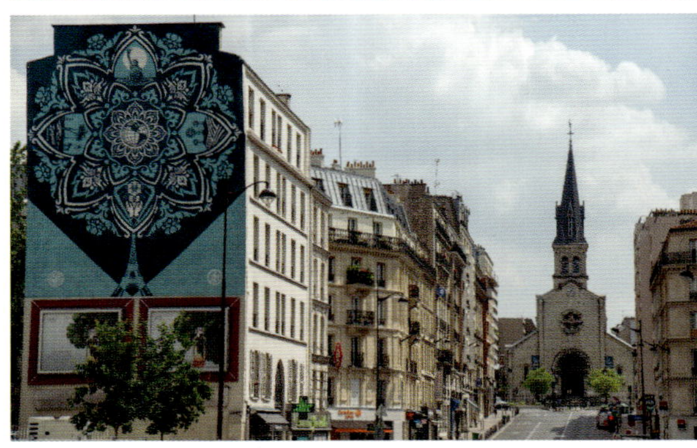
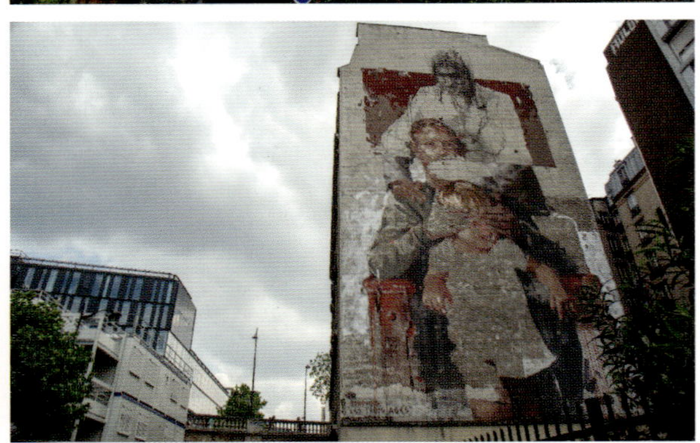
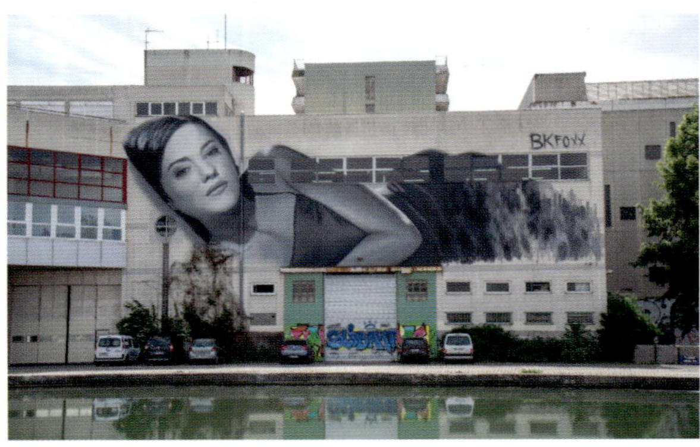
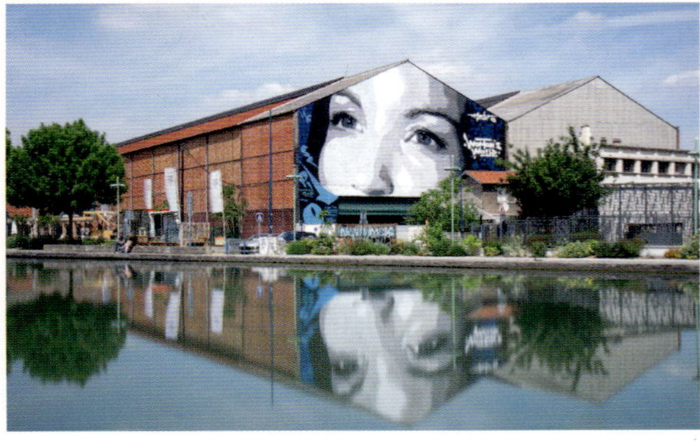

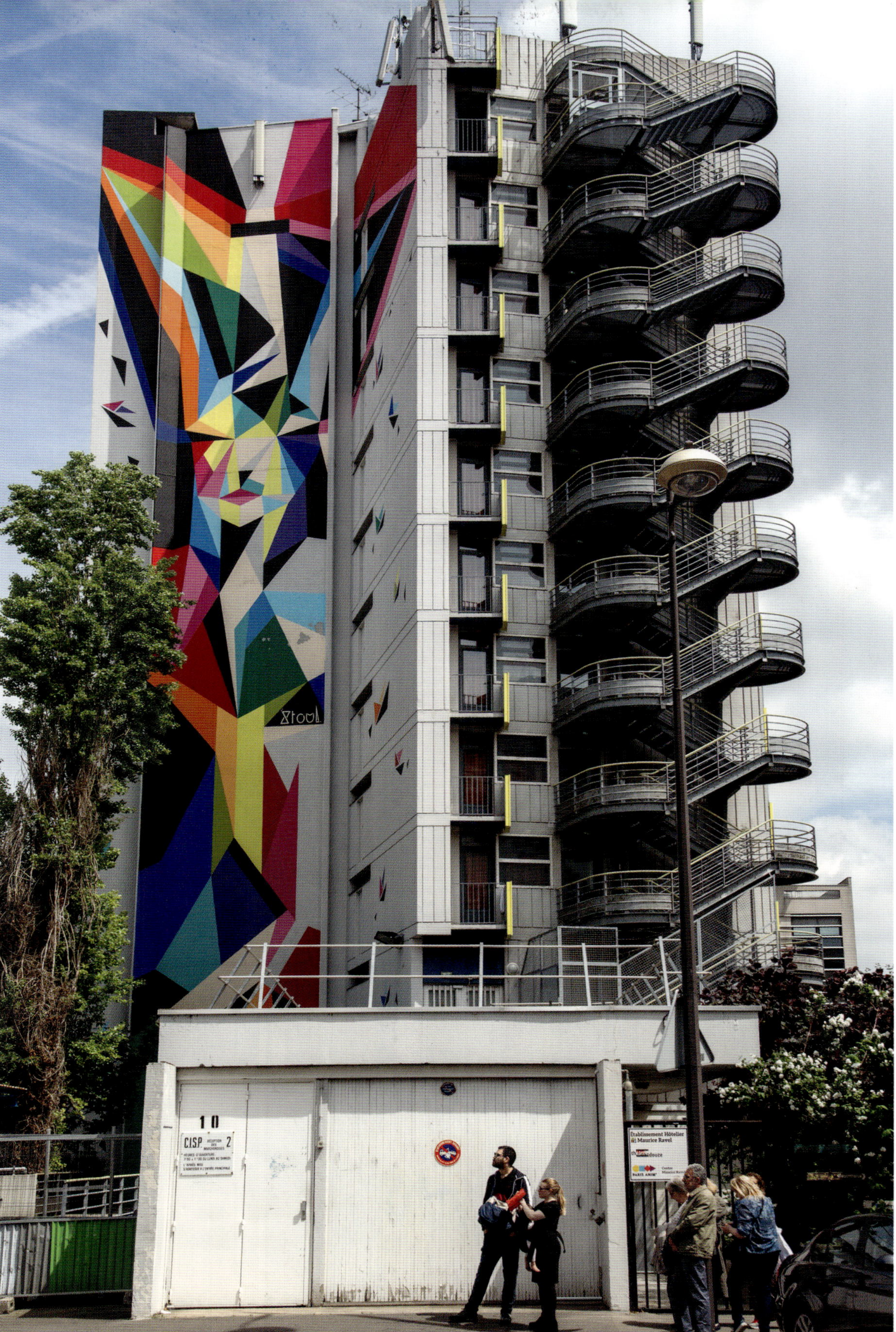

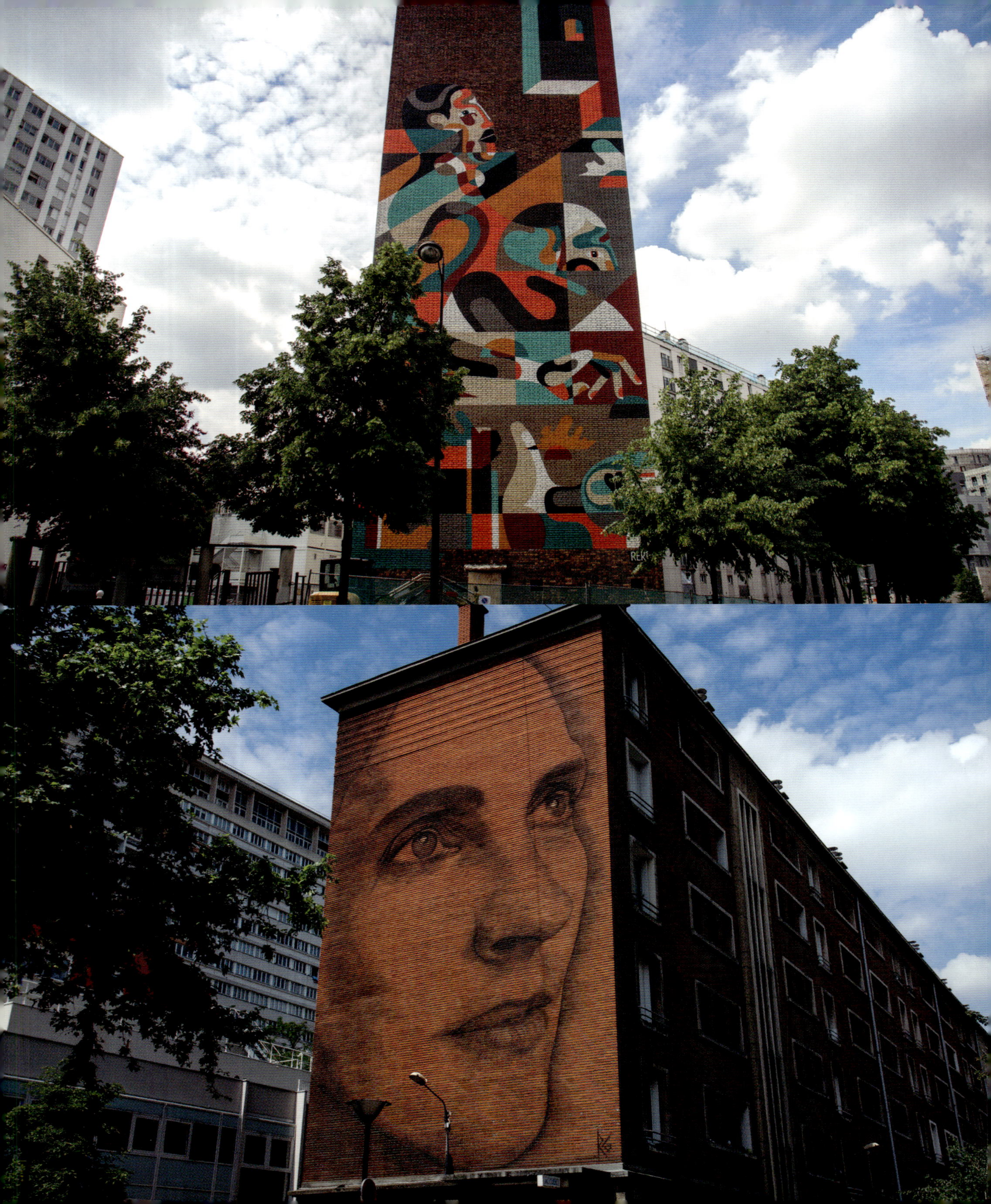

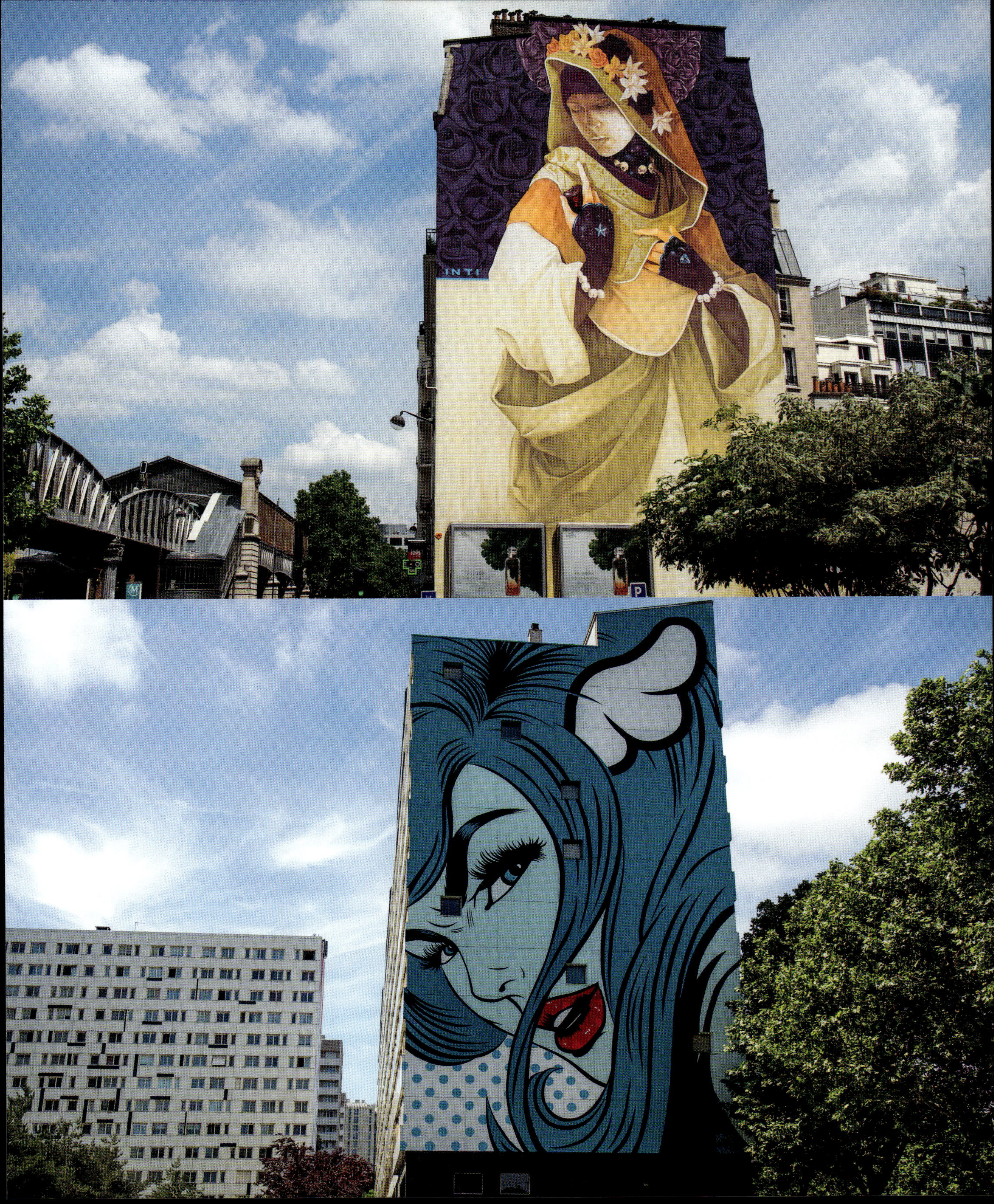

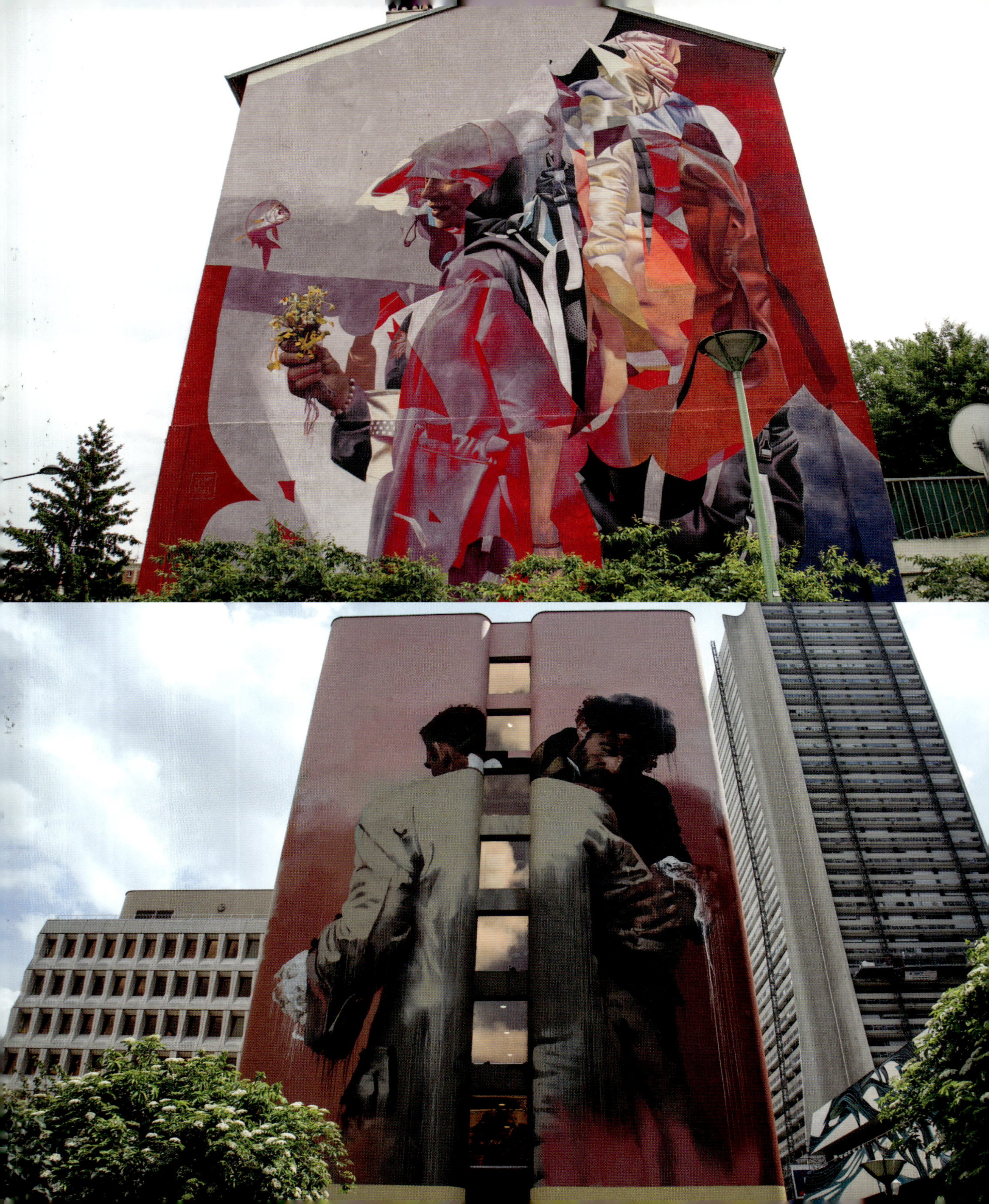

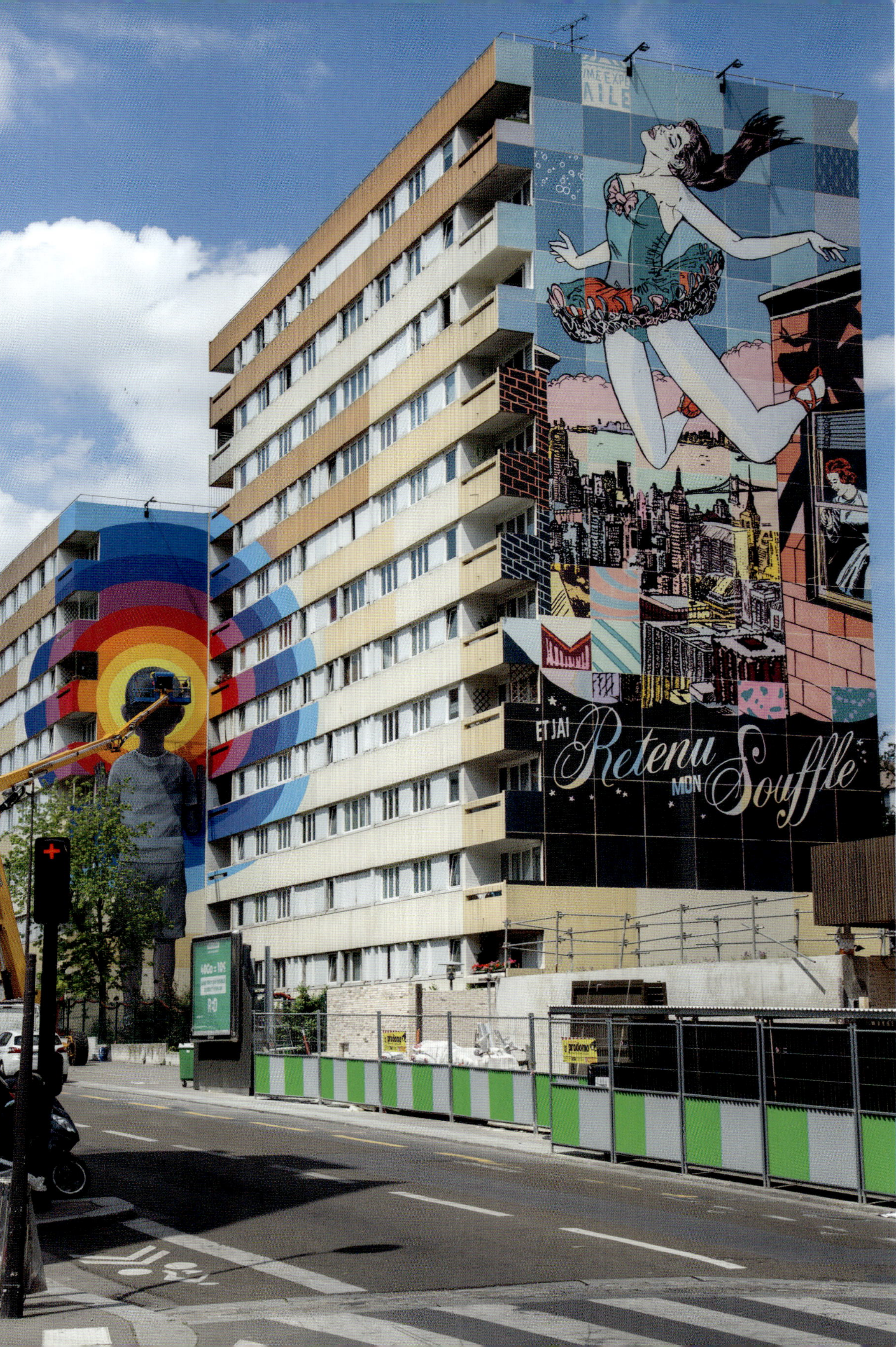

ET J'AI
Retenu
MON Souffle

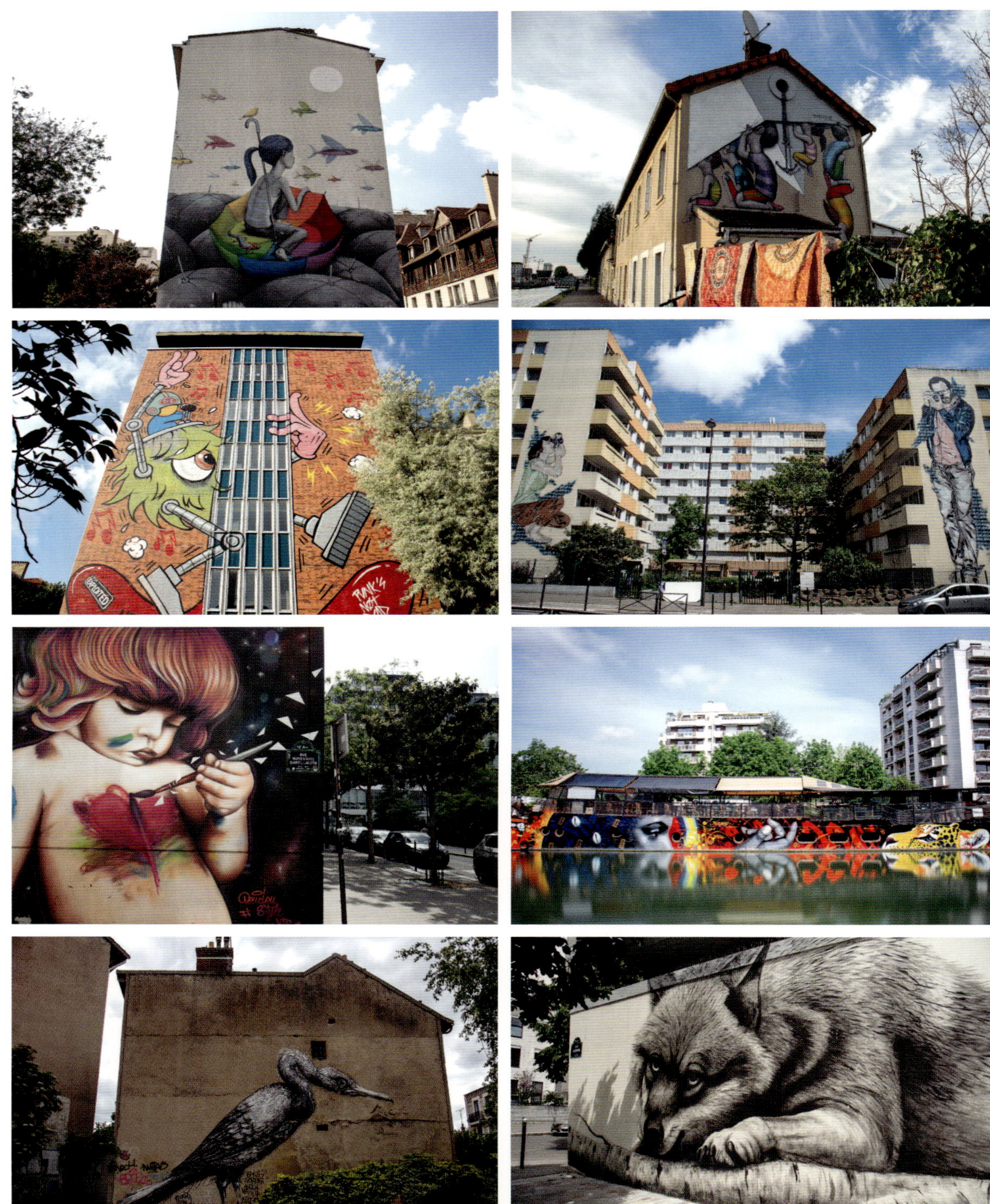

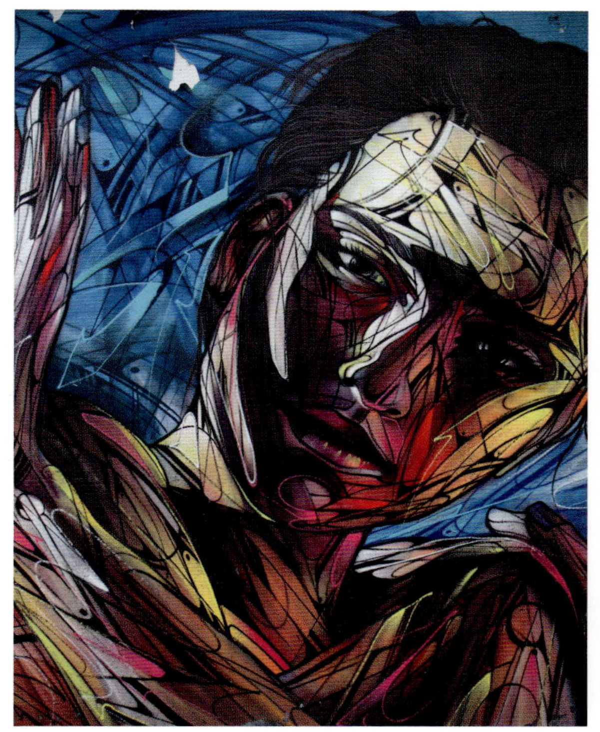

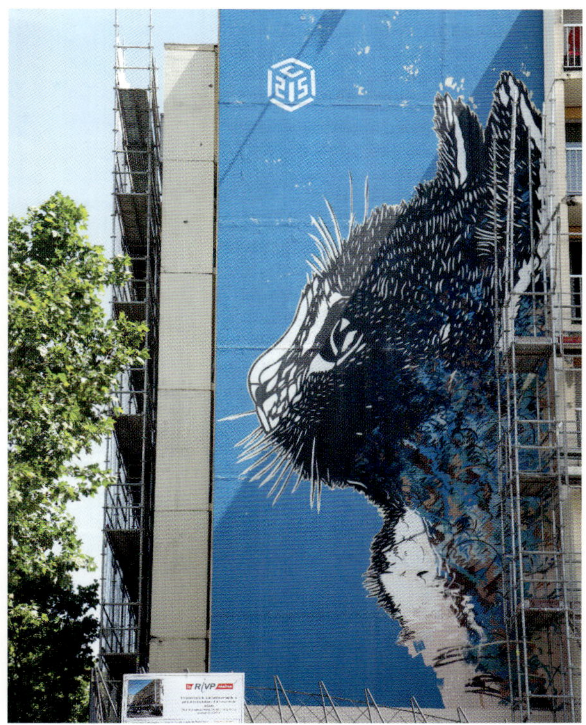

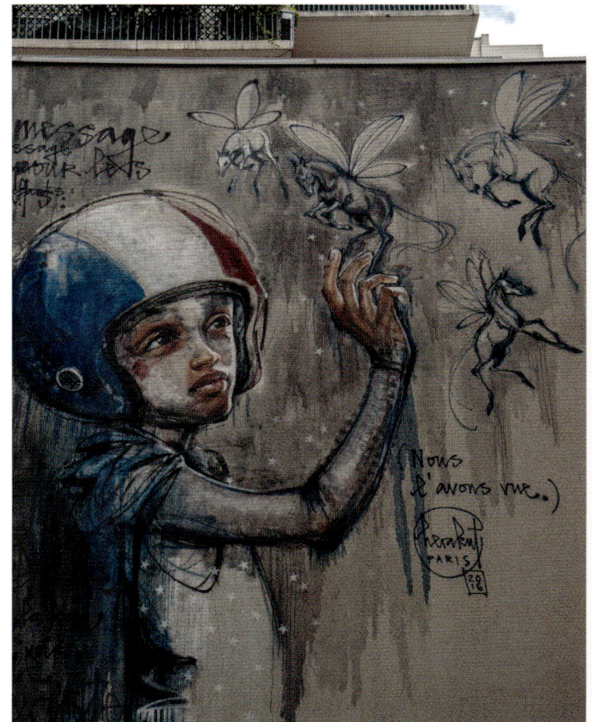

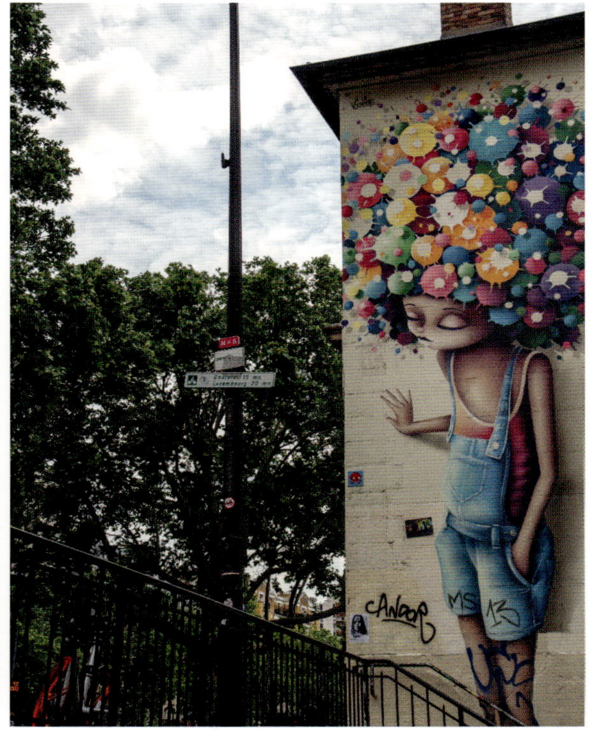

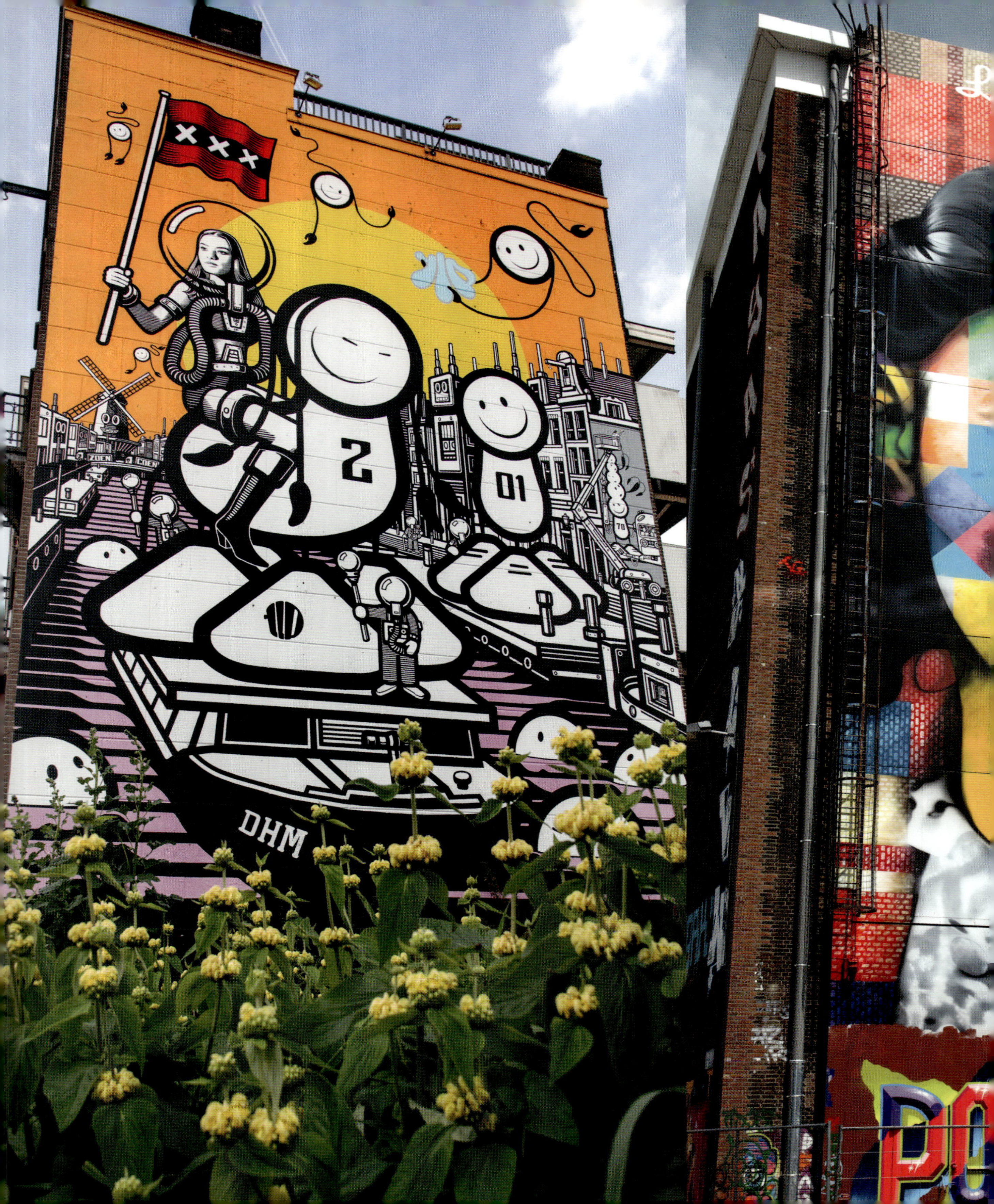

XXX
2
01
10
DHM

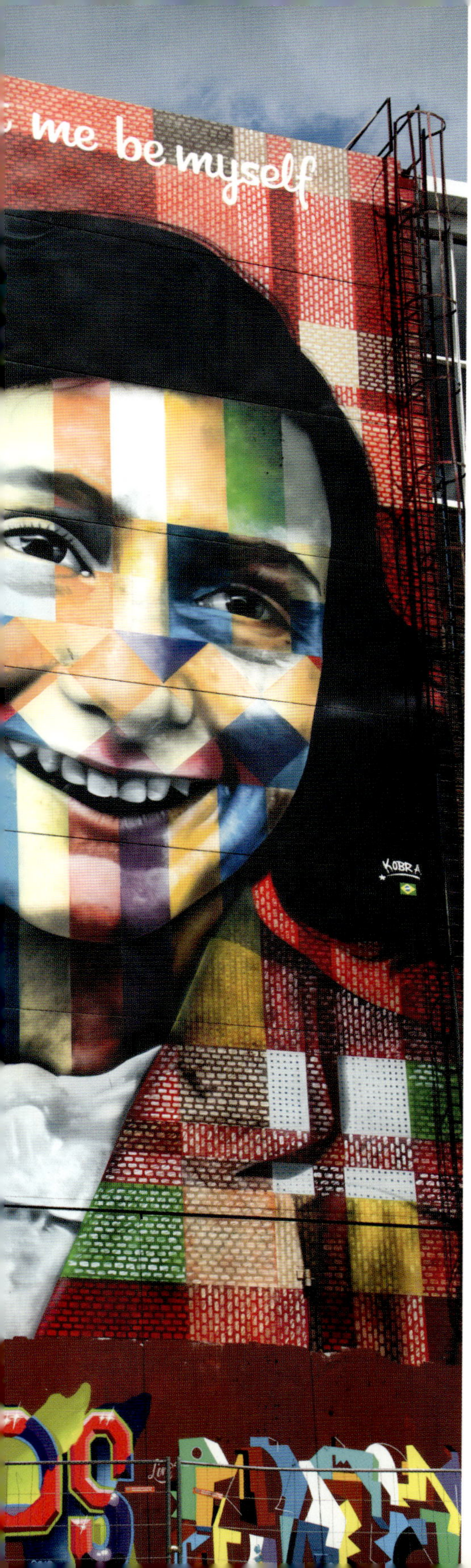

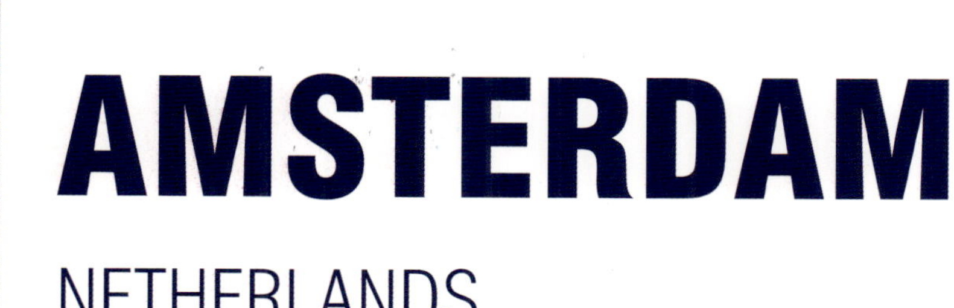

AMSTERDAM

NETHERLANDS

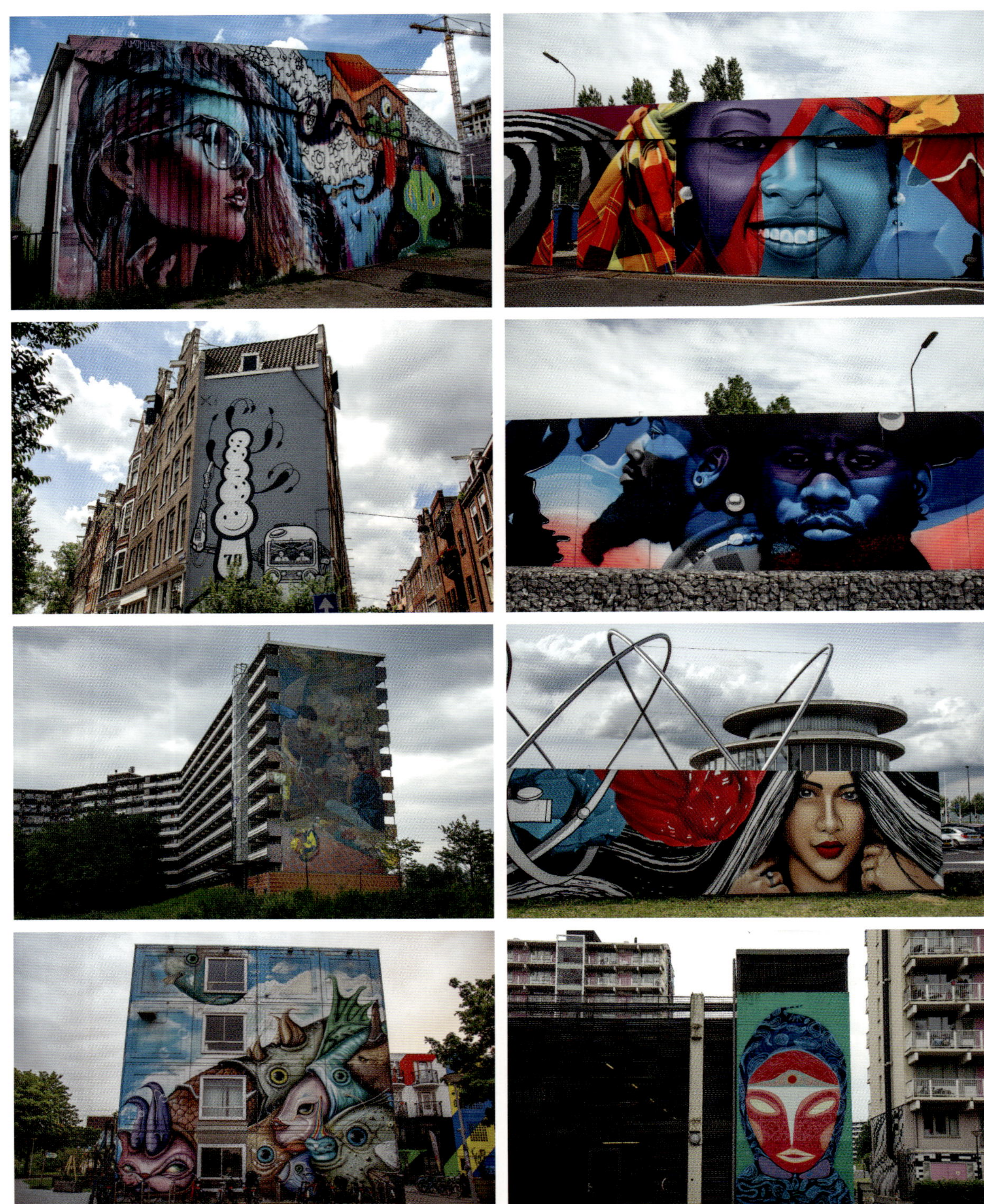

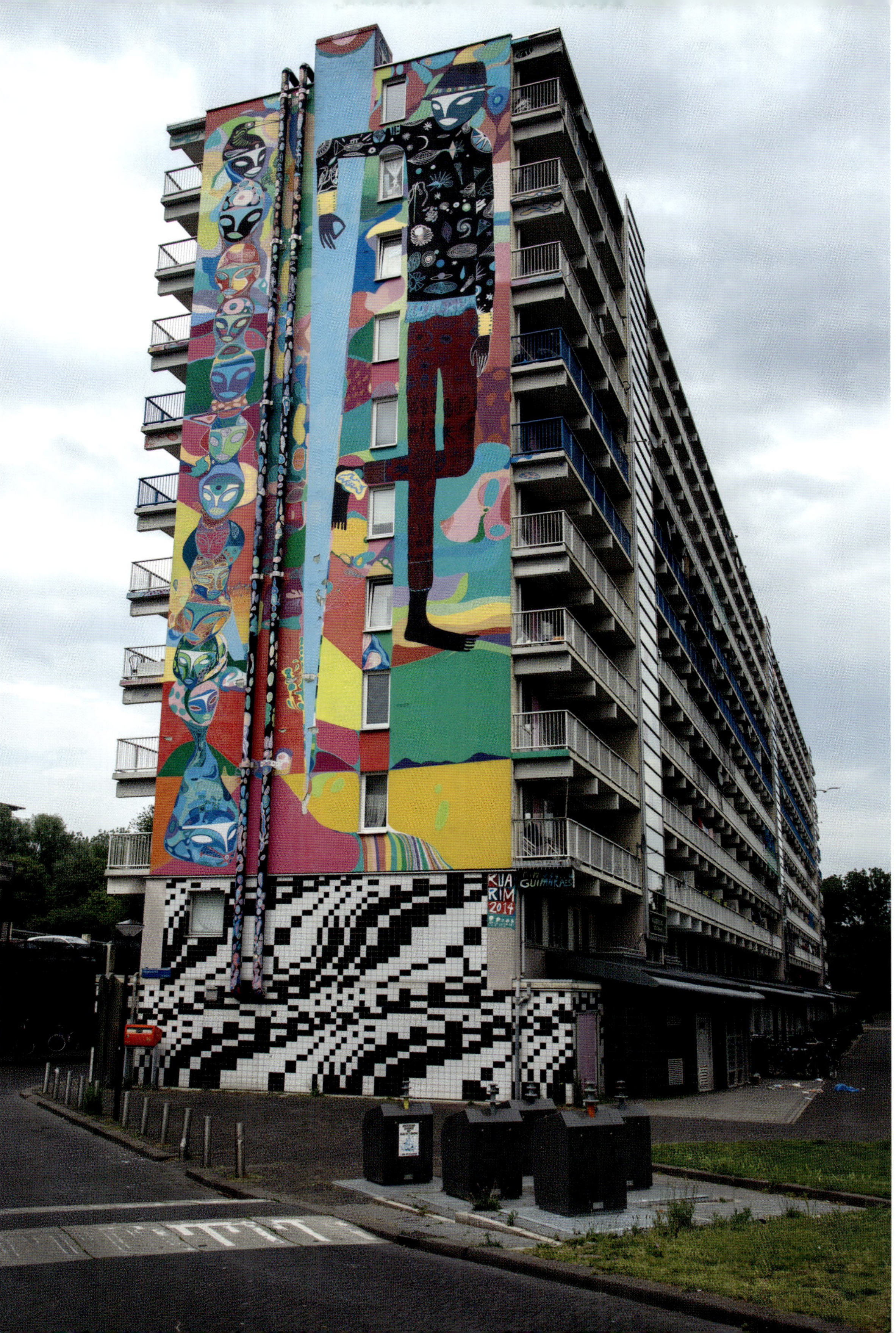

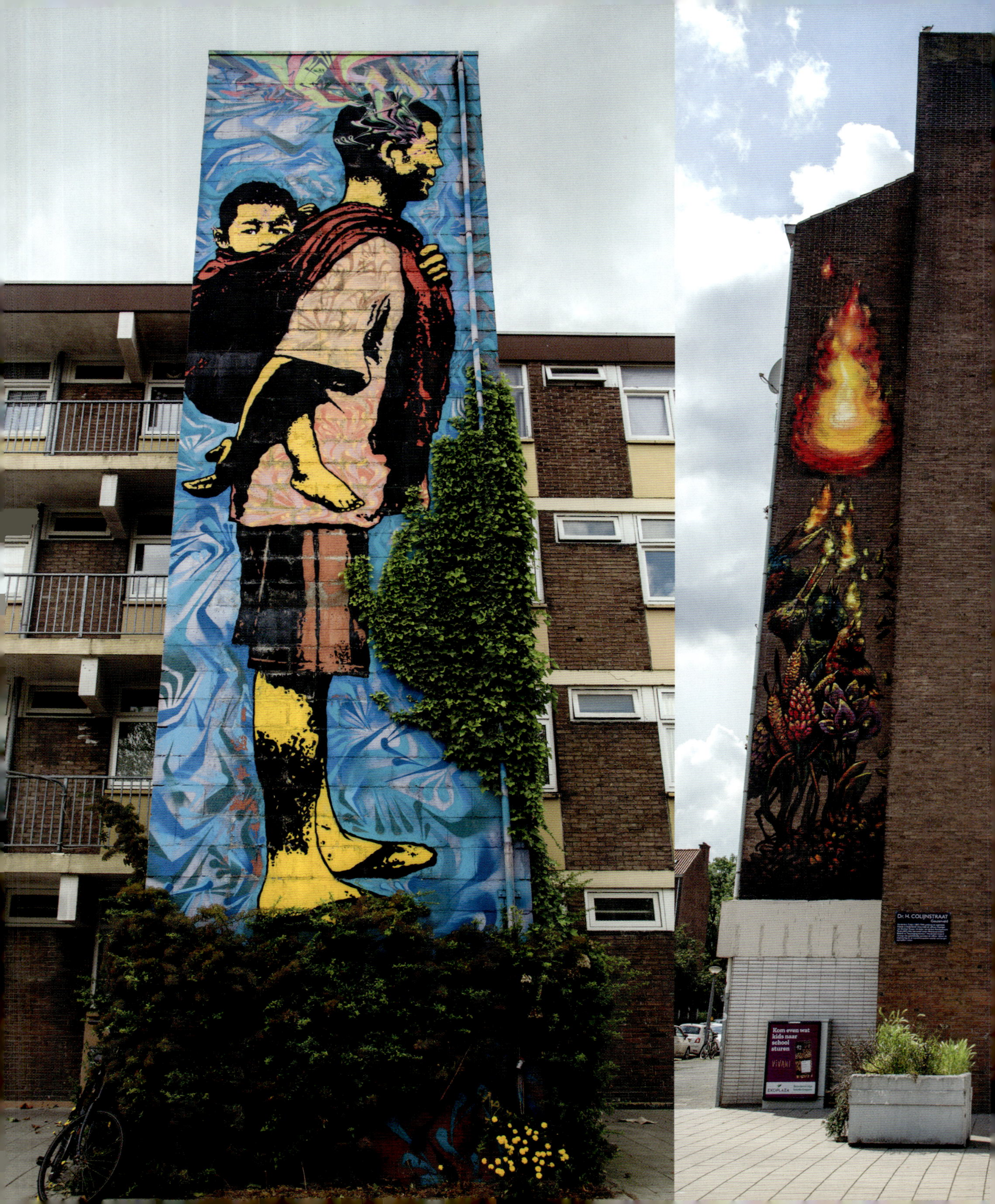

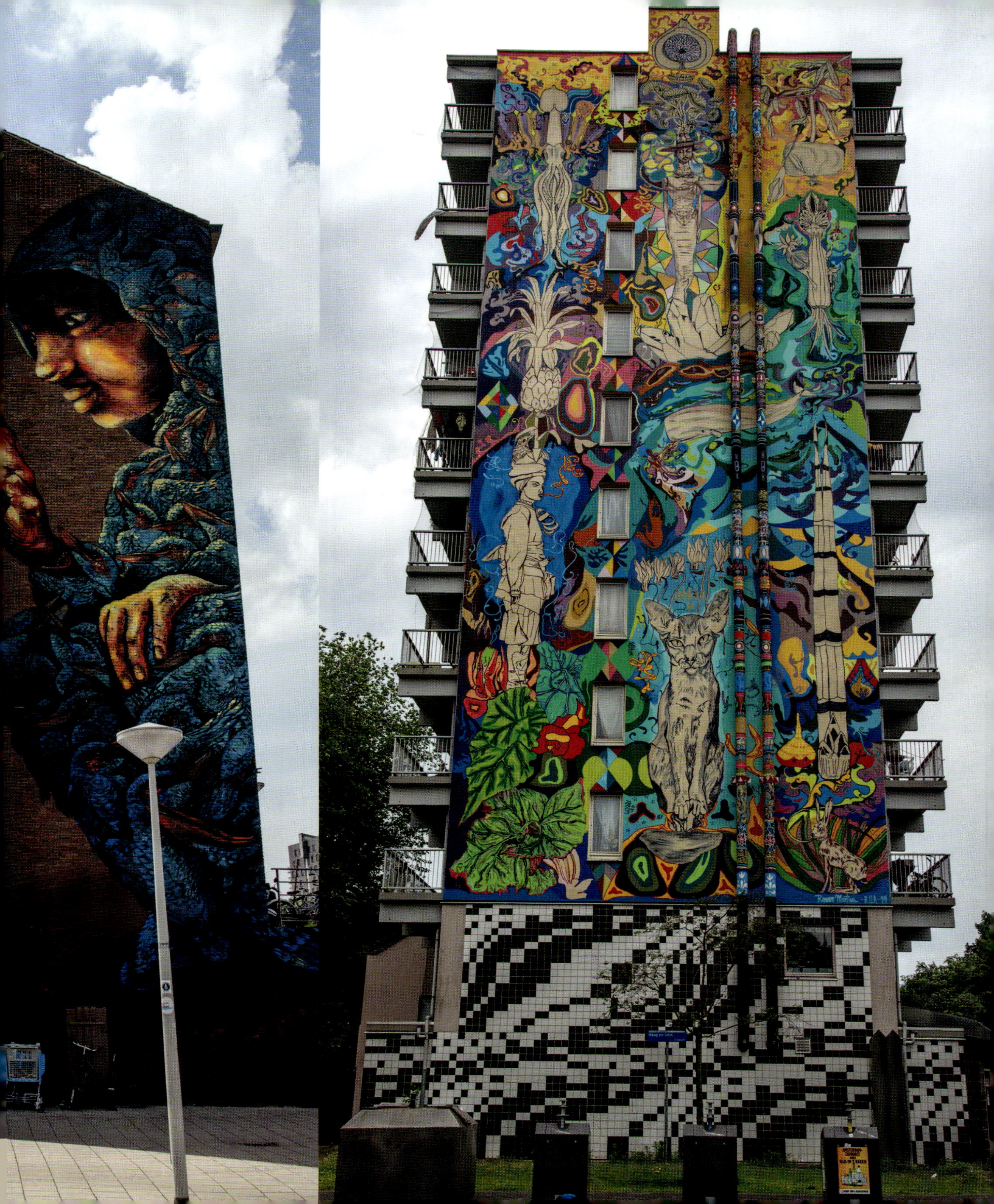

LONDON

ENGLAND

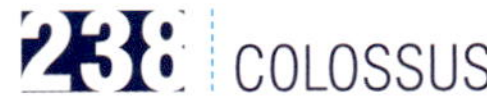

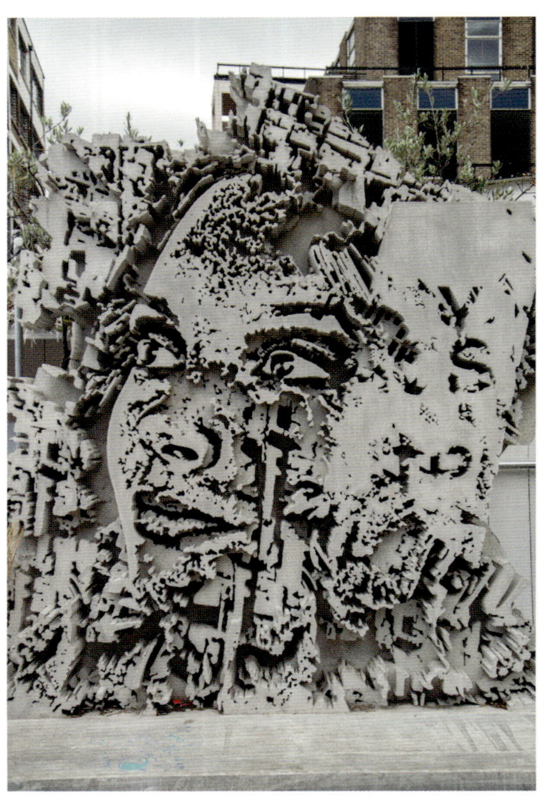

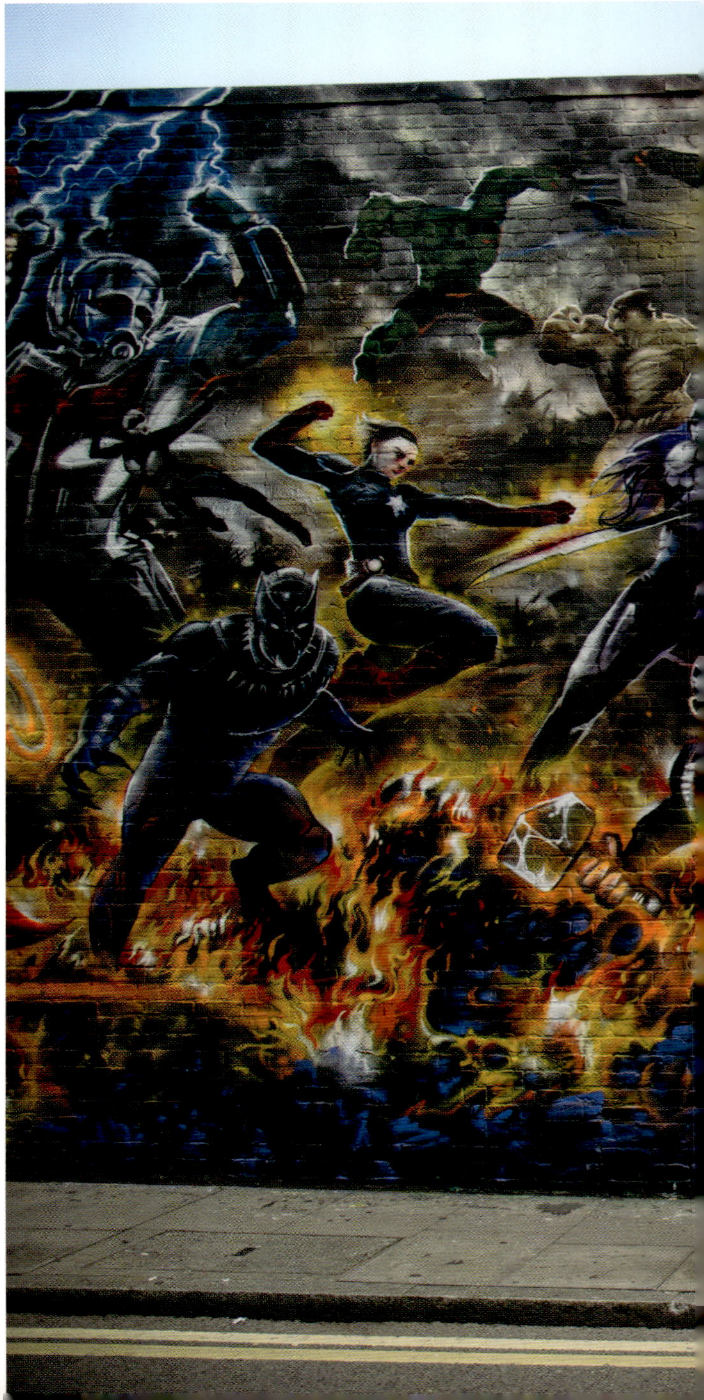

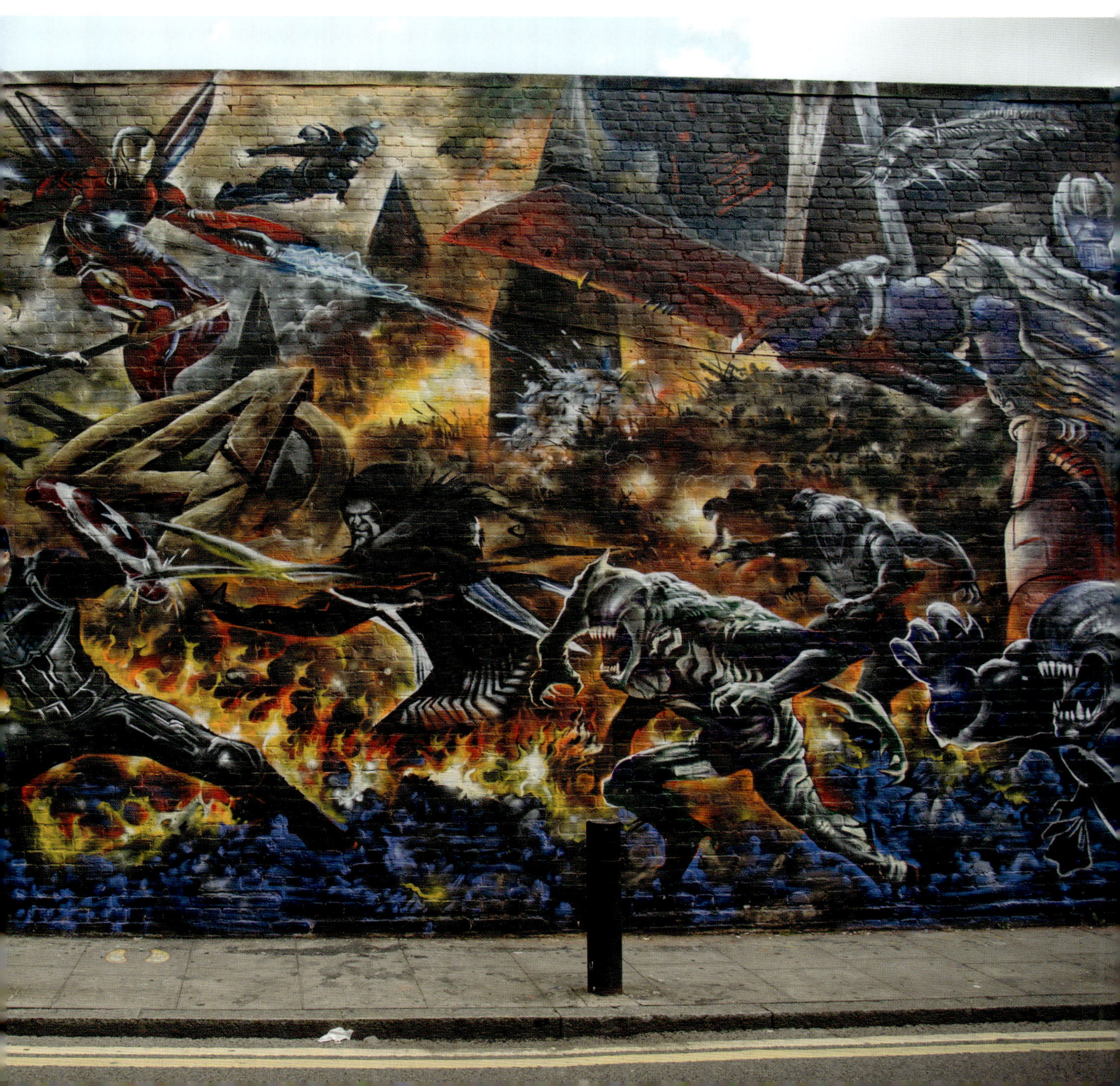

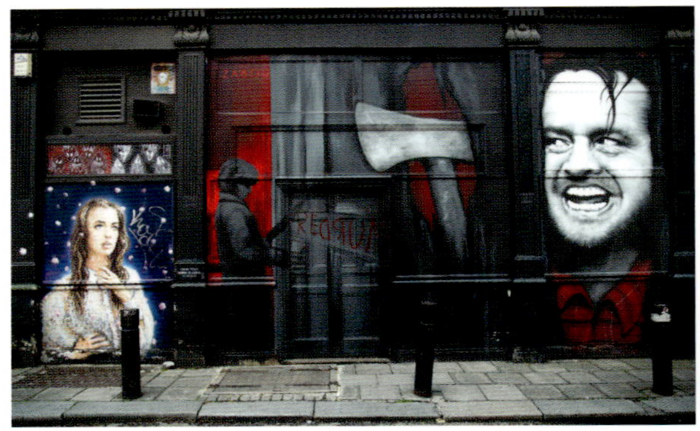

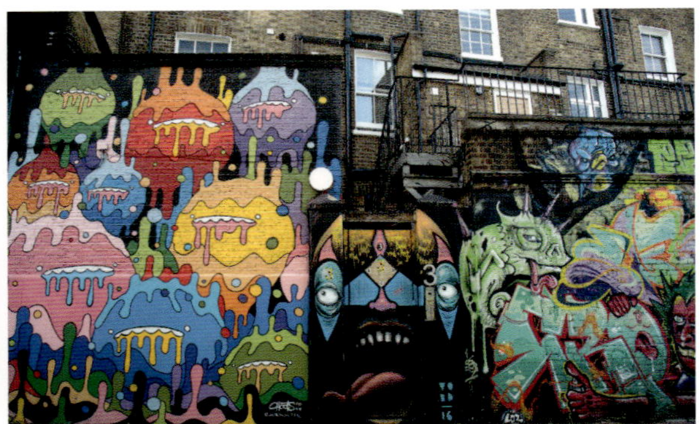

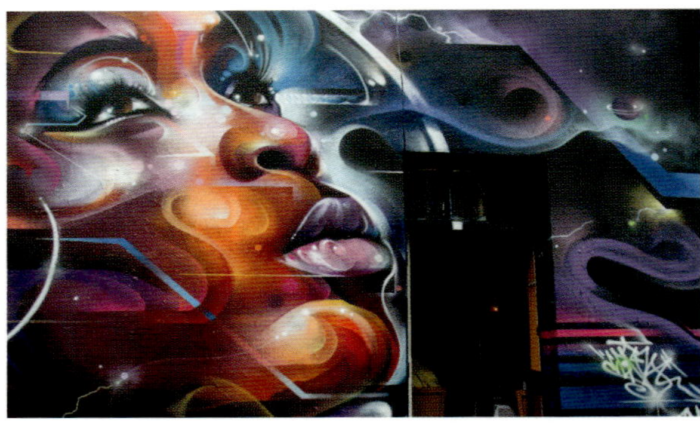

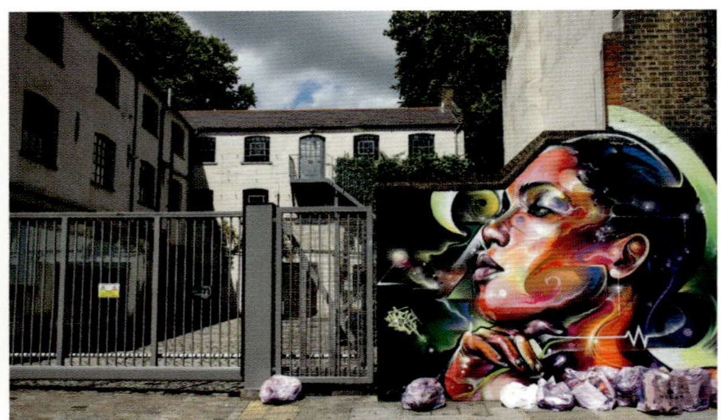

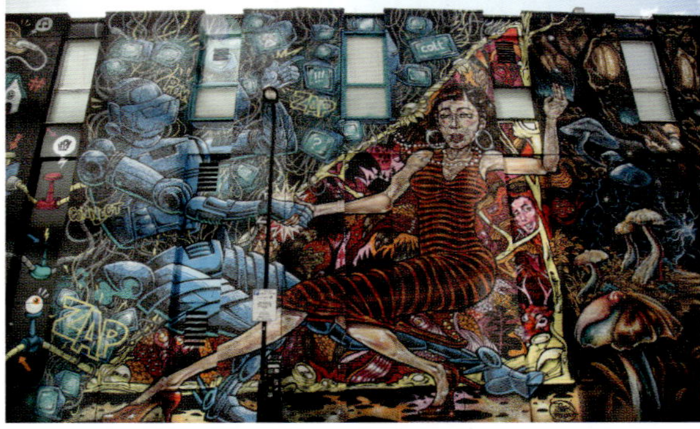

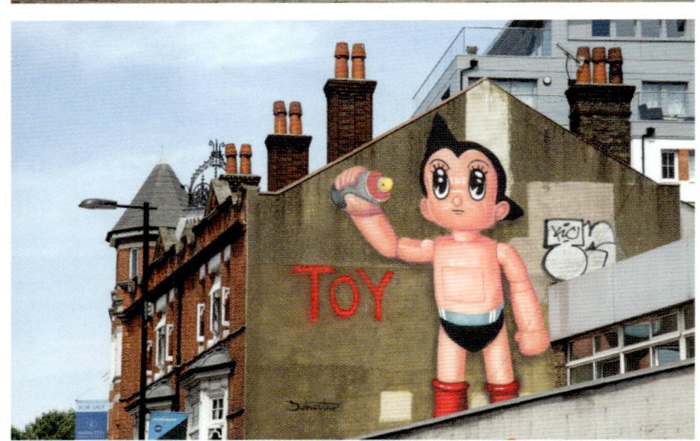

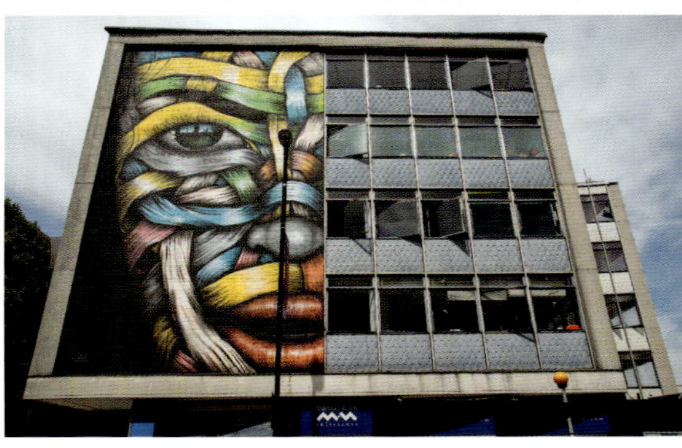

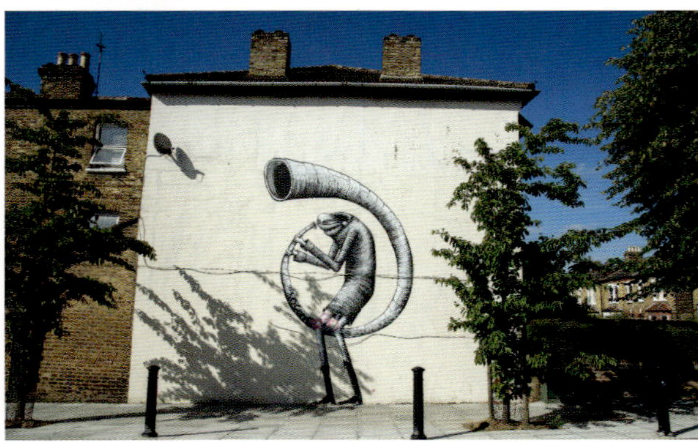

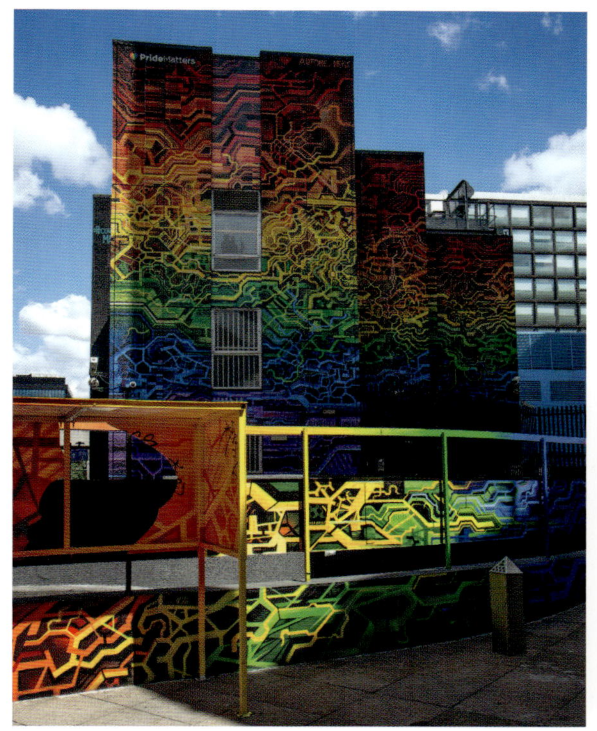

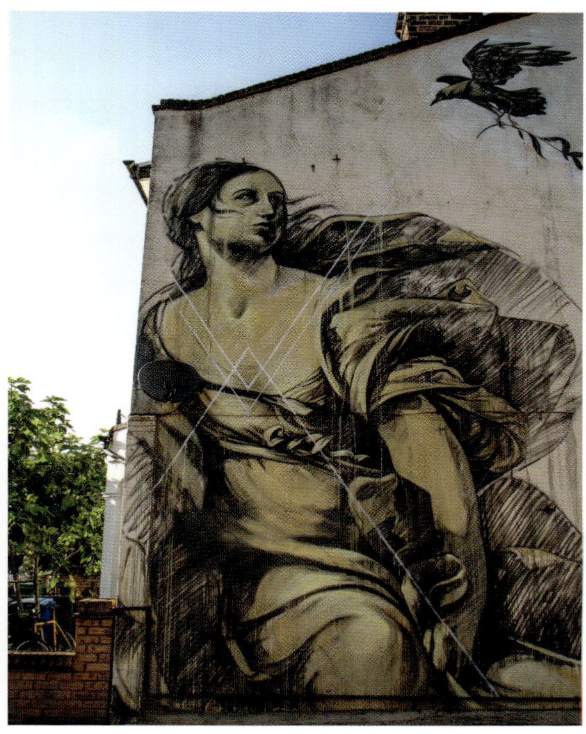

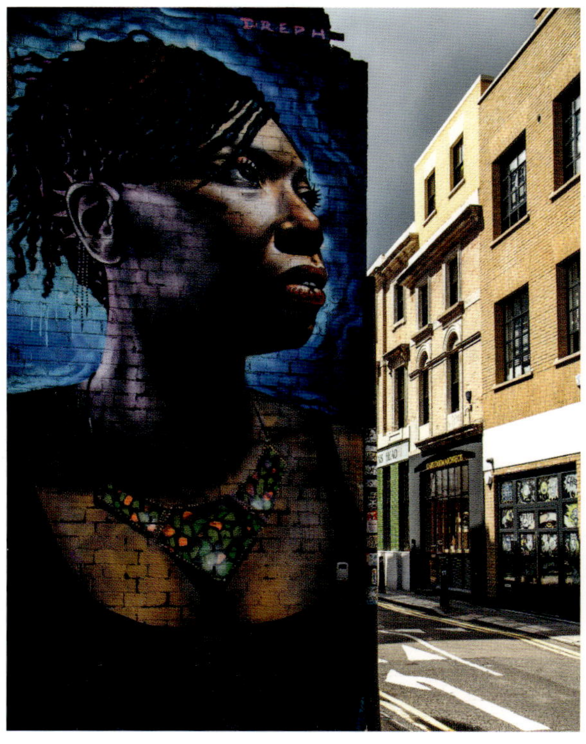

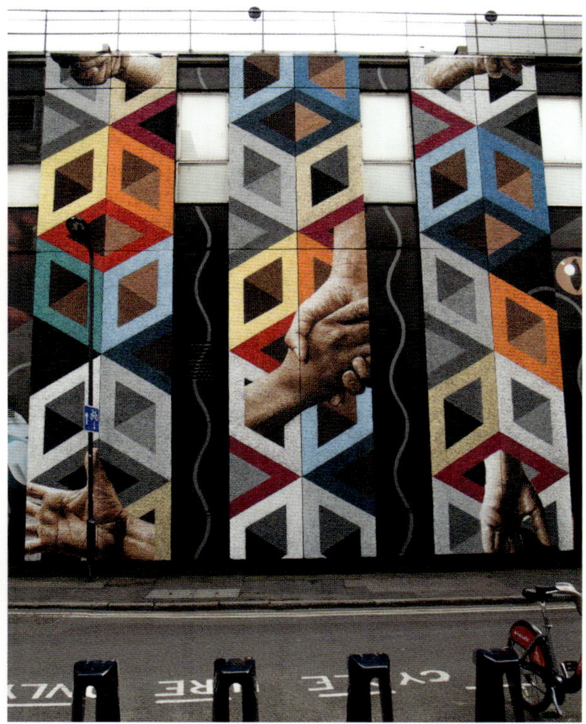

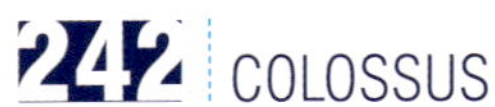

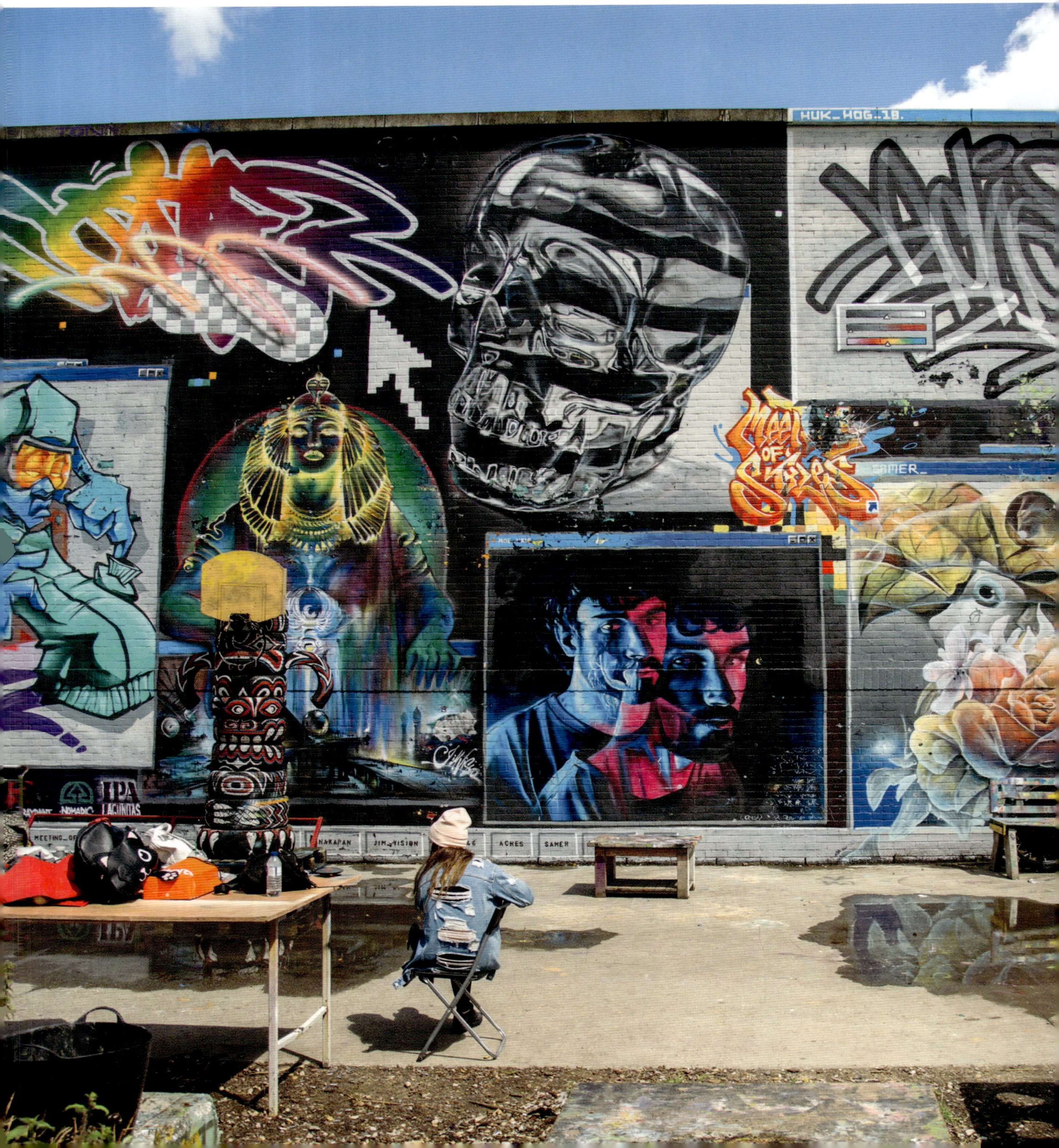

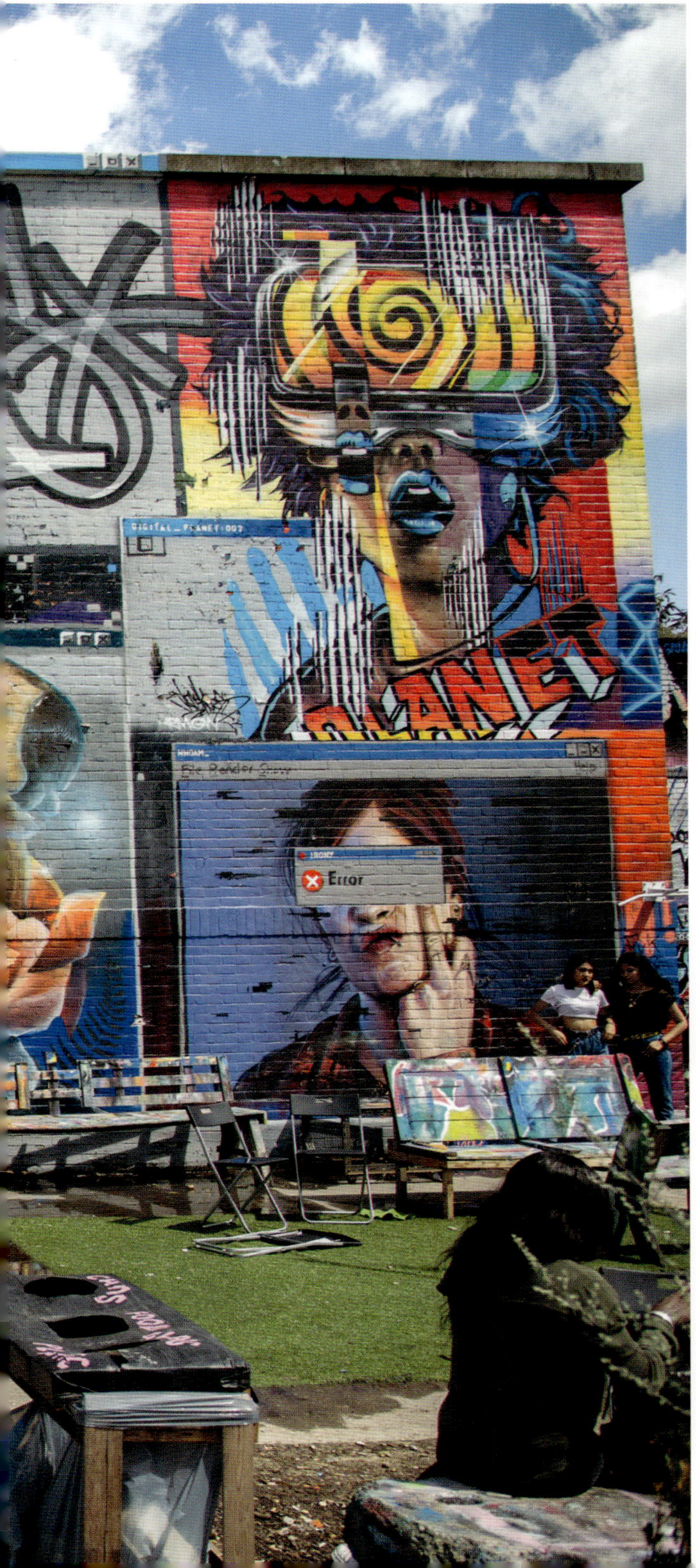

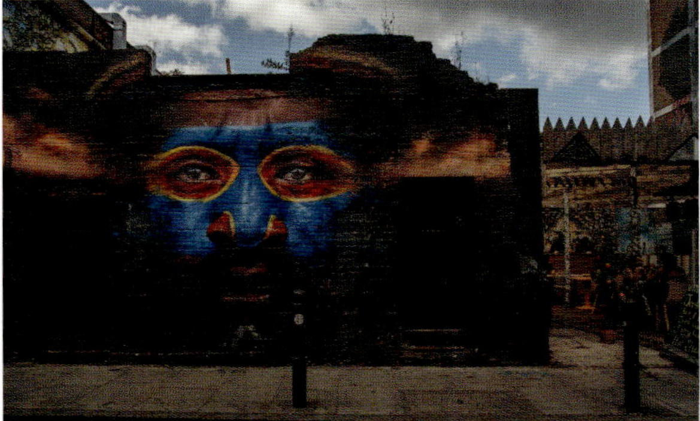

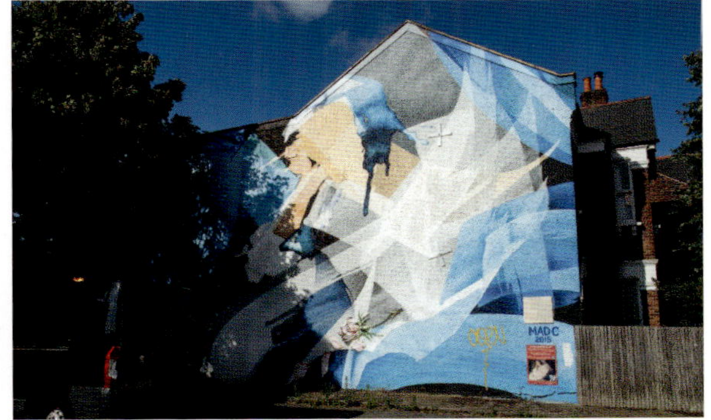

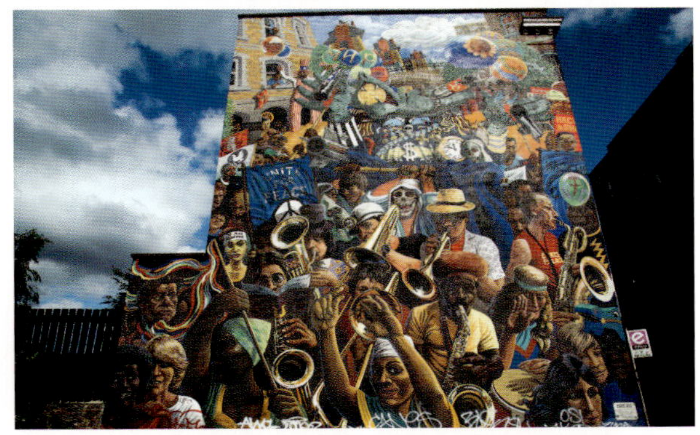

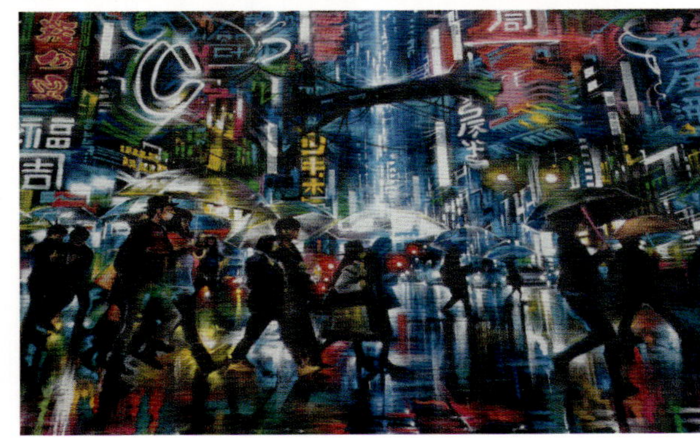

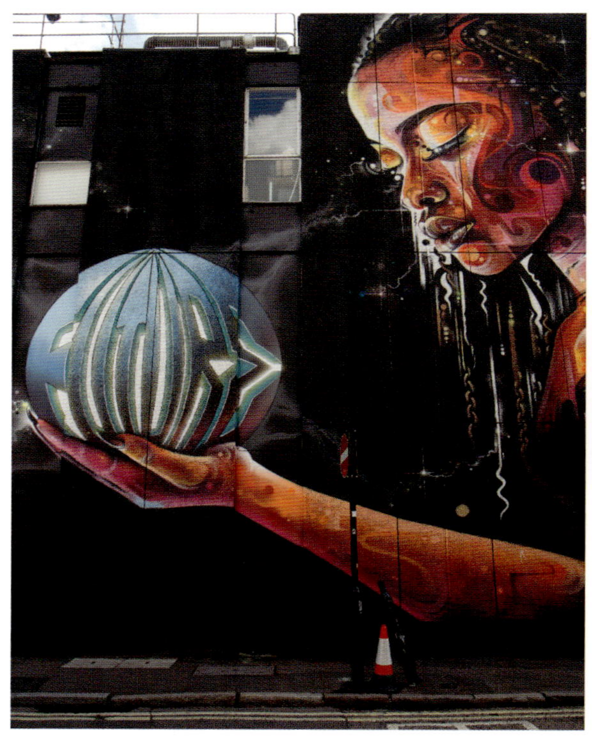

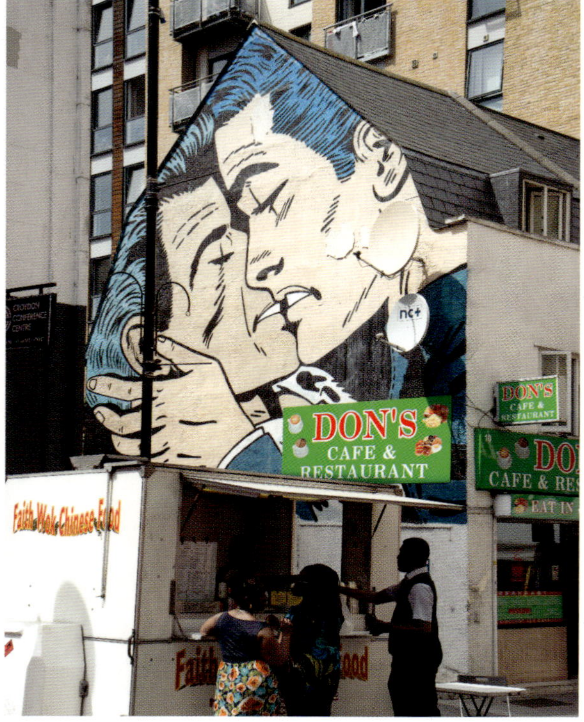
DON'S
CAFE &
RESTAURANT
DON'S
CAFE &
RESTAURANT
EAT IN
Faith Wok Chinese Food

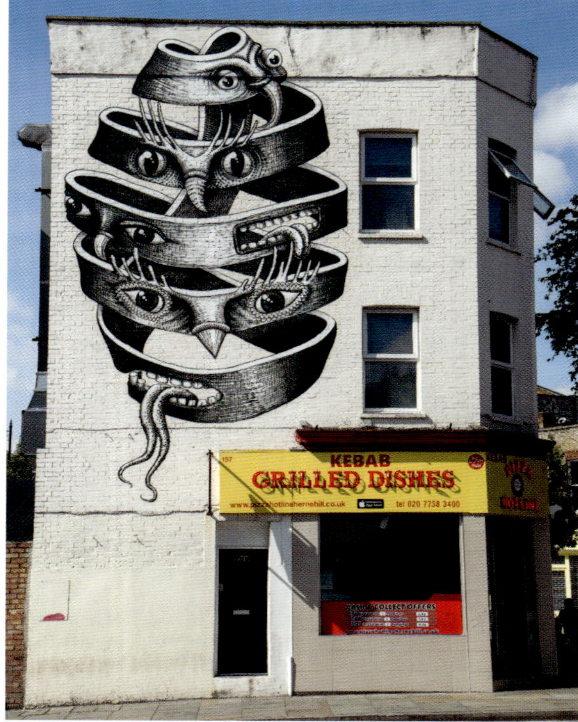
KEBAB
GRILLED DISHES

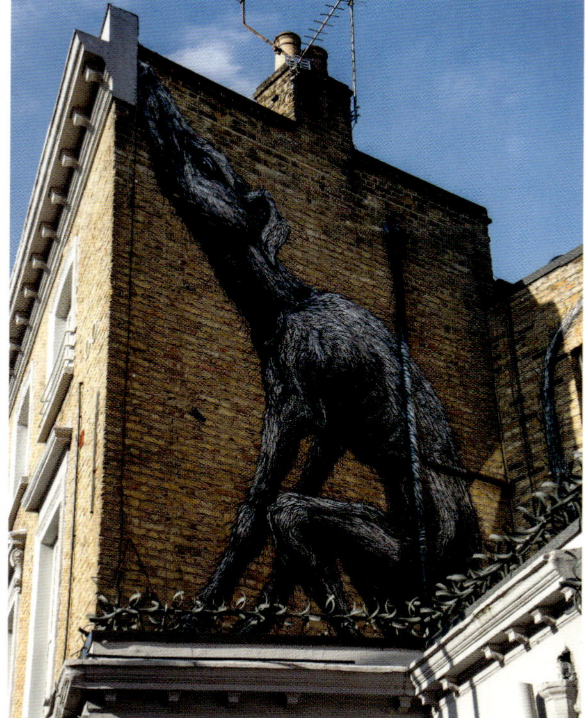

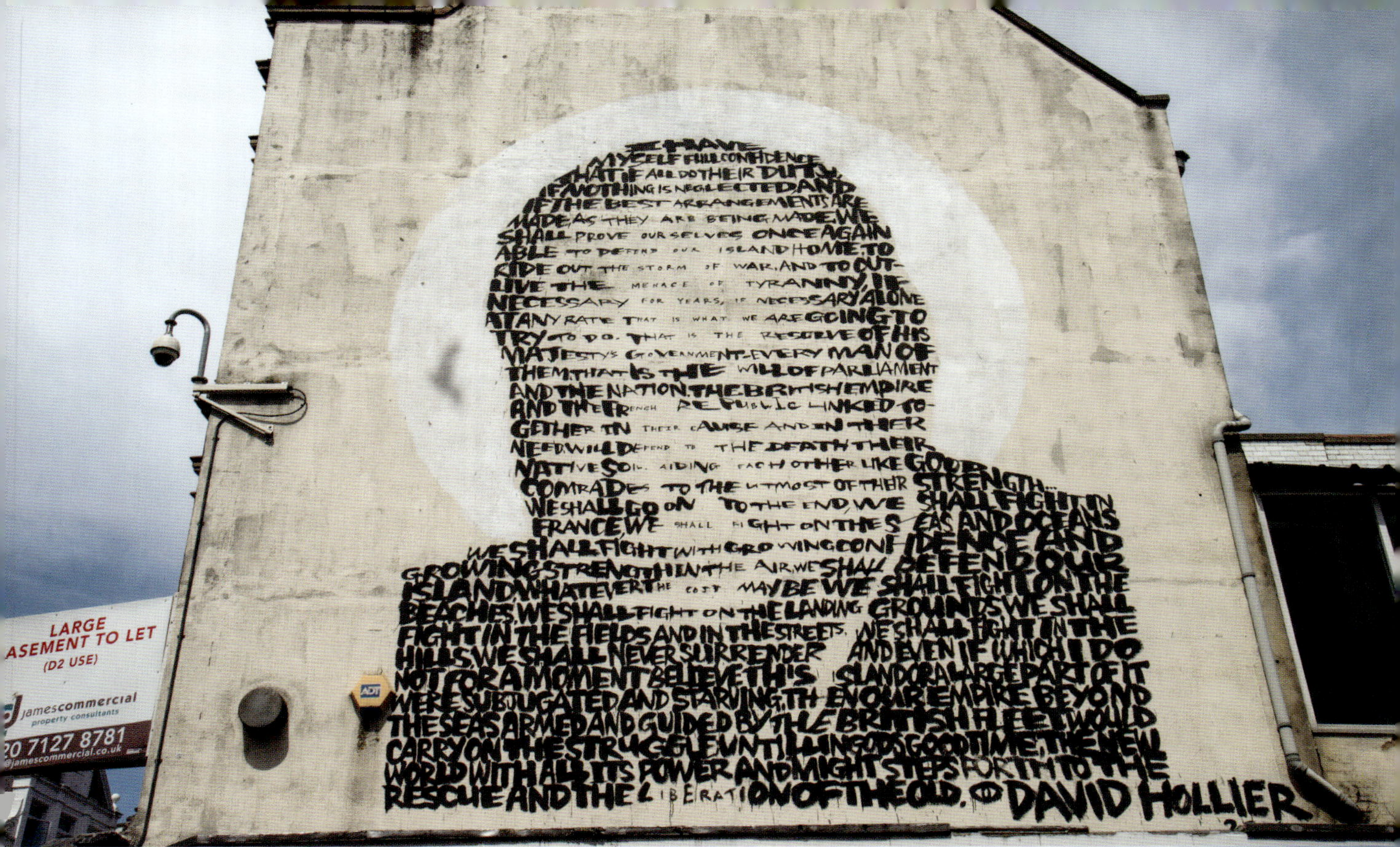

LARGE
ASEMENT TO LET
(D2 USE)
jamescommercial
property consultants
20 7127 8781
jamescommercial.co.uk

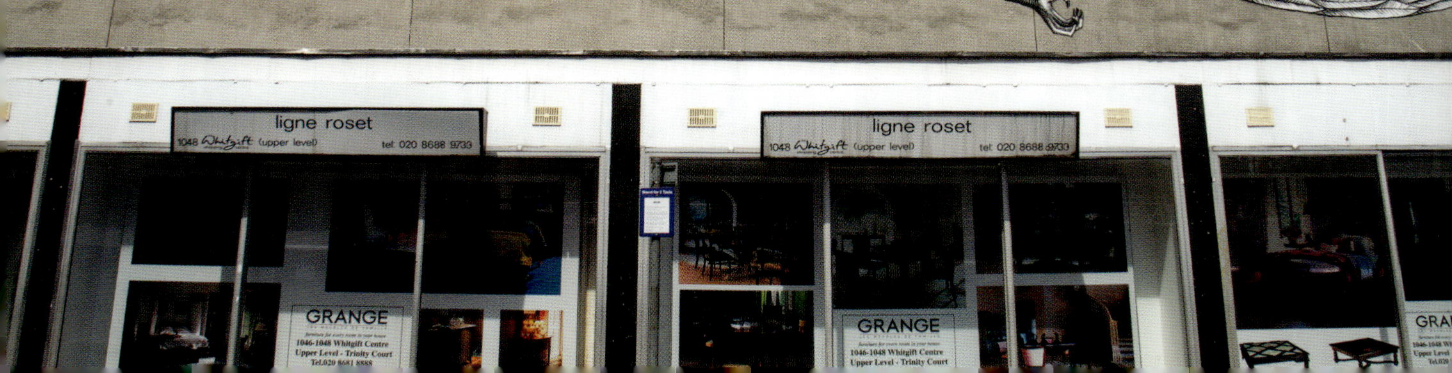
ligne roset
1048 Whitgift (upper level)   tel 020 8688 9733
ligne roset
1048 Whitgift (upper level)   tel 020 8688 9733
GRANGE
1046-1048 Whitgift Centre
Upper Level · Trinity Court
Tel.020 8681 8888
GRANGE
1046-1048 Whitgift Centre
Upper Level · Trinity Court
GRAN

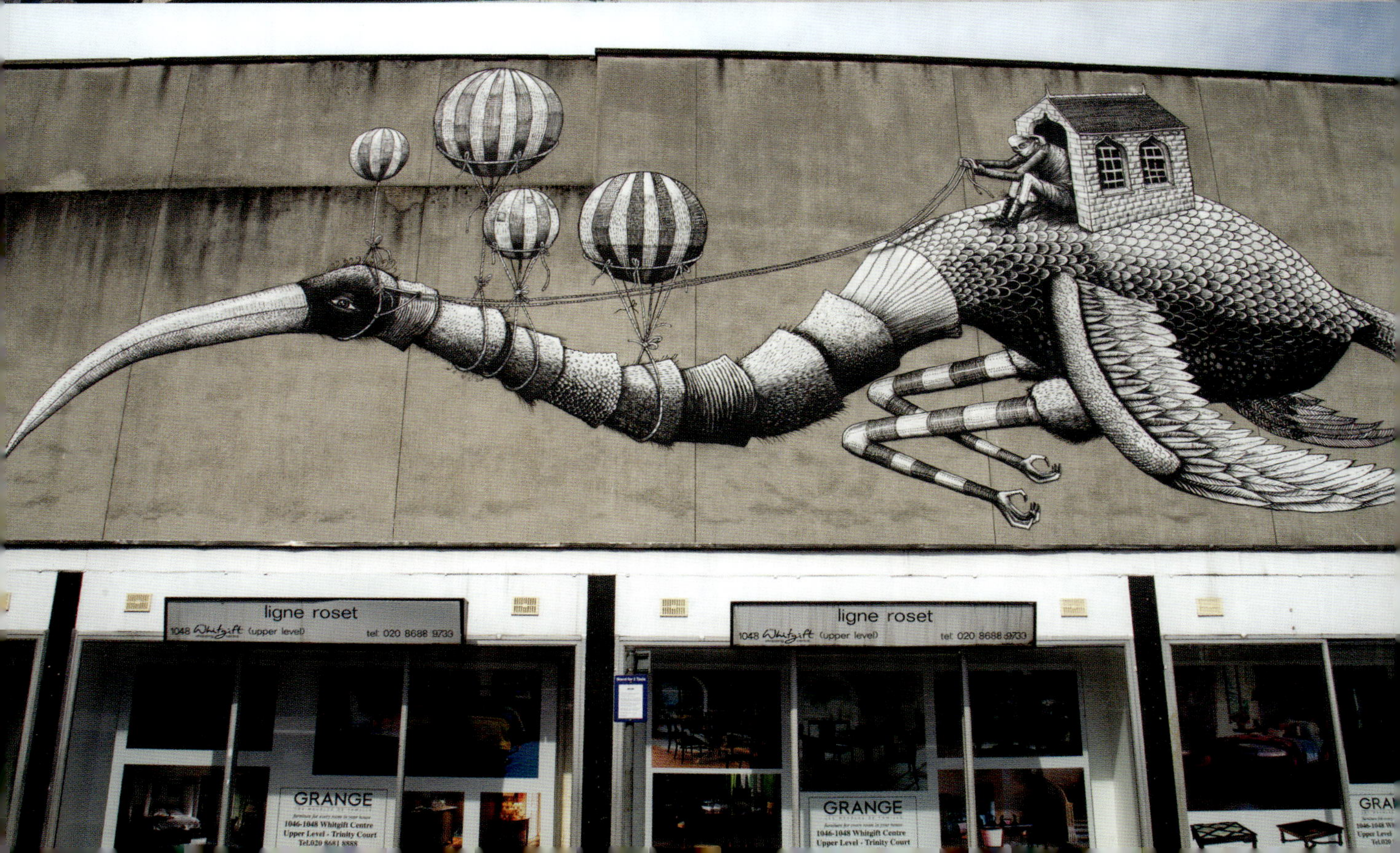

BRISTOL

ENGLAND

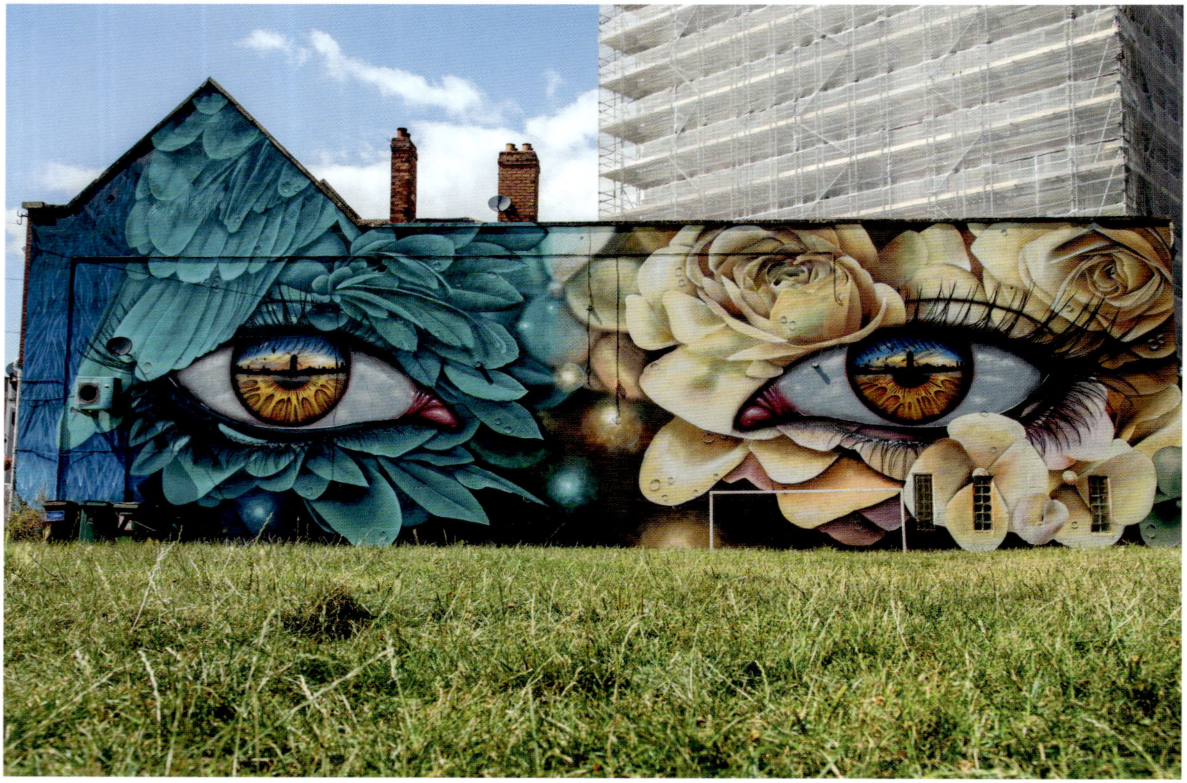

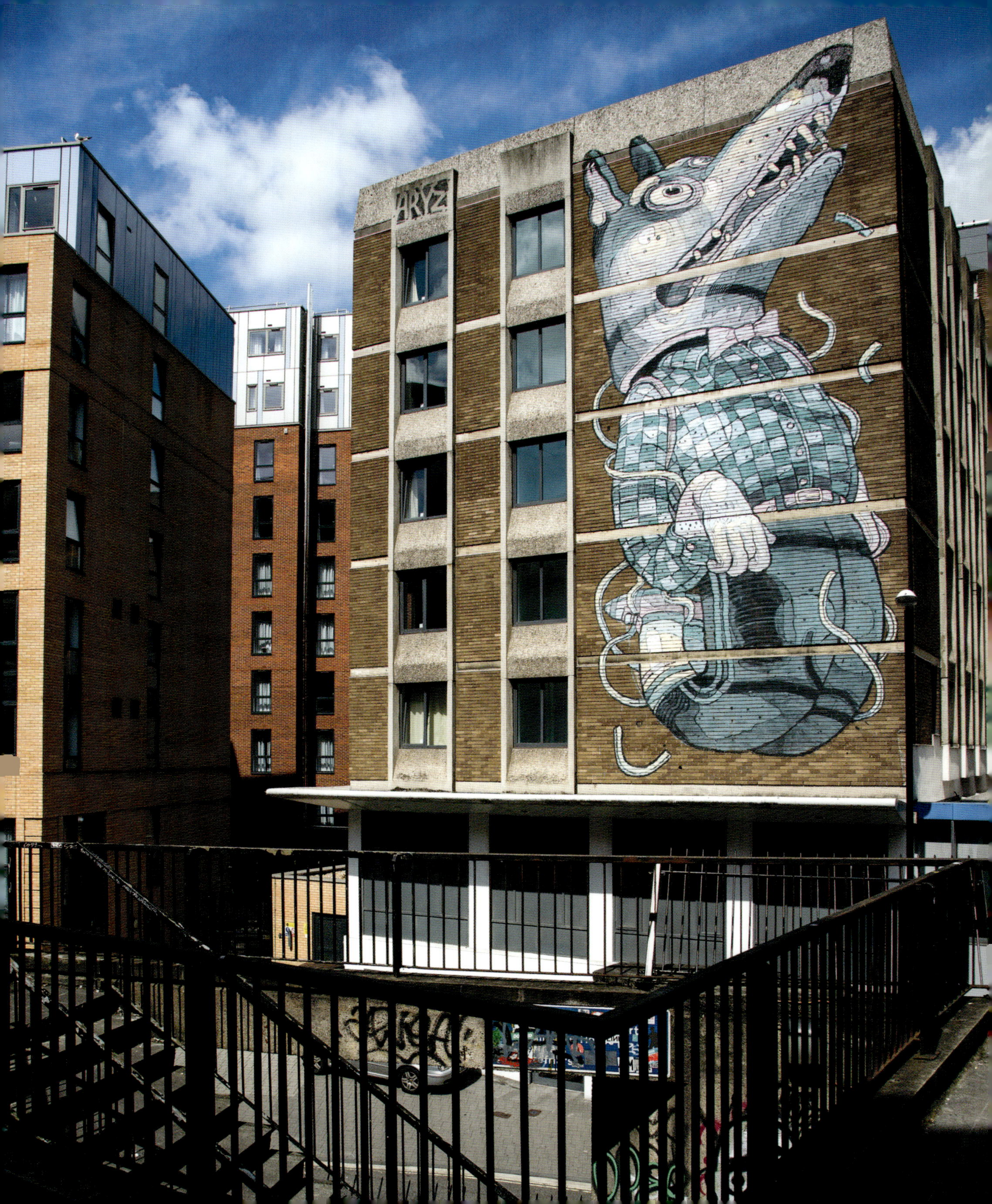

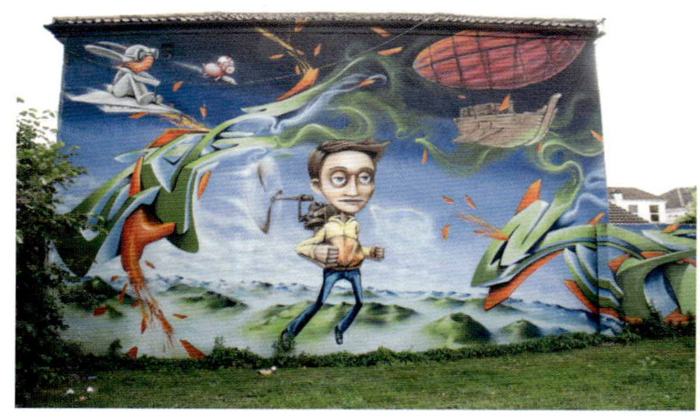
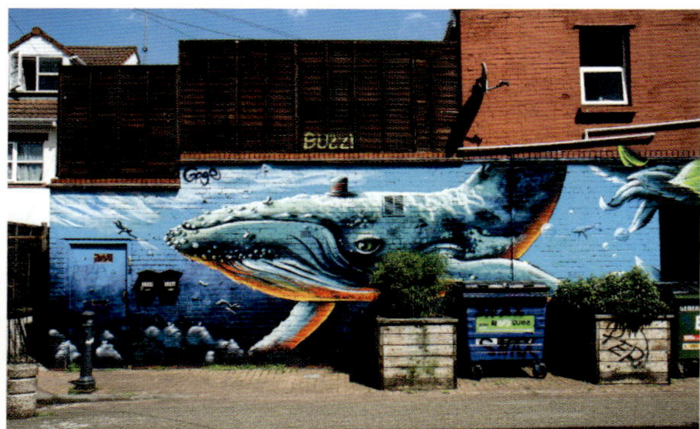
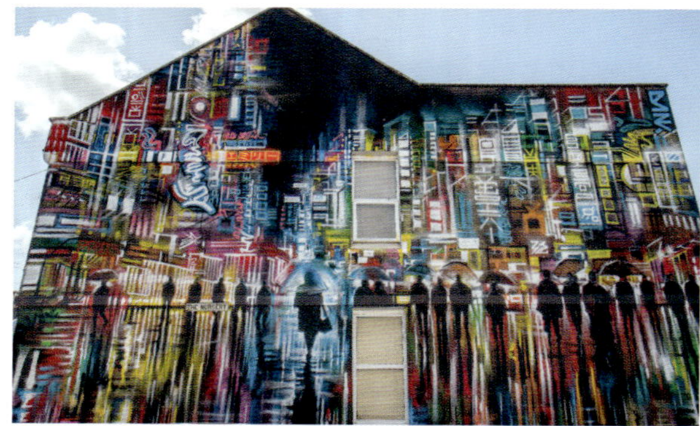
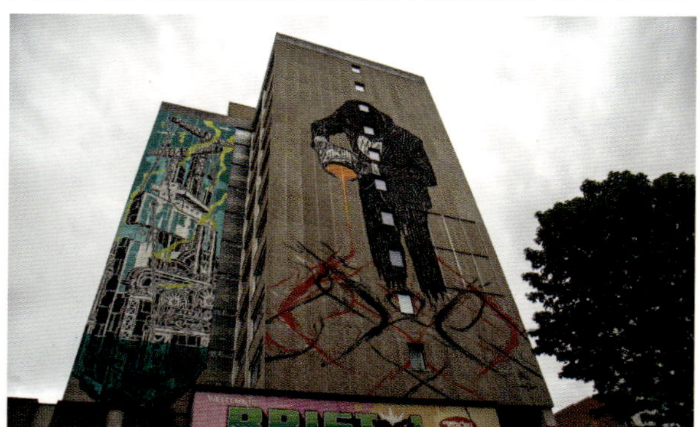
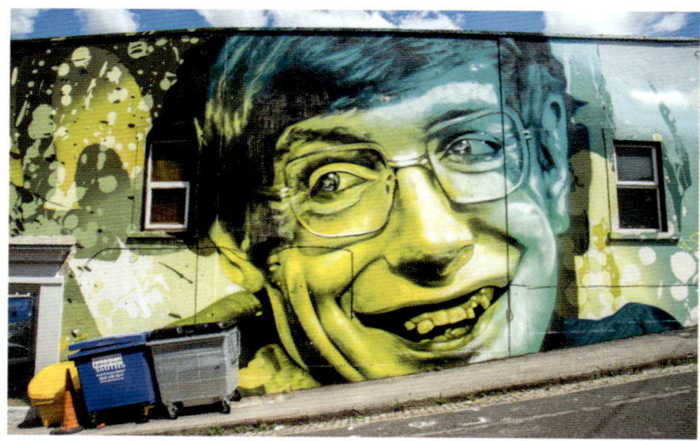
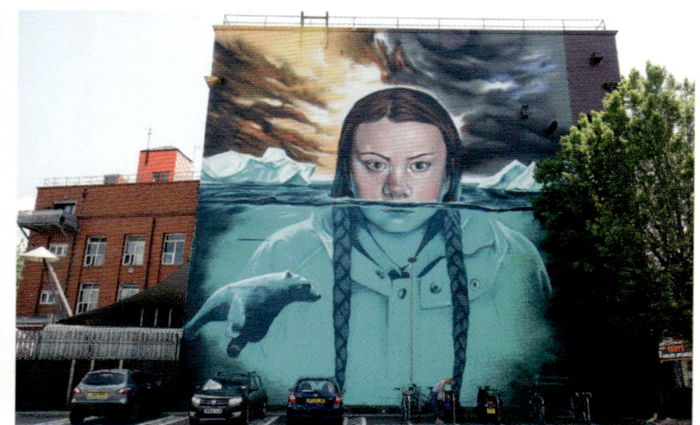
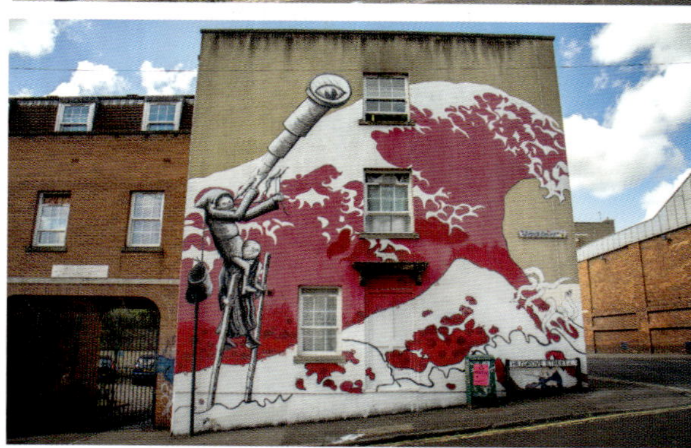
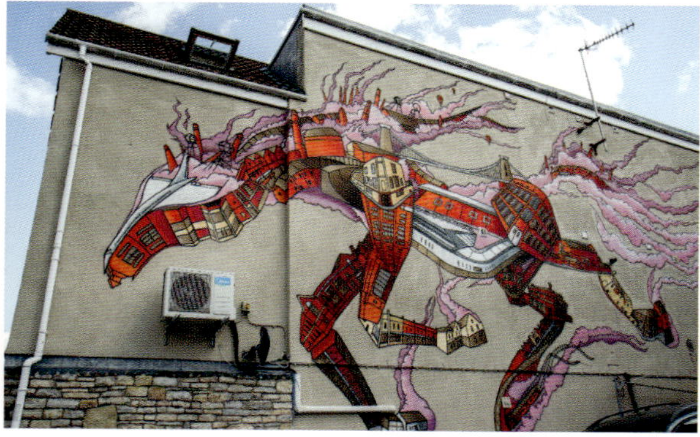

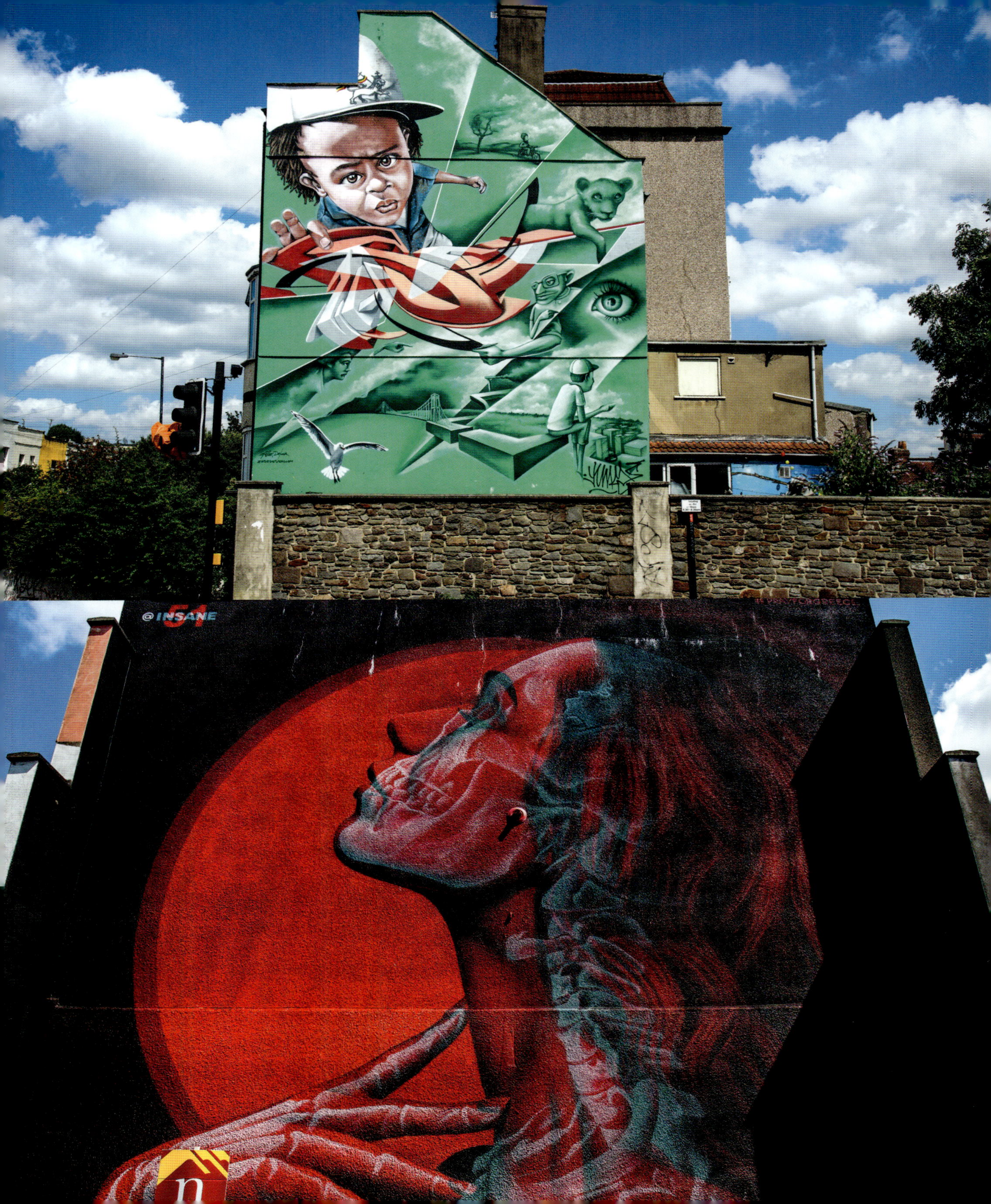

@INSANE51

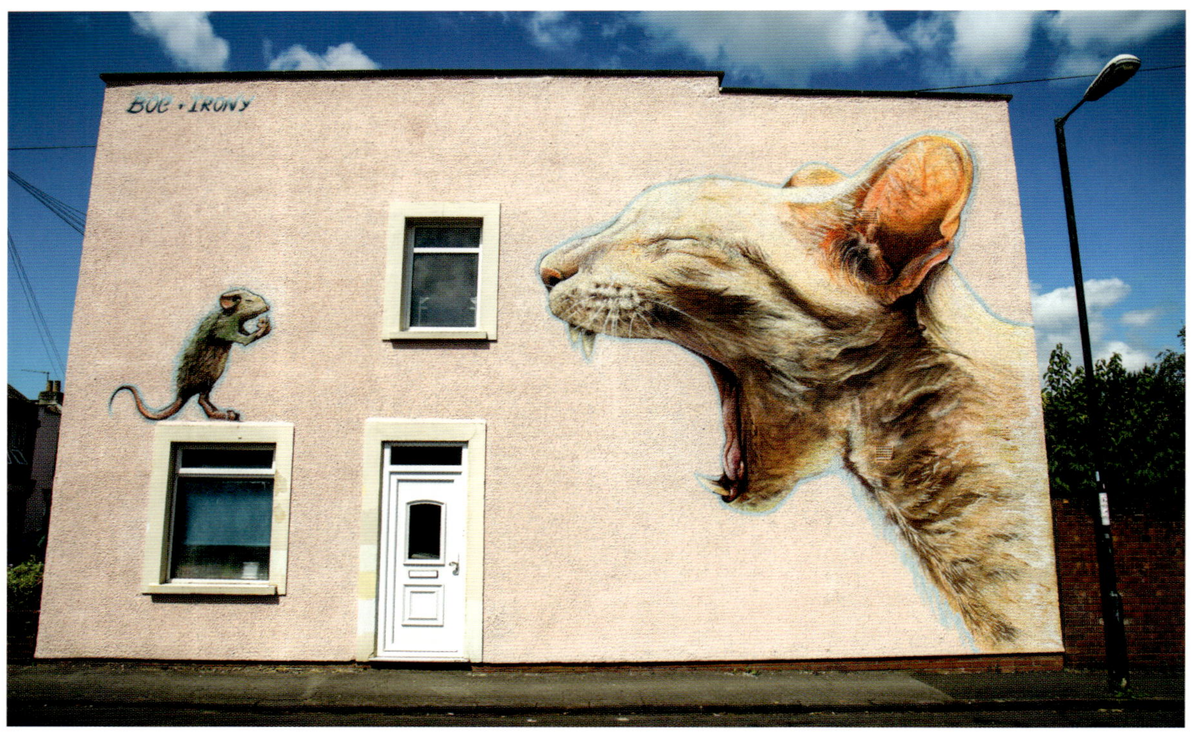

BOE ·IRONY

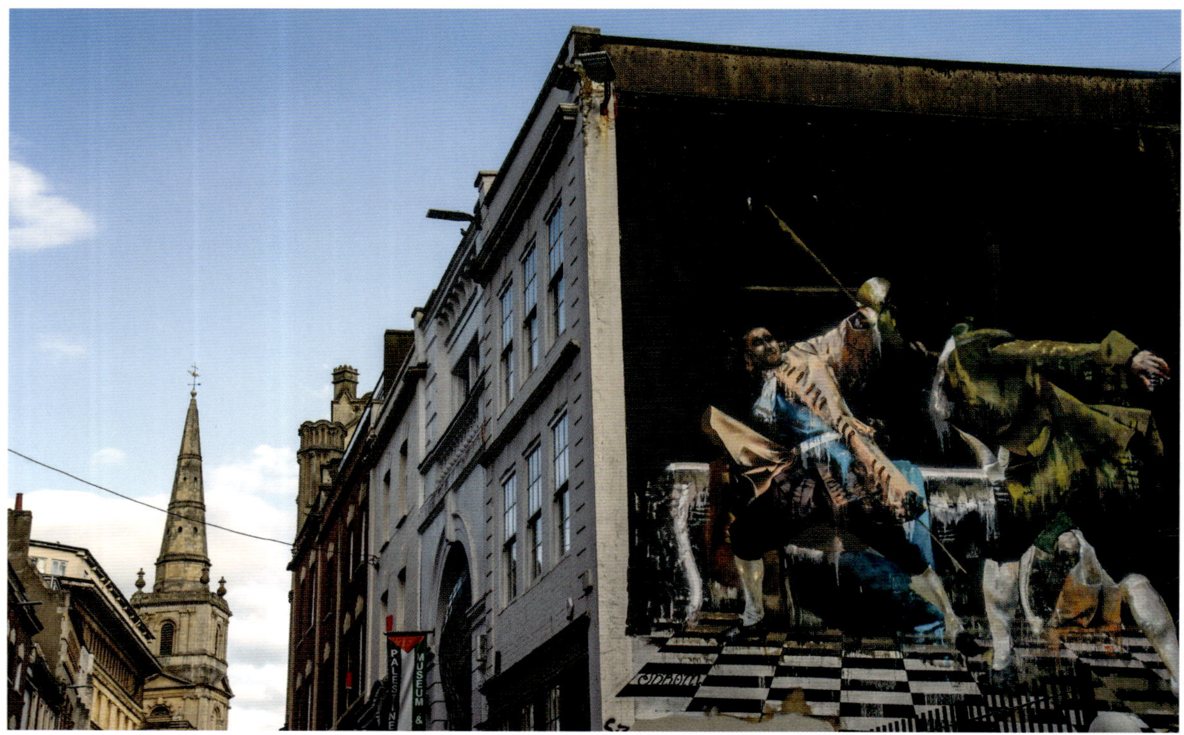

PALESTINE &
MUSEUM &

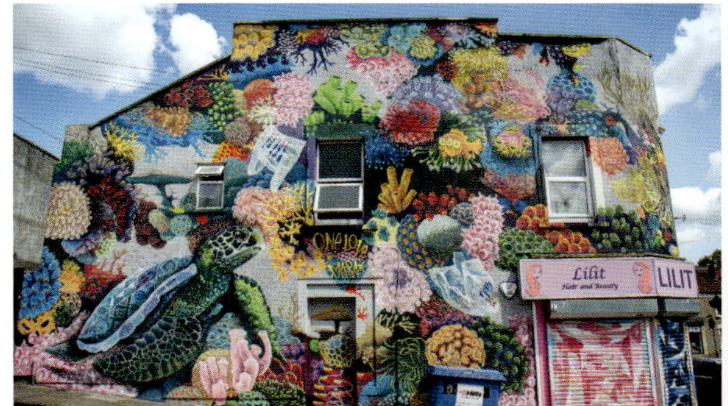
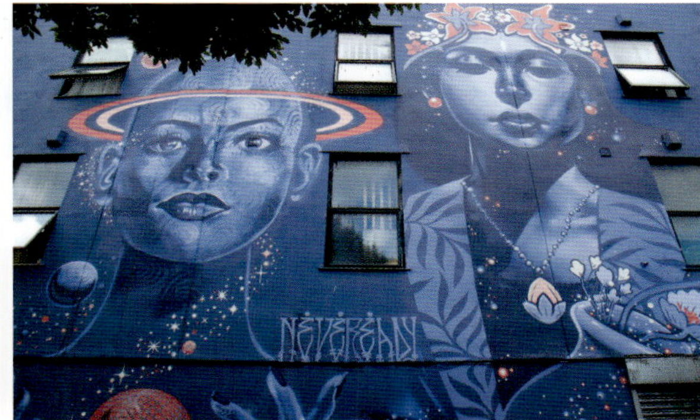
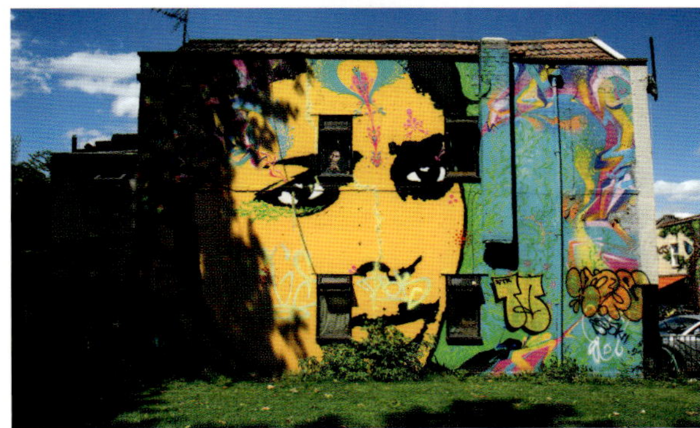
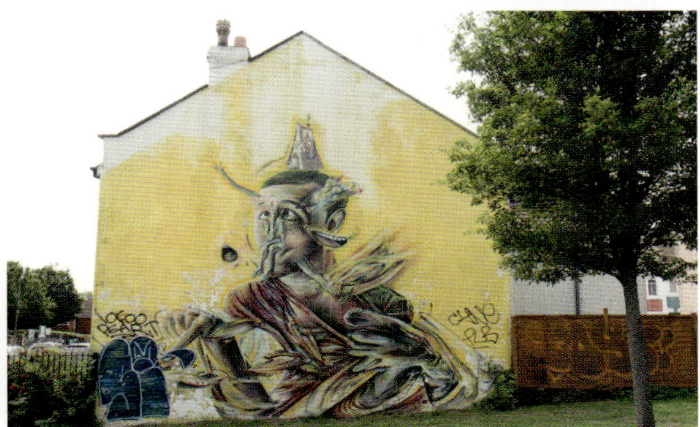
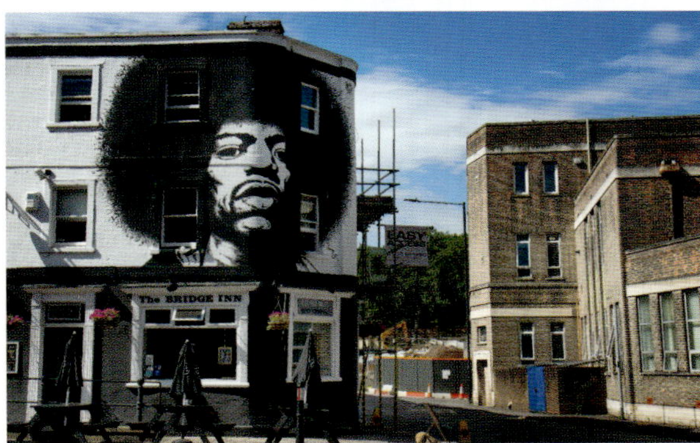
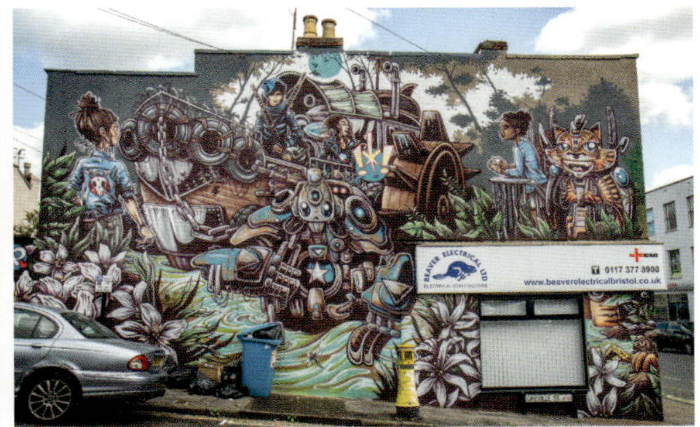
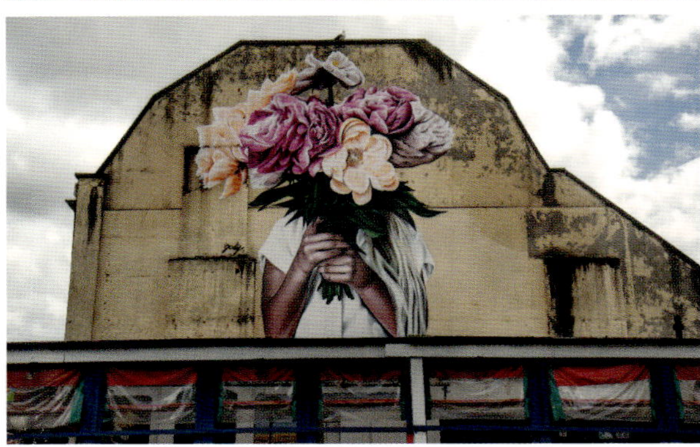
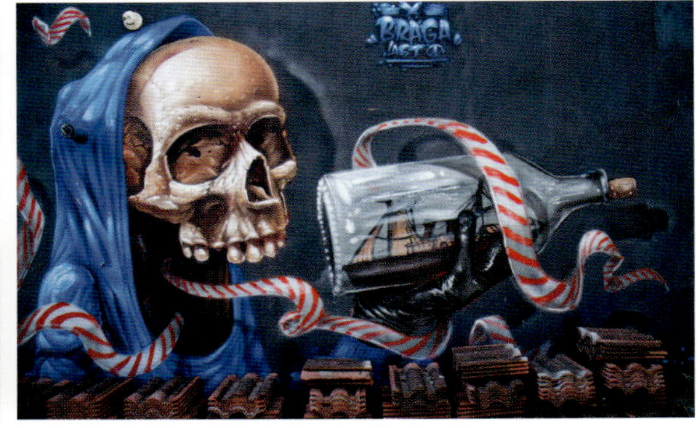

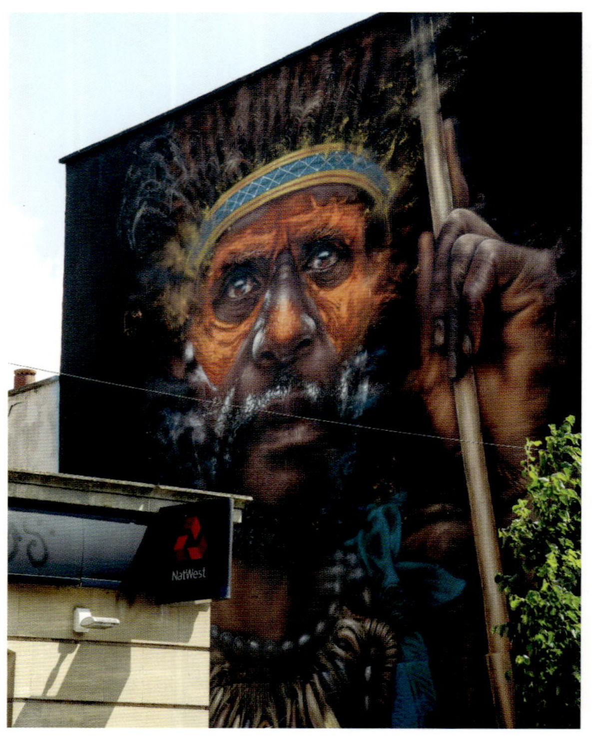

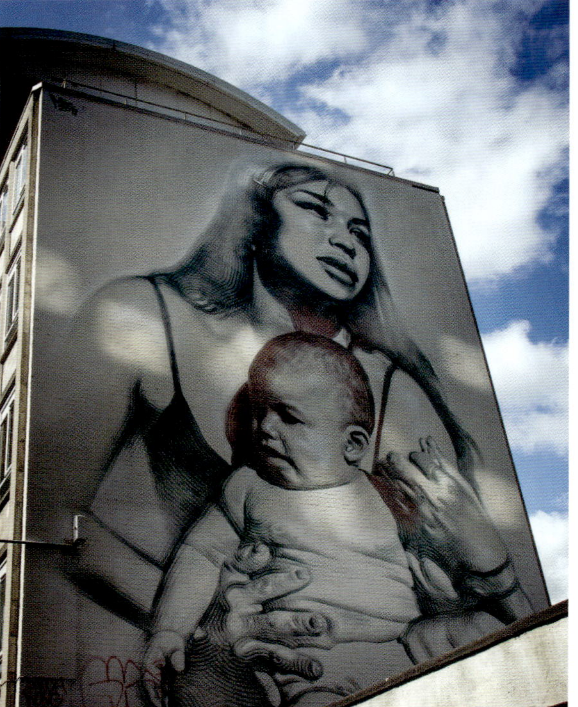

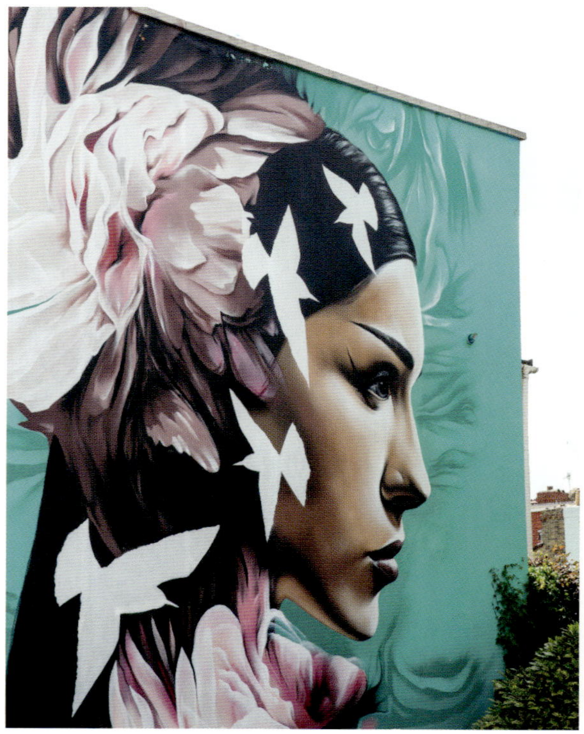

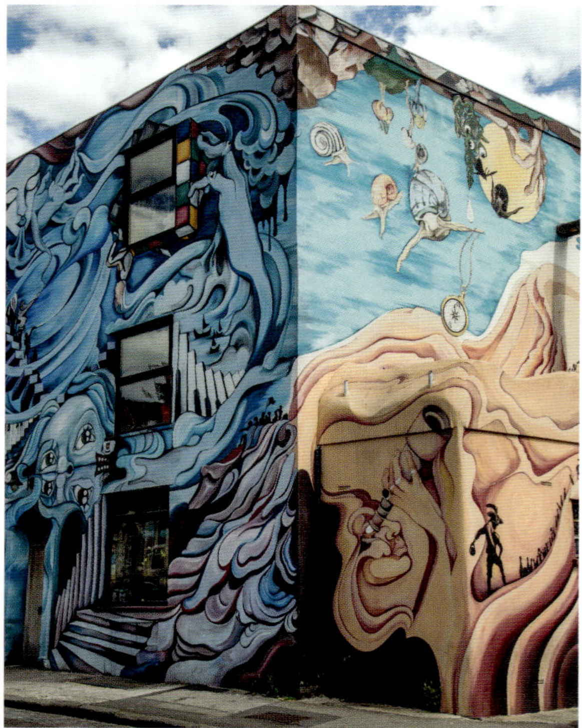